John Donne

and the

Protestant

Reformation

John Donne and the Protestant Reformation

new perspectives

Edited by Mary Arshagouni Papazian

Wayne State University Press
Detroit

Copyright © 2003 by Wayne State University Press,
Detroit, Michigan 48201. All rights are reserved.
No part of this book may be reproduced without formal permission.
Manufactured in the United States of America.
07 06 05 04 03   5 4 3 2 1

Library of Congress Cataloging-in-Publication Data

John Donne and the Protestant Reformation : new perspectives / edited by
Mary Arshagouni Papazian.
     p. cm.
Includes bibliographical references and index.
   ISBN 0-8143-3012-6 (cloth : alk. paper)
  1. Donne, John, 1572–1631—Religion. 2. Christianity and literature—
England—History—17th century. 3. Protestantism and literature—History—
17th century. 4. Christian literature, English—History and criticism.
5. Reformation—England.   I. Papazian, Mary Arshagouni.
   PR2248 .J595 2003
   821'.3—dc21
                                                      2003002565

∞ The paper used in this publication meets the minimum requirements of the
American National Standard for Information Sciences—Permanence of Paper
for Printed Library Materials, ANSI Z39.48-1984.

For Dennis, Ani, and Marie

CONTENTS

Introduction   1
MARY ARSHAGOUNI PAPAZIAN

1
Polemist or Pastor?: Donne and Moderate Calvinist Conformity   12
DANIEL W. DOERKSEN

2
"Speaking Openly and Speaking First": John Donne, the Synod of Dort, and the Early Stuart Church   35
JEANNE SHAMI

3
The Augustinian Donne: How a "Second S. Augustine"?   66
MARY ARSHAGOUNI PAPAZIAN

4
John Donne and Paolo Sarpi: Rendering the Council of Trent   90
JEFFREY JOHNSON

5
Donne's Protestant *Paradiso:* The Johannine Vision of the *Second Anniversary*   113
RAYMOND-JEAN FRONTAIN

6
"Souldiers of one Army": John Donne and the Army of the States General as an International Protestant Crossroads, 1595–1625   143
PAUL R. SELLIN

7
Unmeete Contraryes: The Reformed Subject and the Triangulation of Religious Desire in Donne's *Anniversaries* and *Holy Sonnets*   193
CATHERINE GIMELLI MARTIN

8
From "Tav" to the Cross: John Donne's Protestant Exegesis and Polemics 221
CHANITA GOODBLATT

9
Pathopoeia and the Protestant Form of Donne's *Devotions Upon Emergent Occasions* 247
BRENT NELSON

10
Breaking Down the Walls That Divide: Anti-Polemicism in the *Devotions Upon Emergent Occasions* 273
ELENA LEVY-NAVARRO

11
Reforming Baptism: John Donne and Continental Irenicism 293
ANNETTE DESCHNER

12
True Purification: Donne's Art of Rhetoric in Two Candlemas Sermons 314
MARIA SALENIUS

13
"Not upon a Lecture, but upon a Sermon": Devotional Dynamics of the Donnean Fisher of Men 335
GALE H. CARRITHERS, JR., AND JAMES D. HARDY, JR.

Contributors 361

Index 365

INTRODUCTION

Mary Arshagouni Papazian

In hopes of enriching our understanding of the complex relationship between John Donne and the Protestant Reformation, this collection of thirteen essays by an international—and internationally known—assembly of scholars focuses squarely on the question of the impact of the Reformation on Donne's life, theology, poetry, and prose. While the arguments presented in these essays represent the finest and most recent scholarship on Donne and the English Reformation, an attempt has been made to present the essays in a form that is also accessible to and of interest to students and nonspecialist readers as well as to specialists in the field.

In 1517, Martin Luther, a German Augustinian monk, posted his Ninety-five Theses on indulgences on the door of the castle church at Wittenberg, thereby initiating what history refers to as the Protestant Reformation. Luther's act would result in the breakup of Catholic Europe into warring Catholic and Protestant states, and its consequences would ripple throughout Europe, including England, for the next 150 years. By 1521, Luther's ideas—which were drawn from a careful reading of St. Paul's epistles and the anti-Pelagian works of St. Augustine, and which focused on the effects of original sin on man's nature, man's inability to respond to God without divine grace, and the belief that man can be justified only through faith—began to influence English universities. While King Henry VIII initially resisted the influence of the Protestant reformers, thereby gaining from Pope Leo X the title "Defender of the Faith" for his attack on heresy and defense of papal authority, ultimately dynastic interests—represented in Henry's desire to divorce his Spanish Catholic wife Catherine of Aragon in order to marry Anne Boleyn—led him in 1534 to issue the Acts of Succession and Supremacy. The Succession Act legitimized Henry's marriage to Anne and declared that her children would be legitimate successors to the Crown. The Supremacy Act declared Henry "supreme head" of the Church of England, thereby completing England's schism with Rome. A series of additional laws severed all financial, judicial, and administrative bonds with Rome.

Although King Henry's 1534 declaration formalized England's transformation from a Catholic to a Protestant nation, the transition was neither sudden nor smooth. Indeed, upon the king's death in 1547, at a critical time for the Church of England, Henry's only son, the ten-year-old Edward VI, who had been educated by strongly Protestant tutors, succeeded his father to the throne. During Edward's reign, the Church of England, led by Archbishop Thomas Cranmer, became solidly Protestant, as illustrated in the First and Second Protestant Books of Common Prayer (1549 and 1552) and the Forty-two Articles of Religion (1553), which contained the statement of doctrine for the now independent and Protestant Church of England. Upon Edward's early death in 1553, his eldest half-sister, Mary Tudor—as the daughter of Henry and his first wife, Catherine of Aragon, Mary had been raised Roman Catholic—became queen, despite efforts by the dying Edward and his Protestant advisers to install his cousin, Lady Jane Grey, on the throne. Despite some initial leniency toward the leading Protestants in England, Mary soon began persecuting English Protestants and restored papal supremacy, thereby reconciling the country, at least temporarily, to Rome.

Upon Mary's death in 1558, the Protestant Elizabeth I, daughter of Henry VIII and Anne Boleyn, took the throne and established England once again as a Protestant nation. Early in her forty-five-year reign, Elizabeth restored the 1552 Book of Common Prayer, which had been adopted under Edward VI. She also oversaw the adoption in 1563 of the Thirty-nine Articles of the Church of England, a modified version of the Edwardian Articles, which included some compromises with Catholic-leaning, conservative Englishmen. While the Elizabethan compromises attempted to integrate Catholics into the new Protestant English society, England under Elizabeth remained decidedly Protestant, both in its religious theology and in its political and cultural associations with other Protestant states throughout Europe. England's Protestant orientation became particularly clear in the 1580s and 1590s, when Elizabeth turned more decisively against English Catholics, a consequence in part of her growing fear of Catholic plotting. The defeat of the Spanish Armada in 1588 allowed Elizabeth to declare once and for all God's favor for his Protestant followers in England. Protestant England, in short, saw itself as nothing less than God's chosen nation and saw the Protestant English people as his chosen people.

Upon Elizabeth's death in 1603, the English throne passed to her cousin, the Stuart James VI of Scotland, who became James I of England. James had been raised by Calvinists in Presbyterian Scotland. In keeping with his upbringing, James continued the Protestant orientation of the Church of England established under Elizabeth. Indeed, as recent church historians have demonstrated, the Church of England remained strongly Calvinist throughout the first two decades of James's reign. It was only in the late 1620s that the rise of Arminianism under Archbishop William Laud began to pull the English church away from its Protestant roots.

John Donne, born in London in 1572, entered the world at a time of continuing religious controversy, reached adulthood at the close of Elizabeth's reign, and lived his mature years during the reign of James I, a time referred to in English history as the Jacobean period. While the established and legitimate Church of England throughout Donne's childhood was Protestant in theology, many individuals in England nevertheless remained loyal to Roman Catholicism. These "recusants"—English Catholics who worshiped at home rather than attend services in the Protestant Church of England—included members of Donne's own family, and particularly his mother, who maintained her recusancy until the end of her life. The Roman Catholic influence on Donne during his formative years is undeniable, for according to his modern biographer, R. C. Bald, Donne's tutor during his early years "was a good Catholic, perhaps even a seminary priest" (39). Because Donne was raised in a Roman Catholic household, one tradition in Donne scholarship has been to see in his later life loyalties to the Roman Catholic Church that defined his family during his childhood. Those looking to emphasize Donne's Catholic upbringing generally remind their readers of his Jesuit uncles, his mother's brothers Jasper and Ellis Heywood, who came to England secretly in 1581 as Jesuit missionaries at a time when Jesuits were banned from England.

Despite the continued loyalties of his mother's family to Catholicism, however, it is also undeniable that Donne, like many of his countrymen, came to accept Protestantism, a conversion symbolized most explicitly by his ordination in 1615, at the age of forty-three, as a clergyman in the Church of England. Indeed, in the years preceding his ordination, Donne publicly identified himself with the Protestant consensus that defined the early Stuart English church and that was most clearly expressed in the Thirty-nine Articles adopted during the reign of Elizabeth I. While no scholar has as yet identified conclusively the exact moment of Donne's conversion from Catholic youth to Protestant adult, there is no doubt that such a conversion did take place. Indeed, in the preface to his *Pseudo-Martyr*, a polemical attack on the Jesuits specifically and on Roman Catholicism more generally (1611), Donne refers to this conversion:

> I had a longer work to doe then many other men; for I was first to blot out, certaine impressions of the Romane religion, and to wrastle both against the examples and against the reasons, by which some hold was taken; and some anticipations early layde vpon my conscience, both by Persons who by nature had a power and superiority over my will, and others who by their learning and good life, seem'd to me iustly to claime an interest for the guiding, and rectifying of mine vnderstanding in these matters. (sig. B2v, qtd. in Bald 39)

And, in his *Essays in Divinity*, which probably reached their final form in 1614, just before Donne was ordained (Bald 281), Donne similarly makes clear his commitment to the Church of England rather than the Roman Catholic Church of his childhood, for he asserts that "the form of Gods worship, established in the Church of *England* be more convenient, and advantageous then of any other Kingdome, both to provoke and kindle devotion, and also to fix it" (*Essays* 51).

Once we recognize Donne's commitment to the Church of England as demonstrated both in his words and his deeds (and we have no reason cynically to believe that his conversion was anything but sincere), we must then consider what the Protestant Reformation meant for someone like Donne—Catholic youth, law student at the Inns of Court, soldier in the wars against Catholic Spain, secretary to Lord Egerton, poet, defender of Protestantism in the polemical debates of the early Jacobean period, and, finally, ordained clergyman in the Church of England who became one of the most popular preachers of his day. We must also consider how a deeper understanding of Donne's indebtedness to the Reformation increases our sensitivity to and understanding of his emotional and often moving poetry and prose.

The present collection includes essays that place Donne broadly in the context of the English and European Reformation traditions; essays that consider aspects of Donne's divine poetry in the context of Reformation traditions and concerns; essays that consider the broad influence of the Reformation on Donne and the milieu—or coterie—in which he lived, wrote, and preached; essays on Donne's moving prose work, the *Devotions Upon Emergent Occasions*; and a group of essays specifically on Donne's sermons. Because this collection highlights Donne's relationship to the Reformation, which was primarily—though not exclusively—a theological, cultural, and political movement, little attention is given in these essays to Donne's well-known secular poems, particularly his *Elegies*, *Songs and*

Sonnets, and *Satires*. The collection was not intended to cover Donne's entire oeuvre but rather to provide readers with a more nuanced understanding of Donne's response to the profound theological, cultural, and political changes that, in the name of the Reformation, were transforming the world of early modern England.

As we shall see, many of these essays extend our discussion of Donne beyond the boundaries of England, reminding us that the Protestant Reformation was a broad European movement and that the international dimensions of Protestantism affected England as well. Thus we have to look beyond England's shores to understand the full context in which Donne lived, wrote, and preached. Still, while recognizing that Donne must be seen as a figure of the Continent as well as of England, the essays in this collection also contribute to the current controversies surrounding Donne's theological commitments.

These essays also reveal a Donne who cared much for the idea of moderation. Donne viewed the world as a practical, pastoral preacher and poet, not a systematic theologian. Thus, although much debate over the years has centered on Donne's relationship to Calvinism and Calvinist predestinarian thinking, Donne seems clearly to have embraced the moderate Calvinism that defined the English church, while at the same time moderating the negative effects of a harsh Calvinism for the benefit of his listeners. Moreover, despite the often polemical nature of the term "moderation," which often was used strategically in the early modern period to cast opponents as extremists, Donne emerges from this collection as one deeply committed both to the Reformation heritage of the Church of England and as a preacher deeply committed to effective pastoral care of his flock.

While some of the essays in this collection address broad questions regarding Donne and Protestantism, others focus more narrowly on specific texts or problems. The collection begins with the broad essays in order to establish the impact of the Protestant Reformation on Donne as citizen, soldier, poet, and clergyman of the late Elizabethan and early Jacobean period. These essays provide an important context for reading the collection's remaining essays that share a more specific focus, thereby providing the terminology and explanation of specific issues that emerge in the subsequent essays.

The collection's opening essay, Daniel W. Doerksen's "Polemist or Pastor? Donne and Moderate Calvinist Conformity," addresses the question of Donne's theological position within the early Stuart Church of England during Donne's years as a clergyman and what this meant for him as poet and preacher. Doerksen pays particular attention to the labels that have been applied to Donne over the years, taking issue with the traditional use by scholars of the term "Anglican." According to Doerksen, Donne identifies closely with the conformist Calvinist piety that characterized the pre-Laudian Jacobean church. Doerksen's essay builds on recent scholarship in church history, which has shown that the term "Anglican" did not have real meaning until after Donne's death and that puritans continued to play an important role in the church until the rise of Archbishop Laud in the late 1620s and early 1630s. In short, Doerksen concludes, Donne is a moderate predestinarian and a moderate Calvinist, a position very much in line with the consensus in the Jacobean, pre-Laudian church and one that Donne embraced despite his Roman Catholic upbringing.

In "'Speaking Openly and Speaking First': John Donne, the Synod of Dort, and the Early Stuart Church," Jeanne Shami begins with a detailed discussion of Donne's election at the 1626 Convocation of English clergy, held at Westminster Abbey, to the office of prolocutor—the official representative of the lower house to the upper house of the Convocation—a position requiring both political and theological sensitivity. According to Shami, Donne's election to this important office during a period of tension between the Calvinist conformists of the early Jacobean church and the rising followers of Archbishop Laud, who represented an Arminian position, illustrates the respect accorded Donne by his peers. She also argues that the Latin oration Donne gave on this occasion links him to the "blessed sobriety"—or tactfulness and discretion—exhibited earlier in 1619 by the English delegates to the Synod of Dort, an international gathering of Protestants held in The Hague. As Shami demonstrates, Donne articulates in this oration and throughout his sermons a position of inquiry rather than of dogmatic pronouncement, and he looks for consensus. With a similar moderate spirit, Shami explains, Donne maintains his affinity for Calvin while at the same time engaging "in a program of reinterpreting Calvin to support his own generous interpretations of the Thirty-nine Articles, which he accepts as the foundational articles of the doctrine of the Church of England." At the same time, Shami reminds us, Donne's primary interest is that of a preacher rather than a systematic theologian, and hence he is interested in the practical consequences of doctrines like predestination.

My essay, "The Augustinian Donne: How a 'Second S. Augustine'?," considers Donne in the context of his indebtedness to St. Augustine, the church father most highly esteemed among the Protestant reformers. In this essay, I consider Donne's relationship to Augustine not simply with respect to the pattern of Donne's life, which often has been related to the pattern of Augustine's life as narrated in his *Confessions*, but in terms of Augustine's predestinarian theology. It was to Augustine's predestinarian theology, together with close reading of St. Paul's epistles, that the fathers of the Reformation turned in developing their conception of man as fallen, sinful, and incapable of moral and good action without the undeserved gift of God's abundant mercy. My essay, which places Donne squarely in the tradition of Augustine, analyzes seventeenth-century responses to Augustine as well as Donne's many references to Augustine in his sermons—and particularly those occasioned by Sir Tobie Matthew's 1620 "popish translation" into English of Augustine's *Confessions*. It concludes with a close look at several of Donne's *Holy Sonnets* in order to demonstrate the Augustinian dimensions to these divine poems.

In "John Donne and Paolo Sarpi: Rendering the Council of Trent," Jeffrey Johnson addresses the relationship between Sarpi, who became state theologian to the Venetian Republic and wrote against the Council of Trent, and Donne, who had in his art collection a portrait of Sarpi and may have met Sarpi during a 1605 trip to Venice. Johnson analyzes the different approaches Donne and Sarpi take in their criticisms of the Council of Trent. He demonstrates that "Donne and Sarpi, in fact, arrive at some similar conclusions"—that is, conclusions critical of the Council of Trent and its theological positions—but "from profoundly distinct philosophical and theological foundations." In Sarpi's *History of the Council of Trent*, Johnson explains, he laments the failure of the council both in moving the church toward further reform and in putting aside self-interest and failing to achieve the conciliarism that the council promised. Donne's strong criticism of the Council of Trent occurs not only in *Pseudo-Martyr*, his polemical prose tract that reacts to the abuses in papal authority that Donne sees as characterizing the Roman Catholic Church in general and the Council of Trent in particular, but also in a series of sermons. Johnson's essay provides further texture and context to our understanding Donne's unequivocal criticism of the Roman Catholic Church from his Protestant perspective.

Raymond-Jean Frontain's essay, "Donne's Protestant *Paradiso*: The Johannine Vision of the *Second Anniversary*," provides a new look at Donne's relationship to Dante, particularly in the context of Donne's *First* and *Second Anniversaries*, poems written to commemorate the death of Elizabeth Drury, the daughter of Donne's patron, Sir Robert Drury. Frontain, tracing in rich detail his comparison between Dante's *Divine Comedy*, and especially his *Paradiso*, and Donne's *Anniversary* poems, demonstrates that although both Dante and Donne "model themselves upon the vision enacted in the Revelation of Saint John the Divine, Dante fashions himself as the passive witness to a divine drama, whereas Donne emphasizes that his prophetic vision occurs in his mind's eye, the result of his devotional meditation." Frontain goes on to explain how Donne's transformation of the meditative vision "posits a Reformed fiction of the poet's spiritual authority," one in which the poet's role becomes that of a visionary prophet.

In "'Souldiers of one Army': John Donne and the Army of the States General as an International Protestant Crossroads, 1595–1625," Paul R. Sellin reminds us that the Protestant Reformation involved not only religious issues but also political alliances and relationships. His essay brings to our attention the often-neglected political reality that characterized England from the time of Elizabeth through Donne's own life—namely, that English troops were stationed in the Netherlands throughout most of the years of Elizabeth's and James's reigns and that Donne, like many of his contemporaries, spent some years in military service for the purpose of defending England and its Protestant allies against the threat from Catholic Spain. Donne himself spent two years in military service (1596–97) under the earl of Essex, during which he participated in the military campaigns against Cádiz and the Azores, islands off the coast of Spain. Many of Donne's closest friends, such as Sir Henry Wotton, were knighted as a result of these campaigns. Sellin's essay, which draws on a wide array of archival resources, re-creates the rich network of relationships that formed the British military abroad, one that maps out the rich personal nature of the international Protestant community of which Donne himself was a member. Sellin's essay is another reminder to us that the Reformation in England affected all sectors of British life, including England's relationship with the Continent.

Catherine Gimelli Martin's essay, "Unmeete Contraryes: The Reformed Subject and the Triangulation of Religious Desire in Donne's *Anniversaries* and *Holy Sonnets*," considers the heart-wrenching anxieties and conflicts that characterize many of Donne's divine poems in terms of the competing models of social and religious salvation that perplexed his day. Drawing on the work of theorist René Girard, who is generally concerned with the psychological effects typically produced by large-scale cultural transitions, Martin's essay reminds us that the emotional effects of the social, political, and theological upheavals caused by the Reformation continued to plague many members of Donne's age, leading Donne to give voice to these psychological upheavals and transformations in memorable, moving, and angst-ridden poetry.

In "From 'Tav' to the Cross: John Donne's Protestant Exegesis and Polemics," Chanita Goodblatt extends our understanding of Donne's relationship to Christian Hebraism (the way Christians relate to the Hebrew Bible or Old Testament) and the Hebrew exegetical tradition and of Donne's distinctly Protestant method of biblical exegesis. As Goodblatt demonstrates, Donne, in his exfoliation of biblical texts, draws on original Jewish sources such as the Targum (the Hebrew term used for the Aramaic translations or paraphrases of the Hebrew Bible), medieval Jewish exegetes such as David Kimhi, Solomon ben Isaac, and Abraham Ibn Ezra, and mediating Christian Hebraists such as Tremellius and Pagninus. Goodblatt also reminds us of the importance, for reading and interpreting Donne's sermons, of the Geneva Bible and the Authorized Version in their continual citing of earlier Hebrew exegetes. She also helps us begin to understand the differences between Catholic and Protestant engagement with the Hebrew Bible and the rich Hebrew exegetical tradition.

In "*Pathopoeia* and the Protestant Form of Donne's *Devotions Upon Emergent Occasions*," Brent Nelson demonstrates how Donne drew upon his resources as a preacher in preparation of his *Devotions*, a long prose work written in response to his near-fatal illness of December 1623. Nelson explicates the similar rhetorical purposes and strategies that Donne's sermons and *Devotions* share through consideration of the similar strategies of *pathopoeia*—or the arousing of emotions—seen in both. In his analysis, Nelson concentrates on the audience orientation and the emotional appeal of the *Devotions*, which traditionally has been categorized as meditation or spiritual autobiography. Noting that much of the emotional appeal in the work arises from its very Protestant concern with patterns of fall and redemption, Nelson explains that "Donne thought of himself not as a teacher but as a preacher. And as a pastor-preacher, his aim was not simply to convey personal experience or even to teach by example, but to *move* his audience to greater devotion." This is a method and concern, Nelson argues, that motivated Donne's writing and publishing of his *Devotions* in early 1624.

Elena Levy-Navarro's essay, "Breaking Down the Walls That Divide: Anti-Polemicism in the *Devotions Upon Emergent Occasions*," argues that Donne "takes an anti-polemicist position in order to renew and revitalize '*true Religion*' in England." In language reminiscent of Shami's discussion of Donne's role as prolocutor at the 1626 Convocation, Levy-Navarro similarly presents a Donne who attempts to moderate his language during a period of growing polemicism in England while he simultaneously stresses his commitment "to the fundamentals of the Reformation heritage of the Church of England" during the later years of James I's reign. Levy-Navarro develops her view of Donne as anti-polemicist through a close analysis of the latter half of his *Devotions*, contrasting Donne's position throughout from that of the avant-garde conformists who shared James's positions apropos the Spanish Match and the Thirty Years' War and who rose to power under Buckingham and Laud in the mid-1620s. At the same time, as Levy-Navarro demonstrates, Donne does not embrace the position of the anti-ceremonial puritans either. Rather, he argues for the acceptance of the concept of *things indifferent*—that is, things not necessary for salvation—such as the famous ceremony of bells in the *Devotions* that upset some puritans as too Catholic, while at the same time promoting his own commitment to the Reformation heritage of the Church of England.

In "Reforming Baptism: John Donne and Continental Irenicism," Annette Deschner considers Donne's views on baptism in order to explicate what she argues is his irenic orientation. Like the Dutch jurist and statesman Hugo Grotius and other followers of the European irenic movement, Donne, Deschner argues, worked toward the unity of all Protestants. Donne's was a position that, as Levy-Navarro has also suggested, turned away from polemicism and embraced instead the fundamental articles of religion to which all churches in the Reformed tradition could agree. Part of this movement, according to Deschner, is the return both to early Christianity as a role model for a Reformed Christianity and to Scripture, famously referred to as the *sola scriptura* principle that characterized all Reformed churches. Deschner considers Donne's views on baptism specifically as expressed in Donne's Heidelberg sermon, the sermon he preached in 1619 while a part of Doncaster's delegation at the outset of the Thirty Years' War. In an environment fraught with religious and political land mines, Donne preached on baptism, which was not at the center of doctrinal debate but which nonetheless allowed him to advance his irenic mission, celebrating throughout the role of the early Christian church. At the same time, Deschner argues, Donne avoided discussion of the more volatile issue of original sin that would make his irenic mission more difficult. With consideration of numerous additional Donne sermons, Deschner concludes that "Donne makes baptism theologically indispensable for irenicism."

Maria Salenius, in "True Purification: Donne's Art of Rhetoric in Two Candlemas Sermons," attempts to move beyond the question of Donne's church allegiance and concentrates instead on attempting to identify Donne's "true faith" through an analysis of two of his Candlemas sermons, generally dated 1624 and 1627. Thomas Wilson's *Art of Rhetoric* (1560) provides Salenius with a backdrop for articulating a Protestant theory of language that enables her to analyze the rhetorically Protestant ways in which Donne reaches out to his audiences in these sermons. In demonstrating the linguistic dimension of the Reformation, represented most powerfully in Scripture itself—the sermon was meant to explain God's Word to its audience—and in her careful analysis of these two Candlemas sermons, Salenius reminds us that the Reformation affected Protestants such as Donne in a complicated set of ways—from theology, to language, to political orientation, and to emotional experiences. In short, Salenius concludes, Donne's Protestant linguistics demonstrate his sincere vocation as "a preacher by the grace of God and under the direction of the Holy Spirit" who preaches "for the edification of his hearers, to 'move men to glorifie the Father.'"

In the final essay in the collection, "'Not upon a Lecture, but upon a Sermon': Devotional Dynamics of the Donnean Fisher of Men," Gale H. Carrithers, Jr., and James D. Hardy, Jr., explicate the experience of a Donnean sermon on both readers and listeners. Focusing on three concepts—liturgy, ecclesiology, and justification—Carrithers and Hardy consider specifically Donne's "fishers of men" sermon, in reference to Christ's call to the fishermen Peter and Andrew to "follow Me," a sermon originally delivered in The Hague in 1619 and expanded to two sermons in 1630. In their essay, Carrithers and Hardy focus on the questions of calling and community as amplified in these sermons. Stressing the need for humility and the concern for fostering the relationship between believer and Christ that characterized Protestant as opposed to Roman Catholic preachers, Carrithers and Hardy provide a sense of Donne's practical divinity, his concern as preacher for the audience(s) hearing his words.

Readers of the essays in this collection will gain both an enriched understanding of Donne's place in the broad European and more narrowly English Reformation traditions and a greater recognition that the concerns of the Reformation—whether political, theological, or poetical—inform both Donne's personal poetry and his public preaching. While it also becomes clear that in adopting the values of the Reformation, Donne does not reject out of hand everything from his Catholic background, readers nevertheless will see a Donne committed to the fundamental articles of the protestant Church of England, a commitment that underlies his deep pastoral concern for his flock and his commitment to his nation and his God.

Works Cited

Bald, R. C. *John Donne: A Life*. Oxford: Clarendon, 1970.
Donne, John. *Essays in Divinity*. Ed. Evelyn M. Simpson. Oxford: Clarendon, 1952.

1

Polemist or Pastor?

Donne and Moderate Calvinist Conformity

DANIEL W. DOERKSEN

Where exactly does John Donne the churchman, the author of the *Sermons*, belong within the early Stuart church? And what difference does it make? I will argue in this essay that in his sermons and other late prose writings, Donne identifies in his own way with the conformist Calvinist piety that prevailed in the leadership of the Jacobean Church of England (as it had done in the later Elizabethan church) and that this helps to account for some distinctive elements in what he preached and wrote. Specifically, I will argue that Donne's position within the spectrum of his church profoundly affects his approach toward his task as preacher, influencing not only the nature of his polemics but even his purposeful avoidance of some kinds of polemics.

Donne used to be classed as "Anglican," but modern historical scholarship has given us a picture notably different from the old one—of an English church simply divided on Anglican-Puritan lines—that still prevailed when the latest full editions of Donne's sermons (1962) and his *Devotions Upon Emergent Occasions* (1975) were completed. It is now generally recognized, by historians if not by all literary critics, that there was no "Anglican" party or church by that name until after Donne's death and that most puritans remained an active part of the Church of England into the 1630s. Because these puritans shared common doctrine (as in the Thirty-nine Articles) with the other church members and, like most of them, regarded church government and those aspects of ritual not specified in the Bible as secondary though significant matters, some (such as

Robert Hill and Richard Sibbes) conformed fully, while Calvinistic bishops made some allowances for conscientious scruples in others (Doerksen, *Conforming* 19–20). The idea that a Calvinist consensus including both conformists and moderate puritans existed during the late Elizabethan and the Jacobean years has received considerable acceptance by church historians, although with a recognition that this consensus was itself not stable but rather was being undermined during the reign of King James by processes such as court politicking and propaganda (Milton 395–426).[1] Lori Anne Ferrell, in a fascinating but controversial thesis *(Polemic)*, goes so far as to argue that at the royal court, polemic, and more specifically antipuritan polemic, became more important than substance. I will maintain, however, that this was certainly not true for Donne, one prominent court preacher.

Nonpuritan religious leaders of Donne's time, formerly lumped together as "Anglican," are now generally recognized to have occupied a range of positions or opinions, but most can usefully be classed as "conformist," the term designating "a divine who not only conformed to the ceremonies of the English church, but did so with alacrity, and was prepared both to make an issue of ceremonial conformity and points of church government, and to use the epithet of 'puritan' against his opponents" (Milton 8). This label fits Donne the preacher, with one significant exception: Donne objects to the use of derogatory labels for other members of his own church, and therefore to a remarkable extent avoids using the term "puritan" in an unfavorable way[2] (more on this below). Milton, in spite of his emphasis on change and flexibility in the early Stuart church, still finds it useful throughout his book to further designate various church leaders as either Calvinist conformists, avant-garde conformists (before the time of full-fledged Laudianism), or Laudians.[3] Of course any such classifications should be made with care, and the limitations of any kind of classification must be understood.

Most modern writers recognize that Donne is a conformist, but there are sharp disagreements as to what kind of conformist he is; in some quarters there is a reluctance to further classify Donne at all because of his distinctive background or qualities.[4] While Paul Sellin, Kate Narveson, David Norbrook, and I link Donne with English Calvinism, Lori Anne Ferrell ("Donne") and Richard Strier recently have argued for his alignment with the anti-Calvinist "avant-garde" conformity and Laudianism, which they both associate with a deliberately polemical style. To resolve these differences of opinion, it will be helpful first of all to clarify what these classifications actually mean. Milton, a specialist on Laudianism (he wrote a Cambridge doctoral thesis on it), applies the term "Laudian" in his book very specifically, to

> all those clerics . . . closely associated with Laud and . . . unequivocal in their support for his ecclesiastical policies in the 1630s. This agenda included anti-Sabbatarianism; the placing of the communion table at the east end of the church; the freeing of the clergy, their courts and their maintenance from lay control; and a general de-emphasis on preaching and forms of voluntary religion in favour of the "beauty of holiness," greater ceremonial and more lavish church adornment. . . . [T]his was a group perceptible both to themselves and to outsiders. (9)

Milton excludes here "mere conformists" or more specifically "those who merely acquiesced in the policies adopted, or offered conditional support." When such criteria are applied, Donne cannot be classified as a Laudian. "Avant-garde conformity" is a convenient term that Milton accepts from Peter Lake as designating "new patterns of ceremonialist and sacerdotal conformist thought" such as those of Hooker and Andrewes" (Milton 8–9). These patterns in effect anticipate the full-blown Laudianism of the 1630s, and surely the term implies dissatisfaction with the Calvinist-dominant state of affairs in the church of James I—a contrast to what Kate Narveson calls "contented" conformity (110) and associates with Donne.

When it comes to ceremony and ritual, Donne clearly differs from the stance of the anti-Calvinists. Unlike them, he shows no preoccupation with matters of outward worship. I have found no reference in the sermons to any concern about the location of the communion table. Milton notes that Hooker and the avant-garde acclaimed the excellence of the Book of Common Prayer and became more and more reluctant to concede that English ceremonies were matters "indifferent" (495). Donne as a conformist of course approves of the Book of Common Prayer, and echoes it at times, but he seldom mentions it. This contrasts with his treatment of the Scriptures, which he repeatedly praises and constantly cites. One should note his measured tone when, in a St. Paul's sermon of 1629, he ranks the English church between the Lutheran and Calvinist continental churches with regard to ceremony: "That Church, which they call Lutheran, hath retained more of these Ceremonies, then ours hath done; And ours more then that which they call Calvinist; But both the Lutheran, and ours, without danger, because, in both places, we are diligent to preach to the people the right use of these indifferent things" (8:331). This is the tone of the Calvinist conformist at a time when the Laudians were making much stronger claims for English ceremonies. In all his sermons Donne seems only once to sound rather Laudian in statements about the communion table as an altar on which a sacrifice is made (7:429),[5] but he carefully qualifies what he means, insisting at the end of this 1627 sermon that the disputed ceremonies are "things, in their nature, *indifferent*" (7:433). Also, unlike the Laudians, Donne never explicitly extols the "beauty of holiness." Specifically, in his thousands of scriptural references he never alludes to the four biblical texts that use the term, although two are in his favorite book of the Bible (the Psalms) and are near texts that he does mention (1 Chron. 16:29; 2 Chron. 20:21; Pss. 29:2, 96:9). When Donne thinks of beauty, he is more apt to recall "How beautifull are the feet of them that preach the Gospel!" (2:173). Like all English Protestants (and Calvin), he regards both Word and sacraments as essential features of the church, but unlike the Laudians and like the other Calvinists, he has a "word-centered" rather than "sacrament-centered" view of the church.[6]

In considering whether Donne belongs with the group of Calvinist conformists, it is helpful to bear in mind Milton's broad use of the term "Calvinist" "in common with current historiography, to denote a general sympathy with the continental Reformed tradition in all its purely doctrinal aspects [i.e., including predestination but excluding church polity and those ceremonies unspecified in Scripture], and a sense of identification with the West European Calvinist Churches and their fortunes" (8). This term includes both puritans and nonpuritans; I maintain that Donne fits in with the latter, along with people like Archbishop George Abbot, Bishop John King, Bishop Joseph Hall, and a majority of the leading bishops under King James I (Collinson 82; Fincham, *Prelate* 250–76). But I also specify that in contrast to a number of puritans and some bishops, such as John Whitgift, Donne was a moderate Calvinist, holding more moderate views on predestination and the means of grace. Even within this smaller grouping we should not expect cookie-cutter likenesses but rather differences from person to person. Beyond simply establishing a classification, I want to show the usefulness of such a grouping—for example, for understanding Donne's attitude toward the puritans within the church or his very positive attitude toward Calvin, of whom he always (in his sermons) writes with respect.

In his study of the early Stuart church as it relates to the Roman Catholic Church and to other Protestant churches, Milton depicts a clearly Protestant church in which those most opposed to the Roman church were the Calvinists, while their opponents—the Laudians and the avant-garde conformists—had more conciliatory attitudes toward Rome.[7] Since Donne came from a strongly Roman Catholic family background and, according to some writers (e.g., Dennis Flynn), maintained a lifelong affinity with that communion, one might have expected him in joining the English church to ally himself with the anti-Calvinists. But from what we know of Donne the churchman, he appears in actuality to have associated most closely with Calvinist churchmen like John King (who ordained him), Henry King, Archbishop George Abbot, and Thomas Mountford.[8] His known links with Laud were primarily with Laud as the bishop of London and thus his unavoidable superior in the London diocese. However, the best evidence for Donne's place in the church spectrum of his time is to be found in his own writings.

Throughout the sermons, Donne reveals that he is a conformist, a loyal supporter of the Church of England and its practices; but, as has been shown, this does not make him a member of the "avant-garde" or Laudian group.[9] Donne repeatedly preaches against "singularity" and separatism (departure from the church), conventicles (unauthorized religious gatherings),[10] extempore prayers or preaching, and unjustifiable complaints about matters merely indifferent of themselves.[11] But as Milton, Lake, and Fincham show, Calvinist clerics like John Prideaux, Robert Sanderson, and Arthur Lake similarly opposed puritan practices.[12] Previously, Archbishops Whitgift and Bancroft had combined Calvinist theological views with vigorous antipuritanism. Donne, like other non-Laudian conformists, is quite willing to enforce the rules of the church. Instead of engaging in polemical attacks, however, he regularly tries to bring nonconformists around with pastoral persuasion, and more than once he associates himself publicly with what he considers favorable aspects of puritanism, something the Laudians or their pre-1625 predecessors would never do (see below).

But what of Donne's views on predestination? Ferrell and Strier, acquainted with the recent work of church historians, both proclaim that Donne is theologically anti-Calvinist in his opposition to predestinarian teachings (Ferrell, "Donne" 61–62; Strier 99). While Strier offers no evidence for his claim, Ferrell supports hers as follows:

> Donne's dislike [for Calvin's soteriology] was concentrated upon the doctrine of predestination. Preaching on Matthew 19.17, the narrative of the rich young man, Donne declares:
> "When he enquired of Christ after salvation, Christ doth not say, There is no salvation for thee, . . . I have locked an iron doore of predestination between salvation and thee; when he enquired of him, what he should do to be sure of heaven, Christ doth not say, . . . you must look

into the eternal decree of Election first, and see whether that stand for you or no" (6:229)

Donne's objections to the doctrine of predestination are revealing. He does not reject it outright as untrue or unorthodox, but as impractical. He eschews the doctrine of election as too arbitrary to produce anything but despair; what Christ "doth not say" identifies what Donne refuses to teach. (61–62)

There are serious problems with this reading, and since they may be representative of what other readers think, they call for clarification here. First of all, Donne nowhere in the sermons rejects or even objects to the doctrine of predestination as such, which as he knows is clearly affirmed in positive form in the seventeenth of the church's Thirty-nine Articles (Church of England, *Constitutions*). Donne regards those articles as foundational to the church, not matters indifferent (Doerksen, *Conforming* 71, 75). Far from eschewing the doctrine of election in his sermons,[13] he often refers in positive terms to the elect or election (I count over sixty such references, found in all ten volumes of the Potter and Simpson edition), and at one point, in a sermon that Potter and Simpson identify as most likely preached at St. Paul's shortly after Donne was appointed dean there in 1621/22, he publicly rejoices in "the glorious Doctrine of our Election by Gods eternall Predestination" (3:377). I regard Donne as consistent and sincere, not hypocritical, in such affirmations.

Donne does indeed object to what he considers false or harmful predestinarian teaching. Ferrell is right to say that Donne has "pastoral concerns" when he treats of election here and elsewhere. He is keenly aware of the dangers of despair that Article 17 also warns against. For these reasons Donne often cautions in his sermons against concluding that one has been predestined to damnation, and in so doing he is acting more as a concerned pastor than as a debating polemist. After all, the people he is trying to help are likely right there in his congregation. Unlike Article 17, Donne specifically acknowledges reprobation by name (e.g., *Sermons* 2:319, 4:305, 5:54, 9:81), but he repeatedly and vigorously takes a stand against a supralapsarian view of it—the idea that God even before the Fall and without regard to an individual's sin decides on a person's damnation. Donne's view is sub- or infralapsarian, holding that the decree of reprobation takes into account the Fall and individual sin (see Sellin, *Donne* 12–15). Far from being an antipredestinarian or even an anti-Calvinist view, this was a significant option in English Calvinism of Donne's time. Those who chose it also included the majority at the Synod of Dort (Sellin, *Donne* 14, 32), an international gathering of Calvinist church leaders held in the Netherlands in 1618. More specifically, the Calvinist delegates that King James sent to that synod in 1618 put forward a view called "hypothetical universalism," stressing the scriptural teaching that Christ died for all men (Lake, "Calvinism" 53, 57). In a 1626 sermon before King Charles, Donne commends the "blessed sobriety" of these English delegates, who "delivered their sentence, That all men are truly, and in earnest called to eternall life, by Gods Minister; And that whatsoever is promised or offered out of the Gospel by the Minister, is to the same men, and in the same manner promised and offered . . . by God himselfe" (7:127). Donne goes on to remind his hearers of the conclusion of Article 17, which he paraphrases thus: "That we must receive Gods promises so, as they be generally set forth to us in the Scriptures; And that for our actions and manners, for our life and conversation, we follow that will of God, which is expressly declared to us in his Word." In other words, one should not try to probe into God's eternal decrees, which are hidden, but instead follow the explicit invitations and promises in the Scriptures. To view such a pastoral approach as anti-Calvinist is mistaken. One reason why Donne could feel so positive about Calvin himself is that that reformer was similarly concerned about the pastoral implications of predestinarian teaching. Calvin taught predestination because he found it expressed in the Bible and confirmed by experience, but he made the same distinction that Donne and the Thirty-nine Articles do between God's hidden eternal decrees, which are not known and should not be probed into, and the revealed will in the gospel, which is that people should repent, believe, and live the Christian life (*Inst.* 3.21.1–2).

There is also a serious problem with how Ferrell interprets the last part of her quotation from Donne, given above: "Christ doth not say . . . you must look into the eternal decree of Election first, and see whether that stand for you or no." Ferrell takes this as an implied denunciation of the style of preaching that "urged hearers to examine their lives for signs of election rather than to trust divine guidance in matters of salvation" (62). Donne would not have pitted the one against the other; instead, much like Calvin (*Inst.* 3.21.1–2), he is cautioning against dangerous curiosity and rash or prideful speculation about the decrees. Donne agrees with Calvin (3.24.4) about the right and wrong ways to attain confidence in one's election. The right way is not to think about the decrees in themselves, apart from Scripture or experience, but instead "I looke upon Gods Decrees, in the *execution* of those Decrees, and I try whether I be within that Decree of Election, or no, by *examining my selfe, whether the marks of the Elect be upon me, or no*, and so I appropriate the wisdom of the Scripture to my selfe" (3:331, emphasis added).

The Church of England in Article 17 declares the beneficial value of good predestinarian teaching: the "godly consideration of Predestination, and our Election in Christ is full of sweet,[14] pleasant, and unspeakable comfort to godly persons, and such as feel in themselves the working of the Spirit of Christ, mortifying the works of the flesh ... and drawing up their mind to high and heavenly things, as well because it doth greatly establish and confirm their faith ..., as because it doth fervently kindle their love towards God." Donne's positive preaching on election fits well with these goals of reaping the benefits of predestination even in the earthly life. While the language of Article 17 and of Donne on such matters may sound puritan to some ears, this does not necessarily put Donne into the camp of the puritan "experimental predestinarians" of whom R. T. Kendall writes, since neither Donne nor Calvin deals significantly with William Perkins's doctrine of temporary faith (Kendall 67–76). There is, however, significant common ground. Identifying the "marks" of election is a *pastoral* response to the apostle Peter's advice to "give diligence to make your calling and election sure, for if ye do these things, ye shall never fall" (2 Pet. 1:10).

It is as a pastor and not as a polemist that Donne preaches on the marks of election, not just for the puritan-loving benchers of Lincoln's Inn (2:323–24) but on prominent public occasions where it can bring appropriate comfort. In a sermon before the court at Denmark House just after the death of King James I, Donne tells his hearers that they can discover the "marks" of election "in a rectified conscience, in thy selfe." They will then find comfort in knowing that "no murmuring at Gods corrections, no disappointing of thy hopes, ... no *impatience in sicknesse*, and in the agony of death, can deface those marks" (6:286). At St. Paul's on Christmas Day 1625, Donne ends his sermon by asking who are the "elect of God," and replying (in part), "He that departs so far, as to repent former sinnes, and shut up the wayes, which he knows in his conscience, doe lead him into tentations, he is of this *quorum*, one of us, one of them, who are adopted by Christ, to be the sonnes of God" (6:347).[15] At Magdalen Danvers's commemoration service in 1627, Donne assures his listeners that "*Wee* are they, who have seene the markes of [God's] *Election*, in their first *edition*, in the Scriptures; and seene them againe, in their second *edition*, as they are imprinted in our *consciences*, in our *faith*, in our *manners;* and so *wee* cannot mistake, nor bee deceived in them" (8:70). As late as Easter Day 1630, Donne tells his St. Paul's congregation that it is not possible for death to hold him, "because God hath afforded me the marks of his Election"

(9:204). (Earlier in this same sermon Donne mentions Calvin four times.) As frequently in the sermons, Donne in speaking in the first person is modeling a stance that he invites his hearers to share.[16]

While Donne is aware of the controversy that predestinarian teaching has provoked in some quarters of the English church, and consequently is vigilant to warn against the dangers of false teaching or emphases,[17] he personally responds positively, especially to the assurance that the doctrines of grace provide.[18] It is notable that Donne asserts a "modest infallibility" of assurance in both his first and last known sermons. In a 1615 sermon, which Potter and Simpson consider the first we have from Donne, he speaks of God's restoring his image in us in "our conformity to him" until we come "to that transmutation, . . . which is a modest, but infalible assurance of a final perseverance." This, Donne says, "is the ladder, by which we may try, how far we are in the way to heaven" (1:164; see also 167). In his final sermon, "Deaths Duell," delivered at Whitehall before King Charles in 1631, Donne dares to speak of election, although one year earlier Bishop John Davenant had been brought before the Privy Council and rebuked by the Laudian bishops present for doing exactly the same thing—touching on the forbidden topic of predestination in a sermon before the king! (Doerksen, *Conforming* 41–42 and n. 25). Midway through his sermon, Donne alludes to the decrees:

> We looke no further for *causes* or *reasons* in the *mysteries of religion*, but to the *will* and pleasure of *God*. . . . The humble soule (and onely the humble soule is the religious soule) rests himselfe upon *Gods* purposes, and his decrees . . . which he hath declared and manifested. . . . *Gods decrees* are ever to be considered in the *manifestation* thereof. All *manifestation* is either in the *word* of *God*, or in the *execution* of the *decree;* And when these two concur and meete, it is the strongest *demonstration* that can be: when therefore I finde those *markes* of *adoption* . . . which are delivered in the *word* of *God*, to be upon me, when I finde that reall *execution* of his *good purpose* upon me, as that *actually* I doe *live* under the *obedience*, and under the *conditions* which are *evidences* of *adoption* . . . ; then, and so long as I see these *markes* and live so, I may safely comfort my selfe in a *holy certitude* and a *modest infallibility* of my *adoption*. (10:237)

Donne may have guarded his language a little, referring to "adoption" rather than "election," but the meaning is unmistakable, reflecting his own clearly predestinarian views, applied as they were intended to be in Article 17. Like Bishop Arthur Lake and Dort delegate Samuel Ward (Lake,

"Calvinism" 54–60), Donne is a *moderate* predestinarian, a moderate Calvinist.

Amid general agreement, Donne has some points of difference with Calvin on this topic. One is that he does not agree with Calvin's supralapsarian assertions, even though they are qualified by insistence on God's justice, however inscrutable (*Inst.* 3.23.4). Also, whereas Calvin interprets 1 Timothy 2:3–4, which announces that God wills all men to be saved, as applying to orders and nations rather than strictly to all people, Donne disagrees. He says those who would thus restrict God's general propositions in Matthew 11:28 and 1 Timothy 2:4 are "too good husbands, and too thrifty of God's grace" (5:53).[19] Nevertheless, as Donne doubtless knew, Calvin regularly prayed for the salvation of all people,[20] and Kendall documents from the commentaries that reformer's strongly held view that Christ died for all (14). And when Donne says "no man can say to another, God meanes not thee, no man can say to himselfe, God meanes not me" (5:53), he is in accord with Calvin, who expresses a pastoral concern about the fit way to teach about election and specifically counsels against, in effect, cursing those not sure of their faith. Both Donne and Calvin agree with Augustine's saying that "as we know not who belongs to the number of the predestined or who does not belong, we ought to be so minded as to wish that all men be saved" (*Inst.* 3.23.14).

In dealing with English Calvinism, one should avoid certain misconceptions. One of these is that it consists only, or even chiefly, of predestinarian teaching, or (worse yet) of only *extreme* predestinarianism. Nicholas Tyacke's research into anti-Calvinism was a very important study, clearing some ground; however, it assumed too simply that predestination was *central* to Calvinism and that there were only two positions on Calvinism: pro and con. Tyacke (182, 261) calls Donne an Arminian on the basis of only two passages that oppose extreme or faulty predestinarianism. Anthony Milton's *Catholic and Reformed* is much more satisfying in suggesting a range of views and some changes of views among Calvinist conformists (407–26). Scholars of Calvin himself, such as François Wendel (357–58), have pointed out that neither predestination nor presbyterian order is central in Calvin's teaching but that instead he strove primarily to be a biblical expositor, focusing on what God has done for us through Christ. Calvin was influential not only by means of the *Institutes* but also through the many sermons and commentaries on most parts of the Bible, which were well circulated in England, both in English and in their original Latin and French. Donne knew of these other works, such as the sermons on Job (4:207), not just the *Institutes,* and doubtless consulted some of them. Both on the Continent and in England, Calvinism was a movement of the learned, and its high regard for the Bible (and preaching) included attention to the literary aspects of Scripture, something Donne also cares deeply about.

On predestination, too, one must not assume that English Calvinism was inflexible. Although Beza and other followers of Calvin (e.g., Perkins) notoriously narrowed and rigidified[21] Calvin's teachings, people such as George Hakewill, a royal chaplain with links to Donne and George Abbot (Shami, "Pulpit Crisis" 8–9), could accept Calvin's own writings as authoritative in the Church of England without regarding them as a straitjacket. Acknowledging Calvin's mere humanity, his being subject to error and frailty, Hakewill nevertheless expresses great respect for this "chief Captaine in the Lords battailes." The English, he says, "maintaine nothing with him because he affirmes it, but because from infallible grounds [the Scriptures] he proves it." They "imbrace *Caluin* as himselfe doth authors not diuine . . . so farre foorth as with diuine hee accordeth, and no farther" (285, 135). This is exactly the spirit in which Donne and other Calvinist conformists (though not some puritans, perhaps) accept the writings of Calvin, and why Donne can recognize Calvin's excellence as a biblical commentator, praise the reformer's undogmatic attitudes, and occasionally differ with him (*Sermons* 3:177, 10:128, 6:301, 7:286, 8:359).[22]

One might ask, if Donne really is a part of English Calvinism, why does he not say so more clearly? Similarly, why did not more church leaders like Hakewill or Bishop Anthony Rudd (also known to Donne)[23] overtly acknowledge the theology of the English church to be Calvinist? In part the answer is that any kind of such labeling was accepted only under protest. Calvin himself objected to "Calvinism" as a label (Prestwich 2), and Donne on occasion wishes that all labels except that of "Christian" could be done away with (*Sermons* 2:111–12, 7:310). Yet because labels are useful, Donne employs them too, as in locating the English between the continental Lutheran and Calvinist churches in terms of ceremony (8:331). And in a sermon preached "to the Earle of Carlile, and his Company, at Sion," the residence of the earl of Northumberland, which Potter and Simpson date in 1622, Donne apparently accepts the designation of "Calvinists" as applying to "us," the Church of England (5:255). While Calvin obviously was not a founder of the English church, it is nevertheless true that a Reformed theology that can conveniently be called Calvinism eventually dominated its leadership in the later Elizabethan and early Stuart years. This included not only soteriology (aspects of which were the doctrines of grace, including predestination) but also a generally similar set of views on the Scriptures and the sacraments.[24] For instance, Calvin's views on infant baptism were very welcome in England, and his views of the Lord's Supper were seen as closer to those of the English than were those of the Lutheran churches (Milton 383–86) or of Zwingli.

Donne's attitudes toward the churches of the Reformation are typical of those church leaders now called Calvinist conformists. Like all members of his church, he knows it to be Protestant, but while the Laudians minimize or regret this (Milton 377–78),[25] Donne joyfully acknowledges it, calling the Reformation a deliverance, a victory, a glorious ascent, a miracle, one of the mercies of God (10:142, 9:348, 10:52, 6:158, 8:302). Like other Calvinist conformists, Donne in 1619 expresses his concerns for the fortunes of the continental Reformed churches (2:248–49),[26] and in 1627 he speaks at St. Paul's of the need for a Christian king to care about other kingdoms as well as his own, and the establishing of "Religion abroad too" (8:117). Very much unlike the Laudians,[27] Donne views favorably England's participation in the Synod of Dort, a gathering of Calvinist churches.[28]

Now to the topic of Donne's polemics. We should first note that as a rule Donne the preacher refrains from making polemical attacks on Luther, Calvin, or the continental Protestant churches, though he is aware of their differences from the English church and at times points them out. By contrast, as Potter and Simpson have noticed, "A very large number of Donne's sermons contain controversial passages against the Church of Rome" (10:14n. 32). Donne repeatedly refers to the latter as the "enemy" or the "adversaries."[29] The reason for the difference cannot be that Donne is simply trying to ingratiate himself with the "powers that be" in the English church, because at times he makes such attacks on Rome when King James or Bishop Laud would not desire them.[30] Instead, I would argue that Donne has completely and wholeheartedly become a member of the Church of England and views matters largely as his fellow Calvinist conformists see them. Of course, he brings with him much that he has earlier learned as a member of a Roman Catholic family and as a lifelong searcher for religious truth.[31] Recognizing where Donne belongs in his church should open some new avenues of inquiry without closing others that have been proven useful.

In a recent essay, Jeanne Shami[32] takes a somewhat different position, claiming for Donne an "ongoing relationship with the Church of Rome" (137). She rightly credits Donne with a "deliberate and carefully chosen style of divinity" (138)—here consistent with what Helen Gardner, citing the preface to *Pseudo-Martyr*, claims (xviii). Donne is not one, Shami says, who "forgoes principled religious choices," "wears his religion lightly as his 'lifestyle,'" or advocates "blind and implicit obedience" (140). These are all reasons that can support my view of Donne as someone who on careful consideration of "the whole body of Divinity, controverted betweene ours and the Romane Church," decisively turned from his "previous impressions" of Rome and accepted the Church of England ("ours").[33] Such a responsible choice, not involving a loss of Christian faith, need not be labeled with the odious term "apostasy."[34] Donne, by the way, was like *all* the English and continental reformers (except the Anabaptists) in regarding his baptism into the small-c catholic church as valid.[35] Though the changeover process took a considerable time and was marked by struggles such as those pictured in some of the *Holy Sonnets*, the writings of Donne after his ordination in 1615 reflect a man who has reached a mature confidence in having made the right choice. The sermons show us a very human Donne but not (here I agree with Shami) a hypocrite or mere timeserver. Of course, accepting a position in the church and fully supporting its Protestant position did not necessitate a renouncing of friendships such as with the duke of Northumberland, and certainly not an unfilial treatment of his aging mother, even if she persisted in recusancy. Donne's advice in a 1625 sermon may reflect his attitude toward his mother: in families there should be peace, "mutuall support of one anothers infirmities," and the composing and determining of "all emergent differences" "within doores" (6:255, 259).[36]

Shami's essay sheds some significant light on the topic of "anti-Catholicism" in the sermons. Thus, she reminds us (with Anthony Milton) of the complexities of the spectrum of views within the Church of England and the polemical nature of much of the religious language used at this time (137–38)—though she goes too far in suggesting that antipapal rhetoric was "rarely a statement of belief" (139). She points to evidence linking Donne with Abbot, Hall, and the "conforming Calvinist consensus" rather than with promoters of the avant-garde (138). She brings in a great deal of detail, demonstrating some of the main features of Donne's anti-Roman pronouncements, as in his focus on the Council of Trent and the Jesuits. She faithfully reports some of Donne's severest comments but also aptly calls attention to his "technique of redefining his terms so that they lose their polemical baggage, and are understood in their spirit as well as their letter" (150). And she is right to recognize Donne's "irenical" impulse, his desire to "mitigate the consequences of destructive religious warfare" (141)

All these points are well supported, but Shami's arguments against Donne's complete conversion from Rome are unconvincing. One problem is that the authorities she cites, such as Flynn and Hester, have actually little to say about Donne the Church of England priest and dean, let alone offering proofs of his commitment to Roman Catholicism in that stage of his life.[37] Another problem is that in frequently shortening "Roman Catholic" to simply "Catholic," Shami does not carefully distinguish Donne's use of "catholique" (in the sense of "universal") from his references to the Roman church. With only a few exceptions (3:128, 179), Donne employs the term to refer to the universal church, as in the creed regularly recited at morning prayer, according to the Book of Common Prayer, and he specifically rejects the claims of Rome to be *the* Catholic church (2:280). To avoid confusion, writers about the English church should follow the admirable practice of Anthony Milton in always clearly distinguishing references to the universal church from those to the Roman Catholic communion.[38] While "Catholic" is handy modern parlance for "Roman Catholic," in dealing with Donne and his contemporaries, its use can cause unrecognized confusion and even faulty argument. Like all great Christians, including Calvin, Donne cares deeply for the universal church.[39] In becoming a convert to the English church, which Donne himself knew to be Protestant, he of course continued in his loyalty to the universal church, of which he and his fellow church members considered the Roman church also to be a part, though a diseased one.[40]

"We must not proceed alike with friends and with enemies," Donne approvingly quotes Luther as saying (3:144). Donne's clearly distinguishing himself and his church from Rome has important consequences. While King James, as a monarch thinking politically, chose to regard papists and puritans as virtually equal threats to his rule, Calvinist religious leaders like Donne knew that papists (as recusants) put themselves outside the Church of England, while most of those considered puritan shared the doctrinal position of the Thirty-nine Articles and were fellow church members. Following the lead of King James, Donne sometimes pairs the handily alliterated terms. Significantly, though, on two occasions when he refers to "puritan" in this way as a polemical term, first in an early Lincoln's Inn sermon and then in a 1630 discourse before Charles I, he counsels *against* the use of either "puritan" or "papist" as a label to "defame" devout church members (2:58, 9:214). When referring to those *outside* the Church of England, consistent with his views, Donne does not have the same scruples. He employs plenty of polemical ammunition against the Church of Rome, but the people at the other extreme whom he similarly feels free to attack are the separatists or schismatics—that is, not simply "nonconformists"[41] within the church but those who have actually broken away from the church, either forming conventicles or physically departing from England in order to make such a separation.[42]

In a Paul's Cross sermon of 1616/17 preached "to the Lords of the Council, and other Honorable Persons, . . . It being the Anniversary of the

Kings coming to the Crown, and his Majesty being then gone to Scotland," Donne spoke on a text from Proverbs: "He that loveth pureness of heart, for the grace of his lips, the king shall be his friend" (1:183). One can imagine what an anti-Calvinist, strongly antipuritan polemist like Andrewes would have made of this "political" situation. Donne does indeed raise the issue of puritanism, but he attaches the term "puritan" first to Catharists, surprisingly identified as Roman Catholics; second to modern Cathari, hypocrites and refusers of the Lord's Prayer (insincere and nonconforming puritans who earn the disapproving name); and third to devout, conscientious people within the church, falsely accused by that name.[43] With the third group, whom we could recognize as conforming puritans (these would include people like his father-in-law, Sir George More, or Thomas Adams, who in 1623 dedicated his published Paul's Cross sermon *The Barren Tree* to his patrons, Donne and the prebendaries of St. Paul's Cathedral),[44] Donne gladly identifies (though I do not claim he was actually one of them, only that he was aware of the strong bond between them and moderate conformists like himself). For the first and second groups he advises not vituperation but leaving "no such means untryed, as may work upon their Understandings, and remove their just scruples" (1:186)—and only after that applying sterner means. The first section (more than half) of this long sermon consists of an insightful and searching analysis of moral purity that would delight at the same time as it challenged true puritans within the church. Donne's warnings, as about the danger of hypocrisy, should not be seen (in Potter and Simpson's term) as "attacks" (1:127) but rather recognized as helpful admonitions in which the preacher includes himself: "Our heart is naturally foul; And our heart may be cleansed" (1:191). In approaching people within his church not by polemics but in pastoral concern, Donne differs significantly from the approach Ferrell attributes to the anti-Calvinist court preachers. Specifically, this sermon directly counters Ferrell's claim that the term "puritan" "was unequivocally a term of abuse when broadcast from the official pulpits of Jacobean England" (*Polemic* 16). According to Ferrell, the anti-Calvinists were not interested in sorting out good from bad puritans, but instead were quite willing to lump Calvinist conformists in with the bad lot (140–41). If "James's England [was not] a haven for religious consensus, but . . . the rhetorical laboratory for the development of an increasingly powerful and strident anti-Reformation politics," as Ferrell claims (6), then Donne obviously worked for that consensus and directly against such a development.

Donne is a great and distinctive writer, certainly also distinctive in coming from a strongly Roman Catholic family background, but that should not stop us from recognizing where this author of the *Sermons* belongs on the spectrum of views and positions in the English church. Laud, I would suggest, as his immediate superior in London, did clearly perceive that Donne was not a Laudian. As Milton says, "this was a group perceptible both to themselves and to outsiders" (9). That is surely the main reason why this outstanding and eligible churchman—a former prolocutor of Convention and a royal chaplain "in ordinary" belonging to the very group from which such appointments were made—was not named a bishop[45] at a time when, as Fincham demonstrates, Charles I created "one churchman, Laud, as privileged adviser to the king on clerical promotions" ("Laud and Patronage" 92). Although fully loyal to the Church of England, Donne was a part of the Calvinist consensus that first the avant-garde and then the Laudians sought to undermine and destroy.

In his excellent study of the "Religious Politics of the Mean," Joshua Scodel calls Donne's "middle way" between "the Arminians and their 'Puritan' critics" "unique" (67). It was *not*, however, unique, but shared by moderate Calvinist conformists like Bishop Arthur Lake, not to mention Donne's friends George Abbot and Joseph Hall. These were church leaders who were more concerned with what Fincham (*Prelate* 250) calls the ideal of the preaching pastor than with being custodians of external order (Doerksen, "Preaching Pastor"). Unlike the Laudians, Donne reserved his polemics for people outside the Church of England—Rome and the separatists—and exercised pastoral care in his sermons for those within the church who differed from his understandings of what the church should be like. It is to be hoped that more Donne scholars will, like Jeanne Shami, pay attention to those conformists (and even conforming puritans like Thomas Gataker) with whom, in the Church of England, Donne's true affinities lay.

Notes

1. All my references to "Milton" in this essay are to current historian Anthony Milton, not to John Milton, the seventeenth-century writer. See also Tyacke; Collinson 81–82; Lake, "Calvinism"; Fincham, *Stuart Church* 3–13; and Ferrell, *Polemic*. White offers a contrasting opinion, to an earlier version of which Lake responds; for an analysis of problems with White's full study, see my *Conforming* 142n. 23 and my review of White's book. Milton and Lake emphasize the instability and imply inevitable change. Like other writers on this topic (e.g., Lake, "Calvinism" 33–34), I concentrate on church leadership, ignoring possibly large numbers of indifferent people or recusants.

2. See Donne, *Sermons* 2:111; and my *Conforming* 112.

3. Milton promises a "detailed analysis of individual positions, and of the personal and polemical situations which shaped them" (6), but this has not yet appeared.

4. E.g., George and George 68–69 and Scodel 60–70. Scodel prefers to call Donne's views Augustinian, a designation that, though obviously correct, does not fit Donne very precisely into the English church situation of his time.

5. He also refers to the communion table as an altar in his 1626 St. Paul's Christmas Day sermon (7:286), but his advocacy of the priesthood of all believers at this point is not at all Laudian.

6. See Doerksen and Hodgkins, *Centered on the Word*, which has four essays on Donne. Achsah Guibbory, in *Ceremony and Community from Herbert to Milton*, interestingly studies the tensions between puritanism and ceremonialism but seems to eclipse the moderate Calvinist option, especially that of conformists. Thus she tends to see opposing tendencies in George Herbert as ultimately "contradictory" (78) rather than effectively balanced. I would claim that Donne the preacher, though feeling the pressures around him, was firm and consistent in his own integrative understanding of the relationship of Word and sacrament.

7. See Milton 10, 3–35, 52–55, 59, 63–72.

8. Shami, "Pulpit Crisis" 8–10; Doerksen, *Conforming* 14–15, 54. This is not to say he had no friends who were Laudians: one was the future Laudian bishop Brian Duppa.

9. Potter and Simpson called Donne an "Anglo-Catholic" (which I take to be roughly equivalent) because of his opposition to puritan practices and teachings and in spite of his anti-Roman writings (1:113), probably because they assumed his writings demonstrated he was anti-Calvinist.

10. Such gatherings were perhaps just as likely to be Roman Catholic as puritan—see McCullough 74.

11. See, e.g., 2:279–81, 7:61, and 10:174.

12. Milton 326; Lake, "Sanderson"; Fincham, *Prelate* 260–61.

13. See Papazian, "Donne, Election, and the *Devotions Upon Emergent Occasions*," esp. 604–13. Sellin (*Donne* 1–2) claims that Donne did not fully reveal his theological orientation in his preaching because (among other reasons) clergy were forbidden by royalty from "meddling in controverted points" of religion.

14. The word "sweet" echoes Calvin's reference to "the very sweet fruit" of this doctrine (*Inst.* 3.21.1).

15. Donne here, as elsewhere, equates election and adoption. So does Calvin (*Inst.* 3.24.1).

16. Donne also refers elsewhere to the marks of election, e.g., 6:286, 6:347–48, 9:204, 8:70.

17. Nicholas Tyacke's citation (261) of a sermon in which Donne warns

against a false sense of security is thus not an example of anti-Calvinism. Donne's caution against presumption may usefully be compared with Calvin (*Inst.* 3.23.12). Calvin, like Donne, knew the doctrine could be abused by antinomians.

18. See also Narveson 113, who deals with assurance but dissociates Donne from what she considers the puritan emphasis on "marks of faith." She seems unaware here that Robert Hill, whom she cites as being like Donne, was a conforming puritan (Doerksen, *Conforming* 55–56, 59).

19. Note that Donne chooses not to name Calvin, whereas if he were an anti-Calvinist he might, like the later Laudians, delight in doing so (Milton 429–33).

20. See, e.g., Calvin's sermons on Job, the English translation of which went through four editions. Donne knows of this work, in which each sermon ends in a prayer that includes a petition for all men.

21. One of those more "rigid" followers of the more flexible Calvin was Johannes Piscator (Fischer). In citing him twice in a sermon, Donne identifies him as belonging to "the most rigid sub-division of the Reformation" (8:144), but later (151) he notes the distinction between him and Calvin in this respect. Sellin points out that the English delegates at the Synod of Dort "worked for the condemnation of the expressions" of Piscator (*Donne* 8).

22. Jeffrey Johnson points out both many similarities between Donne and Calvin and also some differences (such as Donne's threefold division of the soul, including memory, following Augustine, and his strenuous denial of supralapsarianism). However, see my review of this book in *Renaissance and Reformation*, which notes some inaccurate terminology and contextual misreadings.

23. See Bald 69–70 for the Donne connection and Milton 397 for Rudd's acknowledgment of English Calvinism.

24. On similarities between the approaches of Calvin, Donne, and the English Protestants to the sacraments, see DiPasquale 12–14.

25. John Cosin even reportedly derided the Reformation as a "Deformation" (Doerksen, *Conforming* 41, and n. 23).

26. The occasion here is Donne's Sermon of Valediction on his going to Germany, preached at Lincoln's Inn on April 18, 1619. Cf. Milton 400, 402. See also Shami, "Pulpit Crisis" 8–9, and Papazian, "Donne and the Thirty Years' War."

27. Cf. Milton 421–22, 429–30.

28. In fact, Sellin argues that Donne evidently "accepted Reformed ministry and Calvinist ordination as valid, . . . considered national synods called by the Reformed church as binding, [and] expected Presbyterian ministers [on the Continent] to conform to synodal decisions" ("*So Doth*" 172–73).

29. The term "enemy" or forms of it occur a hundred times in the Psalms, frequently recited or read in the English church. Both terms are mentioned in the Second Collect for Peace, in the service for morning prayer (Booty 59–60).

30. E.g., Sellin, "*So Doth*" 169.

31. One example of a legacy from his earlier days might be his use of the Vulgate in all ten volumes of his sermons. Donne's choice of targets within the Roman Catholic Church, such as the Jesuits (Shami, "Anti-Catholicism" 145), may result in part from his earlier Roman Catholic experiences as well as, of course, from his pre-preaching days spent on anti-Roman controversial writing.

32. "Anti-Catholicism in the Sermons of John Donne." I thank Jeanne Shami for supplying me with an advance copy of this essay and also for some useful discussions of matters in her essays and mine.

33. Quoted from *Pseudo-Martyr* 13.

34. See Flynn, "Donne the Survivor" (15), where use of the term is attributed to John Carey, *John Donne: Life, Mind, and Art*, and to Roman Catholics responding to Donne's conversion. Unlike Flynn, I would take "apostasy" not as a theological term, implying "denial of God's revelation," but in the modern dictionary definition as the "renunciation of a religious faith." To my mind the word nowadays does not connote "vague disapproval," as Flynn suggests, but instead implies desertion, becoming a turncoat.

35. In his will written within a few years of Donne's birth (Bald 560), Donne's father describes himself as "a parisheon*er*" of the Church of England "Saint Nicholas Olive in Bredstreat," and it is most likely that John was baptized there. Donne is therefore not inconsistent in a Lincoln's Inn sermon, when in an anti-Roman passage he counsels, "Let none divorce himself from that religion . . . which he embraced in his Baptism" (3:129).

36. One may also compare Donne's attitude toward other English Roman Catholics, such as in his preaching against recusancy to Queen Anne of Denmark (see McCullough) and his somewhat daring allusion in a sermon to King Charles to the religion of his queen (7:409). On the latter see also Scodel 68–69. All of these are consistent with a completely Protestant, moderate Calvinist outlook on Donne's part.

37. Flynn's biographical studies deal mainly with the early life of Donne and deliberately involve conjectures; Hester's cited works concentrate on Elegy XIX and on the satires, which Hester dates in the 1590s.

38. Unlike Shami and a number of other writers, including Dennis Flynn, Milton almost never describes the Roman Catholics as simply "Catholics," instead often referring to Rome or the Church of Rome. The title of Milton's book, therefore, refers not to the alternatives outside the Church of England but to the nature of the church itself (5). Shami (163n. 8) explains that she has avoided the term "papist" in her essay title because of its polemical resonances, but she nevertheless usefully employs it elsewhere. Even her title is potentially confusing, because Donne never was "anti-catholic" in the sense of "opposed to the universal church."

39. In the Apostle's Creed, Donne, like Augustine and Calvin, prefers the wording "I beleeve the holy Catholique Church" to the other possible reading, "I believe in . . . The holy Catholick Church" (5:249; cf. Booty 58 and *Inst.* 4.1.2).

40. Cf. Milton 378–79. Shami claims that for Donne "the Church of Rome is a true Church" (158). What Donne actually says at the point she cites is that Rome is "truly a Church," just as a "Pest-house is a house"—a significantly different statement (9:344).

41. Shami's equation of separatists with "nonconforming divines" ("Anti-Catholicism" 150) is inaccurate. Donne and his fellow churchmen (see Milton 326) regard forsaking the church as a much more serious matter than refusing (because of conscience) to comply with some of its nonscriptural rituals.

42. Therefore Shami should rephrase her language in speaking of "*internal* threats posed by the more radical separatist *wing of the Church of England*" ("Anti-Catholicism," 162, emphasis added).

43. On p. 189 Donne somewhat muddles his threefold classification by putting modern contentious puritans in with the first group.

44. Doerksen, *Conforming* 20, 56; Bald 394. See also Friedman.

45. Shami comments on Donne's being prolocutor and his not being named bishop in her forthcoming essay, "Labels, Controversy, and the Language of Inclusion in Donne's Sermons."

Works Cited

Bald, R. C. *John Donne: A Life.* Oxford: Clarendon, 1970.
Booty, John, ed. *The Book of Common Prayer 1559.* Charlottesville: UP of Virginia, 1976.
Calvin, John. *Institutes of the Christian Religion.* Ed. John T. McNeill, trans. F. L. Battles. 2 vols. Philadelphia: Westminster, 1960.
———. *Sermons of Master Iohn Calvin, vpon the Booke of Iob.* Trans. Arthur Golding. N.p., 1574.
Carey, John. *John Donne: Life, Mind, and Art.* New York: Oxford UP, 1981.
Church of England. *The Constitutions and Canons Ecclesiastical. To Which Are Added The Thirty-Nine Articles . . .* London: S.P.C.K., 1908.
Collinson, Patrick. *The Religion of Protestants: The Church in English Society, 1559–1625.* Oxford: Clarendon, 1982.
DiPasquale, Theresa. *Literature and Sacrament: The Sacred and the Secular in John Donne.* Pittsburgh: Duquesne UP, 1999.
Doerksen, Daniel W. *Conforming to the Word: Herbert, Donne, and the English Church before Laud.* Lewisburg, PA: Bucknell UP, 1997.

———. "Preaching Pastor versus Custodian of Order: Donne, Andrewes, and the Jacobean Church." *Philological Quarterly* 73 (1994): 417–29.

———. Review of Jeffrey Johnson's *The Theology of John Donne*. *Renaissance and Reformation* 24.1 (2000): 100–102.

———. Review of Peter White's *Predestination, Policy, and Polemic: Conflict and Consensus in the English Church from the Reformation to the Civil War*. *Seventeenth-Century News* 51 (1993): 54–55.

Doerksen, Daniel W., and Christopher Hodgkins, eds. *Centered on the Word: Literature, Scripture, and the Tudor-Stuart Middle Way*. Newark: U of Delaware P, 2003 (forthcoming).

Donne, John. *Devotions Upon Emergent Occasions*. Ed. Anthony Raspa. McGill-Queens UP, 1975.

———. *Pseudo-Martyr*. Ed. Anthony Raspa. Montreal: McGill-Queen's UP, 1993.

———. *Sermons*. Ed. George R. Potter and Evelyn M. Simpson. 10 vols. Berkeley: U of California P, 1953–62.

Ferrell, Lori Anne. "Donne and His Master's Voice, 1615–1625." *John Donne Journal* 11 (1992): 59–70.

———. *Government by Polemic: James I, the King's Preachers, and the Rhetorics of Conformity, 1603–1625*. Stanford: Stanford UP, 1998.

Fincham, Kenneth, ed. *The Early Stuart Church, 1603–1642*. Stanford: Stanford UP, 1993.

———. *Prelate as Pastor: The Episcopate of James I*. Oxford: Clarendon, 1990.

———. "William Laud and the Exercise of Caroline Ecclesiastical Patronage." *Journal of Ecclesiastical History* 51 (2000): 69–93.

Flynn, Dennis. "Donne the Survivor." *The Eagle and the Dove: Reassessing John Donne*. Ed. Claude J. Summers and Ted-Larry Pebworth. Columbia: U of Missouri P, 1986. 15–24.

———. *John Donne and the Ancient Catholic Nobility*. Bloomington: Indiana UP, 1995.

Friedman, Donald M. "Thomas Adams and John Donne." *Notes and Queries* n.s. 23 (1976): 229–30.

Gardner, Helen, ed. *John Donne: The Divine Poems*. Corr. ed. Oxford: Clarendon, 1959.

George, Charles H., and Katherine George. *The Protestant Mind of the English Reformation, 1570–1640*. Princeton: Princeton UP, 1961.

Guibbory, Achsah. *Ceremony and Community from Herbert to Milton: Literature, Religion, and Cultural Conflict in Seventeenth-Century England*. Cambridge: Cambridge UP, 1998.

Hakewill, George. *An Answere to a Treatise written by Dr. Carier*. London, 1616.

Johnson, Jeffrey. *The Theology of John Donne*. Cambridge, Eng.: D. S. Brewer, 1999.
Kendall, R. T. *Calvin and English Calvinism to 1649*. Oxford: Oxford UP, 1979.
Lake, Peter [P. G.]. "Calvinism and the English Church 1570–1635." *Past and Present* 114 (1987): 32–76.
———. "Serving God and the Times: The Calvinist Conformity of Robert Sanderson." *Journal of British Studies* 27 (1988): 81–116.
McCullough, Peter. "Preaching to a Court Papist? Donne's Sermon Before Queene Anne, December 1617." *John Donne Journal* 14 (1995): 59–81.
Milton, Anthony. *Catholic and Reformed: The Roman and Protestant Churches in English Protestant Thought, 1600–1640*. Cambridge: Cambridge UP, 1995.
Narveson, Kate. "Piety and the Genre of Donne's *Devotions*." *John Donne Journal* 17 (1998): 107–36.
Norbrook, David. "The Monarchy of Wit and the Republic of Letters: Donne's Politics." *Soliciting Interpretation: Literary Theory and Seventeenth-Century English Poetry*. Ed. Elizabeth D. Harvey and Katharine Eisaman Maus. Chicago: U of Chicago P, 1990. 3–36.
Papazian, Mary A. "Donne, Election, and the *Devotions Upon Emergent Occasions*." *Huntington Library Quarterly* 55.4 (1992): 603–19.
———. "John Donne and the Thirty Years' War." *John Donne Journal* 19 (2000): 235–66.
Potter and Simpson. See Donne, *Sermons*.
Prestwich, Menna, ed. *International Calvinism, 1541–1715*. Oxford: Clarendon, 1985.
Scodel, Joshua. "John Donne and the Religious Politics of the Mean." *John Donne's Religious Imagination: Essays in Honor of John T. Shawcross*. Ed. Raymond-Jean Frontain and Frances M. Malpezzi. Conway: U of Central Arkansas P, 1995. 45–80.
Sellin, Paul. *John Donne and "Calvinist" Views of Grace*. Amsterdam: VU Boekhandel, 1983.
———. *"So Doth, So Is Religion": John Donne and Diplomatic Contexts in the Reformed Netherlands, 1619–1620*. Columbia: U of Missouri P, 1988.
Shami, Jeanne. "Anti-Catholicism in the Sermons of John Donne." *The English Sermon Revised: Religion, Literature and History 1600–1650*. Ed. Lori Anne Ferrell and Peter McCullough. Manchester: Manchester UP, 2000. 136–66.
———. "Labels, Controversy, and the Language of Inclusion in the Sermons." *John Donne's Professional Lives*. Ed. David Colclough. Cambridge: D. S. Brewer, 2003. 135–57.
———. "'The Stars in their Order Fought Against Sisera': John Donne and the Pulpit Crisis of 1622." *John Donne Journal* 14 (1995): 1–58.

Strier, Richard. "Donne and the Politics of Devotion." *Religion, Literature, and Politics in Post-Reformation England, 1540–1688*. Ed. Donna B. Hamilton and Richard Strier. Cambridge: Cambridge UP, 1996. 93–114.

Tyacke, Nicholas. *Anti-Calvinists: The Rise of English Arminianism c. 1590–1640*. Oxford: Clarendon, 1987.

Wendel, François. *Calvin: The Origins and Development of His Religious Thought*. Trans. Philip Mairet. London: Collins, 1963.

White, Peter. *Predestination, Policy, and Polemic: Conflict and Consensus in the English Church from the Reformation to the Civil War*. Cambridge: Cambridge UP, 1992.

2

"Speaking Openly and Speaking First"

John Donne, the Synod of Dort, and the Early Stuart Church

JEANNE SHAMI

On February 7, 1626, the clergy of the province of Canterbury met in Convocation at Westminster Abbey and elected John Donne to the position of prolocutor, the official representative of the lower house to the upper house of the Convocation. On Wednesday, February 8, Donne delivered a Latin oration to the full Convocation, to which Dr. Leonard Mawe, master of Peterhouse, Cambridge, responded. In the absence of the archbishop of Canterbury (George Abbot) and the bishop of London (George Montaigne), Dr. Samuel Harsnett, bishop of Norwich, responded to the speeches by Mawe and Donne. An eyewitness evaluated the entire event. Little significance, however, has been attached to this information.[1] R. C. Bald, Donne's modern biographer, knew only of Donne's oration, which was first published in the 1650 *Poems*, and he included it as appendix D, part VII, of *John Donne: A Life* (573–75). Bald describes the oration in remarks more notable for their condescension than their insight ("It is to be feared that Donne was showing off" [482]), and he doubts that many in attendance could have understood fully what Donne was saying. In the end, Bald dismisses the oration as "hyperbolically extravagant," designed only "to impress the simple-minded" (482–83). To be fair, Bald did not know of two contemporary documents: the text of Mawe's address and an eyewitness reaction to all three speakers. But, as Bawcutt and Kelliher remark, neither indicates a "simple-minded" audience (443). At issue for Bawcutt and Kelliher is the extent to which the hyperbolical discourse recorded by the eyewitness can

35

contribute to our knowledge of Donne. In this vein, they conclude that the unmistakable praise of Donne documented by both Mawe and the contemporary witness in these two additional sources "demonstrates the status and reputation he [Donne] had achieved at this stage in his career" (444). Nonetheless, Bawcutt and Kelliher, too, suggest an embarrassing discrepancy between Donne's supposedly "high attainments" and his official role as "little more than a messenger" (442) between the two houses.

Bald also knew of, but rejected, church historian Thomas Fuller's claim that Donne had also been elected prolocutor of the 1624 Convocation, assuming, it seems, that only one of these dates—1624 or 1626—could be correct.[2] Recently, Gerald Bray has discovered that John Young, dean of Winchester, acted as prolocutor in 1624.[3] However, Donne's name continued to be associated with Convocation, and in both the 1628 and 1629 Convocations he was named as one of the sponsors of the new prolocutors, Walter Curll and Thomas Winniffe, respectively.[4]

Much that was occurring in these early months of 1626 suggests the political and religious significance of Donne's election to this position. The York House debates on Arminianism in February, Parliamentary efforts to impeach Buckingham,[5] and Parliamentary proceedings against Richard Montagu for his alleged Arminianism were consuming public interest and threatening serious internal divisions within the Church of England.[6] During these months, "an Army" of books (Heylyn 155)[7] was published against Montagu, alleging that his views were nothing but new-style Pelagianism. But the doctrinal issues raised by his books were not brought to a vote by the clergy assembled in Convocation, where they might more properly have been discussed.[8] By the time Parliament was dissolved in 1626, impeachment proceedings against Buckingham had been attempted but failed, the Commons had condemned Montagu for "publishinge doctryne contrarie to the Articles of the Religion established in the Churche of England" (Tyacke 128), and a proclamation for peace and unity in the church and Commonwealth had been issued, effectively muzzling public predestinarian dispute for some time to come. Although Donne and Montagu were both royal chaplains in the months preceding these events, Donne assumed the position of spokesperson for the lower clergy in Convocation, while Montagu was conspicuously absent from the proceedings altogether.

This essay argues that Donne's election by the lower clergy as their prolocutor in 1626 signals his importance and reputation as a middle voice on matters of religious controversy in these months. Furthermore, Donne's oration betrays his anxieties about speaking publicly in this controversial atmosphere. Nonetheless, comments in his oration and in sermons of the first half of 1626 reveal Donne's conviction that these public, conciliar processes are the best means for handling controversial matters, in part because open debate conducted according to agreed-upon rules was fairer, in part because it was easier to manage. This was especially true for accomplished linguists and exegetes such as Donne, but the position was less attractive to hard-line disputants of any persuasion who saw such debate as encouraging equivocation and rhetorical deception and who did not want to place the clear words of Scripture in competition with human interpretations of them. I will argue that the doctrinal positions Donne articulates for the Church of England in these sermons are very similar to those of the English delegates to the Synod of Dort (1618–19), situated between the rigid Calvinist positions of some Dort delegates and the anti-Calvinist positions of others who had been labeled by the majority of Dort delegates as new-style Pelagians.[9] Furthermore, the middle way that Donne articulates for the Church of England is located in these sermons more in their processes of inquiry than in dogmatic pronouncements, an attractive approach to those whose goals might be inclusive but one infuriating to those, consequently labeled as extremists, who held firmer, less compromising, and, they would argue, more principled positions. This language accords both with Donne's public roles—as prolocutor to Convocation and Court preacher—and with his stated commitment to orderly and constructive processes of debate. So while Donne articulates in these sermons a doctrinal position for the Church of England on the sensitive matters raised by Montagu's books, he does so on the model of "blessed sobriety" offered by the English delegates to Dort. Donne contrasts the "sobriety" of this synod's processes with the contentious model of the Council of Trent, and, by analogy, with contentious men gathered in any public forum who offer their convictions as principled religious foundations not open to debate in the public sphere but who, Donne suggests, are subordinating doctrinal matters to personal convictions.

Let us return, first, to Donne's election by his peers as prolocutor to Convocation in 1626. By 1380, Convocation had been divided into two houses: an upper house, made up of the archbishops and bishops, which alone could initiate canonical legislation; and a lower house, comprising deans, royal chaplains, and representatives of the clergy, which acted in an advisory or consultative capacity to the upper house. As a consequence of the separation, the prolocutor's office was created "to refer all decisions of the Lower House to the Upper House and to act as a channel of communication between them" (Smethurst 16). It seems significant that Donne was deemed the ideal "Internuncius" (Bawcutt and Kelliher 442) between the upper and lower houses, praised for his accomplishments as a poet, orator, controversialist, and preacher, one versed in "civil, canon, and common law, prudent in the handling of current affairs, and a trustworthy Church administrator" (Bawcutt and Kelliher 442). Despite the hyperbolic conventions of praise used by those introducing and responding to his oration, it seems unwise to dismiss the occasion as a ceremonial opportunity for flattery and ostentation or the position as inferior.[10] For one thing, the prolocutor's position was not merely honorary. Upon the charge of the archbishop to choose a person fit for the office, the name had to be submitted for approval of the archbishop.[11] In fact, the prolocutor was responsible for conducting the business of the lower house, reporting to the upper house, and moderating debates. As the voice of the united sense of the lower house, he was charged with presenting their opinions and positions to the upper house and with conveying the upper house's commands and admonitions to his peers. It was a diplomatic position requiring the utmost trust of both houses, for "He [the prolocutor] conveys to the Bishops the petitions and opinions of their clergy, and carries back to the clergy the advice and direction of their bishops; and so by this office the inconveniences of debating together are avoided, and yet the synod remains in effect as united as ever" (Gibson 51). Conveying the "united sense" of the lower house's views was clearly a difficult task in 1626, given the heightened climate of religious controversy surrounding the alleged Arminianism of Montagu's publications. Bishop Carleton, leader of the English delegation to Dort, wanted Convocation to discuss and approve the Dort articles, in this procedural respect, at least, supporting the Durham House group who believed the issue was jurisdictional as much as doctrinal and who feared that Convocation's right to establish canons of orthodoxy was being threatened (White 241–44).[12] In particular, they wanted King Charles to resist determining doctrine in Parliament. However, while Convocation was the most obvious and proper place for such doctrinal discussion to take place, the debate took place at York House instead. Some evidence suggests that Montagu, in fact, feared Convocation, believing it to be sympathetic to the Dort articles, a fact supported by William Loe's remark that some forty-five members of the lower house had banded together against Pelagianism and semi-Pelagianism in the 1626 Convocation (Loe 241). As late as 1629, John Davenant still believed Convocation to be against Montagu (Bodleian MS Tanner 72, fol. 310), and Carleton publicly connected Montagu with the Pelagian heresy against which Loe and his colleagues had banded.

Charles took advice from several quarters about how to proceed. Lancelot Andrewes, the anti-Calvinist bishop of Winchester, in particular, was consulted, but he determined that Convocation should not debate the Dort articles. Fearing that Arminianism would be publicly opposed and discredited by a majority, Andrewes went so far as to hold it not "fit for any thing to be done in that particular, as the case then stood; the truth in those Opinions not being so generally entertained amongst the Clergy, nor the Archbishop and the greater part of the Prelates so inclinable to them, as to venture the determining of those points to a *Convocation*" (Heylyn 153). However, clergy of all shades urged prohibition of doctrinal debate. Some, like Joseph Hall (Calvinist rector of Waltham in 1626), wanted to silence controversy on both sides by preventing debate, even in Convocation; others, like James Ussher (Calvinist archbishop of Armagh), wanted to silence only the Arminians—not because he supported either side, he claimed, but because he viewed Arminians as disturbers of the peace. Hall, for one, urged Charles to prohibit dispute on the grounds that matters of faith differed from "scholastical disquisitions" (9:498). The proclamation issued by Charles in June 1626 mandated a "Rule of sobrietie" as the basis regarding further public statements of doctrinal orthodoxy (Larkin 2:92–93).

Donne himself would have held several views on the question of debate of the Dort articles. On the one hand, Donne in his sermons continued to articulate distinctions between Pelagianism and Church of England doctrine. On the other hand, he understood the need for "sobriety," a quality he attributed to Dort for its way of handling dispute and a quality conspicuously absent from most discussions of Montagu in these months. Donne would have been required to exercise considerable tact in expressing the consensus of the lower house where there was clearly division. Moreover, discretion was also essential in conveying the instructions of the upper house. That Donne was considered acceptable to both houses, themselves internally divided, confirms his reputation for learning, fairness, and eloquence and, more importantly, for independence from increasingly sectarian allegiances.

The oration Donne delivered that day betrays anxieties about his fitness for the position and, more importantly, about the burden of the highly public profile of the prolocutor. To this point, commentators have not taken seriously the extent of these anxieties, concluding that they are hyperbolic, self-dramatizing tropes, perhaps designed to enhance Donne's status in a job that no one else considered very important. In his oration Donne says, "I see myself cast down, suddenly placed under a Burden, unequal and ill-adapted to my strength, and from the shore, where I might have thought to have done my duty satisfactorily by praying to all and assenting to the more rational, [I see myself] thrust into the public arena into the raging of a sea of speaking openly and speaking first, of Conciliating and Consulting, Collecting and Referring, Bringing forth proofs and Accusations. . . ."[13] This anxiety is alleviated to some extent by his professed confidence that Convocation is a consultative body, modeled on God's consultative Trinity.[14] Donne suggests further that a religious "athlete" rather than a man "out of shape" ("homine inexercito") would have been a better choice, but he shoulders what he takes to be his public duty in confidence that God can use weak means to accomplish his ends. Donne's anxiety about "speaking openly and speaking first" might seem exaggerated or insincere, especially since he also asserts that there is "no Goliath" rising against us, "for neither are there heresies for us to contend against, nor are schisms occurring to be minded."[15] This is a remarkable statement given the ongoing public debate over Montagu's allegedly Arminian books and, more specifically, the public attacks on Buckingham. Such a comment could be—and likely was—interpreted as a statement supporting these men. But what Donne suggests here—and consistently in his sermons—is that these labels ought not to be applied subjectively or lightly. Donne makes the same point in his oration, saying that it is in the power of the assembled clergy to avoid unproductive controversy: "just as books are in the comprehension of their readers, so deeds in the minds of their recipients have their fate."[16] So he invites his audience, particularly those of the upper house, to "remember weaker stars from the kindly point of view of the stronger"[17] and to remember that heresies and schisms are serious charges, not to be alleged frivolously in a "sober" body charged with debating difficult religious points.

    The metaphor of greater and lesser stars seems to have attracted some attention on the occasion itself. Dr. Mawe's speech introduces the metaphor as part of a series of comparisons that define Convocation as "the vehicle for transmitting the will of the bench of bishops to the deans and minor clergy" (Bawcutt and Kelliher 442). Bawcutt and Kelliher find the comparison of bishops to greater stars "shedding light and warmth on a cold and cloudy lower world" more acceptable than an earlier one comparing the bishops to "Moses on Mount Sinai speaking directly to God" and the lower clergy to the Israelites "waiting for the tables of the law to be brought down to them" (442). This latter comparison, they claim, "seems near to blasphemy" (442). Donne's oration picks up on the comparison to orders of stars, urging the bishops to invigorate the efforts of the lower clergy by their rays "that our Embryos may come to life in your bosom."[18] The eyewitness notes, wryly, that both Mawe and Donne had used this analogy to stars, but he interposes his opinion that their comparison is faulty: he balks to hear "that from theese Bps wee must receaue all our directions, that wee must be obseqious to their commandes, that by their light wee must bee illightened (at wch woordes I said to one that stoode by mee, I hope he will not deale with the Bps as Dr Mus did with the Popes Legate in Con: Trident: to giue them the office of the holy Ghost, spirituall illumination: neither did this sute with their comparison of maiores and minores stellae, for the lesser doe not receaue their light from the greater starres, but greater and lesser all from one of the great ones, the sunne)" (Bawcutt and Kelliher 443).[19]

In the interpretive spaces opened by repetition of this comparison we can catch a glimpse of some of the dynamics governing this body and, in particular, the sensitivity to jurisdictional issues that all three documents reveal. Dr. Mawe's comparison of clergy to greater or lesser stars is part of the "considerable emphasis" (Bawcutt and Kelliher 442) Mawe places on the public function of Convocation as a vehicle for conveying the will of the bishops. Presumably, the eyewitness had these comparisons in mind when he noted that Mawe "did extraordinarilie flatter the Bishops and Prolocutor, leauing the lower howse of clergie nothing but what they should receaue from the Bishops, in which also did concurre the Prolocutor" (Bawcutt and Kelliher 443). Interestingly, despite the eyewitness's feeling that Mawe had exceeded decorum by flattering Donne "before his face and beyond measure," he says that all of this praise was "truly" said (Bawcutt and Kelliher 443). Of course, the comparison of ministers to stars had been made much earlier by Donne, when he defended James's *Directions to Preachers* in a 1622 sermon with the text "the stars in their courses fought against Sisera" (4:179).[20] In that sermon, Donne had said that to maintain his spiritual war, God had established preaching as his ordinance and "hath made *Preachers Stars*" (4:192), "called to the *Ministery* of the *Gospell*, and appointed to *fight*, to preach there" by fighting "within the discipline and limits of this Text" (4:196), but on this occasion at least one eyewitness interpreted him to mean that the lower clergy must function not within the discipline of strict scriptural exegesis but within the discipline of episcopal authority.

In fact, the sermons for the first half of 1626 articulate a fairly coherent set of principles for governing public religious debate. In the preface to the king preceding a February 24, 1626, Whitehall sermon, Donne says, "Wee are in Times when the way to *Peace* is *Warre*, but my Profession leades not me to *those Warres;* And wee are in Times when the *Peace* of the *Church*, may seeme to implore a kinde of *Warre*, of *Debatements* and *Conferences* in some points; but my disposition leades mee not to that *Warre* neither" (7:72–73). England in 1626 was on the brink of open war with both France and Spain, and Donne seems to be referring to that political situation in the first part of his statement. The second part, however, alludes directly to a number of current church "warres," specifically the York House debates on Arminianism. Just seven days before this sermon was preached, the second of the York House debates had been concluded. The subject of the debates on February 11 and 17 had been Montagu's published views, particularly those regarding perseverance and justification. Donne's friend Thomas Morton was one of the chief spokesmen on the Calvinist side against Bishop Buckeridge of Rochester and Montagu himself, who attended the second meeting. Accounts of the debates written from both sides show that the doctrinal issues raised were not resolved conclusively, and Tyacke sees the conference as "the approximate point at which the circle of clerics patronized by Bishop Neile of Durham emerged as the effective spokesmen of the English Church" (180). As prolocutor to Convocation, a body that, by rights, should have been debating these issues, Donne must have felt considerable pressure from both sides.

We know from Donne's oration that he preferred to observe from the shore rather than to speak first but that occasionally he entered the controversial "fray." When he does so, however, as in his "merely Polemicall" (7:166) sermon of May 21 against the Catholic doctrine of purgatory, he feels called upon to justify this "handling of a Controversie" in the light of James's former *Directions*—which he had publicly defended—against "all impertinent handling of Controversies, meerly and professedly as Controversies, though never by way of positive maintenance of Orthodoxall and fundamentall Truths" (7:166). The earlier directions, he maintains, had been in favor of "a discreet and temperate forbearing of personall, and especially of Nationall exasperations," made precarious by the prince's journey to Spain when he was "then taken in their pits" (7:166). Things having changed, however, so that the prince, now king, is safely returned and all peace with Spain is removed, Donne shifts the focus to the "supplanting, and subverting of [Romish] error" by the "beating of our Drums in the Pulpit" (7:167). This religious war, he contends, is the decorous counterpart of the beating of the drums abroad and a fitting turn from civil dissension to the common enemy, Rome. In his sermon defending the *Directions*, Donne had justified James's pacifist policies by suggesting that the way to war was peace and that in spiritual wars, "Cursed bee they that goe about to make Peace, and to make all one," for "It is an opposition against God . . . to reconcile opinions diametrally contrary to one another, in fundamentall things" (4:193). In this May 21 sermon, Donne seems to be arguing that the way to peace is war and that the enemy is not internal—

a Montagu, a Buckingham—but external, the "Catholique and Militant Church" (7:166).

In commenting on the dangers of internal religious division, Donne's sermon preached April 18, 1626, asks its hearers to contrast the "blessed sobriety" (7:127) with which doctrines were delivered by the English delegates at the Synod of Dort with the contentious wrangling of the Council of Trent. Primarily an attack on Trent's premature determination of many points that Donne says are as yet "in debatement and disputation" (7:124), the sermon concludes, "Therefore have so many sad and sober men amongst them, repented, that in the Councell of Trent, they come to a finall resolution in so many particulars; because how incommodious soever some of those particulars may prove to them, yet they are bound to some necessity of a defence, or to some aspersion if they forsake such things as have been solemnly resolved in that manner" (7:125). Donne is willing to grant the Trent delegates "a prudent, and discreet abstinence" in forbearing to determine precisely "how far the secular Lawes of temporall Princes binde the Conscience of a Subject" (7:125), but he nevertheless charges them with putting too much authority in the pronouncements of the pope.[21] At the same time, he accuses the pope of failing to determine the cause because he saw it more to his advantage to hold it undetermined. Donne is equally critical of the pope's refusal to determine "the concurrence of the Grace of God, and the free will of man" (7:125), especially since he forbids writers on either side of the debate to publish their works, preferring to reserve all to the prerogative of the pope and his "secret judgement" (7:126) rather than to Scriptures. By contrast with the absolutism of the pope and this council, Donne offers the example of the English divines at Dort who modified the narrow views of those "over-good husbands of Gods large and bountifull Grace" (7:126), the Gomarist Calvinists, with their sentence "That all men are truly, and in earnest called to eternall life, by Gods Minister" (7:127). Unlike the articles of faith, which Donne says were invented just "the other day" (7:202) at the Council of Trent, the Dort decrees are characterized as the product of sober and painstaking deliberation, the kind of deliberation vetoed by the prerogative of the pope at Trent. In particular, the doctrine of hypothetical universalism to which the English delegates had led the entire synod, after much deliberation, was an example of the constructive consequences of debate and compromise (Patterson 271–75; White 187–92), constructive, at least, to those delegates interested in expanding the English church and in limiting the number of conscientious objectors to that church's doctrine and discipline.

The Synod of Dort may have been Donne's model of temperate discussion and consultation on contentious doctrinal issues, but Donne's own experience with the foreign synod, and perhaps more recently with Convocation, Parliament, and the York House conference, had made him acutely aware of the difficulty of sustaining decorum even in such sober councils. On April 18, Donne had already attacked the privy whispering of the backbiting Pharisees as outside the proper sphere of discourse (which included "Legal and Juridical Accusation" or "private reprehension done with discretion, and moderation" [7:151]).[22] Now, in June, when articles of impeachment against Buckingham and charges of heretical opinion against Montagu had been aired in Parliament, Donne extends this discussion to comment on how councils ought to handle controversy. Specifically, he comments on the inappropriateness and ineffectiveness of personal revilings in the handling of disputed matters, suggesting that "occassionall displeasure" against particular adversaries should not obscure a "holy zeale" for "the maine doctrinall points" (7:203). Even Augustine, he concedes, may have been "transported sometimes with vehemency against his present adversary, whether Pelagian, or Manichean" (7:203), a statement that makes clear the degree to which Donne was committed to hating the sin rather than the sinner. Donne goes on to say that

> even some great Councels in the Church, and Church-affaires have felt, that for collaterall and occasionall, and personall respects, which were risen after they were met, the maine doctrinall points, and such as have principally concerned the glory of God, and the salvation of soules, and were indeed the principall and onely cause of their then meeting there, have been neglected. Men that came thither with a fervent zeale to the glory of god, have taken in a new fire of displeasure against particular Heretiques, or Schismatiques, and discontinued their holy zeale towards God, till their occasionall displeasure towards those persons might be satisfied, and so those Heresies, and Heretiques against whom they met, have got advantage by that passion. (7:203)

The concurrence of Donne's references to Augustine versus the Pelagians and great councils versus heretics makes it hard not to conclude that Donne is alluding here to one aspect of the Synod of Dort that had appalled the English delegates, namely, the virulent, personal denunciation of the Remonstrants that accompanied the Dort articles, not least by associating them directly with the Pelagian heresy.[23] Donne's own strategy of using the names of ancient heretics—Pelagians and Catharists—to describe contemporary holders of heretical opinions is, from one point of view, a thin veneer of civility in an otherwise highly polemical assault. However, it accords with Donne's own rejection of "personal revilings" and can be interpreted as an invitation to apply the example only if it fits and as an illustration of the "nearenesse" that is the aim of Donne's homiletics.[24]

Historical scholarship on the role of the English delegation at the synod is clear on several points. Foremost among these is the labor of consensus enacted by most of the delegates, and particularly the English delegates, who reported on the degree of courtesy, harmony, and compromise with which decisions on doctrine and wording were achieved (Milton 418–24; Patterson 276). Donne's point is not one in defense of the Dutch Arminians but rather in defense of a clear rhetorical focus against heresies rather than against heretics. Donne elaborates on the point by explaining that in great councils as well as in councils of state, "an immature and indigested, an intempestive and unseasonable pressing of present remedies against all inconveniences, may suffocate the heart of the businesse, and frustrate and evacuate the blessed and glorious purpose of the whole Councell" (7:204). In great councils, "every man puts off his owne person" and comes with a purpose to promote "the safety of the State, and the good of the Church" (7:204). Again, Donne is not urging blindness, indifference, or lack of zeal. Rather, he is advocating the sharp-sightedness of the eagle (who looks to "evident" dangers of the state and church) rather than that of the basilisk, a mythical reptile which sees so "that he may kill" (7:204). The significance of the distinction is that it redefines the quality—sharp-sightedness—as a function of intention, either to espy dangers (i.e., to be watchful) or to destroy enemies (i.e., to kill). There is some evidence, then, that Donne's main objection to the way controversies were handled in England's public institutions is the practice of "personal revilings." These rhetorical and procedural questions rather than substantive doctrinal subtleties remain constant for Donne and frame these 1626 sermons. The matter of rhetorical moderation was one theme of his sermon defending the *Directions* in 1622, where Donne defines peace not as an "indifferencie to contrary Opinions in fundamentall doctrines . . . but a peace with persons, an abstinence from contumelies, and revilings" (4:196). It is included in the May 21, 1626, call for a "discreet and temperate forbearing of personall, and especially of Nationall exasperations" (7:166). Only ten days before, Buckingham himself had been named as "the principall patron and supporter of the Semi-Pelagian[s]," an identification he had stoutly denied, claiming he had never heard of the Pelagian opinion before.[25] So, too, in his efforts to cast off the name "Arminian," Montagu had denied reading Arminius, while Calvinist bishops rejected the name "puritan" applied to them by Montagu and his supporters (Milton 447, 538–39).

In the April 18, 1626, sermon, Donne continues his articulation of the appropriate style of public religious debate by offering the examples of Luther and especially Melanchthon. Melanchthon is an expositor whom Donne praises on several occasions, primarily for being "a man freest of any from contention" and "a man of more learning and temperance then perchance have met in any one, in our perverse and froward times" (7:206–7). Donne's admiration of Melanchthonian Lutheranism is entirely consonant with his comments on the discursive and interpretive practices appropriate to controversial debate: Melanchthon is "no bold, nor rash, nor dangerous expressor of himself" (3:94). And, in fact, it is Melanchthon's rhetorical handling of controverted matters, what W. B. Patterson calls his "unpolemical and conciliatory Protestantism" (138), that earns from Donne respect for the substance of the matters discussed. Melanchthon's commentary on 1 Corinthians 15:50, for example, is an interpretation of the nature of the resurrected body that "no man denies" (3:118). Melanchthon is also named in the controversy over the Sabbath and ceremonies as "that man, who assisted the Reformation of Religion, with as much learning, and modesty, as any" (4:315). However, Donne's endorsement of Melanchthon focuses primarily on the interpretive practices of this Lutheran reformer rather than on his doctrine, commenting on the Augsburg Confession (1530) that it "was written after all things were sufficiently debated, and had siftings, and cribrations, and alterations enow" (7:181). Donne's support for this achievement also recalls that the English delegates to Dort were cautioned by James not to say anything that would preclude reconciliation with Lutherans (and ultimately with Catholics).

It must be observed that Montagu also cited Melanchthon as representing "moderate and temperate" reformers on the question of free will (*Appello Caesarem* 95, 83). And Anthony Milton notes that during the interregnum some Laudians "associated the Church of England more directly and systematically with Melanchthonian Lutheranism's moderate views of predestination" (444). Heylyn, for one, "placed the Church of England's doctrine on many issues alongside 'the Moderate or Melancthonian Lutherans' " (Milton 444). As Dewey Wallace has demonstrated, however, members of the English church who wanted to distinguish themselves from "rigid Calvinistic Protestants" naturally appealed to Lutheran sources, and the "English coupling of Melanchthon with moderate predestinarianism had surfaced long before the Arminian controversy" (358–59). Melanchthon's reputation as a "moderate, ethical, ceremonious, and patristic-inspired" Protestant (Wallace 366) made him appealing to a variety of churchmen along the religious spectrum, especially "conformist theological writers" (Wallace 357). These included those conformists whom Wallace describes as "Anglican Arminians" (360); "Laudian Arminians," especially during the interregnum (men such as Peter Heylyn and Thomas Pierce); Calvinists such as Joseph Hall and Robert Sanderson; and many others.[26]

An important consideration here, however, is that any interpreter receives Donne's approbation if he can avoid what Donne sees as the greatest obstacle to religious reform: "personal revilings" and "vehemency against his present adversary" (7:203). Calvin is also cited in one of Donne's sermons for his willingness to compromise for the sake of confessional unity, even on important matters that had not been locally determined, such as how the Eucharist ought to be administered. The significance of one's quoting from Calvin requires careful interpretation. Donne's increasing use of Calvin does not necessarily prove that Donne remained a Calvinist, but it does show that Donne, unlike Montagu and other Arminians, was not "anxious to denigrate him" (Milton 427). Milton argues that in the 1620s Calvinists objected that "in Laudian hands, the boundary between 'controlling' and 'traducing' Calvin was too readily breached" (453). Donne, on the other hand, is engaged in a program of reinterpreting Calvin to support his own generous interpretations of the Thirty-nine Articles, which he accepts as the foundational doctrinal articles of the Church of England. In this case, Donne explains that Calvin believed the sacrament might be administered in prisons but departed from his own opinion because the church in Geneva thought differently, thus supporting Donne's view that national churches might develop very different interpretations of such important disciplinary questions. In this respect, Calvin becomes Donne's authority against what he calls "*Morositatem*": "a certain peevish frowardnesse, which, as he calls in one place *deterrimam pestem*, the most infectious pestilence, that can fall upon a man, so, in another, he gives the reason, why it is so, *semper nimia morositas est ambitiosa*, that this peevish frowardnesse, is always accompanied with a *pride*, and a *singularity*, and an ambition to have his opinions preferred before all other men, and to condemn all that differ from him" (10:175).[27] The example reinforces how far Donne thought men should be willing to go, and how broad a latitude he allowed for matters indifferent. The example of Calvin's compromise on the adminstration of the sacrament in Geneva also allows Donne to observe that "greater matters then are now thought *fundamentall*, were then thought but indifferent, and *arbitrary*" (7:175) and to castigate "men, who trouble the Church now, about things of lesse importance, and this of private Sacraments in particular" for making themselves believe that "they are *his Disciples*, and always conclude that whatsoever is practised at *Geneva* was *Calvin's* opinion" (10:175–76).

The references to Augustine's controversy with the Pelagians and Manichaeans, to Melanchthon's modesty and sobriety, and to Calvin's reproof of singularity point not so much to a confessional allegiance as to a rhetorical style and a willingness to distinguish opinion from dogma that Donne holds as the only practice of a "civill man" at a council table (10:175). The conciliating efforts of Calvin, of Melanchthon, and of the English delegates to Dort contrast sharply with the opinions of Montagu, who publicly attacked Calvin, the church in Geneva, and even the Synod of Dort, dismissively referring to the council as an irrelevance and to the Dort doctrines as the private opinions of the individual delegates. I think it is important in interpreting all of these comments on private, personal revilings versus a publicly developed rhetoric of consensus to read them as comments not on the substance of the debates but rather on their manner. It seems clear that Donne favors what Luther, and especially Melanchthon, achieved with the Augsburg Confession and what the English delegates achieved in their efforts to modify the rigors of the extreme Contra-Remonstrant (Calvinist) position at Dort. Donne recognized that a public rhetoric of conciliation and civility was not only a style to which he was more temperamentally suited but also an effective means of marginalizing those few genuinely separatist and factious clergy whose overzealous labeling (of heretics and schismatics) actually produced the conditions within which heresies and schisms might occur. The charges of contention, personal revilings, and labeling apply equally, it seems, to those opposed to Montagu and his "innovations" as to Montagu himself, who provocatively enlarged the category of "puritan" to include doctrinal Calvinists such as the Dort delegates. Like Augustine, neo-Augustinian opponents of "Pelagian" heretics lose sight of their doctrinal focus and become "transported" with vehemency against their "present adversaries," the Pelagians (who "overadvanced" man's free will) and the Manichaeans (who "annihilated" it).[28]

For all Donne's dislike of heated debate, however, his sermons for this period comment explicitly on controverted doctrine. Committed to debating doctrinal issues in the public sphere, Donne was bound by his office to achieve pastorally effective statements of those doctrines necessary to salvation. As Achsah Guibbory has shown, many of these sermons qualify rigid Calvinist positions on election, the Atonement, and perseverance.[29] Donne's theological qualifications of Calvinism at this time have been interpreted to mean that Donne was taking advantage of the space opened by the publication of Montagu's works to express his own pro-Arminian views more openly. Peter McCullough has argued that Donne was doctrinally an Arminian while rejecting political association with them. However, Donne's public statements on these doctrinal issues suggest that Donne, like the English delegates to Dort, was working with "blessed sobriety" to temper the practical consequences of predestination (a doctrine he accepts) and to articulate for the Church of England a place on the spectrum between those who limit God's scriptural offers of grace unnecessarily and those who exaggerate human free will.[30] This place is not identified with any specific reformer or church father or with any other national church; rather, it is one that answers the specific needs of the English church and is interpreted in that particular context. Donne believes that the proper place for this doctrinal discourse is in synods or convocations, not in the press. His articulation of the "mediocrity" with which religious and civil debate should be conducted is demonstrated in these sermons of early 1626 in his comments foregrounding interpretation and in his rhetorical efforts to balance doctrinal with experiential (or "experimental") belief.

To take "mediocrity" of interpretation, first, we can look at a Whitehall sermon preached on April 18, 1626, that urges hearers to read the Scriptures in a way that falls between two extremes, a way particular to "our own Church" (7:119). The issue in question—election—is raised in relation to two "distempers": "both theirs, that think, That there are other things to be beleeved, then are in the Scriptures, and theirs that think, That there are some things in the Scriptures, which are not to be beleeved" (7:119). Donne cautions that the best interpretation is to read God's public records (the Scriptures) rather than the traditions of men or the unrevealed decrees, stressing that here, in Scriptures, God's word in the mouth of Christ is "digested" and that here we will find "The rule of all Doctrines": "If I have not told you so, it is not so, and if I have, it is so as I have told you" (7:119).

Donne's negotiation of controversy and religious debate in these sermons is also an extraordinarily clear statement of his interpretive principles. A series of sermons on 1 Corinthians 15:29[31] brings together his strongest objections to Catholic rules and practice of interpretation, especially since Trent. Donne rejects a number of commentaries on this text because they are figurative, and at several points he reminds his hearers that "We [i.e., divines in the English church] have a Rule, . . . which is, Not to admit figurative senses in interpretation of Scriptures, where the literall sense may well stand" (7:193). Donne's thorough examination of expositions of this text shows that only by allowing figurative senses—and many of those farfetched—can this text be made to provide evidence for purgatory. This exercise takes Donne through various church fathers, among Catholics of the Counter-Reformation, and then "our owne men (Expositors since the

Reformation)" (7:206). He selects for comment two of these men: Luther and Melanchthon. What distinguishes their comments for Donne is that they adhere to the "plaine, the naturall, and the true signification of the place" (7:207). Lest these literal interpretations be calumniated because their followers "follow as Sheepe," Donne draws upon another, somewhat different, literal interpretation by Piscator, "a learned and narrow searcher into the literall sense," who, though very far from communion with Lutherans, "yet out of a holy ingenuity, and inclination to truth, he professes this place to be . . . the most sincere and naturall interpretation" (7:207). Both interpretations rely, however, on a historical recovery of burial practices in the apostles' time, practices that Donne cannot corroborate but which "may be proved by some, whom those reverend persons have read, and I have not" (7:208).

In these sermons, Donne seems determined to reject Catholic (and particularly Jesuitical) interpretations, advocating a principled literalism to offset the liberties these expositors have taken with figurative interpretations. Donne even corroborates the Lutheran interpretations with evidence of deathbed baptisms in the early church. In the application of his text to his hearers, however, Donne moves deftly from the literal and historical to the figurative, urging his hearers to acquire a habit of repentance before the deathbed, for "if thou leave all till then, it may prove a heavy businesse" (7:214). Donne's process may serve several controversial purposes. Beginning with his contention that Catholic controversialists (as opposed to expositors) argue primarily to "rayse money, and advance their Revenue," Donne makes this distinction: "as they are but Expositors, they may have leave to be good Divines, and then, and in that capacity, they may give the true sense of that Scripture: But as they are Controverters, they must be good Subjects, good Statemen, good Exchequer men, and then, and in that capacity, they must give such senses as may establish and advance their profit" (7:191). The profit, of course, rests on figurative interpretations that obfuscate the literal sense and, in the case of this text, support the doctrine of purgatory (and the indulgences sold to gain entrance to it). Donne's use of Lutheran expositors is also difficult to interpret, but it seems to be a consistent feature of Donne's irenic, accommodating gestures, a way of establishing Protestant credentials, and perhaps a way of deflecting attention from Calvinist associations at a time when Montagu and other Laudians were trying to dismiss Calvinists as puritans. Despite Donne's support of these expositors, however, his construction of a massive foundation of the doctrinally literal is erected, in the end, to support a practical application of this text to the figurative "resurrection from sin" which is the thrust of his sermon. It ends with a call to action in the exhortation to "be therefore S. *Cyprians Peripatetique*, and not his *Clinique* Christian; A walking, and not a bed-rid Christian" (7:214).[32]

In these sermons of early 1626, Donne's stress on a wise mediocrity of interpretation culminating in a practical or experiential faith is accompanied by a mediocrity of expression, signaled by Donne's overriding insistence that what we are reading are God's public records rather than his unrevealed decrees, records that admit of several interpretations. Donne speaks openly of differences in interpretation that can be accommodated within "our" church, noting for example that the English delegates disagreed with the other participants at the Synod of Dort on the issue of Christ's descent into hell but could agree to the articles nonetheless. On a more controversial issue such as election, however, achieving mediocrity of expression is not only Donne's rhetorical strategy but the foundation of his belief. Echoing Luther once more, Donne agrees that "how" and "why" are "dangerous syllables" (5:206; 6:188) when it comes to discussing this doctrine, and we can see clearly that when Donne expresses his views on election he does so in a way that resists absolute statements of cause and effect. His statements in these months are the best examples of his handling of controverted doctrine. They also indicate why it is especially harmful to label the Donne of these early months of 1626 as Arminian. As historians—especially Peter Lake—have amply shown, a methodology to determine religious allegiances has to go beyond observations that a particular divine "sounded like" another.[33] Precisely the same language and assumptions about the accepted views of the Church of England against heretical and schismatical extremists or factions were used by the Dort delegates who wrote against Montagu and by Montagu himself. Whereas Montagu marginalized these mainstream churchmen as "puritans," they attacked Montagu as a Pelagian heretic. Lake warns explicitly against passing off Montagu as "some moderate, irenical figure, surprised by the extremity of response which his works had stirred up" ("Calvinism" 67). Lake says it would be "difficult to find a more bitterly polarized view of contemporary theological opinion" than that presented by Montagu in his letters. He calls Montagu's gloss on the Thirty-nine Articles "a highly partisan and polemically aggressive act, undertaken against the school of opinion dominant in the Church" ("Calvinism" 69), views that left Montagu feeling isolated and vulnerable within the English church.

Donne's comments on election in his sermons for early 1626 are one index of the kind of interpretive space, both doctrinal and rhetorical, that Donne was claiming for his theology of grace within an increasingly contentious public sphere. This middle way, I am arguing, is not a fixed or absolute doctrinal point but rather a position still being negotiated within the Church of England and altering under the pressure of historical circumstances (Scodel 63–67). A January 29, 1626, sermon, for instance, broaches the subject of election by distinguishing between God's saving grace and his helping grace: "God hath elected certaine men, whom he intends to create, that he may elect them; that is, that he may declare his Election upon them. God had thee, before he made thee; He loved thee first, and then created thee, that thou loving him, he might continue his love to thee" (7:62–63). God has been our "help," Donne says, a term that "presumes an endevour and co-operation in him that is helped" (7:63). And yet, lest that statement smack too much of will worship, Donne states explicitly: "God did not elect me as a helper, nor create me, nor redeeme me, nor convert me, by way of helping me; for he alone did all, and he had no use at all of me. God infuses his first grace, the first way, meerly as a Giver; intirely, all himselfe" (7:63). A clearer statement of the orthodox doctrine of election cannot be imagined. Yet, like the experimental predestinarians at Dort (i.e., those espousing an evangelical Calvinism predicated on a Calvinist doctrinal position but seeking to "inculcate an active piety in the laity" [Lake, "Calvinism" 114]), Donne stresses how important it is that believers accept God's subsequent or "helping graces." So he can conclude that "All inchoations and consummations, beginnings and perfectings are of God, of God alone; but *in the way* [emphasis added] there is a concurrence on our part, (by a successive continuation of Gods grace) in which God proceeds as a Helper" (7:64).

This same space for repentance "in the way" is articulated in his sermon on February 24, 1626. Here, Donne counters the "singularity" of much controversial divinity by figuring it metaphorically as hearing with only one ear. The metaphor is brilliant for the way in which it figures interpretation as something requiring not only two ears but also the capacity to hear—and comprehend—the whole meaning resonating between them. Donne says that expositors of his text for that day sometimes hear only one thing in this text, "wee must perish," though God is no cause of our perishing (7:74). Hearing with one ear, a strict Calvinist ear one might say, is to preserve God's honor ("we our selfes, and not *God*, are the cause of that desperate irremediablenesse" [7:74]) but still to leave souls in desperation. Those who hear with two ears—in stereo—extend the text "fairely," Donne says, to suggest that "There is no necessitie that any Man, any this or that Man should perish" (7:74). This stereophonic interpretation clearly mitigates the rigors of an emphasis on God's absolute decree of reprobation. But the extension, however fair, cannot cancel the notion of election, a doctrine of which Donne speaks as entirely mainstream, not the marginal view of some few radicals, as depicted by Montagu. Both ears together "hear" the whole or right doctrine, as Donne invites his hearers "from one Text [to] receive both Doctrines" (7:74). Neither one on its own—neither absolute predestination (even that predicated on man's sinfulness rather than God's unfathomable decree) nor the view that "any this or that Man" can be saved who "will"—is sufficient, Donne says, urging his hearers to "open both eares" to him (7:74). Donne's position here seems orthodox, very similar to that of the English delegates to Dort who rejected the Gomarist doctrine of double predestination but distinguished their position from those whose emphasis on man's free cooperation effectively denied election entirely. The point Donne comes to stress, however, is not what God has done (a mystery that cannot be resolved through discourse or dispute) but what we can know or experience. So Donne says "That, not disputing what *God*, of his *absolute* power might doe, nor what by his *unreveald Decree* hee hath done, God hath not allowed *me*, nor *thee*, nor *any* to conclude against our selves, a necessity of perishing" (7:85). Suspicion of God's divorce comes from reading a few misunderstood sentences from the Bible rather than the whole book. But, "of an eternal *decree* of thy *divorce*, thy *conscience*, (thus misinformd) can be no *witnesse*, for thou wast not call'd to the making of those *decrees*" (7:90). Of the seals God has given, Donne cites baptism and the Eucharist, "But *Seales* of *Reprobation* at first, or of irrevocable *Separation* now, there are none from GOD" (7:90). In addition, while Donne acknowledges the huge debt of sin, he also asserts that one drop of Christ's blood was sufficient to atone for all of it, a statement of the hypothetical universality of the Atonement which the English delegates to Dort, Ward and Davenant, had first of all persuaded the other English delegates, and then the entire synod, to accept. This statement is a very clear exposition of the orthodox English position against election to reprobation, but we are very far here from the Arminian views articulated by either the Dutch Arminians or Montagu.

Donne's sermon for Easter 1626 continues his articulation of the experience rather than the doctrine of election. So, with Ezekiel, he says that "thou Lord, who knowest whose names are written in the Book of Life, and whose are not; whose bones are wrapped up in the Decree of thy Election, and whose are not, knowest whether these bones can live, or no; for, but in the efficacy and power of that Decree, they cannot" (7:116). Yet, as the Dort delegates had concluded, "As dry, as desperate, as irremediable as they are in themselves, God shall send his servants unto them, and they shall hear them" (7:116).

However, Donne's April 18, 1626, sermon on John 14:2 shows most clearly how his rhetorical handling of election positions the Church of England between rigid Calvinist and Arminian views, primarily by focusing on the experience rather than the doctrine. The text is "In my Fathers house are many mansions; if it were not so, I would have told you." In this sermon, Donne reminds his hearers that controversy over election is not a new thing. Even before the Reformation the church was divided over election: most before Augustine, Donne explains, "placed the cause of our Election in Gods foresight, and foreknowledge of our faith and obedience" (7:123), while most after "placed it in the right Center, that is, onely in the free goodnesse and pleasure of God in Christ" (7:123). Of course, holding that election proceeds from foreseen faith is the charge levied against Montagu and the Arminians, their opponents claiming the victory at York House by making White "disclaim" and Montagu "retract" this view (Tyacke 179). In the contemporary Roman Catholic Church this controversy is played out between Jesuit and Dominican opponents, and the Council of Trent, which erred in coming "to a finall resolution in so many particulars," failed to resolve this crucial difference "about the concurrence of the Grace of God, and the free will of man" (7:125). In contrast to this council, Donne notes the "blessed sobriety" of the English delegates to the Synod of Dort, who "delivered their sentence, That all men are truly, and in earnest called to eternall life, by Gods Minister" (7:127). They knew, he said, "That we must receive Gods promises so, as they be generally set forth to us in the Scriptures; And that for our actions and manners, for our life and conversation, we follow that will of God, which is expresly declared to us in his Word" (7:127). The scriptural evidence, appropriated from the seventeenth of the Thirty-nine Articles, allowed the English delegates to retain their interpretive independence and to make any doctrine confirmed by any synod dependent on that interpretive consensus. What the Synod of Dort confirmed for English divines, according to Donne, was the freedom to establish doctrine according to their interpretation of Scriptures, and the "sobriety" of the synod lay as much in ensuring that the articles established latitude of interpretation as it did in arriving at any particular doctrinal formulation. The point, for Donne, is that—in the Church of England—the details of doctrine are left to ministers to interpret, although the fundamentals remain. This both legitimates his own idiosyncratic doctrinal formulation of a theology of grace and marginalizes those more inflexible interpreters who would have branded his own statements as dangerously heretical or, perhaps, merely incomprehensible. Only following that moment of "blessed sobriety" does Donne paraphrase the synod's statement on election: "conditionall salvation is so far offered to every man, as that no man may preclude himselfe from a possibility of such a performance of those Conditions which God requires at his hands, as God will accept at his hands, if either he doe sincerely endevour the performing, or sincerely repent the not performing of them" (7:127–28). That is, while no one can be absolutely assured of his election, neither can one be so certain of his reprobation as to justify his spiritual inertia. This statement expresses the theology of grace in conditional rather than absolute terms. The key words here are "no man may preclude himselfe," with their focus not on what God has done or can do but on what human beings can know. Ironically, human ignorance of God's unrevealed decrees becomes a ground for faith in the "possibility" of election.

A similar point is reiterated in Donne's April 30, 1626, sermon on Matthew 9:13: "I am not come to call the righteous, but sinners to repentance." Foremost is Donne's distinction between calling and meeting, offered in the context of his explanation of Christ's purpose in coming. Here Donne uses the discussion of "repentance" to mediate between Calvinist and anti-Calvinist positions. As in the previous sermon, the balance between these will identify the doctrine of "our" church. Donne begins this section with the foundational Calvinist doctrine that salvation does not depend on man's will: "Man had no power, no will, no not a faculty to wish that Christ would have come, till Christ did come, and call him . . . yet where was I, when God call'd me, when I was not, as though I had been, in the Eternal Decree of my Election? . . . He came not to meet them who were, of themselves, set out before" (7:155–56). Donne is careful, however, to balance this orthodox Reformed notion of election against the claims that God's grace was irresistible and that he came to force or compel rather than to call. Donne's point here is clear—and anti-Calvinist: "Christ saves not man against his will" (7:156). This forcing of men to religion is associated with the Inquisition and even with harsh penal laws against recusants. "Force and violence, pecuniary and bloudy Laws, are not the right way to bring men to Religion" (7:156), Donne says, although he is careful to distinguish between the unjustified bloodiness of the Inquisition and the justified treatment of English Catholics whose allegiance (as much as their religion) was in question. Donne further qualifies this position along the explicit lines of the Synod of Dort by acknowledging that the Word preached is the right way of calling (although he grants to the Word read at home a "pious" status). So he concludes in a move that is more Calvinist than anti-Calvinist: "if there be a discontinuing or slackning of preaching, there is a danger of loosing Christ" (7:157).

When Donne turns to discussion of who are called (i.e., sinners), he treads on another Calvinist doctrine: perseverance. Donne says, "Even the

Elect themselves have not a constant righteousness in this world: such a righteousness, as does always denominate them, so, as that they can always say to their own conscience, or so as the Church can always say of them, this is a righteous man" (7:58–59). The point of the text, Donne says, is to challenge those who rely upon their righteousness, so he rejects in this section the Pelagian righteousness of those who "thought Nature sufficient without Grace," or the righteousness of the Cathari, who thought the stock of grace given them "sufficient, and that upon that stock they were safe, and become impeccable, and therefore left out of the Lords Prayer, that Petition, . . . *Forgive us our tresspasses*" (7:159). The balance Donne strikes in his interpretation of election is entirely one between God's unknowable decrees and the means by which these decrees are executed, between formal and efficient causes. "Our Glorification was in his intention, as soon as our Election: in God who sees all things at once, both entred at once," Donne concedes, but "in the Execution of his Decrees here, God carries us by steps; he calls us to Repentance" (7:162). The steps are not necessary to achieve election, which was a stamp made all at once from eternity, but are rather the charitable means by which God draws us in time to his purposes. So Donne concludes in this middle ground, asserting that Christ is "Come, not to meet us, who were not able to rise, without him; but yet not to force us, to save us against our wills, but come to call us, by his Ordinances in his Church" (7:163). The active piety to which he exhorts his hearers modifies the absolutism of some Calvinist formulations so that the position of "mediocrity" that Donne defines comes between Calvinist and anti-Calvinist doctrinal formulations, refusing finally to settle on a fixed rhetorical point.

It is important to see Donne's rhetorical handling of election in the context of debates on these issues in both Convocation and the Synod of Dort. As Anthony Milton observes, "Despite all the conflicts of Dort, . . . the Synod still gave clear expression to the harmony of the Confessions of the different Reformed Churches" (421). Although condemning much anti-Calvinist doctrine, for example, the English delegates vehemently opposed published, personal condemnation of the Remonstrants, and Bishop Carleton contrasted the delegates' care of "mutuall consent sought" (Milton 422) with Montagu's attacks on the Contra-Remonstrant Calvinists. W. B. Patterson describes the decrees as "discursive," "aimed more at edifying the faithful than at resolving intractable philosophical and theological compromise" (276). As a "deliberate and judicious compromise" (Patterson 276), these decrees (and the process by which they were approved) provide the model for Donne's balance between doctrine and discourse, between absolute decrees delivered all at once in eternity and human experience of these decrees in steps, over time. This rhetorical dilemma was precisely that articulated by Francis White, one of the divines on the Arminian side of the York House debates: "it is a matter very difficult and peradventure imposible in this life, exactly and distinctly to declare the whole manner and order of divine election, and how the same being one aeternall and simultaneous act in God is to be conceaved according to severall acts in our apprehension" (Tyacke 179). White had overcome this dilemma to some extent by distinguishing between election to grace and election to glory, but Donne does not resort to this distinction, preferring to focus on what his hearers can know rather than what God has done. Donne's sermons of early 1626, then, focus on the experience of election in time rather than on God's eternal decree. The result is not simply a series of absolute statements that balance or contradict one another, such as the ones discussed earlier, but an elaboration of the temporal process of justification figured conventionally as a chain.

A sermon for Whitsunday, dated 1626, examines justification as an interlinked chain in which faith is "but one of those things, which in severall senses, are said to justifie us" (7:228). The efficient cause is God, so it can be truly said that only God justifies us, since "nothing can effect it, nothing can worke towards it, but only the meere goodnesse of God." Christ is the material cause, since "nothing enters into the substance and body of the ransome for our sins, but the obedience of Christ." It is equally true to say that faith alone justifies, since "nothing apprehends, nothing applies the merit of Christ to thee, but thy faith." Works are the declaratory justification, since "Only thy good life can assure thy conscience, and the World, that thou art justified" (7:228). All of these are interconnected, so "Neither of these can be said to justifie us alone, so, as that we may take the chaine in pieces, and thinke to be justified by any one link thereof; by God without Christ, by Christ without faith, or by faith without works; And yet every one of these justifies us alone, so, as that none of the rest enter into that way and that meanes, by which any of these are said to justifie us" (7:228). However, Donne's treatment of the metaphor is unique in its effort to explain the "right signification of that word, cause" (7:227) as it applies to salvation. "Alas," he begins, "let us be content that God is the cause and seek no other" (7:227). But in the end, what justifies is the contractual process—*Crede et vives*—a chain of which the nearest link is "A good life" of good works. Donne's practical advice is to "keepe a fast and inseparable hold upon that" (7:228). The motion is twofold: "God comes downeward to us; but we must go upward to God; not to get above him in his unrevealed Decrees, but to go up towards him, in laying hold upon that lowest linke" (7:229). In Donne's treatment, the chain is not a static thing but rather a living chain of causality in which the works of faith—the "good life"—though most removed from God's eternal decree, make salvation most accessible.

Later in 1626, after Parliament and Convocation had been prorogued, Charles issued his proclamation intended to maintain the "circle of order" in church and state intact, and Donne, who had just completed his time as prolocutor, now embraced the "good life" in another manifestation, as one of the governors of the Charterhouse in London. From 1626 until 1631, Donne attended each assembly of the governors of this charitable "hospital" for educating and lodging needy men and boys. As Robert Evans has shown, Donne was an active participant in the administration of this institution, which handled many issues—some routine, some controversial—in the five years of his tenure. Evans indicates that this hospital was seen in its day as "a symbol of the philanthropy of the reformed religion" (134). Interestingly, Thomas Winniffe, who was sponsored by Donne as prolocutor of the 1629 Convocation, was named to replace Donne at the Charterhouse in 1631. Donne's commitment to service—in government, in the pulpit, and, lastly, in the Charterhouse—can be added to our picture of Donne in his last years as a person taking hold firmly of the "good life," that lowest link on the chain of salvation.

At least in the first half of 1626, in the heated controversial context established by Parliamentary debate, by doctrinal debate in Convocation, and by the public medium of print—and Richard Montagu—we find John Donne focusing on a place of "mediocrity" for the Church of England not simply between Catholics and radical Protestants (the older, Jacobean extremes) but between Calvinists and Arminians, a considerably smaller space. It was a pulpit space Donne hoped to model on the "blessed sobriety" of the English delegates at Dort rather than on the contentious wrangling of the Council of Trent. In understanding this place, we have attached insufficient significance to Donne's role as prolocutor. This was a position built on the foundation of Donne's reputation for conciliation and for sensitivity both doctrinal and rhetorical to current controversial issues. He seems to have been ideally suited in abilities, if not inclined temperamentally, to these sensitive rhetorical situations, providing a voice of discretion at a time of increasingly zealous attacks on personal adversaries.[34] It seems unlikely that Donne was moving toward the new-style Pelagianism of Montagu and his supporters. The qualifications of Calvinism that he articulates in his sermons are not simply subtle or cautious statements of Arminian theology. Nor is it simply a difference in rhetorical means that separates Donne and Montagu from similar doctrinal ends (i.e., enlarging God's grace). Donne's means are his ends, and his theological rhetoric of early 1626 suggests that he is outlining positions remarkably similar to those of the English delegates to Dort, especially the hypothetical universalism to which the synod agreed primarily because of the efforts of these delegates. By expressing his reservations about the perseverance and assurance of the elect as discursive rather than doctrinal formulations, he rejects absolutist language (this person has not been elected) in favor of a practical or commonsense affirmation (we don't know who the elect are, or we cannot be sure). The consequence of this concentration on human beings rather than on God, on what is possible as far as we know rather than on what God knows absolutely, on election as experienced in time rather than as existing in eternity, is an affirmation of salvation resonating between God's decrees and human perceptions—the good news "heard" with both ears in a public sphere that had grown increasingly contentious and, to Donne's mind, unstable in 1626. It is also a focus on the links of the chain of salvation, with emphasis on seizing and practicing the "good life" of public service. Donne's public religious identity as constructed in his sermons, his role as prolocutor, and his charitable service with the Charterhouse express how completely discreet service was for him the politics, the rhetoric, and, most importantly, the ethics of his vocation as one of the foundational voices of the Church of England in the 1620s.

Notes

1. I would like to thank Tom Cain for calling my attention to the eyewitness account in the Scudamore Papers at the British Library. The documents referred to in this study were first reported and discussed in the note by Nigel Bawcutt and Hilton Kelliher.

2. Fuller reports under the year 1623: "As for the convocation contemporary with this [the 1624] parliament, large subsidies were granted by the clergy, otherwise no great matter of moment passed therein. I am informed doctor *Joseph Hall* preached the *Latine Sermon*, and *Doctor Donne* was the Prolocutor" (5:566).

3. Bodleian MS Tanner 114, fols. 127^r–128^v. I owe this information to the kindness of Dr. Gerald Bray.

4. I would like to thank Dr. Gerald Bray for his help in understanding the workings of Convocation, and in particular for his transcription of the relevant folios (for Convocations from 1624 to 1629) of Bodleian MS Tanner 282 and

Lambeth Palace Library (LPL) MS WD 54. The full records for these Convocations were burned in the great fire of London (1666), but LPL WD 54 is the index to the Convocation book from 1584–1629, recently rediscovered by Dr. Bray in St. Paul's Library and now in Lambeth Palace Library. The same material can be found in microfilm in MS Tanner 282, fols. 30^{r-v}.

5. By 1626, Buckingham, as Charles's chief minister, had come to represent "the main grievance" of the Commons. According to Russell, grievances against the duke can be grouped under three heads: "monopoly of counsel, monopoly of patronage, and inefficient discharge of his duties" (295).

6. Arminians, so named as followers of the Dutch theologian Jacobus Arminius, attempted to mitigate the theological rigors of the Calvinist theology of grace. These anti-Calvinists asserted universal grace and the cooperation of man's free will in conversion against Calvinist doctrines of absolute predestination.

7. Heylyn names those who had written against Montagu, observing that "the Encounter seemed to be betwixt a whole Army and a single Person" (155). Tyacke observes that "In the course of the 1626 Parliament at least five books were published attacking Richard Montagu as an Arminian" (155).

8. Peter White makes the jurisdictional argument (238–44). "If Montagu's books were considered to require examination, then Convocation was from the clergy's point of view the appropriate forum" (243).

9. For a discussion of Donne's use of the name "Pelagian" in his sermons following the Synod of Dort and in the context of contemporary usage, see my "Labels." The books attacking Montagu "all define Arminianism in terms of the doctrines condemned by the Synod of Dort" (Tyacke 155). In particular, Bishop Carleton, who had headed the English delegation to Dort, alleged that Montagu "hath with confidence delivered the doctrines of the Pelagians and Arminians for the doctrines of the Church of England" (sig. A3^v).

10. The importance of Convocation to bishops who "staunchly defended the clergy's exclusive right to enact ecclesiastical law" is noted by Kenneth Fincham (64). A full study of Convocation, including the workings of the lower house and its prolocutor, is needed.

11. Donne's relations with Abbot were closer than Bald has suggested (440). See my "Pulpit Crisis" for evidence supporting this claim.

12. The Durham House group comprised anti-Calvinist divines under the leadership of Richard Neile, archbishop of Durham. Under the patronage of the duke of Buckingham, they were instrumental in advancing the Arminian cause at two conferences held February 11 and 17, 1626, at Buckingham's residence, York House in the Strand.

13. "Dejectum me video, Oneri, viribus meis impari, & importuno, repente suppositum, & a litore, ubi omnibus adprecando, & sanioribus annuendo, satis officio meo fecisse putari possem, in arenam, in aestum maris jam protrusum, pro-

loquendi & praeloquendi, Conciliandi & Consulendi, Colligendi & Referendi, Argumentandi & Arguendi . . ." (Bald 574). I would like to thank Annabel Robinson of the Department of Philosophy and Classics at the University of Regina for her able and ready assistance in translating Donne's prose.

14. This topic is discussed by Nicholls, Johnson, and Gray and Shami.

15. "(nec enim haereses a nobis debellandae, nec schismate occurunt resarcienda)" (Bald 575).

16. "sicut & libri a captu lectorum, ita & opera ab animis recipientum, sua fata habere" (Bald 575).

17. "ut meminisse dignentur, imbecilliores stellas, a benigno fortiorum aspectu" (Bald 575).

18. "& in sinu vestro animari Embryones nostros" (Bald 575).

19. I would like to thank Dr. Hilton Kelliher for kindly providing me with his transcription of supplementary passages, not published in his note, from MS Add. 11044, fol. 10^r.

20. All quotations from Donne's sermons are taken from the Potter and Simpson edition. Future page references are to this edition and are given parenthetically in the text.

21. In "Anti-Catholicism in the Sermons of John Donne," I argue from this passage that Donne saw this failure to fulfill the responsibility of a visible church as unequivocally negative. Donne's willingness to concede that in this matter their "abstinence" might have been "discreet" is important, however, and shows the kinds of practical, moral distinctions he makes constantly in his sermons.

22. Donne uses the "Pharisees" to stand in for puritans, particularly in his Caroline sermons.

23. The Remonstrants were Dutch Arminians whose five anti-Calvinist articles had been published in 1610 and to which the Synod of Dort responded specifically.

24. Peter McCullough discusses Donne's apparently irenical treatment of controversial religious doctrine in one sermon by showing how Donne takes "the argumentative form of reconciling opposites (here, unconditional election), but filled with opposites from within his own position in the larger debate (conditional election) (195)." For "nearenesse," see my "John Donne and the Absolutist Politics of Quotation" (391–92).

25. Tyacke cites the words of Christopher Sherland and Buckingham's reply (165).

26. Wallace is still using the term "Anglican," as opposed to "puritan," to describe those churchmen who cited Melanchthon to support views that modified rigid predestinarianism, and it would be fair to say that most of the examples he adduces create a Melanchthon who "had given greater scope to the freedom of the will in the process of salvation than had the Calvinist reformers, and had taught

views on predestination and falling from grace similar to those of the Arminians" (364). But the examples he uses also admit of a more subtle interpretation, particularly of citations of Melanchthon from the 1620s, before the extreme polarization of doctrinal debate of later decades had occurred.

27. The issue of singularity is treated in Shami, "Labels" (16–18), and is noted as characteristic of Donne's religion by Doerksen in "Donne's 'Puritan' Imagination" (352). Forrest shows how contemporaries associated singularity with puritans, but Donne associates it with schismatics of any description, including recusants.

28. I discuss Donne's evenhanded treatment of all those who engage in "opprobrious and contumelious speeches" (3:240) more fully in "Labels."

29. I am grateful to Achsah Guibbory for many productive discussions on these issues and for sharing with me her important essay "Donne's Religion: Montagu, Arminianism, and Donne's Sermons, 1624–30."

30. Donne's views on election have been discussed by several scholars, in particular Sellin, Papazian, Johnson, and Doerksen *(Conforming)*.

31. "Else, what shall they doe which are baptized for the dead? If the dead rise not at all, why are they then baptized for the dead?"

32. See my "Labels" for a fuller discussion of Donne's "experimental" predestination. Peter Lake ("Calvinism" 56) says that "the stress of the English delegation [to Dort] was always pastoral and edificational. They played up those aspects of the Calvinist case which left room for an element of human responsibility and effort and which avoided the possibility of fatalism and desperation in the laity." Lake calls attention to this "experimental predestinarianism" which "can be seen operating on and subtly changing the doctrinal core of 'credal Calvinism' at Dort" (58). I am not arguing that Donne was an "experimental predestinarian" but only that his rhetorical approach emphasizes practical piety and devotion rather than abstract doctrine.

33. See Lake's articles on Sanderson, Hall, and Skinner.

34. For discussion of this topic see Shami, "Donne on Discretion" and "Anti-Catholicism" (140–42).

Works Cited

Bald, R. C. *John Donne: A Life*. Oxford: Clarendon, 1970.
Bawcutt, Nigel, and Hilton Kelliher. "Donne through Contemporary Eyes: New Light on His Participation in the Convocation of 1626." *Notes and Queries* n.s. 42.4 (1995): 441–44.

Carleton, George. *An Examination of those Things wherein the Author of the late Appeale holdeth the Doctrines of the Pelagians and Arminians to be the Doctrine of the Church of England.* London, 1626.

Doerksen, Daniel. *Conforming to the Word: Herbert, Donne, and the English Church before Laud.* Lewisburg: Bucknell UP, 1997.

———. "'Saint Pauls Puritan': John Donne's 'Puritan' Imagination in the Sermons." Frontain and Malpezzi 350–65.

Donne, John. *Sermons.* Ed. George R. Potter and Evelyn M. Simpson. 10 vols. Berkeley: U of California P, 1953–62.

Evans, Robert. "John Donne, Governor of Charterhouse." *John Donne Journal* 8 (1989): 133–50.

Fincham, Kenneth. *Prelate as Pastor: The Episcopate of James I.* Oxford: Clarendon, 1990.

Forrest, James F. "Malvolio and Puritan 'Singularity.'" *English Language Notes* 11 (1973–74): 259–64.

Frontain, Raymond-Jean, and Frances M. Malpezzi, eds. *John Donne's Religious Imagination: Essays in Honor of John T. Shawcross.* Conway: U of Central Arkansas P, 1995.

Fuller, Thomas. *The Church History of Britain.* 6 vols. Oxford, 1845.

Gibson, Edmund. *Synodus Anglicana; or, The constitution and proceedings of an English Convocation, shown from the acts and registers thereof, to be agreeable to the principles of and Episcopal Church.* London, 1702.

Gray, Dave, and Jeanne Shami. "Political Advice in Donne's *Devotions*: 'No Man is an Island.'" *Modern Language Quarterly* 50.4 (1989): 337–56.

Guibbory, Achsah. "Donne's Religion: Montagu, Arminianism, and Donne's Sermons, 1624–30." *English Literary Renaissance* 31.1 (2001): 412–39.

Hall, Joseph. *The Works of the Right Reverend Joseph Hall, D. D., Bishop of Exeter and Afterwards of Norwich.* Ed. Philip Wynter. 10 vols. Oxford: Clarendon, 1863.

Heylyn, Peter. *Cyprianus Anglicus: or, The History of the Life and Death of the most Reverend and Renowned Prelate William by Divine Providence, Lord Archbishop of Canterbury,* London, 1668.

Johnson, Jeffrey. *The Theology of John Donne.* Cambridge: D. S. Brewer, 1999.

Lake, Peter. "Calvinism and the English Church 1570–1635." *Past and Present* 114 (1987): 32–76.

———. "Joseph Hall, Robert Skinner and the Rhetoric of Moderation at the Early Stuart Court." *The English Sermon Revised: Religion, Literature and History 1600–1750.* Ed. Peter McCullough and Lori Anne Ferrell. Manchester: Manchester UP, 2000. 167–85.

———. "The Moderate and Irenic Case for Religious War: Joseph Hall's Via

Media in Context." *Political Culture and Cultural Politics in Early Modern Europe.* Ed. Susan Amussen and Mark Kishlansky. Manchester: Manchester UP, 1995. 55–83.

———. "Serving God and the Times: The Calvinist Conformity of Robert Sanderson." *Journal of English Studies* 27 (1988): 81–116.

Larkin, James F., ed. *Stuart Royal Proclamations.* 2 vols. Oxford: Clarendon, 1983.

Loe, William. *A Sermon preached at the Funeral of Daniel Featley.* Oxford, 1645.

McCullough, Peter E. "Donne as Preacher at Court: Precarious 'Inthronization.'" *John Donne's Professional Lives.* Ed. David Colclough. Cambridge: D. S. Brewer, 2003. 179–204.

Milton, Anthony. *Catholic and Reformed: The Roman and Protestant Churches in English Protestant Thought, 1600–1640.* Cambridge: Cambridge UP, 1995.

Montagu, Richard. *Appello Caesarem: A Just Appeal from Two Unjust Informers.* London, 1625.

Nicholls, David. "Divine Analogy: The Theological Politics of John Donne." *Political Studies* 32 (1984): 570–80.

———. "The Political Theology of John Donne." *Theological Studies* 49 (1988): 45–66.

Papazian, Mary Arshagouni. "Donne, Election, and the *Devotions Upon Emergent Occasions.*" *Huntington Library Quarterly* 55.4 (1992): 603–19.

Patterson, W. B. *King James VI and I and the Reunion of Christendom.* Cambridge: Cambridge UP, 1997.

Russell, Conrad. *Parliaments and English Politics, 1621–1629.* Oxford: Clarendon, 1979.

Scodel, Joshua. "John Donne and the Religious Politics of the Mean." Frontain and Malpezzi 45–80.

Sellin, Paul. *John Donne and "Calvinist" Views of Grace.* Amsterdam: VU Boekhandel, 1983.

Shami, Jeanne. "Anti-Catholicism in the Sermons of John Donne." *The English Sermon Revised: Religion, Literature and History 1600–1750.* Ed. Lori Anne Ferrell and Peter McCullough. Manchester: Manchester UP, 2000. 136–66.

———. "Donne on Discretion." *English Literary History* 47 (1980): 48–66.

———. "John Donne and the Absolutist Politics of Quotation." Frontain and Malpezzi 380–412.

———. "Labels, Controversy, and the Language of Inclusion in the Sermons." *John Donne's Professional Lives.* Ed. David Colclough. Cambridge: D. S. Brewer, 2003. 135–57.

———. "'The Stars in their Order Fought Against Sisera': John Donne and the Pulpit Crisis of 1622." *John Donne Journal* 14 (1995): 1–58.

Smethurst, Arthur F. *Convocation of Canterbury: What It Is; What It Does; How It Works*. London: Society for the Promotion of Christian Knowledge, 1949.

Tyacke, Nicholas. *Anti-Calvinists: The Rise of English Arminianism c. 1590–1640*. Oxford: Clarendon, 1987.

Wallace, Dewey D. "The Anglican Appeal to Lutheran Sources: Philipp Melanchthon's Reputation in Seventeenth-Century England." *Historical Magazine of the Protestant Episcopal Church* 52 (1983): 361–67.

White, Peter. *Predestination, Policy, and Polemic: Conflict and Consensus in the English Church from the Reformation to the Civil War*. Cambridge: Cambridge UP, 1992.

3

The Augustinian Donne

How a "Second S. Augustine"?

MARY ARSHAGOUNI PAPAZIAN

In his 1640 *Life of Donne*, Isaak Walton refers to the pattern of Donne's life rather than his theology when he remarks with praise that in Donne "the English Church had gained a second S. Augustine," a figure who, like the Augustine described in the *Confessions*, had survived a reckless youth to become unparalleled in "learning and holiness" (sig. B2). In these comments, Walton gives first expression to what traditionally has come to be known as Donne's transformation from the rake Jack Donne, a licentious youth who wrote elegies in the Ovidian tradition, to the serious and devout Dr. John Donne, dean of St. Paul's Cathedral in London and one of the foremost preachers of his day.[1] More recently, George Potter and Evelyn Simpson, the modern editors of Donne's sermons, suggest not only that Donne resembled Augustine in the pattern of his life but that his thought owed much to Augustine's writings. As they demonstrate in their edition of the sermons, Donne's "quotations cover almost the whole field of Augustine's thought" and "deal with such immense subjects as the Nature of God, the Creation of the Universe, the relation between soul and body, the fall of Adam and its consequences, original sin, the saving work of Christ in all its aspects, death and immortality, and the authority of Scripture." Yet, even though they recognize throughout that Donne "owed much of value to Augustine," they nevertheless "wonder whether Augustine's influence on him was altogether healthy." Their complaint is that Donne was concerned too much with Augustine's doctrine of original sin and predestination, a pejorative influence that, in their view, caused Donne to place "too much emphasis on sin and its punishment," to "meditate too long on human guilt and frailty," and, consequently, to "distort the Christian message" (10:354-58).[2]

While Walton may well be right in terming Donne a "second S. Augustine" and thereby calling our attention to the importance of the *Confessions* for understanding Donne's transformation from youth to maturity, one can also argue that the indebtedness that Potter and Simpson bewail lies not merely in the pattern of Donne's life but rather in the close relationship between Donne, the *Confessions*, and Augustine's late predestinarian theology. Rather than see this influence as an unfortunate blemish on Donne's thought, it was, I think, this very predestinarian theology that endeared Augustine to Donne and many of his contemporary English reformers, not to speak of the Reformed churches on the Continent. Indeed, as John Stachniewski has argued, Donne's "vital ideological exposure was to Pauline and Augustinian teaching as it was interpreted, modified, and translated into experience in his own time" (262).[3] Augustine's *Confessions* had a profound influence on Reformation theology. Indeed, as we shall see below, the essentials of Augustine's predestinarian theology, with its emphasis on original sin, election, perseverance, and grace, represent a continuation of—not a break from—the underlying theology of the *Confessions*.

As we begin our discussion, we must remember that Augustine was an important church father for both the Roman Catholic Church and for Protestant churches of many denominations. Indeed, as I commented some years ago, "it was the venerable Augustine who not only embellished the Roman Catholic tradition, but who also provided a foundation for Protestantism" ("Things Indifferent" 328). As David Steinmetz reminds us, every Western theologian is Augustinian in one way or another (13-16). The question is, in what way? Numerous church historians have shown that the Reformation was influenced primarily by Augustine's late works, while the Roman Catholic tradition grew out of Augustine's earlier views on the church. In speaking of Augustine's influence on Donne in his sermons, Potter and Simpson refer primarily to Augustine's *Confessions* and his late anti-Pelagian works. These works, which include *De Gratia et Libero Arbitrio (On Grace and Free Will)*, *De Correptione et Gratia (On Rebuke and Grace)*, *De Praedestinatione Sanctorum (On the Predestination of the Saints)*, and *De Dono Perseverantiae (On the Gift of Perseverance)*, provide Augustine's response to what he considered the Pelagian heresy and are the same works to which the churches of the Reformation, including the English church, turned in their responses to Rome during the sixteenth and seventeenth centuries. While defenders of the Roman Catholic

Church promoted Augustine's conception of the authority of the church in matters of theology, church practice, and structure, Protestant reformers from Luther and Calvin forward exfoliated Augustine's predestinarian theology, focusing particularly on Augustine's late anti-Pelagian works, in their various efforts to define themselves as different from Roman Catholicism (cf. Pelikan 258–59).[4] Or, as William Placher explains, "Historians have with some justice described the Reformation as a struggle between two sides of Augustine: Protestantism began with his doctrine of grace, and Roman Catholic response grew out of his doctrine of the church" (108). Moreover, as William Halewood reminds us, the "Augustinian revival" of the early seventeenth century has its roots in St. Paul, and particularly in St. Paul's Epistle to the Galatians. In Halewood's words,

> There can be no mistaking what Augustine and the Reformers found in Galatians: Augustine cites it regularly; we have full commentaries on it by both Luther and Calvin; and its support of essential Reformation positions is self-evident. In this epistle, Paul admonishes a congregation which is tempted to the error of reviving the law, and he sorts out their alternatives along a clear line of division: on the one side God, Spirit, Faith, Salvation; on the other Man, Flesh, Law, Damnation. The essential point is that the Christian should accept Christ as the agent of his salvation, and the only agent possible for him. To hope for salvation under the law is to put faith in the saving power of human effort, which in Paul's view is a ridiculous blasphemy and denial of the miracle of God's grace. (36)

Halewood adds, "For Augustine, Paul was the pencil, *stylus dei*, through whom God had communicated truth to Augustine himself.... The grace which in Paul works to liberate the Christian from Hebrew law appears in Augustine to liberate the soul from sin" (37). And, "Such a view of man and man's relation to God provides the central pillars of Augustine's theology, thoroughly restored at the Reformation, and the structure of his vivid spiritual autobiography [the *Confessions*]—an account of a confused struggle and flight from God until stunningly overtaken" (38).[5]

The derivation of Augustine's predestinarian theology from his *Confessions* is much at issue in the early seventeenth century. It emerges not only in the controversy that surrounded the first translation of the *Confessions* into English (by Sir Tobie Matthew in 1620) but also in the context of Donne's own references to the *Confessions* in his sermons. Awareness of this connection between the *Confessions*, late Augustine, and the Reformation will enable us to define more fully an important backdrop for interpreting the emotions Donne displays throughout his divine poetry and in works such as his *Devotions Upon Emergent Occasions*. These emotions, as we shall see, place Donne squarely in the theological mainstream of the Church of England.

A proposition like this entails two concerns. Let us proceed first by considering the relationship between Augustine's *Confessions* and his late anti-Pelagian tracts. We can then examine what Augustine meant to loyal members of the Church of England—and John Donne in particular. Augustine composed his late works in response to a British monk, Pelagius, who had been troubled by some of the implications in the *Confessions*. Pelagius's criticism centered on Augustine's view of predestination and free will, a concern that erupted into renewed controversy during Donne's years. As Potter and Simpson remind us, Augustine's theology lay behind Donne's use of the term *massa damnata* (the mass of the damned) as a reference to doubt and original sin, a term that aligns Donne with Augustine's—and later Calvin's—views of man's essentially sinful nature rather than with those of Pelagius.[6] Augustine's modern biographer, Peter Brown, describes the differences between Augustine and Pelagius as follows:

> The basic conviction of Pelagius and his followers, was that man's nature was certain and fundamentally unchanging. Originally created good by God, the powers of human nature had, admittedly, been constricted by the weight of past habits and by the corruption of society. But such constriction was purely superficial. . . . To Augustine, man's nature was at a nadir of uncertainty. . . . For Pelagius, self-control was sufficient: it was sufficient to guard the citadel of free decision by choosing good and rejecting evil. Augustine was less sure. . . . Only the transformation of this deadness could heal men of the deep cause of their sins. (365–66)

Many of the issues Augustine addresses in these late anti-Pelagian works—election, predestination, perseverance, grace and free will (man's will remains free, but without God's grace he can do little but sin), the importance of the heart, God's undeserved mercy, humility and complete self-abnegation, original sin, the problem of assurance, pride, and God's inscrutability—emerge first in the *Confessions*, as Augustine himself noted in his treatise *De Praedestinatione Sanctorum*. As Augustine explains in chapter 53,

> Although I published [the *Confessions*] before the Pelagian heresy had come into existence, certainly in them I said to my God, and said it frequently, "Give what Thou commandest, and command what Thou willest." Which words of mine Pelagius at Rome . . . could not bear. . . . And, moreover, in those same books, . . . [I] certainly declared that God

> by His grace converted the wills of men to the true faith, not only when they had been turned away from it, but even when they were opposed to it. Further, in what manner I besought God concerning my growth in perseverance, you know, and you are able to review if you wish. Therefore, that all the gifts of God which in that work [the *Confessions*] I either asked for or praised, who can dare, I will not say to deny, but even to doubt, were foreknown by God that He would give, and that He could never be ignorant of the persons to whom He would give them? This is the manifest and assured predestination of the saints, which subsequently necessity compelled me more carefully and laboriously to defend when I was already disputing against the Pelagians. (222–23)

As these comments make clear, Augustine himself saw a close link between his *Confessions* and his predestinarian theology—a theology that grew out of his belief in man's sinful nature and absolute dependence on God's grace. Indeed, Augustine's words suggest that the *Confessions* itself occasioned the Pelagian controversy, for Pelagius "feared that Augustine justified all this spiritual laziness by telling how he had been unable to reform his life, radically unable to do anything about his sin, until God seized him in the midst of his sins" (Placher 116).

In his later treatise *De Correptione et Gratia*, Augustine presents his essential anti-Pelagian theology of salvation as follows:

> . . . all these do not stand apart from that mass which, we know, was sentenced to the loss of God; all of them, by reason of one, fell under condemnation. And they are singled out *not* [emphasis added] by their own merits, but by the grace of the Mediator; . . . As for those who by the bounty of divine grace are singled out of that original body of the lost, there is no doubt that the opportunity to hear the Gospel is arranged for them; and, when they hear, they believe, and persevere unto the end in the faith which worketh by charity; and, if ever they go off the tract, they are chastised by *admonitions* [emphasis added]; . . . and some, too, having received grace at various ages, are withdrawn from this life by a swift death. All these things are done in them by Him who made them vessels of mercy, and who also chose them in His Son before the foundation of the world by a gracious choice. (259–60)

Furthermore, Augustine adds in the *De Correptione*, "for such who love Him"—that is, for the elect, whose very identity that separates them from the *massa damnata* comes from God—"God makes all things work together unto good—absolutely all things, even to this extent, that if some of them swerve and stray from the path, He makes their very wanderings contribute to their good, because they come back wiser and more humble" (274). In short, because man can do good only through God's grace, and because God will chastise his own, "the man of God who takes pride is to take pride in the Lord, not only because he has obtained mercy, with the result that he hath faith, but also because his faith does not fail" (293). It is a process, as we shall see, to which Donne's *Holy Sonnets* and *Devotions*, not to mention his many sermons, testify, and to which Donne responded deeply.

By and large, Donne's fellow divines in the 1620s—whether termed Anglican, Reformed, or puritan—similarly turned to Augustine's *Confessions* as an example of his predestinarian theology. Moreover, they read it as a work in great harmony with their own Reformation spirituality and considered its theology in line with that of the Church of England. Indeed, the tenth of the Thirty-nine Articles echoes Augustine's language: "The condition of Man after the fall of Adam is such, that he cannot turn and prepare himself, by his own natural strength and good works, to faith, and calling upon God: Wherefore we have no power to do good works pleasant and acceptable to God, without the grace of God by Christ preventing [leading] us, that we may have a good will, and working with us, when we have that good will" (Gibson). The strong affinity that Donne and his fellow divines shared with Augustine's late anti-Pelagian theology and their certainty that the early-seventeenth-century Church of England had as its foundation Augustine's beliefs as expressed in these treatises become clear in the controversy that followed Sir Tobie Matthew's 1620 translation into English of the *Confessions*. Already a controversial figure—despite having a puritanically minded mother, Matthew converted to Roman Catholicism, a conversion that had people like Donne, Henry Goodyere, Dudley Carleton, Francis Bacon, and even James I concerned about his backsliding (Bald 187–89)—Matthew's translation of the *Confessions* came on the heels of the outbreak of the Thirty Years' War, a conflict that pitted Protestant Europe, including England, against Catholic Spain and its numerous possessions.[7] Negative responses to this edition, which was condemned vehemently as a "popish translation" and as an attempt by Catholics to usurp the Reformation tradition, appeared steadily throughout the 1620s.

A brief description of Matthew's "popish translation" and the powerful responses it engendered among Protestants enables us to suggest an early-seventeenth-century view of the relationship between Augustine, his *Confessions*, and the essentials of his predestinarian theology to Church of

England divines contemporary with Donne. The responses to Matthew's translation also highlight the essential differences between Roman Catholicism and all churches in the Reformed tradition. Dedicating his translation to the Virgin Mary, a point that stirs strong negative reaction in his Protestant respondents, Matthew begins his "Preface to the Pious and Courteous Reader" by presenting "both Catholikes, and Protestants, with a Translation of the *Confessions* of S. Augustine; which may extradordinarily serve to the setting out of Mans extreme misery, and the manifesting of Gods unspeakable mercy" (1). Early on in the preface, Matthew criticizes the Protestants for mistranslating works by Augustine other than the *Confessions* in a way that favored the Protestant churches and at the expense of Roman claims of indebtedness to Augustine, claiming that "the Church of [Augustine's] time, were fully agreeable to that of the Catholik *Roman Church* at this day; as that of our Adversaryes is wholly different" (7). Matthew's comments highlight the need, as noted above, to define the "Augustine" to which we refer during these years, the post-Tridentine Roman or the Protestant Augustine. Donne's use of Augustine—and particularly Augustine's view of man and grace, as noted by Potter and Simpson—followed in number only by his references to Calvin, suggests that Donne followed the view of his fellow divines that their present Church of England is in the Augustinian tradition, with Luther and Calvin as intermediary steps. Most important in Matthew's work for our purposes is the vehemence of his attack on the Calvinists as usurpers of Augustinianism, a response by Matthew which suggests that the view that the Calvinists—and not the Roman Catholics—represent Augustine's true followers indeed was accepted and stated frequently in the England of James I. Indeed, throughout his commentary, Matthew tried to undermine what he considered the Protestant's misreading of Augustine. It is important to add, as well, that throughout his commentary Matthew freely interchanges "Protestant" and "Calvinist" when speaking of the Church of England in 1620, thereby implying that in his mind there was no difference. The Church of England and its divines, one of the most prominent of which is Donne, are perceived, in short, to be "Reformed" or "Protestant" in terms of the paradigm of salvation, a model that derives from Augustine as defined in his late anti-Pelagian works.

The first of the two most vehement attacks on Matthew's translation was that of William Crompton, aptly titled *Saint Austin's Religion: Wherein is manifestly proved out of the Workes of that Learned Father, who lived neere twelve hundred yeares before the time of Luther; that he dissented from Poperie, and agreed with the Religion of Protestants, in all the main Poynts of Faith and*

Doctrine: Contrary to that Impudent, Erronious, and Slanderous Position of the bragging Papist of our Times, who falsly affirme, Wee had no Religion, before the Times of Luther and Calvine. . . . (1625). The second was that of Matthew Sutcliffe, entitled *The Unmasking of a Masse-monger. Who in the Counterfeit Habit of S. Augustine hath cunningly crept into the Closets of many English Ladies. Or, The Vindication of Saint Augustines Confessions, from the false and malicious Calumniations of a late noted Apostate* (1626).[8] Both of these works reveal an insistence during the 1620s of the importance of Augustine for the Reformation, with a clear conception of the modern reformed Church of England—which Donne faithfully served—as following in the tradition of Augustine.

A brief description of these powerful responses to Matthew's "popish translation" enables us to suggest a contemporary seventeenth-century view of the relationship between Augustine, his *Confessions,* and the essentials of his predestinarian theology to Church of England divines contemporary with Donne. First, both Crompton and Sutcliffe assert the importance of Augustine for their present church and criticize the Roman Catholics for their attempts to usurp Augustine for themselves.[9] Crompton, for example, argues that in contrast to the Roman Catholic Church, the Church of England continues the religion of the early church fathers, especially Augustine. As he addresses points of controversy such as the differences between the Protestant and Roman Catholic Bibles, Bible translation, and, perhaps most importantly, that all things necessary to salvation are contained in Scripture, Crompton returns each time to Augustine's words in order to prove that Augustine anticipates the Protestants on nearly every central point. Sutcliffe similarly questions the view that Augustine's religion is at odds with that of the Church of England. "Doe wee then thinke," he asks in the dedicatory epistle, "that the Translator of St. Austine's Confessions a notorious Renegate from the Faith of the Church of *England,* hath reason out of that Father to draw his Romish Doctrine? Sure no, the poyson of his Heresie cannot be found in that holy Fathers Workes" (page prior to A1r). Like Crompton, Sutcliffe identifies himself explicitly with the Church of England throughout his work. "But the more excellent hee [St. Augustine] is, the more is our gaine; the lesse the Apostates advantage," Sutcliffe says to his "Christian Reader," "for this I affirme, and I doubt not but to make it good against all the packe of Jesuites, and not only against this silly Translator, whose soule is lately turned and translated popish; First, that S. Augustine never beleeved the Popes infallible judgement in matters of Faith . . . ; and secondly, that hee holdeth nothing as a matter of Faith and necessary to bee beleeved, that is contrary to the Articles of Religion publikely professed in the Church of England" (A2v).

Second, on the issue of grace versus works, Crompton writes: "The Papists teach, *Some good workes may bee done by Infidels through the strength of nature onely*. We say, Nay. And for proofe of our Negative in this, we alledge Saint *Austine*" (10). Sutcliffe agrees, for he argues too that Augustine anticipates the Church of England in placing grace over works. In Sutcliffe's words, "S. *Austine* . . . doth expressely condemne mens Merits, 'esteeming all our sufferings vile, and not worthie of that which we receive.'" Indeed, in criticizing Matthew on the issue of free will and grace, Sutcliffe claims that Matthew "concurreth rather with Pelagius, then holdeth with S. Austine" (11). Crompton places the debate as to the nature of "true religion" firmly in the context of sin and salvation, thereby suggesting that the focus of his discussion on the churches' respective theology and Augustine will be that of the questions of salvation—original sin, free will, grace, predestination, and perseverance. In response to all of these questions, Crompton affirms that "there is no difference between Saint *Austin* and the Church of England." In his response to the explicitly predestinarian question: "Whether doth S. *Austin* teach, that God is no Author of sinne, and that hee did reprobate some to damnation?," Crompton explains that "One company of men are predestinated to raigne eternally with God; another, to undergo eternall punishment with the Divell." "And did not God then reprobate some to damnation?" he continues, for "the sonne of perdition was predestinated to perdition, saith *Austin*." Crompton concludes this point as follows: "Now to ask a reason, why God chooses this man and passes by that, is forbidden by Saint *Austin*. . . . [yet] thus farre, you see, Saint *Austins* Religion goes hand in hand with the Religion now taught in the Church of England; yea, and most of your own [Roman Catholic] Writers confesse as much as I have said" (9–13). According to Crompton, in short, there is no difference between the positions of Augustine and the Church of England on the reprobate, those rejected by God and left to wallow in sin. This makes the Church of England one with the Reformed establishments on the Continent.

Third, Crompton marks a distinction between Adam's free will and fallen man's inability to choose the good without God's grace, again making explicit the links between Augustine and the theology of the Church of England:

> God fore-saw from the beginning, that man would abuse the liberty of his will; and yet being not tyed to give him his assisting grace, gave him Comandements; as if he had been to have continued in his created abil-

ity: which, God knowing hee would not, and that afterwards hee would be unable to fulfill the Law, (which cries out in a thundering Dialect; Doe this, or dye) hee provided another remedy, even the death and passion of his owne Son, who was sent from Heaven to Earth, ecchoing forth the calme sound of mercy; Beleeve onely, and thou shalt live. They therefore that can fulfill the Law, have no need of the death of Christ; but all that have need of Salvation, have need also of the death of Christ: and therefore, since the fall of *Adam,* none can actually fulfill the Law. (15–16)

These comments, Crompton suggests, are proof that "thus you see what Saint *Austins* Religion was, concerning the fulfilling of the Law; which is in nothing contradicted by the Church of England" (16–17). Indeed, he asserts in response to the question, "Whether doth Saint Austin teach, that man hath free-will now, to doe good of himselfe?" that "The opinion of the Church of *England* concerning this question, is laid down in the 10. Article of her Religion: That the condition of man after the fall is such, that he cannot turne and prepare himselfe by his owne naturall strength, etc. Wherefore we have no power to doe good workes acceptable to God, without the grace of God, etc. And Saint *Austin* teaches the very same" (141). And, in saying that "Lastly, Saint *Austin* teaches, that a mans best workes cannot justifie him before God . . . : All must bee imputed to his grace, not our merit: thou shalt not receive life eternall for any merit, but onely by grace," Crompton concludes that "yet there is no difference in Religion betweene Saint *Austin* and the Church of *England*" (149).

All in all, both Crompton and Sutcliffe anatomize—that is, consider point by point—the connection between Augustine and predestination that characterizes mainstream Reformation theology. For example, Crompton declares, "I hope, I have made it plaine unto thee, (judicious Reader, whosoever thou art) that it is both a false and slanderous position of our adversaries, when they say, That the Religion profest now in the Church of *England,* was never taught before the dayes of *Luther* [for] in the chiefe points of Religion, there is no difference between Saint *Austin* and the Church of *England*" (203). Indeed, as Sutcliffe argues, "those principall points of Romish Religion which we reject, are also rejected and contradicted by S. Austine" (6). "And this, I trust," Sutcliffe concludes, "will suffice to vindicate the holy Father Saint *Austine* from the violence and wrong offered to him by this impure Apostate" (14). "As for the wrong that he [Matthew] hath offered to Religion, and the Church of *England,*" he adds, "I trust our Superiors will in time vindicate: and albeit they neglect it, or cannot redresse it, I doubt not but God will revenge his owne Cause his owne selfe" (84).

Since, as noted above, "historians have with some justice described the Reformation as a struggle between two sides of Augustine" (Placher 108), the relevant question is, to which side of Augustine does Donne respond? That is, does he follow Matthew in his "popish translation," or does he conform to the position taken by his fellow divines such as Crompton and Sutcliffe, and if so, how does this inform his works? In the light of Augustine's own linking of the *Confessions* to his paradigm of salvation, a relationship asserted in contemporary seventeenth-century responses to Augustine and his *Confessions*, Donne's many references to Augustine's *Confessions* in his sermons—the most frequently quoted work from his most frequently quoted source[10]—provide a useful place to begin. In this context, it should not surprise us that Donne's references to the *Confessions* in his sermons emerge consistently in passages that address the very issues that Augustine identifies as his essential predestinarian theology: human sinfulness, affliction, and absolute dependence on God's grace for anything good.

As the sermon passages that follow will show, Donne turned to Augustine's *Confessions* as far more than simply a pattern for his own life. Rather, the *Confessions* enabled Donne to do nothing less than define man's nature and his relationship to God. In his sermon "Preached to Queen Anne, at Denmarke-house, December 14, 1617," for example, Donne encourages his listeners to turn to God, as Augustine had in his *Confessions*, with thanksgiving for the prevenient grace that enables us to ask to be lifted from the *massa damnata*, something we cannot do on our own. He says to his parishioners:

> Canst not thou remember that he sought thee yesterday, that is, that some tentations besieged thee then and he sought thee out by his Grace, and preserved thee? . . . How early did he seek thee, when he sought thee in Adam's confused loynes, and out of that leavened and sowre loaf in which we were all kneaded up, and out of that *massa damnata*, out of that grain which thou shouldst be; yea millions of millions of generations before all this he sought thee in his own eternall Decree. . . . Therefore shall every one that is godlie make his Prayer unto thee O God, in a time when thou may'st be found: we acknowledg this to be that time, and we come to thee now early, with the confesssion of thy servant "*Augustine* [emphasis added]. . . ." (1:249–50)

In his sermon "Preached at Lincolns Inne" (1618), Donne's reference to the *Confessions* follows a long expostulation on the inevitability of affliction and murmuring, even in the most godly, a passage that anticipates Donne's

Devotions Upon Emergent Occasions (1624), a long devotional prose-poem written in response to Donne's own near-fatal illness. As Donne explains in this sermon, "such an impatience in affliction, as brings us toward a 'murmuring' at Gods proceedings, and almost to a calling of God to an account, in inordinate expostulations, is a leaven so kneaded into the nature of man, so innate a tartar, so inherent a sting, so inseparable a venim in man, as that the holyest of men have scarce avoided it in all degrees thereof" (2:51–52). Donne next describes that "nature of man" in Augustinian terms, where man is characterized by sinfulness and complete dependence on God: "There we lost our 'Immortality,' our 'Impassibility,' our *assurance* [emphasis added] of Paradise, and then we lost 'Possibilitatem boni,' says S. Augustine: all possibility of recovering any of this by our selves" (2:55). In another sermon "Preached at Lincolns Inne," Donne again draws on Augustine's *Confessions* to mark distinctions in man's sinfulness. Moreover, he calls Augustine to the minds of his listeners as an example of the right way to confess sin:

> But except we doe come to say, "Our sins are our own," God will never cut up that root in us, God will never blot out the memory in himselfe, of those sins. Nothing can make them none of ours, but the avowing of them, the confession of them to be ours. Onely in this way, I am a holy lier, and in this the God of truth will reward my lie; for, if I say my sins are mine own, they are none of mine, but, by that confessing and appropriating of those sins to my selfe, they are made the sins of him, who hath suffered enough for all, my blessed Lord and Saviour, Christ Jesus. Therefore that servant of God, S. Augustine confesses those sins, which he never did, to be his sins, and to have been forgiven him . . . ; Those sins which I have done, and those, which, but for thy grace, I should have done, are all, my sins. (2:102)

Augustine's notion that one must confess sins that one would have committed but for the grace of God informs not only Donne's sermons, as we have seen, but his *Devotions* and divine poems as well. Again, in this sermon, Donne turns to Augustine in order to define original sin: "For though Saint Augustine confesse, that there are many things concerning Originall sin, of which he is utterly ignorant, yet of this he would have no man ignorant, that to the guiltiness of originall sin, our own wills concurre as well as to any actual sin" (2:106). Finally, in a sermon preached at The Hague on December 19, 1619, on the heels of the Synod of Dort and its reaffirmation of Calvinist predestinarian thinking over Arminianism,[11]

Donne calls on Augustine to help explicate the relationship between pride, sinfulness, and the importance of humility:

> So early so primary a sin is pride, as that, out of every mercy, and blessing, which God affords us, (and "His mercies are new every morning") we gather Pride; wee are not the more thankfull for them, and yet we are the prouder of them. Nay, we gather Pride, not onely out of those things which mend and improve us, (God's blessings and mercies) but out of those actions of our own, that destroy and ruine us, and yet we are proud of our sinnes. How many men have we heard boast of their sinnes; and, (as S. Augustine confesses himselfe) belie themselves, and boast of more sinnes then ever they committed? (2:295)

Again, this concern for pride, as we will see, which Donne draws from Augustine (and Augustine from St. Paul before him), helps us define the predicament of the speaker in Donne's divine poems and his *Devotions*.

As example after example makes clear, Donne generally turns to Augustine and his *Confessions* in order to reassert for his parishioners Augustine's predestinarian theology—a theology based on original sin and man's dependence on divine grace, an emphasis that recurs throughout the sermons. Note, for example, the following passage from Donne's "Sermon Preached at White-Hall, April 19, 1618." In this sermon, Donne speaks powerfully—and in metaphoric language that is reminiscent of his divine poems—of the strength of God's grace to overcome our inherited and inevitable sinfulness, as well as the importance of our living by our knowledge of both God's grace and man's sinfulness. After remarking on "the good use of our own Will, after God hath enlightned us in this Paradise, in the Christian Church, and so restor'd our dead will again, by his Grace precedent and subsequent, and concomitant," Donne continues:

> For without such Grace and such succession of Grace, our Will is so far unable to pre-dispose it selfe to any good, as that . . . we have no interest in our selves, no power to doe any thing of, or with our selves, but to our destruction. Miserable man! a Toad is a bag of Poyson, and a Spider is a blister of Poyson, and yet a Toad and a Spider cannot poyson themselves; Man had a dram of poyson, originall-Sin, in an invisible corner, we know not where, and he cannot choose but poison himselfe and all his actions with that; we are so far from being able to begin without Grace, as then where we have the first Grace, we cannot proceed to the use of that, without more. But yet, sayes Saint *Augustine*; The Will of a Christian so rectified and so assisted, is *lignum scientiae*, the Tree of knowledge, and he

shall be the worse for knowing, if he live not according to that knowledge. (1:292–93)

It seems clear that Donne valued Augustine and his *Confessions*, as is evident in reference after reference to Augustine throughout Donne's more than 160 extant sermons—the work in which Augustine himself claims that he laid the groundwork for later attacks on Pelagius—not for his conversion experience primarily but rather for the very understanding of man's sinful nature about which Potter and Simpson express such exaggerated regret. In this regard, Donne followed Augustine as the true father of the Reformation, the father to whom Luther, Calvin, and the founders of the newly reformed Church of England similarly turned. At the same time, it is worth noting, Donne does not call on Augustine's *Confessions* as an example of the conversion pattern of his life, the angle highlighted by Walton and by Donne's modern biographer, R. C. Bald (Bald 235).

As I have argued above—and as I have shown elsewhere in the context of my study of Donne's *Devotions* and Bunyan's *Grace Abounding* (see "Things Indifferent")—Augustine's theology formed the basis of the Reformed "literature of the heart" tradition that became so widespread during the early seventeenth century and that underlies the experience of Donne's speakers in his *Holy Sonnets* and *Devotions*. It is my contention that, as the 1620s controversy and Donne's own references to the *Confessions* in his sermons suggest, the Church of England that Donne loyally served must be considered positively in terms of Reformed Augustinianism, despite the distaste of modern scholars like Potter and Simpson for so doing. Indeed, it was the venerable Augustine who not only embellished the Roman Catholic tradition but also provided a foundation for Protestantism, particularly with regard to his conception of the fallen nature of humankind. As Diarmaid MacCulloch explains, "overarching all Calvin's theological ideas, as with Augustine, Luther and the earlier Swiss reformers before him, was the constant emphasis on the incomparable majesty of God and the total 'fallen-ness' of humankind, on which ideas he erected the most comprehensive picture of salvation which the Reformation had so far produced" (73–74). Indeed, we must not forget that Protestantism's embrace of a conception of man as completely dependent on God's mercy for salvation, a view that, as noted above, has its roots in St. Paul's epistles and Augustine's late anti-Pelagian works, defines a fundamental divide between Roman Catholicism and all forms of Protestantism, at least until the rise of Arminianism in the Laudian Church of England.

How, then, can our understanding of Augustine's importance for Donne help in our response to his divine poems such as his *Holy Sonnets*?[12]

As I already and in detail have focused on the Augustinianism of Donne's *Devotions* (see "Things Indifferent"), the remainder of this essay will focus on Donne's divine poems, and particularly his *Holy Sonnets*, in the context of the Augustinian backdrop described above. As Halewood asserts, Donne's divine poems "demonstrate a precise understanding of the issues in the debate over the nature of grace and come out unequivocally on the Protestant side" (74).[13] Most Donne scholars agree that the majority of Donne's *Holy Sonnets*, with the exception of "Since she whome I lovd," "Show me deare Christ," and "Oh, to vex me," date from the first decade of the seventeenth century.[14] In these remaining sonnets, Donne presents speakers who embody Augustine's views of sinful man yearning for the grace that only God can give. In this context, one can argue that Donne's poems, which predate his taking orders in the English church, exhibit the spirit of Reformed Augustinianism, or the late Augustine to which the Protestant churches in England and on the Continent turned, in their understanding of man's fallen nature, questions of grace and mercy, sin and damnation.[15] In these sonnets, as Paul Sellin has argued, Donne presents speakers at various stages of certainty or fear regarding their election, a concern central to Augustine's views on predestination.[16] Drawing on the Articles of the Synod of Dort (1619),[17] which derive in their essence from Augustine's anti-Pelagian treatises, Sellin outlines three broad categories of speakers in Donne's divine poems and *Songs and Sonnets:* the elect; "Christians 'seriously converted unto God' who, as they are desperately aware of their need to stand in grace, suffer great Angst at the thought of reprobation because they do not feel assurance of election" (164); and irreligious transgressors. The speakers in the *Holy Sonnets*, Sellin argues, generally derive from the first two categories. Only a few of the *Holy Sonnets* can be described as sonnets of assurance, in which the speakers feel their election and express it in powerful language. Poems in this category include "Death be not proud," in which the speaker expresses confidence of heart; "Why are wee by all creatures waited on?," in which the speaker is "presented in the act of marveling before our eyes at a Christ who 'For us, his Creatures, and his foes, hath dyed'" (14) (Sellin 164); and "What if this present were the worlds last night?" (Sellin 164–65). The remaining *Holy Sonnets* are poems of religious discomfort and anxiety, in which a sinful speaker, in language that calls to mind Augustine's concern with sinfulness and the desire for God's mercy, worries about the status of his relationship to God. Or, in Sellin's words, "the other Holy Sonnets are poems of religious Angst, soliloquies portraying a person in a closed moment of venting intense feelings occasioned by anxieties past or present about the state of his soul and the availability of grace" (165).

Perhaps the best-known of the poems of assurance is the sonnet "Death be not proud," which opens in defiance of the powers of death, a defiance made possible only through assurance of God's undeserved gift of mercy:

> Death be not proud, though some have called thee
> Mighty and dreadfull, for, thou art not soe,
> For, those, whom thou think'st, thou dost overthrow,
> Die not, poore death, nor yet canst thou kill mee. (1–4)

After rehearsing all manner in which men are translated from this life to the next, reminding readers that "one short sleepe past, wee wake eternally" (13), Donne's speaker then proclaims the death of death itself, for after we gain eternal life through the generous and undeserved gift of God and "we wake eternally," then "death shall be no more, Death thou shalt die" (13–14).

Although Donne's poems of assurance—poems in which the speaker expresses confidence in his election and thanksgiving to God for raising him or her up from the *massa damnata* who remain anxious over their election—represent the feelings of peace and triumph that accompany the assurance of election that Augustine defines, Augustine's presence can be felt most poignantly in Donne's holy sonnets of religious angst. These poems, as indicated above, represent the majority of Donne's holy sonnets—his powerful and moving poems of religious anxiety that express in strong feeling the emotions that result from the Augustinian predestinarian theology that characterized the early-seventeenth-century Church of England and to which, as we have seen, Donne responded so powerfully in his sermons. In responding to the Augustinian elements in Donne's *Holy Sonnets*, it is important to remember that, contrary to the overarching despair that Stachniewski describes, "the Protestant emphasis on sin is not in itself morbid or negative . . . and is not aimed at inducing despair. Indeed Augustine and the Reformers quite explicitly offer their doctrine as a specific against hopelessness." In other words, "while man deserves destruction, he receives mercy instead, and such mercy as God must exert himself to give" (Halewood 53–54). On the contrary, as readers of Donne's divine poems of religious anxiety—if not the speakers themselves—know, the very ability of these speakers to contemplate their sinfulness is itself a sign of God's presence within them, a tension that produces some irony in the poems themselves. An interesting poem in this context is the sonnet "At the round earths imagin'd corners." In this poem, which divides neatly into the octave and sestet structure, the speaker in the opening shares the assurance of the speaker in "Death be not proud," that is, until he considers his own sinfulness and the presence of grace within him. In other words, after imagining the triumphant moment of Christ's second coming, a time when the angels will "blow your trumpets" and the "numberlesse infinities of soules" will "arise, arise from death" (1–4), the speaker pauses as he considers his own sinfulness, his own place in the *massa damnata*, a concern that he may not yet be of the elect:

> But let them sleepe, Lord, and mee mourne a space,
> For, if above all these, my sinnes abound,
> 'Tis late to aske abundance of thy grace,
> When we are there. (9–12)

Rather, in full awareness of his nature as a sinful son of Adam, this speaker shows the humility toward God so important in Augustinian theology, requesting God to "teach mee how to repent" (13), a lesson that signifies God's gift of grace, for, as the speaker concludes, "that's as good / as if thou'hadst seal'd my pardon, with thy blood" (13–14). In a moment of dramatic irony, these final lines provide a sign to the reader that the speaker is, in fact, of the elect, although he does not yet have confidence in his own election.

In each of these holy sonnets, Donne's speakers are overwhelmed with guilt for their own sinfulness, aware of the need to submit themselves completely to God, and fully desirous of God's grace. Indeed, in many of these cases the speakers' emotions are especially moving both in their awareness of the grace that Augustine so eloquently defines and aware that as a result of man's sinfulness, not all will be rescued through grace. A goodly part of the *massa damnata*, in other words, will be left to wallow in their own sinfulness, with no ability on their own to do anything good. Whether reprobate from eternity or simply left to wallow in their own sinfulness, these speakers fear such reprobation and cry out to God for his saving grace. Ironically, the very ability of these speakers to call out to God generally is a sign of the first stirrings of grace within them. Consider, for example, the holy sonnet "As due by many titles I resigne." Here, the speaker desires to turn to God, to "resigne / My selfe to thee" (1–2), and recognizes the long history of man's relationship to God, from Adam's fall to Christ's sacrificial gift of life. Still, "knowing himself a divine creature purposely created to share in the glorious destiny that Scripture promises, he is extremely agitated at finding himself still in the power of Satan and fears mightily what he suspects may be reprobation" (Sellin 165). This agitated concern emerges strongly in the poem's closing sestet:

> Why doth the devil then usurpe in mee?
> Why doth he steale, nay ravish that's thy right?
> Except thou rise and for thine owne worke fight,
> Oh I shall soone despaire, when I doe see
> That thou lov'st mankind well, yet wilt not chuse me,
> And Satan hates mee, yet is loth to lose mee. (9–14)

In near despair, the speaker recognizes that only God can triumph over sin. His anxiety emerges from his fear that perhaps God will not "chuse" him, that he will be left in the clutches of Satan, reprobate for eternity. A similar emotion emerges in "Oh my black Soule," in which the speaker, recognizing his own sinfulness, yearns for that grace that only God can give. Yet, although the speaker recognizes that "grace, if thou repent, thou canst not lacke" (9), he worries about "who shall give thee that grace to beginne" (10), a question that reminds us of Augustine's belief in man's complete dependence on God for the grace necessary to overcome sin. This sonnet ends with an admonition to the speaker's soul to humble itself and turn to Christ in fervent hope that such true humility will lead to the cleansing of the soul from sin:

> Oh make thy selfe with holy mourning blacke,
> And red with blushing, as thou art with sinne;
> Or wash thee in Christs blood, which hath this might
> That being red, it dyes red soules to white. (11–14)

The emotions expressed in these and the remaining holy sonnets vacillate between hope and near-despair, all resulting from the recognition of sin and desire for grace that defines Augustine's predestinarian theology. As Halewood asserts, these poems proceed "through self-induced despaires and devastations to a mood in which it is possible to talk with God . . . and be assured of his mercy" (79).

As William Bouwsma explained some years ago, Augustine's views led to a greater emphasis on grace and its effect on the heart. In other words, "the Augustinian conception of man . . . inevitably meant that life must be fraught with conflict, an external struggle with other men, but also an inner struggle with destructive impulses in the self that can never be fully overcome" (50). This last point highlights the place of affliction in Augustine's theology, a position that characterizes the drama of Donne's *Devotions Upon Emergent Occasions* (see "Things Indifferent") and his divine poems as discussed above. In short, Donne can be considered a "second S. Augustine" not simply because his life, in Walton's eyes, followed an Augustinian pattern, but, more importantly, because he put into poetry as powerful as that of Augustine's own *Confessions* the emotions behind the predestinarian theology that was Augustine's legacy to the English church.

Notes

1. See Bald on the pattern of Donne's life. See also Sellin for an interesting approach to mending the Jack Donne/Dr. John Donne divide.

2. According to Halewood, "Donne is perhaps the greatest Augustinian enthusiast in the history of English preaching" (47).

3. I owe much to Halewood's important study *The Poetry of Grace*, which was one of the first books to take a positive view in defining Donne's relationship to Augustine in terms of Augustinian views of grace, a position that is very much in harmony with that presented in this essay. Stachniewski (261–69), in his analysis of Donne's *Holy Sonnets*, similarly argues for Donne's strong indebtedness to both Augustine and Calvin, emphasizing the strong points of coincidence between the two.

4. We should note that "among the great Reformers, it is Calvin . . . whose influence worked most strongly in the English Reformation and who can be held most directly responsible for the Augustinianisn of the Elizabethan church—as revealed, for example, in Articles IX through XVIII of the *Thirty-nine Articles of the Church of England*, which established as national belief the 'corruption of the nature of euery man . . . whereby man . . . is of his owne nature inclined to euyll [and] dserueth God's wrath and damnation,' prevenient grace, and justification 'only for the merite of our Lord and sauior Jesus Chrisste, by faith, and not for our owne workes or deseruynges'" (Halewood 56).

5. As Halewood acknowledges, "the vision of man helpless and errant and of God distant but overwhelming in his solicitude, is, of course, an orthodox Christian vision and can be found in every period and setting in the history of Christianity" (40). Still, differences of emphasis are clear in the way Augustine was invoked by members of the Roman versus Reformed churches. See Young on the broadly Christian—and hence not strictly Reformed—dimension to Donne's views of grace.

6. The Arminians and Laudians who gained influence during the 1620s articulated a position on free will and grace that was very similar to that of Pelagius in his attacks on Augustine.

7. For an analysis of the impact of the Thirty Years' War on Englishmen, and particularly Donne, see my essay "John Donne and the Thirty Years' War."

8. The *Dictionary of National Biography (DNB)* characterizes Crompton as a "puritan divine," a label that seems to have resulted from his growing association with the anti-Laudian party during the late 1620s and 1630s. In 1624, when Crompton wrote his first treatise, *Saint Austins Religion*, he was a young "'preacher

of God's word' at Little Kimble." Although he was called before King James after his publication of *Saint Austins Religion*, the *DNB* explains that "the interview . . . ended in the king being satisfied with the orthodoxy of the treatise and in his rewarding the author with 'forty pieces of gold'" (5:150).

Sutcliffe, a conformist divine who became dean of Exeter in 1588 and remained in that position for forty years, was perhaps best-known for his role in the founding of "a polemical college at Chelsea" (*DNB* 19:175) whose establishment "was intended for a spirituall garrison, with a magazine of all books for that purpose; where learned divines should study and write in maintenance of all controversies against papists" (*DNB* 19:175). James I nominated the members of the college, which was to be called "King James' College at Chelsey," and Sutcliffe was its first provost (19:176). Sutcliffe was also active in the Virginia Company during the years of Donne's involvement, and "in July 1624 he was one of the commissioners appointed to wind up [its] affairs" (*DNB* 19:176). Sutcliffe, a longtime supporter of King James, fell out of favor with the king as a consequence of his opposition to the Spanish Match (19:176). Throughout his career, Sutcliffe was also known as "the scourge of presbyterians in the 1590s" (Milton 33). Milton also notes that "Sutcliffe and George Carleton similarly claimed that Calvin's views were being misrepresented, and that he was being wrongly accused of arguing that men were damned without respect to sin" (416), thus indicating Sutcliffe's rejection of the more extreme—and non-Augustinian—supralapsarianism position. Perhaps most important, as Milton notes, "these writers [including Sutcliffe and Carleton] sought to *defend* Calvin and Beza against accusations, rather than depicting themselves as explicitly dissenting from the Calvinist tradition, or denying the Church of England's place within it" (416).

Sutcliffe's attack was followed by a new translation of the *Confessions* by William Watts in 1631, which similarly is critical in its attack of Matthew's earlier translation. As his title page indicates, Watts certainly intended his translation as one in which "divers Antiquities are explained; and the marginall notes of a former Popish Translation, answered."

9. In his *Cygnea Cantio*, Crompton's contemporary Daniel Featley recounts King James's reaction to Crompton's attack on Matthew's "popish translation." According to Featley, the volume as it appears was considered entirely within the bounds of the Church of England's soteriology, though some disagreement emerged on questions of discipline. See 10–16.

10. As Halewood explains, "it is overwhelmingly clear that St. Augustine is Donne's most heavily used nonscriptural source and that St. Paul is his favorite source in scripture. This pattern of preference in authorities could probably be shown to be almost a standard Reformation pattern and reflects the characteristic Reformation intensity of interest in the great Pauline and Augustinian themes of man's sin, God's mercy, and the process by which mercy acts on sin" (60).

11. According to most church historians, the Calvinist/Arminian debate on questions of predestination and grace that took place at the Synod of Dort was in many ways a seventeenth-century reenactment of the fifth-century Augustinian/Pelagian debate. In other words, like Pelagius, the Arminians argued for a role for free will in man's salvation, a role that was denied by both Augustine in his responses to Pelagius and by Calvin and his followers in the sixteenth and seventeenth centuries.

12. Although reading Donne in the context of Augustinianism is not new, the majority of readings have focused on Donne's transformation from Jack Donne, the rake, to Dr. John Donne, dean of St. Paul's, in a transformation that resembles that of Augustine as described in his *Confessions*. Other essays on Donne and Augustine focus on Augustine's views on reason and faith (Sherwood), his importance in helping define a methodology of rhetoric and interpretation (Shuger, Todd), Augustine and rhetorical strategies (Quinn), Augustine and Protestant poetics and biblical genre theory (Lewalski), and Augustine and time (Brooks).

13. Here Halewood—correctly, I believe—argues against the position on meditation taken by Louis Martz in his influential study *The Poetry of Meditation*, a position that continues to have some influence with readers of Donne's poetry and prose. See Stachniewski's essay for commentary on the limitations of applying the Ignatian model popularized by Martz to Donne's divine poems.

14. Gardner considers 1609–10 the probable date of composition of Donne's *Holy Sonnets*, with the exception of these three from the Westmoreland manuscript (xlii–l). As Stachniewski reminds us, "acceptance of this dating means that Donne wrote the poems long before the ascendancy of Laud—before, that is, those who promoted Calvinist dogma were, by the expedient of identifying them with supposedly disreputable 'puritans,' polarized to an ideological extremity, and before this manoeuvre enabled a critique of Calvinism, in some circles, to be confidently developed" (287).

15. Although Grant's essay on "Augustinian Spirituality and the *Holy Sonnets*" does read Donne's *Holy Sonnets* in the context of Augustine, the Augustine whom Grant presents is not the late anti-Pelagian Augustine to which Donne's contemporaries Sutcliffe and Crompton, as well as Donne himself, responded. Rather, Grant presents a Donne who takes a balanced, *via media* position with regard to a medieval and Reformation Augustine which rejects the severity of the late Augustine. Grant's understanding of *via media*, essentially, as something between Rome and Geneva, presents a view that has received much rethinking in the years since his article appeared. In many ways, Grant's position resembles that of Potter and Simpson, for while Grant remarks that "it is hard to ignore the stress Donne places on the Fall, and his obsession with sin" (550), Grant associates Donne with the "seventeenth-century latitudinarian desire to repudiate the harsh doctrinal derivations

from Augustine, such as they were to be found, for example, among the Reformers" (544). I see no evidence that Donne repudiates Augustine's essential predestinarian theology, though one can argue that in his role as pastor Donne attempted to minister to his parishioners in language that might be mistaken for such a repudiation. Thus, while Grant focuses on how Donne's poems represent a medieval Augustinian spiritual tradition, this essay argues that Donne's poems grow out of a distinctly Protestant encounter with Augustine that defined Protestantism in the early modern era. In his brief note, Ware affirms Donne's indebtedness to Augustine while at the same time reminding us that Donne was his own thinker who in his sermons would modify Augustine and all other church fathers and church commentators to serve his purposes. While Ware's brief reminder of the independence of Donne's thinking is useful, his argument does not question Donne's overall indebtedness to Augustine, particularly with regard to the latter's predestinarian thinking.

16. Sellin defines several classes of speakers using as his guide the 1619 Articles of the Synod of Dort, a document that shares much with classic predestinarian thinking derived either directly or through intermediaries from Augustine's late anti-Pelagian tracts. Hence these categories are useful to us as we explore the Augustinian dimensions of Donne's *Holy Sonnets*.

17. For a description of the Synod of Dort, including the English participation in it, see Shami (in her article in this collection), Cogswell, and Sellin. As Sellin reminds us, "both the genesis of the synod [of Dort] in the clash between Perkins and Arminius and its aftermath that after 1619 led in England to the rise of Laud ran exactly parallel with Donne's life from his young manhood in the early 1590s to his full maturity as a divine, and he commented on the synodal process and findings both repeatedly and positively" (163).

Works Cited

Augustine, Saint, Bishop of Hippo. *De Correptione et Gratia*. Trans. John C. Murray. Fathers of the Church series, vol. 4. New York: Cima Publishing, 1947.
———. *De Praedestinatione Sanctorum*. Trans. Peter Holmes and Robert Ernest Wallis. *The Anti-Pelagian Work of Saint Augustine, Bishop of Hippo*. Vol. 3 Edinburgh: T. & T. Clark, 1926.
Bald, R. C. *John Donne: A Life*. Ed. W. Milgate. London: Oxford UP, 1970.
Bouwsma, William J. "The Two Faces of Humanism." *Itinerarium Italicum: The Profile of the Italian Renaissance in the Mirror of Its European Transformations*. Ed. Heiko A. Oberman and Thomas A. Brady. Leiden: Brill, 1975. 3–60.
Brooks, Helen B. "Donne's 'Goodfriday, 1613. Riding Westward' and Augustine's Psychology of Time." Frontain and Malpezzi 284–305.

Brown, Peter. *Augustine of Hippo: A Biography*. Berkeley: U of California P, 1967.

Cogswell, Thomas. *The Blessed Revolution: English Politics and the Coming of War, 1621–1624*. Cambridge: Cambridge UP, 1989.

Crompton, William. *Saint Austins Religion: Wherein is manifestly proved out of the Workes of that Learned Father, who lived neere twelve hundred yeares before the time of Luther; that he dissented from Poperie, and agreed with the Religion of Protestants, in all the main Poynts of Faith and Doctrine: Contrary to that Impudent, Erronious, and Slanderous Position of the bragging Papist of our Times, who falsly affirme, Wee had no Religion, before the Times of Luther and Calvine. Whereunto is newly added, Saint Austin's Summes; in Answer to Mr. John Breerely, Priest*. London, 1625.

Dictionary of National Biography. Ed. Sir Leslie Stephen and Sir Sidney Lee. London: Oxford UP, 1917.

Donne, John. *John Donne: The Divine Poems*. Ed. Helen Gardner. 2nd ed. Oxford: Clarendon, 1978.

———. *Sermons*. Ed. George R. Potter and Evelyn M. Simpson. 10 vols. Berkeley: U of California P, 1953–62.

Featley, Daniel. *Cygneea Cantio: Or, Learned Decisions and most Prudent and Pious Directions for Students in Divinitie; Delivered by our late Soveraigne of Happie Memorie, King James, at White Hall a few weekes before his Death*. London, 1629.

Frontain, Raymond-Jean, and Frances M. Malpezzi, eds. *John Donne's Religious Imagination: Essays in Honor of John T. Shawcross*. Conway: U of Central Arkansas P, 1995.

Gibson, Edgar C. S., ed. *The Thirty-nine Articles of the Church of England*. 2 vols. London: Methuen and Co., 1897.

Grant, Patrick. "Augustinian Spirituality and the *Holy Sonnets* of John Donne." *English Literary History* 38 (1971): 542–61.

Halewood, William. *The Poetry of Grace*. New Haven: Yale UP, 1970.

Lewalski, Barbara. *Protestant Poetics and the Seventeenth-Century Religious Lyric*. Princeton: Princeton UP, 1979.

MacCulloch, Diarmaid. *The Later Reformation in England: 1547–1603*. New York: St. Martin's P, 1990.

Martz, Louis. *The Poetry of Meditation: A Study in English Religious Literature of the Seventeenth Century*. 2nd ed. New Haven: Yale UP, 1962.

Matthew, Sir Tobie. *The Confessions of the Incomparable Doctour S. Augustine, translated into English*. London, 1620.

Milton, Anthony. *Catholic and Reformed: The Roman and Protestant Churches in English Protestant Thought, 1600–1640*. Cambridge: Cambridge UP, 1995.

Papazian, Mary A. "John Donne and the Thirty Years' War." *John Donne Journal* 19 (2000): 235–66.

———. "Literary 'Things Indifferent': The Shared Augustinianism of Donne's *Devotions* and Bunyan's *Grace Abounding*." Frontain and Malpezzi 324–49.

Pelikan, Jaroslav. *Reformation of Church and Dogma (1300–1700). The Christian Tradition: A History of the Development of Doctrine.* Vol. 4. Chicago: U of Chicago P, 1984.

Placher, William C. *A History of Christian Theology: An Introduction.* Philadelphia: Westminster P, 1983.

Potter and Simpson. See Donne, *Sermons.*

Quinn, Dennis. "Donne's Christian Eloquence." *English Literary History* 27 (1960): 276–97.

Sellin, Paul R. "The Mimetic Poetry of Jack and John Donne: A Field Theory for the Amorous and the Divine." *Sacred and Profane: Secular and Devotional Interplay in Early Modern British Literature.* Ed. Helen Wilcox, Richard Todd, and Alaistair MacDonald. Amsterdam: VU UP, 1996. 163–72.

Sherwood, Terry. "Reason, Faith, and Just Augustinian Lamentation in Donne's Elegy on Prince Henry." *Studies in English Literature* 13 (1973): 53–67.

———. "Reason in Donne's Sermons." *English Literary History* 29 (1972): 353–74.

Shuger, Debora. *Habits of Thought in the English Renaissance: Religion, Politics, and the Dominant Culture.* Berkeley: U of California P, 1990.

———. *Sacred Rhetoric: The Christian Grand Style in the English Renaissance.* Princeton: Princeton UP, 1988.

Stachniewski, John. *The Persecutory Imagination: English Puritanism and the Literature of Religious Despair.* Oxford: Clarendon, 1991.

Steinmetz, David. *Luther and Staupitz: An Essay in the Intellectual Origins of the Protestant Reformation.* Durham: Duke UP, 1980.

Sutcliffe, Matthew. *The Unmasking of a Masse-monger. Who in the Counterfeit Habit of S. Augustine hath cunningly crept into the Closets of many English Ladies. Or, The Vindication of Saint Augustines Confessions, from the false and malicious Calumniations of a late noted Apostate.* London, 1626.

Todd, Richard. *The Opacity of Signs: Acts of Interpretation in George Herbert's "The Temple."* Columbus: U of Missouri P, 1986.

Walton, Issak. *Life of Donne. Eighty Sermons.* Ed. John Donne, Jr. London, 1640.

Ware, Tracy. "Donne and Augustine: A Qualification." *Notes and Queries* 30.5 (1983): 425–27.

Watts, William. *Saint Augustines Confessions translated and with some marginall notes illustrated.* London, 1631.

Young, Robert V. "Donne's Holy Sonnets and the Theology of Grace." *"Bright Shootes of Everlastingnesse": The Seventeenth-Century Religious Lyric.* Ed. Claude J. Summers and Ted-Larry Pebworth. Columbia: U of Missouri P, 1987. 20–39.

4

John Donne and Paolo Sarpi

Rendering the Council of Trent

JEFFREY JOHNSON

When John Donne made out his will on December 13, 1630, he bequeathed to Henry King, his close friend and executor, "the twoe Pictures of *Padre Paolo* and *Fulgentio* wch hange in the Parlo*ur* at my howse at Pauls" (Bald 563). The paintings of these two Venetians, the one of Paolo Sarpi (who in 1606 was appointed state theologian to the Republic of Venice) and the other of Fulgenzio Micanzio (Sarpi's initimate associate), are unusual among Donne's art collection because they are portraits of contemporary subjects, and he displayed them in the parlor, the most public room in the deanery of St. Paul's. It seems likely that the portrait of Sarpi and the companion picture of Micanzio were copies of the ones known to have been made in 1607 at the request of Sir Henry Wotton. During this time Wotton was the English ambassador to Venice, and after his return to England he was in the habit of presenting copies of these paintings to his friends.[1] The portrait of Sarpi, in particular, may or may not have been the now familiar image showing the black spot on his right temple that represents the wound he suffered from a murderous assault commonly thought to have been ordered by the pope in October 1607.

According to the historical accounts by R. C. Bald and, more recently, by Dennis Flynn, it seems probable that Donne met Sarpi during his trip to Venice in 1605. Donne had been licensed to travel abroad with Sir Walter Chute on February 16, 1605,[2] and it was during this trip that Donne visited with his friend Henry Wotton, who would surely have put him in contact with Sarpi. Although by 1605 Sarpi had not yet become theological counselor to the Republic of Venice, he was, as Bald points out, by the time of Donne's visit "already a man of influence in affairs of state, and was in contact with many learned Protestants throughout Europe" so that Sarpi was "such a man, in other words, as a visitor to Venice like Donne would be eager to meet" (151). The likelihood that, through Wotton, Donne did meet so prominent a figure as Sarpi, coupled with the portraits noted above (and their prominence in Donne's art collection), seems to indicate that Donne held the Venetian in rather high esteem. However, the lack of any mention of Sarpi in Donne's extant writings (other than his will) raises questions concerning the nature of Donne's apparent admiration for Sarpi and the extent of any influence Sarpi may have had on Donne.

One discernible, and intriguing, point of intersection for Donne and Sarpi is their mutual criticism of the Council of Trent. Sarpi (in his *History of the Council of Trent*) and Donne (throughout his extant sermons) both condemn the council on the grounds that it not only failed to reunite Christendom in western Europe but that it finally only succeeded in establishing irreconcilable divisions between Roman Catholics and Protestants. At first blush, Donne and Sarpi seem to share decidedly similar views regarding both conciliarism and, as a consequence, the council's failure to discover an alternative policy to the controversies that necessitated the council, other than the one that simply protected and reaffirmed papal absolutism.

Such significant points of similarity lead Frances Yates to espouse that Donne "held a theological position similar to that of Sarpi" (135). A closer examination, however, reveals otherwise. Donne and Sarpi, in fact, arrive at some similar conclusions from profoundly distinct philosophical and theological foundations. Sarpi's deep pessimism regarding the limitations of the human intellect and the affinities he has for the doctrines of predestination and human depravity stand in contrast to Donne's own brand of philosophical idealism and conflict theologically with Donne's insistence on the unity that is attained in the visible Church as it conforms itself to the Trinity. The purpose of this study, therefore, is not only to highlight the similarities between Donne and Sarpi as interpreters of the Council of Trent but finally to disclose the departures in their renderings of the council and its rulings. Both Sarpi and Donne argue for religious reform, yet neither pursues a Reformation that can be strictly identified as either Protestant or Catholic/Counter; each seeks, in his own way, a reformation of a more fundamental nature that transcends the bounds of sectarian allegiance. Such a clarification of the thought of Donne and Sarpi provides a lens through which to gauge the complexity of responses to the Council of Trent and the religious controversies it sparked.

I

There is little doubt that Sir Henry Wotton used the opportunity afforded him as English ambassador to Venice to exercise his zeal for introducing Protestantism in Italy, and his characterizations of and interactions with Sarpi reflect this mind-set. In a letter to the earl of Salisbury (September 13, 1607), Wotton describes Sarpi as "a sound Protestant, as yet in the habit of a friar" (Smith 1:399). While in retrospect Wotton's assessment certainly appears overblown, he seems to have had good reasons at the time for his optimism. For example, after Wotton's initial arrival in Venice, the Republican government granted his request to hold religious services according to the Church of England ritual, and a significant number of Venetians soon began to attend. In addition, we also know that during this time (probably through Wotton) Sarpi procured and read Calvin's *Institutes* and that late in 1607, on the advice of Sarpi and Micanzio, Wotton arranged for the Genevan pastor Giovanni Diodati to visit Venice. Further, in 1609 Micanzio preached a series of Lenten sermons in which he urged the large crowds that gathered to embrace a belief in justification by faith and to read and interpret the Scriptures without the gloss of human tradition. Finally, one of Sarpi's suggestions to Wotton was the establishment of a Protestant seminary on the borders of Italy, as a Protestant counterpart to the Jesuit College at Rheims, and during Wotton's second embassy he successfully negotiated with the Grison Republic to found just such a college, though the project was short-lived.[3]

There are, however, good reasons to believe that Sarpi's actions had less to do with affirming Protestantism than with displaying his own distrust of the papal absolutism that he believed defined the Roman Catholic Church. William Bouwsma contends that Sarpi's willingness to collaborate with English Protestants (as well as with Lutherans and Calvinists from the Continent) for ends both political and religious is grounded in his distrust in human capabilities to produce a rational and coherent definition of faith. As a result, Bouwsma explains, "rather than an expression of *politique* indifference or the consequence of a direct inspiration from Protestant doctrines," Sarpi could not exclude any of these Protestant "heretics" on dogmatic grounds, "for no human authority could be considered intellectually competent to determine their orthodoxy" ("Papacy"

371). It is just this emphasis on the limitations of human intellect and efforts, along with the complementary need to place one's trust wholly in divine grace, that informs Sarpi's recounting of the Council of Trent.

Throughout his *History of the Council of Trent*, Sarpi laments the opportunity missed at Trent for reforming the church, such as when he writes in the opening pages of the work that "It will not be inconuenient therefore to call it [the Council of Trent] the Iliade of our age" (2).[4] In this context, David Wootton concludes that "Much of the *History of Trent* is concerned with exposing the hypocrisy of the papacy, and indeed as far as Sarpi is concerned the whole of scholastic theology is no more than an elaborate mask devised to conceal papal self-interest" (112). Bouwsma reaches a similar conclusion, stating, "Again and again Sarpi appears to discern in the deliberations of the Council only the complicated interplay of passion and self-interest" that reveals "the antagonism between papalism and conciliarism," and that these concerns place Sarpi clearly on the side "of charity and open discussion rather than force in dealing with error" (*Defense*, 574, 588).

Displaying the dismay of an idealist, such as one often finds in Donne's work, Sarpi laments throughout his *History* the opportunity lost at Trent for putting self-interest aside in order to achieve the conciliarism that the council promised. For example, Sarpi explains that in 1545, after a long series of carefully orchestrated delays, the papally appointed legates at Trent finally pronounced that the council would be assembled for three causes: "for the extirpation of heresie, [the] restitution of Ecclesiastical discipline, and [the] regaining of peace" (130). Because of the unwillingness by the Catholics to work toward any type of church reunification, Sarpi warns in the third paragraph of the work that "the causes and managings" he will relate are those "which hath gotten a forme and conclusion contrary altogether of the deseigne of them that procured it, and to the feare of those that with all diligence disturbed it; a cleare instruction for vs to referre our selues to God, and not to trust in the wisedome of man" (1). As a result, Sarpi contends that the council "hath so established the Schisme, and made the parties so obstinate, that the discords are become irreconcilable" and "hath caused the greatest deformation that euer was since Christianity did begin" (2). In fact, Sarpi doubts the validity of the council as a spiritual body at all, believing it to have been utterly under papal control rather than the guidance of the Holy Spirit, "by repeating (or inventing) the joke," as Wootton writes, "that it was evident that the Holy Spirit travelled back and forth between Rome and Trent in a despatch box" (110).[5]

Donne's comments on and reactions to the Council of Trent, when viewed against the backdrop of his friendship with Sir Henry Wotton, of his probable meeting with Sarpi, and of Sarpi's writings themselves, reveal the parallels Donne perceived between the situations of Venice and the English church with respect to the question of papal authority. Anthony Raspa, in the introduction to his edition of Donne's *Pseudo-Martyr*, states, "Donne's request to contemporary popes in *Pseudo-Martyr* was that they should be as conciliatory to England as they had been to the Venetian, to the Spanish and to the German rulers, and to free the English-Catholic conscience from having to refuse to swear fealty to James," and he later adds, "Of the three controversies between the Catholic rulers of Venice, Sicily and Germany, and the papacy, that Donne used to illustrate his argument about swearing to English Catholics, the Venetian affair provided him with the most detailed parallel with the English cause" (xxiv, xxvii). Further, Dennis Flynn argues that "it seems inescapable that at about the time Donne met Sarpi, and subsequent to their meeting, Donne devoted considerable study to the literature surrounding the Venetian interdict, including Sarpi's writings," and that "in the writing of *Pseudo-Martyr*, Donne reveals a complete familiarity with the terms and published record of the interdict controversy," to which Donne alludes in *Pseudo-Martyr* "more than to any other" (353, 346).[6]

It is evident in *Pseudo-Martyr* that Donne sees the Council of Trent as the source of abuses in papal authority directly affecting the religious controversies related to Venice and the Church of England. In particular, Donne reacts to a variety of the council's rulings that, from Donne's perspective, were innovations that redefined orthodoxy. For example, in Book 12 of *Pseudo-Martyr* Donne writes:

> When *Paulus* 4. had a *purpose* to take in, and binde more sorts of men, by that oath which was framed according to the *Trent Councell*, for them onely who were admitted to spirituall dignities, and some few others, and so to swear all those men fast to the Doctrine of that Councel, and to the obedience of the Church of Rome, it is expressed in so exquisite and so safe wordes, as can admit no escape. For, how ignorant soever he be in controverted *Divinity*, every one which takes that oath, must sweare, *That there are seven Sacraments instituted by Christ*; which any of their Doctors might have doubted and impugn'd an houre before; as it appears by *Azorius*, that *Alensis* and *Bonaventure* did *of Confirmation*, *Hugo Victor* and *Bonaventure* of *extreame unction*, *Hostiensis* and *Durandus* of *Matrimony*, and other of others: and he must sweare, *That he beleeves Purgatory, Indul-*

gences, and veneration of Reliques: and hee must sweare, *That all things contrary to the Councell are hereticall.* And this oath is not onely *Canonized* (as their phrase is) by being inserted into the body of the *Canon* law, but it is alloweed a roome in the Title, *De Summa Trinitate, & fide Catholica,* and so made of equall credite with that. (243)

Although Donne published *Pseudo-Martyr* in 1610, which predates by five years his taking Holy Orders, the assessments of the Council of Trent's *de fide* rulings in the passage above inform his comments on the council found throughout his extant sermons.[7]

In the *Sermons,* Donne joins Sarpi in his questioning of the validity of the Council of Trent (see 5:71–72).[8] There is little doubt that for Donne "the fundamental obstacles to communion with the Roman Church are the Jesuits and the Council of Trent" (Shami, "Anti-Catholicism" 145), as Donne himself states unamibiguously in his 1622 Ascension Day sermon: "we had received the Reformation before the Council of *Trent,* and before the growth of the Jesuits: And if we should turn to them now, we should be worse then we were before we receiv'd the Reformation; and the Council of *Trent* and the Jesuits have made that Religion worse then it was" (4:139). The condemnation Donne levels against Trent resides primarily in the new articles of faith affirmed by the council that Donne sees as additions to what the primitive church taught was necessary for salvation (see 3:209). Throughout the *Sermons,* Donne explains that "certainly nothing endangers a Church more, then to draw indifferent things to be necessary," and he conjectures that the Roman Catholic Church must surely regret to have made "so many particular things, which were indifferent, and problematically disputed before, to bee had necessarily *De fide,* in the Councell of Trent" (2:204). Again, in the conclusion to his Lincoln's Inn sermon preached on Ascension Day 1622, Donne laments the faulty reasoning that leads to the *de fide* rulings at Trent:

> And so thou maist fall into the first snare, it hath been done, therefore it may be done; and into another after, It may be done, therefore it must be done: When thou art come to think that some men are saved that have done it, thou wilt think that no man can be saved except he do it: From making infirmities excusable necessary (which is the bondage the Council of *Trent* hath laid upon the world) to make Problematical Things, Dogmatical; and matter of Disputation, matter of Faith; to bring the University into *Smithfield,* and heaps of Arguments into Piles of Faggots. (4:144)

What clearly disturbs Donne about these innovations is how ephemeral and delimiting they are: "Threescore yeares agoe, a man might have beene sav'd at halfe the price hee can now: Threescore yeares agoe, he might have beene saved for beleeving the *Apostles Creed*; now it will cost him the *Trent Creed* too" (6:249).[9] Yet, Donne also objects to the ways in which such rulings are unnaturally self-propogating, such as he explains in his 1621 Christmas sermon:

> As in the heavens the stars were created at once, with one *Fiat*, and then being so made, stars doe not beget new stars, so the *Christian doctrine necessary* to salvation, was delivered once, that is, intirely in one spheare, in the body of the Scriptures. And then, as stars doe not beget stars, Articles of faith doe not beget Articles of faith; so, as that the *Councell of Trent* should be brought to bed of a *new Creed*, not conceived before by the *holy Ghost* in the Scriptures, and, (which is a monstrous birth) the child greater then the Father, as soon as it is borne, the new Creed of the *Councell of Trent* to containe more Articles, then the old Creed of the Apostles did. (3:369)

As a result, Donne believes that the council's pronouncement of "this sureness upon so many new Articles" is a counterfeiting of "the language of the Holy Ghost" (6:300) and, as such, heresy, for "if all the particular doctrines be not *Hereticall*, yet, the doctrine of inducing new Articles of faith is *Hereticall*, and that doctrine runs through all the Articles, for else they could not be Articles" (3:132). While he never dismisses the Roman Catholic Church as a whole, Donne nevertheless condemns the Council of Trent for operating without faith and at cross-purposes with the Holy Spirit. As such, Shami correctly assesses that "despite Donne's uncovering of the corruptions of the contemporary Roman Church, then, there are signs that reconciliation with it is possible, although never on Tridentine terms" ("Anti-Catholicism" 158).

The particular articles that Donne rails against consistently throughout the *Sermons* are the first two decrees from the Fourth Session at Trent (held on April 8, 1546), the former dealing with the notion of tradition (in which the writings of the church fathers are afforded equal authority with the canonical scriptures)[10] and the latter with the issue of biblical interpretation (which specified that orthodox renderings of the Scriptures required the unanimous consent of the church fathers).[11] In his sermon to Charles I at Whitehall on April 18, 1626, Donne explains the motivations he believes to be at work regarding this issue of ecclesiastical authority and biblical interpretation. In fact, Donne asserts that the *Arcana Imperii* of the Roman Catholic Church are easily discovered and result, he writes, "not because they [the Catholics] absolutely oppose the Scriptures, or stiffly deny them to be the most certain and constant rule that can be presented" (7:124), but because of the self-interest the papacy extended itself in affording the traditions of the church fathers the same authority as Scripture:

> But because the Scriptures are constant, and limited, and determined, there can be no more Scriptures, And they should be shrewdly prejudiced, and shrewdly disadvantaged, if all emergent cases arising in the Christian world, must be judged by a Law, which others may know beforehand, as well as they; Therefore being wise in their own generation, they choose rather to lay up their Rule in a Cupboard, then upon a Shelfe, rather *in Scrinio pectoris*, in the breast and bosome of one man, Then upon every deske in a study, where every man may lay, or whence every man may take a Bible. (7:124–25)

Thus, Donne doubts the validity of the Council of Trent and interprets the underlying motivations for the rulings of the synod precisely in the same vein as Sarpi. The conciliatory possibilities of Trent, Sarpi and Donne both arrgee, were undermined to preserve papal absolutism.

II

It is clear that Donne and Sarpi share common judgments in their renderings of Trent, especially concerning the papal self-interest that governed the council and which, they believed, established the Counter-Reformation by thwarting the possibilities for conciliarism. As thinkers, however, Sarpi and Donne begin from very different premises that finally reveal their distinct aims and ideals, and their respective epistemological and theological differences are most clearly seen in their views of the Church.

William Bouwsma offers a characterization of Sarpi as "an empiricist, skeptical about all speculative thought, concerned with the utility and the merely human meaning of what can be known, and hostile to the construction of rational systems" (*Defense* 518–19). Sarpi's own metaphoric explanation in his *History of the Council of Trent* reflects his distrust of general principles as the foundations of rational inquiry by means of his insistence that human reasoning must proceed from the concrete and particular: "To someone reading this report, its attention to trivial things and causes may seem excessive. But the writer of the history, taking a different view, has thought it necessary to show what tiny rivulets caused the great lake that occupies Europe."[12]

Sarpi's methodological approach in the *History* is complemented by the first of his *Pensieri*, in which he enumerates the modes of human knowledge. In their descending order of excellence, the first mode is the knowledge acquired through action, by which one can know both the essence and the cause of things; the second is the knowledge acquired through observation, by which one can know the essence but not the cause; and the third is the knowledge acquired through conjecture, by which one may know what is possible but not always what is true. Later in his *Pensieri*, Sarpi reiterates his epistemological approach in a slightly altered form:

> There are four modes of philosophizing: the first with reason alone, the second with sense alone, the third with reason first and then sense, the fourth beginning with sense and ending with reason. The first is the worst, because from it we know what we would like to be, not what is. The third is bad because we many times distort what is into what we would like, rather than adjusting what we would like to what is. The second is true but crude, permitting us to know little and that rather of things than of their causes. The fourth is the best we can have in this miserable life.[13]

The wording that concludes this passage illustrates Sarpi's pessimism concerning the limits of human understanding and, by extension, his inherent objection to all systematized religious belief, including the scholasticism that the Council of Trent established as dogma.

A portion of Sarpi's account of the Fourth Session at Trent provides an excellent example of the "tiny rivulets" of the council proceedings that, instead of producing a conciliatory pursuit of truth, codified papal self-interest. In 1546 the council debated the Lutheran contention "that to vnderstand the Scripture well, or to alledge the proper words, it is necessary to haue recourse to the texts of the originall tongue in which it is written, and to reprooue the Latine translation; as full of errors" (150). Sarpi notes, not without satiric effect, that the issue was considered "betweene some few who had good knowledge of the Latine, and some tast of the Greeke, and others who were ignorant in the Tongues" (155). Sarpi then provides the argument offered by Friar Aloisius of Catanea, who begins the debate by drawing upon "the iudgement of Cardinall *Caietan*" (155). The friar points out that while Cajetan had "no knowledge himselfe" of Hebrew and Greek, nevertheless "he imployed men of vnderstanding, who made construction of the text vnto him word by word" (155). According to Sarpi, Aloisius then asserts "That good Cardinall was wont to say, that to understand the Latine text, was not to vnderstand the infallible word of God, but the word of the translator, subiect and obnoxious vnto errors. That *Hierome* spake well, that to prophesie and write holy bookes proceeded from the holy Ghost, but to translate them into another tongue, was a worke of humane skill" (155). A few pages later in this same section of the *History*, Sarpi reiterates a similar point in the argument offered by the Benedictine abbot D. Isodorus Clarus: "Saint *Hierome* saith plainely that no interpreter hath spokon by the holy Ghost. The Edition which wee haue is his for the most part: it would bee strange to attribute the assistance of God to him that knoweth and affirmeth hee hath it not. Whereof no translation can bee compared to the text in the originall tongue" (157). As a solution, Friar Aloisius further argues that the council could correct a translation according to the original languages and urges that "the holy Ghost, which assisteth Synods in matters of faith, would keepe them from erring; and such a translation, so examined and approoued, might be called authenticall" (155). Sarpi's satiric method in the *History* and his deep pessimism regarding the limitations of human reasoning are revealed in the concluding words of Friar Aloisius, who, admitting the difficulties of producing a corrected, authentic translation, concedes, "But this beeing a worke of ten yeeres, and impossible to be vndertaken, it seemed better to leaue things as they had remained 1500. yeeres" (155–56).

In spite of Aloisius's undermining of his own argument, Sarpi contends that the friar's view was a minority opinion. The majority, Sarpi explains, believed it was necessary, without apology or commentary, to promote the Vulgate, "which formerly hath beene read in the Churches, and vsed in the schooles," as divinely inspired and authentic, for "otherwise they should yeeld the cause to the Lutherans, and open a gate to innumerable heresies hereafter, and continually trouble the peace of Christendom" (156). Sarpi adds that the council majority also feared that a reliance on the Hebrew and Greek originals of the Scripture would require and foster a newly trained group of grammarians and that "these new Grammarians would confound all, and would be made Iudges and arbiters of faith" (156). Further, Sarpi includes the additional position by the majority that "The Inquisitors will not be able to proceede against the Lutherans, in case they know not Hebrew and Greek" (156). Finally, on this matter, Sarpi reports, "The difficulties were not so great, but that the vulgar edition was approued, almost by a generall consent, the discourse hauing made deepe impression in their mindes, that Grammarians would take vpon them to teach Bishops and Diuines" (159). This brief overview of one part of Sarpi's account of the Fourth Session at Trent is typical of his approach and intent throughout the *History*. Sarpi believes that a truthful interpretation of Trent can only be attained by examining the particulars of the proceedings and that aggregately the particulars form the "great lake" of deception and self-interest in which all of the rulings at Trent were submerged.

In the light of Sarpi's epistemological perspective, his theological preference for a distinctly Reformed position concerning human depravity and divine grace is understandable. Although Sarpi's theological tendencies are not easily determined (probably as a consequence of his rejection of systematic thought), David Wootton argues that "if one looks across the whole scope of Sarpi's writings this [the doctrine of predestination] is really the only theological issue on which he expressed a clear commitment" (108). Sarpi's characterization in his *History* of the debate over Zwingli's doctrine of predestination reveals his belief in human depravity and the utter dependence on God that individuals have for receiving grace. Sarpi characterizes those at the council who argued for the doctrine as "keeping the mind humble and relying on God, without any confidence in it selfe, knowing the deformity of sinne, and the excellency of diuine grace," while those arguing against the doctrine (those who finally succeeded in having the Zwinglian view declared heretical) only proposed, according the Sarpi, that which "was plausible and popular, cherishing human presumption, and making a good shew," and this view, Sarpi continues, "using humane reasons, preuailed against the others, but comming to the testimonies of the Scripture, they were manifestly ouercome" (212). Here Sarpi expresses not only his belief that human sinfulness keeps individuals from playing any role in receiving divine grace but also his reliance on the Scriptures as the sole authority in matters of doctrine.

Sarpi's view of the Church, then, is a logical extension of these epistemological and theological foundations. It is a view that finds expression primarily in the particular and localized experience of the individual, as well as within individual church communities. Bouwsma summarizes that "Sarpi's concept of the Church is based on his insistence upon the fundamental importance of the individual believer," and thus the Church becomes, he continues, "merely an aggregation of individuals, *convocatio fidelium*" ("Papacy" 371). Sarpi can only conceive of the Church in terms of the "tiny rivulets" of the individual members within it. This concept of the Church, Bouwsma believes, accounts for the fact that Sarpi "showed little enthusiasm for any formal reconciliation and institutional unification between Catholics and Protestants," for to Sarpi "unity savored too much of authoritaian uniformity, and it was therefore the absolute negation of that freedom to which he so much aspired" ("Papacy" 372–73). Thus, it seems that Sarpi pleads for conciliarism in order to validate individual voices and expressions of religious belief and, thereby, to expand the limits of orthodox Christianity. Further, Sarpi even goes so far as to understand the practice of Christianity in extremely individual, private terms. Again, Bouwsma contends that "Divine grace seems also to have operated, for Sarpi, with a minimum of assistance from the visible church; he evidently preferred to derive both nourishment for the Christian life and the assurance of salvation directly from the Scriptures" (*Defense* 532). These views of the Church, and the individual in relation to it, are profoundly different from those of Donne.

III

The contrasts between Sarpi's thought and Donne's are readily perceived in a series of three sermons Donne preached in the spring and early summer of 1626, all using as their text 1 Corinthians 15:29 ("Else, what shall they do that are baptized for the dead? If the dead rise not at all, why are they then baptized for the dead?").[14] While these three sermons do not in and of themselves establish the epistemological and theological foundations for Donne's views on the Church, they do confirm the scope of his thought in these contexts as discovered throughout his *Sermons*.

Donne preached the first of the three sermons at St. Paul's on Easter 1626, in the evening, and although Potter and Simpson characterize the sermon as "curious rather than eloquent" (7:7), Donne is clear in his purpose and design. In the opening paragraph he states explicitly that although the Roman Catholic Church has used this text "to the maintenance of their Purgatory," he adds, "yet all agree, that these words are an argument for the Resurrection, and therefore proper to this day" (7:94). He then enumerates in the *divisio* the "two steps" that will govern the structure of the sermon: "Glory in the end, And Grace in the way; The Glory of our bodies, in the last Resurrection then, And the Grace upon our souls, in their present Resurrection now" (7:95). Donne then immediately adds, by way of elaboration, that this doctrine of the Resurrection, therefore, touches both the future (in the Church triumphant) and the present (in the Church militant). Further, he explains that although the knowledge and assurance of the resurrection of the body is presented and illustrated by reason,

> the roote and foundation thereof is in Faith; though Reason may chafe the wax, yet Faith imprints the seale, (for the Resurrection is not a conclusion out of actuall Reason, but it is an article of supernaturall Faith; and though you assent to me now, speaking of the Resurrection, yet that

is not out of my Logick, nor out of my Rhetorique, but out of that Character, and Ordinance which God hath imprinted in me, in the power and efficacy whereof, I speak unto you, as often as I speak out of this place.) (7:95)

Donne's views on faith and reason have been well argued by Terry Sherwood,[15] so let it suffice here to assert, as the passage above indicates, that Donne is no enemy to reason. In contrast to Sarpi's pessimism, Donne sees reason as necessary for confirming, although never in establishing, the truths revealed through faith. Reason and faith, in Donne's thought, complement one another in the ways in which reason is able to grasp and apply those truths that it could never arrive at without faith. As a result, the complementary exchange of reason and faith also affirms the enabling presence of the corporate body of the Church in the present, as Donne himself imagines in the preaching of this sermon to his auditors at St. Paul's on Easter evening 1626.[16]

Donne preached the second of the three sermons on 1 Corinthians 15:29 at St. Paul's on May 21, 1626. In the opening paragraph he asserts that in the words comprising the Scripture text "the whole Circle of a Christian is designed and accomplished" (7:164), for the spiritual birth of baptism is the first point in the circle, then the point diametrically opposed to the first is death, and finally, the circle is completed in another birth, the resurrection. Donne then immediately reinterprets this circle of experience for the individual in terms of the common body of the Church. In contrast to Sarpi, Donne cannot conceive of the Christian life outside the Church as a corporate body; individual Christians can only find their completion and fulfillment, for Donne, by participating in the shared and public liturgy of the Church.

Later in the rather lengthy introduction to this second sermon, Donne states that "this Dayes Exercise will bee meerely Polemicall, the handling of a Controversie; which though it be not always pertinent, yet neither is it always unseasonable" (7:166). Donne then clarifies the political occasion for engaging in such anti-Catholic commentary, namely the passing of King James, who during his reign had forbidden the preaching of this type of aggressive polemic. Donne then provides, in an uncharacteristically abbreviated *divisio*, the three points he will examine: first, what he labels the grandmother error, which is prayer for the dead; second, the mother error, the doctrine of purgatory; and finally, the children, that is, indulgences. Donne's mentioning here of the death of James I, and its subsequent implication of the new reign under Charles I, opens a window for understanding the broader context of these three sermons. On April 3, 1625, Donne was invited to preach his first sermon to the newly crowned King Charles, and in that sermon, one that Jeanne Shami asserts "is arguably one of the most important sermons Donne preached" ("Anti-Catholicism" 155), Donne delineates the foundations, both religious and political, for the Church in England at that historical moment. Roughly a year later, Donne preached his three-sermon series on 1 Corinthians 15:29. Because of the polemical function of these sermons and because of the principles of biblical interpretation articulated, even belabored, throughout them, it seems prudent to read these three as extensions of and complements to his "foundations" sermon of the previous year. The foundations for biblical interpretation that Donne articulates throughout this trio of sermons embody the discourse of conciliarism he wishes to promote between Protestants and Catholics.

In the middle of this second sermon, during his argument against the doctrine of purgatory, Donne raises an issue that looks back to a concern he touches on in the first sermon and also forward to the rendering of Trent he elucidates in the third of the series. In particular, Donne comments in this middle sermon on the references to purgatory found in the church fathers and the variety of meanings this concept has in their writings, and concludes, "For from how many things, which passe through the Fathers, by way of opinion, and of discourse, are they in the Roman Church departed, onely upon that, That the Fathers said it, but said it not Dogmatically, but by way of discourse, or opinion" (7:178). Donne is concerned here not only with the ruling of Trent that made the tradition of the church fathers of equal authority with the Scriptures but also with the collapse of distinction between things fundamental and things indifferent that makes impossible the discourse over these issues that Donne believes is essential for reconciliation in the Church. In the last sermon in the series, Donne expresses similar concerns in drawing a distinction between the *matter* of religious belief, to which "we are all bound, and bound upon salvation, to think alike," and the *manner* of that belief, by means of which "we may think diversly, without forfeiture of salvation, or impeachment of discretion; For, he is not presently an indiscreet man, that differs in opinion from another man that is discreet, in things that fall under opinion" (7:96–97). It is this same concern over the question of authority and for the principle of discreet discourse that so powerfully informs the third, and clearly the most significant, sermon of the series.

Donne preached the last of his trio of sermons on 1 Corinthians 15:29 on June 18, 1626,[17] and in the brief opening paragraph, instead of offering his usual *exordium*, Donne describes his purpose in an especially truncated manner:

> Wee are now come at last, to that which wast first in our intention, How these words have been detorted, and misapplied by our Adversaries of the Roman Church, for the establishing of those heresies, which we have formerly opposed, And then, the divers wayes, which sounder and more Orthodoxall Divines have held in the Exposition thereof; that so from the first Part, wee may learne what to avoid and shun, and from the second, what to embrace and follow. (7:190)

Then with the second paragraph Donne initiates his objection to Cardinal Bellarmine's interpretation of the Scripture text that shapes Donne's thought throughout this sermon. Although Bellarmine died in 1621, Donne clearly thinks of him as the foremost polemicist for the Roman Catholic Church. This third sermon of the series, as a response to Bellarmine's writings, provides a lesson in biblical interpretation and as such reaffirms Donne's theology of dialogic unity.[18]

The precise nature of Donne's complaint against Bellarmine's interpretation of this text is that the Jesuit cardinal asserts that purgatory is discovered principally in this verse from 1 Corinthians. While Donne first describes his own interpretive methology that "the sense which should ground an assurance in Doctrinall things, should be the literall sense" (7:192), he then expresses his astonishment not only that Bellarmine insists on reading the word "baptism" as "a Baptisme of teares" (a figurative use of the word by which Donne explains that Bellarmine means penance, discipline, suffering) but also that Bellarmine contends that this reading is "the true and naturall sense of the place" (7:192). Donne goes on to explain that Bellarmine supports his argument for this reading by referring to Matthew 20:22 and Luke 12:50, both of which provide examples of Christ using the word "baptism" to describe his passion. Donne then asks, "But what then? Was the Passion of Christ himselfe, such an affliction, as *Bellarmine* speaks of here, and argues from in this place, that is, an affliction so inflicted upon himselfe, and undertaken by himselfe, as that then when he did beare it, he might have forborne it, and refused to beare it?" (7:194). He dismisses Bellarmine's reasoning by concluding that "never any but Christ, in the Scriptures, called Affliction, Baptisme" (7:194).

In response to what he considers the absurdity of Bellarmine's position, Donne reminds his auditors of the basis for biblical interpretation ("We have a Rule, by which that sense will be suspicious to us, which is,

Not to admit figurative senses in the interpretation of Scriptures, where the literall sense may well stand" [7:193]), as well as the article of interpretation established at Trent that should have governed Bellarmine ("And he himselfe hath a Rule, [if he remember the Councell of Trent] by which that sense cannot be admitted by himselfe, which is, That they must interpret Scriptures according to the unanime consent of the Fathers; and he knowes in his conscience, that he hath not don so" [7:193]). In the context of urging sound principles of interpretation and of the controversy over *sola scriptura*, Donne raises what for him is *the* interpretive question of this particular Scripture text:

> For what were all this to the Resurrection of the body, which is S. *Pauls* scope, and purpose in the place, *If men were baptized*, that is, (as *Bellarmine* would have it) if they did suffer voluntarily, and unnecessarily affliction *for the Dead*, that is, to deliver their soules out of Purgatory; what would all this conduce to the proofe of the Resurrection of the body? (7:195)

As a result, because Bellarmine persists in an interpretation that blinds itself to the commonsense and literal reading of the passage, to the complications in ascribing the unique instances of Christ's application of the word "baptism" in the Gospels to this letter from St. Paul, and to the context in which this verse appears, Donne finds Bellarmine's argument specious. In addition, Donne soundly condemns Bellarmine for ignoring the Trent ruling of unanimous consent that should have governed the cardinal's own interpretation:

> Since then it is the Exposition of a few onely, *Alii dicunt, Aliqui dicunt,* Others have said so, Some few have said so, and those few are late men, new men, and of those new men, Jesuits, and Readers, and Cardinalls have differed from that opinion, this Jesuit, and Reader, and Cardinall *Bellarmine* needed not to have made that victorious acclamation, *Hic locus*, we desire no more then this place, for the evident proofe of Purgatory. (7:196–97)

Donne is keen to point out—to the extent that Bellarmine claims his explanation of the Scripture text to be "the evident proofe of Purgatory," and to the extent that this position is by no means derived from the unanimous consent of the church fathers—that Bellarmine's interpretation "leaves out the Fathers themselves out of the Arke, and makes them Heretiques" (7:197). What galls Donne here is the pride and arrogance of a reading that by logical extension, as Donne works so hard to demonstrate, must leave any reading that disagrees with Bellarmine's open to the suspicion of heresy. Here Donne objects not only to the Trent articles regarding principles for biblical interpretation but especially (in this case) to the duplicitous waiving of the Trent rulings that Bellarmine, in so many other instances, staunchly upholds in sniffing out heterodoxy.

When Donne comes to discuss the church fathers in this last sermon of the series, it is to highlight their differences in interpreting the phrase "baptism for the dead" in order to establish that there is no unanimous consent. He begins by noting that Tertullian reads the phrase as "Baptisme by an Atturney, by a Proxy" (7:198); followed by Theodoret, who understands it as "a baptisme of Representation" (7:199); then by Chrysostom and Theophylact, who believe the phrase signifies "a baptisme for the hope of Resurrection" (7:200); and finally, moving "from the Fathers to the Schoole," by Aquinas, who imagines the dead specifically as "Dead works, sins, and so *to be baptized for the dead*, is to be baptized for our sins" (7:200). Prior to offering his own reading of the passage, one that relies on the literal approach he has been urging throughout the sermon, Donne also includes in the second half of this sermon an array of interpretations from modern theologians, both Catholic and Protestant.

Recent articles by Paul Stanwood and Mark Vessey shed interesting light on Donne's appropriation of the church fathers. In his essay discussing "Donne's Art of Preaching and the Reconstruction of Tertullian," Stanwood cites this very passage from Donne's third sermon on 1 Corinthians 15:29 to illustrate how Donne has received inspiration from Tertullian's ideas, although, as Stanwood writes, "often in elaborately misleading ways" (164). He concludes that Donne's references to Tertullian in this sermon "provide only a strange shimmer of patristic authority, a superficial yet amplifying ornament in the sermon as a whole" (165). Vessey's article analyzing Donne's sermon on Psalm 51:7 ("Purge me with hyssope") has paved the way for a critical reevaluation of Donne's use of the church fathers. In particular, Vessey describes Donne's homiletic approach as "his presumptuous deference—or deferential presumption—with respect to the Church Fathers" (100). He concludes that because the references to the fathers have so little effect in assisting or directing Donne's exegesis, "much of what we have taken for erudition is more rightly considered a form of display" (107). Finally, in his article on "Donne's Reinvention of the Fathers," Stanwood finds that "Donne seldom confers with his patristic sources directly," quoting them "inaccurately and out of context," and that Donne thus reinvents the fathers by preaching with their company, "but not really with their exclusive support" (195, 197). While Donne's patristic references provide a veneer, an illusion, of erudition and perhaps of intellectual and rhetorical display, there is little doubt that his use (or misuse) of the church fathers undermines the position of authority the Council of Trent afforded them. In other words, Donne appropriates the writings of the church fathers in ways that illustrate his disdain for the ruling from the Fourth Session of Trent that placed them on the same authoritative plain as Scripture. Thus, in this final sermon on 1 Corinthians 15:29 Donne's inclusion of the fathers all the more clearly establishes his complaint against Bellarmine on these doctrinal grounds. The point here is that Donne incorporates the fathers in this sermon in the same manner he does the other religious thinkers, to engage them in dialogue. Scripture alone is authoritative for Donne; all else is open for discussion and revision, for all else is subject to error.

The method Donne employs throughout the sermons suggests that Bellarmine's interpretation of the Scripture text is the result of theological pride and self-interest in simply upholding, for their own sake, the Roman Catholic positions regarding prayers for the dead, purgatory, and indulgences. This is not conciliarism; this is, instead, the same kind of absolutism that defined the Council of Trent, as Donne seeks to bring to the memory of his auditory at St. Paul's. In fact, it is the communal implications of Donne's theological position that inform the closing section of his last sermon on 1 Corinthians 15:29 and that finally distinguish him theologically from Sarpi.

Following his own literal reading of the Scripture text as St. Paul's argument to prove the resurrection of the body, Donne warns his auditors of the effects that this verse will have on them:

> All S. *Pauls* words work as lightning, *Et capit omne quod tetigerit*, It affects, and it leaves some marke upon every thing that it touches; And if hee have touched thee now, his effect is not onely to make thee beleeve a future resurrection of thy body, but to feele a present resurrection of thy soule, and to make mee beleeve that thou feelest it, by expressing it in thy life and conversation. (7:211)

This is not Sarpi's view of the Church, the singularity of an individual attending to the Scriptures alone. Donne's plea here is for unity, of body and soul, and of individual Christians to one another in their words and actions, for this unity affirms the truth of the Scripture text. Donne then concludes by urging his auditors not only to abstain from their sins but, more importantly, to find joy in seeking the one who will resurrect them body and soul:

> A Resurrection is such an abstinence from the practice of the sin, as is grounded upon a repentance, and a detestation of the sin, and then it is a setling, and an establishing of the soule in that state, and disposition: It is not a sudden and transitory remorse, nor onely a reparation of that which was ruined, and demolished, but it is a building up of habits contrary to former habits, and customes, in actions contrary to that of sin, that we have been accustomed to. (7:213)

In contrast to Sarpi, Donne espouses the belief that the action of grace is itself communal, requiring both the initial, prevenient grace offered by God and the subsequent grace of human efforts that completes the relationship.[19] While Sarpi contends, as he states in his *Pensieri*, that God "acts without discourse" (qtd. in Bouwsma, *Defense* 521), Donne's theology is grounded on a communal understanding of the Church that finds its model in the dialogic unity of the Trinity. In other words, for Donne the godhead itself is a council, and the divine conciliarism of the Trinity serves as the model from which the Church realizes its identity. The profoundly different views of grace held by Donne and Sarpi result in profoundly different views of the Church and of the type of conciliarism that each believes necessary to unify the Church.

In their renderings of the Council of Trent, both Donne and Sarpi are interested in enlarging the fold of orthodox Christianity, and it is with this end in view that they condemn the council. These two are keenly aware of the knotty problem of biblical interpretation and how decidedly the rulings at Trent, through the papal self-interest that they believe engendered them, affected the divisions between Catholics and Protestants. Nevertheless, a comparison of Donne and Sarpi reveals the profound, though not irreconcilable, differences between thinkers who each had his own vision of reform for the Church and of the possibilities for conciliarism.

Notes

I wish to extend my gratitude to Kathleen Gibson, who was gracious in assisting my research, and to Dennis Flynn, who generously shared his scholarship.
    1. See Smith 2:478–79.

2. For overviews of the details establishing Donne's trip to Venice at this time, see Bald 148–53 and Flynn.

3. Smith explains that "in the summer of 1620 the Catholic inhabitants of the Valtelline [which lay in the dominion of the Grison Republic] rose and slaughtered the Protestants; the country was occupied by Spanish troops, and the little seminary seems to have disappeared amid the armies and battles and disasters which filled for years that unhappy valley" (1:162).

4. All references to Sarpi's *History*, unless specified otherwise, are from the English translation by Nathanael Brent.

5. Donne seems to allude to this joke in his 1628 Whitsunday sermon, preached at St. Paul's, when he writes, "The Holy Ghost is no longer Omnipresent, as in *David's* time, (*Whither shall I goe from thy Spirit?*) but he is onely there, whither he shall be sent from Rome in a Cloakbagge, and upon a Post-horse, as it was often complained in the Councell of Trent" (8:265).

6. See also Anthony Raspa's edition of *Pseudo-Martyr* (xxvii).

7. Jeanne Shami concurs on this point, arguing, "Donne's rejection of the decrees of the Council of Trent, however, appears to remain consistent throughout his career" ("Stars" 46n. 30). See also her "Anti-Catholicism," esp. 143–47.

8. All references to Donne's *Sermons* are from the Potter and Simpson edition and are cited by volume and page numbers.

9. See also 3:211 and 6:98.

10. Anthony Milton notes, "Cf. Henry Roger, *The Protestant Church Existent* (1638), p. 111, where he stresses that it was the first decree of Trent, Session 4, which enthroned unwritten traditions. To dissent from this point was 'to be Protestant in the maine point,' since all errors of faith followed from this" (243n. 60).

11. See also 3:176 and 8:357–58. The first decree, on the acceptance of the sacred books and apostolic traditions, reads in part,

> The council clearly perceives that this truth and rule are contained in written books and in unwritten traditions which were received by the apostles from the mouth of Christ himself, or else have come down to us, handed on as it were from the apostles themselves at the inspiration of the holy Spirit. Following the example of the orthodox fathers, the council accepts and venerates with a like feeling of piety and reverence all the books of both the old and the new Testament, since the one God is the author of both, as well as the traditions concerning both faith and conduct, as either directly spoken by Christ or dictated by the holy Spirit, which have been preserved in unbroken sequence in the catholic church.

And the second decree, the rule on the manner of interpreting sacred scripture, reads in part,

> The council further decrees, in order to control those of unbalanced character, that no one, relying on his personal judgment in matters of faith and customs which are linked to the establishment of christian doctrine, shall dare to interpret the sacred scriptures either by twisting its text to his individual meaning in opposition to that which has been and is held by holy mother church, whose function is to pass judgment on the true meaning and interpretation of the sacred scriptures; or by giving it meanings contrary to the unanimous consent of the fathers, even if interpretations of this kind were never intended for publication. (Tanner 2:663, 664)

12. Qtd. in Bouwsma, "Papacy" 360. In the original the text reads, "Ad alcuno nel leggere questa relazione potrebbe parere che, essendo di cose e ragioni leggiere, tenesse del superfluo; ma lo scrittore dell'istoria, con senso contrario, ha stimato necessario far sapere da quali minimi rivoletti sia causato un gran lago che occupa Europa" (Sarpi, *Istoria del Concilio Tridentino* 1:145). In his English translation, however, Nathanael Brent removes the metaphor and simply states, "Whereof that I may the better tell what was commonly spoken, it is necessary to relate briefly the contents of the Oration" (132).

13. Qtd. in Bouwsma, *Defense* 519–20. Later in this same work, Bouwsma goes on to explain:

> Three general principles underlay his conception of the nature and purposes of historical composition, including his own work. He conceived of historical study, first of all, as a kind of empirical investigation designed to tell the truth about the past. He also regarded historical truth, no matter what its subject, as autonomous, governed by nothing beyond the internal structure of events and illuminated by the historian's general understanding of human nature and human affairs. Finally, he considered knowledge of history potentially useful and occasionally urgent; historical composition was to be judged above all by its utility for the purposes of men. (593)

14. Simpson and Potter edition, vol. 7, nos. 3, 6, and 7.

15. Sherwood, *Fulfilling the Circle*, esp. chap. 2, 21–62.

16. For a clear-sighted explanation of the interdependence of faith and reason, see Brown 61–65.

17. Concerning the date of this sermon, Simpson and Potter note, "It seems probable that June 21 [the date indicated on the printed sermon] is a mistake for June 18, owing to faulty reckoning from May 21, which was the Sunday after Ascension Day. May 28 was Whitsunday, and June 4 Trinity Sunday. If Donne really preached the second sermon on June 21, he preached it on a Wednesday, an unusual day of the week for a long and elaborate sermon" (7:13n. 29).

18. See Johnson 1–36.

19. For an argument outlining the parameters of Donne's views on grace, see chap. 5 of my *The Theology of John Donne*, esp. 123–27.

Works Cited

Bald, R. C. *John Donne: A Life.* Oxford: Clarendon, 1970.
Bouwsma, William. *Venice and the Defense of Republican Liberty.* Berkeley: U of California P, 1968.
———. "Venice, Spain, and the Papacy: Paolo Sarpi and the Renaissance Tradition." *The Late Italian Renaissance, 1525–1630.* Ed. Eric Cochrane. New York: Harper, 1970. 353–76.
Brown, Meg Lota. *Donne and the Politics of Conscience in Early Modern England.* Leiden: Brill, 1995.
Donne, John. *Pseudo-Martyr.* Ed. Anthony Raspa. Montreal: McGill-Queen's UP, 1993.
———. *Sermons.* Ed. Evelyn M. Simpson and George R. Potter. 10 vols. Berkeley: U of California P, 1953–62.
Flynn, Dennis. "Donne's Politics, 'Desperate Ambition,' and Meeting Paolo Sarpi in Venice." *Journal of English and German Philology* 99 (2000): 334–55.
Johnson, Jeffrey. *The Theology of John Donne.* Woodbridge, Eng.: D. S. Brewer, 1999.
Milton, Anthony. *Catholic and Reformed.* Cambridge: Cambridge UP, 1995.
Sarpi, Paolo. *The Historie of the Councel of Trent.* Trans. Nathanael Brent. London, 1620.
———. *Istoria del Concilio Tridentino.* Ed. Giovanni Gambarin and Renzo Pecchioli. 2 vols. Firenze: Sansoni, 1966.
Shami, Jeanne. "Anti-Catholicism in the Sermons of John Donne." *The English Sermon Revised.* Ed. Lori Anne Ferrell and Peter McCullough. Manchester and New York: Manchester UP, 2000. 136–66.
———. "'The Stars in their Order Fought Against Sisera': John Donne and the Pulpit Crisis of 1622." *John Donne Journal* 14 (1995): 1–58.
Sherwood, Terry. *Fulfilling the Circle.* Toronto: U of Toronto P, 1984.
Smith, Logan Pearsall. *The Life and Letters of Sir Henry Wotton.* 2 vols. Oxford: Clarendon, 1907.
Stanwood, P. G. "Donne's Art of Preaching and the Reconstruction of Tertullian." *John Donne Journal* 15 (1996): 153–69.
———. "Donne's Reinvention of the Fathers: Sacred Truths Suitably Expressed." *Sacred and Profane: Secular and Devotional Interplay in Early Modern British*

Literature. Ed. Helen Wilcox, Richard Todd, and Alastair MacDonald. Amsterdam: VU UP, 1996. 195–201.

Tanner, Norman P., S.J., ed. *Decrees of the Ecumenical Councils*. 2 vols. London: Sheed & Ward; Washington, DC: Georgetown UP, 1990.

Vessey, Mark. "Consulting the Fathers: Invention and Meditation in Donne's Sermon on Psalm 51:7." *John Donne Journal* 11 (1992): 99–110.

Wootton, David. *Paolo Sarpi: Between Renaissance and Enlightenment*. Cambridge: Cambridge UP, 1983.

Yates, Frances A. "Paolo Sarpi's 'History of the Council of Trent.'" *Journal of the Warburg and Courtauld Institutes* 7 (1944): 123–43.

5

Donne's Protestant *Paradiso*

The Johannine Vision of the *Second Anniversary*

RAYMOND-JEAN FRONTAIN

John Donne's familiarity with the *Divine Comedy* of medieval Italian poet Dante Alighieri is too often treated simply as a curiosity of literary history.[1] But while the imaginative bases of his identification with Dante have received some comment,[2] the extent of Donne's experimentation with Dantean self-presentation has yet to be documented and explored. Donne's *Second Anniversary* (*SA*)—one of two poems written in 1611–12 in response to the death of Elizabeth Drury, the daughter of Donne's patron Sir Robert Drury—posits a Reformed alternative to Dante's *Paradiso*, one that practices an "art of knowing Heaven" (*SA* 311) that Donne hopes is, unlike Dante's, not too "pert" to be "beeleeved."[3] Like the pilgrim in Dante's *Paradiso*, the speaker of Donne's *Second Anniversary* witnesses a soul's progress to heaven, watching it shoot like a bullet through the nine spheres and into the empyrean. But whereas it takes Dante the pilgrim nearly thirty-three cantos to reach the seat of God with Beatrice, Donne gets Elizabeth Drury's soul to heaven in a scant thirty-seven lines. And while both poems model themselves upon the prophecy of vision enacted in the Revelation of Saint John the Divine, Dante fashions himself as the passive witness to a divine drama, whereas Donne emphasizes that his prophetic vision occurs in his mind's eye, the result of his devotional meditation. By climbing his "watch-towre" (*SA* 294)—a traditional medieval image for the mind, but one that Donne invests with allusions to Isaiah and Habakkuk—Donne posits a new authority for the devotional poet as visionary prophet.

113

Donne's *Second Anniversary*, in short, posits a Reformed fiction of the poet's spiritual authority, one designed specifically to undercut Marian "mis-deuotion" and put that "pert" Italian Dante in his place.[4] Dante's reliance in the *Divine Comedy* upon the mediation of the Blessed Virgin and a host of saints created and worshiped by the (for Donne) misguided Church of Rome is replaced as the primary source of spiritual authority in the *Second Anniversary* by the devout Christian's meditative activity. While Dante's vision depends upon saintly assistance, Donne's poem models how the soul can achieve a progress independent of some mediating agency, through one's own meditative powers.

Dante's Visionary Poetic

In *Paradiso* 17 of the *Divine Comedy*, Dante, nearing the end of his journey, speaks with his great-great-grandfather, Cacciaguida, who had come down from the giant cross of the Warriors of God as a shooting star in canto 15. After hearing his forebear's prophecy that he eventually will be exiled from his beloved Florence, Dante admits his reluctance to return to the mortal realm and tell others what he has seen in the course of his journey lest it incite them against him. At the same time, he understands that failure actively to publish the truth that has been revealed to him may endanger his eternal soul.

> Down in the world of endless bitterness,
> and on the mountain from whose lovely peak
> I was drawn upward by my lady's eyes,
>   and afterward, from light to light in Heaven,
> I learned that which, if I retell it, must
> for many have a taste too sharp, too harsh;
>   yet if I am a timid friend of truth,
> I fear that I may lose my life among
> those who will call this present, ancient times. (*Par.* 17:112–18)

Cacciaguida resolves Dante's dilemma by providing him with a mandate to sing his comedy.

> "A conscience that is dark—
> either through its or through another's shame—
> indeed will find that what you speak is harsh.

>   Nevertheless, all falsehood is set aside,
> let all that you have seen be manifest,
> and let them scratch wherever it may itch.
>   For if, at the first taste, your words molest,
> they will, when they have been digested, end
> as living nourishment." (124–32)

Commenting on this scene, Marguerite Waller notes that "buried in this apparently figurative description of the responsibility borne by the reader of the poem to make good its 'vision,' there is an allusion which is virtually a quotation from Scripture. What appears at first to be a metaphorical elaboration, a movement away from plain speaking, actually draws us further inward toward the center of the poem's 'meaning'" (31). The allusion she cites is to Revelation 10:9, where the angel hands John a scroll and orders him to "Take it and eat it up"; and, John notes, "it was in my mouth sweet as honey: and as soon as I had eaten it, my belly was bitter." This is itself a recasting of the command given to Ezekiel by the Lord: "Son of man, cause thy belly to eat, and fill thy bowels with this roll that I give thee." This Ezekiel does, "and it was in my mouth as honey for sweetness" (Ezek. 3:2). Cacciaguida associates the message that Dante must bring back to earth with the often bitter but nevertheless spiritually nourishing message of the prophets. Like Jonah, Dante initially is reluctant to undertake the mission imposed upon him; knowing that prophets are rarely heeded and, indeed, are often persecuted, he questions whether he is up to the task. But like John of Patmos and Ezekiel, Dante has been given a vision both mighty and strange that he is commanded to relate to others in order that they may know the will of God. Its mandate cast in biblical language, Dante's poem implies that its authority derives from, and thus carries a weight similar to, the Word of God.[5]

Dante presents himself in prophetic terms elsewhere in the *Divine Comedy*, drawing upon the visionary experiences of Elisha, John, and Ezekiel. In *Inferno* 26:34–39, he compares his action of looking down upon an amazing sight to Elisha's watching Elijah's ascension to heaven in a fiery chariot; moments later in the biblical narrative, of course, Elisha inherits Elijah's prophetic mantle. In *Purgatorio* 9:19–33, Dante dreams that he is "seared with the visionary fire" when he is carried upward by an eagle from the sphere of flame. The dream suggests both Isaiah's being transported to heaven, where his lips are burnt with a fiery coal, and John of Patmos's revelation, the eagle being a symbol of John and of Christian prophecy in general.[6] And in *Purgatorio* 29:97–105, Dante compares his own vision of the heavenly beasts to Ezekiel's and John's, noting however that as to number "John's with me / as to their wings; with . . . [Ezekiel] he disagrees." He identifies with Ezekiel, however, by repeating that prophet's situation; Dante is walking along a riverbank when the vision occurs (cf. Ezek. 1:1 with *Purg.* 29:8).

The emphasis in each of these prophetic moments is upon the visionary act of witnessing, Dante, in effect, making an epic of witnessing.[7] "I am not Aeneas, am not Paul," he protests to Virgil when first told of the journey he must undertake (*Inf.* 2:31). His denial, of course, only highlights the ways in which he will duplicate and even exceed the accomplishments of each of his heroic predecessors before his poem ends. Like the *Aeneid*, the *Divine Comedy* is the epic of a heroic journey to a new home, to the "promised land" as it were. Books 2 and 3 of the *Aeneid*, in which Aeneas tells his story to Dido and her court, provide Dante with a model of the hero's awareness of his role as witness to significant events, a model of "I"-ness as the foundation of credibility. And, like Paul, Dante will make an arduous journey to the Eternal City which is typologically related to Aeneas's. More significantly, Dante will be quite literally "caught up" or lifted by Beatrice, not to the third heaven, as Paul reports in what became for the Middle Ages the paradigm of mystical experience, but through all nine of the spheres.

> I knew a man in Christ above fourteen years ago, (whether in the body, I cannot tell; or whether out of the body, I cannot tell: God knoweth;) such an one caught up to the third heaven.
> And I knew such a man, (whether in the body, or out of the body, I cannot tell: God knoweth;)
> How that he was caught up into paradise, and heard unspeakable words, which it is not lawful for a man to utter. (2 Cor. 12:2–4)[8]

Unlike Paul, Dante speaks unambiguously of himself rather than of some unidentified "man," and of his own immediate recent experience, not of something that occurred at a fourteen-year distance. And while Dante continually puzzles over the physics of how his mortal body can be transported through incorporeal realms, there is never any doubt as to whether his experiences occur to him "in" or "out" of the body; soul after soul whom Dante meets while on his epic journey calls attention to his corporeality. Most importantly, Dante the pilgrim is not only permitted, but commanded, to tell in as much detail as possible what he has seen and heard.

This is the biblical pole of Dante's epic—to see as Paul, John, Elisha, Isaiah, and Ezekiel saw. And, if the letter to Can Grande della Scala (the powerful lord of Verona and Vicenza to whom Dante dedicated his *Paradiso*) can be trusted as Dante's, this biblical pole had a stronger pull on him than the classical pole, as represented by Virgil's *Aeneid*. Writing, as Paul does, of himself in the third person, Dante reports that the "author" "says that he was in the first heaven and that he wishes to relate of the heavenly kingdom whatever, like a treasure, he was able to retain in his mind" (41).[9] Dante's biblical self-presentation is also his most extraordinary and daring attempt at fabulation: to claim to have penetrated to the very throne of God and to have witnessed the face of the Holy while still in the body. Isaiah saw the throne of the Lord in its heavenly temple, as well as the seraphim that make up the Lord's train (Isa. 6:1–3); and while Deuteronomy asserts upon Moses' death that "there arose not a prophet since in Israel like unto Moses, whom the LORD knew face to face" (34:10), Moses is elsewhere famously reported to have been allowed to see only the "back parts" of God (Exod. 33:23). Dante seizes upon the personal testamentary function of the "I" inherent in biblical prophecy, in which testifying is attestation to what the inspired self has uniquely experienced.[10]

Dante is cautious, however, in asserting his prophetic power, and careful to validate the source of his vision with an authority other than that of the self. Most obviously, he sets his epic—which he began writing around 1308—in the year 1300, thus allowing himself to "foresee" accurately many of the events that occurred before the time of the poem's actual composition but, to all appearances within the text, after the time of the poem's supposed action. By this means he encouraged his initial readers to believe that the poem's other predictions would eventually be fulfilled just as these already seemingly had been. More complicated is the machinery of the fiction itself. Dante is led to heaven by a relay team comprised of Lucia, Beatrice, Virgil, Statius, and Mathilda that is commanded by the Virgin Mary; even an eagle of fire is implicated in the process, if only in a dream. This chain of command—stretching directly from Mary, the penultimate figure in heaven, down to Dante himself—suggests a process of inspiration: if Dante sees things that have not been seen by other men, it is because of this complicated machinery that has allowed them to be acted out before him. But however "pert" his assertion of prophetic identity, Dante is careful not to commit blasphemy: it is Cacciaguida who provides him with his mandate to sing the *Divine Comedy*, not God.

However much later poets might be indebted to Dante's promotion of a prophecy of witnessing, Donne—at the climax of the Reformation, and at a moment in his own life when he was meditating upon the deficiencies of the Catholic faith in which he had been raised[11]—was frustrated by Dante's reliance upon the machinery of mediation. In his *Second Anniversary*, Donne seems determined, like Dante, to appropriate the voice and vision of the biblical prophet. But rather than locate the source of his inspiration in a process controlled by Mary and the saints, as did Dante—for such an approach strained Donne's credulity—Donne turned to the private act of spiritual devotion. Donne's prophetic vision is the result of meditation, not mediation.

"The Trumpet at Whose Voice the People Came"

"Quod vidimus, testamur," John of Patmos is told by he who is both alpha and omega (Rev. 1:19). And John's command to testify to what he sees provides the most important link between Dante's *Divine Comedy* and Donne's *Second Anniversary*. Most medieval and Renaissance commentators considered John the "prince" of prophets, both because of his having seen in such detail the unfolding of the Last Things and because of the placement of his Book of Revelation as the capstone of the entire Bible. Studying Renaissance attitudes toward the Book of Revelation, Joseph Anthony Wittreich notes that "since it represents the culmination of scriptural prophecy and is a vision not just of a prophet but of the prince of prophets, the Apocalypse—the purest and highest example of prophetic poetry—was thought to contain the great code of Christian art—to be the source book, as it were, for a Christian poetic" (*Visionary* xiv).[12] Indeed, as Gabriel Harvey notes,

> as well for the singularitie of the manner, as the Divinitie of the matter, I hearde once a Divine, preferre Saint Johns Revelation before al the veriest Metaphysicall Visions, and jollyest conceited Dreames or Extasies, that ever were devised. . . . And truely I am so confirmed in this opinion, that when I bethinke me of the verie notablest, and most wonderful Propheticall, or Poeticall Vision, that ever I read, or hearde, me seemeth . . . that there hardly appeareth anye semblaunce of Comparison: no more in a manner (specialy for Poets) than doth betweene the incomprehensible Wisedome of God, and the sensible Wit of Man. (qtd. in Borris 9)

Curiously, Wittreich's survey of sixteenth- and seventeenth-century poetic attempts to distill a visionary poetic from the Book of Revelation, limits the mainstream practice of such a poetic in England to Spenser and Milton. Donne's *Second Anniversary* predates Milton's *Paradise Lost* by some fifty years as an imitation of a Johannine vision, and his literary model is not Spenser's *Faerie Queene* (as Wittreich posits was Milton's) but Dante's *Divine Comedy*. In the *Second Anniversary* Donne absorbs, and then transforms, Dante's Johannine prophecy of witnessing the conversion of mortal things into immortal ones. In the process Donne provides Milton with a far more valuable potential model than Spenser for the poet as visionary spectator, not of what miraculously has been revealed, but of what the reformed Christian discovers in meditation.[13]

Donne associates himself with John of Revelation at the conclusion of the *Second Anniversary* where the speaker identifies himself as "The Trumphet, at whose voice the people came" to hear the proclamation that is Elizabeth Drury (527–28). The trumpet image has a rich and varied biblical background that complements as well the concern with memory and law expressed in the *First Anniversarie* (*FA*), the *Second Anniversary*'s companion poem.[14] But ultimately the trumpet signature establishes the speaker's identity as a modern prophet and in particular associates him with the Revelation of St. John the Divine, the culminating instance of the biblical prophetic tradition and clearly the primary source of Donne's engagement with the trumpet motif. In order to appreciate the remarkably complex field of associations that Donne's use of the image incorporates into his poem—and to illuminate Donne's attempt to reform Dante's figure of the poet as visionary prophet—the full range of the biblical trumpet motif, and the specific resonance that each instance has for the prophetic operation of the *Anniversaries*, needs to be mapped.

The trumpet's general role in the Israelite community is defined in Numbers 10, where the Lord orders Moses to make two trumpets of hammered silver:

> And if ye go to war in your land against the enemy that oppresseth you, then ye shall blow an alarm with the trumpets; and ye shall be remembered before the LORD your God, and ye shall be saved from your enemies. Also in the day of your gladness, and in your solemn days, and in the beginning of your months, ye shall blow with the trumpets over your burnt offerings, and over the sacrifices of your peace offerings; that they may be to you for a memorial before your God; I am the LORD your God. (Num. 10:1–10)

Thus the trumpet initially serves a memorial function, both reminding God of the Israelites' need of divine assistance and assuring the people of God's providence in times of prosperity or "gladness." The trumpet whose sound disclosed God's presence was called the "strophar" and was sounded every seven years to call the twelve tribes of Israel together to hear the Law read.[15] The signatures of Donne's speaker possess in this regard an important simultaneity, the trumpet at the conclusion of the *Second Anniversary* calling the people to hear the Law contained in the song at the end of the *First*, thus confirming Elizabeth Drury as an example "equal to law" (*FA* 48).

But the Hebrew prophets used the trumpet just as commonly as the symbol of God's protective presence, investing it with more than a memorial function. In Jeremiah, the Lord orders the people to stop at the crossroads and look for the ancient paths, promising that when the people are incapable of finding—or perversely refuse to follow—the paths themselves, he will set a watchman over them who will guide them by the blast of a trumpet (6:16–18; cf. Jer. 4:5). Similarly, in Ezekiel 33:1–6, the watchman himself is warned that if he sees the enemy approaching and blows his trumpet to warn the Israelites, then the Israelites themselves, not he, will be responsible for their sins should they die unprepared. Here the trumpet has associations with memory, the trumpeter being appointed as guardian of a potentially lazy or forgetful people—the very audience that Donne projects in the *First Anniversarie*—and suggests some of the responsibility that Donne felt as poet-prophet (Frontain, "Mosaic Voice") and would subsequently take on as a preacher.

When the trumpet sounds in Ezekiel 7:14 and nobody goes to war, the instrument becomes a symbol of the people's unpreparedness when suddenly tested (cf. Jer. 6). The trumpet thus becomes associated with the advent of that moment of chastisement, apocalyptic in its severity, known as "the Day of the Lord." In Joel 2:1, for example, the prophet is commanded: "Blow ye the trumpet in Zion, and sound an alarm in my holy mountain: let all the inhabitants of the land tremble: for the day of the LORD cometh, for it is nigh at hand" (see also Joel 2:15). Likewise, when prophesying against the wickedness of Israel, Hosea is commanded to "set the trumpet to thy mouth," at which sound the avenger of the Lord shall come "as an eagle against the house of the LORD, because they have transgressed my covenant, and trespassed against my law" (Hos. 8:1; see also Amos 3:6).[16] The prophet's voice of chastisement and admonition itself serves in some instances as the sounding trumpet, as when Isaiah is instructed by the Lord to "Cry aloud, spare not, lift up thy voice like a trumpet, and shew my people their transgression, and the house of Jacob their sins" (Isa. 58:1). In describing the day of the Lord's judgment, Isaiah exults that "it shall come to pass in that day, that the great trumpet shall be blown" and those who have rejected the Lord shall reform and "worship the LORD in the holy mount at Jerusalem" (Isa. 27:13). The apocalyptic imagery of the *First Anniversarie* suggests that just such a moment of divine judgment has arrived: the speaker protests "how poore a trifling thing man is" (*FA* 184) and "how lame a cripple," "how vgly a monster," "how wan a Ghost," and "how drie a Cinder this world is" (*FA* 238, 326, 370, 428) because the people have forgotten the name of Elizabeth Drury.

However, in the *Second Anniversary*, which traces the progress of a soul to heaven and challenges the process by which Dante was supposedly transported to heaven while still in the body, Paul's "mystery"—and its accompanying trumpet blast—is crucial.

> Behold, I shew you a mystery; We shall not all sleep, but we shall all be changed, in a moment, in the twinkling of an eye, at the last trump: for the trumpet shall sound, and the dead shall be raised incorruptible and we shall be changed. For this corruptible must put on incorruption, and this mortal must put on immortality. So when this corruptible shall have put on immortality, then shall be brought to pass the saying that is written, Death is swallowed up in victory. O death, where is thy sting? O grave, where is thy victory? (1 Cor. 15:51–55)

Paul figures a Christian appropriation of the Hebraic motif, the trumpet no longer functioning to announce that the retributory Day of the Lord is at hand but rather to celebrate the soul's final transformation at the Last Judgment. The trumpet, its function suspended as an omen of the punishment that is to be wreaked upon those who have forgotten the Law, now signals the soul's movement to glory. Thus, while Elizabeth Drury's death is lamented in the *First Anniversarie*, the progress of her soul to heaven is celebrated in the *Second*; Donne's diptych illustrates in its very structure Paul's "mystery," the trumpet sounding at the conclusion of the second poem signaling to the people Drury's "change" as she puts on incorruption, which is emblematic of the resurrected Christian soul's achieving victory over the grave.

But however important these earlier versions of the trumpet motif are for understanding Donne's attempt to fashion himself as a Reformed prophet, it is John's associating the trumpet with a vision of the old order's dissolution and of the new order's emergence that possesses the deepest resonance for Donne and his speaker's self-presentation in both *Anniversary* poems. John's vision on Patmos of the seven angels sounding a trumpet immediately before the moment of final revelation is the most significant analogue for companion poems that anatomize the dead or dying world and that follow the progress of a soul to heaven. In the Book of Revelation, six angels sound their horns and the seven thunders speak after the seventh seal is broken. John is about to write down what they say when a voice commands him to seal his scroll, for it is not yet time for the people to be given full knowledge of the world's end: "But in the days of the voice of the seventh angel, when he shall begin to sound [his trumpet], the mystery of God should be finished, as he hath declared to his servants the prophets" (Rev. 10:7). The voice goes on to explain that when the seventh trumpet is finally sounded, the heavens will be ripped asunder, the heavenly temple will open, and a portent will appear in the skies: "a woman clothed with the sun, and the moon under her feet, and upon her head a crown of twelve stars" (Rev. 12:1).

Typologically, John's is the ultimate trumpet blast, the various Hebraic soundings of a trumpet proving but veiled anticipations of this one, which ushers in the final revelation of God's plan for humankind. In terms of Christian eschatology, the Old Testament trumpets signaled God's action within history, whereas John's marks the end of the temporal, human order and the return to the (prelapsarian) divine, eternal order. Similarly, whereas Paul's trumpet blast revealed the transformation of an individual soul, John's reveals the fate of all humankind. The extraordinary power that this Johannine moment had in Donne's imagination (and Donne's willingness to conflate the Pauline moment with the Johannine) is suggested by his use of Revelation's apocalyptic trumpet in "Holy Sonnet: At the round earths imagin'd corners," in which the speaker meditates upon the trumpet call that will signal the end of time and the individual's reunion of body and soul. In that sonnet the speaker's meditation recreates John's enforced postponement of the cosmic drama's denouement, for just as John was forbidden to break open the final seal, the speaker suddenly halts the dramatic action that his meditation has stimulated, professing himself content to repent further of his sins before being summoned to the Last Judgment.

> But let them sleepe, Lord, and mee mourne a space,
> For, if above all these, my sinnes abound,
> 'Tis late to aske abundance of thy grace,
> When wee are there; here on this lowly ground,
> Teach mee how to repent.... (lines 9–13)

The reader of Donne's sonnet is left in a state of suspension, prepared in the octave for a vision of ultimate things that in the sestet is, as though at the last minute, denied.

Donne's presentation of himself at the conclusion of the *Second Anniversary* as "The Trumpet, at whose voice the people came" thus signals the speaker's functioning as a Johannine prophet, as the prophet who testifies to what he has seen and who, in turn, calls upon the people to see mortality transformed into immortality, the corruptible body mysteriously changed into the incorruptible soul.[17] Donne's concluding his seven-part *Progres*[18] with a speaker sounding a trumpet and summoning the people to behold a glorified Elizabeth Drury may be seen as his attempt to generate poetic and spiritual authority by positioning himself rhetorically at the moment in Revelation when the final trumpet sounds and the woman clothed with the sun appears. But it is also part of his attempt to replace Dante's Virgin Mary, the penultimate figure of his revelation, with the Protestant image of any regenerate Christian soul. Little wonder that Ben Jonson, a Roman Catholic convert, complained that "Dones Anniversarie was profane and full of Blasphemies / that he told Mr. Donne, if it had been written of ye Virgin Marie it had been something" (qtd. in Manley 7). Roman Catholics identified the woman of Revelation with the Virgin Mary, and Donne insists that Elizabeth Drury died a virgin (*FA* 106–7). Addressing Elizabeth as "blessed maid" (*FA* 443) who is "fild with grace" (*SA* 465) and later as "Immortal Maid" (*SA* 516) (both of which are traditionally Mary's soubriquets), Donne is clearly writing a reformist revelation to meet the challenge of the Roman Catholic Mary, a revelation that imitates John's but counters "pert" Dante's. For, significantly, Donne's "Mary" lacks the special powers of a mediatrix that, reformers long protested, made her the equal of Christ in Roman Catholic devotion.[19] Rather, Drury represents the potential of any "regenerate Christian as the restored image of God" (Lewalski 140), which, as Barbara Lewalski has demonstrated, was central to Protestant belief (chap. 4).

Donne's use of the trumpet signature, then, functions similarly to Dante's being told to eat the Word, each biblical allusion working to associate its poet with John of Revelation and to establish his poem as a visionary prophecy. Likewise, Donne shares with Dante the vision of a soul's progress to or through heaven. Thus, the very singularity of their descriptions of such movement demands that their poems be compared; few other writers were so audacious as to claim they too possessed what Donne calls "th'Art of knowing Heauen" (*SA* 311). The differences between the two poems (and their informing theologies), however, are telling. First, as already noted, Donne has replaced Dante's Mary with a Protestant Everywoman. Second, whereas Dante complains that he finds the passage from sphere to sphere so swift that he cannot record in detail what he and Beatrice pass, Donne shrugs off any interest in celestial sightseeing, so eager is his regenerate soul to get to heaven. Third, as already noted, whereas Dante requires thirty-three cantos to make the trip, Elizabeth Drury completes her voyage in a mere thirty-seven lines (*SA* 181–218). And finally, whereas Dante is continuously in the spotlight in his poem (it is, after all, his body that is transported through the nine realms of the saints, and his experience of witnessing that is at the heart of his poem), Donne carefully effaces himself. Elizabeth Drury is the proclamation or message; he is only the trumpet used to call people's attention to her. He speaks, in the root meaning of "prophecy," for or on behalf of another. Little wonder, then, that Donne's description of Drury's soul speeding to heaven like a bullet seems a parody of Dante's more careful, almost encyclopedic, mapping of all nine heavens. In heaven Drury joins the choir of reformed souls where she is translated into song—where, like Sir Philip Sidney and the countess of Pembroke in "Upon the translation of the Psalmes," she is both the singer and the song that can now be sung by those remaining on earth.[20]

The View from Donne's Watchtower

The speaker of Donne's *Second Anniversary* is, thus, a prophet who testifies to what he has seen; his testimony, which is the poem itself, functions as a trumpet calling everyone to witness the revelation that is Elizabeth Drury. Like the Revelation of St. John and Dante's *Divine Comedy*, the *Second Anniversary* is a poem of spiritual vision, celebrating Elizabeth Drury for her attainment of such vision, instructing the reader in how to grow in such proficiency him- or herself, and in the process demonstrating to the reader the spiritual sharp-sightedness of poet-prophet Donne for recognizing Elizabeth Drury as an example equal to the Law. As Frank Manley points out in the introduction to his edition of the *Anniversaries*, in Renaissance thinking, both Protestant and Catholic, grace was considered an "infusion . . . , *de sursum descendens*, which allowed the soul to perceive the beauty of god" (27). As an example Manley cites Pico's praise of such vision in *On the Dignity of Man:* "with this sight Moses saw, Paul saw, and many other of the elect saw the face of the Lord; and this is the sight our theologians call intellectual cognition, intuitive knowledge; with this sight, St. John the Evangelist says the just will see high God, and this is the whole of our reward" (qtd. in Manley 27). What remains to be considered is how radically different the source of Donne's inspiration is—that is, the different way in which Donne is able to see the soul's progress to heaven. This is represented by the speaker's action of climbing into the watchtower of his own mind, a biblical metaphor that Donne refashions to represent the essentially Protestant action of meditation. For if Donne's *Second Anniversary* repeats the essentially visual nature of both the *Divine Comedy* and the Book of Revelation, then his imperatives to his reader to look and see, as he encourages the reader to follow him in his meditation, transform the nature of the prophet from one to whom is granted an extraordinary vision that he is commanded to share with others, to any devout person committed to meditating upon the Word of God.

A failure to see the extent to which the *Anniversaries* are concerned with the importance of spiritual vision remains, paradoxically, perhaps the greatest blindness among modern critics of the poems.[21] From the outset Donne's speaker insists that Elizabeth Drury is to be celebrated because of the depth of her spiritual vision. "Sight is the noblest sense of any one," the speaker asserts in the *First Anniversarie* (353). And it is the first requisite of those souls that will be permitted to make their progress home, as the speaker insists in an aside at the very opening of the poems:

(For who is sure he hath a soule, *vnlesse*
It see, and Iudge, and follow worthinesse,
And by Deedes praise it? He who doth not this,
May lodge an In-mate soule, but tis not his.) (*FA* 3–6, emphasis added)

Inasmuch as Elizabeth Drury's body is corrupted and her soul has departed for heaven, goodness remains the only way for those left on earth "to see" her (*FA* 16–18). The fading of light and color, however, signals the fading of the very goodness and spiritual intelligence from the world that, paradoxically, people need in order to be able to see and follow her example (*FA* 70–73, 260). A good portion of the *First Anniversarie* is given to chronicling failure of vision and absence of color—"how wan a Ghost this our world is" when people are blind to Drury, who was "all color, all Diaphanous" (*FA* 370, 366).[22] And, in an increasingly destructive chain of causes and effects, the failure of physical sight can only lead to diminished comprehension as well:

Th'Ayre showes such Meteors, as none can see,
Not onely what they meane, but what they bee. (*FA* 387–88)

"[C]an wee / Who liue, and lacke her, here this vantage see?" the speaker plaintively asks in "A Funerall Elegie" (47–48), the poem that Donne printed as a segue from the *First* to the *Second Anniversary*.

The speaker in the *First Anniversarie* is painfully aware of the limitations of human vision and the resulting diminishment of goodness in the mortal world. In the course of her progress, conversely, Elizabeth Drury grows to be "all Eye" (*SA* 200), her perfection of self equaling her perfected vision (I/eye).[23] So unflagging was her vision that even "Hee that charm'd Argus, sweet Mercury," could not cause her to close her eyes (*SA* 199); like the Wise Virgins of the parable, she refused to sleep lest she miss the Bridegroom's arrival. In life, the young girl's

> eies enspheard
> Star-light inough, t'haue made the South controll,
> (Had shee beene there) the Star-full Northern Pole. (*SA* 78–80)

"What eie was casuall, may euer bee" (*SA* 482), the speaker says, celebrating Drury's translation from "casual" or "accidental" sights to "permanent" or "essential" ones. In death she knows the "essentiall ioye" of "The sight of God, in fulnesse" (*SA* 440–41).

"[W]e vnderstood / Her by her sight," the speaker comments (*SA* 243–44), alerting the reader to the expanding circle of vision that the *Anniversaries* are constructed to initiate. The visionary is known by her vision; Elizabeth Drury concentrated so intensely on pursuing the sight of God that her own eyes became a light powerful enough to guide others who, in turn, may themselves guide still more people to heaven. The purpose of Donne's *Anniversaries* is to encourage the reader in just such vision as Drury displayed while on earth.[24] In the poems' two-part audience (see Frontain, "Mosaic Voice" 167–70), those who have already seen and judged Drury's worthiness are already following her example; their interest in the girl's progress is as much an interest in seeing the route that their souls will eventually travel as it is in bearing witness to her transformation. But those who do not know that they have souls, and who have forgotten Elizabeth Drury's name, need first to be taught to see the example of worthiness that she provided while on earth, just as they need in the *First Anniversarie* to be taught that the world is not well but in a lethargy. Addressing them in the *Second Anniversary*, the prophet-speaker both castigates and commands:

> Thou look'st through spectacles; small things seeme great,
> Below; But vp into the watch-towre get,
> And see all things despoyld of fallacies:
> Thou shalt not peepe through lattices of eies,
> Nor heare through Laberinths of eares, nor learne
> By circuit, or collections to discerne. (*SA* 293–98)

Documenting in the *First Anniversarie* just such a world of inverted perspective, the prophet-speaker attempts in the *Second* to raise his readers' sights from earth, which is impermanent and disintegrating, to heaven, which is permanent and immutable. "Looke vpward," he exhorts (*SA* 65) as he attempts to shift their attention from accidental to essential joys and teach them to "read" the multilayered proclamation that was Elizabeth Drury:

> for shee rather was two soules,
> Or like to full, on both sides written Rols,
> Where eies might read vpon the outward skin,
> As strong Records for God, as mindes within. (*SA* 503–6)

The very title of the poem suggests movement that visually can be discerned ("progress"), while the physical movement narrated within the poem encourages the reader in those activities necessary to knowledge that one has a soul: seeing, judging, following, and praising worthiness.

Significantly, Donne's exhortation is addressed not only to the reader but to his own "drowsie soule," which, like a Foolish Virgin, is in danger of closing its eyes rather than becoming, like Elizabeth Drury, "all Eye." And his self-exhortation is not to pray for divine assistance, such as Dante received when he became lost in the Dark Wood, but to rely upon his own powers of meditation. Unlike John of Patmos, to whom an angel is sent "to shew unto his servants things which must shortly come to pass" (Rev. 1:1), and unlike Dante, whose cumbersome machinery guaranteeing the poet-pilgrim's inspiration we have already discussed, Donne allows for no miraculous intervention or supernatural aid. As one of those regenerate souls who had the perspicacity to see, judge, and follow worthiness in the form of Elizabeth Drury, Donne praises her in his two-part poem. His "Deede" of praising worthiness is to prophesy about her and thereby manifest that he has a soul worthy of salvation. When encouraging the spiritually weak to follow Drury's example and lift their eyes to heaven, Donne is encouraging himself as well. His soul, "standing outside" itself in an ecstasy as he contemplates the girl's goodness and progress, is far removed from the base earth, concentration on which would throw it into a lethargy.

> Returne not, my soule, from this extasee,
> And meditation of what thou shalt bee,
> To earthly thoughts. . . .
> Vp, vp, my drowsie soule. . . . (*SA* 321–23, 358)

Rather, like "those Prophets, which now gladly see / Their Prophecies growen to be Historee" (*SA* 347–48), the speaker's "extasee" (in which he sees the progress of Elizabeth Drury's soul to heaven) is a "meditation of what thou [i.e., his own soul] shalt bee" (*SA* 321–22). The prophet becomes his own prophecy; his vision becomes a self-fulfilling artifact.

Donne, in effect, has redefined the identity and operation of the biblical prophet. To understand the extent of Donne's daring, one must consider carefully the speaker's exhortation "But vp vnto the watch-towre get" (*SA* 294), which both Manley and Shawcross gloss with references to the medieval conceit of the watchtower as the human mind. Its additional allusion to the biblical prophet's watchtower, however, allows Donne to conflate the practitioner of the intellectual-spiritual exercise of meditation with the divinely inspired visionary. And this is the greatest reform that Donne acts upon Dante, to redefine the prophetic visionary as any Christian in meditation.

Watchmen and watchtowers appear throughout biblical narrative, as in 2 Kings 9:17–20 where a watchman communicates to King Joram the approach of Jehu's army. Throughout the prophetic oracles, however, provision for a watchman is associated with Yahweh's loving protection of his people. In Isaiah's parable of the vineyard, for example, the Lord sets a tower in the field from which a watchman can ensure the crop's protection (Isa. 5:1–7). Likewise, as part of the covenant reestablished after Jerusalem's destruction, the Lord sets watchmen over the city's walls (Isa. 62:6). Repeatedly the watchman is associated with the prophet. Ezekiel's commission to serve as prophet is figured as the watchman being charged with sounding a warning (Ezek. 3:17), that warning sometimes figured as a trumpet (Ezek. 33:1–7; cf. Jer. 6:17). And the watchman's view of a foreign army advancing upon the city figures as Isaiah's oracle of the destruction about to be wreaked upon sinful Israel (Isa. 21).

But the passage that has the greatest resonance for Donne's climbing his watchtower is Habakkuk 2:1–3, in which the prophet says,

> I will stand upon my watch, and set me upon the tower, and will watch to see what he will say unto me, and what I shall answer when I am reproved.
>
> And the Lord answered me, and said, Write the vision, and make it plain upon tables, that he may run and readeth it.
>
> For the vision is yet for an appointed time, but at the end it shall speak, and not lie: though it tarry, wait for it; because it will surely come, it will not tarry.

The watchtower thus symbolizes the prophet's readiness to receive a revelation from the Lord, and his willingness to keep a written record of the vision accorded him until the *kairos* or "appointed time" when he is instructed to share it with the people. Such a delay, as we have seen, is recognized by Donne to be an essential feature of John's visionary experience as well. And, apparently, it is of a piece with the curious suspension of action that characterizes so many of Donne's major poems, both amatory and religious (Frontain, "Make all this All" 15–19).

Significantly, Habakkuk's ascending the stairs of his tower was thought in patristic tradition to indicate devotional activity or meditation. In his *Homilies on the Psalms*, for example, Jerome concludes: "Such is the meaning also of the prophet Habacuc in: 'I will stand at my guard post, and keep watch to see what the Lord will give me and what answer I will give Him,' and I will hear what the Lord God proclaims within me. The words: 'I will hear what the Lord God proclaims within me,' refer, therefore, to what the Lord speaks in the heart—in the understanding" (130). Elsewhere, discussing the episode in which the harlot Rahab secrets on her roof two Israelite spies sent by Joshua to reconnoiter the hostile city of Jericho (Josh. 2), Jerome takes the rooftop or watchtower to represent the power of faith: "If Sion is taken to mean a watch tower, our soul ascends to a contemplation even more sublime" (143). In Christian tradition, thus, Habakkuk's climbing his watchtower is implicitly an emblem of meditation, of the soul in communion with its creator, of the devout person in prayer.[25]

Both Dante's *Divine Comedy* and Donne's *Anniversaries*, then, unfold dramas of the making of a visionary. Dante the pilgrim must be led by Virgil and a procession of others out of the Dark Wood to the realm of pure light, while Donne's speaker must learn to concentrate his or her sight upon

> A glimmering light,
> A faint weakeloue of vertue and of good
> [that] Reflects from her, on them which vnderstood
> Her worth. (*FA* 70–73)

No fiction of divine inspiration is necessary to a Reformed poet-prophet like Donne, however. It is Donne's ability to meditate, to climb the watchtower of his own mind, that calls him to be a prophet. Donne's "art of knowing heaven" (*SA* 311) comes to him, not through the miraculous intervention in his life of any of those Roman Catholic "saints, whose very names / The ancient Church knew not, Heauen knowes not yet" (*SA* 512–13) with whom Dante peoples his *Paradiso*, but by the power of his own meditative acts and spiritual vision. He, rather than Dante, is the prophet of true devotion.

Conclusion: The Prophet of True Devotion

In a letter to sometime ambassador to Venice Sir Henry Wotton that editors Helen Gardner and Timothy Healy speculate was written around 1600, Donne meditates upon the value of reading "other mens works" and reports that "Even when I begun to write these [lines to Wotton] I flung away Dant the Italian, a man pert enough to bee beloved and too much to bee beleeved" (110). Donne complains specifically about Dante's placement of Pope Celestine V—he "who made, through cowardice, the great refusal" (*Inf.* 3:60)—in the antechamber of hell where those who in life blew neither hot nor cold are condemned through eternity to chase an empty banner.

> [I]t angred me that Celestine a pope [so] far from the manners of other popes, that he left even their seat, should by the court of Dants witt bee attached and by him throwne into his purgatory. And it angred me as much, that in the life of a pope he should spy no greater fault, than that in the affectation of a cowardly securyty he slipt from the great burthen layd upon him. Alas! what would Dant have him do? Thus wee find the story related: he that thought himself next in succession, by a trunke thorough a wall whispered in Celestines eare counsell to remove the papacy: why would not Dant be content to thinke that Celestine tooke this for as imediate a salutacion and discourse of the holy ghost as Abraham did the commandment of killing his sonn? If he will needs punish retyrednes thus, what hell can his witt devise for ambition? (Donne, *Selected Prose* 110)

Donne's exasperation with Dante's failure to understand Celestine's renunciation of the papacy stems from two separate but related complaints. The more immediate one concerns the moral scheme of the *Divine Comedy*, particularly Dante's attitude toward the papacy. For a medieval Christian like Dante, whose commitment to a hierarchical understanding of the cosmos presumed respect for the idea of ecclesiastical authority (however ambivalent his personal feelings about certain popes, and however strong his resentment of papal usurpation of temporal authority), Celestine's resignation of the papacy after only five months in office, in order to resume a contemplative life, was indeed "the affectation of a cowardly securyty," a presumptuous placing of his own salvation before the good of the church; his slipping "from the great burthen layd upon him" signaled an irresponsible refusal of a divinely imposed task. But in a Reformed Christian of Donne's stripe, Celestine's abjuring the corruption and "ambition" of the papacy inspires only admiration.

Donne's disdain for the papacy is manifested by his reference to the intrigue by which the papal succession could be, and so often was, manipulated. The man who would succeed Celestine as Boniface VII was rumored to have driven Celestine from Peter's throne by the Machiavellian device of "a trunke thorough a wall" through which he whispered suggestions in unsuspecting Celestine's ear.[26] But Donne resents Dante's failure to consider the possibility that Celestine might genuinely have thought himself moved by "as imediate a salutacion and discourse of the holy ghost as Abraham did the commandment of killing his son"; in such a scenario Boniface would prove as unsuspecting an agent of divine providence as Milton's Satan does in *Paradise Lost*. Abraham's willingness to sacrifice Isaac was understood in the Middle Ages and Renaissance, of course, to prefigure God the Father's giving his only begotten Son up to be crucified for the redemption of humankind. Dante, according to Donne, should at least have considered the possibility that Celestine genuinely believed his renunciation to be a divinely ordained sacrifice by which Celestine redeemed both himself and others, as a Christlike renunciation of earthly glory in order to win a crown of heavenly glory.

Thus, against Roman Catholic "ambition"—that is, the love of power, ceremony, and display—Donne sets a reformer's love of "retyrednes," of a simple meditative existence. And against Dante's "fiction" of Celestine as a moral coward, Donne posits an alternative, reformist fiction of Celestine possibly only "affect[ing] . . . a cowardly securyty" in order to free himself of the corrupting power of the papacy. At the same time, Donne suggests that Dante's overconcern with the earthly institution of the papacy left him insensitive to the possible workings of divine inspiration. This criticism of Dante's fiction-making powers implies Donne's second, more subtle and, finally, more important area of contest with his predecessor. Dante, in Donne's epigrammatic summation, is a writer "pert enough to bee beloved and too much to bee beeleeved." That is to say, Donne does not actually object to the audacity of the fiction on which Dante hangs his moral, for how could a writer of Donne's own "pertness" fail to admire Dante's claim that he alone was permitted, while still in the body, to tour the three realms of the medieval Christian afterlife?[27] Indeed, Dante's "pertness" actually seems to arouse admiration, and possibly even begrudging affection, in Donne, who willingly acknowledges that Dante is "pert enough to bee beloved." Donne objects, rather, that Dante's fiction is so "pert" that it strains Donne's credulity as a reader.

It is not Dante's controlling fiction *per se* but rather the effort of Coleridgean "suspension of disbelief" that Dante's poem requires which disturbs Donne. This accords with the criticism that Donne makes of Dante in "Satyre 4" when, trapped in that "Purgatorie" which is the court, Donne's speaker falls into what he calls "a trance / Like his, who dreamt he saw hell" (lines 157–58). From Donne's point of view, Dante deludes both himself and his reader when he insists that his "trance" or dream vision was an actual occurrence.[28] Not surprisingly, when the time came for Donne to write his own "Inferno," in *Ignatius His Conclave* (1611), Donne's speaker promises to "relate what I saw" while "in an Extasie" (*Ignatius* 5)—that is, in a dream vision, the unreliability of which the satirist calls the reader's attention to, in effect winking a warning that the reader not take literally the satirist's claim to have been transported to another realm.[29] Donne, unlike Dante, insists upon the fictionality of his fiction, making no pretense that the events he narrates in *Ignatius* were witnessed in actuality.

Donne's quarrel with Dante illuminates one of the most significant issues of his poetic canon. The speaker of Donne's "Satyre 2" is troubled to recognize that "my words none drawes / Within the vast reach of th'huge statue lawes" (lines 111–12). How, in effect, does one assert poetic and moral authority? What fiction can one invent to authorize one's poetic and spiritual vision? How far does one dare go before that fiction arouses incredulity? In the *Anniversaries* Donne assumes a prophetic identity analogous to the one assumed by Dante in the *Divine Comedy*. But whereas Dante presents himself in the passive role of witness, Donne is spiritually active in meditating upon the significance of Elizabeth Drury's life and death. Donne presents himself as an un-"pert" prophet, and the fiction of his *Second Anniversary* as believable rather than exasperating. His poem is a Reformed *Paradiso*.

Donne's rejection of a Dantean narrative of saintly intervention and his reliance, rather, upon meditation is in keeping with a particular thrust of English religious reform. As Ernest Gilman notes,

> Both Perkins and Baxter distinguish between the blasphemous crucifixes and pictures of the Roman church and the vibrant images of divine things that display themselves inwardly to the eye of faith: "get the liveliest picture of them in thy mind that possibly thou canst." The Word spoken by the preacher, the Word planted in the faithful, carries its own radiant

visual potential; properly "seen," it not only compensates for the loss of pictures as a help to devotion, but also satisfies the imagination so fully that only those mired in the carnal would still have resort to external images. (151)

Donne, of course, had no difficulty with the crucifix or with religious art *per se* (see Frontain, "Donne's Emblematic Imagination"), but "the Word spoken by the preacher" would become increasingly important in his thinking after the *Anniversaries*. Indeed, the companion poems may be seen as his first attempt to identify himself as a Reformed preacher, anticipating the "progress" of his career in later life.

The trumpet signature that concludes the *Second Anniversary* places the poems within a Protestant tradition of admonition and sermonizing that spans the Tudor and Stuart eras. Robert Crowley's *The Voyce of the laste trumpet, blowen bi the seventh Angel . . . calling all estates of men to the ryght path* (1550), for example, is a spirited Reformation tract whose very title makes clear the apocalyptic dimensions of its author's reformist zeal. Similarly, not quite a century later, John Milton justifies his challenge to episcopacy in terms of a revelation brought about by a divinely commanded trumpet call: "But when God commands to take the trumpet and blow a dolorous or a jarring blast, it lies not in man's will what he shall say or what he shall conceal" (666). Not surprisingly, once Donne overcame his doubts concerning ordination, he regularly presented himself in the pulpit as a trumpet being sounded by God: "God shall send Prophets, Trumpets, and Trumpetors, that is, preachers of his word, and not the word of men; and they shall be heard willingly too; for as they are Tubae, Trumpets, so they shall be musicum carmen, acceptable musick to them that hear them" (*Sermons* 2:169).[30] The *Anniversaries* themselves follow German theologian (and the primary author of the influential Augsburg Confession) Phillip Melanchthon's strictures for the Protestant preacher (see Shuger 68), the *First Anniversarie* awakening the reader's fear and terror of judgment, and the *Second* eliciting faith in the mercy and promises of Christ. As noted at the outset of this essay, Donne's speaker professes himself to be intensely aware of writing the *Second Anniversary*

> Here in a place, where mis-devotion frames
> A thousand praiers to saints, whose very names
> The ancient Church knew not, Heaven knowes not yet. (*SA* 512–14)

The *Anniversaries* suggest a great deal about Donne's evolving devotional intentions, about his recognition of how his meditation may inspire others in an expanding circle of praise and prayer. The *Anniversaries* aim at the re-formation of community after he anatomizes it, at the restoring or re-membering of the body of the world.

Notes

All quotes from the Bible in this essay are from the Authorized (King James) Version.

    1. Although a recent spate of books on Dante and Chaucer amply testifies to Chaucer's reading of Dante (see, e.g., Richard Neuse, who summarizes in his introduction a number of books and articles published in the 1980s on Chaucer's engagement with Dante), by the seventeenth century the Italian poet was relatively unknown in England. Irene Samuel claims that Milton's knowledge of Dante was itself "exceptional" in that "Dante enjoyed little favor, even in Italy, during the seventeenth century. Whereas the Cinquecento had argued violently about him, the Seicento largely ignored him, and outside Italy he was scarcely named" (33). While both Chaucer and Milton clearly display in their work knowledge of and indebtedness to Dante, Donne is the first English poet to write specifically about the experience of reading Dante's text.

    Throughout this essay I quote Dante in Allen Mandelbaum's translation. Donne's *Anniversaries* appear in his *Complete Poems*.

    2. Most mention of Dante in Donne criticism juxtaposes their respective love poetries, Dante's idealization of the *donna angelica* held up as an example of the tradition that Donne appropriated and against which he reacted; see, e.g., both Freccero and Fleissner on the relation of Donne's compass conceit in "A Valediction forbidding mourning" to Dante's depiction of love as a circle. Likewise, Hester has suggested the hill obstructing the path of the pilgrim in *Inferno* 1 as a possible source for the Hill of Truth in Donne's "Satyre 3." A number of readers, even, have paralleled Donne's Elizabeth Drury with Dante's Beatrice, although in each case the parallel has been made only in passing; see, e.g., Manley 38–40, Hardison 182, Lebans 557–58, and Warnke 78.

    3. So Donne describes Dante's *Inferno* in a letter written around 1600, to which I return in my conclusion, below.

    4. Significantly, Donne was one of the first Englishmen to use Dante as a Reformation straw man. As Frances Yates reports (38–47), Dante's defense of an imperial counterclaim to the worldwide authority of the papacy in *De Monarchia* actually endeared him to a number of Tudor reformers, Bishop John Jewel citing him in *Defence of the Apology of the Church of England* and John Foxe in *Acts and Monuments*, while John Bale went so far as to include *De Monarchia* in a collection of imperialist tracts that he edited in 1559.

Whenever possible, I use the term "Reformed" rather than "Protestant" because I mistrust Lewalski's assertion of a specifically Protestant poetic and think it more accurate to argue instead for Donne's employment of a Reformed, Bible-centered poetic. "Reformed" does not reduce the occasionally polemical nature of Donne's intentions or operations; rather, it attempts to reduce the polemical nature of our critical terminology when writing about Donne.

5. As Hawkins points out, Cacciaguida's mandate to Dante makes explicit "the gradual unfolding of a call to divine prophecy hinted at from the very beginning of the poem" (73). The "cumulative effect" of Dante's self-affirmation, Hawkins concludes, "is almost breathtaking. No other poet or apostle in either Testament of Scripture was ever more fully commissioned; nor (I would venture) has any poet so daringly underwritten his own literary enterprise" (75). The entire of Hawkins's chapter 4 in effect deals with Dante's prophetic self-fashioning.

6. Accordingly to the medieval *Bestiary*, an aging eagle renews its failing vision by flying "up to the height of heaven, even unto the circle of the sun," which "evaporates the fog of his eyes. Then at length, taking a header down into the fountain, he dips himself three times in it, and instantly he is renewed with a great vigour of plumage and splendour of vision" (White 105). The eagle, then, was associated with spiritual renewal achieved by the cleansing of vision. The eagle was thought to be the only bird capable of looking directly at the sun for great lengths of time without being blinded, and so in medieval art it came to represent the evangelist who wrote of Jesus as the light of the world, who was assumed to heaven in a blinding blast of light (Metford 144), and to whom alone was vouchsafed a vision of the end of the world.

7. I am grateful to Allen Mandelbaum for first encouraging me to think in these terms. Significantly, whereas Dante could more easily say *vidi* in Italian, he always chooses to write *io vidi*. Italian does not require, as English does, that the subject "I" be stated, yet Dante always includes it as though to emphasize his singular identity as prophetic witness. As Hawkins has subsequently noted, Dante "gives us what he has made up as if it were what he had received through experience, what he had seen with his own eyes, what had been revealed to him" (93). And because some of the information that Dante provides is available neither in Scripture nor in the writings of the church fathers, Dante seems to be suggesting that his personal witnessing accords him an authority equal to, if not superior to, both Aquinas and the Bible (Hawkins 92–93).

8. Donne's awareness of the Pauline analogue is clear from the language he uses in *Ignatius*, where he says that "In the twinckling of an eye" all the rooms in hell were open to him (7). Kathryn Kremen (chap. 2) analyzes the Pauline language of Donne's resurrection theology, much of which is indebted to 1 Corinthians.

9. As Hawkins notes, Dante's assertion in the letter to Can Grande that the *Divine Comedy* is to be read according to the four "senses" of Scripture is

"breathtaking": "Because only God could write according to this 'allegory of the theologians,' any claim of such fourfold exegesis by a human author is astounding, perhaps even blasphemous. Could Dante possibly mean that his poem was the Bible?" (55).

10. Dante's testamentary voice allows him otherwise to function as a prophet in his castigation of ecclesiastical and political powers as he vehemently demands reform and attempts to initiate spiritual renewal; in his deliberately cryptic language, hiding his teaching "beneath the veil of verse so obscure" (*Inf.* 9:61–63); and in his knowledge of things incomprehensible to other men, such as the prophecy of the greyhound, and the figure of the Old Man of Crete.

Rabelais's testamentary voice is similarly modeled on the Book of Revelation's command, Alcofribas asserting his authority and the authenticity of Pantagruel by insisting, "Car ne croyez pas que j'en parle comme les Juifz de la Loy J'en parle comme saint Jehan de l'Apocalypse: quod vidimus, testamur" [Do not believe that I speak like the Jews of the Law. I speak of it like Saint John of the Apocalypse: testify to what you have seen] (169n. 5). As Edwin Duval observes, "The obvious parallelism between these two sentences establishes a clear and direct opposition between the Law and Revelation—that is, between the Old Testament, in which truth and divine intention were revealed only imperfectly, indirectly, and figuratively, and the New Testament, in which the partial revelations of the Old are completed and its veiled meanings unveiled in a complete, direct revelation of the Truth" (6). Duval's summary of the Christian humanist juxtaposition of Moses' obscure Truth with John the Divine's "complete unveiling—that is, a 'revelatio,' or 'apocalypse'—of the perfect, seen truth" (9) bears directly on Donne's choice of a Mosaic signature at the conclusion of the *First Anniversary* and a Johannine signature at the conclusion of the *Second*.

11. "The first thing to remember about Donne is that he was a Catholic; the second, that he betrayed his Faith," writes John Carey (14) at the start of the strongest polemic concerning Donne's rejection of the Roman Catholic tradition in which he was raised. See, however, Dennis Flynn's important challenge to Carey, which demonstrates that Donne's associations with the ancient Catholic nobility persisted long after the period of his supposed apostasy, thus undermining both Carey's and Lewalski's presumption that Donne's reformist religion be read as militantly Protestant—that is, as an outright rejection of, rather than a Reformed engagement with, the Catholicism of his youth. Among the possessions that Donne thought worth mentioning in his will and bequeathing to his executor (and later bishop of Exeter), Henry King, are portraits of antipapal historian and Protestant hero Paolo Sarpi and of Sarpi's biographer, Fulgenzio, which Donne kept in the parlor of the St. Paul's deanery (see Gilman 120). This seems as telling a testimonial to his differences with Roman Catholicism as his publishing *Pseudo-Martyr*.

12. See also Wittreich's excellent article in *Milton and the Line of Vision*. See as well Michael Lieb (181–90) on the Book of Revelation's "christianization" of Ezekiel as the model for visionary prophecy, and passim for an excellent historical analysis of the biblically inspired tradition of visionary prophecy.

13. On Spenser's understanding of the visionary poet's "double perspective" that allows him "to hold the eternal and the ephemeral in simultaneous copresence, balancing stable principle against unstable reality," see Fletcher (4–5). Borris extends to Book 5 Spenser criticism's already formidable purchase on the apocalyptic or Johannine operations of Book 1.

14. As I have pointed out elsewhere ("Mosaic Voice"), the signatures occurring at the conclusion of each poem indicate the comprehensive prophetic identity adopted by the speaker of the *Anniversaries*. I will not repeat that argument here except to note that in the *First Anniversarie* Donne is an Old Testament, specifically Mosaic, prophet through whom God, understanding the likelihood that his chosen people will forget "The Law, the Prophets, and the History" but remember divine teaching that has been cast in verse, delivers "A last, and lastingst peece, a song" (*FA* 457–66) about Elizabeth Drury, who is identified as "a strong example equall to law" (*FA* 48). In the *Second Anniversary*, I am arguing here, Donne is a New Testament or Johannine prophet of vision. Thus, the *First* and *Second Anniversaries* must be read, like the Old and New Testaments, as complementary halves that together make a coherent whole. And the speaker of the *Anniversaries* functions typically as a biblical prophet does, chastising God's sinful and forgetful people in the *First* while offering comfort and a promise of impending succor in the *Second*.

15. On the "strophar" see Muilenburg 61. Donne refers to the use of the trumpet, citing Numbers 10, in Expostulation XVI of the *Devotions Upon Emergent Occasions*. Additionally, Leviticus 25:8–10 prescribes that the trumpet be blown in the seventh month of the forty-ninth year (which, the passage notes, is seven times seven) to allow people to prepare for the Jubilee year that follows. The significance of the number seven, both in terms of the seven trumpets of the Book of Revelation and of the seven-part division of the *Second Anniversary*, is discussed below.

16. Hosea 8:12 continues use of the trumpet as a reminder that the Law is being forgotten. Together these references reinforce the prophetic moment dramatized by the speaker's signature at the conclusion of the *First Anniversarie*—that is, that Donne's speaker is speaking at that moment foretold to Moses by the Lord when the people would forget the Law (see Frontain, "Mosaic Voice").

17. On religion, in Donne's thought, as the only "antidote against the natural pattern of decay and decline" witnessed everywhere in nature, see Achsah Guibbory (chap. 3; 98). Guibbory is particularly strong when showing how the resurrection of the soul and its reunion with its creator, as witnessed in Donne's *Second Anniversary*, reverses the process of the body's dissolution recorded in the *First*.

18. Although Lewalski disagrees with Louis Martz on where the first section ends and the second begins, both emphasize the seven-part structure of the *Second Anniversary*; see Lewalski 284–85 for a summary of their generally compatible views of the poem's structure, but her ultimate divergence from him.

19. In terms of making Elizabeth Drury a Protestant Mary, Donne goes further than this. Elizabeth, like Mary, is the antithesis of Eve (*FA* 100–102, 106–7), driving out the poisonous tincture that entered the world with Eve and the serpent (*FA* 179–82). And just as Mary is held up in Roman Catholic teaching as the model of all womanhood, Elizabeth is praised as "Shee that was best, and first originall / Of all faire copies" (*FA* 227–28). Elizabeth is even described as perfuming the world (*FA* 229–34), an association with Mary made through the latter's typological association with the Shulemite maiden in Song of Solomon (Warner, chap. 8; see, e.g., p. 130 for Bernard of Clairvaux's application to Mary of the description in Song of Sol. 3:6 of the Bride as "perfumed with myrrh and frankincense"). Significantly, when Mary does appear in the *Second Anniversary*, it is as "the blessed Mother-maid" who "is exalted more for being good, / Than for her interest, of mother-hood" (*SA* 341–44). That is, her goodness rather than her status as the Mother of God makes her a worthy object of devotion. Donne, in one passing couplet, transforms Mary into a Catholic Elizabeth Drury.

20. See Frontain, "Translating Heavenwards," for an analysis of how the biblically inspired circle of praise that Donne maps in "Upon the translation of the Psalmes" illuminates the literary dynamic of the *Anniversaries*.

21. Ironically, Joseph Hall, the poems' first commentator, clearly recognized the importance of both Elizabeth Drury's spiritual vision and its relation to Donne's poetic vision. "Wel dy'de the world, that we might liue to see / This world of wit, in his Anatomee," runs Hall's opening couplet in the prefatory "To The Praise of the Dead, and the Anatomy," emphasis falling upon the verb "to see" at the end of line one. Likewise, in "The Harbinger to the Progres," which precedes the *Second Anniversary*, Hall reiterates the poems' various schemes of seeing. In her progress, Drury "still aspires to see / The worlds last day" (5–6), just as Hall, regretting that his vision is not yet so refined that "I can . . . thy glory see" (18), praises Donne for having long ago "lost the vulgar sight" and developed "the better eyes" that allow him to follow the progress of Drury's soul to heaven (23–26).

Johnson, chap. 3, analyzes the importance of vision in Donne's theology but curiously ignores the Johannine revelation that is Elizabeth Drury in the *Anniversaries*.

22. Being "all color, all Diaphanous," Elizabeth Drury is the rainbow, symbol of God's restorative covenant with humankind.

23. Lieb (233) quotes the fourth-century monastic Macarius the Egyptian as exhorting his followers to attain a state in which "thy whole soul has become a spiritual eye, and thy whole soul light."

24. If the *First Anniversarie* laments the failure of human vision, the *Second* plays with the sight of the dead. The poem opens with the involuntary motions made by a corpse that the viewer "saw" (*SA* 17), including the twinkling of the decapitated man's eyes (*SA* 13). The reader is asked to imagine Death as a groom bringing a taper into a darkened room (*SA* 85–88), and him- or herself as a corpse whose eyes are closed by an attendant (*SA* 109). Survivors' mistrust of "a dead man's eye" is juxtaposed with the angels not needing to "couer" their eyes (*SA* 111–12). Indeed, it was the failure of the rebellious angels to look at God that caused their fall (*SA* 446).

25. John King (218) calls attention to the Johannine association of Redcrosse Knight's climbing the Mount of Contemplation in *Faerie Queene* I.x. Reformation thought associates the Christian who perfects meditative practice with John climbing the mountain on Patmos from which he was traditionally thought to have seen the unfolding of the Last Things.

26. Donne gives no indication of exactly where "wee find the story related." Singleton (47–51), however, quotes at length the chronicles of Giovanni Villani for the period, which tell how Cardinal Caetani (who would succeed the eighty-year-old Celestine as pope) "succeeded in hiding himself at night in the pope's chamber. He placed a long tube just above the bed of the pope, and spoke through it, saying: 'I am the angel sent to speak with you, and I command you, in the name of glorious God, to renounce the papacy immediately, and return to being a hermit.' He did this for three nights in a row, so that the pope believed in the deceitful voice, and renounced the papacy" (50).

27. On one level at least, Donne is as much the English voice of audacious solipsism as Dante is the continental. As Mandelbaum points out, Dante's "io sol uno" ("I myself alone") in *Inferno* 2:3 is "the first triple repetition of an 'I' that we have in Western writing" (*Inf*. xiii), and so one of the earliest indications of modern self-consciousness. Likewise, Donne can write poems in which the speaker asserts of his lover and himself that "She'is all States, and all Princes, I, / Nothing else is" ("Sunne Rising," lines 21–22) or, conversely, that "I am every dead thing, / In whom love wrought new Alchimie" ("Nocturnall," lines 12–13). I suspect that, in general, as a reader Donne must have found Dante's strength of self-assertion entirely engaging.

28. Boccaccio recorded the credulity of certain of Dante's contemporaries who "took the poet at his literal word, and thought his dark complexion was the result of the time he had spent in the 'heat and smoke down there': 'Do you see the man who goes down into hell and returns when he pleases, and brings back tidings of them that are below?'" (qtd. in Hawkins 13).

29. "The Extasie," of course, is the title of one of the most famous of Donne's *Songs and Sonets*, which depends upon the presence of an uncertain observer called upon to interpret the indecipherable, trancelike state of the lovers, which he is

privileged to witness. Donne thus seems to use the word "extasie" to signal a state that cannot be rationally or reliably ascertained—that is, a state that requires the viewer's interpretation, which the text itself refuses to confirm. In Dante's high medieval culture, the very otherworldliness of a dream or dream vision allowed it to function effectively as a metaphor for inspiration, whereas for Donne the uncertainty of a dream or of an ecstatic fit made them markers for early modern hermeneutical instability. As I indicate above, Paul's famous description of his ecstasy in 1 Corinthians is the biblical prototype of both Dante's and Donne's visionary poetics.

30. Donne's sermon preached at Whitehall on February 12, 1618/19 (*Sermons* 2:164–78), has attracted the attention of several commentators seeking to analyze Donne's understanding of his role as preacher; see, e.g., Johnson (116) and Hughes (252–54). Hughes (252–54), Lewalski (278–80), and Rowe (171–72) likewise recognize the relation of Donne's self-presentation as a preacher to his signing himself as a prophet-trumpet at the conclusion of the *Second Anniversary*. "The Trumpet of God is the loudest voice that we conceive God to speak in," Donne says in another sermon, prefatory to analyzing the trumpet blast in Revelation that will raise the souls of the dead (*Sermons* 4:70). Significantly, in the verse epistle "To the Countesse of Huntington (Man to Gods image)," a poem that Shawcross speculates "was written at least close to Donne's ordination" (404), Donne anticipates the prophetic function that he will undertake in the *Anniversaries*, calling the world's attention to the presence of God in the countess (lines 61–70) just as he summons readers to hear the divine proclamation that is Elizabeth Drury.

Works Cited

Borris, Kenneth. *Spenser's Poetics of Prophecy in "The Faerie Queen" V.* English Literary Monograph Series 52. Victoria, BC: English Literary Studies, 1991.

Carey, John. *John Donne: Life, Mind, and Art.* New York: Oxford UP, 1981.

Dante Alighieri. *The Divine Comedy.* Trans. Allen Mandelbaum. 3 vols. Berkeley: U of California P, 1980–84.

———."Letter to Can Grande." Trans. Nancy Howe. *Essays on Dante.* Ed. Mark Musa. Bloomington: Indiana UP, 1964. 32–47.

Donne, John. *The Complete Poetry of John Donne.* Ed. John T. Shawcross. Garden City, NY: Doubleday-Anchor, 1967.

———. *Ignatius His Conclave.* Ed. T. S. Healy, S.J. Oxford: Clarendon, 1969.

———. *Selected Prose.* Chosen by Evelyn Simpson. Ed. Helen Gardner and Timothy Healy. Oxford: Clarendon, 1967.

———. *Sermons.* Ed. Evelyn M. Simpson and George R. Potter. 10 vols. Berkeley: U of California P, 1953–62.

Duval, Edwin M. *The Design of Rabelais's Pantagruel.* New Haven: Yale UP, 1991.
Fleissner, Robert F. "Donne and Dante: The Compass Figure Reinterpreted." *Modern Language Notes* 76 (1961): 315–20.
Fletcher, Angus. *The Prophetic Moment: An Essay on Spenser.* Chicago: U of Chicago P, 1971.
Flynn, Dennis. *John Donne and the Ancient Catholic Nobility.* Bloomington: Indiana UP, 1995.
Freccero, John. "Donne's 'Valediction: Forbidding Mourning.'" *English Literary History* 30 (1963): 335–76.
Frontain, Raymond-Jean. "Donne's Emblematic Imagination: Vision and Reformation of the Self in 'The Crosse.'" *PAPA: Publications of the Arkansas Philological Association* 20 (1994): 27–51.
———. "Law, Song, and Memory: The Mosaic Voice of Donne's *First Anniversarie.*" *Literature and Belief* 19 (1999): 154–74.
———. "'Make all this All': The Religious Operations of John Donne's Imagination." *John Donne's Religious Imagination: Essays in Honor of John T. Shawcross.* Ed. Raymond-Jean Frontain and Frances M. Malpezzi. Conway: U of Central Arkansas P, 1995. 1–27.
———. "Translating Heavenwards: 'Upon the translation of the Psalmes' and John Donne's Poetics of Praise." *Explorations in Renaissance Culture* 22 (1996): 103–25.
Gilman, Ernest B. *Iconoclasm and Poetry in the English Reformation: Down Went Dagon.* Chicago: U of Chicago P, 1986.
Guibbory, Achsah. *The Map of Time: Seventeenth-Century English Literature and Ideas of Pattern in History.* Urbana: U of Illinois P, 1986.
Hardison, O. B., Jr. *The Enduring Monument: A Study of the Idea of Praise in Renaissance Literary Theory and Practice.* 1962. Westport, CN: Greenwood P, 1973.
Hawkins, Peter S. *Dante's Testaments: Essays in Scriptural Imagination.* Stanford: Stanford UP, 1999.
Hester, M. Thomas. "John Donne's 'Hill of Truth.'" *English Language Notes* 14.2 (1976): 100–105.
Hughes, Richard E. *The Progress of the Soul: The Interior Career of John Donne.* New York: William Morrow, 1968.
Jerome. *Homilies on the Psalms* (1–59). Trans. Sr. Marie Liguori Ewald, IHM. Washington, D.C.: Catholic U of America P, 1964.
Johnson, Jeffrey. *The Theology of John Donne.* Cambridge: D. S. Brewer, 1999.
King, John. *Spenser's Poetry and the English Reformation.* Princeton: Princeton UP, 1990.
Kremen, Kathryn R. *The Imagination of the Resurrection: The Poetic Continuity of a Religious Motif in Donne, Blake, and Yeats.* Lewisburg, PA: Bucknell UP, 1972.
Lebans, W. M. "Donne's *Anniversaries* and the Tradition of Funeral Elegy." *English Literary History* 39 (1972): 545–59.

Lewalski, Barbara Kiefer. *Donne's "Anniversaries" and the Poetry of Praise: The Creation of a Symbolic Mode.* Princeton: Princeton UP, 1973.

Lieb, Michael. *The Visionary Mode: Biblical Prophecy, Hermeneutics, and Cultural Change.* Ithaca: Cornell UP, 1991.

Manley, Frank, ed. *John Donne: The Anniversaries.* Baltimore: Johns Hopkins UP, 1963.

Metford, J. C. J. *Dictionary of Christian Lore and Legend.* London: Thames and Hudson, 1983.

Milton, John. *Complete Poems and Major Prose.* Ed. Merritt Y. Hughes. New York: Macmillan, 1957.

Muilenburg, James. *The Way of Israel.* New York: Harper and Row, 1960.

Neuse, Richard. *Chaucer's Dante: Allegory and Epic Theater in "The Canterbury Tales."* Berkeley: U of California P, 1991.

Rabelais, Francois. *Oeuvres Completes.* Ed. Jacques Boulenger and Lucien Scheler. Paris: Editions Gallimard, 1955.

Rowe, Frederick A. *I Launch at Paradise: A Consideration of John Donne, Poet and Preacher.* London: Epworth P, 1964.

Samuel, Irene. *Dante and Milton: The "Commedia" and "Paradise Lost."* Ithaca: Cornell UP, 1966.

Shuger, Deborah. *Sacred Rhetoric: The Christian Grand Style in the English Renaissance.* Princeton: Princeton UP, 1988.

Singleton, Charles S. *Inferno, 2: Commentary.* Princeton: Princeton UP, 1970.

Waller, Marguerite. *Petrarch's Poetics and Literary History.* Amherst: U of Massachusetts P, 1980

Warner, Marina. *Alone of All Her Sex: The Myth and Cult of the Virgin Mary.* 1976. New York: Vintage Books, 1983.

Warnke, Frank. *John Donne.* Boston: Twayne, 1987.

White, T. H., ed. and trans. *The Bestiary: A Book of Beasts, Being a Translation from a Latin Bestiary of the Twelfth Century.* 1954. New York: Capricorn Books, 1960.

Wittreich, Joseph Anthony, Jr. "'A Poet Amongst Poets': Milton and the Tradition of Prophecy." *Milton and the Line of Vision.* Ed. Joseph Anthony Wittreich, Jr. Madison: U of Wisconsin P, 1975. 97–142.

——. *Visionary Poetics: Milton's Tradition and His Legacy.* San Marino, CA: Huntington Library, 1979.

Yates, Frances. *Astraea: The Imperial Theme in the Sixteenth Century.* London: Routledge and Kegan Paul, 1975.

6

"Souldiers of one Army"

John Donne and the Army of the States General as an International Protestant Crossroads, 1595–1625

PAUL R. SELLIN

> Though we must be blown with strange winds, . . . yet it is the Spirit of God that blows all this wind, and shall blow away all contrary winds of diffidence or distrust in Gods mercy; where we shall be all Souldiers of one Army, the Lord of Hostes.
> *John Donne, "A Sermon of Valediction at my going into Germany,"*
> *April 18/28, 1619*

> Voyez, voyez les Anglais, qui tournent à la charge!
> *Maurits of Nassau at the Battle of Nieuwpoort, July 2, 1600*

Literary scholarship is vaguely aware that during the 1570s and 1580s Queen Elizabeth of England came to the aid of the rebellion in the Netherlands against the extirpative religious and absolutist civil policies relentlessly pursued by *el rey católico*, Philip II of Spain. However, we often fail to realize how substantial the English military contribution actually was to the eighty years of warfare set off by the Reformation and the anathemas of the Council of Trent in the Low Countries. As a consequence, the Dutch, Huguenot, English, Scottish, and other worthies who fought on the rebel side during that cruel and bloody struggle have seldom been examined in the context of a broad, international network of Protestant military that was common to them all regardless of personal confession, whether Protestant or Catholic. As the subject is too huge for a small space, the following pages are intended to provide a minimal start in profiling the religious, political, and cultural milieu in which British military personnel abroad found themselves in the Netherlands. Essentially, they served in the army of a popular insurrection that began around 1566. Under William the Silent's leadership the revolt stabilized as a conservative endeavor to preserve ancient autonomies and liberties while maintaining a religiously tolerant Catholic government in all seventeen of the Low Countries. By 1590, though, the original aim had perforce evolved into a de facto pluralist Dutch republic in the seven unconquered provinces in the north. It was based on more or less traditional oligarchic civil and church establishments, but ones in which the Reformed had by then come officially to dominate.

The first Scottish and English volunteers to serve in Holland and Belgium under the prince of Orange arrived in 1572. Even though these early auxiliaries were intended as a form of merely covert aid, the contingents were nonetheless regimental in size, numbering around nine hundred men each. With the Treaty of Nonesuch in 1585, Elizabeth formally allied England with the Dutch, lending overt military and financial support against Spain in return for certain "cautionary" towns—The Brill in Holland, Vlissingen (Flushing) and Fort Rammekens in Zeeland—that she held as security. The *secours* that England now sent to swell the Dutch army amounted to upward of seven thousand foot and horse (Ten Raa and de Bas 1:80), no small force in times when even large armies seldom exceeded ten thousand men in the field. After the accession of King James, the States General reorganized its forces to include five regiments of British infantry—two Scottish and three English—each consisting of up to a dozen or more companies with strengths ranging from less than a hundred to more than two hundred men (Ten Raa and de Bas 2:99–164). There were also some half dozen cavalry squadrons plus assorted companies serving as garrisons in the cautionary towns. When the Dutch redeemed these cities in 1616, the garrisons were combined with other miscellaneous units into a fourth English regiment, and this situation obtained until shortly after the accession of Charles I, when the States General again expanded its now very renowned army with additional regiments of English and Scots (Ten Raa and de Bas 3:170). In fact, throughout Donne's entire lifetime the heart of the infantry forces with which the United Provinces resisted the zealously Catholic House of Habsburg consisted of about equal numbers of native provincial and British regiments, and the list of officers commanding Scottish and English units during the first quarter of the seventeenth century reads like a military honor roll of Protestant chivalry involving the first families governing England and the Dutch republic. To puritans and patriot hispanophobes of Donne's generation, certainly, these were the English and Scottish heroes who by risking their lives on behalf of the Reformed religion abroad had compelled Spain to sue for the Twelve Years' Truce of 1609 and ultimately in 1648 grant the independence for which the United Provinces had striven for eighty years.

Throughout the course of Donne's adult life, English military involvement in the Low Countries' wars deeply impinged on him and his. Whether he served under Parma in Flanders and Brabant in 1585 (Flynn, *Donne* 136–46, 170–72, 228n. 6), held a captaincy in Dutch forces in 1597 (Bald, *Life* 92n. 1), or went with Drake in 1589 is conjecture based on tenuous or no hard evidence. However, there is little doubt, as both the earliest of known prose letters demonstrably his (August 1597) and some fascinating descriptive poetry show ("The Storme," "The Calme," and three epigrams), that he sailed with at least two joint Anglo-Dutch expeditions, that against Cádiz in 1596 and then the Azores in 1597. Around 1600–1601, his letters show him closely following the siege of Oostende, not to speak of the second front that the Spanish had opened in Ireland to divert England from aiding the Dutch, and it seems more than sufficiently clear that he seriously considered joining in the Anglo-Dutch raids that went out against various Spanish harbors in the spring of 1602—this again under the very Dutch admiral who led the republic's flotilla against Cádiz in 1596.[1] In 1610 he composed a verse letter honoring Sir Edward Herbert's service at the siege of Juliers, when the Dutch sent an expeditionary force to resist Spanish exploitation of the disputed succession there. A few months later he began a suite of poems commemorating the late daughter of Sir Robert Drury, one of the English heroes of the Battle of Nieuwpoort (1600), in which the States General's foot and cavalry for the first time defeated the Spanish in pitched battle on the open field. As the acting secretary of Viscount Doncaster's abortive peace mission of 1619 to stave off the Thirty Years' War, more or less the second half of the Dutch revolt against the Spanish that was sure to come when the truce expired in 1621, Donne visited The Hague, where some thirty of the British infantry and cavalry officers in Dutch service gathered at Haarlem to swell the ambassador's huge train during its ceremonious progress from Haarlem to Rotterdam via the Dutch capital (Sellin 63–64 et passim). For several years after hostilities resumed, Donne closely followed the progress of military operations in the Palatinate and Holland, and recounted them in great detail, as if a staple of news for his friends regarding such matters as the fall of Heidelberg or the siege of Bergen op Zoom in 1622 (Papazian 236–66; Sellin 177–84). Inasmuch as Donne himself had as a young man taken part in this very struggle, some of the officers on whom he reports had at one time literally been fellows-in-arms, and it is no wonder that later he should follow their careers or maintain contact with them, their friends, or their relatives.

Between 1603 and the expansion of Dutch forces in 1626, the captains and colonels of the British contingents amounted to at least 238 Scottish and English who held infantry company or cavalry commands in the Army of the States. What were these men like, what social milieu did such people afford a poetical diplomat and divine like Donne, and what might their confessional alignments suggest about the nature of the international Protestant community to which Donne belonged by virtue of his very occupation? The records of his stay with Doncaster at Haarlem in 1619 provide a convenient starting point. The ranks specified in inn reckonings show that the British officers who attended on emissaries like Lord Hay and Donne included regimental commanders (colonels), their seconds-in-command (lieutenant colonels), regimental sergeant-majors (captains), and commanders of the British cavalry troops and infantry companies (captains) then serving as volunteers in the Army of the States, all under command of the prince of Orange by authority of the States General. Although many of the highest-ranking staff and cavalry commanders spent time at home during the winter months when there was no campaigning, their understudies had to stay in the Netherlands to attend to daily garrison life *sur les lieux*. As a group these men were an international lot, and they included some of the most renowned soldiers in the Protestant world of Donne's time. Many of the older officers still in service in 1619 had lived through—some barely—the worst fighting of the Eighty Years' War, and from the time of Elizabeth's intervention in the Low Countries, gallantry like theirs and their fathers' had secured the joint safety of Britain and the Netherlands from the Catholic Habsburg threat. So far as concerns the internal stability of the Dutch republic, which had been seriously threatened during the recent strife between Arminians and orthodox in the Dutch church, the British units in Dutch service had also had much to do with both preserving the political integrity of the United Provinces and maintaining uniformity of the Reformed religion in the republic.

The two Scottish regiments deserve pride of place because, as reputedly the earliest auxiliaries to come to the aid of the Dutch, they claimed precedence over all foreign troops serving the States General. Although they had often borne the brunt of ground fighting, they prided themselves on never having lost a stand of colors, and even the English yielded place to them (Ferguson 1:xix). Indeed, one cannot ignore them if for no other reason than that it was the patronage of one of their leading countrymen,

James Hay, Viscount Doncaster, that brought Donne to The Hague in 1619. Scholarship has devoted surprisingly little study to the Scots as a group even though they afforded Donne his most constant source of moral, material, and spiritual support during the second decade of the seventeenth century. That is, four Scottish lords—the two Robert Kers or Carrs, Lord Hay himself, and the marquis of Hamilton—were in varying degrees central to the career that Donne pursued during his middle and late years, and they all had close links with the Scottish commanders and their service on behalf of the Reformed cause in the Netherlands. Consider two specific examples. Not long after Donne's return to England after Hay's embassy, his friend Sir Robert Ker, earl of Ancrum, was exiled for dueling. Where did Sir Robert take refuge, except among these very military circles in the Netherlands? What is more, the experience of hearing the Genevan Psalms sung in both Dutch and French in Holland inspired him to translate the psalter according to the meters and tunes that he had encountered in the Dutch churches (Sellin 14). Second, when the States General expanded their forces in 1626 to include a third Scottish regiment, the colonel appointed to lead it in the field was no one less than Sir George Hay of Kinfauns, son of the first earl of Kinnoul, lord high chancellor of Scotland (Ten Raa and de Bas 4:26, 29, 41–42). As these Hays and Donne's Viscount Doncaster, himself overtly "fort Puritain, et qui fait le subtil dans ca [sic] religion" (Raylor 50), were descended of Peter Hay of Megginch, Viscount James was actually Sir George's first cousin. Through Doncaster—by 1627 earl of Carlisle and lord proprietor of all colonies in the West Indies—Donne's son George and either Sir George Hay or another Hay kinsman, probably Colonel William Hay (his regiment was dissolved in 1629—cf. Ten Raa and de Bas 4:279–80, 196), were both sent out to St. Kitt's, with Captain Donne as commander of the forces and possibly either Colonel George or Colonel William as governor.[2] However, they had to surrender the island to a Spanish armada that surprised them soon after their arrival in 1629. Donne's son and one of these Hays were taken to Cádiz, ironically, and held as hostages, George not escaping from captivity until after his father's death (Bald, *Life* 519–20, 553).

The "first and oldest regiment of foreign volunteers in The Netherlands," one that rendered not just the Dutch but the Reformed cause "so many notable and excellent services, as the chronicles show, and as are still fresh in the memory of everybody, and will continue certainly to be so till death," was the regiment of Colonel Sir William Brog (Ferguson 1:285; SvO 1605, 1610, 1620; SP 84/98). Doughty, able, experienced, and diligent, he had been commissioned sergeant major of the regiment in 1588. At the Battle of Nieuwpoort in 1600, where the army of the States General routed the Spanish, Count Maurits of Nassau, stadholder of Holland and captain general of the Dutch forces, won a glittering victory. By throwing a much-outnumbered Scottish force against an advancing enemy that took the besiegers by surprise, he gained sufficient time to order his forces and win the day, although at terrible cost to the Scots. Indeed, the regiment sacrificed half of its company commanders and five entire companies of a total of thirteen. Brog survived to distinguish himself at the famous siege of Oostende (July 5, 1601–September 22, 1604), where he was wounded. (When shot felled the Comte de Châtillon, son of the martyred Admiral Coligny, who commanded the Huguenot regiment, fragments of the skull struck him in the face.) In 1600, probably as the result of the losses at Nieuwpoort, Brog volunteered to perform the duties of lieutenant colonel without promotion or extra pay, and he was so commissioned not long after. At the decease of the regimental commander in 1606, Count Maurits personally requested the States General to let Brog have the regiment. Although King James had repeatedly attempted to retire him in favor of the former commander's son, young Walter Scott, created earl of Buccleugh in 1619, the stadholder would not allow court influence to oust a valorous officer of proven competence. Brog must have been nearing sixty when Donne visited Holland, but he nevertheless spent another full decade and a half in some of the hottest fighting of the Thirty Years' War, yet managed to outlive the poet by nearly five years (Ferguson 1:285 et passim).

In the Brog regiment, one rose by merit, not influence. His early seconds-in-command, Lieutenant Colonel Allan Coutts (SvO 1605, 1610, 1620; SP 84/98) and the sergeant major, Captain Andrew Donaldson (SvO 1605, 1610; SP 84/98), were likewise distinguished veterans who had seen firsthand what the struggle against Spain meant. Descended of an ancient family of Aberdeenshire, Coutts too survived Nieuwpoort while Donaldson received a company as early as 1604. Coutts went on campaign with Maurits immediately after the outbreak of the Thirty Years' War and died in 1631. Donaldson perished in 1627, probably killed at the siege of Groll, when the Scottish companies repulsed a Spanish attempt to relieve the place (Ferguson 1:285, 310–11 et passim). However, when Donne arrived in The Hague with Doncaster in 1619, the regiment had a new sergeant major with connections to favorites like the earl of Ancrum or Sir David Murray (formerly attached to Prince Henry's household) on the one hand, and with Scottish poets like Sir Robert Ayton or William Alexander of Stirling on the other. He was William Dromont, or Drummond, son of Alexander Drummond of Midhoop (SvO 1605, 1620). As such, he was a direct cousin to Sir John Drummond, the father of the poet Sir William of Hawthornden. Whether and what sort of contacts existed between Major William and his Hawthornden kinsman I do not know. They are likely, since Sir John had come south to London upon King James's accession, where he served in his sovereign's household as a gentleman usher, and the poet Drummond of Hawthornden's at first glance slightly incongruous interest in military technology points in the direction of his kinsman's profession and common interests. Resumption of the war in 1621 cost Major William dearly, for he too was killed at the siege of Groll.

The other Scottish regiment was commanded by Colonel Sir Robert Henderson (SvO 1605, 1610; SP 84/98). Second son of James Henderson of Fordell, he survived the intense fighting of the 1590s as well as the Battle of Nieuwpoort. In 1603 he was transferred to a new regiment of Scots brought over complete by Lord Buccleugh the elder (SvO 1604, 1605, 1610; SP 84/98) and rose to second-in-command as lieutenant colonel in 1609. The next year he was appointed acting colonel of the Scottish contingent that distinguished itself in the campaign for Juliers and Cleves, echoes of which, as we pointed out, recur in Donne's poetry. At Buccleugh's death in 1612, the States General, fearing lest King James recommend someone "not having necessary skill and experience," asked Maurits for a "fit colonel at once." Despite James's meddling on behalf of young Buccleugh, who tried to secure this command too, Prince Maurits recommended Henderson as one "whom he knows as a good soldier, and who is well fitted" for the position, and the States General so appointed him in 1612 (Ferguson 1:258–59). Henderson's private attitudes were hard-core puritan. Informing the English ambassador to The Hague, Sir Dudley Carleton, of a deserter not long after the execution of Van Oldenbarnevelt, for example, he termed the man a "debauched papist and a meddler with jesuits" (Ferguson 1:223), and it was precisely on Henderson's troops that Prince Maurits relied when he surprised the Remonstrants and disarmed their militia *(waardgelders)* in a bold move at Utrecht in 1618. Indeed, after the Synod of Dort, Henderson's units were employed to suppress "Arminian" conventicles in the country. For example, he personally commanded the "extraordinary" troops sent to Alkmaar in June of 1619 to suppress Remonstrant "tumults," and, as he was accompanying the deputies of the States General who had come to forbid one of these meetings, the people assaulted him with knives, "not without some danger to himself and the deputies," until a troop of soldiers came up and beat them away "though without blood" (Ferguson 1:223–24). When the Catholic commander Spinola laid siege to Bergen op Zoom (July 18–October 3, 1622), a move that suddenly threatened the heart of Holland, Henderson was sent to take command of the British troops in the garrison. In a "terrible" sally that lasted a whole night and the next morning, Henderson fell, shot in the thigh while leading a charge on enemy trenches with pike in hand. The romance of his end exceeded even Sir Philip Sidney's. After receiving the sacrament, he drank five healths—one to King James, one to Prince Charles, one to the queen of Bohemia, one to the prince of Orange, and one to a former fellow-in-arms, Sir James Erskine, earl of Marre (cf. SvO 1610)—and only then did he die. It would have comforted him immensely to know that after supposedly losing ten thousand men (Ferguson 1:309), Spinola was ultimately forced to raise a siege that Donne anxiously followed very closely (Donne to Goodere, September 22, 1622 [O. S.], *Letters* 198–200)—a suspenseful event anxiety over which prompted Donne's informant, Constantijn Huygens, then in Britain as a secretary to a Dutch embassy, to compose "De uitlandighe herder" ("The Shepherd Abroad"), one of the most remarkable pastoral elegies of its kind in any language.

In 1619, Henderson's brother, Sir Francis, was second-in-command (SvO 1604, 1605, 1610, 1620; SP 84/98). Like Sir Robert, he had fought in the original Scottish contingent, then was transferred to the new Buccleugh regiment where he became sergeant major in 1604. After his brother's promotion to the colonelcy, he succeeded to the vacant post of lieutenant colonel. During the civil turmoil over religion in the Dutch republic during 1618, an "infortunat maleur" fell out, as he put it. Attacked by an angry father and son, who insulted him, he had unintentionally killed the son with the pommel of his sword (Ferguson 1:394). He obtained pardon, however, and succeeded to the command of the regiment when his brother perished at Bergen op Zoom. He died in 1628 (Ferguson 1:65 et passim), probably in battle under Frederik Hendrik, prince of Orange, who succeeded his half-brother in the title after the latter's passing in 1625. As for the regimental sergeant major, this was Sir John Halkett (SvO 1610, 1620; SP 84/98). Second son of George Halkett of Pitfirrane, a family that had served the Netherlands in remarkable capacities for nearly two centuries, he had been personally knighted by King James while still James VI of Scotland. As the younger heir who had to seek his fortune in the military, he went into the service of the republic and served faithfully in actions such as Nieuwpoort. After the death of Sir Robert, he became lieutenant colonel, succeeded Sir Francis in the colonelcy in 1628, and fell himself at the famous siege of s Hertogenbosch the following year (Ferguson 1:xxiv, 308, 311). In this connection it is especially interesting that several poems in the apocrypha attributed to Donne by Jasper Mayne in fact stem from this campaign.

Three Scots commanded cavalry between 1610 and 1620 (Ten Raa and de Bas 3:155–57). They are worth noting because cavalry commands were very prestigious posts and normally went to gentlemen of high birth and influence. Little is known of Captain William Urrie (SvO 1620), commander of Troop 29 (cuirassiers), except that he was a blood relative of the duke of Lennox. Since he asked leave in 1632 to retire because of age, he may have been serving the Dutch rebels as early as Leicester's governor-generalship of the Netherlands in the late 1580s (Ferguson 1:443–51). Alexander Wishart (SvO 1610, 1620; SP 84/98), captain of Troop 22 (also cuirassiers), had been commissioned by Leicester for "vaillantsie et preudhomie au faict de la guerre" and "fidelite et experience" (Ferguson 1:81). A clue to his loyalties became evident in the religious turmoil between Arminians and Contra-Remonstrants at Utrecht in 1612, for when some members of his company "revolted" against Maurits's authority, presumably in support of heterodoxy, Wishart proceeded vigorously to secure immediate discharge of the ringleaders (Ferguson 1:270–72, 276–77 et passim). The third, Sir William Balfour (SvO 1610, 1620; SP 84/98), commander of Troop 24 (harquebusiers), is the one identifiable Scottish officer whom we know for sure to have waited on Doncaster at Haarlem. He is also the most interesting of the three. His father, Colonel Henry Balfour of Pitcullo,[3] had been one of the first commanders of Brog's regiment in the very beginning of its service, well before the earl of Leicester's arrival in the Netherlands as governor-general. He was killed near The Hague at Wassenaar in 1580. Sir William received his commission as captain of infantry in 1594 and served under Henderson as sergeant major of the composite Scottish contingent sent to invest Juliers in 1610. Not all was harmony among these Scottish commanders when Doncaster visited the Netherlands, however. Balfour once applied for the lieutenant colonelcy under Brog but had been refused. He had also quarreled violently with Captain Wishart at Leith in 1616, and both were imprisoned for dueling in Edinburgh (Ferguson 1:48, 57, 107, 245, 294, 438). In 1617–18 he served as an emissary for Ambassador Carleton and Sir Thomas Lake, then secretary of state (Ferguson 1:223n. 1; Sellin 69). After the outbreak of the Thirty Years' War, he was taken prisoner by the Spanish at Emmerich in 1622, returned to England in 1627–28 in order to serve King Charles in military capacities, and upon the assassination of the duke of Buckingham went back to the United Provinces, where he received a handsome reward for his twenty-five years of service (Ferguson 1:70 et passim). As Doncaster could undoubtedly attest, Balfour was a courtier of great influence. Among his friends he could number the king himself,

Prince Charles, Charles's sister the exiled queen of Bohemia living in Holland, and the duke of Buckingham, who had shown him special favor, and he had also served on the Privy Council. Unlike Donne, he lived on into the period of the Puritan Revolt, and his choices suggest the dilemma that the poet might have faced had he too lived to see the upheaval. After retiring from Dutch service, Balfour was made lieutenant of the Tower, but despite the favors he had received from the royal family, he did not stand by the king in the civil war. Characterized as violently antipapist and probably too much of a patriot to stomach Charles's imposition of bishops on Scotland, let alone the insult of an English army on Scottish soil under command of a Catholic like the earl of Arundel, Balfour resigned his post rather than take bribes and allow Strafford to escape. After the Scots allied with Parliament in 1643–44, he became lieutenant general of the parliamentary horse. Despite his age, he led the cavalry reserve at Edgehill, breaking several regiments of the king's foot and capturing the royal artillery. At the second battle of Newbury, he commanded the right wing of the cavalry. He retired when Oliver Cromwell, who had learned the shock effect of horse under him, put the New Model Army into the field. Fittingly, he passed away the year of the Restoration.

In addition to the regimental staff and cavalry officers, there were many other Scottish captains with infantry commands, not counting artillery officers, quartermasters, and provosts. Although it would be tedious to list them all, some are worth mentioning because of their connections with James's court and Scots who patronized Donne. Such was Thomas Erskine, or Arskin, evidently the first earl of Kellie (SvO 1603, 1605, 1610, 1620; SP 84/98). A childhood companion of King James's, he accompanied James to England where he succeeded Ralegh as Captain of the Yeomen of the Guard, received the Order of the Garter, and was elevated to the earldom in 1618. Similarly the David Lindsey named in the Staten van Oorlog for 1620 was perhaps the second son of John Lindsey, Lord Menmuir, secretary of state in Scotland and instrumental in reestablishing limited episcopacy. Whether the Abraham Morton in Dutch service (SvO 1610, 1620) was related to Sir Albertus Morton or had anything to do with William Douglas, earl of Morton, lord high treasurer of Scotland, is highly dubious, although the earl's commanding a regiment during the expedition against La Rochelle in 1627 points to similar military background. Others were Jacques Sandilandis (SvO 1620), probably the grandnephew of Sandilands of Calder, First Lord Tophichen; Sir John Seton of St. Germain (SvO 1610, 1620; SP 84/98), youngest son of Robert, first earl of Winton, who had been a great favorite of the king; Walter

Bruce (SvO 1603, 1604, 1605, 1610, 1620; SP 84/98), likely a descendent of Edward, Lord Kinloss, whose eldest son was killed in a duel at Bergen op Zoom by Donne's friend and patron, Edward Sackville, later fourth earl of Dorset; Mongo Hamilton (SvO 1610, SP 84/98), perhaps related to Hugh Hamilton, First Baron Hamilton of Glenawley; James Livingstone (Ten Raa and de Bas 3:181–82, 237; MacLean, *Huwelijksintekeningen* 341; SvO 1620), third son of Alexander, first earl of Linlithgow, who had been guardian of Prince Henry and Princess Elizabeth; and one Robert "Schot" (SvO 1604, 1610, 1620; SP 84/98; MacLean, *Huwelijksintekeningen* 343), possibly family of Sir John Scot of Scotstarvet, in which case he enjoyed kinship not only by blood with the Drummonds of Hawthornden but by literary interests that culminated on the one hand in publication of Arthur Johnston's *Delitiae poetarum scotorum* at Amsterdam in 1637 and on the other in Blaeuw's Atlas of Scotland—not to mention Johnston's *Opera*, which appeared at Middelburg in 1642. The religious loyalties of the Scottish auxiliaries in the United Provinces are easy to guess. The chaplain common to both regiments was the Reverend Andrew Hunter (SvO 1610, 1620), a veteran Presbyterian who since 1597 had the onerous task of serving Scottish units scattered all over the garrison towns and frontier camps throughout the United Provinces. A conscientious, indefatigable, and modest pastor burdened by an excessive number of children and a supposedly mean salary (Ferguson 1:xxix, 57 et passim),[4] he had faced many of the same dangers as the line officers and commanded the respect and affection of his martial countrymen. When Donne visited Utrecht with Doncaster in 1619, he may well have heard Hunter officiate at Sunday service in the Scottish garrison church at St. Pieter's, or possibly he himself preached to Hunter's congregation (Sellin 43).

When it comes to officers of the four English regiments in Dutch service, relations with Donne are more direct. This was not merely because he was English and a Londoner. Of the three leaders of Doncaster's mission, Donne was, I believe, the only ex-soldier actually to have seen action with the forces of the States General, and some of the commanders with whom we are about to deal had either been at one time companions-in-arms, however briefly, or were friends, relatives, or fellow soldiers of Donne's friends and patrons. Doubtless they were the source of much of the astonishingly detailed information that regularly turns up in Donne's letters regarding military and political affairs in the Low Countries. To one's surprise, the religious and political profiles of the English regimental staff officers are less indicative of staunch Anglican or Laudian sympathies than some might expect. Indeed, as a group they inclined rather toward puritan nonconformism, both latent and rampant, and with just one exception the theology they publicly endorsed was pronouncedly orthodox Calvinian. But of course, when one thinks about the matter, their salaries, and those of their chaplains, came from the Reformed establishments governing the towns and provinces to which their units were repartitioned (cf. Sprunger, *Churches* 162, 180, 197, 212–13, 262–69, 275–83).

Donne had many ties with officers in the senior regiment of English in the Netherlands, and they adumbrate the web of interrelationships linking the military in the Low Countries with supporters of the Dutch among his friends and patrons in London. Although at the time of Donne's 1619 visit to The Hague, General Sir Edward Cecil (SvO 1603, 1605, 1610, 1620; SP 84/98) was actually in England soliciting command of the force being raised to serve in the Palatinate, his career illustrates the point. Grandson of William Cecil, First Lord Burghley, he was, according to Dalton (passim), the son of Sir Thomas Cecil and Mary Cheeke, daughter of the learned Sir John, that Protestant tutor of Edward VI in Greek. (One wonders whether the captain Hatton Cheeke recorded in the SvOs for 1603, 1605, and 1610 was related to her family.) Cecil's father, Thomas, had distinguished himself during the early days of the Dutch rebellion—Thomas and his half brother Sir Robert had served as volunteers in the English fleet in 1588—and just as Sir Philip Sidney became governor of Vlissingen, so Sir Thomas received commission as the first English governor of The Brill when the Dutch relinquished these strategic strongholds to Elizabeth as cautionary towns in 1585 (Ten Raa and de Bas 1:246, 280). In early 1599, Sir Edward's uncle, Robert Cecil, later Lord Salisbury, procured him a company of foot. After conducting himself well at the siege of Bommel (1599), he obtained appointment as captain of the 27th troop of horse on June 13, 1600. Nine days later, Maurits marched for Nieuwpoort. Here Cecil established his reputation as a professional soldier, for his unit was combined with those of the famous Sir Horace Vere and the noted Dutch cavalry leader Godard van Balen in a "regiment" of reserve that, under the command of the seasoned Dutch officer, was to save the army from total defeat. At the climax of the battle, when the pressure of the Spanish advance forced the troops to fall back, Maurits committed the reserve just as the English infantry began to falter, and the three squadrons of cavalry delivered the famous charge that gave the day to the Dutch. Indeed, when Cecil's unit repulsed the enemy in the downs and dispersed part of them, the infantry stopped retreating, and the tide of battle turned into the most glorious victory the Dutch rebels had ever enjoyed on land.

Cecil was likewise at the siege of Oostende. When English reinforcements were rushed to relieve the fortress at the end of June 1601, Cecil commanded the contingent (Bald, *Drurys* 46; Dalton 1:71–78), while Sir Robert Drury, Donne's friend and patron, was one of the company commanders under him (cf. "Lijsten," Oldenbarnevelt 2946).[5] Upon Cecil's return to England, Queen Elizabeth knighted him. Both gentlemen participated in Maurits's campaign of 1602, but whereas Drury felt resentment for want of advancement (Bald, *Drurys* 46–47)—his father, Sir William, had been appointed governor of Bergen op Zoom in 1588 (Ten Raa and de Bas 1:244–45)—the States General and Count Maurits raised Cecil to colonel of horse, in which capacity he served at the siege of Grave, which was taken that year at great cost. At the accession of King James in 1603, who entrusted Cecil's uncle Sir Robert with the chief affairs of the nation, Sir Edward was named Gentleman of His Majesty's Privy Chamber. However, he returned to the Low Countries the next year to fight in the siege of Sluys. About 1605, after James abandoned the triple alliance and made a separate peace with Spain, the status of the British regiments in Dutch service was completely revised. At this time, the English companies were permanently divided into set regiments, and Cecil received the one that he still commanded when Donne traveled through the United Provinces with Doncaster in 1619. After participating in other hard actions, he was chosen over such eminent juniors as Sir Horace Vere as general in command of the British contingent at the investment of Juliers in 1610 (Ten Raa and de Bas 3:18, 179).

Bold and ambitious, Cecil was a diligent, judicious, and thoroughly effective commander in the field. Among the many volunteers he thus attracted as apprentices in the art military were men close to Donne such as Grey Bridges, Lord Chandos (who was the husband of the step-daughter of Donne's erstwhile employer, Sir Thomas Egerton), and Sir Edward Herbert, Baron Herbert of Cherbury, who went over to serve at Juliers too. As we know, Donne seized the occasion and composed a verse epistle to Herbert, observing

> As brave as true, is that profession than
> Which you doe use to make; that you know man.
> This makes it credible, you have dwelt upon
> All worthy bookes; and now are such an one.
> Actions are authors, and of those in you
> Your friends finde every day a mart of new.
> ("To Sir Edward Herbert, at Julyers," Shawcross, lines 49–50)

If anyone fully understood exactly what Donne was alluding to in his praise of Cherbury's "actions" at Juliers, it was Cecil, for the general allowed Herbert to share his quarters, and Herbert's accounts of his escapades with Sir Edward provide some of the most vivid testaments to the bravery and care Cecil exhibited as commander and tactician (Cherbury, *Autobiography* 112–16).

As Cecil's presence in the Netherlands during the Twelve Years' Truce was not so mandatory as before, he spent much time in England after 1611 seeking to improve his fortunes, and there are noteworthy links with sources of Donne's patronage during this period. The soldierly Prince Henry had extended Cecil his favor, and to Sir Edward the sudden death of the prince on the eve of the Palatine wedding must have been much the blow that Donne's elegy describes. As Sir Edward also became treasurer to Princess Elizabeth, whom he escorted to the Palatinate upon her marriage to the elector in 1613, the loss of Henry and the Palatine wedding were both occasions of great import to him, not the least because the Harringtons—the parents of Donne's patroness, Lucy, countess of Bedford—had brought the princess up in their puritanical ways and had played leading roles in her removal to Germany. Obviously, one is not very far in this context from poems in and around these occasions, including Donne's elegy on the death of the countess of Bedford's brother.

When the death of Sir Edward's uncle, the earl of Salisbury, opened the way for new favorites at court in 1612, Donne turned immediately to both his Scottish friends and the Cecils for advancement. The first prospective patron of this sort was of course Sir Robert Ker, earl of Somerset, a cousin of Donne's friend Sir Robert of Ancrum, at whose behest he wrote his epithalamion on Somerset's notorious marriage with Frances Howard. While Donne was lucky enough to have had no discernible part in Somerset's criminal involvement with Lady Essex, nevertheless he was associated for years afterward in both the Netherlands and England with the murdered keeper of the Tower, Sir Thomas Overbury, through his contributions to the *Overburian Characters* (Sellin 29–30)—cynical reflections on the court and Crown that others have called "the most dangerously scandalous writings ever attributed to Donne" (Flynn, "Problematic" 101). Supposed by some to be pieces that "could never safely have been allowed to get out of hand," the fact is that they quickly began to circulate among literary Netherlanders such as Huygens, Lodewijk Rosaeus, probably P. C. Hooft (to whom Huygens later forwarded his translations from Donne), or Jacob vander Burgh—with Huygens a member of Hooft's so-called Muiden circle—who as late as 1636 recalled Overbury in his preface to Hooft's poetry (Bachrach, "Acquaintance" 114; Sellin 17–30; Vander Burgh sig.[*] r-v;

Hooft *Werken*). As for Donne's very last bid for civilian employment in August 1614, he directed it on invitation to the wife of Sir Edward's cousin William, to whom the earldom of Salisbury had passed, terming Catherine Howard an angel of light in whom he professed "all goodnesse" to "have discern'd, / And though I burn my librarie, be learn'd" ("To the Countess of Salisbury, *August*, 1614," Shawcross, lines 83–84). The countess's receptivity, thus, may have been due to considerably more than simply, as we usually think, the offices of Donne's friend George Garrard, who had taken service with the earl.

Both Colonel Cecil and Donne sat as members in the Addled Parliament, Donne serving on several of its important committees, while on February 27, 1618—just as the religious troubles in the Netherlands were culminating in the Synod of Dort—Sir Edward took to wife none other than Diana Drury, the third and youngest sister of Donne's former patron, Sir Robert. As it happened, Diana was the second of the Drury sisters to marry into Edward's branch of the family (her middle sister, Elisabeth, had become the spouse of Edward's brother William back in 1598), and it seems reasonable to think that long-standing contacts through the Dutch military did not hinder these matches, to say the least. Oddly enough, had her niece, the Elizabeth lamented in Donne's *Anniversaries* and funeral elegy, survived, would not Drury's daughter, not her Cecil aunts, have inherited the Drury wealth when Sir William Drury, the only surviving son, died in 1615? Similarities in style and theme between Donne's lines to the countess of Salisbury and the *Anniversaries* may suggest more than style or coincidence, for in such a social context one can readily understand why Donne was especially sensitive about comparison of what he wrote for the new countess of Salisbury with his laments over the Drury maiden.

Sir Edward's reactions during the theological strife between the orthodox party and the Remonstrants in the United Provinces during the second decade of the seventeenth century are quite in line with opinions reigning in the circles to which Donne had been appealing for patronage just before entering the ministry. Although all companies under Cecil's command were under oath to the States General, some were under repartition to—that is, paid by—the Estates of Utrecht, and they were stationed in and around that city. The situation offered the Arminians a good chance at two kinds of subversion. One was to ruin the forces by withholding pay, the other to undermine the authority of the regular garrison by replacing or integrating it with municipal *waardgelders*, or civic militia, raised by the Remonstrant Municipal Council. As the struggle between the Remonstrants and their opponents reached its climax, a captaincy in one of Cecil's companies fell vacant. The pro-Arminian Estates of Utrecht seized the opportunity and bestowed the post on an officer of their own choosing. One can thus imagine what Sir Edward thought of the Remonstrants and their ideas of free will and predestination. His company was but "in prison at Utrecht," he observed sarcastically, it being powerless to oppose the municipal and provincial authorities, and so, when Maurits, now prince of Orange, forcibly disarmed the Arminian levies there the following year, Cecil's company was the one he was "more sure of than any other" (Dalton 1:269 et passim).

For subordinate officers, Cecil relied on Sir Philip Packenham (SvO 1603, 1605, 1610, 1620; SP 84/98) as his lieutenant colonel and on Captain William Proude (SvO 1603, 1604, 1605, 1620; SP 84/98) as sergeant major. Both are indicative of the spiritual climate prevailing in the regiment. Of Packenham, we know little more than that he was appointed to his post shortly after Cecil took command of the regiment and that King James had knighted him at Theobalds in 1617. Evidently he too was anti-Remonstrant. At least, while acting as commandant during Cecil's absence in 1619, he made sure that Carleton was kept up to date about "Arminian practises," and he served as liaison between the British ambassador and Sir Edward in London (Dalton 1:251, 300; Ten Raa and de Bas 2:160, 3:179; Markham 440). When the States General in displeasure relieved Cecil (then Viscount Wimbledon) in 1631, Packenham rose to command the regiment and led it into battle at the siege of Maastricht (1632). Under his leadership, the regiment held to its tradition of maintaining strongly puritan preachers (Dalton 2:312; Sprunger, *Ames* 216).

Proude died with Packenham at Maastricht. Having entered service as early as Drake's expedition against Lisbon and campaigned in Brittany in support of Henry IV in 1591, he too had participated in both the Cádiz and the Islands' voyage, as Donne surely knew, and thereafter he joined Essex's expedition in Ireland. "A patterne of true Nobility," he volunteered as a private gentleman at Oostende, and his gallantry there—he was wounded in a sally—secured him exactly the sort of commission that had eluded Donne at Cádiz. Noted "for valour, for diligence, for insight in his Office," Proude succeeded Packenham as sergeant major in 1614, and he also received command of eight companies sent to Juliers under Sir Edward that year. As one might expect, Proude was a pious man, attending church faithfully on "lecture daies" and the Sabbath to hear God's Word, and his wont was to pray in his chambers "heartily, and fervently to God on his knees" and daily to "read his Bible and other good books" (Dalton 2:314; see Ten Raa and de Bas 3:179). At his death, he received a public funeral in the Cathedral Church of Christ at Canterbury (Rogers, sig. D^r–D2^v).

As for religion in Cecil's command, there had been considerable friction about the time of the Synod of Dort between the colonel and the States General about granting a stipend to Adrian (Andrew) Hughes (Hewes), a minister whom Cecil desired as his regimental chaplain. It seems plausible that Arminian factions opposed the nomination because of the attitudes that he and Colonel Cecil manifested toward their doctrines, but the reason given was that Hughes was too often absent in England with the colonel to minister properly to the troops. Right in the midst of the religious controversy rocking the land, that is, Cecil had recommended Hughes as a minister who "hath done [the United Provinces] more honor and servis then all the other [regimental chaplains] have, for he hath prayed for [the States General] in many churches in this kingdom, which others have not done, but they have given him cause to leave it" (Cecil to Carleton, London, December 11, 1617, and March 26, 1618, Dalton 1:256–63; Hewes to Carleton, SP 84/93).[6] It was in fact not until just a short time before Donne's arrival in The Hague that Sir Dudley persuaded the States General to grant Cecil's request, and the difference was resolved just as Doncaster reached Haarlem.[7] Whether this Hughes was in any way related to Jacobus Hughes (Hugenus), who (according to some sources) served at the Synod of Dort, is thus an interesting question. Andrew's efforts as a pro-Dutch propagandist from pulpits in England run parallel to those of Jacobus in the Netherlands. Jacobus was responsible for rendering into Dutch some of the puritan alarms against King James's pacifist, pro-Spanish policies ascribed to a former royal chaplain, the indomitable Thomas Scot, namely, the courageously outspoken *Vox populi* (1620) and *Vox dei* (1624). To the rage of the king, Pastor Scot, who was a protégé of William Herbert, earl of Pembroke, refused blindly to accept Solomon's judgment on such matters of foreign policy as English neutrality, the Palsgrave's right to the throne of Bohemia, and the survival of the Reformed cause on the Continent without speaking out. Fleeing England barely a step ahead of the hue and cry after him, he found refuge in the Netherlands as a Reformed chaplain ministering to British garrisons at Utrecht and Gorinchem, and it was at Utrecht ("Printed in Paradise") that most of this voluminous stream of publications against English neutrality saw light. Inasmuch as these pamphlets include a speech purportedly delivered by Cecil in 1621 urging the House of Commons to provide speedily for war in "defence of Religion, and the safetie of the land," one guesses that, given what must have been both Scot's and Hughes's dependency on the good graces of Sir Edward at Utrecht, Cecil's at least tacit endorsement stood behind such thunderings against Stuart policy (Scot, *Speech*; cf. Schrickx 157).[8]

The second of the English regiments was even more flagrantly inclined toward puritanical practices and policies than Cecil's. These companies were led by the field general of the English regiments in Donne's time, Sir Horace Vere (SvO 1603, 1605, 1610, 1620; SP 84/98), whose name, according to the epigram on Vere by Ben Jonson—himself a veteran of the Low Countries' wars—not only bears "A *romane* sound, but *romane* virtue weares". Again, Cádiz forms a common ground. When Donne embarked on that joint Anglo-Dutch venture against the king of Spain, the earl of Essex technically held command of the land forces, while Sir Horace's elder brother, Sir Francis Vere, then brigade commander of all the English regiments serving in the Low Countries, seconded him as lieutenant general and lord marshal. As the most successful Protestant field commander of his time, Sir Francis was, for all practical purposes, in charge of shore operations, and his 2,200 Dutch and English veterans drawn from the army of States General formed the heart of the force that made the actual assault on the citadel. Of adventurers like Donne, there were about a thousand volunteering, and like the rest of these auxiliaries, Donne must have been farmed out to one of the regular companies already in Dutch service (Ten Raa and de Bas 2:301–304; Markham 217–35; Bald, *Life* 80–85). After the taking of the city on June 21 and the funeral five days later of Sir John Wingfield, who atoned the loss of Gertruidenberg with his death in the streets of Cadiz, Donne most aptly commemorated him in the finest of his epigrams:

> Beyond th'old Pillers many'have trauailed
> Towards the Suns cradle, and his throne, and bed.
> A fitter Piller our Earle did bestow
> In that late Iland, for he well did know
> Farther then Wingefield no man dares to go—[9]

The victory was celebrated by the dubbing of no fewer than sixty-four knights, including William Herbert, future earl of Pembroke, Miles Corbet, Arthur Throckmorton (Sir Walter Ralegh's brother-in-law, whose younger brother Nicholas was married to the sister of Donne's wife),[10] and friends and acquaintances of Donne later like Robert Radcliffe, earl of Sussex, Maurice Berkeley, and Edward Conway (Kinney 83–84; cf. Bald, *Life* 84). Unfortunately for Donne, he was not among them, but for many of those who distinguished themselves sufficiently to qualify for spurs, the occasion launched fine military careers in the Low Countries, particularly in this regiment.

Chief of these was Sir Horace himself (SvO 1603, 1605, 1610, 1620; SP 84/98). From his auspicious beginning at Cádiz, he soon came to hold key commands. At Sluys he so won the confidence of the States General that when a second English regiment was formed in 1599, he obtained the colonelcy, and his cool heroics on battlefields like Nieuwpoort, Oostende, and Mühlheim brought international fame. When Sir Francis retired in 1609, Sir Horace was made field general of the English brigade and governor of The Brill. In 1610 he served at Juliers at the head of his force, and when the pensionary of Holland, Johan Van Oldenbarnevelt (in effect the prime minister of the republic), redeemed the cautionary towns in 1616, Vere was the officer who handed The Brill back to its native masters. During the civil unrest of 1618 and 1619, Sir Horace's main services had been to support the authority of the States General and Prince Maurits on behalf of the orthodox cause. Just as the stadholder had relied on Henderson and Cecil, so he had also used Vere's troops to disarm the Arminian levies at Utrecht. Indeed, the States General named Sir Horace temporary governor expressly to secure the city and province from Remonstrant subversion, and when Maurits made his grim progress through the republic to purge various municipal governments of Remonstrant influence, Sir Horace had accompanied him (Markham 391–92). Vere was not in The Hague when Donne arrived with Doncaster, for he had gone off to England in hopes of a commission to recruit another army of Englishmen, this time for the relief of Bohemia and the Palsgrave. It was Vere's performance as leader of this tiny force sent off to martyr itself in defense of Heidelberg, Mannheim, the interests of the Elector Palatine and his consort the Queen of Hearts—England's own former Princess Elizabeth—in their homeland, and the Reformed church in Germany that brought him eternal fame not only in British military annals but in the hearts and minds of admiring contemporaries, including, as Donne's letters indicate, the poet himself (Donne, *Letters* liii:142–43; lxxxiii:198–201, lxxv:182–83). As Sir Edward's loud complaints show after the Bohemian government gave the nod to Vere as commander of the expeditionary force, the two colonels disliked each other and there was much friction between them.

Sir Horace's second-in-command was Lieutenant Colonel Sir Edward Vere (SvO 1603, 1605, 1610, 1620; SP 84/98), his regimental sergeant major Sir George Hollis (SvO 1603, 1605, 1610, 1620; SP 84/98). Although Sir Edward's precise relationship to Sir Horace, who had no male heirs (Markham 385), is not clear, he had served with great distinction under his kinsman ever since boyhood, rising from page to sergeant major in 1605 and then to his higher place in 1614. Sir Horace's subalterns were men of letters, and this Vere was no exception. An accomplished scholar, he produced a translation of Polybius sufficiently worthy to elicit a witty "character" after his fall at's Hertogenbosch in 1629 to the effect of "all summer in the field, all winter in his study; in whose fall fame makes this kingdom a great loser" (Markham 437–38; Ten Raa and de Bas 2:160, 3:180). Hollis, next brother to Sir John Hollis, earl of Clare, was kin to the Veres and had long been their companion-in-arms. His brother Sir John had gone on the Islands' voyage—it was his last exploit—and as Sir George commanded a company at Nieuwpoort, Donne's patron, Sir Robert Drury, had also fought with him in that memorable battle.[11] Now Hollis's brother Sir John held much of the property in and around the very houses occupied by Donne and Sir Robert in Drury Lane, so they were probably no strangers to him. No longer young and somewhat maimed by several bad wounds, Sir George had lost his left eye in action. Yet, as sergeant major was a post asking "valiant men, an old soldier, and one experienced in the way of his profession," a place that "on all occasion" gave access to the captain general of the forces, Prince Maurits, or to the marshal of the field, Hollis was ideal for it (Hexam 2:1639, 5; cf. Markham 54–55). Whatever his rank, his reputation far exceeded it. Tall, slender, ruddy with dark brown hair and a "sanguine complexion," his countenance "stout and very spiritfull," he had been "very wilde" in his youth, and his readiness to challenge anyone over the slightest point affecting his honor reminds one of captains like Shakespeare's Gower, Fluellen, or Macmorris. When Maurits once tried to settle a quarrel between Hollis and another, Sir George dared upbraid the then stadholder to his face and storm from the room—a slight that he accepted, for Hollis was in the right. Hollis profoundly disliked Cecil. Having begun his service as a lieutenant to Sir Edward, he had quit in disgust at Cecil's arbitrary ways. On one occasion he arrived late at a "meeting . . . of diverse principall officers in the Low Countries at a feast" and learned that the colonel had "trenched upon him" in his absence. Supposedly he strode up to end of the table where Sir Edward had his place, clapped his hand on Cecil's shoulder, proclaimed that he lied like a villain, and added that he would kick him out of the room if company were not present. We are asked to believe that Cecil took the braving (Holles 72–80).

When it came to matters of the gospel, Sir Horace and his wife, Lady Mary Vere, the widow of William Hoby, were "famous for their religion." Like that of the countess of Bedford, it was outspokenly Reformed, with a strong tendency toward nonconformism. Accordingly, puritans "celebrated the Veres' godliness and marveled that the Lady Mary could turn her home [in The Hague] so effectively into a little sanctuary." Prayer and Bible reading were her rule: "Each night the Veres read a psalm, on Fridays the family was catechized, and on Saturdays they made preparation for the Sabbath." "She was a faithful woman," her eulogist quoted from Nehemiah, "and feared God above any." Samuel Clarke, the puritan hagiographer, included Lady Mary Vere in his *Lives of Sundry Eminent Persons in This Later Age*, while Richard Sibbes dedicated his *Bruised Reede* to Sir Horace and Lady Mary, saying, "The world hath a long time taken notice of you, in whom both religion, and military imployment, meeknesse of spirit with height of courage, humility with honor, by a rare and happy combination have met together. Whereby you have much vindicated your profession from common imputation, and shewed that Piety can enter into Tents, and follow after camps, and that God hath his *Iosua's* and his *Cornelius'es* in all ages" (Sprunger, *Ames* 31, 34–35).

Not surprisingly, Sir Horace had a habit of employing nonconforming chaplains to minister to his regiment, many of them outspoken refugees from English bishops. One of the first had been John Paget, that refugee puritan preacher leading the Scots-English Presbyterian church in the Begijnhof at Amsterdam. Another was John Burgess, who, having refused to subscribe to Bancroft's canons, dared to preach against ceremonies before the king himself and so fetched up with Vere's flock at The Hague, ministering the Word and sacraments without kneeling, employing the cross in baptism, or donning the surplice (Sprunger, *Ames* 30). At the time of the Synod of Dort and Doncaster's embassy to The Hague, Vere's regiment had just lost its previous minister, but whether the subsequent candidate, one Reverend John Hassel (Hessel), had yet been appointed is unclear.[12] In any event, Vere's chaplain when Donne visited The Hague in 1619–20 was none other than that unloving anti-prelatical son of the Church of England, William Ames, who had mightily assisted the orthodox cause from the sidelines at Dort and now stood upon the threshold of a professorship of theology at the anything but heterodox University of Franeker in Friesland (Sellin 110–11, 215n. 11). The extent to which the spiritual milieu obtaining in the officers of Vere's regiment at the outbreak of the Thirty Years' War conformed to Scot's crusading puritanism is amply evident in the foreword of Scot's *A Tongue Combat* (1623), penned by Vere's quartermaster, Henry Hexam (SvO 1620), who dedicated it to his fellow "Servant to Truth," the "honorable Sir George Holles Knight." "It is now time or never," this warlike compiler of the first truly substantial Dutch-English lexicon for the use of "Divines, students, and others" (Osselton 34–57) intoned,

> to declare ourselves, and stand together for the truth of Religion herein oppugned: which he that shrinkes from, for any worldly or politicke

respect, or any Anti-christian and temperarie temptation, shall surely be denied hereafter of *Christ Jesus*, who will publiquely professe to be ashamed of them before God, who are ashamed of him here before men; and to spare those lukewarme persons out of his mouth, whom the sudden and unexpected alarum of bold, daring, and desperate opposition for Falshood, will not awaken from that stupid Lethargie, or reserved Foxe sleepe of Policie, wherein they lie bedrid, to be as couragious for Truth, as other men are for lyes, in this Age of Atheisme.

The Lord by his Spirit kindle this zeale in our hearts for his Cause, and honour the millitarie Profession so farre, that as *Phineas* the Priest, hath heretofore taken his pike and led us ... so *wee* may now leade *Phineas* against that *Babylonish Strumpet* and her Brood, who *commits fornication with the greatest Princes of the earth*, and would impudently presse into our Tents to do, and cause the like villanie to be openly and universally committed by us and all men. (Sig. A2v)

This is a remarkable echo of similarly fervent puritan protest against lukewarm, self-serving, even criminal Presbyterian "Atheisme" that another hotly antipapist protégé of both the Veres and Cecil in Dutch service, Cyril Tourneur, dramatized a decade or so before in *The Atheists Tragedy*. Indeed, Tourneur characterized his Huguenot hero as a brave defender of Oostende against the Spanish and arranged the action of his drama accordingly. For men like Hexam, the Veres, and Tourneur, it was imperative that aiding the "mutinous Dutch," as Donne put it, must be driven not by fleshly concerns, however courageous, but by "all our Soules devotion" to "our Mistresse faire," "true religion" ("Satire III," Shawcross, lines 5–43)—Una, thus, as Spenser has it, not Duessa. Skeptics questioning whether such Scotto-Tourneurian idealism has any relevance to Donne should keep in mind another captain in this regiment who also received his spurs at Cádiz. This was Donne's friend Sir Edward Conway, later Viscount Conway and one of the principal secretaries of state, who has been discussed elsewhere in connection with Donne and the Netherlands (Sellin 28; Sellin and Veenendaal 236–50). Son and heir of Sir John Conway by Eleanore Greville, a younger sister of Sir Fulke, Sir Edward boasted fine ancestry in Anglo-Dutch arms and letters alike. His father, who had been a member of the Areopagus with Sir Philip Sidney and Sir Edward Dyer, had gone off like both of them to the wars in the Low Countries, where he had served as governor of Oostende in 1586 until joining Drake's attack on Portugal in 1589. Later he became lieutenant governor under the elder Vere at The Brill. A trusted confidant of the Veres, Sir

Edward had gone on the expedition against Cádiz where, unlike Donne, he received his knighthood (Kinney 84) and stayed in Dutch service, soon rising to follow his father as lieutenant governor at the same cautionary town. For a good part of the time that Donne had known him—that is, from at least as early as 1598 up through the return of the towns to Dutch control in 1616—Conway spent much of his time in The Brill (Sellin 18), taking good care, as the Dutch acknowledged, of that strategic citadel just to the west of Rotterdam.

Such religiosity as Hexam's would not have been at all strange to a Conway in the Vere regiment. In 1570 and 1571, Sir Edward's father, Sir John, published a set of meditations and prayers that received a second edition as recently as 1611 under the title *Poesie of Floured Praiers*. As for Sir Edward's piety, he had a great deal in common with the Veres, for he had married Dorothy Tracy, Lady Vere's sister. In other words, the puritan saint heralded by Clarke was no less than the sister-in-law of one of Donne's trusted familiars, and their relationship with Vere was such that the Conways had actually arranged the match between Lady Mary and Sir Horace. When one recalls that Donne seems to have acted as an intermediary for Sir Edward with common friends in England like Sir Henry Goodyer, then piety and letters begin to overlap dramatically. In fact, from Donne's correspondence it seems clear that he had been sending holographs of compositions like *Biathanatos* and the *Problems* across the Channel to Conway at The Brill "during one of the most profoundly spiritual and creative periods in his life" (Sellin 17–30). Indeed, since at one time the Conways "seem to have possessed a [manuscript] collection of Donne's poetry organized in somewhat the same fashion as those possessed by other noble families like the Egertons or the Percys" (Sellin and Veenendaal 235–36), there is reason to think that Donne's literary endeavors—like the lost Latin epigrams, *Conclave Ignati*, or "Newes from the very Country," which certainly seem to have circulated in the Netherlands before 1621; as well as other pieces such as "A Litanie," say, the *La Corona* sequence, *Pseudo-Martyr*; the first twelve of the *Holy Sonnets*, the elegies, or some of the *Songs and Sonets*—formed part of the traffic between Donne and the Conways at The Brill up until at least the time that Sir Edward relinquished his post there in 1616. Some of the politico-religious works that Donne composed in this period, thus, may well have had in mind a military audience abroad much more specific in politics and religion than we have imagined, one that probably shared outlooks not far removed from the countess of Bedford and her family, with whom the *Holy Sonnets* have long been connected. Certainly, any number of eyes and ears among the zealously Protestant Veres and their officers stuck in dreary Dutch garrison towns during the winter would have been eager for works like *Ignatius His Conclave*, the elegy and *Anniversaries* on the late daughter of an erstwhile companion-hero-in-arms at Nieuwpoort, the elegy on Prince Henry, the *Essays in Divinity*, or the *Divine Poems* and the passionate religiosity that informs them, not to speak of the enjoyable, rough *jeux* of soldierly wit in Donne's cruder love elegies or the *Overburian Characters*. When one also calls to mind the fact that after leaving Dutch service, Sir Edward would succeed Nethersole as agent to the king of Bohemia, then we begin to suspect not only that a Dutch impulse like Constantijn Huygens's to translate Donne has deep roots in the Dutch Council of State and English military serving in The Hague and Dutch garrison towns, but that behind high points of related Dutch literature such as Huygens's *Heylige Dagen*, a magnificent cycle of rich feast-day sonnets in Donnean mode, lies a common piety that can as certainly be called Reformed as Anglican.

Donne also had connections with the third English regiment, although its political orientation was quite different from Vere's. The colonel, Sir John Ogle, a younger son of Thomas Ogle of Pinchbeck, Lincolnshire, was a brave soldier who rose quickly after joining Dutch service probably in the late 1580s (SvO 1603, 1605, 1610, 1620; SP 84/98). By 1591 he was acting sergeant major general under Sir Francis Vere, participated in Maurits's great campaigns of the 1590s, and soon attained the lieutenant colonelcy of the Vere regiment under Sir Francis (Ten Raa and de Bas 2:159–61). He wrote a brief account of the English charge that finally broke the Spanish at Nieuwpoort, and the heroism he displayed there together with that of Sir Robert Drury immortalized both in military annals. As second-in-command over the English, Ogle stood in the thick of the fighting throughout the day, so much so that at one point Cecil and Vere had been obliged to rescue him lest he be captured. Together with young Sir Horace and Sir Charles Fairfax (SvO 1603),[13] Ogle rallied the British at a crucial moment and delivered the charge that won the day. His most notable deed of personal bravery was the rescue of Sir Francis. As the English began to buckle under pressure from the main attack, the general's horse was shot dead under him. Together with Drury and the latter's servant Thomas Higham, Ogle extricated the wounded Sir Francis from under his mount in the teeth of the enemy advance and put him up behind Drury as Vere's blood flowed over him (Dillingham 102–6, 110; Markham 299). In the attempts to relieve Oostende, Ogle was used to recruit forces in England and bring them over to Flanders. In 1603 he was knighted at Woodstock and took command of the English defending Oostende that same year. When the over-strength

English regiments were divided to form a third, the States General named him colonel in 1605, once the rival candidate, Thomas, Lord Grey de Wilton, was convicted, along with Ralegh and Lord Cobham, of conspiring against James's accession.[14]

Though a hero of the Dutch revolt, Ogle had been compromised by events in 1618 and 1619. Nominated governor of Utrecht in 1610, he had no sooner assumed his post than rioting broke out against the "libertine" policies of the Remonstrant regents and the perceived despotism of Remonstrant-minded Gillis van Ledenberg, the provincial secretary of Utrecht who controlled political power there. As commander of the citadel, Ogle turned out to be a "reliable adherent of the ruling party" at Utrecht, naturally, but as a consequence, orthodox Calvinists began to view him as standing in the way of change (Den Tex 2:517–19), even to the point of organizing a conspiracy to seize him, occupy the town hall, and assassinate two unwanted Arminian pastors. When the then Arminian colored Estates of Holland adopted Van Oldenbarnevelt's "Sharp Resolution" of 1617, a measure that called for the cities to take on their own militias and demanded loyalty from the regular military to the Estates of Holland and local governments regardless of oaths to the States General (Den Tex 2:517–19), Ogle's situation became untenable. Under contradictory instructions to maintain order at Utrecht on the one hand and yet to cooperate with the Estates of Utrecht and the Town Council on the other, he was relieved of his post even though he had refused to bar Prince Maurits from the city when the stadholder and his troops arrived to disband the Utrecht militia and put an end to such attempts to undermine the regular army (Sanderson 466).

The charges against him were serious enough. Ogle, whose wife was Dutch, was fond of life in Utrecht, so much so that one of his daughters—Huygens, who also composed many songs, esteemed her for her lovely singing voice—was named Utricia, the other Trajectina. Over the years leaders of the Remonstrant faction had become his cherished friends. Not only did he make no secret of his admiration for Van Oldenbarnevelt, but he had revealed confidential documents to Ledenberg and lobbied for the Remonstrants with sympathizers in England like Lancelot Andrewes (Dalton 1:269; Vervou 128). He had even allowed himself to be led by friends of his wife into foolishly belittling directives from the States General and allowing disputed levies of the Arminian militia to share the watch with the regular garrison manning the walls and gates at Utrecht (Den Tex 2:518, 596–98, 607, 636–38; Ten Raa and de Bas 3:55–69; Markham 391–93; Dalton 1:246–60, 263–71). Fletcher and Massinger included this matter in their dramatization (act II, scene i) of the fall of Van Oldenbarnevelt (Sellin 86–87). Although the play gives full credit to Ogle's troops for delivering Utrecht into Maurits's hands, the portrayal of unseemly Arminian women meddling in Utrecht politics was surely designed to pillory Lady Ogle and her theologically progressive Dutch gossips as well as ridicule Sir John for his failure to rule his foreign mate as a proper Englishman should. When Count Ernst Casimir, field marshal of the Army of the States as well as vice-stadholder and captain general of Gelderland, was put on in his stead, Sir John resigned "voluntarily" and left for England.

Thus, all was not well among the English commanders in the Netherlands after the business at Utrecht. Ties between Ogle and Vere were strained because Vere had been appointed when Sir John was relieved, while Cecil was filled with bitterness and contempt because during his dispute with the Estates of Utrecht regarding rights to his company, the Utrecht authorities had not only pelted Cecil with slights and insults but had given the commission to Ogle's nephew Thomas (SvO 1620) in order to woo Sir John.[15] Once the command had been bestowed, neither the prince of Orange nor King James was willing to discharge young Ogle, and Cecil still felt an anger that was anything but reconciled. The recent troubles even infected Ogle's own regimental staff. Sir Charles Morgan, his lieutenant colonel (SvO 1603, 1610, 1620; SP 84/98), seems to have fallen out with his superior over the matter (Dalton 1:331–32), a serious business because Sir Charles also belonged to the gallery of heroes who had distinguished themselves for gallantry at Nieuwpoort, where, like Drury and Hollis, he had charge of a company. Indeed, while Drury was busy rescuing Ogle, Sir Charles joined Sir Horace Vere and Fairfax in rallying broken units and forming up the body that would deliver the famous charge (Markham 301). Donne must once have witnessed his prowess firsthand. During the attack on the walls of Cádiz, Morgan commanded a company of the assault force under Wingfield, and the capable execution of the operation was something that a martial young poet could scarcely have forgotten, certainly not if Donne's epigram "Fall of a Wall" on the death of a "too-bold Captaine" is at all suggestive of how the poet valued courage in battle (*Variorum* 8:7). Morgan also belonged to the Dutch Calvinist elite by virtue of a remarkable marriage. Knighted at Whitehall in 1603, Sir Charles had taken to wife no one less than Elizabeth van Marnix, the fourth daughter of a former student of Calvin at Geneva, Philips van Marnix, lord of St. Aldegonde, one of the most multifaceted figures animating the early Dutch Reformation. He was a revered defender of iconoclastic zeal, author of the powerful antipapist satire *Byencorf der Heilige*

Roomsche kercke (well known in English as "Beehive of the Romische Church"), translator of the Bible, composer of memorably poetic Psalms and perhaps the Dutch national anthem the *Wilhelmus*, a seasoned soldier who commanded the garrison at Antwerp before its fall, prudent counselor to William the Silent, and forceful publicist for the cause of Calvinism internationally. Sir Charles's union with Elizabeth undoubtedly came about through connections between Marnix and another valorous Welshman in Dutch service who, like Sir Charles's father, Edward, was a Pencard Morgan hailing from Glamorganshire. This was Colonel Sir Thomas Morgan, nicknamed "The Warrior", who captained the very first band of English volunteers to serve in the cause of William of Orange (cf. "Lijsten," Oldenbarnevelt 2943). He had been one of Marnix's associates and subordinates from the start of English intervention right up through the siege and surrender of Antwerp; a street name at Bergen op Zoom still commemorates his service as governor. By virtue of eloping—somewhat more successfully than Donne and his Anne—with Anna, daughter of Jan, Baron van Merode, Sir Thomas (though nearly fifty) managed, however unacceptably, to marry into Dutch nobility and have children. Accordingly, the social circles in which Sir Charles and his wife moved in The Netherlands included such luminaries as the great anglophilic cavalry leader Sir Marcelis Bax, the Huygenses, and noble in-laws of theirs such as the Boetzelaars (see Bachrach 57), Marnix's family orbit, obviously, and the likes of Justinus van Nassau, a natural son of William the Silent, whom Lady Anna took as her second husband after Sir Thomas's death in 1595 (SvO 1610, Ten Raa and de Bas 1:186). Needless to say, Elizabeth and Charles were unlikely to turn their backs on the Dutch revolt for theological "novelties" that charmed their colonel commanding. As for the regimental sergeant major, Captain Thomas Panton (SvO 1603, 1605, 1610, 1620; SP 84/98), we know only that he briefly commanded the English companies at Oostende and held a company repartitioned to Holland around 1610 (Ten Raa and de Bas 2:279n. 3).

While information about the theological colors of William Douglas, Ogle's regimental chaplain at this time, is too scanty to permit sure conclusions,[16] Ogle's could have been the only British regiment with clergy possibly sympathetic to the heterodox. Although Douglas had originally ministered to Cecil's regiment, his going over to Ogle as early as 1612 suggests a piety less rigorously Calvinist than Ames's. Certainly an Arminian taint clung to his name thereafter, though he always denied the allegation. Evidence leans in both directions, for the States General evidently had no objection to Douglas's remaining in service at Utrecht after Ogle's disgrace,[17] and in fact Donne may have met him and seen him officiate there on the Sunday when he was in Utrecht with Doncaster (Sellin 204n. 34). As far as Ogle personally was concerned, religious considerations were probably paramount. Inasmuch as his ambition upon retiring from the military was to enter the church (Dalton 2:127 and note), Sir John's interest in the Reverend Johannes Uytenbogaert, the spiritual leader of the Remonstrant party after the death of Arminius (Welsby 168), as well as his readiness to cooperate with Remonstrant authorities both suggest that he may have played a role in the emergence of Arminianism as a force in English ecclesiastical polity during the 1620s. In such matters, though, caution is the watchword. After all, the Arminian ministers so recently censured by the Dutch Reformed churches and the States General as well as by the English Crown were all pious sons ordained in the Presbyterian Reformed Church. As the Arminian theology of some current American Pentecostal churches serves to illustrate, such "liberalism" is not necessarily synonymous with Laudian tastes in church government or worship. Donne knew Ogle in other contexts as well. As the colonel was an enthusiastic member of the Virginia Company, he must have had some acquaintance with Donne from at least the time when the poet sought the company secretaryship. Sir John was present at virtually all the various courts of the company that Donne attended after he became a member (Kingsbury 2:224, 244, 300; 3:66, 300, 390), and by 1622 the new dean of St. Paul's Cathedral must have known something firsthand about Ogle's struggles in the Netherlands.

    The commander of the last English regiment was striking for his strong physical resemblance (Jonson 27) to a legendary soldier, statesman, and poet once in Dutch service. He was Sir Philip Sidney's nephew, Sir Robert Sidney, Viscount Lord Lisle (SvO 1620), eldest surviving son of Sir Robert Sidney, second earl of Leicester, Sir Philip's brother. A ripe twenty-four when he accompanied Donne and Doncaster to Germany in 1619, he had been created Knight of the Bath four years before, and inasmuch as Robert's father had succeeded his renowned uncle as governor of Vlissingen after Sir Philip died of the wounds he received outside Zutphen, young Robert obtained a company in the Dutch army at an early age. At twenty-one, he found himself a colonel in command of the new regiment that was formed from the combined garrisons of the cautionary towns when these reverted to the States General on June 10, 1616 (Ten Raa and de Bas 3:46, 178–79 and note, 180–81). Ambitious of military glory, he found the day-to-day administration of the regiment irksome, though, and the difficulties that the States General experienced in securing pay for his troops constantly hampered efforts to maintain the companies properly. By 1622 he became so disgruntled that he sold off his rights, and the command passed to his lieutenant colonel (Dalton 2:1–3, 15–16).

Although biographers make little of the fact, Lord Lisle knew Donne personally (cf. Novarr 154–55), if for no other reason than that he had accompanied Doncaster's train throughout the 1619 embassy to Germany (Bald, *Life* 344; Doncaster to Naunton, Munich, July 2/12, 1619, Gardiner 98:148, document 78). As he had taken to wife Dorothy Percy, the daughter of Henry Percy, ninth earl of Northumberland, Sidney and Doncaster were brothers-in-law. That is, Lord Hay himself had recently espoused (albeit to the ire of the peppery earl, who detested "Scotch-jigs") Dorothy's sister Lucy Percy. Although a violent quarrel was soon to ensue between Sidney and the normally genial Hay, the principals were still close at the time of the embassy. Northumberland, of course, was the friend whom Donne called upon to break the news of his marriage to Sir George More back in 1601–2, a favor the bridegroom-poet claimed at practically the very moment when the pro-Ralegh Northumberland (who once served with Leicester in the Low Countries) returned from beleaguered Oostende, where he had had the audacity not merely to offend General Sir Frances Vere about his conduct of operations there but even challenged him to a duel (Schrickx 162). Moreover, Donne's patroness Lucy, countess of Bedford, was, after all, Sidney's second cousin, while Earl Henry was the husband of Dorothy, sister of Robert Devereux, second earl of Essex. It was her nephew Robert, the third earl, whom Frances Howard married in 1606, only shamelessly to abandon him for Donne's prospective patron Somerset. Lord Robert III, thus, was a principal in the events that occasioned many witty addenda to the Overbury *Wife* of 1614, including one by Donne that especially interested Huygens in 1621 (Sellin 23). Despite the scandal, Essex's military career proceeded as if unhindered even by the later disclosure of Overbury's sensational murder at the hands of his former wife and her lover. When new regiments were formed in 1624 to strengthen the Dutch infantry, he received one of them (Ten Raa and de Bas 3:121 et passim). As everyone knows, he ultimately served Parliament as captain general of the puritan armies during the first years of the Great Rebellion.

Sidney's choice of lieutenant colonel suggests that at least some of the devotion and Reformed idealism that had animated his revered uncle and his father still lingered in Lord Lisle's heart. In Sir Edward Harwood (SvO 1605, 1610, 1620; *CSPD* 10:392, 600 [June 8] et passim; Ten Raa and de Bas 3:180–81) he had one of the most experienced and competent English officers in Dutch service. Born at Norfolk about 1586, Harwood entered the employment of the States General as a lad of thirteen or so, received a company after gallant service at Oostende, and rose to captain for brave actions at Rijnberg in 1606. Evidently, Sir Edward was well acquainted with the countess of Bedford, for he paid her visits on and off during the years of Donne's association with her. Harwood was a known puritan, and like the countess and her husband—Bedford had also served in the Dutch military—he supported nonconformist ministers of the gospel (Sellin 117–22). Hugh Peter, founder of the puritan congregation at Rotterdam and one of the first generation of New England preachers, lauded him as a "good man, a good soldier, a good Christian," and in appealing to Prince Maurits on behalf of William Ames in 1622, Sir Edward was instrumental in counteracting opposition to the learned doctor's appointment as professor of theology at Franeker (Sprunger, *Ames* 73). Indeed, in 1623 Lady Carleton reported to her husband, Sir Dudley, that Harwood would marry a certain Lady Smith "if she were Puritan enough" (Sprunger, *Ames* 73). As for the sergeant major, Captain Sir William Zouche (SP 84/98; SvO 1620), he had long held a company of infantry and received his staff post on June 12, 1617. Assuming that he was a kinsman of Captain Allan Zouche (SvO 1620), he may have been of the family of the very hispanophobic Edward, eleventh Baron Zouche of Harringworth. Besides numbering among his literary friends Ben Jonson, his cousin Richard Zouche, and William Browne, and having moreover Thomas Randolph's father as his steward, Baron Zouche was, like Ogle and Donne, involved with the Virginia Company during the 1620s. Sergeant Major William drowned crossing the Channel in the summer of 1620 (Ten Raa and de Bas 3:180–81; *CSPD* 165) and was replaced first by Edward Prichard (SvO 1620) and then by Henry Herbert (SvO 1620; Ten Raa and de Bas 3:180–81).

A month before Doncaster arrived in Holland, Carleton managed to secure subsidy for a chaplain to serve Sidney's regiment in conformity with practices obtaining among the other English units. This was one Walter Wytston (Whetston). Regarding Whetston's religion, Carleton and Sir Robert obviously thought the choice acceptable to the then outspokenly Contra-Remonstrant establishment, and the States General evidently had no hesitation in granting Sidney's chaplain the salary that under the Holland Remonstrants had eluded Cecil's for so long.[18] If this obscure pastor was kindred of Bernard Whetstone, which is likely, then he too had special ties with the countess of Bedford as well as Sidney. That is, not only had Bernard served with Sir Philip in the Low Countries, but his even better-known kinsman, George Whetstone, that Calvinian soldier-poet encomiast of Sir Philip, who provided Shakespeare with the plot of *Mea-*

sure for Measure, had amply celebrated the parents and grandparents of the earl of Bedford as favorers of Geneva.

Lord Lisle's behavior during the Great Rebellion reinforces these notions. Although older biographers are sometimes quick to deny any taint of "Puritanism," Sidney's role as what some have euphemistically called a "popular Protestant" shows that he was anything but a blind devotee of Canterbury regardless of its theology, nor was he ready to concede to the Crown such rights as arbitrary exercise of royal prerogative on the basis of divine right of kings. His intransigent support of the Calvinist Huguenots in France aroused Laud's dislike from the beginning. Rather than declare for the king, he resigned his post in 1643, and by refusing to endorse the letter from the peers petitioning the Scottish Privy Council not to invade England in support of the Presbyterians, he forfeited all chance of royal preferment. Being a "speculative rather than a practical man," as Clarendon—in a somewhat odd characterization of an erstwhile regimental colonel—put it (370), he retired to Penshurst, took the negative oath, and spent the rest of the interregnum uncommitted to either side, ultimately voting in the Long Parliament for the Restoration. In referring to the death of the queen of Bohemia on February 13, 1662, in a letter four days later to his brother-in-law, Northumberland's son, Algernon Percy, now tenth earl, he associated her instantly with Donne. It was a pity, reads one of Sidney's first reactions to the news, that the Queen of Hearts had not lived a "few Houres more" so as to die on her "Weddingday" and "that there is not as good a Poet to make her Epitaph, as Doctor *Donne*, who wrote her *Epithalamium* upon that Day unto St *Valentine*" (Collins 2:723). Though more than thirty years in his grave, Donne and his verse came immediately to Sidney's mind when he thought back on the Palatine wedding of 1613, a match that then had seemed to guarantee the security of the Reformed cause on the Continent, one that had been celebrated in strains somewhat other than those he later heard for the queen and court of Charles I.

Of English cavalry, there were at least three troops of cuirassiers, all of them prestigious commands. Cecil held Troop 12, Vere retained Troop 27 (Ten Raa and de Bas 3:152–54; cf. Bachrach 57n. 1), and the third, Troop 16, belonged to one "Robert Carry" (SvO 1610, 1620; SP 84/98). This must have been Sir Robert Carey, Queen Elizabeth's only blood cousin and guardian of the prince of Wales, whom Charles created first earl of Monmouth the day after his coronation in 1626 (see Carey 5–7, 12–15; Markham 112n. 1; Ten Raa and de Bas 3:154 and n. 2). Youngest son of Henry, first Lord Hunsdon, Sir Robert was born about 1560.

Although he is chiefly remembered for attending the duke of Alençon in his attempt to succeed the martyred William the Silent as leader of the Dutch rebels and marry Queen Elizabeth, riding posthaste to inform James of the queen's death in 1603, and accompanying Buckingham and Prince Charles to Madrid two decades later, his career was in fact studded with military adventures abroad. Hence Carey, who was Charles's chamberlain and gentleman of the bedchamber, interspersed playing the courtier in London during the winter with stints on battlefields across the Channel in the spring and summer, which explains hitherto unknown sources of much-needed income after the death of Queen Anne brought impecunity upon his household. Sir Robert had charge of a company of foot in Dutch service before acquiring his cavalry command, but by 1620 the Carey holding an infantry command was Ferdinand Carey, who became sergeant major of the Sidney regiment under Harwood in 1624 (SvO 1620; Ten Raa and de Bas 3:181). Moreover, one of Sir Robert's brothers, Edmund ("Lijsten," 1587, Oldenbarnevelt 2943), had held a company under Leicester, and Sir Robert joined him in earlier actions at Oostende and at Bergen op Zoom in the summer of 1587. An experienced soldier, this Carey went with Essex to assist Henry IV in Normandy, where he not only led a company but succeeded Edward Cromwell ("Lijsten," 1587, Oldenbarnevelt 2943)—another name in Dutch service that glitters along with that of Fairfax—as commander of a regiment at the siege of Gournay. Edmund's company probably devolved to Sir Robert sometime after 1600, and on September 15, 1616, Sir Robert acquired the troop of horse at issue. His was an influential voice at the Jacobean court, and people in The Hague like Carleton counted on him to incline the king toward courses that they advocated in Holland (Carey 72–76; Bald, *Life* 73, 248–49; Donne, *Complete Poetry* 237n, 247n, 404; Carleton to Carey, The Hague, November 28, 1619, Carleton, *Lettres* 216–19; Ten Raa and de Bas 2:366–67).

The Cockington Hunsdons did not have a monopoly on Careys warring abroad, however. Dutch army records of this period draw a clear distinction between the Hunsdon "Carrey" family and their blood kin, the "Careuw" family of Haccombe. Sir Walter Ralegh's kinsman and close friend Sir George Carew, created Baron Carew of Clopton in 1603 and earl of Totnes in 1625, had taken prominent parts in the expeditions against Cádiz and the Azores, and subsequently he commanded a large strength infantry company repartitioned to Holland (SvO 1605; Ten Raa and de Bas 2:367). Another kinsman who had long been in French and Dutch service was Sir Henry "Careuw" from the Falkland line, later lord deputy of Ireland. He had fought and been captured at Oostende, and as late as 1620, the year Sir Henry was created First Viscount Falkland, he still retained his company (SvO 1603, 1605, 1610, 1620; SP 84/98). Obviously, Donne had ties to both families. Whether the "Elegie on the L. C." was meant to honor Sir Robert's father, Henry, Lord Hunsdon, who died just as Donne returned from Cádiz, or Sir Lionel Cranfield, Hay's predecessor as Master of the Great Wardrobe, there is a connection of some sort with the Cockington-Hunsdon Careys, for Sir Lionel's daughter married into the family, and of course Donne addressed his elegant verse epistle "Here where by All All Saints invoked are"—composed while the poet was with Drury in France—to Lettice Carey, née Rich, who was married to the former treasurer at war and lord deputy in Ireland, Sir George Carey of the Cockington branch. As for the Haccombe Carews of Devon, Donne served under Sir George Carew and his kinsman Ralegh at Cádiz and on the Islands voyage. Little could he then have anticipated that he would become an in-law to both when Sir Nicholas Carey-Throckmorton took Ann More's sister to wife. It is doubtless no accident that when Donne died, a scion of the Falkland branch, Sir Lucius "Carie," was the only nobleman of high title who not only stooped to compose "An Elegie on Dr. Donne" but deigned to allow its publication—and that in the same year in which he succeeded his father as Viscount Falkland.

Besides regimental staff and cavalry officers, there were upward of fifty other English captains in charge of companies of foot at any given time. Because the Dutch "States of War," on the basis of which the Council of State (*Raad van State*) cast the annual military budget, are organized according to the provinces to which the companies were repartitioned and the size of the units, one cannot be certain as to which regiment the company of a given captain may belong. Nevertheless, some of these officers should be mentioned because of their prominence, their connections with Donne or his friends, or their places in literary history.

A good example of such an officer, one virtually unknown but well worth some speculation, was Captain Michiel Everarts. Dutch as the name may sound, he is listed among the English commanding infantry in 1610 and later, and one cannot help but wonder whether there were ties with Donne's friend Everard Guilpin, author of *Skialetheia* (1598). After all, the maiden name of Everard's mother was Thomasin Everard; both families were from the Norfolk area, where there was a large Dutch community; and possibly the English Captain Everarts and Guilpin were related. However this may be, it is an incontrovertible fact that the grand uncle of Donne's fellow satirist, George Guilpin (1514[?]–1602), was an English merchant at Amsterdam. Having studied civil law at Mechelen in the southern provinces and later matriculating at Leiden, he was one of Queen Elizabeth's most trusted agents in her negotiations with the Low Countries. He knew the country and the language very well, and during Leicester's governor-generalship he sat on the Dutch Council of State, first as one of its three secretaries (Christiaan Huygens, the father of Donne's translator Constantijn, was another) and then as a full member. What is more, he was responsible for an excellent translation (dedicated to Sir Philip Sidney) of Marnix's classic satire *De Byencorf* that we mentioned above: namely, the *Beehive of the Romishe Church*, a kind of Dutch forerunner (but antipapist, of course) of Martin Marprelate popular enough to see five editions in English between 1579 and 1636. Able, trustworthy, and influential, Guilpin enjoyed much goodwill in the States General and was particularly interested in military matters. Together, his nephew Everard Guilpin, Donne, and Marston constitute a veritable triumvirate of late Elizabethan poetic satire, just as Marnix's *Beehive* and Martin Marprelate mark high points of prose ridicule. We should also note that one Emmanuel Gilpin (SvO 1610) was a member of Prince Maurits's elite, handpicked guard, famous in both story and art for its soldierly prowess and spectacular drills as a school of war that Donne at least once witnessed in person (Sellin 154–55nn. 97, 98). Was it through friends like Everard and such families as the Guilpins that Donne was first induced to enlist in the Anglo-Dutch expeditions against the king of Spain in 1596 and 1597? One will probably never know, but such ready avenues of contact definitely existed.

Four officers of lesser rank of whom one should take special note may be reasonably associated with the Vere regiment. Besides Sir Edward Conway the elder, quondam secretary of state whom we discussed above, there were also Conway's sons, Sir Edward the younger (SvO 1620) and Sir Thomas (SvO 1620), who both held companies under oath to the States General. Sir Edward, who succeeded his father as second viscount, was a friend of Donne's too, and the manuscripts of Donne's poems in Additional MS 23229, British Library, derive from his papers (Sellin and Veenendaal 236–43). In 1619, two Lovelaces, William the father (SvO 1620) and Sir William the grandfather (SvO 1603, 1605, 1610, 1620; SP 84/98; Kinney 86) of the poet, held infantry companies under Holland. Although students of literature are vaguely aware that Richard Lovelace was born and raised in the Netherlands, they seldom realize how far back his roots in the Dutch military went. Indeed, Sir William the younger was killed at the siege of Groll, leaving a widow and a large family that included Richard the "Cavalier" poet. Two gentlemen worth noting are likely to have served under Ogle. One was Richard Knightely (SvO 1620), possibly a grandson or nephew of Sir Richard Knightely, patron of puritans and abetter of Martin Marprelate. A second was Sir Warham St. Leger (SvO 1620), son of Sir Warham the elder, Sir Walter Ralegh's comrade in the Irish wars (Kinney 85; Edwards 1:38). Sir Warham the younger accompanied Ralegh as his lieutenant general, or second-in-command, on that fateful last voyage of 1617–18 to Guyana (Harlow passim). Although he survived the voyage, the sickness scourging the fleet put him on what was like to be his deathbed, and the charge of leading the expedition up the Orinoco and recovering Sir Walter's elusive gold mine fell instead to Ralegh's nephew, George Ralegh (Edwards 1:567, 615). In this context, one should also take note of a lesser-known but experienced Scottish officer, John Pigott (SvO 1603, 1605, 1610; SP 84/98; Edwards 1:610), who likewise served on Ralegh's second voyage to Guyana as sergeant major in charge of land operations (Harlow passim). When he too died of the terrible illness that devastated the fleet, the remains were buried at sea, but Ralegh kept his heart for interment at Cayenne (Ralegh 190). Major Pigott's charge devolved to Ralegh's son Walter, whose confused assault at San Thomé not only cost young "Wat" his life but ruined the little chance of success his father still had left.

Other distinguished names associated with the Sidney regiment include two Herberts, one being Sir Henry (Pembroke-Conington line), who succeeded Zouche as sergeant major (SvO 1620), the other Sir Gerard, still another distant relative of Sir Edward and the poet George (SvO 1610, 1620; SP 84/98). Donne commemorated his valor to the death with a tellingly compact yet powerfully vivid piece of virtually professional battlefield reportage in his letter to Goodyer of September 24, 1622, saying, "Now we are sure that *Heidelberge* is taken, and entred with extreme cruelties. Almost all the defendors [sic] forsook their stations; only Sir *Ger.* Herbert maintained his nobly, to the repulsing of the enemy three times, but having ease in the other parts, 800 new fresh men were put upon his quarter, and after he had broke 4 Pikes and done very well, he was shot dead in the place" (Donne, *Letters* 116). So too Sir Henry Killigrew (SvO 1620). He was probably the younger son of Sir Henry the elder, who had served on the Dutch Council of State under Leicester and was—not surprisingly in that milieu—a strong Calvinist as well as an important catalyst in Anglo-Dutch relations thereafter. Now among the lords and knights accompanying Doncaster to Germany in 1619 there were two members of the Killigrew family, Sir Robert and Peter (Bald, *Life* 344). It was also at the house of Sir Robert and Lady Killigrew four years later, one recalls, that young Constantijn Huygens had a remarkable encounter with Donne that he described effusively in his verse memoirs much later (Bachrach 114; Bald, *Life* 432, 441–42).[19]

Of officers whom I cannot link with specific regiments, several require notice. The first is one of Donne's most important early friends, Sir Thomas Egerton, son of Sir Thomas Egerton, lord chancellor and keeper of the great seal, who retained Donne in his employment until the young poet eloped with Ann More. Whether young Egerton enlisted like Donne for Cádiz I do not know, but he certainly went along on the Anglo-Dutch voyage against the Azores in 1597, being one of the only four or so knights that Essex created there (Kinney 85). Instead of soldiering in the Low Countries, he went off to Ireland and died of his wounds on August 23, 1599, at the age of twenty-five. I perceive little mystery as to why Donne should have occupied a position of "considerable honour" at his funeral in Chester cathedral (Flynn, *Donne* 176–77). Donne's being a friend of the deceased and an erstwhile fellow campaigner of about the same age, it seems wonderfully appropriate that the Egertons chose to have him bear their son's sword in the funeral procession, preceded only by the king of arms and the bishop of Chester. We have already mentioned Sir Robert Radcliffe, earl of Sussex. Son of Sir John Radcliffe, to whom the States General entrusted cavalry squadron 26 in 1606 (Ten Raa and de Bas 2:125)—Robert Sidney the elder had commanded it until 1599, and it had devolved, as we have seen, to Sir Robert Carey in 1615—Sussex was at Cádiz too, where he reportedly commanded a regiment of foot, and was the first to receive knighthood at the hands of Lord Admiral Howard (Kinney 83). A patron of Elizabethan poets such as Robert Greene, Lodge, Emmanuel Ford, Henry Lok, and Chapman, Sir Robert associated around 1607 with a convivial group in London that included Donne and some of his friends such as Christopher Brooke and Henry Goodyer (Bald, *Life* 189ff.).

Another such officer is Sir Thomas Gates (SvO 1620), whom Donne may have known in connection with the Virginia Company. Also knighted at Cádiz (Kinney 84), Gates went on to serve in the Low Countries up until the time of the Twelve Years' Truce, when he left for the new colony where he acted as governor. As every student of Shakespeare knows, he suffered shipwreck in a terrible storm in the Bermudas (Smith 1:635–39), the story of which has gone down in history as a possible source of *The Tempest*. Gates returned to England in 1614 and sometime thereafter went to the Netherlands to claim arrears of pay. He resumed service with the States General and thus held a company in 1619 when Doncaster and Donne visited The Hague. An officer who should be noteworthy to anyone interested in North America is Captain Joseph Duxberry. In his *True*

Travels (1630), John Smith claimed that "peace being concluded in France [1596], he went with Captain Ioseph Duxbury into the Low-countries, under whose Colours [he] served three or foure yeeres" (Smith 2:822). However, the Dutch Council of State did not commission "Joseph Duxberi" a "captain" until March 30, 1599 ("Commissieboek" folio 205 verso). Evidently he fought and died at Nieuwpoort (June 2, 1600).[20] However, Smith had left Duxberry to take other service before that battle, and he could never have been under the captain's "colours" in "the Low-countries" for as long as "three or four yeeres." At best, Duxberry was his company commander for but a matter of months, during which period Smith could only have seen serious combat, if any, between May 15 and June 13, 1599, when Count Maurits repelled Mendoza's attempt to seize Bommel. Because "I know not how Desert more great can rise," one of several poems commending Smith's *General Historie of Virginia* (1624), is signed "Io: Done" (Smith 1:284–85), scholarship is divided as to whether the verse is Donne's (Roberts, nos. 309, 312, 318, 322, 328–30, 333, 537; cf. Emerson 33, 64). In view of the poet's involvement in the Virginia Company about this time (Bald, *Life* 434–38), the record of Smith's service with the States General, or rather lack thereof, perhaps helps explain "Done's" cryptic disclaimer, "though I but little know / To what t'hast seene" (lines 21 and 22), if the poem actually is by the dean of St. Paul's.

Since we have touched on an American context, let us not forget Captain Francis Willoughby either (SvO 1620), who was probably kin through common ancestors to Peregrine Bertie, Lord Willoughby de Eresby, and his son Robert Bertie, Baron Willoughby. Peregrine's name stems from the fact that his parents were abroad as Marian exiles when he was born at Wesel, and accordingly he was staunchly Protestant. Not only had he long commanded English forces in the Low Countries, but he had sat with Sir Henry Killigrew on the Dutch Council of State and succeeded Leicester as general of the English auxiliaries in the Netherlands (Ten Raa and de Bas 1:93–94 et passim). Peregrine's son, Sir Robert, took part in the expeditions against Cádiz and the Azores, supposedly receiving his spurs at Cádiz (not listed in Kinney 83–85), and went on to become colonel of still another new English regiment in 1624 (Ten Raa and de Bas 3:121). As for Sir Francis in 1620, specifically, he had just replaced Sir Thomas Dale (SvO 1604, 1605, 1610, 1620; SP 84/98), also of Virginia colony fame. Having had a long career as a soldier and naval officer in the Low Countries, Captain Dale brought Pocahontas and her spouse Thomas Rolfe over to England from Jamestown in 1616 (Smith 525). He died of fever in 1619 while besieging . . . Jakarta!

The literary-minded should also be aware of another officer in Dutch service, Sir John Spencer (SvO 1620), son of Sir Richard Spencer, who, together with Sir Ralph Winwood, had conducted negotiations for King James in arranging the Twelve Years' Truce. This brings us back to the Careys, for the eldest of Sir John's aunts was Elizabeth, Lady Carey, wife of Sir George Carey, heir of the first Lord Hunsdon. Edmund Spenser, who dedicated *Muiopotmos* to her, claimed her as a kinswoman. Besides Spenser, she patronized figures like Nashe and Dowland, and her circle in society, particularly her granddaughter, brings one close to Shakespeare's sonnets and *A Midsummer Night's Dream*. The second was Anne, who took Robert Sackville, second earl of Dorset, as her (third) husband. It was to his heir, the third earl, that until fairly recently scholarship assumed Donne to have dedicated some of his *Holy Sonnets*. After the loss of the third sister's husband, the earl of Derby, whom Spenser lamented in *Colin Clout's Come Home Again* (1595), Alice, the youngest of the three, remarried in 1600, taking as her spouse Donne's early patron, Lord Keeper Egerton, afterward Lord Chancellor Ellesmere. With her, of course, one begins to touch on the young Milton and the world of *Arcades* and *Comus*.

A second Sackville, Sir John Sackville, was likewise under oath to the States General (SvO 1620). Descended of John Sackville and Margaret Boleyn through Sir Christopher Sackville, he was the second cousin of Robert, second earl of Dorset, whom we have mentioned above. Not only did he thus spring from a family that in *A Mirror for Magistrates* and *Gorborduc* had virtually set Elizabethan tragedy going, but he undoubtedly owed his position to the favor that Thomas Sackville, the first earl of Dorset, had won in the Low Countries as successor to Leicester and later as a special emissary to the Netherlands. Sir John was close to his "nephews," the third and fourth earls, whose friendship and favor (as Donne's living at St. Dunstan's and the dedication of the *Holy Sonnets* witness) the poet enjoyed over many years. As we have seen, Edward, later fourth earl, was at Bergen op Zoom during the siege in 1621, and he too was to have received a command in the expeditionary regiment that Vere recruited in 1619 to defend Heidelberg and the Palatinate. In 1624 the States General extended Sir John special leave to stay in England to care for the Dorset estates until Edward could return and receive the title, and one of his last acts was to defend arms belonging to the earl at Synnock in Kent against a raid of Parliament men in 1642.

One should also remember that Sir John Throckmorton (SvO 1620) was lieutenant governor under Sidney at Vlissingen. Unlike the companies belonging to Vere and the elder Conway, which were detached from the garrison and assigned to Vere when the cautionary towns were given back to the Dutch (1616), Sir John's was incorporated into the new Sidney regiment, and when Doncaster arrived in The Hague, he was still in command (Ten Raa and de Bas 3:46, 178, 274). Descended of one of the eight or so sons of George Throckmorton, he was a cousin not only of Job Throckmorton, who is generally regarded as the author behind Martin Marprelate, but also of Elizabeth Throckmorton, Lady Ralegh, and of Sir Nicholas Carey-Throckmorton, who, as we pointed out above, was married to the sister of Donne's wife, Ann More. It is quite in keeping with the character of the Sidney regiment that this Throckmorton too was a confirmed puritan sympathizer, as well as an enemy of Van Oldenbarnevelt and the Remonstrant faction in Holland.

There was, finally, one other well-born "Englishman" whose career provides a fitting close to this sketch. The gentleman who held a full general's rank at the time of Doncaster's visit to Germany and the United Provinces was neither the renowned Sir Horace Vere nor Edward Cecil, who are the officers usually glorified in English military annals before the Civil War between Crown and Parliament. Rather, it was the highly worthy Sir Adolf van Meetkerken (SvO 1603, 1605, 1610, 1620; SP 84/98), or à Meetkirk, as Anthony à Wood styles the family. Despite his neglect by British historians, van Meetkerken bore an illustrious name that "patriots" in Donne's time could hardly contemplate with indifference. Sir Adolf's father, Adolf the elder, had been another of the outstanding Flemish humanists flourishing in Belgium before the civil unrest began there, and the seventeenth century still remembered him for a particularly fine translation of Theocritus into Latin. Adolf the elder had also been one of the foremost statesmen leading the early stages of the insurrection against Spain. President of the Council of Flanders at Ghent, he had fled before the duke of Parma's reconquest of the south during the 1570s and 1580s. Like most zealous Calvinist exiles from the south, he vigorously espoused the cause of English intervention in the Netherlands. Indeed, during Leicester's tenure as governor-general, he so compromised himself as a principal spokesman for the earl in the Council of State that, after the earl's withdrawal in disgrace back to England, van Meetkerken left Holland to escape prosecution under Van Oldenbarnevelt. He finished his days in London, where he was buried in St. Paul's Cathedral in 1591 (Bachrach 151–54).

Of some six sons, all but the youngest sought to recoup their fortunes by arms. The eldest, Anthony, fought under Leicester, receiving his death wound in the same operations around Zutphen that cost Sir Philip Sidney his life. Nicholaas, also a precocious classicist, was not only a soldier but a promising statesman, and despite his youth he commanded the troops on board when Drake sailed from Plymouth in 1589 in support of the Portuguese pretender whom the Spanish had ousted during the mid-1580s. He fell at Deventer in 1591, aged scarcely thirty (Ten Raa and de Bas 2: 18,301). Essex knighted his sibling, Boudewijn, at Cádiz (Kinney 84) a few days before this "brave personnage, et bien experimenté" died of wounds while storming the gates (*Description* 139).[21] Another brother, Guido, also served in the assault forces at Cádiz, as he would again in similar raids during 1599 (Ten Raa and de Bas 2:215), and so did our Adolf the younger. Adolf's actions as commander of a company of foot so distinguished him that Essex knighted him too (not in Kinney 83–84; cf. *Description* 141). Accordingly he shared the stage at Nieuwpoort and Oostende, where Vere entrusted him with defending one of the key routes by which the enemy would advance. Whereas a man like Drury vented his frustration with Vere for not leaving a single "corner of his army for any man to lay hold upon" (Bald, *Drurys* 47), sound officers like van Meetkerken rose quickly, attaining the lieutenant colonelcy in Sir Horace's regiment in 1605 (Ringoir 145). In 1614–15, the Dutch Council of State appointed him sergeant major general of the entire army (Ten Raa and de Bas 3:180, 266, 268), letting him retain his company, of course. As Hexam puts it, the post was one "of high degree, whose Commaund, is full of action, and therefore ought to be an able, a wise, a grave, and a valiant person" (2:7). He became, in effect, the chief operational officer of all the Dutch ground forces, with enormous responsibility for transmitting to the various units the orders of the captain general, Prince Maurits, and seeing to their implementation. Although historians have wondered why Sir Horace never received a permanent generalship like the one his brother Francis had held in earlier times, the fact is that the States General promoted his lieutenant colonel over him to a rank on a par with that which Vere's elder brother, the illustrious Sir Francis, had earlier enjoyed. In short, van Meetkerken occupied one of the most elevated posts ever to be entrusted to a British officer in Dutch service after Leicester.

Remarkably enough, the paths of Donne's family and the van Meetkerkens intersected in quite a different sphere back in England during the 1620s. The youngest son of the family, gifted little Edward, who was born at London in 1590, was destined for the church instead of battle. Having proceeded B.A. at Oxford in 1610, he became a tutor at Christ Church about the time that Donne took orders, received his M.A. at Cambridge in 1617, and then returned to Oxford to pursue his D.D. Enjoying a fine reputation as a precise and conscientious teacher, he was soon guiding some remarkable young men, including Meric Causaubon, who entered Christ Church in 1619, and by 1620 Edward succeeded Richard Kilbye as Regius Professor of Hebrew (Wood, *Athenae* 2:287, 3:934; *Fasti* 1:423). Whether he had any contact with Donne's younger son George, who is surmised to have entered Broadgates Hall in 1615, is doubtful, but there seems to me no question about the elder son, John Donne, Jr. The future editor of his father's works, John was elected to Christ Church in 1622, and it seems unlikely that a divinity student prominent enough to contribute to commemorative volumes at the university would have had no contact with such a distinguished young academic at his own college (Bald, *Life* 546–55).

Such then were some of the leading British officers who conducted the Low Countries' wars under oath to the States General for two generations during Donne's lifetime. Together, these men constituted a remarkable network of institutions, relationships, common interests, and experiences that linked them together willy-nilly, and their very looks in both life and portraiture undoubtedly exercised an eloquent, living rhetoric on the warlike Protestant mind of the age. To a vivid poetic imagination that like Donne's could picture a battered veteran

> weatherbeaten ... come back; my hand
> Perchance with rude Oares torne, or Suns beams tand,
> My face and breast of hayre cloth, and my head
> With Cares rash sodain horines orspred,
> My body a sack of bones, broken within
> And powders blew staines scatterd on my skin
> ("His Picture," Shawcross, lines 4–10),

surely the impulse was overwhelming to identify with men like these and if nothing else to see their scars, their glories, their status, and their—yes—privileges and wealth as things that would have accrued to the poet himself had sullen providence not willed otherwise. Certainly, the chivalric ideals of Protestant knight-errantry that animated many of these men to defy death, if necessary for a mere "eggshell" that "hath in it no profit but the name" if honor were at stake, never left Donne, even in later life. For what profession did he pronounce himself "content" for his beloved soldierly George to follow except precisely the art military that he himself had attempted unsuccessfully to pursue in 1596 and 1597 (Bald, *Life* 510)? George's was a career that he strove very hard to advance through his philo-Reformed Lord Hay, and his efforts were crowned with remarkable success during the 1620s. The entire context—from, that is, Donne's earliest lines on serving in the Low Countries' wars to Buckingham's ill-fated attempts to relieve the Huguenots at La Rochelle, in which George supposedly participated as nothing less than a regimental sergeant major!—argues a typical veteran's sense of kinship with and concern for the body of comrades with whom he had upon a time campaigned, and with whom he once banqueted as Doncaster's chaplain-secretary at the Inn of the Golden Fleece in Haarlem. In such Hals-like, "cavalier" settings—whether in London or the Low Countries, whether in palaces, parlors, ships, or camps—it is difficult to think that the cause for which these brave men fought and died in Flanders, the United Provinces, Germany, America, and even the East Indies was not, as Donne himself once explicitly claimed, as fervently his "to promove" with "the same prayers as I present for myne owne soule to the ears of Allmighty God" as theirs (Sellin 11), the queen of Bohemia as much "the eclipse and glory of her kind" to his heart as to Henderson's or Wotton's ("On His Mistress, The Queen of Bohemia" line 20).[22] Indeed, I dare wonder: Had Donne's enlistments for Cádiz and the Islands' voyage been crowned with a knighthood like those that had boosted several of his fellows-in-arms like van Meetkerken, Horace Vere, Proude, and many others up into their first commands, might he not have been as likely as any number of them to have ended his days as a valorous captain or colonel in Dutch service, rather than as a failed soldier–civil servant reluctantly turned poetical clergy late in life?

Notes

Special thanks are owing to the Algemeen Rijksarchief and to the Instituut voor Nederlandse Geschiedenis, The Hague, and especially to two of its members, Dr. A. J. Veenendaal, Jr., for coaching me through Dutch archives over many years, and Dr. J. Roelevink for helping refine my dating of SP 84/98. I am also grateful to my colleagues David Kunzle, Department of Art History, and Reginald Foakes, Department of English, UCLA, and to Professors Keith Sprunger, Department of History, Bethel College, and Jean R. Brink, Huntington Library, for critiquing the essay. None of these friends are in any way responsible for the inevitable inaccuracies, invalid propositions, or other shortcomings inhabiting the argument. Since it requires too much space to annotate every detail obtained from standard biographical dictionaries such as A. J. van der Aa, *Biographisch woordenboek der Nederlanden*, 12 vols. in 6 (Haarlem: J. J. van Brederode, 1876–78); *Dictonary of National Biography*, ed. Leslie Stephen and Sidney Lee, 66 vols. (London: Oxford

UP, 1885–1900); *Nationaal biografisch woordenboek*, gen. ed. J. Duverger (Brussels: Paleis der Academiën, 1964–); or *Nieuw Nederlandsch biografisch woordenboek*, ed. P. C. Molhuysen and P. J. Blok, 10 vols. (Leiden: A. W. Sijthoff, 1911–37), readers should consult these works as needed.

1. After destroying the Spanish Armada, England and the United Provinces decided to go after the Spanish in their own harbors. Between 1589 and 1604, when James I made peace with the king of Spain and the archduke, the English and Dutch undertook a number of joint raids—1589 against Lisbon under Drake; 1596, Cádiz under Essex, Howard, Ralegh, and the Dutch admiral Jonkheer Johan van Wassenaar, Lord (of the manor of) Warmond; 1597, the Azores under Essex, Francis Vere, and Warmond; 1599, Ireland; 1601, another Spanish armada heading for the Channel; and finally 1602, enemy warships based in various Spanish and French harbors, once again with Warmond (Ten Raa and de Bas 2:299–306). The dates of Donne's letters to Sir George More at this time—ca. March 1601/2 ("but though I be not headlongly destroyed, I languish and rust dangerously. From seeking preferments abroad, my love and conscience restrains me" [Gosse 1:113]) and March 1, 1601/2 ("It is now late for me . . . to begin that course which some years past I purposed to travel, though I could now do it, not much disadvantageously. But I have some bridle upon me now more than then by my marriage of this gentlewoman, in providing for whom I can and will show myself very honest, though not so fortunate" [Gosse 1:114–15])—show that were he still single, as he had been in 1596 and 1597, he would have gone off once again on the Warmond foray of 1602, as he thought that he still had good chance to win advancement in the same way that had indeed worked well for him until he lost his position by eloping with Ann More. The phrase "seeking preferments abroad" thus refers to neither "some" vague "branch of English foreign service" nor undefined "*catholic* preferment in *exile*" (Flynn, *Donne* 173–74) but to the last Anglo-Dutch enterprise of its kind before the accession of King James and his pacifist attitudes put an end to them.

2. Note that Ten Raa and de Bas (1:204) also indicate that Wishart received the cavalry unit of a late "kapitein Hay" in 1589; SvO 1605 lists a Captain William Hey (infantry, repartitioned to Holland).

3. For a detailed family tree, see MacLean, "Balfour."

4. Salaries of Reformed chaplains like Hunter conformed with pay in the Dutch churches. See Van Deursen 72–73.

5. "Drury" is canceled and "Waldegrave" substituted.

6. Hewes is not yet carried in the SvO 1620.

7. W. W. van Driel to Sellin, The Hague, May 31, 1978, indicates that later SvOs identify Cecil's "Hewes" as "Adriaen Hewes."

8. According to *Calendar of State Papers, Domestic Series* (*CSPD*) 10:220, document 71, Colonel Cecil did address the House of Commons on February 5, stressing the danger to England from the ambition of the king of Spain, his aspiration to

universal monarchy, his aggressive militarism abroad, and the connivance of domestic papists, and he urged the necessity of providing against the threat by raising forces for foreign service and strengthening defenses at home (*CSPD* 10:220, document 1; Wright 149–55; Breslow 74–94).

 9. Donne, *Variorum* 8:8. Donne's verse assumes a militarily aware audience familiar with Sir John's story. In the course of his brief rule in the Netherlands, Leicester appointed Wingfield governor of Geertruidenberg. A strategic citadel guarding access to the Maas (Meuse) as it empties into the Rhine estuary (Biesbos), the town was garrisoned by a large number of English and some Dutch troops (Ten Raa and de Bas 2:272). When pay did not arrive on time, the English mutinied, Wingfield sided with the malcontents (Ten Raa 2:8), and the city was "sold" to Parma in 1589 (*Description* 139). From then on the Dutch viewed the Geertruidenberg English as "merchants" and "berg"-sellers," the traitors they could catch they summarily hanged, and they proscribed Wingfield, putting him under ban as well (*Description* 139). However, Queen Elizabeth forgave Sir John, and, to the indignation of Dutch officers serving in the joint Dutch-Anglo expedition against Cádiz, the disgraced Wingfield was allowed to participate (Ten Raa and de Bas 2:8). So it happened that as English troops stormed the city gates, Sir John—entering the fight without proper armor, rather like Sidney at Zutphen—behaved valiantly, running through one of the Spanish officers with his pike before receiving a wound in his uncovered thigh (Bald, *Life* 84). Once inside the walls and unable to walk, he mounted a captured horse. Although offering a most conspicuous target, he refused the exhortations of his commander in chief, Sir Francis Vere, to don his armor or withdraw (*Description* 139) and rode out into the midst of the street fighting with his sword in hand until an inevitable musket shot found his unprotected head. Anything but an act of vainglorious rash bravado, Sir John's gesture was in fact a desperate effort to atone for his "unnoble swerving" of 1589, and his burial in the cathedral of Cádiz with full military pomp by teary eyed companions in arms (Bald, *Life* 84) proved the success of his endeavor. Donne's lines thus commemorate not simply the heroic fall of a too brave captain but the self-redemption of a revolted, disgraced traitor, whose ultimate love of lost honor over base life turned his grave at Cadiz into an "unsurpassable" monument of English chivalry. For initiates in the lore of the Low Country wars, at whom I think Donne primarily aimed his poem, the last three lines end with a marvelously epigrammatic snap of laconic understatement, Stoic glorification laden with pathos nobly implied, not expressed.

 10. SvO 1620, Ten Raa and de Bas 2:46, 178, 180, 274, list a John "Throgmorton" as a company commander; one conjectures a possible scion of one of the eight uncles of Arthur and Nicholas.

 11. Markham's statement (434) that Hollis was sergeant major general must be in error. This post would have put him at third in command of the whole army, behind only Prince Maurits and Count Willem Lodewijk van Nassau, stadholder

of Friesland. Ten Raa and de Bas (3:266) indicate that Jonkheer Pieter, Baron Sedlinitzky, held this position from 1592 to 1610. Hollis did not rise to sergeant major of the regiment until 1615, when Sir Edward Vere obtained the lieutenant colonelcy (Ten Raa and de Bas 3:180).

12. Van Driel to Sellin, The Hague, May 31, 1978, informs me that the Staten van Oorlog for 1618–21 (1619 is missing) indicate that "Johan Hassel" does not appear among the ministers assigned to English regiments until 1621.

13. He briefly took command of the English companies at Oostende, where he was killed on September 17, 1604 (Ten Raa and de Bas 2:278).

14. Heir of Arthur, Lord Grey de Wilton, lord deputy in Ireland, whom Spenser served there, according to Professor Brink, as personal secretary. Regarding Thomas's service as a cavalry officer up to 1603, see Ten Raa and de Bas 2:56, 106, 131, 160–61; regarding Donne's aspiration in 1608 for an Irish secretaryship, see Bald, *Life* 160.

15. He replaced one captain De[n]- or De[w]hirst (SP 84/98; SvO 1620; Ten Raa and de Bas 3:56n. 4).

16. Cecil to Carleton, London, March 26/April 5, 1618 (Dalton 1:264), states specifically that Ogle had no chaplain before "I turned over to him that which he hath not." Van Driel to Sellin, The Hague, May 31, 1978, establishes that the one English preacher officially in service of the States General besides Vere's chaplain was William Douglas, and that Douglas held such a post in 1612 but apparently not in 1610 (records for 1611 are missing).

17. SvO 1620 (folio 27) cancels the name "Willem" (Douglas) and replaces it with "Jhon." A William or Willem Douglas had commanded a company of infantry repartitioned to Holland (SvO 1610; SP 84/98). Evidently thinking of the company commander rather than the regimental *predicant*, the scribe's first impulse was to put down "Willem." He then canceled the name and substituted "Jhon."

18. Van Driel to Sellin, The Hague, May 31, 1978, indicates that "Walter Wytston" or "Wolter Wytston" received subsidy as chaplain to Sidney in 1621 and 1626. Dalton (2:312n) calls him Cecil's chaplain erroneously. Regarding the subsidy, see SG, Resolutiën, October 29, November 2 and 6, 1619, rubric "Colonnel Sidneij."

19. As Lady Killigrew was Anne Woodhouse, it is worthwhile noting that two Woodhouses, "Franchois Woldhouse" (SvO 1605, 1610; SP 84/98) and "Henry Wodhuysen" (SvO 1610), commanded companies in Dutch service between James's accession and the siege of Juliers (see Schrickz 139–40). According to Ten Raa and de Bas (2:277), Franchois headed a regiment of ten companies in the spring of 1604.

20. SvO for 1601 (1600 seems to be missing) fails to list him, although it does carry the other three officers whom the "Commissieboek" records as having taken

the oath at the same time and under identical circumstances (Hendrick Sutton [SvO 1603, 1605], Charles Schot [?], and Henry Holcraft [SvO 1610, SP 84/98]).

21. *Description* states (139) that "Le Capitaine Nicholas de Metkercke fils d'Adolf y fut blessé, & mourut quelques jours aprés [*sic*] de sa blessure," thus evidently mistaking Boudewijn with his late brother, who died in 1591. Markham (101, 174, 181, 325) also confuses Adolf and Nicholaas. "Le Capitaine Metkercke qui estoit blessé," mentioned later among the Dutch officers Essex knighted (*Description* 141), undoubtedly refers to Boudewijn, but it is just possible that Adolf the younger is meant.

22. Immediately upon her exile to Holland, Donne sent her in 1622 a copy of his sermon on King James's *Directions for Preachers* to comfort her in affliction; at the beginning of 1624, he forwarded copies to The Hague of *Devotions Upon Emergent Occasions* as soon as it was published for "her Majesty, who is ever joined by me with my own soul in all" my "prayers" (Donne's "Madam," n.p., February 1, 1623/24, Gosse 2:205); and in 1625 she received his first sermon preached before King Charles, her brother, as a kind of "anniversary importunity" pushed by "zeal to appear" in her "Majestie's presence" (Donne to the queen of Bohemia, n.p. [1626], Gosse, 2:233).

Works Cited

Manuscript

Abbreviations

ARA	Algemeen Rijksarchief, The Hague
I	Eerste Afdeling
III	Derde Afdeling
Inv	Inventaris
PRO	Public Record Office, London
SG	Staten Generaal
SP	State Papers
SvO	Staten van Oorlog

ARA I. Archief SG, Inv no. 12.589.11: "A certen List of her Ma[ties] Forces Horse and Foote ymploied in y[e] Lowe Countries. Signed by the Lo: Willoughbie her Ma[ties] Lieutenant Generall the 27th of Februar 1588 with the Alterations Since the said tyme: and Where in Garrison," 1589.

———. Archief SG, SvO, Inv no. 1525: "Commisseboek van den Raad van State der Verenigde Nederlanden beginnende met den 10 Mei 1591 tot 6 Decemb 1599."
———. Archief SG, SvO, Inv no. 8040: 1595.
———. Archief SG, Resolutiën, Inv no. 3178: 1619.
———. Archief Generaliteits Rekenkamer, Inv no. 1232: SvO, 1603, 1604, 1605.
———. Archief Raad van State, Inv no. 1226: SvO, 1579, 1601, 1609, 1610.
———. Archief Raad van State, Inv no. 1236: SvO, [1607–]1610.
———. Archief Raad van State, Inv no. 1244: SvO, 1620.
ARA III. Archief van Johan van Oldenbarnevelt 1586–1619, Inv no. 2943: "Lijsten van Engelse compagnies infanterie en regimenten cavalerie die in 1587 en in [1588] in dienst van de Republiek zijn, 1587 en [1588]; afschriften."
———. Archief van Johan van Oldenbarnevelt 1586–1619, Inv no. 2946: "Lijsten van bevelhebbers van compagnies infanterie en regimenten cavalerie in dienst van de Republiek, [1580], [1586], en [1591]; concepten."
PRO. SP 84/93: Andrew Hewes to Dudley Carleton, Breda, December 10/20, 1619.
———. SP 84/98, folios 176r–181v: "A List of the horse and foote-Companies, wch are now in service of ye States Gñll; vizt, those of the English, and Scottish nation," [1610].

Printed

Bachrach, A. G. H. "Constantijn Huygens's Acquaintance with Donne: A Note on Evidence and Conjecture." *Litterae textuales/Neerlandica manuscripta: Essays Presented to G. I. Lieftinck*. Ed. J. P. Gomberts and N. J. M. de Haan. Amsterdam: n.p., 1976. 112–17.
———. *Sir Constantine Huygens and Britain 1596–1687: A Pattern of Cultural Exchange*. Leiden and Oxford U. Presses, 1962.
Bald, R. C. *Donne and the Drurys*. Cambridge: Cambridge, 1959.
———. *John Donne: A Life*. New York: Oxford UP, 1970.
Breslow, M. A. *A Mirror of England: English Puritan Views of Foreign Nations, 1618–1640*. Cambridge: Harvard UP, 1970.
Calendar of State Papers, Domestic Series. Ed. M. A. E. Green. Vol. 10: 1619–1623. London: Longman, Brown, Green, Longmans, and Roberts, 1858.
Carey, Robert. *The Memoirs of Robert Carey*. Ed. F. H. Mares. Oxford: Clarendon, 1972.
Carleton, Dudley. *Lettres, memoires et negociations du chevalier Carleton, Ambassadeur ordinaire de Jacques I. Roi d'Angleterre, etc. aupres des Etats-Generaux des Provinces Unies. Dans le tems de son ambassade en Hollande depuis le commence-*

ment de 1616. jusqu'a la fin de 1620. Translator anonymous. 3 vols. The Hague and Leiden: Chez Pierre Gosse, Jr., and Elie Luzac fils, 1759.

Cherbury, Edward, Lord Herbert of. *The Autobiography of Edward, Lord Herbert of Cherbury*. Ed. Sidney Lee. London: J. C. Nimmo, 1886.

Clarendon, Edward Hyde, earl of. *The History of the Rebellion and Civil Wars in England*. Oxford: Oxford UP, 1843.

Collins, Arthur, ed. *Letters and Memorialls of State*. 2 vols. London: T. Osborn, 1746.

Dalton, Charles. *Life and Times of General Sir Edward Cecil, Viscount Wimbledon, Colonel of an English Regiment in the Dutch Service, 1605–31, and One of His Majesty's Most Honorable Privy Council*. 2 vols. London: S. Low, Marston, Searle, and Rivington, 1885.

Den Tex, Jan. *Oldenbarnevelt*. 5 vols. Haarlem and Groningen: H. D. Tjeenk Willink & Zoon, 1960–72.

Description & representation de toutes les victoires tant par eau gue par terre, lesquelles Dieu a octroiees Aux Nobles, Hauts & Puissants Seigneurs, Messeign[eu]rs Les Estats Des Provinces Unies du Païs-bas, Souz la conduite & gouvernement de son Excellence, le Prince Maurice de Nassau. Leiden: Par Iean Ieanszoon Orlers, & Henry de Haestens, 1612.

Deursen, Arie Th. van. *Bavianen en slijkgeuzen: Kerk en kerkvolk ten tijde van Maurits en Oldenbarnevelt*. Assen: Van Gorcum, 1974.

Dillingham, William, ed. *The Commentaries of Sr. Francis Vere, Being Diverse Pieces of Service, Wherein He Had Command, Written by Himself in Way of Commentary*. Cambridge: printed by John Field, 1657.

Donne, John. *The Complete Poetry of John Donne*. Ed. John Shawcross. Garden City, NY: Doubleday, 1967.

———. *Letters to Severall Persons of Honour*. 1651. Reprinted with an introduction by M. Thomas Hester. Delmar, NY: Scholars' Facsimiles and Reprints, 1977.

———. *Paradoxes and Problems*. Ed. Helen Peters. Oxford: Clarendon, 1980.

———. *The Variorum Edition of the Poetry of John Donne*. General ed. Gary A. Stringer. Vols. 2 and 8. Bloomington: Indiana UP, 1995, 2000.

Edwards, Edward. *The Life of Sir Walter Ralegh Together with His Letters; now First Collected*. 2 vols. London: Macmillan and Company, 1868.

Emerson, Everett H. *Captain John Smith*. Boston: Twayne, 1971.

Ferguson, J., ed. *Papers Illustrating the History of the Scots Brigade in Service of the United Netherlands, 1572–1782*. 3 vols. Edinburgh: At the University Press, 1899–1901.

Fletcher, John. *The Tragedy of Sir John Van Olden Barnavelt*. Intro. Robert Fruin. Reprint of Bullen edition. The Hague: Martinus Nyhoff, 1884.

Flynn, Dennis. *John Donne and the Ancient Catholic Nobility*. Bloomington: Indiana UP, 1995.

———. "A Problematic Text." *John Donne Journal* 3 (1984): 99–103.

Gardiner, S. R. *Letters and Other Documents Illustrating the Relations between England and Germany at the Commencement of the Thirty Years War.* Second Series: From the Election of the Emperor Ferdinand II to the Close of the Conferences at Mühlhausen. Vols. 90 and 98. Westminster: Camden Society, 1865, 1868.

Gosse, Edmund. *The Life and Letters of John Donne.* 2 vols. New York: Dodd, Mead, and Co., 1899.

Harlow, Vincent T. *Ralegh's Last Voyage.* London: Argonaut P, 1932.

Hexam, Henry. *The Principles of the Art Military.* 3 vols. London: Robert Young et al., 1637–40.

Holles, Gervase. *Memorials of the Hollis Family, 1493–1656.* Ed. A. C. Wood et al. Camden Society Third Series, vol. 55. London: Offices of the Society, 1937.

Hooft, Pieter Corneliszoon. *Alle de gedrukte werken 1611–1738.* Vol. 3, *Gedichten 1636.* Ed. W. Hellinga and P. Tuynman. Amsterdam: Universitaire Pers, 1972.

Jonson, Ben. *Conversations with Drummond of Hawthornden.* Ed. R. F. Patterson. London: Blackie and Son, 1924.

Kingsbury, Susan M., ed. *The Records of the Virginia Company of London: The Court Book, from the Manuscript in the Library of Congress.* 4 vols. Washington, DC: Government Printing Office, 1906–35.

Kinney, Arthur F. *Titled Elizabethans: A Directory of Elizabethan State and Church Officers and Knights, with Peers of England, Scotland, and Ireland, 1558–1603.* Hamden, CN: Archon, 1973.

MacLean, D. J. *De huwelijksintekeningen van Schotse militairen in Nederland, 1574–1665.* Zutphen: De Walburg Pers, 1976.

———. "Sir William Balfour." *De Nederlandsche Leeuw* 94 (1997): 146–80.

Markham, Clements R. "The Fighting Veres." *Lives of Sir Francis Vere, General of the Queen's Forces in the Low Countries, Governor of The Brill and of Portsmouth and of Sir Horace Vere, General of the English Forces in the Low Countries, Governor of the Brill, Master-General of Ordinance, and Baron Vere of Tilbury.* Boston: Houghton Mifflin and Company, 1888.

Novarr, David. *The Disinterred Muse.* Ithaca: Cornell UP, 1980.

Osselton, N. E. *The Dumb Linguists: A Study of the Earliest English and Dutch Dictionaries.* Sir Thomas Brown Institute. Leiden: Leiden and Oxford UP, 1973.

Papazian, Mary Arshagouni. "John Donne and the Thirty Years' War." *John Donne Journal* 19 (2000): 235–66.

Ralegh, Walter. "Journal of His Second Voyage to Guiana." In *The Discovery of the Large, Rich, and Beautiful Empire of Guiana.* Ed. Robert H. Schomburgh. London: printed for the Hakluyt Society, 1989. 177–208.

Raylor, Timothy. *The Essex House Masque of 1621: Viscount Doncaster and the Jacobean Masque.* Pittsburgh: Duquesne UP, 2000.

Ringoir, H. *Hoofdofficieren der infanterie van 1568 tot 1813.* The Hague: Sectie Militaire Geschiedenis van de Landmachtstaf, 1898.

Roberts, John R. *John Donne: An Annotated Bibliography of Modern Criticism, 1912–1967.* Columbia: U of Missouri P, 1973.

Rogers, Francis. *A Sermon Preached at the Funerall of William Proud.* London: By John Norton, 1633.

Sanderson, W. *A Compleat History of the Lives and Reigns of Mary Queen of Scotland, and of her Son and Succesor James.* London: For Humphrey Moseley, 1656.

Schrickx, Wilelm. *Foreign Envoys and Travelling Players in the Age of Shakespeare and Jonson.* Rijksunversiteit te Gent, Faculty of Letters, Vol. 173; Wetteren: Drukkerij Universa, 1986.

Scot, Thomas. *A Speech Made in the Lower House of Parliament, Anno. 1621. By Sir Edward Cicill, Colonell.* N.p., 1621.

———. *A Tongue-Combat, lately happening between Two English Souldiers in the Tilt-boat of Gravesend, the one going to serve the King of Spaine, the other to serve the States Generall of the United Provinces. Wherein the Cause, Course, and Continuance of Those Warres is debated and declared.* Ed. H. Hexam. London, 1623.

———. *The Workes of the Most Famous and Reverend Divine Mr. Thomas Scot, Batcheler in Divinitie: Sometimes Preacher in Norwich.* 1624 edition reprinted as No. 621; Amsterdam: Da Capo P, 1973.

Sellin, Paul R. *"So Doth, So Is Religion": John Donne and Diplomatic Contexts in the Reformed Netherlands, 1619–1620.* Columbia: U of Missouri P, 1988.

Sellin, Paul R., and A. J. Veenendaal, Jr. "A 'Pub Crawl' through Old The Hague: Shady Light on Life and Art among English Friends of John Donne in the Netherlands, 1627–1635." *John Donne Journal* 2 (1987): 235–60.

Smith, John. *Works, 1608–1631.* Ed. Edward Arber. 2 vols. Westminster: Archibald Constable and Co., 1895.

Sprunger, Keith. *Dutch Puritanism: A History of English and Scottish Churches of the Netherlands in the Sixteenth and Seventeenth Centuries.* Leiden: Brill, 1982.

———. *The Learned Doctor William Ames: Dutch Backgrounds of English and American Puritanism.* Urbana: U of Illinois P, 1972.

Ten Raa, F. J. G., and F. de Bas. *Het staatsche leger, 1568–1795.* 8 vols. to date. Breda: De Koninklijke Militaire Academie, 1911–.

Vervou, Frederik van. *Enige aenteekeningen van 't gepasseerde in de vergadering van de Staten-Generaal, anno 1616, 1617, 1618, 1619, 1620.* Leeuwarden: H. Kuipers, 1874.

Welsby, Paul. *Lancelot Andrewes, 1555–1626.* London: S.P.C.K., 1958.

Wood, Anthony à. *Athenae oxonienses: An Exact History of All the Writers and Bishops Who have had their Education in the University of Oxford. To which are added the Fasti, or Annals of the Said University.* Ed. Philip Bliss. London: For F. C. Rivington *et al.*, 1813–15.

Wright, Louis B. "Propaganda against James I's 'Appeasement' of Spain." *Huntington Library Quarterly* 6 (1942–43): 149–55.

7

Unmeete Contraryes

The Reformed Subject and the Triangulation of Religious Desire in Donne's *Anniversaries* and *Holy Sonnets*

CATHERINE GIMELLI MARTIN

> I will finde out another death, *mortem raptus*, a death of rapture, and of extasie, that death which S. *Paul* died more than once.
>
> Donne, *Sermons* 2:210

At least for later observers, the Stuart masque reveals more ideological fractures than it conceals. For in attempting to identify the heavenly covenant with that of the earthly king, it shows its audience's deep need for "transcendent" reassurance on questions ranging from the divine right of kings to the divine presence in the sacramental host. The masque's reliance on theatrical magnificence is equally symptomatic of both the period's deep insecurities and the competitive impulses that drive them, which according to Lawrence Stone were often marked by a "personal recklessness of behaviour whose cause was more psychological than social" (582). In this essay, I argue that the aesthetic instability of Donne's *Holy Sonnets* and *Anniversaries* reflects the reckless competition for psychic and social assurance prevalent throughout a "culture of anxiety," which in his case was greatly aggravated by the competition between rival theological models of salvation. As Eamon Duffy shows in *The Stripping of the Altars*, Henry VIII set the stage for this theological competition through his varying commitment to ecclesiastical reform. Later, it was greatly intensified as Protestant Edward gave way to Catholic Mary and Protestant Elizabeth to the Counter-Reformation sympathies of the Stuart court. But in his note "Of Ceremonies" in the 1549 Book of Common Prayer, Cranmer was already well aware of the growing crisis "in this our time, [where] the minds of men are so diverse, that some think it a great matter of conscience to depart from a piece of the least of their ceremonies, they be so addicted to their old customs; and again on the other wise, some be so new-fangled, they would innovate all things."

Aside from the obvious social, political, and religious turmoil that these conflicts produced, they often stimulated the grave internal doubts about certitude and rectitude early registered both in Donne's *Satyres* and Francis Bacon's *Essays*. Bacon's essay "Of Atheism" goes straight to the heart of the problem: although God's natural and divine revelation is self-evident, skepticism results whenever there are too many religious divisions; "for any one main division addeth zeal to both sides; but many divisions introduce atheism," as does "scandal of priests" in moral and spiritual matters (*Essays* 372). Donne's *Satyre 3* takes up the same theme: doctrinal conflict among Protestants so severely pits them against one another that some are driven back to the dubious "embrace" of "mother" Rome, a reversion most Protestants considered equivalent to atheism. Not without a certain inevitable irony, then, does Richard Hooker remark that "I doubt not but God was mercyfull to save thousandes of our fathers lyvinge in popish supersticions in as muche as they synned ignorantly" (*Learned Discourse* 1:26). In Donne's *Holy Sonnets*, the same irony is tinged with envy at the "faithfull soules" now "alike glorifi'd" in heaven while their sons have been left behind, struggling and perhaps failing to find "signes" of salvation "that be / Apparent not in us immediately" (*HS 8*).[1]

As Robert Jackson observes, the anxieties inherent in Donne's envious competition not only with the present and future elect but also with those of the past drove him to rest his most "constant" assurance on his own inconstancy (*HS 19*, "Oh to vex me" 2–3), on the ironic "confidence that doubt is itself the vehicle of salvation" (152). Yet in making insecurity its own ostentatiously insufficient answer to his constant "crisis" of faith, Donne also supplementally stabilizes his spiritual turmoil through a dramatic triangulation of religious desire. This strategy is most clearly evident in *Holy Sonnet 11* ("Spit in my face you Jewes"), where the speaker archetypally imagines himself torn between three competing perspectives: that of Christ on the Cross, that of the crucifying Jews, and that of his own Jacob-like persona, the "supplanter" of both (12). But again, his purpose in creating these baroquely conflicting perspectives is not resolution but irresolution, a tactic that keeps him at the perpetually unstable apex of the sacrificial crisis they dramatize. Donne's *Anniversaries* and *Sermons* employ essentially the same strategies, so that as in *Death's Duell*, we find a dialectic rooted first "in self-dependency," but "as the motions of the self are one by one stilled, we grow gradually less self-sufficient, until we are finally left, hanging, 'in dependency.' And yet this dependency is blessed, for although by means of it we are rendered powerless (*dis*abled), our powers are increased in the person of Him on whom we depend." As these remarks by Stanley Fish go on to show, Donne's mirroring of Christ's *"blessed dependancy"* leads to an exchange that paradoxically promotes rather than demotes the "dependant" to the center or apex of the duel with death. For Fish, the point of this exchange is Christian kenosis: like his sermon itself, Donne becomes "a vessel filled by and wholly dependent on the Lord," not a self-dramatizing baroque artist, but his own self-consuming artifact (*Self-Consuming Artifacts* 69–70).

This assessment has its merits, but it ultimately overlooks the alternate pole of Donne's dialectic: his construction of the vital and highly *present* persona whom Joshua Scodel rightly characterizes as neither an empty or "decentered subject nor the fully autonomous person imagined by the Enlightenment but rather a distinctive early modern *tertium quid*" (60). As Scodel further shows, this *tertium quid* is the direct by-product of Donne's attempt to forge a viable *via media* between the two unmeet "contraryes" or religious poles which "vext" his entire generation (*HS 19*, 1). Torn between the more familiar and comfortable emphasis on external, communal, and sacramental works of salvation taught by the Roman Catholic Church and the reformers' emphasis upon invisible signs of mysterious grace, first-generation Protestants in particular attempted to forge an increasingly elusive theological "middle path." For as these converts came increasingly to acknowledge only symbols deeply immersed in "the depths which separate visual being from meaning" and only moral acts officially dissociated from religious reassurance or reward, they became increasingly subject to melancholy (Benjamin 165, 138). This melancholy can also be traced to a breakdown in the older allegorical schema, which taught that after answering the question of what to believe *(quid credas)*, one was easily directed to the simpler question of how to act *(quid agas)*. Yet as the new questions of belief increasingly took over the angst-ridden center of a spiritual life officially devoid of salvific action, the release attainable through penitential, sacramental, and charitable works was too often insistently sought and tragically not found.

A major symptom of this "tragic" need for supplemental assurance in newly Protestant lands appears in the simultaneous "mourning," demystification, and re-creation of sacramental symbols characteristic not only of

Donne's metaphysical style but of the baroque-period style it signally reflects and influences (Benjamin; Martin 2–5, 13, 40, 45–46). Moreover, because both sides of the sacramental and ceremonial controversy experienced the common "Protestant struggle to find equivalents of the forfeited Catholic means for assuring personal immortality" (Watson 199), both sides typically sought substitutes for the miracle of transubstantiation, the glimpse of immortality formerly available in the "sacering" of the host (Duffy). Yet as the *First Anniversary* indicates, Donne associates sacramental loss not just with the elimination of holy acts, images, sanctuaries, and relics, but with the loss of the ritual power of language itself:

> What Artist now dares boast that he can bring
> Heaven hither, or constellate any thing,
> So as the influence of those starres may bee
> Imprisoned in an Herbe, or Charme, or Tree,
> And doe by touch, all which those starres could do?
> The art is lost, and correspondence too.
> For heaven gives little, and earth takes lesse,
> And man least knows their trade and purposes. (*FA* 391–98)

The *First Anniversary* is also quintessentially baroque in supplementing the lost sacramental potency of art with a displaced aesthetic substitute, in this case with a quasi-priestly resurrection of the "soule" whose "progress" the *Second Anniversary* witnesses.[2] Hence the poet performs a displaced and/or inverted act of extreme unction as he summons Elizabeth Drury's spirit to "embalme, and spice" the world with a new kind of "everlastingness" (*SA* 2, 39). As critics from Ben Jonson to William Empson have noted, this verbal "mass" tends to make the newly deceased Drury into a new immaculate conception and Christ figure all in one (Jonson 1:133).[3] Yet Donne's priestly "resurrection" of the putatively dying universe from which Drury has departed is even more paradoxical than it first appears to be. Despite this "putrified" world's complete desacralization, the poet semi-parodically, semi-seriously reconstellates the *Divine Comedy*'s depiction of the soul's voyage through a divine cosmos. Whereas the *First Anniversary* had announced that like "the Planets," "the Firmament / . . . Is crumbled out againe to his atomis" (*FA* 210, 212), the *Second Anniversary* describes the stars as "but so many beades / Strunge on one string" of a hypothetical rosary (*SA* 207–8). These paradoxes provide a key to another central element in Donne's triangulation of religious desire: admitting that his own metaphors are contaminated by the blasphemous "recklessness" of a spiritually and sacramentally fallen human world, he must rely on a "donor's" (Drury's) "transubstantiatory" grace, for without it, not only his own effort but the entire universe "would putrify with vice" (*SA* 40). This constant triangulation between iconoclasm and neosacramentalism also explains Donne's connection with the two apparently opposing "radical movements in Jacobean culture"—"Puritan theology and Metaphysical poetry," movements subterraneanly linked by the prominence commonly given to the "radically . . . empowered word," which "overthrow[s] convention by exposing as corrupt illusions the familiar figurations and decorations of the physical universe" (Watson 221).

Donne thus "triangulates" between Calvinist iconoclasm and Counter-Reformation neosacramentalism, so that, as Robert V. Young argues, "Calvinist notions of grace pervade the Holy Sonnets . . . not as a principal theological inspiration, but as a lingering fear of faithlessness haunting the background of poems that in most of their features resemble the Catholic devotional poetry of the Continent" (Young 38). But while Young is obviously right that devices like the "Spanish baroque crucifix" in *Holy Sonnet 13* ("What if this present") hardly sustain the idea that Donne practices an orthodox "Protestant poetics" (Young 34–35), neither the *Anniversaries*, nor the *Holy Sonnets*, nor anything in Donne's life records suggests that his conversion was actually wavering or insincere.[4] Unlike his friend Goodyer, the author of *Pseudo-Martyr* was unmoved by Toby Mathew's arguments for the superiority of a religion he had long since rejected as idolatrous, not merely for personal gain and social acceptance but also on the basis of real conviction. Like his enduring relationship with that paragon of Protestant virtue, Magdalen Herbert (a far more formative influence on him than his own Catholic mother), Donne's iconoclastic impulses testify to his fundamental Protestantism (Watson 239–52).

Thus as strange as *Holy Sonnet 13*'s baroque "picture of Christ crucified" with "Teares," "Blood," and wounds undoubtedly is, it performs an *internal* and "awe-ful" meditation upon the final moments of Christ's life (3, 5–6), without becoming the graven image that Young would make it. This image is thus fully appropriate to the poem's stated theme, "What if this present were the worlds last night?," a point in time when believers must confront either a dispenser of wrath or a vehicle of grace. Since we know that the Last Judgment will somehow unite the two covenants of wrath and grace, the theologically "correct" answer is that grace will predominate as his final "Word." With this reunion in mind, the speaker is then licensed to consider the sight of the dying Son "beauteous" despite the obvious horror and pity of the scene (11, 14). By alluding to his own romantic "idolatrie," he also employs a pun appropriate to his iconoclastic purposes. For in identifying the sacred with the profane sense of the word, he admits that while he had once "idolatrously" assigned outward signs of beauty to compassion and "fouleness only" to "rigour" or "unlovely" chastity, he now realizes that this rigorously horrible or "foul" figure conceals the supremely *inward* beauty of compassion, which, even at the height of his physical agony, could have "pray'd forgivenesse for his foes fierce spight" (8–12).

Yet once again, Donne never fully resolves his Reformed/Roman dichotomies but triangulates between them here as throughout the *Holy Sonnets*. Pitting Catholic crucifixes against Protestant penitentialism, or the wrath of the Old Testament against the grace of the New, the speaker at once indulges his sacramental longings and rejects them for the "true" transubstantiation of compassionate grace. But by so baroquely mixing Catholic with Protestant tropes, as Wilbur Sanders points out, the poet so recklessly flirts with "blatant theological sophistry" that he not only fails to resolve his "spiritual malady . . . [but] seems almost to [want] . . . to make us aware of this fact" (128). Why should he continually indulge in this reckless self-exposure rather than forging a more stable *via media*? One answer (Fish's) is that Donne simply suffered from an incurable form of spiritual bulimia—an insatiable need to project his insecurities and the resulting *mea culpas* on to the universe at large ("Masculine Persuasive Force"). But while there is considerable merit to this argument, it overlooks the vital fact that Donne's conflicts were maintained by the very theology through which he meant to resolve them.

Officially, Donne believed that the Incarnation testified to the possibility of salvation for all, not just for a Calvinist elect: "As all mankinde was in *Adam*, all mankinde was in *Christ:* and as the *seale of the Serpent* is in all, by *originall sinne*, so the *seale* of God, *Jesus Christ*, is on us *all*, by his assuming our *nature*" (*Sermons* 6:159). Officially, he also believed that religion should not be "fettered nor imprisoned. . . . in a *Rome*, or *Wittenburg*, or a *Geneva*; [for] they are all virtuall beams of one Sun" (*Letters* 102). And yet, if Calvin was right about the means if not the ends of grace—that is, if he was wrong about limited atonement for a narrow elect but not about the fact that the elect receive only imputed, not engrafted, grace—then the effects of original sin are no longer wholly removed by baptism and the Eucharist, but only by a wholly internal faith in the "invisible" fact that the Atonement applies to us.[5] Psychologically, the situation is even more demanding than this theological formulation makes it seem, since the correct path to salvation now paradoxically demands both blind faith and exquisite exegetical choice between the conflicting claims of Rome, Wittenberg, and Geneva, whose adherents regularly regarded one another as damned. As the *Holy Sonnets* especially show, believers may then find themselves hopelessly torn between confessing their defective faith and blaming the deity for permitting the conflicting claims that asked them as no previous generation to make such temporally and eternally life-threatening choices.

The insecurities caused by these conflicting claims as well as by the reformers' sole reliance on invisible grace seem to have generally contributed to the extreme Protestant emphasis upon the believer's personal conviction of sin as a certain "sign" of salvation (Haller 150–72), a theme that forms a constant refrain in the *Holy Sonnets*. This uncomfortable conviction also produces their unstable alternation between a wistfully questioning and a wishfully imperative attitude toward grace. From one perspective, grace is a puzzle without a clear key: "Yet grace, if thou repent, thou canst not lacke; / But who shall give thee that grace to beginne?" ("Oh my black Soule!" 9–10). Yet at other moments, the speaker simply demands the key: "Teach mee how to repent: for that's as good / As if thou 'hadst seal'd my pardon, with thy blood" ("At the round earths imagin'd corners," 13–14). But no assured solution to these conflicting stances can be achieved by a speaker whose besetting sin, as he tells us elsewhere, is not pride or even doubt but fear:

> I have a sinne of feare, that when I have spunne
> My last thred, I shall perish on the shore;
> But sweare by thy selfe, that at my death thy sonne
> Shall shine as he shines now, and heretofore;
> And having done that, thou haste done,
> I fear no more. ("A Hymne to God the Father," 13–18)

Donne's "Hymne to God the Father" thus clearly shows how the classic paradoxes of the *Holy Sonnets* originate in his paradoxical God. Steadying his fear by openly expressing his doubt, the speaker dares his God to do the impossible—to take his own name in vain, or to "swear by thy selfe" that what has already been decreed "done" from eternity will be done *for* Donne, that God has exalted his forever shining Son/sun specifically for him. Taking his own name in vain as well, the poet recklessly confesses his need to exchange both the father of justice and wrath and the son of mercy for own his name or "word": "Thou hast done." As in the *Anniversaries*, this punning substitution is the verbal equivalent of making a "donor" perform his own resurrection. For by playing not just upon his own name but also upon the future perfect-tense meaning of "Thou hast done," he can also imagine the work of salvation in the past tense.[6] What is then left is only the future perfect sense of the phrase—"you will have done [or Donne]," a pronouncement that effectively cancels both the soul's fearful present and its equally fearful "flight" at the moment of death. For according to the speaker, if then as now, you (God) have done that (swear and save according to your "Word" or Son), you will have me, and your work will be done. Through this "sophistry," Donne makes his sin of fear vanish into eternal consolation, leaving no present time in which to struggle (like Bunyan's fearful Christian) toward the Celestial City with his faith and his Christian virtues as his guide.[7] Since the Resurrection was usually considered a type of transubstantiation, little salvific *or* transubstantiational work is thereby left for God, who is neither confessor, nor intermediary, nor even savior after Donne's pun on his own name "blasphemously" appropriates all of this work to himself. Yet through this reckless flirtation with blasphemy, that "work" is also undone, to borrow another of the poet's famous puns on his name.

What, then, can possibly be gained by this peculiar strategy? One answer has already been outlined: that Donne is creating a baroquely triangulated *imitatio Christi* to fulfill his Pauline need personally and perpetually to reenact Christ's suffering and death as the most assured way to heaven. His *Sermons*, too, explicitly recommend this means of acquiring a semi-visible "sign" of salvation: "There is nothing so near Immortality, as to die daily; for not to feele death, is Immortality; and onely hee shall never feele death, that is exercised in the continual Meditation thereof; Continuall Mortification is Immortality" (*Sermons* 8:168).[8] But this "mortification" or conviction of sin also fulfills the forbidden longing of his "insatiate soule" for a saving drink from "Gods safe-sealing Bowle," the communion cup which in the past literally washed away sin (*ex opere operato*—by the work worked) rather than (as now) by merely symbolizing the covenant of grace (DiPasquale 12–13). Deprived of this drink, the Protestant convert believes that "th'onely Health [is] to be Hydropique so" (*SA* 45–48): to be constantly thirsty for salvation and continually summoning its semivisible sign, "Continuall Mortification." But unlike the thirst that had afflicted his youth with "an Hydroptique immoderate desire of human learning and languages" (*Letters* 51), this religious desire can *never* be even partially filled because once it is, it would signal the subject's "security" and therefore his *lack* of salvation.[9] Modeling himself on the Creator-God, the good

Calvinist continues to work at his salvation because "God hath not accomplished his worke upon us, in one Act, through an Election; but he works in our vocation, and he works in our Justification, and in our sanctification he works still" (*Sermons* 7:368). For although God knows the elect from all eternity, the faithful experience their election in time as a process in which their constant "thirst" testifies to their necessarily but also mercifully incomplete "steps to the temple."

Nevertheless, Donne exhibits a far more excessive investment in this incompletion than Protestant contemporaries like George Herbert, in part because Herbert seems to have had far less difficulty simply accepting the sacraments as Protestant signs lacking any transcendentally operative *(ex opere operato)* "work." Thus while we regularly find Herbert confessing fear, doubt, weakness, and near despair, and also regularly turning to priestly symbols as supplements for sacramental "presence," we never find the ostentatious excess of the *Holy Sonnets:* the sense that like the self-exorcist he becomes in his bouts with melancholy, "Donne could deal more easily with the invigorating threat of damnation than with the melancholy possibility that there are no authentic supernatural manifestations in his personal universe, only the facts of mortal decay" (Watson 166).[10] Moreover, we never find Herbert's excessive longing for supernatural, nonsymbolic *seals* of grace causing him to reintroduce "real" ritual objects or reenact ritual scenes no longer considered efficacious for Protestants as Donne does. But as we have seen, Donne's fixation on rejoining the theological poles of the period in ways that will reproduce the original Reformation crisis is inherent in his "mixed" theology, which is ultimately incompatible both with Calvin's irresistible, predestined grace and with the Jesuits' emphasis upon justification by works. By replacing both doctrines with the belief that justification by faith is *fulfilled in* works (a doctrine also held by radical Roman Catholics), as Dominic Baker-Smith suggests, Donne creates as many philosophical difficulties as he solves. For in believing that the function of the true Church essentially consists in interpreting the Bible and administering the sacraments, while the final "contact with God . . . remains the responsibility of the individual," Donne can regard the sacrament as neither a full presence nor as a full absence of grace. By refusing to fully internalize faith and thereby neglect the Church, he creates "an extremely delicate relationship between Church and believer designed to allow a maximum of personal responsibility within a framework of Catholic tradition" (Baker-Smith 412); but he also makes himself subject to the notorious anxieties outlined above.

Ultimately, then, Donne's simultaneous longing for and rejection of the Real Presence of grace creates an internal trauma very like what psychoanalysts refer to as a psychological double bind. The religious aspect of this trauma remains largely unexplored since while most literary critics officially recognize the continuities between Donne's psychic anxieties and his spiritual problems in theory, in practice they usually treat them in virtual isolation. As a result, psychoanalytic approaches rarely intersect with theological approaches to the *Holy Sonnets*. But this "schism" is partly the result of unjustly neglecting the work of a critic equally well known for his work on the double bind and on religious triangulation—René Girard. As Girard signally shows, large-scale cultural transitions are especially fertile ground for double binds that exhibit all the characteristic elements of Donne's religious and aesthetic psychology. Their chief symptom is the inability to directly pursue a desired object—either a person or a path to salvation. Deeply disturbed by the possibility of failure or rejection by a real or imagined parental authority, the subject displaces his competitive drives onto another, more immediately powerful presence: a mediator or *tertium quid* ambivalently regarded as more worthy than the subject or even than the apparent object of desire. In the resulting triangulation, the apparent desiderata is not what it seems but

> a merely passive obstacle . . . because the rival is secretly revered. The demigod seems to answer homage with a curse. . . . The subject would like to think of himself as the victim of an atrocious injustice but in his anguish he wonders whether perhaps he does not deserve his apparent condemnation. Rivalry therefore only . . . increases the mediator's prestige and strengthens the bond which links the object to his mediator by forcing him to affirm openly his right or desire of possession. (*Deceit, Desire* 13)

Girard based his theory upon a partial correction of Max Scheler's German romantic theory of *ressentiment*. Following Nietzsche in grounding all human interaction on social competition, Scheler believed that "all jealousy, all ambition, and even an ideal like the 'imitation of Christ' is based on such comparisons" (*Deceit, Desire* 14). While the universality of this model has often been questioned, its application to periods of social crisis is well established. More intriguing for our purposes, however, is Girard's proposal that "Only the great artists attribute to the mediator the position usurped by the object; only they reverse the commonly accepted hierarchy of desire" (*Deceit, Desire*, 14; cf. 59). For if Girard is right, his remark would go far toward explaining the unstable literary reception of Donne's "greatness," which has been simultaneously admired and scorned by literary critics from Samuel Johnson to the present. It should also explain why, like Donne's "Hymne to God the Father," his *Holy Sonnets* "recklessly" reveal and even revel in their competitive *ressentiment* both toward God the Father and God the Son, thereby reversing the "commonly accepted hierarchy of desire" by making the conventional mediator his competitor. Finally, Girard's analysis of how *ressentiment* produces a triangulation of desire helps to explain why the *Holy Sonnets* regularly displace objects of emulation or desire (not only sainted fathers or wives, but the higher objects that they symbolize—the invisible church, grace, and redemption itself) in favor of a paradoxically hostile rival/friendly mediator frankly revealed as the "real" object of desire.

As Girard would predict, in the *Holy Sonnets* this mediator is typically a double: a jealous Son figure visibly and violently linked either to the devil or a false savior, to the visible church as a potentially false spouse, or again to the unworthy/suffering/persecuted subject himself. Due to his daring exposure of a double bind that would normally be displaced or concealed, the subject also reverses the normal hierarchy of desire by openly acknowledging that he can free himself only by *failing* to attain the passive but also prohibited object of assurance. As a result, he becomes his own mediator through a strategy that at once resembles and reverses Fish's "self-consuming" dialectic: he substitutes the healing "Real Presence" of the sacrament for the fallen real presence of the subject himself. In "sacrificially" confessing his deeply conflicted feelings toward his sainted wife and father, he also tacitly confesses his guilty desire for the sacramental "seals" of assurance but then permits himself to "resurrect" them along with himself. For while his father and wife had "easie[r] ways and neare" to heaven, only he himself (not these false and even potentially "idolatrous" objects of religious desire) will truly "merit" divine grace through his Christlike suffering and sacrificial self-exposure.[11]

As noted above, this conflictive sense of sonship or brotherhood is first adumbrated in *Satyre 3*. After expressing his "brave scorn" for the religious controversies of the present age, the speaker mockingly questions whether when "thy fathers spirit / Meete blinde Philosophers in heaven, whose merit / Of strict life may be imputed faith," he might "heare / Thee, whom hee taught so easie wayes and neare / To follow, damn'd?" (1, 11–15). Echoing Hooker, Donne locates the main sources of his *ressentiment* in the contrast between his difficulties and his rival/role model's apparent security: having "easily" arrived in heaven by means of the old faith, his father now watches his son struggle to compete for this ultimate prize with "blinde philosophers," none of whom had to fear that "having left their roots," they might be "givcn / To the streames tyrannous rage" (105–6). But as Girard's model predicts, the speaker chiefly fears and resents not these philosophers but his true rival or mediator, God the Father, who may be "too superior to accept him as a disciple" (*Deceit, Desire* 10) despite his faithful attempt to transcend the mere "idolatrie" of power—the "mere contraries / Equally strong" (98, 102) that "a Philip, or a Gregory, / A Harry or a Martin taught thee" (96–97). So while this *Satyre* optimistically claims that a more firm and "hard knowledge" can be won by the pilgrim who climbs the heights and sees truth "like the Sunne, dazzling, yet plaine to all eyes" (86–88), Donne's characteristic note of anxiety enters in as he reflects on the limitations of a quest that must be completed "before age, deaths twilight, / . . . for none can worke in that night" (83–84).

In the *Holy Sonnets*, that twilight already seems fast upon him as he imagines his own father's redeemed spirit ironically rejoicing at his triangulation between these poles of belief and seeing how "valiantly I hels wide mouth o'rstride" ("If faithfull soules be alike," 4). Equally ironically, his "white truth" (8) is not only far less bright than the dazzling light of the Son/sun, but also far more vaguely "imputed" than the goodness of the blind philosophers. Appearing only through "circumstances, and by signes that be / Apparent in us not immediately" (6–7), his soul's "truth" can no more be transparently "seen" by the heavenly host than his justification by faith can be seen by himself. Clearly, then, like the lovers who with rituals of "weeping" and "mourning" worship the false god of courtly love (9), the merely ritual worshipers of the true God must now be condemned as "vile blasphemous Conjurers" and "Pharisaicall / Dissemblers" whose "feigne[d] devotion" (10–12) earns them the common fate of all Romish "idolaters." Yet what, in fact, are the boundaries of "idolatry"? Does it rule out the desire of the speaker's "pensive soule" to offer his father more clear and "apparent" signs of grace? Or must he propitiate this indirect object of desire with ever more anxious and oblique tokens of "griefe" and affliction (14) to appease his direct object—God? As Girard again would predict, only by embracing rather than eluding the toils of *ressentiment*—only by openly affirming "his right or desire" to equal the suffering mediator and/or "possessor" of salvation—can the speaker transubstantiate his internal "curse" into an external blessing by effectively cursing himself (cf. "Spit in my face").

Girard's most seminal study of these themes in *Violence and the Sacred* explains why the rival role models manipulated by subjects caught in the double bind of a ritual crisis are so dynamically interchangeable with the subject himself. On the one hand, these rivals will seem strongly differentiated, but on the other, they seem indistinguishable; for "from within the system, only differences are perceived; from without, the antagonists all seem alike." However,

> Only the outside perspective, which takes into consideration reciprocity and unity and denies the difference, can discern the workings of the violent resolution, the cryptic process by which unanimity is reformed against and around the surrogate victim. When all differences have been eliminated and the similarity between two figures has been achieved, we say that the antagonists are *doubles* . . . [whose] interchangeability . . . makes possible the act of sacrificial substitution. (*Violence and the Sacred* 158–59)

While the double initially appears as an overt rival, an enemy twin, monster, or deity—all of which are so interchangeable in the ritual crisis that even gender is irrelevant (although typically, the "idolized antagonist undergoes first a feminine incarnation, then a masculine" one)—"nobody . . . incarnates the true oppressor or the true oppressed." Modern ideological interpretations thus "seriously misconstrue the tragic spirit . . . [by imposing] a static Manichaean confrontation . . . , an unyielding rancor that holds fast to its victims" by wholly divorcing them from their apparent oppressors (*Violence and the Sacred*, 156, 150). Hence while the subject himself is naturally "torn between two opposite feelings toward his model—the most submissive reverence and most intense malice . . . [even] *hatred*"—the great artist or poet knows that he can succeed in his sacrificial aims only by becoming his own enemy—as self-persecuted and abject as mannerist portraits of the Crucifixion depict Christ himself (*Deceit, Desire* 10). Reenacting the ritual crisis therefore involves "an extreme form of alienation" since it involves repeating an original sacrifice that can be seen as a "sickness, cure, or both at once," at once dramatizing or "doubling" the disintegration of the old order and the "new order" emerging from within it (*Violence and the Sacred* 165–68, 272).

Historically, this reenactment of ritual sacrifice will vary in accordance with the particular crisis it seeks to heal, which in the *Holy Sonnets* is clearly the crisis surrounding the Reformation's simultaneous rejection and reinvention of ritual atonement. Whereas Roman Catholic Christianity had conserved its genetic linkage with primitive, ritual systems of sacrifice wherein "no act of punitive justice is performed, [and] . . . the altar can in no way be compared to a tribunal," since "expiation is not a punitive act, but a method of salvation" (Ricoeur 98n. 46; G. von Rad qtd. in *Theologie*), Calvin's virtually "Manichaean" notion of human depravity required his heirs to turn the altar into an actual tribunal. In their highly individualized "forum of conscience," the believer's "sense of divine judgement, as a witness . . . does not allow [them] . . . to hide their sins from being accused" (*Institutes* 3.19.15). In this Calvinistic "courtroom," grace now depends upon the subject's self-prosecution. And Donne himself clearly agrees that the "participation [of the Holy Ghost] manifests itself as a 'sense of sin'" (*Sermons* 7:222) rather than as a mediator and comforter sent to confirm the Son's atoning sacrifice and his defeat of the devil. Hence, the Holy Spirit too becomes a rival role model or conscience whose "afflictions" are easily conflated with those of the old archenemy.

The result is what Debora Shuger refers to as truly "radical monotheism," a form of Christianity in which mediators and rivals are regularly blurred as the believer struggles to maintain his conviction that his soul has received the unstable imprint of imputed grace. In the process, both the scene on the Cross and the day of judgment become interchangeable "doubles" of the individual's own deathbed scene. These temporal doubles are constantly reproduced in an individual consciousness divided between a threatening enemy self or other and an "indwelling Spirit which resembles the Freudian superego, the introjected punitive Other that generates conscience, rationality and guilt." Externally torn between a God who is both "duplicate and supplement," accuser and savior, the internal self is triangulated between the conflicting desire to acknowledge sin and to accept salvation, or as Shuger puts it, between a Christ complex and an Oedipus complex (Shuger 169, 181, 196, 203).

For Donne, these conflicts are considerably exacerbated by the fact that, in line with Reformed doctrine, Anglican contrition is far more demanding than Catholic contrition, which accepts sorrow inspired by fear as evidence of salvation. Converts are thrown into a particularly painful double bind by this shift, since if they are at all apprehensive that their motives for conversion were improper or misguided, they can take no refuge in fearful contrition but must learn to fear fear itself. A related cause of anxiety can be found in Anglicanism's stricter definition of justification, which eliminates even purely internal and emotional tokens of salvation as potential idols that should not be taken as certain signs of grace.[12] Worse still, Donne himself argues that the individual's choice of faith and church form the sole criteria by which he must judge and be judged. The anxieties attendant upon this choice thus tempt him to conflate his own Catholic/Protestant dichotomy with Christ's man/God dichotomy, rejecting the pseudo-martyrdom of the Jesuits for the emotional martyrdom of the true society of Jesus. In the process, he reinvents the sacrificial crisis described by Girard, first, by laying full claim to "Thy griefe, for he put it into my breast" ("If faithfull soules be alike," 14), and then by committing himself to an ever-deeper complicity with the paradoxical "duplicity" he finds in Christ, the Mediator—the faith/doubt of the dying man/God who questions on the Cross, "My God, my God, why hast thou forsaken me?" But while this ultimate triangulation allows Donne to lay hold of the "presence" of salvation (the true object of religious desire), he can do so only by accepting his dying rival's momentary "absence" of transcendence on the Cross. Thus in the end, his Christlike sense of desertion and affliction becomes his most brightly "apparent," quasi-sacramental, yet also fearful sign of salvation.

Again in accordance with Girard's theory of the double bind, the speaker bases his claim of martyrdom on his Christlike "double interest" (*HS 16*, 1) in two opposing spiritual kingdoms, the city of God and the city of man. Triangulating between ever-multiplying enemy twins—"our old subtle foe" (*HS 1*, 11), "gluttonous death" (*HS 6*, 5), his own "sinne" (*HS 7*, 10; *HS 9*, 12), and the Christlike "vehement griefe" of his un-Christlike "black Soule" (*HS 3*, 13; *HS 4*, 1), the speaker finds himself condemned to "dual" with them all. But despite their prominence, these "duals" are only displaced objects or foes substituting for the real rival, the one true Mediator whose matchless superiority simultaneously threatens his villainous alter-ego and his victim-ego. Thus like Jacob, he must compete with a rival who alternately appears as the rightful heir and as the evil twin in the contest for their common birthright, the "bosom" position in the line of Abraham (*HS 11*). For as Donne is well aware, the literal meaning of Jacob's Hebrew name, "supplanter," is also associated with Satan, the semi-concealed "double" of the true Son. The violent contest between these twins precipitates the primal ritual crisis traced even in superficially peaceful sonnets like "Why are wee by all creatures waited on?" Donne answers this question by showing that the Fall has so violently inverted the benign order of nature that the lamb has become indistinguishable from the lion. As a result, the meek can only inherit the earth with a vengeance. For like the Creator-Son, the innocent now die not for their own "sin, nor nature," but for other "Creatures" who are actually "foes" (*HS 12*, 7, 10–14). Christ thus becomes the bearer not of peace but of the sword, reminding us that his suffering is neither simply just nor merciful but also wrathful, a consideration that turns the sonnet into a cruel parody of a manger or nativity scene.

In this way, the *Holy Sonnets* restate the recurring theme of the *Anniversaries:* that the soul's "happiest Harmonee" consists in "division" (92) understood in three separate senses—musical, physical, and teleological. In this new "allegory" of redemption, Christian souls sacrificially mark the events of sacred history in time with a newly negative, discordant "song." In addition to this musical division, they are physically divided by the "total depravity" of sin. Laid in a "poore Inne" (175) without benefit of virgin birth or immaculate conception, like the abjectly suffering animals but unlike Christ, they are the physical children of "their true mother, Age" (178). But their teleological fate is even worse, for they must die without sacramental assistance—ironically, like Christ himself. As a result, all Christian deaths have become as violent, if hardly as exalted, as his:

> Thinke that a rusty peece, discharg'd, is flowen
> In peeces, and the bullet is his owne,
> And freely flies; this to thy soule allow,
> Thinke thy sheell broke, thinke thy Soule hatch'd but now. (*SA* 181–84)

In place of Paul's mystic unity of body and soul figured by the seed organically "sown" into eternity, the disenchanted soul is now violently "flown" to the next life in the form of a quite different pod or shell: a bullet whose double death consists in the simultaneous explosion of the rusty world or gun "peece" and the shell/soul's own "discharge." Along with the loss of the sacramental system's chief assurance—a "good death" eased by the rites of extreme unction and the ritual gathering of family and community—this deeply ironic "release" may also reflect the bullets flying in the contemporary religious wars where a redemptive "discharge" was ironically expected by religious martyrs on both sides of these self- and community-shattering controversies.[13]

Here as in his *Satyres*, Donne's sarcasm is remarkably even-handed or double-edged. He generally objects to controversialists of all stripes, but particularly to those "too stiffe to recant, / A hundred controversies of an Ant" (*SA* 281–89). The word "recant" ironically reverberates throughout his bitter experience of the period's (and his own) theological reversals, and at the same time, suggests an additional rationale behind Donne's deep need for a form of grace that will provide "More Antidote, then all the world was ill" (*SA* 378). In the absence of the traditional "antidote" of death—Eucharistic transubstantiation—true transubstantiation now consists in inversely repeating Christ's sacrificial triangulation between worlds, the theme of "Good Friday, 1613: Riding Westward."[14] Although complete recovery must await the soul's final resurrection (*SA* 485–94), in the supplemental eternity of suffering experienced in this "present last night" of penitential meditation, God's servants can "justify" their sanctification in something *like* the old sacramental manner by paying "Rent" (*SA* 520) on God's true coin, not in good works, but in discovering new miracles of Christlike self-abjection. While these "miracles" are always, like Elizabeth Drury herself, as officially superior to the speaker as the true Mediator himself, Donne never quits competing with them in spirit—"That [which] gave thee power to doe, me, to say this, / Since his will is, that to posteritee, / Thou shouldest for life, and death a patterne bee" (*SA* 522–24). By thus rivaling these "patterns" of Pauline tribulation in "spirit," he gains Johannine predictive powers that allow him to supplement/supplant their voices: "Thou art the Proclamation; and I ame / The Trumpet, at whose voice the people came" (*SA* 527–28). Finally, by offering a new "pattern . . . of [divine] love" in an age whose center will not otherwise hold, he "still keepes" its "full perfection" *within* an irrevocably "peece[d]," divided, and diametrically crossed circle (*SA* 507–8).

Thus like the age itself, the speaker's synthetic powers are as radically incomplete as they are violent. Just as both church and state are no longer "met in one" but find themselves internally and externally at war, both subject and object, poet and patron, are no longer interdependent but "rather . . . two soules," "Or like to full, on both sides written Rols" (*SA* 503–4). These "Rols" seem to refer to at least two varieties of competing "doubles"—the Old and New Testament, and the old and the Reformed religion. In *Holy Sonnets 16* ("Father, part of his double interest") and *13* ("What if this present"), Donne therefore represents the soul as a two-sided scroll or palimpsest reflecting the two opposing images of God: on the one side beauty and pity, on the other duplicity and wrath. But like the Old and New Testaments, these "twins" are only read aright as triangulated reflections of his own tripartite mind/body/soul.[15] Perceiving these redoubled triangulations accurately has the advantage of forcing the subject to acknowledge his own multiple tears or "rents," the endless self-divisions, gaps, and lacerations that also serve as his purgatorial down payment on their final reunion in heaven. Ironically anticipating the Cartesian cogito—"I think, therefore I am"—Donne invents an even more complex mind/body/soul schism based on the antithetical proposition—"I suffer, therefore I shall be."[16]

The dynamism of this suffering is maintained by the sufferer's "supplanting" or appropriating crimes that Christ could never have committed himself. Relentlessly exploring his *less*-than-Christlike "doubleness" of every kind, Donne's self-sacrificial iconoclasm effectively re-creates *while renouncing* all twelve stations of the cross. In part, this superhuman effort is rooted in his belief that

> the most precious things which God hath afforded us here, for the agony and exercise of our sense and spirit, are often envenomed and putrified, and stray into a corrupt disease; for as God doth thus occasion, and positively concur to evil, that when a man is purposed to do a great sin, God infuses some good thoughts which make him choose a less sin, or leave out some circumstance which aggravated that; so the devil doth not only suffer but provoke us to some things naturally good, upon condition that we shall omit some other more necessary and more obligatory. And this is his greatest subtlety, because herein we have the deceitful comfort of having done well, and can very hardly spy our error because it is but an insensible omission and no accusing act. (*Life and Letters* 1:190–91)

Although these reflections still lie well within the mainline Christian tradition of meditation, examination of conscience, confession, and penance, Donne's exaggeratedly self-divided suspicions both of divine providence and of the highest of the "precious things" that it provides further illuminate his ambivalence about the life to come. For in his view, this good is so tempting that it becomes a potential source of sin—a forbidden desire quickly to conclude this endlessly anxious race for eternal life. Since this option is foreclosed, as the epigraph to this essay indicates, he mimics immortality by eternally prolonging his own suffering. Conceding that only the true Son of God could experience such extreme fears of unworthiness and/or desertion without sin, his *imitatio Christi* alternates between losing and winning his contest with his Mediator: between abandoning all outward signs of grace and sacrificing his own "idolatrous" or enemy-self on the common altar that ironically allows it lowest to become its *most* authentically worthy victim.

Donne had earlier experimented with a similar dialectic in his anti-Petrarchan love lyrics, which similarly strip exalted images of their conventional, ritual meaning to expose potentially debased motives that, from a confessional perspective, can also be taken as redemptive. This pattern is particularly plain in "The Canonization," where the lover's very profanation—his graying hair, his gout, palsy, and ruined fortune—leads directly to the sacrificial, phoenix-like resurrection of himself and his beloved. Yet as in the *Holy Sonnets*, he can only succeed by first abandoning all tangible signs of justification and/or sanctification. Afterwards, the "well wrought urn," which preserves the lovers' ashy or inky remains for canonization, provides their "hermitage" only because they have eschewed not only external honors and rewards but also the fame that it secretly "enrolls." Thus finally, both urn and fame exist only as a hypothetical "covenant" between poet and readers who have similarly triumphed over their many rivals not by winning, but by losing all for love.

Holy Sonnet 3 ("Oh might those sighes and teares") takes virtually the same approach to the poet's earlier "sacrifices" to profane love, which only through the loss of his utterly wasted sufferings in love's service "proves" that his days of "vaine" mourning are over (4–5). While those earlier sufferings cannot "count" as true penance, by reminding him of the true "paine" (8) of sin, they can still "shrive" or absolve him by acting as a *continual* penance. Finally, since he now has no "reliefe" (11) from pain, his vehement sufferings raise him incomparably above all of his rivals in sin: "th'hydroptique drunkard, and night-scouting thiefe / The itchy Lecher, and selfe-tickling proud" (9–10), all of whom have a "remembrance of past joyes" (11) prohibited by his own "vehement griefe." Because this Christ-like pain simultaneously acts as "The'effect and cause, the punishment and sinne" (14), he can once again cancel out all rival claims to redemption by discovering the one "secure" ground of hope in his irrefutable dis-ease, the "holy discontent" that permits him to "Mourne with some fruit" or "rent" acting as the earnest money of his resurrection (3–4).

But Donne's self-exposing "solution" to the double bind is most notoriously apparent in "Batter my heart," his most reckless re-creation of the ritual crisis in the sonnet sequence. For here the "three person'd God" most plainly acts as a sexual rival to the speaker's "betroth'd" enemy (10), from whom his "true" lover can save him only by violently "ravishing" him. Through an outrageous pun on the Latin root *(raptus)* as ravishment *or* rape (since the verb *rapere* means to seize in both negative and positive senses), the poet converts the contamination of rape into the "rapture" of transfiguration. Yet to "carry off" this transfiguration, he must first identify a competing object—a critic, elder brother, a "chider" or other "enemie" who upbraids him for his enthrallment to his rival—for the mediator or ego-ideal to destroy and, in the process, become his twin. Yet this suspicious doubling permits only a tentative release from the other pole of triangulation, the false or satanic mediator to whose influence and power he remains most susceptible, as the more accessible, earthly, and "earthy" role model. Thus when confronted with these conflicting "faces" of supernatural power, the speaker passively represents himself as a woman "betroth'd unto . . . [her] enemie" unless her Lord "breake that knot" by which "she" is bound to their common rival. Here the "knot" at once refers to her external bond and her virgin knot, which must be broken if she is to "wed" either her betrothed's rival or her true betrothed. From the inner perspective, this "wedding" seems more like the capture/rapture of the Sabine women than the marriage of the Christian Bridegroom and bride (10–14); but from the more distanced, outer perspective, these pagan "relics" clearly serve the speaker's need for a "transcendent" self-abjection equivalent to sacramental transubstantiation.

The final and most "knotty" sonnet of the 1635 sequence comes even closer to revealing the strategy and motives behind Donne's precarious triangulation by comparing the Son's inevitable "duplicity" as man/God to two other closely related "knots": the violent union-in-division that characterizes both the triune godhead and triune human nature. In man, the inner soul still provides the invisible "knot" linking the potential "whiteness" of his condition to his actual foulness, the link between his angelic nature and his animal nature. When Adam fell, it was by ceding his angelic, masculine *sapientia* (wisdom) to the middle or "feminine" aspect of his nature, *scientia* (active will), which then delivered both over to the senses, his "serpentine" or animal nature (Grant 12–13). But since the human aspect of Christ's nature bore this same threefold structure sinlessly, he was able to defeat the infernal triad and rejoin the heavenly one. According to the Calvinist theology of imputed as opposed to engrafted grace, his sons can at best imitate only *half* of his victory: through faith, they may defeat the world and the flesh (the old serpent or flesh and the old Eve or worldly will), but never the devil, who still retains the authority ceded to him by original sin. Thus as *Holy Sonnet 16* states, Christ's heirs can at best hope to fulfill only half of his two dispensations or "two Wills," but they may fulfill neither if imputed grace does not redeem "what law and letter kill" (7, 12). As a result, "men argue yet / Whether a man [either of] those statutes can fulfill" (9–10).

Conventionally, of course, the two wills are the old law of Moses and the new law of Christ, although the former has already been largely abrogated for Christians, who with Paul agree it was unfulfillable. Here, however, not just the prior cancellation of the first will but the identity of both is called into question when the poet says that both have been put into place by the Lamb slain "from the worlds beginning" (5–6) and remain debated to this day. Moreover, even if the two wills simply refer to Christ's redaction of the ten commandments into two—to love God with one's whole soul and to love one's neighbor as oneself—then *neither* the faithful of Geneva or Rome (i.e., neither Reformed nor Counter-Reformation "martyrs") can be said to fulfill them both. In England as all across Europe, there now exists only rivalry, even hatred, among those bearing Christ's name, which doubly problematizes both Donne's willing sonship and his inheritance or "will." This crux leads directly to the speaker's plea to let "Thy lawes final abridgement" and "last Will stand" by "all-healing grace and spirit" (11, 13–14): that is, to uphold the "feminine" law of love that restores what Eve lost. Yet this plea also suggests that he finds any purely internal transubstantiation of rivalry, *ressentiment*, legalism, and religious hatred into the composite "bride" of piteous Christian love profoundly problematic unless he can discover another, more masculine supplement or "will."

Both the absence of this discovery and the corresponding necessity of triangulation are frankly revealed in the sonnets excluded from the 1635 sonnet sequence and included only in the Westmoreland manuscript.[17] In the sonnet to his deceased wife ("Since she whom I lov'd"), Donne again presents himself as a sinner torn between two impossibly divided divine wills: rivalry between her saintly inspiration and the love he owes to his heavenly Father. These conflicts produce no solution but only the "holy thirsty dropsy" that typically melts and makes him "begg more Love" (8–9). For while his wife's death *should* have canceled this sacred/profane "competition" for love by diverting it back into the "head" from which her "streame" flowed, the speaker still must be "wooe[d]" by a heavenly rival who (once again mixing genders and metaphors) competes not only with his wife's soul but with other "Saints and Angels[,] things divine" (10, 12) in his "tender jealosy" and "doubt / Least the World, fleshe, yea Devill putt thee out" (13–14).[18] The speaker also fears that the competing "fires" of love will completely dry up the waters with which his shepherd "my thirst hast fed" (7), thus turning all desired objects, even his beloved wife, into even more overt rivals. Inverting the conventional hierarchy of desire, he then recognizes that all of these objects represent simultaneously worthy and unworthy "wills." Thus once again, his solution is to set these "twins" against each other, making himself the true Mediator's bride, and entering the "bosom position" of Abraham where he equals the bridegroom himself.

Donne's most reckless revelation of his need to usurp the bridegroom's role occurs in the Westmoreland sonnet entitled "Show me deare

Christ, thy spouse." Here the schisms currently dividing Rome, England, and Germany at first seem to be canceled by the anticipated wedding of Christ's true bride, which is corporately conceived not as the visible but as the invisible church. But the many disguises in which the bride "peepes up" (5) instead suggest the bitter confusion that Donne actually associates with the incongruous "wills" that the Father of the bride has bequeathed to the suitors of his time. For these hapless knights, Christ's bride alternately appears as a prostitute or "maid Marian," a "richly painted" whore (3); then as a fairy-spouse snoring for a thousand years (5); next as a worldly-wise woman of fashion whose brightness is "now new, now'outwore" (6); and finally as an enchantress pursued both by the speaker and other "adventuring knights" (9) seeking her "grail." Because the same radical ambiguity surrounds all of her appearances and not merely her more recent European sightings—"On one, on seaven, or on no hill" (7–8)—as a rival mediator, this spouse is ironically "redeemed" only when she is least coy and most inconstant, for only then is she most "open" and able to "betray" most men.

Since the word "betray" at once means to "show herself to" and to deceive or seduce "most men" (11, 13), in this most profound of all Donne's paradoxes, the true bride who courts and wins his "amorous soule" becomes *both* the tempting wife *and* the "Idolatr[ous]" mistress earlier rejected in "O might those sighes." As such, she also becomes a *permanently* ambivalent object of desire who once again leaves the speaker with two potentially unfulfillable wills. For if this mediator/bride's "virtue" consists only in iconoclastically exposing *and* sustaining the amorous jealousy of all the fathers and brothers "dualing" one another in the renewed ritual crisis, it also maintains her ironically "true" or "constant" faithlessness. This potentially scandalous scenario (which Donne in part adapts from the wedding of the prophet and prostitute in Hosea) reveals the inherently unsatisfactory nature of his ritual search and sacrificial "wedding" at the same time that it reenacts and/or indulges these impulses. In and through this confusion, the two bridegrooms—that is, the true Mediator and his unworthy rival/victim—again become "one."

This situation is fully rehearsed in the signature piece of this essay, "Oh, to vex me, contraryes meete in one," which freely acknowledges that like the bride of "Show me deare Christ," the speaker can be "constant" or "true" only through an inconstant conversion that follows the predicable pattern of his earlier amours: "as humorous . . . / As my prophane Love, and as soone forgott" (5–6). Yet this apparently damning admission also allows him to conjecture that although his spiritual love "unnaturally" resembles the lusts of the flesh with its "distemper, cold and hott" (6), like them it is as real as it is illusory, "as infinite, as none" (7). Thus like the "brotherly" mark or curse of Cain he may have earned from his betrayal of his Roman or "profane" yet mercifully "common" religion, and like his once-illicit passion for his wife, Donne's Adamic "curse" or heel-wound may also "heal" or bless him by dissolving him into the true "streames" of divine love. Once again balancing a theology of invisible election against a longing for sacramental signs, he ceaselessly wavers between holy dread and semi-profane penance, between not daring to "view heaven yesterday; and to day / In prayers, and flattering speeches . . . [to] court God" (9–10). Finally, the speaker bases his hope of salvation on a condition that he understands as heterodox from one perspective, but from another, as orthodoxly "true" to Christ's dual nature. At this point, the curse can also become a healing or cure: "So my devout fitts come and go away / Like a fantastique Ague: save that here / Those are my best dayes, when I shake with feare" (12–14).

The "true feare of his rod" (11) thus provides the unstable center of Donne's iconoclastic and triangulated form of sacramentalism. Ultimately rejecting all outward appearances of the visible church as potentially false idols, he constantly crucifies and resurrects himself as the "idolatrous" icon of its crucified Christ. To atone for his primal sins of self-division and inauthenticity—sins outrivaling those of both the old and the new Adam—he ritually rehearses the violence that he has or fears "to have done" by repeatedly blaspheming his ever-redoubling mediators (father, son, and bride) in order to judge himself as he would be judged: as a "righteous" sinner.[19] But as such, he can be saved only by a quasi-sacramental form of violence in which he himself has become the Real Presence, a synthesis not just of the host's body and blood but of mediator and victim, bride and ravisher, cuckold and spouse, Jesus and Judas, Mary and Mary Magdalene.[20] In this "eternal" movement, Donne reenacts not only the sacrificial crisis surrounding the Crucifixion and the primitive ritual behind it but also the hope for religious renewal outlined by Girard:

> The surrogate victim dies so that the entire community, threatened by the same fate, can be reborn in a new or renewed cultural order. Having sown the seeds of death, the god, ancestor, or mythic hero then dies himself or selects a victim to die in his stead. In doing so he bestows a new life on men. Understanding this process, we can also understand why death should be regarded as the elder sister, not to say the mother and ultimate source, of life itself. (*Violence and the Sacred* 255)

Notes

1. Since the sonnets are numbered differently in different editions, the first phrase from each opening line will be cited unless the reference is already clear.

2. Thus as Peter Rudnytsky similarly observes, "In the face of the breakdown of 'correspondence' between heaven and earth, Donne had to meet the task of reinvesting his poetic art with the stamp of essential metaphor" (187). And as Richard Wollman reminds us, "far from being restricted to the *Sermons*, Donne's claim that 'the art of *salvation*, is but the art of *memory*' helps explain how the poet came to think of his poetic conceits as serving both the earthly and heavenly purposes contained in the word 'salvation.' For when connected to the memory, 'salvation' retained the meaning—from Aquinas onward—of preserving an image in human memory *and* making a soul fit for heaven" (121).

3. As Empson remarks in identifying Elizabeth Drury with the Logos or Christ, "the break-up of the unified world of medieval thought" provides the poem's framework, "but the frame is itself . . . [its] symbol. . . . He could hardly have used it had he not felt, with that secret largeness of outlook which is his fascination, that the ideas he handled did not necessarily belong to the one Jesus" (82–83).

4. As Young also shows (21), Barbara Lewalski's work on *Protestant Poetics* and on *Donne's "Anniversaries"* inconsistently claims that Donne's *Holy Sonnets* are a typical example of a genre that avoids external images of the Nativity and Passion in order to depict the work of redemption operating "solely and directly upon the speaker's heart." For while, as Lewalski claims, the poems' speaker does replace Christ as "the proper subject of the crucifixion," it does not follow that Donne overlooks the external aspects of this event (*Donne's "Anniversaries"* 106–7).

5. For a fuller summary of the doctrine of imputed grace and its differences from "engrafted" grace, see Lewalski, *Donne's "Anniversaries"* 122–33. My discussion above also relies on the reader's understanding that Protestants generally came to prefer the word "seal" to "sacrament," since "sacrament" (derived ultimately from the Greek word *mysterion*) suggests the mystery of the Real Presence. Richard Hooker's position on this issue is the standard one: sacraments "are called seals of God's truth" because "the spirit affixes unto those elements and words, [a] power of operation within the soul" that is not outward or instrumental but inward and "impossible to be exprest" (*Lawes* 6.6.10). However, Donne's "original, theological synthesis" (Lewalski, *Donne's "Anniversaries"* 132) is actually closer to Calvin than to Hooker on many points, which makes it darker if not quite as "despairing" as John Stachniewski suggests. Stachniewski's analysis of the reasons for Donne's attraction to the Calvinist orthodoxy of the Anglican Church are partly convincing, but they should be balanced against his difficulties with the

Calvinist doctrines of sin and imputed grace; see Hughes 177 and Grant 60–72, 201. Grant convincingly suggests that Donne's natural affinity was with the broader, more compassionate Augustine of the Franciscan tradition, of St. Bernard and St. Bonaventure, whom he frequently cites, than with Calvin's reading of Augustine (59–60).

6. On Donne's need to perform his own resurrection in the love sonnets, see Watson 218.

7. However, for some intriguing parallels between the theology of Bunyan and Donne, see Papazian.

8. For a psychoanalytic approach to Donne's need to cancel death by constantly (re)subjecting himself to its experience, see Watson 165–75; for a theological approach, see Sherwood, "'Ego videbo,'" and *Fulfilling the Circle*, 117–18, 127–29.

9. "Security" in the sense favored by Calvinists is the opposite sin to despair: imperviousness to spiritual peril. On this point, see Haller.

10. See also Watson 178–79. However, Watson's explanations seems to rely too narrowly on the "traumas" of Donne's childhood, including his inferior maternal nurturance, and too little on the inherited martyr complex discussed by Carey (15–59, 213).

11. Donne's sense of spiritual danger is also obliquely reflected in his later "self-exposure" in advising other Christians not to change churches; see Carey 35.

12. See Peterson and Baker-Smith 412–24.

13. On the "good death," see Duffy; on Donne's recognition of its unavailability in "A Valediction: Forbidding Mourning," see Watson 193.

14. Donne personally inverts this triangulation by riding westward rather than eastward, just as his "sacrament" inverts the traditional doctrine summarized by Paul Tillich, where "Christ gives . . . both the knowledge of immortality and the drug of immortality, which is the sacrament. Ignatius called the Lord's Supper the remedy against our having to die, the *antidoton to me apothanein*[,] . . . meaning . . . that the sacramental materials of the Lord's Supper are, so to speak, drugs or remedies which produce immortality. . . . [This] shows that the apostolic fathers did not believe in the immortality of the soul . . . otherwise it would be meaningless for them to speak about immortal life which Christ offers. They believed that man is naturally mortal, just as the Old Testament held that in paradise man was able to eat from the food of the gods, called the 'tree of life,' and to keep alive by participating in this divine power" (23–24).

15. On the Augustinian trinities the dominated Donne's thought, see Tayler 106 ff.

16. On Donne's anticipation of Descartes, see Carey 234–35.

17. As Patrides explains (*Complete Poems* 445, 522), these last three *Holy Sonnets* were first printed by Gosse in 1899 from the Westmoreland manuscript.

18. Since, as Baker-Smith observes, "the entire system of the Roman Church appears to him as built on a confusion of the metaphorical and the literal" (415), the poet again finds himself guiltily reflecting this confusion in his "passion" for punning.

19. This attitude is in many ways more characteristic of the Counter-Reformation than of mainline Anglicanism, bearing significant affinities with Jansenism, the Calvinistically inflected Catholic movement contemporarily under way in France. There, too, we find the birth of that most "paradoxical being *par excellence*, the *juste pêcheur* (righteous sinner)," who, as Goldmann observes, provides "the most important and difficult problem for the student of Jansenism" (160).

20. Watson finds it significant that portrait of Mary Magdalene hung in Donne's study; Baker-Smith finds it equally suggestive that Paolo Sarpi (the counter Counter-Reformation Catholic) received similar honors.

Works Cited

Bacon, Francis. *The Essays or Counsels Civil and Moral* (1625). *Francis Bacon: A Critical Edition of the Major Works*. Ed. Brian Vickers. Oxford: Oxford UP, 1996.

Baker-Smith, Dominic. "John Donne's *Critique of True Religion*." *John Donne: Essays in Celebration*. Ed. A. J. Smith. London: Metheun, 1972. 404–32

Benjamin, Walter. *On the Origin of German Tragic Drama*. Trans. John Osborne. London: New Left Books, 1977.

Calvin, John. *Institutes of the Christian Religion*. Ed. John T. McNeill, trans. F. L. Battles. 2 vols. Philadelphia: Westminster, 1960.

Carey, John. *John Donne: Life, Mind, and Art*. New York: Oxford UP, 1981.

DiPasquale, Theresa M. *Literature and Sacrament: The Sacred and the Secular in John Donne* Pittsburgh: Duquesne UP, 1999.

Donne, John. *The Complete English Poems*. Ed. C. A. Patrides. New York: Knopf, 1985.

———. *Letters to Severall Persons of Honour (1651)*. Intro. M. Thomas Hester. Delmar, NY: Scholars' Facsimiles and Reprints, 1977.

———. *Life and Letters of John Donne: Dean of St. Paul's*. 2 vols. Ed. Edmund Gosse. New York: Dodd, Mead, 1899.

———. *Sermons*. Ed. George R. Potter and Evelyn M. Simpson. 10 vols. Berkeley: U of California P, 1953–62.

Duffy, Eamon. *The Stripping of the Altars*. New Haven: Yale UP, 1992.

Empson, William. *Some Versions of Pastoral: A Study of the Pastoral Form in Literature*. Harmondsworth: Penguin Books, 1966.

Fish, Stanley E. "Masculine Persuasive Force: Donne and Verbal Power." *Soliciting Interpretation: Literary Theory and Seventeenth-Century English Poetry*. Ed.

Elizabeth D. Harvey and Katharine Eisaman Maus. Chicago: U of Chicago P, 1990. 223–52.

———. *Self-Consuming Artifacts: The Experience of Seventeenth-Century Literature.* Berkeley: U of California P, 1972.

Frontain, Raymond-Jean, and Frances M. Malpezzi, eds. *John Donne's Religious Imagination: Essays in Honor of John T. Shawcross.* Conway: U of Central Arizona P, 1995.

Girard, René. *Deceit, Desire, and the Novel: Self and Other in Literary Structure.* Trans. Yvonne Freccero. Baltimore: Johns Hopkins UP, 1965.

———. *Violence and the Sacred.* Trans. Patrick Gregory. Baltimore: Johns Hopkins UP, 1977.

Goldmann, Lucien. *The Hidden God.* London: Routledge and Kegan Paul, 1964.

Grant, Patrick. *The Transformation of Sin: Studies in Donne, Herbert, Vaughan, and Traherne.* Montreal: McGill-Queens UP, 1974.

Haller, William. *The Rise of Puritanism.* New York: Harper & Row, 1957.

Hooker, Richard. *Lawes of Ecclesiasticall Politie. Works.* Ed. John Keble. 7th ed., rev. R. W. Church and F. Paget. New York: Burt Franklin, 1970.

———. *A Learned Discourse of Justification.* London, 1586. Rpt. in *The Laws of Ecclesiastical Polity.* 2 vols. London: J. M. Dent & Sons, 1907.

Hughes, Richard E. *The Progress of the Soul: The Inner Career of John Donne.* New York: William Morrow, 1969.

Jackson, Robert S. *John Donne's Religious Vocation.* Evanston: Northwestern UP, 1970.

Jonson, Ben. "Conversations with William Drummond of Hawthornden." *Works.* Ed. C. H. Herford and Percy M. Simpson. Oxford: Clarendon, 1925. Vol. 1: 128–78

Lewalski, Barbara K. *Donne's "Anniversaries" and the Poetry of Praise: The Creation of a Symbolic Mode.* Princeton: Princeton UP, 1973.

———. *Protestant Poetics and the Seventeenth-Century Religious Lyric.* Princeton: Princeton UP, 1979.

Martin, Catherine Gimelli. *The Ruins of Allegory: "Paradise Lost" and the Metamorphosis of Epic Convention.* Durham: Duke UP, 1998.

Papazian, Mary Arshagouni. "Literary 'Things Indifferent': The Shared Augustinianism of Donne's *Devotions* and Bunyan's *Grace Abounding*." Frontain and Malpezzi 324–49.

Peterson, D. L. "John Donne's *Holy Sonnets* and the Anglican Doctrine of Contrition." *Studies in Philology* 56 (1959): 504–18.

Ricoeur, Paul. *The Symbolism of Evil.* Trans. Emerson Buchanan. New York: Harper & Row, 1967.

Rudnytsky, Peter. "'The Sight of God': Donne's Poetics of Transcendence." *Texas Studies in Literature and Language* 24.2 (1982): 185–207.

Sanders, Wilbur. *John Donne's Poetry.* Cambridge UP, 1970.

Scodel, Joshua. "John Donne and the Religious Politics of the Mean." Frontain and Malpezzi 45–80.

Sherwood, Terry G. "'Ego videbo': Donne and the Vocational Self." *John Donne Journal* 16 (1997): 59–113.

———. *Fulfilling the Circle: A Study of John Donne's Thought.* Toronto: U of Toronto P, 1984.

Shuger, Debora. *Habits of Thought in the English Renaissance.* Berkeley: U of California P, 1990.

Stachniewski, John. "John Donne: The Despair of the *Holy Sonnets.*" *English Literary History* 48 (1981): 677–705.

Stone, Lawrence. *The Crisis of the Aristocracy: 1558–1641.* Oxford: Clarendon, 1965.

Tayler, Edward W. *Donne's Idea of a Woman: Structure and Meaning in the "Anniversaries"* New York: Columbia UP, 1991.

Tillich, Paul. *A History of Christian Thought: From Its Judaic and Hellenistic Origins to Existentialism.* Ed. Carl E. Braaten. New York: Simon and Shuster, 1967.

Watson, Robert N. *The Rest Is Silence: Death as Annihilation in the English Renaissance* Berkeley: U of California P, 1994.

Wollman, Richard. "Donne's Obscurity: Memory and Manuscript Culture." *John Donne Journal* 16 (1997): 115–35.

Young, Robert V. "Donne's *Holy Sonnets* and the Theology of Grace." *"Bright Shootes of Everlastingness": The Seventeenth-Century Religious Lyric.* Ed. Claude J. Summers and Ted-Larry Pebworth. Columbia: U of Missouri P, 1987. 20–39.

8

From "Tav" to the Cross

John Donne's Protestant Exegesis and Polemics

CHANITA GOODBLATT

> I am not all here, I am here now preaching upon this text, and I am at home in my Library considering whether *S. Gregory*, or *S. Hierome*,[1] have said best of this text, before.
>
> Donne, *Sermons* 3:110

> The parts are, first, the Literall, the Historicall sense of the words; And then an emergent, a collaterall, an occasionall sense of them. The *explication* of the wordes, and the *Application, Quid tunc, Quid nunc*, How the words were spoken then, How they may be applied now, will be our two parts.
>
> Donne, *Sermons* 4:181

These quotations, taken from two of Donne's sermons on the Hebrew Bible,[2] distinctly evoke this Protestant preacher's method of biblical exegesis. The vivid depiction of Donne's scholarly searching for—and weighing of—revered interpretations of a biblical text is the concern of the first passage, with a particular emphasis on the early church fathers. The second passage directly declares his partaking of the Reformation's preoccupation with the literal or historical sense of the biblical text as a basis for a more contemporary, even figurative application of its significance (B. Hall 76–78). Taken in tandem, these quotations define the features of Donne's biblical hermeneutics, moving (though not necessarily in equivalence) between Catholic and Protestant and between the literal and the figurative.

The particular parameters of Donne's biblical hermeneutics remain, however, somewhat vague. Critical attention to this matter has occupied several seminal essays that focused on Donne's use of scholarly sources and traditions (Allen; Potter and Simpson 10:295–401) as well as on his deft balancing of the literal, historical exposition of the biblical text with the more medieval meanings of tropological (moral), anagogical (spiritual), and allegorical variants (Mueller 89–92; Quinn; Schleiner 185–200). It is, however, Evelyn M. Simpson's comment, made on Donne's series of six sermons on Psalm 6 (originally published as nos. 50–55 in *LXXX Sermons* of 1640),[3] which provides an apt key to understanding Donne's exegetical strategy. In her editions of both Donne's *Essays in Divinity* (xx–xxi) and his sermons (5:26–30), Simpson demonstrates that sermons 50–53 "contain passages which strongly resemble parts of the *Essays in Divinity*, written by Donne at some time before his ordination in 1615" (5:26). More than serving to give these sermons an early date of composition,[4] this resemblance is important—as Dennis Quinn has demonstrated (1962)—in establishing Donne's use of biblical commentaries. For as the (oftentimes) flamboyantly erudite, "sometimes meditative, sometimes homiletic" *Essays in Divinity* (M. Hall 425) are recast in Donne's sermons,[5] they provide the scholarly addenda to the no less erudite but more admonitive and hortatory demands of the later, public genre. In other words, the text and marginal notes in the *Essays in Divinity* indicate Donne's exegetical sources, which are often missing or less accurately recorded in the *Sermons*.

What is more, this attention to Donne's scholarly references will naturally remind an astute reader, as Don Cameron Allen has demonstrated (213), that the text and marginal notes of the Geneva Bible can also indicate the exegetical sources of Donne's sermons, for they are distinctly echoed in many of Donne's biblical readings. First published in 1560 by Protestant exiles from the Catholic Queen Mary's persecutions, the Geneva Bible contains three distinct types of marginal notes: those that provide a "Protestant, Calvinist, anti-Catholic" interpretation of the biblical text (Hammond 94), and which were accordingly suppressed by royal agreement in the King James Bible of 1611 (Anderson 368–72); those that provide alternate possibilities of translations for problematic Hebrew terms; and those that provide narrative and thematic links to other parts of the Bible. Together, these varied scholia open up a window onto the fascinating way in which Donne integrates various exegetical sources and traditions.

Drawing encouragement from Jeanne Shami's more recent and pivotal recommendation that "more work needs to be done on the complex exegetical strategies" used in Donne's sermons (15), the present essay therefore seeks to update and elaborate upon the terms of this critical discourse. Three major points distinguish this effort. First, that the discussion of Donne's study of the Hebrew Bible must include an investigation into the complex Jewish exegetical tradition as well as into its direct and indirect Christian transmission. Second, that any discussion of Donne's biblical hermeneutics must also encounter the textual and religious polemic—both Catholic versus Protestant and Jewish versus Christian—involved in biblical exegesis. And third, that a flexible understanding of exegetical connections should be maintained, reflecting the intertwined and resolutely dialogic character of both the Jewish and Christian exegetical projects.

Donne's Hebraism

It will be helpful at this point to quote somewhat at length David Daiches's insightful comment on the sources of the King James Bible:

> To determine exactly and in detail the sources of A.V. [the Authorized or King James Version] would be an impossible task, as the combinations of possible sources which would have yielded the same results are almost infinite in number.... Thus, though we know the declared principal sources of A.V., it is impossible to give definitely the source of an A.V. rendering which differs from most or all of the declared principal sources but yet agrees with, say, Tremellius and the commentary of David Kimchi;[6] or with Pagninus and the Targum;[7] or with Leo Juda[8] and one of the French versions.... [I]t is this wealth of possible sources for the rendering of any given difficult passage which makes any definite conclusions about A.V. sources impossible—at least impossible without a painstaking textual collation which no individual could hope to achieve in a lifetime. (171–73)

Daiches's comment is of importance to a reader of Donne's sermons, first and foremost because of the latter's reference to the very sources used by the King James translators. Whether it is the original Jewish source—the Targum ("Chaldee paraphrase," as Donne calls it)[9] as well as Solomon ben Isaac and Abraham Ibn Ezra,[10] who are medieval Jewish exegetes like Kimhi—or the mediating Christian Hebraists (Tremellius and Pagninus), Donne's continuous citing of such an array of textual authorities bespeaks his participation in a "tradition of literal exposition originating in the Middle Ages and culminating in the great exegetical works of the Reformation" (Rosenblatt 85). Second, Daiches's evaluation of the problematic nature of source criticism in the King James Bible adumbrates Allen's corresponding statement on the impossibility of tracing Donne's use of the "scholia of theologians" (214); in this manner these critics bring to the forefront the complex interweaving of sources, both cited and uncited, that characterizes this exegetical tradition.

Donne's standing as a Christian Hebraist is further substantiated when he is viewed within the context of Matt Goldish's important conception of Christian Hebraism in the sixteenth and seventeenth centuries. Goldish proposes a gradation of Hebrew knowledge, in which Donne certainly can be said to belong to the "third-order Hebraists . . . who could read *some* Hebrew, but who knew and used significant amounts of Jewish literature in Latin and vernacular translation" (18). Furthermore, as Goldish explains, "most English Hebraists of the seventeenth century either learned only the rudiments of the language in grammar school or university and studied further on their own or were complete autodidacts" (21). This accords well with the biographical information from Donne's letters concerning his adult studies of "the Eastern tongues," perhaps with the Hebraist Dr. John Layfield, himself one of the translators of the King James Bible.[11]

This cogent account of Christian Hebraism in England, albeit necessarily abridged in the present essay,[12] can put to rest a debate about Donne's knowledge of Hebrew, which has been brought to the forefront in an exchange between Anthony Raspa and Judith Scherer Herz. As Herz rightly points out (98), the biographical sources do indeed support the fact that Donne knew Hebrew, which is sustained by his continuous translations and explanations of single Hebrew words throughout his sermons (10:329–44). Yet Raspa just as rightly asserts that in Donne's prose works before the *Sermons*, "literally all of Donne's references to past and present Hebrew writers are to the Latin translations of mainly German, Italian and Spanish translators" (97). Though previously discussed in various essays (Allen; Potter and Simpson 10:295–344; Newman; Hill; Goodblatt, "Intertextual Discourse"), this exchange about Donne's Hebraic knowledge particularly calls for the solution provided by the conception of him as a third-order Christian Hebraist. Such a conception realigns the terms of the debate to allow for both Raspa and Herz to be correct in their assertions; there is nothing contradictory, after all, about Donne's possessing a basic, lexical grasp of the Hebrew language while acquiring the more sophisticated semantic nuances from commentators such as Nicholas of Lyre (heavily influenced by Solomon ben Isaac) as well as Johannes Reuchlin and Pietro Columna Galatinus (as Raspa notes).[13]

Donne is most assuredly a product of his time, exploring along with other Christian Hebraists Jerome's "Hebraica veritas" (Hebrew truth) of the Bible (Pelikan, Hotchkiss, and Price 17). This is clearly evident in his sermon on Job 16:18, preached in 1630 (and published as sermon 13 in *LXXX Sermons*), in which Donne comments as follows on the biblical phrase "O Earth cover not thou my blood":

> Difference of Expositions makes us stop here, upon this inquisition, in what affection *Iob* spake this. . . . Amongst our later men, *Cajetan*,[14] (and he, from a Rabbi of the Jews, *Aben Ezra*) takes this to be an adjuration of the Earth, as *Gregory* does, but not, as *Gregory*, does, in the person of Christ, but of *Iob* himselfe. . . . S. *Chrysostome*,[15] I think, was the first that gave light to the sense of this place. He saies, that such men, as are (as they thinke) overpunished, have naturally a desire, that the world knew their faults; that so, by comparing their faults with their punishments, there might arise some pitty and commiseration of their state. . . . This light, which *S. Chyrsostome* gave to this place, shined not out, (I think) till the Reformation. . . . But, since our Authors of the Reformation, have somewhat generally pursued that sense, (*Calvin* hath done so, and so *Tremellius*, and so *Piscator*[16] and many, many more) now, one Author of the Romane Church . . . the Capuchin *Bolduc*,[17] hath also pursued that sense. That sense is, that in this adjuration, or imprecation, *O Earth cover not thou my blood*; Blood is not literally bodily blood, but spirituall blood, the blood of the soule, exhausted by many, and hainous sins, such as they insimulated *Iob* of. (9:221–22)

In reading the biblical phrase, Donne responds to two (perceived) semantic gaps in the biblical text "that must be filled in" by the reader (Perry and Sternberg 276): the first concerns the identification of the speaker, while the second concerns the meaning of the word "blood." He makes his way through Jewish, Catholic, and Protestant explanations, ultimately combining their various readings to define the speaker as literally the prophet Job and "blood" as figuratively the "spiritual blood, the blood of the soule."

In his discussion of the "difference of Expositions" that characterizes the various exegetical responses to this text, Donne first turns to Pope Gregory I, one of the early church fathers. For this Catholic exegete, the semantic gap involves the identification of the speaker as Christ, which stands in opposition to the later Catholic Cajetan's returning to the Jewish Ibn Ezra's literal reading of the speaker as Job himself ("if I have seen it in my heart, God will not listen"; *Biblia Rabbinica*).[18] While Allen disparagingly remarks that Donne's reference to Ibn Ezra "comes through Cajetan and hardly counts" (220n. 5), this reference actually uncovers the line of transmission from the twelfth-century Jewish exegete to the sixteenth-century Catholic commentator, and then to the seventeenth-century Protestant preacher.[19] What is equally important is Donne's evocation (albeit circuitous) of the authority installed in Ibn Ezra's commentary, which in this rare instance in the *Sermons* lays bare one of the direct sources of Donne's own continuous reference to Jewish sources. In this manner Donne marks out the transition from a heavily symbolic, christological interpretation of the Hebrew Bible produced by the early church fathers to a more contemporary preference for the literal meaning of the biblical text; this even at the expense of producing at times a more perilous—because a more "Jewish"—reading that excises Gregory's decidedly Christian one.

In a subsequent passage of this sermon, Donne crosses Catholic and Protestant partisan lines. For the early church father John Chrysostom, the semantic gap in understanding the biblical text involves the interpretation of the word "blood" as "faults"—most likely in conjunction with the previous passage "not for any injustice in my hands" (Job 16:17). Donne ascertains that his audience is quite aware of the mistaken readings of interim commentators by stating that this meaning "shined not out till the Reformation." He further substantiates this reading by recognizing a shared exegetical concern—a "pursuing of that sense"—that links Chrysostom with the seventeenth-century Catholic commentator Bolduc, as well as more generally with Protestant commentators and translators of the sixteenth and seventeenth centuries (Calvin, Tremellius, and Piscator). Finally, Donne's own rhetorical extension of this meaning continues this figurative interpretation by focusing on "the spirituall blood . . . exhausted by many, and hainous sins."

Donne's loose tracing out of shared exegetical concerns can readily include the explanations put forward by both Ibn Ezra and the Geneva Bible; the Jewish exegete interprets "blood" as "wickedness" *(Biblia Rabbinica)*, while the marginal note of the Geneva Bible interprets it as "sinne."[20] Like the translators of the King James Bible, those of the Geneva Bible made constant and consistent—though definitely uncited—use of the Hebrew biblical text and of Jewish exegetes (Daiches 178–81; Greenslade 155–59). What is jointly marked here is a particular interpretation of the biblical text, one that elides the violence and vengeance associated with the solely literal image of uncovered blood[21] to emphasize instead the continued Jobian drama of suffering and sin. In summary, then, Donne's preaching on this verse from Job confirms his evocation of the authority of Jewish exegesis. What is more, his intertwining of Jewish, Catholic, and Protestant interpretations of the Hebrew Bible invites a paraphrase of Daiches: Is there a declared principal source of the sixteenth- and seventeenth-century interpretations? Is it actually possible to give definitely the source of this rendering? Donne quite carefully seems to indicate that there is not always a ready answer.

This Is That Name

There is no more interesting way to examine such complicated exegetical interconnections than to focus on Donne's discussion of the semantic and christological implications of God's ineffable name, (mis)pronounced as "Jehovah." Not surprisingly, Donne's fullest treatment of this name is to be found in several of his sermons on Psalm 6. For echoing as they do the scholarship of the *Essays in Divinity*, and preached as they were before "the smaller, homogeneous congregation of lawyers and other learned men" of Lincoln's Inn (J. Shapiro 55), this series of sermons comprises one of the "high points" in Donne's use and exploration of Hebrew language and exegesis (Allen 214; Simpson, *Psalms and Gospels* 5n. 13).

In two corresponding passages from the *Essays in Divinity* (25) and from sermon 50 on Psalm 6:1 (5:324–25)—which are rather too long and laborious for quoting—Donne concentrates on the lexical and semantic implications of what he correctly terms the "Name of four letters"—the tetragrammaton—"YHWH." This is the sacred name of God in the Hebrew Bible (erroneously pronounced as "Jehovah"), which the translators of both the King James and Geneva Bibles reverently write throughout Psalm 6 as "Lord" (most probably following the Jewish custom of preserving the holiness of this name; see Hirsch).[22] The form and meaning of the tetragrammaton is explained on the basis of God's designation of himself in Exodus 3:14 as "**Ehyeh**-asher-**Ehyeh**"—variously "I Am That I Am," "I Am Who I Am," or "I Will Be What I Will Be" (*Tanakh* 88). This wordplay on the Hebrew root "hyh/hwh/hvh" (to be/exist) accounts for God's designation as "YHWH," generated from this root, and confirms that his "characteristic note consists in being, or The Being simply" (Maas, "Jehova").

This seeming digression into the linguistic underpinnings of the tetragrammaton plunges the readers of Donne's prose works into the intellectual milieu of Christian Hebraism, in which linguistic study and strategy led to a more figurative and Christian reading of the Hebrew Bible. This is clearly evident in a passage from sermon 52 in *LXXX Sermons*. Here Donne is concerned with demonstrating the lexical and semantic connection of Jesus' name with the tetragrammaton. In this sermon, he relates to the appeal to God in Psalm 6:4, "O Lord save me":

> But who is that? what Saviour? Doubtlesse he that is proclaimed by God, in the same Prophet [marginal note: Esay 62.11], *Behold, the Lord hath proclaimed unto the end of the world, Behold thy salvation commeth*. For, that word which that Prophet uses there, and this word, in which *David* presents this last Petition here, is in both places *Iashang*, and *Iashang* is the very word, from which the name of *Iesus* is derived; so that *David* desires here, that salvation which *Esay* proclaimed there, salvation in the Saviour of the world, Christ Jesus, and an interest in the assurance of his merits. (5:377)

The name "Jesus" is the Latin form of the Greek "Iesous," a transliteration of the Hebrew "**Ye**i**shu**'**a**," which in turn is a shortened form of the biblical name "**Ye**ho**shu**'**a**" (Joshua; see Maas, "Jesus Christ"). This biblical name is constructed from the first part of the tetragrammaton, "YH[WH]," and the Hebrew root "ysh'a" (salvation), together meaning "God saves." Donne extends this discussion in sermon 52 to include two other forms of "ysh'a" (in his transliteration, "Iashang"),[23] comparing "**ho**sh**i**'**ei**ni" of Psalm 6:4 ("save me"; second person, singular, masculine imperative) with "**yish**'**ei**kh" of Isaiah 62:11 ("your [Daughter of Zion's] salvation"; possessive or genitive form). He thereby reads the Hebrew Bible as being of one Christian piece, declaring "that *David* desires here [Ps. 6:4], that salvation which *Esay* proclaimed there, salvation in the Saviour of the world, Christ Jesus."[24] In this way Donne distinctly echoes the text of the Geneva Bible, which translates and personalizes the term "yish'eikh" in Isaiah 62:11 as "thy Saviour." It further appends a marginal note to this verse that explicitly designates this term as "salvation by Christ."[25] In Donne's sermon this wordplay serves quite obviously to Christianize the Hebrew Bible's vision of salvation in an immediate, Protestant way, presenting Jesus as grammatically the subject of Isaiah's prophecy and theologically the object of David's prayer.

Donne's use of exegetical sources is deeply invested in a religious polemic that resonates first and foremost with the Protestant concern with biblical translation. This is evident, for instance, in Donne's discussion of the title "Zaphnat-Pa'aneah," given to Joseph by Pharaoh (Genesis 41:45). In the *Essays in Divinity* Donne simply notes two different explanations for this title: "Expounder of secrets" and "Saviour of the world" (46). In a second passage from sermon 52, however, he makes use of the disparity between two interpretive traditions to criticize the Latin Vulgate Bible—in his words "that Translation":

> A Saviour of all the world, of all the conditions in the world, of all times through the world, of all places of the world, such a Saviour is no man called, but Christ Jesus only. For when it is said that *Pharaoh* called *Ioseph*, *Salvatorem mundi*, A Saviour of the world [marginal note: Gen. 41.45] . . . there is a manifest error in that Translation, which cals *Ioseph* so, for that name which was given to *Ioseph* there, in that language in which it was given, doth truly signifie *Revelatorum Secretorum*, and no more, a Revealer, a Discoverer, a Decypherer of secret and mysterious things; according to the occasion, upon which that name was then given, which was the Decyphering, the Interpreting of *Pharaohs* Dreame. (5:378)

The Vulgate translation of "Zaphnat-Pa'aneah" is most probably founded on the Greek Septuagint's translation[26] of Egyptian terminology (Ahituv). Alternatively, the Geneva Bible's marginal note explains this term as "the expounder of secrets," at once echoing Solomon ben Isaac's commentary—which clarifies it as "the explainer of hidden things" *(Biblia Rabbinica)*—and calling forth Donne's own final elucidation. Revealed here is Donne's insistence on "Hebraica veritas"—in his own words, "in that language in which it was given"—as a recourse against the Latin text's appropriation of Christ's status as "Salvatorem mundi" for the Israelite Joseph. Ultimately this highly probable reliance on the Protestant Geneva Bible enables Donne to read the Hebrew Psalm 6:4 as an appeal to Christ ("hoshi'eini"; save me) as being the sole "Saviour of all the world."

De Verbo Mirifico

Resounding throughout Donne's discussion of God's nature as "Jehovah" is also a second polemic, one in which his anti-Jewish and anti-Catholic attitudes converge. Distasteful though they are to the modern reader, these sentiments are threaded throughout his sermons, showing him for better and for worse to be a man of his times. Yet it is this very attention to Donne's contemporary situation that can help to confront and clarify (and perhaps caution against) what James Shapiro, in his discussion of representations of Jews in early modern England, presents as the "cultural anxieties felt by English men and women at a time when their nation was experiencing extraordinary social, religious, and political turbulence" (1). What is more, in the context of the present essay, such attention can confront the complex intellectual legacy of Christian Hebraism, that matrix where—in spite of these anxieties—Jewish, Catholic, and Protestant ideas, texts, and interests meet.

Shapiro himself has pointedly, albeit only in passing, noted instances of Donne's refutation of the Jews (e.g., 2, 39, 107, 175), especially in its worst semblance as an accusation of their ritual murder of Christians.[27] Care should be taken to consider the particular circumstances in which the sermon containing this accusation was preached, at St. Paul's on Christmas of 1625, following closely upon an epidemic of the bubonic plague in London (6:31–35). It is reasonable to ask if Donne in this instance is submitting—and indeed contributing—to the general hysteria and scandalous belief that the Jews caused the plague by poisoning wells in order to wipe out Christians (Breuer 140–42). Such a consideration of the wider cultural anxieties (to adopt Shapiro's term) about Jews and ritual murder, possibly evoked by the plague, can partially answer the astonishment (though not the dismay) expressed about Donne by Potter and Simpson (6:35–36), and Shapiro (12). It can also circumscribe the significance of this blood libel in Donne's sermons as a whole, by the absence of a reference to it in his other plague sermons,[28] or in any other of the extant sermons. This ultimately allows Donne's reader to concentrate more fully on the complex interaction between the Christian's problematic conception of the Jew and the Christian Hebraist's use of Jewish knowledge.

Donne's direct reference in the *Essays in Divinity* to Johannes Reuchlin's book on Christian Kabbalah, *De Verbo Mirifico* (On the Wonder-Working Word; 1494), particularly demonstrates such an interaction:

> . . . there are two Names proper, and expressing his Essence: One imposed by us, *God*; The other taken by God, the Name of *four* letters; for the name, *I am* is derived from the same root. . . . Of which Name [marginal note: Tetragra.] one says [marginal note: Reuclin.de verbo Mirifico 1.2.[2] c.6], that as there is a secret property by which we are

changed into God, (referring, I think to that, *We are made partakers of the godly nature* [marginal note: 2 Peter 1:4])²⁹ so God hath a certain name, to which he hath annexed himself to be present. This is the Name, which the *Jews* stubbornly deny ever to have been attributed to the Messias in the Scriptures. (24)

De Verbo Mirifico is composed of three conversations—a more appropriate description would be disputes, leading to penance and baptism—among a Christian, an Epicurean philosopher, and a Jew (Oberman 74). In the marginal notes of the *Essays in Divinity* (24–25), Donne clearly marks *De Verbo Mirifico* as the source for his statement that "there is a secret property by which we are changed into God"; he also closely paraphrases Reuchlin's words that "the master of eternity . . . is striving . . . through a hidden property, to transform into himself by digesting so that man should migrate into God and God should dwell in man" (Reuchlin 42).³⁰ Significantly, this explanation of the mysterious relationship between God and humankind is placed in the mouth of the Jew Baruchias, who is quite likely modeled after Reuchlin's own Jewish teacher, the court physician Jakob ben Jehiel Loans (Oberman 73–75). Taking this in tandem with the second marginal note, which raises the connection between Reuchlin and the second epistle of Peter, Donne thereby effectively encompasses Jewish occult, theosophic thought within a Christian text and context.

That the Protestant preacher shares in the definition of God's nature as sounded out through the Jew Baruchias can be demonstrated by looking at another passage from Book Two of *De Verbo Mirifico* (Reuchlin 53–54): "This name [Ehyeh] Plato had learned in that so-long peregrination of his among the Assyrians, which in the end he translated for the Greeks in two letters 'On' [öv; being]. For in the *Timaeus* he says this: "Therefore, according to my opinion, one must first distinguish what 'On' is; it is the being that forever is, but has no origin."³¹ Baruchias discusses God as "Ehyeh," who is "the fundamental cause, the principle and measure, the Creator, and means the simplest essence in which all is contained, the endowed of all substance" (Maxwell-Stuart 208). Such a description accords quite well with Donne's statement in the lines quoted from *Essays in Divinity*, as well as his statement from sermon 50 that "the name of Iehovah, [is] the name of Essence, and Being" (5:325). Paraphrasing Daiches once again, the acknowledgment of Donne's use of *De Verbo Mirifico* may not be sufficient to declare it as the sole source of such a discussion, but it definitely makes it necessary to consider Reuchlin's influence on and affinity with Donne's emphasis on God as "Essence and Being."

It is crucial to recognize that this influence raises issues concerning the transmission of knowledge within a Christian Hebraist text. The mimetic level of the discourse, which presents Baruchias as the speaker, emphasizes the heterogeneous origins of the Jew's statement about God's nature; his words at once evoke Platonic authority and support the Jewish belief that places the roots of Plato's concepts, and indeed all Greek philosophy—in Judaism and in the cultures of other eastern (e.g., Assyrian) nations (Altman 854; Klausner 236). The narrative level, on the other hand, emphasizes the uncertain origins of such knowledge; is it the Jewish physician who is being quoted as reading Plato, or is it the Christian author Reuchlin who is responsible for such knowledge? As in Donne's evocation of Ibn Ezra through Cajetan, such ambiguity reveals the intellectual hybridism in the Christian Hebraist text, as well as the circuitous routes by which Jewish (and classical) knowledge was transmitted.

In his repeated concern with "Hebraica veritas," Donne participates in what can be described as a "war of the words," drawing out the semantic and theological consequences of the Christian's accusation to the Jew in *De Verbo Mirifico* that "the saving power of the Word [the pentagrammaton][32] has forsaken you: chosen us: accompanies us" (Reuchlin 29).[33] Thus again in sermon 50, Donne repeats—and intensifies—his statement quoted from the *Essays in Divinity*, adding phrases fraught with anti-Jewish polemic by writing: "This is the name [Jehovah] which the Jews falsly, but peremptorily, (for falshood lives by its peremptorinesse, and feeds and armes it selfe with peremptorinesse) deny ever to have been attributed to the *Messias*, in the Scriptures" (5:324).

In a subsequent passage in sermon 50 Donne turns this polemic against the pagan Romans and the Catholics by playing cleverly on the meaning of Jehovah as "Essence and Being":

> *David* therefore comes to God *In nomine totali; in nomine integrali;* He considers God totally, entirely, altogether; Not altogether, that is, confusedly, but altogether, that is, in such a Name as comprehends all his Attributes, all his Power upon the world, and all his benefits upon him. The Gentiles were not able to consider God so; not so entirely, not altogether; but broke God in pieces . . . a clap of thunder made a *Iupiter*; a tempest at sea made a *Neptune*, an earthquake made a *Pluto* . . .[34] Neither as the Gentiles did, nor as some ignorants of the Roman church do, that there must be a stormie god, S. *Nicholas*, and a plaguie god, S. *Rook*,[35] and a sheepshearing god, and a swineherd god, a god for every Parish, a god for every occupation, God forbid. Acknowledg God to be the Author of

thy Being; find him so at the spring-head, and then thou shalt easily trace him, by the branches, to all that belongs to thy well-being. (5:325)

For Donne the name "Jehovah" is an integrative one, meaning "a Name as comprehends all his Attributes." In contrast to this integrative concept of God, Donne denigrates the atomistic concept equally upheld, in his mind, by the pre-Christian Romans ("Gentiles") and the Catholics ("ignorants of the Roman church"). For their similar insistence upon distinguishing a god by a single natural or occupational attribute contravenes Donne's more polemically Protestant explanation of the encompassing divine name and nature. At the very center of his rhetoric stands (somewhat surprisingly for a metaphysical poet) an organic metaphor (Wimsatt), in which Donne introduces and underlines a multifaceted similitude between God and a "springhead." This similitude easily includes their shared natural life-giving potential and universal dissemination, as well as their more figurative and even symbolic meanings such as rebirth, purification, and salvation. Yet Donne then qualifies the emotional power of this metaphor with the almost roguish interjection of "God forbid" and with the borderline pun of "Being/well-being." Apparent here is therefore a convergence of interest between Donne's fascination (as a Christian Hebraist) with the meaning and power of words and his sharp wit as a metaphysical poet.

From "Tav" to the Cross

A passage from another sermon from the series on Psalm 6, published as number 54 in *LXXX Sermons*, provides a fitting conclusion to the present discussion of Donne's Protestant exegesis and polemics. Dealing as it does with the iconic and theological transformation of the Hebrew letter "tav" into the Cross, it further reiterates the move in Donne's reading of the biblical text among Jewish, Catholic, and Protestant interpretations and between the literal and the figurative. What is more, Donne once again takes care to expose the lines of exegesis that support his polemic. This is very much in evidence in his detailed discussion of the Hebrew root "**an**ah" (sigh, moan, groan), which will be quoted at some length:

> This sighing, this groaning, expressed in this word, *Anach, Gemitus*, is *Vox Turturis. Turtur gemit*; It is that voyce, that sound which the Turtle [turtledove] gives.... Then *Vox Turturis audita in terra nostra*, sayes Christ to

his Spouse [marginal note: Can. 2.12], *The voyce of the Turtle is heard in our Land;* And so he sayes to thy soule, This voyce of the Turtle, these sighs of thy penitent soul, are heard *in terra nostra*, in our Land, in the Kingdome of heaven.

And when he heares this voyce of this Turtle, these sighs of thy soule, then he puts thy name also into that List, which he gave to his messenger, (in which Commission this very word of our Text, *Anach*, is used) *Sinabis signum super frontibus virorum suspirantium & gementium* [marginal note: Ezek. 9:4], Upon all their fore-heads, that sigh and groane, imprint my mark; Which is ordinarily conceived by the Ancients to have been the letter *Tau;* of which though *Calvin* assigne a usefull, and a convenient reason, that they were marked with this letter *Tau*, which is the last letter of the Hebrew Alphabet, in signe, that though they were in estimation of the world, the most abject, and the outcasts thereof, yet God set his mark upon them, with a purpose to raise them; yet *S. Hierome*, and the Ancients for the most part assigne that for the reason, why they were marked with that letter, because that letter had the forme of the Crosse . . . so God imprinted upon them, that sighed, and mourned, that *Tau*, that letter, which had the forme of the Crosse, that it might be an evidence, that all their crosses shall be swallowed in his Crosse, their sighs in his sighs, and their agonies in his. (8:197–98)

On the basis of the shared Hebrew root "**anah**," Donne lexically and semantically connects the phrase "yagati be'**anh**ati" (I am weary with my groaning) from Psalm 6:6 with that from Ezekiel 9:4, "vehitvita tav 'al mitshot hane'**enah**im vehan'**enah**im" (put a mark on the foreheads of the men who moan and groan; *Tanakh* 903). The root "**anah**" thus appears both in the term "be'**anh**ati" (my groaning) and in the term "hane'**enah**im" (those who groan). How or where Donne has learned to connect these two verses is uncertain (though this root does appear in the margins of the Complutensian Polyglot for Ezekiel 9:4; see Zuñiga). Yet certainly this link provides the opportunity for his creation of a semantic bridge between the two biblical texts, which includes the Hebrew phrase "vehitvita tav" (set a mark) in its span. Thus the dual meaning of the word "tav" evokes for Jews and Christians a critical semantic gap in the biblical text—whether it is simply a "mark or sign" or whether it specifically denotes the last letter of the Hebrew alphabet (ת). This gap is particularly significant for Christians, as the original form of the letter "tav" is a cross turned on its side (X = †; Chomsky 87).

Quite evident in this passage is Donne's Christianization of the Hebrew text. This is seen first and foremost as he echoes the Geneva Bible in designating Christ as the agent of the biblical narrative in *Canticles* (or *Song of Songs*), with the Genevan introductory argument to this book explicitly Christianizing an earlier Jewish interpretation. The rabbinic biblical exegesis (or midrash) reads the *Song of Songs* "as an allegorical glorification of the relation between God and Israel" (Theodor 564), while the Geneva translators declare that "in this Song, Salomen by most sweete and comfortable allegories and parables describeth the perfite love of Iesus Christ, the true Salomen and King of peace, and the faithfull soule or his Church, which he has sanctified and appoynted to be his spouse, holy, chaste, and without reprehension." Fully developing this allegorical meaning, Donne interprets and extends this biblical pastoral to include the members of his Christian congregation, whose "sighs of thy penitent soul" are indeed those heard by Christ. Finally, Donne follows Jerome's explanation of the mark as "that letter [which] had the forme of the Crosse," thereby iconically fashioning the central symbol of Christian suffering and salvation out of the materiality of the Hebrew language.

Yet Donne does not remain content with this essentially allegorical explanation. Not only does he make explicit use of Calvin's more semantically oriented clarification, but—but by stretching taut the loose lines of transmission—the reader of this sermon can also attend to similar explanations put forth by the medieval Jewish exegete David Kimhi and by the Geneva Bible. This is not at all surprising, since Kimhi's biblical commentary was not only "regarded by [Catholic and Protestant] Christian scholars of the time as the work of the most competent of the Jewish grammarians"[36] (Daiches 173), but as Daiches continues, "there is strong evidence for concluding that the Geneva Bible translators were the first of the English translators to make considerable use at first hand of the Hebrew commentary of David Kimhi" (180). In the present instance, these two implicit sources join Calvin in providing for Donne a counterbalance to the Catholic iconography put forth by Jerome.

The Jewish exegete is quite naturally concerned with the function and semantics of this sign, quoting a talmudic discussion in which two explanations are presented: the "tav" as a protective marking of the righteous against their "destroyers"; and the distinctive marking of the righteous and the wicked by different verbs of which the letter "tav" is a prefix (second-person form).[37] These explanations echo forth in the Protestant commentaries, adumbrating both the attempt to "set forth the plain sensible meaning of a passage" (B. Hall 87) and the preoccupation with the issue of "God's *Election* from all eternity of certain persons to salvation and eternal life" (Lewalski 16). Thus Donne explicitly brings Calvin's explanation that the final letter "tav" marks the "most abject, and the outcasts" to be raised by God. Similarly, the Genevan translators echo Calvin in their comment about "Gods children, whom he marketh to salvation" (marginal note on Ezekiel 9:4), also significantly adding another note that more literally explains the biblical phrase "set a marke" as meaning "marke with [the letter] Thau." Donne himself can therefore be seen as intertwining the concepts of Catholic iconology and Protestant election in his own highly rhetorical and emotionally charged explanation (in the passage quoted above) that "all their crosses shall be swallowed in his Crosse, their sighs in his sighs, and their agonies in his."

Such interpretive differences are not just slight turns of wording. Though seemingly comprising minor examples of exegetic strategy, they raise major questions about interpretation and theology in Donne's sermons. Does he, for instance, maintain an intractable choice of Christian versus Jewish conceptions and interpretations, or Protestant versus Catholic ones? As has been seen in the necessarily small number of examples discussed here, one may cautiously say that he does not. From this question can be derived a second one: How can Donne's often anti-Jewish and anti-Catholic attitudes be reconciled with his constant use of their knowledge? Working once again from limited examples, one can answer: only through a cautious but in no way complaisant understanding of historical and cultural circumstances.

In this essay, then, an initial step has been taken in reconstructing the intellectual, scholarly, and inevitably religious context of Donne's Protestant exegesis and polemics. This is a baffling and perhaps endless task, to be undertaken in curiosity and continued in anticipation of shedding light on the circuitous route by which Donne fuses out of the myriad Jewish, Catholic, and Protestant interpretations a singular way of reading the biblical text that reflects his personal and theological quandaries.

Notes

I would like to thank the following persons for their gracious assistance in my research efforts: Mayer I. Gruber, Daniel Lasker, Victor Avigdor Hurowitz, Georges Slama, and Pinhas Ziv of Ben-Gurion University; Judith Tydor Baumel of Bar-Ilan University; Seth Jerchower of the Center for Judaic Studies, University of Pennsylvania; and Father David Nyhouse of the Pontifical Biblical Institute, Jerusalem. Work on this paper was facilitated by a fellowship from the Center for Judaic Studies in January–February 2000. Earlier versions of this paper were presented at the John Donne Society Conferences in 1995 and 1997.

1. Pope Gregory I (c. 540–604) was one of the early church fathers. In his sermons he presented "mostly simple, popular expositions of Scripture" (Hudleston). Hierome (Jerome: 342–420), also was one of the early church fathers. He translated the Hebrew and Christian Bibles into Latin from the original Hebrew and Greek, also composing commentaries and sermons on these Bibles (Saltet).

2. Sermon 3:3 (on Job 19:26) was preached at Lincoln's Inn, possibly during Easter term 1620. It is number 14 in *Fifty Sermons*. Sermon 4:7 (on Judges 5:20) was preached at "the Crosse" on September 15, 1622, and published separately in that year.

3. These sermons were published in the Potter and Simpson edition in volumes 5 (nos. 16–19), 6 (no. 1), and 8 (no. 8).

4. I. A. Shapiro and Paul Stanwood argue persuasively, supporting Simpson's earliest opinion (*Prose Works* 351) that all Donne's sermons on Psalm 6, though probably reshaped and preached on later occasions, were first preached at Lincoln's Inn in the early period of his ministry (1616–22).

5. Marotti has perceptively remarked that the *Essays in Divinity* can be seen to comprise "a piece of mock- or comical-scholarship, parodying the methods of scriptural exegesis and mystical writing" (91).

6. John Immanuel Tremellius (1510–80) converted from Judaism to Protestantism. He became King's Reader of Hebrew at Cambridge and subsequently professor of Hebrew studies at Heidelberg. Between 1569 and 1579 he translated the Hebrew and Christian Bibles into Latin (Daiches 138; Potter and Simpson 10:400). David Kimhi (c. 1160–c. 1235), was a Provençal-Jewish grammarian and biblical commentator. He is more popularly known as "Radak," an acronym created from the first letters of his Hebrew name: Rabbi David Kimhi. He stressed scientific philological analysis and deemphasized homiletical digression. He also wrote a philological treatise, *Mikhlol*, which contained a Hebrew grammar and dictionary (Talmage).

7. Santes Pagninus (c. 1470–1541), a Dominican, translated the Hebrew and Greek Bibles into Latin (1527); the merit of this translation "lies in its literal adherence to the Hebrew, which won for it the preference of contemporary rabbis" (Reilly). Targum (Hebrew: "translation") is the term used for the Aramaic translations or paraphrases of the Hebrew Bible. The official Targum was included in the Complutensian Polyglot (Zuñiga).

8. Leo Judä (1482–1542) was a German-Swiss Protestant. He took part in producing the Zurich translation of the Bible into German (1524–29) and also produced a Latin translation of the Bible in 1543 (Daiches 20, 138; Loewe 40).

9. Potter and Simpson explain that Aramaic was generally called Chaldee, due to the mistaken belief that the language spoken in Chaldea in the days of the prophet Daniel was biblical Aramaic (10:312).

10. Solomon ben Isaac (1040–1105) was a [northern] French-Jewish grammarian and biblical commentator. He is more popularly known as "Rashi," an acronym created from the first letters of his Hebrew name: Rabbi Shlomo ben Yitshak. The main distinguishing characteristic of his commentary is a compromise between the literal and the midrashic (rabbinic biblical exegesis) interpretation. When basing his comment on the Midrash he chose from the available material, those closest to the literal interpretation of the biblical text (Grossman). Abraham Ibn Ezra (1089–1164) was a Spanish-Jewish grammarian and biblical commentator. He focused on establishing independently the literal meaning of the biblical text, but following the explanation of the talmudic sages in interpreting the legislative part of the Pentateuch (Preschel 1166).

11. In the letter dated July 17, 1613, Donne had written to an unknown addressee: "Except demonstrations (and perchance there are very few of them) I find nothing without perplexities. I am grown more sensible of it by busying myself a little in search of the Eastern tongues, where a perpetual perplexity in the words cannot choose but cast a perplexity upon the things" (Gosse 16). Bald suggests (281) that Donne studied Hebrew with Layfield (d. 1617), who belonged to the group of King James translators that met at Westminster and translated Isaiah to Malachi. Bald bases his assumption on Donne's letter to Sir Henry Goodyear, dated March 14, 1614, in which he writes: ". . . and ask you leave to make this which I am fain to call my good day, so much truly good, as to spend the rest of it with Dr. Layfield, who is, upon my summons, at this hour come to me" (Gosse 39).

12. For more detailed discussions of Christian Hebraism in England, see Jones and Shoulson.

13. Nicholas of Lyre (c. 1270–c. 1349) was a French Franciscan who composed the biblical commentaries *Postillae Perpetuae in Universam S. Scripturam* (1322–30). These commentaries made extensive use of the works of Rashi (Solomon ben Isaac), sharing a mutual emphasis on the literal-historical—rather than allegorical—meaning of the biblical text (Goodblatt, "Christian Hebraists" 111). Donne owned a copy of the Vulgate Bible in six volumes, containing Nicholas of Lyre's commentary (Keynes 279; Potter and Simpson 2:2–3; 3:43). Johannes Reuchlin (1455–1522), a German Hebraist, was one of the architects of the Christian Kabbalah. Among other books, Reuchlin published *De Rudimentis Hebraicis* (1506), comprising a Hebrew grammar and lexicon, and two books on the Kabbalah, *De Verbo Mirifico* (1494) and *De Arte Cabalistica* (1517) (Silverman and Scholem). Pietro

Columna Galatinus (Peter Galatin, 1460–1540) was an Italian theologian, Franciscan friar, and Christian Kabbalist (Potter and Simpson 10:393; Silverman 262).

14. Tommaso de Vio Gaetani Cajetan (1469–1534) was a Dominican cardinal, philosopher, theologian, and exegete. He translated much of the Bible into Latin and wrote commentaries on many books of the Bible (Potter and Simpson 10:390). Of his biblical translation it is explained that "chiefly with rabbinical assistance, it is said, being himself unversed in Hebrew, and with the aid of current Greek versions he prepared a literal translation of the Bible" (Volz).

15. John Chrysostom (c. 347–407), one of the early church fathers, was a renowned preacher. He is the chief representative of the exegetical principles of the School of Antioch, which supported the grammatico-historical method, in opposition to allegorical and mystical interpretation (Baur).

16. John Calvin (1509–64) was a French Protestant theologian of the Reformation. He pursued the study of law, the classics, and Hebrew, as well as systematizing Protestant thought in his *Institutes of the Christian Religion*. On Tremellius, see note 6. Johannes Fischer Piscator (1546–1626) was a German Protestant theologian. He composed a Hebrew grammar and a translation of the Bible (Potter and Simpson 10:397).

17. Jacques Bolduc (d. 1646) was a French Capuchin (Franciscan) and superior of several monasteries, as well as a Christian Hebraist who wrote a commentary on Job (Potter and Simpson 10:390; Loewe 24).

18. The first printed Rabbinic Bible was published by Daniel Bomberg (1483–1553) in 1517 and included the Hebrew text with Targum and rabbinic commentaries (hence the name). The second edition was printed in 1525 and added the Masorah (critical notes on the external form of the biblical text; see Levias); this edition became the textus receptus, "the standard form of the Masoretic text for subsequent scholarship by both Jews and Christians" (Pelikan, Hotchkiss, and Price 106).

19. Whether Donne could—and did—read the medieval Jewish commentaries of Ibn Ezra and Rashi is in doubt. Though both Allen (219) and Potter and Simpson (10:307, 314) suggest that Donne read the Rabbinic Bible, in which these commentaries were readily found, Donne himself makes no mention of this book. In addition, there is little evidence that he would have been capable of deciphering the singular Hebrew script in which these commentaries were printed.

20. The sixteenth-century spelling and punctuation of the Geneva Bible have been preserved in all the quotations brought in this essay. Exceptions are the modernization in the use of long "s," i/j, u/v, and the vowel-macron replacing a succeeding "n" or "m." The complete note reads: "Let my sinne be knowen if I be such a sinner as mine adversaries accuse me, and let me finde no favour."

240 · Chanita Goodblatt

21. Reichert explains (84): "The customary interpretation of this passionate outburst is: May my blood lie exposed that it may call for vengeance. Blood not covered by the earth was understood to have been violently shed, and was regarded as calling for revenge on the murderer (Genesis 4:10; Ezekiel 24:7–8)."

22. The problem of pronouncing "YHWH" seems to have resulted from a variety of factors: its closely guarded use within temple ritual; the desire to avoid profaning the tetragrammaton by voicing it; and the substitution of the word "Adonai" (My Lord) in study and public readings of the Bible (Hirsch; Maas, "Jehova"). As originally the Hebrew biblical text was solely consonantal, there was little written indication about how to pronounce the tetragrammaton; moreover, the vowel points of an alternate designation for God—"Adonai" (My Lord)—were eventually added in the marginal notes of the Masoretic text to indicate such a substitution (Hirsch; Maas, "Jehova"). It is then but a step to the Christian use of these alternate vowels with the original consonants to create the name "Jehovah."

23. Potter and Simpson make note of "a curious feature of Donne's transliteration" in the use of "gn" to represent the Hebrew guttural "ayin" (10:309, 329), represented here by the final "a." The root "ysh'a" is listed in the margin of the Complutensian Polyglot (Zuñiga). Donne explicitly demonstrates his use of the Complutensian and Antwerp (or Kings; see Allen 210) Polyglots in sermon 70 of *LXXX Sermons* (3:232).

24. Chamberlin explains that Donne upheld the authenticity of David's authorship of the Psalms, following the views of the Roman Catholic Church rather than those of the Calvinist commentators on the Bible (137).

25. The complete note reads: "Ye Prophets and Ministers shew the people of this their deliverance: which was chiefly meant of our salvation by Christ, Zach. 9,9. matth. 21,5."

26. The Septuagint was the first translation of the Hebrew Bible, made into popular Greek. According to tradition, it was solicited by Ptolemy II Philadelphius, king of Egypt (287–247 B.C.E.). The name "Septuagint" (seventy) comes from the tradition that seventy-two Jewish interpreters, inspired by God and working separately, produced identical translations (Heeren).

27. Donne writes: ". . . this barbarous and inhumane custome of theirs [the Jews], that they always keep in readinesse the blood of some Christian, with which they anoint the body of any that dyes amongst them, with these words, if Jesus Christ were the Messias, then may the blood of this Christian avail thee to salvation . . ." (6:334).

28. Sermon 6:18: "A Sermon Preached at St. Dunstan's. January 15, 1625 [1625/6]. The First Sermon after our Dispersion, by the Sickness." In addition, as Stanwood states, "it is very probable that he [Donne] composed, or preached, or revised" his sermons on Psalm 6 at the time of the plague (77).

29. Donne actually paraphrases this biblical verse. The Geneva and King James Bibles read similarly, "ye may become [Geneva Bible: should be] partakers of the divine nature."

30. In Latin: "verumetiam proprietate occulata in seipsum digerendo transformare: ut et homo migret in deum et deus habitet in homine." The fifteenth-century spelling of Reuchlin's Latin text has been preserved in all the quotations. Exceptions are the modernization in the use of long "s," i/j, u/v, and the vowel-macron replacing a succeeding "n" or "m."

31. In Latin: "Hoc nomen [Ehyeh] Plato in sua illa tam longa penes Assyrios peregrinatione didicerat: quod ad grëcos tandom duabus literis: On transtulit. Nam in Timæo sic ait: Est igitur secundum meam opinionem primo distinguendum quid sit On: id est ens quod semper est: ortum vero non habet . . ." The *Timaeus* is one of the later, post-*Republic* dialogues, it and "stands alone among the Platonic dialogues in being devoted to cosmology and natural science" (Taylor 19, 436).

32. The pentagrammaton is the word of five letters: YHSWH, which is the unfolded name of God as the tetragrammaton (YHWH) and which represents, according to Reuchlin, the name of Jesus (in Hebrew Yeishu'a; see Silverman and Scholem).

33. In Latin: "Salubris ista potestas verborum, quë vos deseruit: Nos elegit: nos comitatur."

34. Jupiter, Neptune, and Pluto are, respectively, the Roman gods of rain, thunder, and lightning; of the sea; and of Hades, the realm of the dead.

35. St. Nicholas (d. 345 or 352) was one of the most popular saints in the Greek and Latin churches. Born in Asia Minor, he became bishop of Myra. He is a patron of mariners, merchants, and travelers (Ott). St. Rook or St. Roch (1295–1327) was born at Montpelier to the governor of that city. After the death of his parents he distributed his fortune among the poor, took the disguise of a mendicant pilgrim, and devoted himself to the plague-stricken (Cleary).

36. The term "grammarians" was applied to the medieval Jewish exegetes because they focused on reeexamining the Bible by using an analysis of Hebrew grammar and syntax to determine the text's objective, historical meaning.

37. Kimhi writes (*Biblia Rabbinica*, my translation): "MARK A MARK. As for the subject of the sign and writing, he [God] said that he [Ezekiel] should make the sign with ink on the foreheads of the men who groan and moan as a sign that the destroyers should not touch them. This is like the matter of the Passover in Egypt as a symbol and a sign, however this [Ezekiel] was in a prophetic vision. Our Rabbis of blessed memory explained [see the Babylonian Talmud, the Tractate of Shabbat, page 55, side 1] that 'tav' is the letter which is called 'tav' [ת]. The Holy One, blessed be He, said to Gabriel: 'Write on the foreheads of the righteous a "tav" of ink and on the foreheads of the evil a "tav" of blood.' He said: 'How is the

[letter] "tav" different?' Rav [Rav and Samuel are two leading Talmudic masters or 'Amoraim' of the first half of the third century C.E.] said: '"Tav" of "you shall live" [tihyeh] and "tav" of "you shall die" [tamut].' And Samuel said: '[The second "tav" stands for] the merit of the ancestors has come to an end [tamah].'"

Works Cited

Ahituv, Shmuel. "Zaphenath-Paaneah" [Hebrew]. *Biblical Encyclopedia*. Vol. 6. Jerusalem: Bialik Institute, 1971. 759.

Allen, Don Cameron. "Dean Donne Sets His Text." *English Literary History* 10 (1943): 208–29.

Altman, Shimon Tsevi Alexander. "Aristoteles and Judaism" [Hebrew]. *Encyclopedia Hebraica*. Vol. 5. Jerusalem: Encyclopedia Publishing Company, 1953. 853–60.

Anderson, Christopher. *The Annals of the English Bible*. Vol. 2. London: William Pickering, 1845.

Bald, R. C. *John Donne: A Life*. Oxford: Clarendon, 1970.

Baur, C. "St. John Chrysostom." *The Catholic Encyclopedia*. Vol. 7. 1909. Online edition 1999. 4 March 2001. <http://www.newadvent.org/cathen/08452b.htm>.

Biblia Rabbinica. Reprint of the 1525 Venice edition. Ed. Jacob Ben Haim Ibn Adoniya. Jerusalem: Makor, 1972.

Breuer, Mordechai. "The 'Black Death' and Antisemitism." *Antisemitism through the Ages*. Ed. Shmuel Almog, trans. Nathan H. Reisner. Oxford: Pergamon P, 1988. 139–51.

"Calvin, John." *The Columbia Encyclopedia*. 6th ed. 2001. Columbia UP. 15 March 2001. <http://www.bartleby.com/65/ca/Calvin-J.html>.

Chamberlin, John S. *Increase and Multiply: Arts-of-Discourse Procedure in the Preaching of Donne*. Chapel Hill: U of North Carolina P, 1976.

Chomsky, William. *Hebrew: The Eternal Language*. Philadelphia: Jewish Publication Society of America, 1957.

Cleary, Gregory. "St. Roch." *The Catholic Encyclopedia*. Vol. 13. 1909. Online edition 1999. Kevin Knight. 29 March 2001. <http://www.newadvent.org/cathen/13100c.htm>.

Daiches, David. *The King James Version of the English Bible*. Chicago: U of Chicago P, 1941.

Donne, John. *Essays in Divinity*. Ed. Evelyn M. Simpson. Oxford: Clarendon, 1952.

———. *Sermons*. Ed. George R. Potter and Evelyn M. Simpson. 10 vols. Berkeley: U of California P, 1953–62.

Geneva Bible. A Facsimile of the 1599 Edition. Ozark, MO: L. L. Brown, 1990.

Goldish, Matt. *Judaism in the Theology of Sir Isaac Newton.* Dordrecht: Kluwer, 1998.

Goodblatt, Chanita. "Christian Hebraists." *Reader's Guide to Judaism.* Ed. Michael Terry. Chicago: Fitzroy Dearborn, 2000. 110–11.

———. "An Intertextual Discourse on Sin and Salvation: John Donne's Sermon on Psalm 51." *Renaissance and Reformation* 20 (1996): 23–40.

Gosse, Edmund. *The Life and Letters of John Donne.* Gloucester, MA: Peter Smith, 1959.

Greenslade, S. L. "English Versions of the Bible, 1525–1611." *The Cambridge History of the Bible: The West from the Reformation to the Present Day.* Ed. S. L. Greenslade. Cambridge: Cambridge UP, 1963. 141–74.

Grossman, Avraham. "Rashi (Solomon ben Isaac): Main Characteristics of His Commentary." *Encyclopaedia Judaica.* Vol. 3. Jerusalem: Keter, 1972. 1560–62.

Hall, Basil. "Biblical Scholarship: Editions and Commentaries." *The Cambridge History of the Bible: The West from the Reformation to the Present Day.* Ed. S. L. Greenslade. Cambridge: Cambridge UP, 1963. 38–93.

Hall, Michael L. "Searching and Not Finding: The Experience of Donne's *Essays in Divinity.*" *Genre* 14 (1981): 423–40.

Hammond, Gerald. *The Making of the English Bible.* Manchester: Carcanet New Press, 1982.

Heeren, A. Vander. "Septuagint Version." *The Catholic Encyclopedia.* Vol. 13. 1909. Online edition 1999. Kevin Knight. 26 March 2001. <http://www.newadvent.org/cathen/13722a.htm>.

Hill, Eugene D. "John Donne's Moralized Grammar: A Study in Renaissance Christian Hebraica." *Papers in the History of Linguistics.* Ed. Hans Aarsleff, Louis G. Kelly, and Hans-Josef Niederehe. Amsterdam: John Benjamins, 1987. 189–98.

Hirsch, Emil G. "Jehovah." *The Jewish Encyclopedia.* Vol. 7. New York: Funk and Wagnalls, 1916. 87–88.

Holy Bible. An Exact Reprint in Roman Type, Page for Page of the Authorized Version. Published in the Year 1611. Oxford: Oxford UP, 1911.

Hudleston, G. Roger. "Pope St. Gregory I ('the Great')." *The Catholic Encyclopedia.* Vol. 6. 1909. Online edition 1999. Kevin Knight. 4 March 2001. <http://www.newadvent.org/cathen/06780a.htm>.

Jones, G. Lloyd. *The Discovery of Hebrew in Tudor England: A Third Language.* Manchester: Manchester UP, 1983.

Keynes, Geoffrey. *A Bibliography of Dr. John Donne.* Oxford: Clarendon, 1973.

Klausner, Joseph. "Plato" [Hebrew]. *Encyclopedia Hebraica.* Vol. 5. Jerusalem: Encyclopedia Publishing Company, 1953. 223–36.

Levias, Caspar. "Masorah." *The Jewish Encyclopedia.* Vol. 8. New York: Funk and Wagnalls, 1916. 385–71.

Lewalski, Barbara Kiefer. "The Protestant Paradigm of Salvation." *Protestant Poetics and the Seventeenth-Century Religious Lyric.* Princeton: Princeton UP, 1979. 13–27.

Loewe, Raphael. "Christian Hebraists." *Encyclopaedia Judaica.* Vol. 8. Jerusalem: Keter, 1972. 9–72.

Maas, A. J. "Jehovha (Yahweh)." *The Catholic Encyclopedia.* Vol. 8. 1910. Online edition 1999. Kevin Knight. 24 March 2001. <http://www.newadvent.org/cathen/08329a.htm>.

———. "Jesus Christ: Origin of the Name." *The Catholic Encyclopedia.* Vol. 8. 1910. Online edition 1999. Kevin Knight. 24 March 2001. <http://www.newadvent.org/cathen/08374x.htm>.

Marotti, Arthur F. "Donne as Social Exile and Jacobean Courtier: The Devotional Verse and Prose of the Secular Man." *Critical Essays on John Donne.* Ed. Arthur F. Marotti. New York: G. K. Hall, 1994. 77–101.

Maxwell-Stuart, P. G. "De Verbo Mirifico: Johannes Reuchlin and the Royal Arch." *Ars Quatuor Coronatorum* 99 (1986): 206–9.

Mueller, William R. *John Donne: Preacher.* Princeton: Princeton UP, 1962.

Newman, Beth S. "John Donne and the Cabala." *Jewish Quarterly* 23 (1975): 31–36.

Oberman, Heiko A. "Reuchlin and the Jews: Obstacles on the Path to Emancipation." *The Challenge of Periodization: Old Paradigms and New Perspectives.* Ed. Lawrence Besserman. New York: Garland, 1996. 67–93.

Ott, Michael. "St. Nicholas of Myra." *The Catholic Encyclopedia.* Vol. 11. 1909. Online edition 1999. Kevin Knight. 29 March 2001. <http://www.newadvent.org/cathen/11063b.htm>.

Pelikan, Jaroslav, Valerie R. Hotchkiss, and David Price. *The Reformation of the Bible: The Bible of the Reformation.* New Haven: Yale UP, 1996.

Perry, Menahem, and Meir Sternberg. "The King through Ironic Eyes: Biblical Narrative and the Literary Reading Process." *Poetics Today* 7 (1986): 275–322.

Potter and Simpson. See Donne, *Sermons.*

Preschel, Tovia. "Ibn Ezra as Commentator on the Bible." *Encyclopaedia Judaica.* Vol. 8. Jerusalem: Keter, 1971. 1166–68.

Quinn, Dennis B. "John Donne's Principles of Biblical Exegesis." *Journal of English and German Philology* 61 (1962): 313–29.

Raspa, Anthony, and Judith Scherer Herz. "Response." *Renaissance and Reformation* 20 (1996): 97–98.

Reichert, Victor E. *Job.* Hebrew text and English translation, with an introduction and commentary. London: Soncino P, 1946.

Reilly, Thos. A. K. "Santes Pagnino." *The Catholic Encyclopedia*. Vol. 11. 1909. Online edition 1999. Kevin Knight. 1 March 2001. <http://www.newadvent.org/cathen/11394e.htm>.

Reuchlin, Johannes. *De Verbo Mirifico*. Basel: Johannes Amerbach, 1494. Reprint. Stuttgart–Bad Cannstatt: Günther Holzboog, 1964.

Rosenblatt, Jason P. *Torah and Law in Paradise Lost*. Princeton: Princeton UP, 1994.

Saltet, Louis. "Jerome." *The Catholic Encyclopedia*. Vol. 8. 1909. Online edition 1999. Kevin Knight. 18 March 2001. <http://www.newadvent.org/cathen/08341a.htm>.

Schleiner, Winfried. *The Imagery of John Donne's Sermons*. Providence: Brown UP, 1970.

Shami, Jeanne. "Introduction: Reading Donne's Sermons." *John Donne Journal* 11 (1992): 1–20.

Shapiro, I. A. "Notes: Donne's Sermons Dates." *Review of English Studies* 31 (1980): 54–56.

Shapiro, James. *Shakespeare and the Jews*. New York: Columbia UP, 1996.

Shoulson, Jeffrey S. "'Proprietie in this Hebrew poesy': George Wither, Judaism, and the Formation of English National Identity." *Journal of English and Germanic Philology* 98 (1999): 354–72.

Silverman, Godfrey Edmond. "Galatinus, Pietro Columna." *Encyclopaedia Judaica*. Vol. 7. Jerusalem: Keter, 1971. 262–63.

Silverman, Godfrey Edmond, and Gershom Scholem. "Reuchlin, Johannes." *Encyclopaedia Judaica*. Vol. 14. Jerusalem: Keter, 1971. 108–11.

Simpson, Evelyn M. Introduction. *John Donne's Sermons on the Psalms and Gospels*. Ed. Evelyn M. Simpson. Berkeley: U of California P, 1963. 1–27.

———. *A Study of the Prose Works of John Donne*. 2nd ed. Oxford: Clarendon, 1948.

Stanwood, P. G. "John Donne's Sermon Notes." *The Sempiternal Season: Studies in Seventeenth-Century Devotional Writing*. New York: Peter Lang, 1992. 74–83.

Talmage, Frank. "Kimhi, David." *Encyclopaedia Judaica*. Vol. 10. Jerusalem: Keter, 1971. 1001–4.

Tanakh: The Holy Scriptures. The New JPS Translation According to the Traditional Hebrew Text. Philadelphia: Jewish Publication Society, 1985.

Taylor, A. E. *Plato: The Man and His Work*. Cleveland: Meridian Books, 1956.

Theodor, J. "Midrash Haggadah." *The Jewish Encyclopedia*. Vol. 8. New York: Funk and Wagnalls, 1916. 550–69.

Volz, John R. "Tommaso de Vio Gaetani Cajetan." *The Catholic Encyclopedia*. Vol. 3. 1908. Online edition 1999. Kevin Knight. 19 February 2001. <http://www.newadvent.org/cathen/03145c.htm>.

Wimsatt, W. K. "The Structure of Romantic Nature Imagery." *Romanticism: Points of View*. Ed. Robert F. Gleckner and Gerald E. Enscoe. 2nd ed. Detroit: Wayne State UP, 1975. 219–30.

Zuñiga, Diego López de, et al., eds. *Biblia Sacra Polyglotta*. Alcalá de Henares: Arnaldi Guillelmi de Brocario, 1514–17.

9

Pathopoeia and the Protestant Form of Donne's *Devotions Upon Emergent Occasions*

BRENT NELSON

John Donne was at the height of his preaching career when he wrote his *Devotions Upon Emergent Occasions*, a long devotional work occasioned by his illness in December 1623 and published in early 1624. He had been dean of St. Paul's Cathedral in London, arguably the most popular pulpit in England, for just over two years. Despite his considerable administrative responsibilities, Dean Donne took every opportunity to ascend the pulpit. So when he decided to adapt his own meditations on the occasion of his illness to the devotional benefit of a public audience, it was natural for him to draw upon his resources as a preacher. Yet despite Barbara Lewalski's assertion of the "near-identification of sermons and meditation in terms of methods and purposes" (83), only Janel Mueller has looked to Donne's sermons for clues to his method in the *Devotions*.[1] Mueller focuses on the similarity of thought, describing Donne's coupling of "preaching procedures and meditative ones" to account for the predominance of exegesis, both of Scripture and of human experience, in the *Devotions* (3). The sermons and the *Devotions*, I would also argue, share similar rhetorical purposes and strategies as well. In his sermons Donne typically adheres to what Debora Shuger calls the "grand style" of preaching, which is marked by strategies of *pathopoeia*, the arousing of the emotions. He uses similar *pathopoeic* devices in his *Devotions*. Specifically, in both the sermons and the *Devotions*, Donne uses *hypotyposis*, or vivid depictions of emotionally charged circumstances, to incite the passions of his audience and motivate them in devotion. These circumstances typically bear a formal pattern of fall and redemption, a distinctively Protestant emphasis in devotional experience, which aims to move the congregant or reader to feel profoundly his or her complete dependence on God's grace and to respond with faith in Christ.

In looking to the sermon, I hope to account for two key features of the *Devotions* that have been largely overlooked in scholarship: its audience orientation and its emotional appeal. Scholars have identified numerous generic influences on the *Devotions*, usually dividing along Roman Catholic/Protestant lines. An undeniable influence is the *Spiritual Exercises* of Ignatius of Loyola, while proposed Protestant models include spiritual autobiography, the "holy soliloquy," Richard Hooker's paradigm of repentance, and various models of Protestant meditation, including the occasional meditations of Joseph Hall.[2] These sources have accounted for the private, personal quality that is so striking in the *Devotions*, but they have not enabled scholars from either camp adequately to account for the public, rhetorical orientation that is also evident.[3] Those who acknowledge the audience orientation of the *Devotions* have difficulty reconciling the ostensible rhetorical purpose of the work with its apparently confessional, self-expressive nature.[4] Even among those who have acknowledged the public address of the *Devotions*, the emphasis is on what it reveals about its author and his experience rather than the effect it was designed to produce for the reader. Yet despite its obviously personal matter, Donne clearly intended his *Devotions* for an audience's edification.[5] The questions remain, what effect does this text aim to produce in its audience, and what means does it employ to achieve this effect?

Concomitant with this focus on the private, personal orientation of the *Devotions* is an emphasis on its discursive function.[6] And once again, this logical turn typically is seen as a personal reflection of the mind of the author. Murray Arndt, for example, argues that "the emphasis that Ignatius placed upon the intellect in the achievement of willed affirmation unfortunately encouraged Donne's tendency toward rationalization and clever control of experienced materials" resulting in an "intellectualized defense" that enabled Donne to avoid the issues of pain and death (43). Although he acknowledges an emotional element in the "meditations" (the first part of each devotional cycle), Arndt leaves this feature unexamined, hastening instead to focus on what he sees as the rationalizing and spiritualizing of experience that takes place in the "expostulations" (the second part of each cycle).[7] This emphasis on the rational function of discourse (*logos*) has carried over into discussion of the Protestant forms of Donne's *Devotions*. Even though Andreasen emphasizes the Protestant influence on Donne's *Devotions*, she nonetheless finds in it a discursive quality that functions much like that of the Ignatian *Exercises*, such that "both the meditation and the expostulation are analyses, governed by the meditator's reason or understanding" (211). The first meditation, for example, "logically demonstrates the 'miserable condition of Man.'" In this way, says Andreasen, Donne "reason[s] himself through to consolation" (211), expressed in the prayer (the third and final section of each cycle). When critics do attempt to describe the designs of the *Devotions* upon its audience, it is typically in terms of *logos*, or reason, applied to the function of teaching by example. Roger B. Rollins describes it as "exemplary and hortatory" and "a positive lesson in holy dying" (53). Frost sees its autobiographical element serving as *exemplum* to bring understanding of the human condition (332). Narveson also notes its exemplary function, which she similarly limits to the instructional purpose of providing a pattern that the reader can emulate in his or her own self-scrutiny (119, 126–27). Yet Donne thought of himself not as a teacher but as a preacher. And as a pastor-preacher, his aim was not simply to convey personal experience or even to teach by example, but to *move* his audience to greater devotion. For insight into Donne's *pathopoeic* method for accomplishing this effect in his *Devotions Upon Emergent Occasions*, I turn to his habitual literary form as a pastor: the sermon.

Pathopoeia in the Sermons

In *Sacred Rhetoric*, Debora Shuger demonstrates the central importance of *pathopoeic* appeal (*pathos*) in Renaissance preaching, where moving (*movere*) the congregant toward greater devotion was the primary goal.[8] According to Shuger, this new advocacy of the "grand style"—passionate preaching aimed at inciting emotive responses—went hand in hand with a revival of Augustinian ideas on rhetoric and spirituality. Shuger explains that

> [f]or Augustine spiritual existence, with its joy, desire, sorrow, and hope, is affective. In the Renaissance, this Augustinianism develops into the belief that spiritual life is primarily a matter of the heart and will, that love is more important than knowledge. Sin therefore results from defective love rather than ignorance and is healed not by suppressing emotion but by redirecting it. The importance of the grand style in the sacred rhetorics follows from this conviction that man comes to God through love and desire. The association between affective spirituality and the grand style is further strengthened by the Renaissance conviction that all

thought and feeling depend on imagination. Unlike philosophy, rhetoric appeals to the imagination and is therefore able to move and transform the desires of the heart. (8)

Philip Melanchthon (1497–1560), the prominent German church reformer, is representative of those Protestants who advocated the grand style of preaching. In *De modo et arte* (c. 1537–39) Melanchthon writes, "in every sermon of whatever kind, the speech *(oratio)* should aim at [arousing] a certain emotion, namely fear of God or faith, or a related emotion, patience or love" (Shuger's translation 68). Elsewhere he describes the function of oratory (i.e., preaching): "the end of dialectic is to teach, of rhetoric however to move *(permovere)* and incite souls, and to lead them to certain emotion" (120). Johann-Heinrich Alsted in his *Orator* [1612] similarly states, "Teaching is not the principle job *(officium)* of the orator; this he does by means of logic. However, he moves and bends [the soul] by rhetoric. The orator therefore mainly looks to the heart, so that he may stir up in it different emotions" (Shuger's translation 120).

The influence of passionate preaching was felt in England as early as 1577 when John Ludham published his English translation of the first Protestant homiletic, D. Andreas Hyperius's *De formandis concionibus sacris*, which features a section on appealing to the affections. To Hyperius, says Shuger, "the ability to move the emotions is the most important aspect of preaching" (72). For adding affective force to a sermon, Hyperius recommends a method that, as I shall demonstrate, accords well with Donne's procedure in the *Devotions*; this is accomplished "by a vehement imagination or fantasy, when a man with most atte[n]tiue cogitatio[n] apprehendeth, and depaynteth to himselfe the formes and simylitudes of the thinges whereof hee entreateth, which afterwarde he so fireth & setleth in his minde, as if his owne priuate cause were in handling, and as though hee shoulde perpetually muse uppon that thinge alone" (Hyperius 43b). Hyperius goes on to explain that certain types of matter are "of great weight and force to the stirring up of the motions of myndes. For ther happen some thinges of such a nature, that the narration thereof (though it be rude and homely) doe moste swiftely and deeply sincke into the hartes of hearers, and that doe very greatly moue and delight the same" (44b). What Hyperius describes here is *hypotyposis*, a rhetorical figure that covers all forms of vividness—especially in depictions of situations and circumstances—and which Shuger identifies as a key feature of the grand style in Renaissance preaching (cf. Shuger 131, 262).

This appeal to the passions characterizes Donne's method in the sermons and, as we shall see, in the *Devotions* as well. In moving his congregations as a preacher, Donne's first concern was to prick, stir, or agitate his audience out of complacency in preparation for response, so that they would want to change their present condition. In a sermon preached to the court at Whitehall on 12 February 1618/19 on the subject of preaching, Donne asserts that sermons should aim to "move" and "affect" an audience and that preachers should therefore eschew a "drowsie, and cold manner of preaching" (2:167–68). In another sermon, preached in 1627 at St. Dunstan's church, Donne says, "The Preacher stirres and moves, and agitates the holy affections of the Congregation, that they slumber not in a senselesnesse of that which is said" (8:43). Picking up the imagery of the mother eagle from Deuteronomy 32:11, Donne further describes the preacher as one who "makes a holy noise in the conscience of the Congregation, and when hee hath awakened them, by stirring the nest, hee casts some claps of thunder, some intimidations, in denouncing the judgements of God, and he flings open the gates of Heaven, that they may heare, and look up, and see a man sent by God, with power to infuse his feare upon them" (8:44).

The "stirring" function of pulpit rhetoric accords well with Donne's stated concerns in the *Devotions*. Moreover, Donne's vivid and sometimes vehement depiction of the occasions of his sickness belong to Hyperius's category of things that conduce especially well to moving the emotions. As in the sermons, Donne's aim in the *Devotions* is not chiefly to instruct but to motivate—not simply to teach a right way of thinking but also to stimulate the affections and reform attitudes in order to incline his audience to a right way of living. In keeping with Protestant ideas of preaching, the *Devotions* achieves its audience's reorientation and surrender to God's will by first preparing the soul by agitating it in the meditation and the expostulation, making it desirous of relief and ready to surrender in prayer.

In the remainder of this essay I will elaborate the Protestant *pathopoeic* form of the *Devotions* and show how Donne uses this form to stimulate and move his audience toward greater devotion. This form derives from Protestant doctrine.[9] Both Roman Catholic and Protestant preachers (some, not all) valued the grand style and viewed it as central to their common rhetorical purpose of moving their congregations. What distinguishes Roman Catholics and Protestants of the period, says Shuger, is the way in which they attempted to adapt common rhetorical ideals and strategies to their respective doctrine. Melanchthon, for example, builds upon the Protestant emphasis on the imperative of faith by appealing to feelings of fear and faith in his congregation, where "[p]reaching of the law awakens terror, a terror only consoled by faith in the promises of Christ" (Shuger 68). The shaping principle of much Protestant preaching, and in particular Donne's sermons, derives from the new Protestant emphasis on a soteriology of fall (representing human need) and redemption (divine provision). Under the curse of original sin, humankind is humbled and completely dependent on God for his providence. Donne describes these two basic principles of salvation in a sermon on repentance preached at Whitehall in 1626. First, paraphrasing Augustine, he asserts that "[i]f Man had not fallen, and lain irrevocably under that fall, the Son of God had not come to suffer the shame, and the pain of the Cross." Humankind's depravity in turn implies complete dependence on Christ's redemption: "no man hath any such righteousness of his own, as can save him; for howsoever it be his, by that Application, or Imputation, yet the righteousness that saves him, is the very righteousness of Christ himself" (7:158–59).

This theological emphasis has its corollary in the affections, where spiritual agitation over one's fallen state provides the first impulse to devotion.[10] William H. Halewood finds in the seventeenth-century devotional poets a distinctively Protestant emphasis on prevenient grace, "the grace which is required to make men *want* to be saved by softening the stony in their hearts" (75–83). He sees this process at work in Donne's *Holy Sonnets*, where a descent into desolation sets the conditions that cause a desire for an ascent to consolation. Halewood describes this form as a movement from a state of unrest to one of rest. John Calvin describes a similar pattern in relation to his four steps of prayer, where the first three leave one "cast down and overcome by true humility" and prepared for the fourth step of assurance, where "we should be nonetheless encouraged to pray by a sure hope that our prayer will be answered" (*Institutes* 3.20.11). The devotee's dejection prepares him or her to seek aid and comfort in God. Calvin elaborates this pattern, focusing on the experience of agitation as a goad toward devout living:

> [A]ssurance I do not understand to mean that which soothes our mind with sweet and perfect repose, releasing it from every anxiety. For to repose so peacefully is the part of those who, when all affairs are flowing to their liking, are touched by no care, burn with no desire, toss with no fear. But for the saints the occasion that best stimulates them to call upon God is when, distressed by their own need, they are troubled by the greatest unrest, and are almost driven out of their senses, until faith oppor-

tunely comes to their relief. For among such tribulations God's goodness so shines upon them that even when they groan with weariness under the weight of present ills and also are troubled and tormented by the fear of greater ones, yet, relying upon his goodness, they are relieved of the difficulty of bearing them, and are solaced and hope for escape and deliverance. It is fitting therefore that the godly man's prayer arise from these two emotions, that it also contain and represent both. That is, that he groan under present ills and anxiously fear those to come, yet at the same time take refuge in God, not at all doubting he is ready to extend his helping hand. (3.20.11)[11]

The potential relevance of such experience to preaching is made clear by Hyperius, who describes the *pathopoeic* operation of vivid depictions where "the very shape, maner, & other circumstances of [the] same vices, which declare their filthynesse & indignitie" help in the "stirryng up of hatred and detestation of any one or mo[r]e vices" (46a, 45b). He also suggests that "to the procurement of hope and desyre of mercy doe conduce a number of places accustomed to be used in consolations" (47a). These same operations of detestation and desire figure prominently in the cycles of Donne's *Devotions*, which engender dissatisfaction with the human condition and an attendant hope and longing for relief in Christ.

Critics of the *Devotions* cannot help but notice this pattern of fall and redemption, or some variation of this form. Goldberg notes the paradox that falling into sickness is, at the same time, rising to salvation (512). Frost identifies the form of downwardness (prostration in sickness) and upwardness (healing) that echoes the conversion experiences of Hezekiah and St. Paul (28–36). And Papazian finds in the *Devotions* a movement from "anxiety to peace" ("Donne, Election" 610–11). Abrahamson similarly notes a two-part pattern independent of the three-part structure of each devotion: the meditation exhibits a restlessness of mind as Donne struggles with the problem of physical misery, and this restlessness increases in the expostulation, where he confronts the problem of sinfulness. By the end of the expostulation Donne begins to surrender his will, so that in the prayer he is able to find peace of mind in complete submission to God. Goldberg sees this pattern as simply an informing idea in Donne's experience, and Frost goes a step further in describing it as a "lesson" or example for his audience. None of these critics relates this informing idea to the rhetorical activity of the text.

Donne describes the rhetorical effect of this formal pattern of fall and redemption in a sermon preached at St. Paul's Cathedral in 1621 or 1622, where he characterizes the preacher's activity with reference to various Hebrew and Latin equivalents for *Obsecramus*, translated "we pray you" in 2 Corinthians 5:20, his text for this sermon.[12] The first meaning Donne identifies is "to throw down, to deject our selves, to admit any undervalue, any exinanition, any evacuation of our selves, so we may advance this great work" (10:123). He continues, "as Physicians must consider excrements, so we must consider sin, the leprosie, the pestilence, the ordure of the soule" (10:123). The preacher does this, he says, for the purpose of "mak[ing] you see your poverty and indigence," that is, to feel the desperation of our fallen state (10:123). Donne's term further signifies both "*Dolere*, to grieve within our selves, for the affliction of another," and "*vulnerare*, to wound, and afflict another" (10:123). And so, says Donne, "we [preachers] wound your consciences, with a sense of your sins" (10:123). But Donne adds a redemptive element expressed by two Latin equivalents: "*Cruciare*, to vex, and . . . *Placare* too, to appease, to restore to rest and quiet" (10:124). This single word, *Obsecramus*, is thus made to imply a process that includes both fall and redemption and the corresponding experiences of affliction and cure. Donne then makes a direct application to the activity of the sermon:

> And therefore, if from our words proceed any vexation to your consciences, you must not say, *Transeat calix, let that Cup passe*, no more of that matter, for it is the *physick* that must first *stirre* the humour, before it can *purge* it; And if our words apply to your consciences, the soverain balm of the merits of your Saviour, and that thereupon your troubled consciences finde some rest, be not too soon secure, but proceed in your good beginnings. (10:124)

The preacher prepares the congregant by stirring appropriate emotions, by troubling consciences and creating a desire for the relief and rest that comes in redemption. This pattern of agitation and rest is a common theme in the sermons. In the *divisio* of another sermon on preaching, Donne notes that the prophet of his text (Ezekiel 33:32) first sounds "a Trumpet, to awaken with terror," but then he "become[s] . . . a musical and harmonious charmer, to settle and compose the soul again in a reposed confidence, and in a delight in God" (2:199). In his opening prayer to a marriage sermon, Donne attributes a similar procedure to God who has "maryed *Increpation* and *Consolation* in the Holy Ghost" and prays God to "mary in us also . . . a *Love* and a *Fear* of thee" (8:94). In another sermon he adds to the bipartite structure to draw out the process, moving from

"*Commination*" (threat) to "*Commonition*" (instruction) to "*Consolation*" (5:184).[13]

Donne often uses images of upwardness and downwardness to define his audience's sermonic experience along these same affective lines. "The naturall way is *upward*," says Donne, yet sometimes we see better by being brought low. He goes on to explain that "Gods meaning was, that by the sun-shine of prosperity, and by the beames of honour, and temporall blessings, a man should see farre into him; but I know not how he is come to need *spectacles*; scarce any man sees much in this matter, till affliction shew it him" (4:171). Donne often arranges his material to bring his congregation low in order to raise them up again with a new vision. In this sermon Donne exploits the dyslogistic associations of downwardness (a well) and their eulogistic counterparts (associated with a spire) to structure his audience's desire. It is much more desirable, in this case, to appreciate one's prosperity, and to see God at the end of it, than to need humiliation through affliction in order to have one's vision retrained on God.

But all too often, the way of affliction is required. In a sermon preached at St. Paul's (probably in the early 1620s) on Psalm 90:14—"O Satisfie us early with thy mercy, that we may rejoyce and be glad all our dayes"— Donne uses journey imagery to introduce the formal operation of fall and redemption, and he accentuates this imagery with figures of repetition and *hypotyposis* (vividness) to augment these dyslogistic/eulogistic alternatives. In beginning the second partition of his sermon, where he aims to explicate the verse as a particular, illustrative instance of prayer, Donne breaks the verse into semantic units, the first being "*Satisfie*," the second "satisfie *Vs*," the third "Satisfie us *early*," and so on (5:273, emphasis added). Then he figures this approach through the text as a journey, describing the key words in the text as "the land-markes that must guide you in this voyage" (5:273). But the voyage he sets out before his congregation is not one of immediate satisfaction but rather one of frustrated desire designed to engender a longing for satisfaction (i.e., home and rest in heaven). Reiterating his first point, "*Satisfie*," Donne says that he may understand, believe, and see evidence that God will do what he has promised, "but yet this is not a fulnesse, a satisfaction, and this [verse] is a prayer for that, *Satura, satisfie*" (5:273). He returns again to the journey *topos* as he revisits his third subpoint, "*Satisfie us early*," noting that God "will bring Israel out of Egypt, and out of Babylon, but yet his Israel [me and you] may lye long under the scourge and scorne of his and their enemies, 300. yeares before they get out of Egypt, seventy yeares before they get out of Babylon, and so fall into tentations of conceiving a jealousie, and suspition of Gods good purpose towards them, and [so] this is a Prayer of Dispatch and Expedition" (5:273). Donne reads into "early" the possibility of a long and uncomfortable sojourn, which he amplifies with reference to the Egyptian and Babylonian captivities. He goes on to warn that help may come from many quarters, and yet not from God; for this reason he prays, "*Satisfie us* with that, which is *thine*, and comes from *thee*, and so directs us to *thee*" (5:274). Yet even still, God's satisfaction may not be what we expect: "God may multiply corrections, and judgements, and tribulations upon us, and intend to helpe us that way, by whipping and beating us into the way, and this is his way" (5:274). The human experience Donne describes runs contrary to the prayer of this verse and the end it envisions. His journey through the text fosters a sense of frustration that helps the congregation feel with urgency the hope it expresses. The verse thus becomes a felt expression of desire for relief from the rough journey of common experience that Donne so vividly depicts.

As Donne turns to elaborate the first point, he strategically undermines the hope that his text expresses in order to agitate his audience and pique their desire for satisfaction. "*Satura*," he says, "implies a fulnesse, and it implies a satisfaction, A quietenesse, a contentednesse, and acquiescence in that fulnesse; *Satisfie* is, let us bee full, and let us feele it, and rest in that fulnesse" (5:274). He and his congregation must not simply understand this satisfaction; they must also *feel* it. Donne notes that St. Jerome associates the satisfaction of this text with the Resurrection, for "though we shall have a fulnesse in Heaven [after death], as soon as we come thither, yet that is not fully a satisfaction, because we shall desire, and expect a fuller satisfaction in the reunion of the body and soule [at the Resurrection]" (5:274). How much less, asks Donne, can we expect to find real satisfaction on earth? Donne uses *hypotyposis* to drive the point home, amplifying a number of instances of worldly satisfaction, all of which share "the nature of vomit": "hard to get downe, and hard to keep in the stomach when it is there; hardly got, hardly kept when they are got" (5:275). There is, however, "a spirituall fulnesse in this life," says Donne (adopting the first-person perspective), where "[t]he desire of spirituall graces begets a satiety, if I would be, I am full of them, And then this satiety begets a further desire, still we have a new appetite to those spirituall graces" (5:275). But again Donne defies expectation, adding that "even in spirituall things, there may be, there is often an error, or mistaking" (5:276). On the one hand, "there may be a fulnesse, but no satisfaction"; that is, "I may have as much knowledge, as is presently necessary for my salvation, and yet have a restlesse and unsatisfied desire, to search into unprofitable curiosities." On the other hand, "there may be a satisfaction, and no fulnesse"; that is, "a man may be satisfied, and thinke he knowes all, when, God knowes, he knowes nothing at all." Donne further augments this sense of futility with the figure of *isocolon* (successive phrases of approximately equal length and corresponding structure) arranged in *climax:* "for, I know nothing, if I know not Christ crucified, And I know not that, if I know not how to apply him to my selfe, Nor doe I know that, if I embrace him not in those meanes, which he hath afforded me in his Church, in his Word, and Sacraments" (5:276).

Donne offers a brief reprieve from the uncertainty he has been engendering, noting that satisfaction can be found in contentment with one's calling in life and that the "us" of the verse implies "a charitable extention [of this prayer] to others too" (5:278). But then he disrupts any sense of comfort as he introduces the next word of his text, again raising the possibility that "if God doe leave us in an Egypt, in a Babylon, without reliefe, for some time I may proceed to this holy importunity" of calling on God "*early*" (5:280). As Donne draws this point to a conclusion, he returns to the theme of life's difficult journey: "There are testimonies of Gods love to us, in our East, in our beginnings; but if God continue tribulation upon us to our West, to our ends, and give us the light of his presence then, if he appeare to us at our transmigration, certainly he was favourable to us all our peregrination, and though he shew himself late, hee was our friend early" (5:283). The issue is one of emotional and attitudinal perspective. In turning to the final word for this partition of his sermon—"mercy"—Donne brings an emphasis that pervades the *Devotions* as well: "let mee feele the effect of this Prayer, as it is a Prayer of manifestation, Let mee discerne that, that that is done upon mee, is done by the hand of God, and I care not what it be: I had rather have Gods Vinegar, then mans Oyle, Gods Wormewood, then mans Manna, Gods Justice, then any mans Mercy" (5:284). Donne goes on to elaborate this point in terms of human fallenness and divine redemption, corresponding to an experience of affliction followed by relief, where

> God will beat downe, and cut off, and blow up, and blow out at his pleasure; . . . stormes and tempests, ruines and devastations, are not onely in Gods Armories, but they are in his Treasuries; as hee is the Lord of Hosts, hee fetches his judgements from his Armories, and casts confusion upon his enemies, but as he is the God of mercy, and of plentifull redemption, he fetches these judgements, these corrections out of his treasuries, and they are the Money, the Jewels, by which he redeemes and buyes us againe. (5:284)

The way of affliction is God's means of redemption. Then Donne draws an analogy between sin and sickness, saying that "[w]hen God made man, his first intention was not that man should fall, and so need a Messias, nor that man should fall sick, and so need a Physitian" (5:285). But fall he did. And so, throughout this whole second partition of the sermon Donne provides the experience of affliction as a preparative to help his congregation "feel" (as he says twice in the sermon) the desire expressed in this prayer. Having thus agitated his listeners with a desire for relief, Donne prepares them to rest in the promise of the second half of the text, which he expounds in the final partition of the sermon: "*That we may rejoyce and be glad all our dayes.*"

Finally, it is worth noting that through much of this sermon Donne moves very easily between a second-person orientation ("you") and a first-person perspective ("I"), often implicating both himself and his audience with the first-person plural. Specifically, Donne often uses himself as an *exemplum* that also functions as *exuscitatio*, a figure of "awakening or arousing" in the form of an "[e]motional utterance that seeks to move hearers to a like feeling" (Hyperius 77). A famous instance of this is in Donne's funeral sermon for Sir William Cokayne in 1626, where he describes himself distracted in prayer. He begins,

> . . . when we consider with a religious seriousnesse the manifold weaknesses of the strongest devotions in time of Prayer, it is a sad consideration. I throw my selfe downe in my Chamber, and I call in, and invite God, and his Angels thither, and when they are there, I neglect God and his Angels, for the noise of a Flie, for the ratling of a Coach, for the whining of a doore; I talke on, in the same posture of praying; Eyes lifted up; knees bowed downe; as though I prayed to God; and, if God, or his Angels should aske me, when I thought last of God in that prayer, I cannot tell: Sometimes I finde that I had forgot what I was about, but when I began to forget it, I cannot tell. A memory of yesterdays pleasures, a feare of to morrows dangers, a straw under my knee, a noise in mine eare, a light in mine eye, an any thing, a nothing, a fancy, a Chimera in my braine, troubles me in my prayer. (7:264–65)

Donne's vivid depiction of his own circumstances invites those in his audience to imagine themselves in a similar situation and to feel similar disgust at their own inattentiveness. This is a feature that is more thoroughly employed to much the same effect in the *Devotions*, where Donne's emotional experience through the stages of his sickness is not merely expressed, but replicated in the experience of the reader.

Pathopoeia in the *Devotions*

Donne's *Devotions* functions much like so many of his sermons which model and, more importantly, seek to reproduce in their audience a fall and redemption. To understand the rhetorical form of the *Devotions*, we must first understand the devotional problem they address, as Donne sees it: spiritual insensibility. After detailing in the opening meditation the new sensitivity his body has experienced in sickness, Donne in the expostulation begs with equal vehemence (echoing Christ's passion on the Cross),

> *My God, my God*, why is not my *soule*, as sensible as my *body*? Why hath not my *soule* these apprehensions, these presages, these changes, those antidates, those jalousies, those suspitions of a *sinne*, as well as my body of a *sicknes*? why is there not always a *pulse* in my *Soule*, to beat at the approch of a tentation to sinne? why are there not always *waters* in mine eyes, to testifie my spiritual sicknes? (1M; 8)[14]

Donne elaborates the point for several more lines before continuing, "Thou hast imprinted a *pulse* in our *Soule*, but we do not examine it; a voice in our conscience, but wee doe not hearken unto it. We talk it out, we jest it out, we drinke it out, we sleepe it out; and when wee wake, we doe not say with *Jacob*, *Surely the Lord is in this place, and I knew it not:* but though we might know it, we do not, we wil not" (1M; 9). The problem, Donne concludes, is not that God ill-equipped us but rather that we are prodigal with the soul he has given to us. In his first prayer Donne asks that God therefore enable him in the "practise of considering thy mercy" and that God make him considerate so that he "may heare and hearken" and that he may (as in the sermon on Psalm 90:14) "heare that voyce early" (1P; 10).

Throughout the *Devotions*, Donne reiterates his concern at the thoughtlessness, insensitivity, lethargy, and sleepiness of fallen humanity. He seeks a continual "consideration" of each occasion that will bring him to "Contemplation" (17M; 87). In his prayers he asks that a habit of contemplation of Christ "be evermore present to me" as a remedy against sin, which is ever "insensibly insinuating it selfe, into my *Soule*" (10P; 55). He prays for new awareness, so that he can say of any circumstance or occasion, "it is *physick;* if I may discern thy hand to give it, & it is *physick*, if it be a speedy departing of this *Soule*, if I may discerne thy hand to receive it" (9P; 50). In the sixth cycle Donne prays God to give him "tender, and supple, and conformable affections, that as I *joy* with them that *joy*, and *mourne* with them, that *mourne*, so I may *feare* with them that *feare*." He goes on to ask that his fear might conduce to "a present submitting of all to thy will. And when thou shalt have inflamd, & thawd my former coldnesses, and indevotions, with these heats, and quenched my former heates, with these sweats, and inundations, and rectified my former presumptions, and negligences with these fears, bee pleased, *O Lord*, as one, made so by thee, to thinke mee fit for thee" (6P; 34). Although Donne's ultimate goal is to train the soul properly to interpret personal experience and to find rest in submission to God's will, his immediate concern is that the affections be prepared so that the soul will be responsive and ready to submit.

In the fourth cycle, Donne relates this need for affective stimulation to a method of fall and redemption, much as he uses it in the sermons. So important is this first part of the devotional process, the experiencing of affliction, that Donne describes the whole of his *Devotions* to his friend Sir Robert Kerr as a book of "Mortification."[15] Upon the occasion of calling a physician, he notes that animals know how to recognize their own affliction and find their own medicine in nature but that humans do not have this sensibility. To this Donne responds, "Call back therefore thy Meditations again, and bring it downe; whats become of mans great extent & proportion, when himselfe shrinkes himselfe, and consumes himselfe to a handfull of dust; whats become of his soaring thoughts, his compassing thoughts, when himselfe brings himselfe to the ignorance, to the thoughtlesnesse of the *Grave*?" (4E; 21). He must first bring himself low, enact a fall to engender a new sensitivity to his own miserable condition, before he will be prepared to be resurrected to a spiritual cure. In the eleventh expostulation he confesses that his is often a *"stonie"* heart which must be softened (described as *"melting," "troubled," "wounded," "broken,"* and *"contrite"*) before it will return to devotion; then, "If my heart bee *prepared*, it is a *returning* heart; And if thou see it upon the *way*, thou wilt carrie it *home;* Nay, the *preparation* is thine too; this *melting*, this *wounding*, this *breaking*, this *contrition*, which I have now, is thy *Way*, to thy *Ende*" (11E; 59–60).

But more than simple self-scrutiny or self-expression, Donne in the *Devotions*, as in the sermons, replicates this experience in his audience. The rhetorical function of Donne's method is most easily discerned in his use of some common *pathopoeic* figures. He frequently begins each section with a form of *ecphonesis*, an exclamation expressing emotion; sometimes it is in the form of an *apostrophe*. The meditations often begin with an expression of despair: "Variable, and therfore miserable condition of Man!" (1M, 7). Often *ecphonesis* comes in the middle or at the conclusion of a meditation: "O miserable abundance, O beggarly riches" (3M, 20); "O multiplied misery!"; "O perplex'd discomposition, O ridling distemper, O miserable condition of Man!" (1M, 7). In some cases Donne uses *epiplexis*, a rebuke in the form of a question that reproaches or upbraids: "O how little a thing is all the greatnes of man, and through how false glasses doth he make shift to *multiply it*, and *magnifie* it to himselfe?" (11M 57). Typically, a continuation of this agitation is signaled at the start of the expostulation, where Donne addresses God directly with an expression of *ecphonesis*—"*O God, my God*"—that emulates Christ's passion on the Cross. Conversely, every prayer begins with a direct address to God, but one of comfort and assurance, usually "O eternal and most gracious God."

The most important *pathopoetic* device in the *Devotions*, however, is *hypotyposis*, a key characteristic of the passionate grand style of preaching. It is also a quality that Abrahamson (63) finds in Donne's *Devotions* and which Low identifies especially with the reader's experience of a devotional text (37).[16] While the *Devotions* does indeed teach by example, appealing to the faculty of understanding, Donne's vivid portrayal of his experience aims first and foremost to move and motivate by touching the heart. Far from being gratuitous ornamentation, imagery in the *Devotions* does real rhetorical work. Although, as Raspa points out, the specific images vary from set to set, there is a continual pattern of upwardness and downwardness that complements this Protestant form and serves to induce desire. In the third meditation, for example, Donne launches an assault on human dignity that cannot help but agitate an engaged reader. He begins by asserting that the "one priviledge, and advantage to Mans body, above other moving creatures [is] that he is not as others, groveling, but of an erect, of an upright form, naturally built, & disposed to the contemplation of *Heaven*" (3M, 14–15). For several lines Donne amplifies this upward inclination of humankind in contrast to animals, building his reader up for a fall when he then questions, "what state hath he in this *dignitie*?" The answer: "A fever can fillip him downe, a fever can depose him; a fever can bring that head, which yesterday caried a *crown* of gold, five foot towards a *crown* of glory, as low as his own foot, today" (3M, 15). The disturbing effect is accentuated by the suggestion that even a king is so vulnerable. For the rest of the meditation Donne elaborates the fragility of the human condition, focusing on the misery of the sick bed as a type of grave. He allows no one to escape the implications of his own condition as he broadens the application to the common experience of sleep, where "[e]very nights bed is a *Type* of the *grave.*" Donne carries the immediacy of this connection over to a comparison of sleep with sickness, whose misery he elaborates in vivid detail:

> At night wee tell our servants at what houre wee will rise; here [in sickness] we cannot tell our selves, at what day, what week, what moneth. Here the head lies as low as the foot; the *Head* of the people, as lowe as they, whome those feet trod upon; And that hande that signed Pardons, is too weake to begge his owne, if hee might have it for lifting up that hand: Strange fetters to the feete, strange Manacles to the hands, when the feete, and handes are bound so much the faster, by how much the coards are slacker; So much the lesse able to doe their Offices, by how much more the Sinnewes and Ligaments are the looser. (3M, 15)

Donne continues amplifying this condition to the end of the meditation, where he concludes his deflation of human dignity by lamenting, "Miserable, and, (though common to all) inhuman *posture*, where I must practise my lying in the *grave*, by lying still, and not practise my *Resurrection*, by rising any more" (16).

In the expostulation Donne amplifies this reduced condition, visiting several biblical *topoi* that add to the dyslogistic associations of his bedridden state before turning to the spiritual benefit to be derived from this condition: "and therefore am I *cast downe*, that I might not be *cast away*" (17). But the quality of his ultimate spiritual ascent is determined by the depth of his descent. He continues (addressing God),

> Thou couldst take mee by the head, as thou didst *Abacuc* [Habakkuk], and carrie mee so; By a *Chariot*, as thou didst *Eliah*, & carrie me so; but thou carriest me thine own private way, the way by which thou carryedst thy *Sonne*, who first lay upon the *earth*, & praid, and then had his *Exaltation*, as himselfe calls his *Crucifying*, and first *descended into hell*, and then had his *Ascension*. There is another *Station* (indeed neither are *stations* but *prostrations*) lower then this bed; To morrow I may be laid one Story lower, upon the *Floore*, the face of the earth, and next day another Story, in the *grave*, the wombe of the Earth: As yet God suspends mee betweene *Heaven* and *Earth*. (3E, 17)

The effect of this sequence of descents is determined by gravity, the sense of heaviness that comes with the realization of how low this upright form of humankind can fall. This condition, so vividly portrayed, aims at producing anxiety and dissatisfaction and a concomitant desire to rise from this depth. If Donne is right about the upward, contemplative inclination of his audience, this continual assertion of human declination will meet with a resistant desire to ascend by the way of contemplation. He thus prepares his audience to say with him to God, "if I rise againe, thou wilt bee my recompence, all the dayes of my life, in making the memory of this sicknes beneficiall to me" (17).

Donne then turns to a tone of consolation, affirming in his prayer the desire expressed at the end of the expostulation: "O most mightie and merciful *God*, who though thou have taken me off my feet, hast not taken me off of my foundation, which is *thy selfe*" (18). He goes on to say that though he has been laid low, this condition has inclined him to be more spiritually responsive to God. Whereas downward images dominated the meditation and expostulation, in the prayer Donne provides comforting images of ascent as he tells God, "As thou hast made these *feathers* [of his mattress], *thornes*, in the sharpnes of this sicknes, so, *Lord*, make these *thornes*, *feathers*, againe, *feathers* of thy *Dove*, in the peace of Conscience, and in a holy recourse to thine *Arke*, to the Instruments of true comfort, in thy Institutions, and in the Ordinances of thy *Church*" (18).

This misery of man, which dominates the first four cycles, is never far from the text of each meditation and often the expostulation as well. On the occasion of his purging, Donne invites meditation on "the slipperie condition of *man*," who is ever inclined to "*ruine*" (20M, 105). Regarding the act of purging (the mechanics of which he delicately avoids), he exclaims, "O *deare price*, & O *strange* way of *addition*, to doe it by *subtraction*; of *restoring* Nature, to *violate Nature*; of *providing strength*, by *increasing weaknesse*" (20M, 106). All that is involved in this "unnatural process" immediately comes to mind. This realization, says Donne, "is another *step* upon which we may stand, and see farther into the *miserie of man*, the *time*, the *season* of his *Miserie*" (106). Donne amplifies this misery in another *apostrophe*, this time combined with a variation of *anaphora* (in this case the repetition of a word in the first half of a series of compound words) and *synonymia* (amplification by repetition of synonyms); he exclaims, "O *overcunning*, *over-watchfull*, *over-diligent*, and *over-sociable misery* of *man*, that seldome comes alone, but then when it may accompanie other *miseries*, and so put one another into the higher *exaltation*, and better *heart*." He then concludes with a graded series of words (*auxesis*) to express this descent of his misery: "I am ground even to an *attenuation*, and must proceed to *evacuation*, all waies to exinanition [emptying] and annihilation" (106).

In the expostulation Donne picks up on the theme he introduced in the meditation—the necessity of human action—and asks which must come first, faith or repentance, a variation of the soteriological debate of faith versus works. Donne takes the text of Psalm 24:4—"*Who shall ascend to the hill of the Lord? . . . he that hath cleane hands, and a pure heart*"—to indicate that although belief comes chronologically before doing, "in the most eminent, and obvious, and conspicuous place, stands *doing*" (E20, 107). This emphasis on human agency, however, brings no confidence but a rather Hamlet-like frustration at the difficulty of taking action. Donne asks, "Why then, O my *God*, my blessed *God*, in the waies of my *spirituall strength*, come I so slow to *action*? I was whipped by thy *rod*, before I came to *consultation*, to consider my state; and shall I goe no farther?" (107). The distress caused by Donne's physical evacuation, his "*purgative physicke*," provides the stimulus that enables him to act, to proceed with "a free and entire evacuation of [his] *soule* by *confession*" (108). This process is mirrored in the reader, who is similarly distressed by Donne's portrayal of this experience. Donne's depiction here of his own wrestling with repentance, though not explicitly violent, is nonetheless unsettling, even as he determines, "I will fill this *Cup* of *compunction*, as full as I have formerly filled the *Cups* of worldly *confections*, that so I may scape the *cup of Malediction*, and irrecoverable destruction that depends upon that" (108). If the course of remedy is unsettling, the suggestion of the alternative is even more so.

Again, as images of downwardness and decline dominate the meditation and expostulation, images of upwardness and ascent take over in the prayer. An assured tone is established at the outset by his evocation, "O eternall, and most gracious *God*" (20P, 109). Though he describes his soul as "*sea* swoln into the depth of a *Deluge*, above the *Sea*," his devotional journey is figured as a series of ascents toward relief from the assault of sin:

> Thou hast raised up certaine *hils* in *me* heretofore, by which I might have stood safe, from these *inundations* of *sin*. Even our *Naturall faculties* are a *hill*, and might preserve us from *some sinne*. Education, *study, observation, example*, are *hills* too, and might preserve us from *some*. Thy *Church*, and thy *Word*, and thy *Sacraments*, and thine *Ordinances*, are *hills*, above these; thy *Spirit* of *remorse*, and *compunction*, & *repentance* for former *sin*, are *hills* too; and to the *top* of all these *hils*, thou hast brought mee heretofore. (20P, 109–10)

But, says Donne, "this *Deluge*, this *inundation*, is got above all my *Hills;* and I have sinned and sinned, and multiplied *sinne* to *sinne*, after all these thy assistances against *sinne*, and where is there *water* enough to wash away this *Deluge*?" The answer comes quickly: "There is a *red Sea*, greater than this *Ocean*; and there is a *little spring*, through which this *Ocean*, may powre it selfe into that *red Sea*" (109)—that is, his tears of "true *contrition*" (the little spring) are the means by which his sin (this ocean) is absorbed by Christ's blood (the red sea). Donne has, in fact, thus brought his reader to yet a new, higher hill, a fuller realization of the need for true contrition, a place of refuge for sin, however temporary it may be in this ongoing journey of spiritual struggle.

Though journey imagery does not especially dominate the *Devotions*, it is nonetheless a significant iteration of the formal pattern I have been describing, similar to that of the sermon on Psalm 90:14. In devotion 19, Donne similarly begins his meditation with the journey *topos* to communicate a sense of anxiety at God's delayed provision. He observes, "All this while the *Physicians* themselves have beene *patients*, patiently attending when they should see any *land* in this *Sea*, any *earth*, any *cloud*, and *indication* of *concoction* in these *waters*" (19M, 97). The sea is Donne's misery, the land his relief. In meditation 8, sea voyage has already served to represent the miserable condition of man, where Donne says,

> Let [man] be a *world*, and him self will be the *land*, and *misery* the *sea*. His misery, (for misery is his, his own; of the happinesses even of this world, hee is but *tenant*, but of misery the *freeholder*; of happines hee is but the *farmer*, but the *usufructuary* [one who uses something that belongs to another]; but of the misery, the *Lord*, the *proprietary*) his misery, as the *sea*, swells above all the hilles, and reaches to the remotest parts of this earth, *Man*. (8M, 40–41)

Notwithstanding the professional patience of the physician, this same sense of anxiety takes over in meditation 19 as Donne continues, "Any *disorder* of mine, any *pretermission* [passive omission, neglect] of theirs, exalts the disease, accelerates the rages of it; no *diligence* accelerates the *concoction*, the *maturitie* of the *disease*" (19M, 97). Donne goes on to note the impossibility of hurrying the regular course of nature: fruit, he says, comes only in harvest. But he uses this dependable fact not for comfort, but to launch an extended amplification of the frustration of delayed expectation, questioning, "why should wee looke for it [maturity] in a *disease*, which is the *disorder*, the *discord*, the *irregularitie*, the *commotion*, and *rebellion* of the *body*?" (97). He next complements this string of unsettling synonyms with an image that epitomizes the experience of helplessness, that of "a [pregnant] *woman* that is weake, [and] cannot put off her *ninth moneth* to a *tenth*, for her *deliverie*" (98). He then repeats the idea, adding another dyslogistic association as he continues, "nor a *Queene* cannot hasten it to a *seventh*, that shee may bee ready for some other pleasure" (98).

Donne continues developing the theme of frustrated expectation as he matches his natural metaphor with a parallel experience in human affairs: "There are of *them* that will *give*, that will doe *justice*, that will *pardon*, but they have their owne *seasons* for al these, and he that knowes not *them*, shall *starve* before that gift come, and *ruine*, before the Justice, and *dye* before the pardon save him" (98). The reader is invited to identify with the plight of those waiting in utter dependence on the provision of another for their basic human needs. Donne amplifies the point by multiplying instances of this plight, arranged in order of severity and with *anaphora*:

> [S]ome *tree* beares no fruit, except much *dung* be laid about it, and *Justice* comes not from some, till they bee richly manured: some *trees* require much *visiting*, much *watring*, much *labour*; and some men give not their *fruits* but upon *importunitie*; some *trees* require *incision*, and *pruning*, and *lopping*; some men must bee *intimidated* and *syndicated* with *Commissions*, before they will deliver the fruits of *Justice*; some *trees* require the *early* and the *often* access of the *Sunne*; some men *open* not, but upon the *favours* and *letters* of *Court mediation*; some *trees* must bee *housd* and kept within doores; some men locke up, not onely their liberalitie, but their *Justice*, and their *compassion*, till the sollicitation of a *wife*, or a *sonne*, or a *friend*, or a *servant* turne the *key*. (98)

At the end of the meditation, Donne introduces another field of imagery, besiegement, amplifying his own distress by speculating, "O how many farre more miserable, and farre more worthy to be lesse miserable than I, are beseiged with this *sicknesse*, and lacke their *Sentinels*, their *Physitians* to *watch*, and lacke their *munition*, their *cordials* to *defend*, and perish before the *enemies* weaknesse might invite them to *sally*" (98–99).

Donne begins the nineteenth exposition with his famous reflections on his "*metaphoricall God*" before continuing the assault of *pathos* begun in the meditation, returning again to the journey *topos*. Throughout the exposition he raises the possibility of comfort and relief, only to undermine this hope at every turn. Adopting God's metaphorical manner, says Donne, "I am bold to call the comfort which I receive now in this sicknesse, in the *indication* of the *concoction* and *maturity* there of, in certaine *clouds*, and *res-*

idences, which the *Physitians* observe, a discovering of *land* from *Sea*, after a long, and tempestuous *voyage*" (19E, 100). Donne's vivid imagery has made his reader feel the weariness and anxiety of this journey, and now he raises the promise of a destination of rest: land. But he promptly thrusts the reader back into the storm as he questions, "wherefore, O my *God*, hast thou presented to us, the *afflictions* and *calamities* of this life, in the name of *waters*? so often in the name of *waters*, and *deepe waters*, and *Seas* of *waters*? must we looke to bee *drowned*? are they *bottomlesse*, are they *boundless*?" (100). And then relief is promised once again as he continues with the answer, "Thats not the *dialect* of thy *language*; thou hast given a *Remedy* against the deepest *water*, by *water*; against the *inundation* of sinne, by *Baptisme*; and the first *life*, that thou gavest to any *Creatures*, was in *waters*; therefore thou doest not threaten us, with an *irremediablenesse*, when our *affliction* is a *Sea*" (100).

The rest of the expostulation continues like the ebb and flow of the sea, overwhelming the reader with a strong impression of life's afflictions only to offer hope before bringing another wave of life's turmoil. Donne again agitates his reader by confirming that affliction is indeed a sea, "if we consider *our selves*." From a lake, to a sea, to the great sea, to a flood, and finally to the Great Deluge, this life of affliction grows by degrees until it "is above my *strength*" and "*secular Mountaines*; men *strong in power*, spirituall mountaines, men *strong in grace*, are shaken with *afflictions*" (101). Yet God, who controls the waves, calls back the whelming flood "when they have done their *service*, to humble thy *patient*." Similar to yet different from the Hebrews, who "*passed Jordan dry foot*," the redeemed "run into the red Sea (the Sea of thy *Sons bloud*) & the red Sea, that red Sea, drownes none of *thine*." In the atonement, affliction itself is turned to the way of salvation. But, continues Donne, quoting Ecclesiasticus 43:24[26], "*they that saile in the Sea, tell of the danger thereof*" and of God's provision therein. Yet God in his providence is unfathomable, observes Donne, and "Since thou art so, O my God, and *affliction* is a *Sea*, too deepe for us, what is our *refuge*?" (101). The answer is that God uses means on earth: "thine *Arke*, thy *ship*." In the case of sickness, God's means is a physician. But in the great deluge of sin, his ark is the church where the Word is preached. For the next page or so of text, Donne amplifies the image of the ship as a place of refuge, citing several instances in Scripture. But impatience takes over, as it often does on a long voyage, and Donne asks, "O my *God*, my *God*, since *I have my ship* [his physicians], and *they theirs* [religion], I have *them*, and they have *thee*, why are we yet no neerer land?" (102). This longing for final rest finds temporal satisfaction where "the *assurance* of *future mercy*, is *present mercy*." "But what is my *assurance* now?" asks Donne, "What is my *seale*? It is but a *cloud*." This cloud is the indication, observed by the physicians, that the disease is relenting, which Donne likens to the cloud that guided the Hebrews in the wilderness and the cloud that signaled rain to Elijah in a time of drought. Throughout his meditation and expostulation, Donne amplifies the affliction of sickness and, more importantly, the affliction of sin, replicating in his reader the tumult of a sea journey that gives rise to desire for rest in God. When rest finally comes, it is temporary, as he prays, "O *Lord*, let *this daies* comfort be the *earnest* of to *morrowes*, so farre as may *conforme* me entirely to thee, to what *end*, and by what *way* soever thy *mercie* have appointed mee" (19E; 104).

As Sharon Seelig notes, Donne becomes more agitated as the threat of death recedes at the conclusion of the *Devotions*. This is because "[t]he real danger, as one returns to the mundane affairs of everyday life, is of relapsing into sin"; more precisely, Donne aims to prevent his audience from falling back into spiritual insensibility and complacency (108). In the final cycle he rues the "sinfull *carelesnesse*" of relapse and fears "*indevotion, and spirituall coldnesse*," and he prays to the "*God* of *constancie*, and *perseverance*" that his "*Spirit* of *Remorce*, and *Compunction* shall never *depart* from mee" (23M, 122; 23E, 123; 23P, 126–27). Thus Donne ends with cycle 23, a number of incompleteness, so that the larger cycle of the *Devotions* is prevented from coming to a full stop.[17] It must carry on. The soul must always be kept ready to seek peace in God.

Because of this habitual insensitivity of the soul, the Christian must be continually reminded in startling fashion. Donne's *Devotions Upon Emergent Occaions* thus functions much like the poetry of lament described by George Puttenham in *The Arte of English Poesie* (1589). Donne, like the elegiac poet, is himself a Paracelsian physician who "mak[es] the very greef it selfe (in part) cure of the disease" (Puttenham 62). But Donne's cure is even more radical. He introduces grief where there is none, afflicting the well with a sense of spiritual misery by means of a series of meditations on his own physical illness. The remedy comes when the devotee, compelled by a sense of profound need experienced in the agitation of the meditation and expostulation, turns for rest and restoration to the Great Physician in prayer. To accomplish this effect in his congregation of readers, Donne employs his considerable skill as a preacher, using his familiar formal pattern of fall and redemption, vividly portrayed in the circumstances of his illness, to arouse in his audience a renewed desire for the God of all comfort.

Notes

1. It was common for Donne to find sermon material in his private devotional exercises. He tells his congregation in a sermon preached at Lincolns Inn (probably in 1618), "as a hearty entertainer offers to others, the meat which he loves best himself, so doe I oftnest present to Gods people, in these Congregations, the meditations which I feed upon at home" (2:49). Donne makes similar associations in the prefatory letter that accompanied the publication of his sermon to the Virginia Company in 1622 (4:264) and again in 2:167.

2. The Ignatian influence is noted by Thomas F. Van Laan, R. L. Abrahamson, Anthony Raspa (in Donne, *Devotions*), and David Sullivan. N. J. C. Andreasen notes similarities between Donne and the typically Protestant approach of Joseph Hall, and Gerard H. Cox III sees marks of Hooker's notion of steps of repentance. A general Protestant influence is also noted by Janel M. Meuller, Jonathan Goldberg, and Mary Arshagouni Papazian ("Donne, Election" and "Literary 'Things Indifferent'"). Thomas J. Morrissey rightly concludes that Donne borrows from both Catholic and Protestant meditative theory. Kate Narveson categorizes the *Devotions* as a "holy soliloquy," an anatomizing of the self for the full view and edification of others, a generic tradition she traces from Augustine through near-contemporaries of Donne: Thomas Rogers, Sir John Hayward, Bishop Arthur Lake, and Phineas Fletcher. Kate Gartner Frost places the *Devotions* in the tradition of spiritual autobiography of self-scrutiny that is both confessional and exemplary (*Holy Delight*, ch. 2).

3. Van Laan (194) and Andreasen (207) characterize the *Devotions* as subjective, personal, and private. Helen White similarly describes them as "highly personal revelations," ultimately concluding that they are of "much more significance from the literary than the devotional point of view" (253–54). The extreme case of this tendency is John Sparrow, who questions its devotional value, appreciating it instead for its psychological intrigue as "a unique revelation of a unique mind" (Donne, *Devotions* xxiii).

4. Kate Frost describes the autobiographical self-fashioning of the *Devotions*, which, she says, despite its audience consciousness, remains essentially personal in orientation (26). Similarly, Kate Narveson classifies the *Devotions* as holy soliloquy, which, in the conformist tradition, constituted a public sharing of what was nonetheless an inherently personal experience (118–19).

5. See Papazian, "Latin '*Stationes*.'"

6. According to Anthony Low, of the three main faculties involved in meditation—memory, understanding, and will—"most meditative treatises emphasize the second state, exact and discursive use of the understanding" (37).

7. Anthony Raspa similarly argues that Donne selectively adapted the operations of Ignatius's "three powers of the mind"—memory, understanding, and will—to his own purposes by focusing on their discursive function "because he needed such an argumentative structure to satisfy his dialectical cast of mind" (Donne, *Devotions* xxxix).

8. I use the less common term *pathopoeia* instead of *pathos* in order to prevent twenty-first-century connotations that distort the technical sense of the term, especially in its adjectival form, *pathetic*.

9. I use the term *form* rather than *structure* because the former carries the sense of an essential organizing principle. Abrams summarizes R. S. Crane on this point: "The form of a literary work is (in the Greek term) the 'dynamis,' the particular 'working' or 'emotional power' that the work is designed to effect, and that functions as its 'shaping principle.' This formal principle controls and synthesizes the 'structure' of a work—the order, emphasis, and rendering of all its components, materials and parts—into a 'beautiful and effective whole of a determinate kind'" (64–65).

10. For a fuller elaboration of this rhetorical form in Donne's sermons, see chapter 3 in my *Holy Ambition: Rhetoric, Courtship, and Devotion in the Sermons of John Donne* (forthcoming with *Medieval and Renaissance Texts and Studies*).

11. In describing the self-examination of the *Devotions*, Narveson (115) quotes part of this passage and notes in passing Donne's use of a similar pattern in the *Devotions*.

12. The text reads: "We pray yee in Christs stead, be ye reconciled to God." Donne's Latin term *Obsecramus* is the Latin equivalent of the original Greek word δεομεθα, which he does not supply.

13. Potter and Simpson date the delivery of this sermon in either 1621 or 1623 (5:15).

14. Elsewhere Donne says that "I know that in the state of my *body*, which is more *discernable*, than that of my soule, thou dost *effigiate* [make an image of] my *Soule* to me" (22E, 119); and so he prays, "let mee alwaies so apprehend *thee*, as *present* with me, and yet so *follow* after thee, as though I had not apprehended thee" (22P, 120). Playing on a double sense of *apprehend*, Donne seeks to understand God's presence in every occasion, but always to be striving to possess him.

15. Donne asks Kerr "whether there be any uncomlinesse, or unseasonablenesse, in presenting matter of Devotion, or Mortification" to Prince Charles (*Letters to Severall Persons of Honour* 215).

16. Raspa speaks of the "vividness of the reader's experience" (Donne, *Devotions* xxxvii).

17. On the numerological significance of the structure of Donne's *Devotions* see Frost 126–57.

Works Cited

Abrahamson, R. L. "The Vision of Redemption in Donne's *Devotions Upon Emergent Occasions.*" *Studia Mystica* 6.1 (1983): 62–69.

Abrams, M. H. *A Glossary of Literary Terms.* 3rd ed. New York: Holt, Rinehart and Winston, 1971.

Andreasen, N. J. C. "Donne's *Devotions* and the Psychology of Assent." *Modern Philology* 62.3 (1965): 207–16.

Arndt, Murray. "Distance on the Look of Death." *Literature and Medicine* 9 (1990): 38–49.

Calvin, John. *Institutes of the Christian Religion.* Ed. John T. McNeill, trans. Ford Lewis Battles. Vol. 2. Philadelphia: Westminster, [1960].

Cox, Gerard H., III. "Donne's *Devotions:* A Meditative Sequence on Repentance." *Harvard Theological Review* 66 (1973): 331–51.

Donne, John. *Devotions Upon Emergent Occasions.* Ed. Anthony Raspa. Montreal: McGill-Queen's UP, 1975.

———. *Devotions Upon Emergent Occasions.* Ed. John Sparrow. Cambridge: Cambridge UP, 1923.

———. *Letters to Severall Persons of Honour.* Ed. Charles Edmund Merrill, Jr. New York: Sturgis & Walton, 1910.

———. *Sermons.* Ed. George R. Potter and Evelyn M. Simpson. 10 vols. Berkeley: U of California P, 1953–62.

Frost, Kate Gartner. *Holy Delight: Typology, Numerology, and Autobiography in Donne's Devotions Upon Emergent Occasions.* Princeton: Princeton UP, 1990.

Goldberg, Jonathan. "The Understanding of Sickness in Donne's *Devotions.*" *Renaissance Quarterly* 24 (1971): 507–17.

Halewood, William H. *The Poetry of Grace.* New Haven: Yale UP, 1970.

Hyperius, D. Andreas. *The practise of preaching, otherwise called the Pathway to the Pulpet.* Trans. John Ludham. London, 1577.

Lewalski, Barbara. *Donne's "Anniversaries" and the Poetry of Praise: The Creation of a Symbolic Mode.* Princeton: Princeton UP, 1973.

Low, Anthony. *Love's Architecture: Devotional Modes in Seventeenth-Century English Poetry.* New York: New York UP, 1978.

Morrissey, Thomas J. "The Self and the Meditative Tradition in Donne's *Devotions.*" *Notre Dame English Journal* 13.1 (1980): 29–49.

Mueller, Janel M. "The Exegesis of Experience: Dean Donne's *Devotions Upon Emergent Occasions.*" *Journal of English and Germanic Philology* 67 (1968): 1–19.

Narveson, Kate. "Piety and the Genre of Donne's *Devotions.*" *John Donne Journal* 17 (1998): 107–36.

Nelson, Brent. *Holy Ambition: Rhetoric, Courtship, and Devotion in the Sermons of John Donne* (forthcoming with *Medieval and Renaissance Texts and Studies*).

Papazian, Mary Arshagouni. "Donne, Election, and the *Devotions Upon Emergent Occasions*." Huntington Library Quarterly 55.4 (1992): 603–19.

———. "The Latin '*Stationes*' in John Donne's *Devotions Upon Emergent Occasions*." *Modern Philology* 89.2 (1991): 196–210.

———. "Literary 'Things Indifferent': The Shared Augustinianism of Donne's *Devotions* and Bunyan's *Grace Abounding*." *John Donne's Religious Imagination: Essays in Honor of John T. Shawcross*. Ed. Raymond-Jean Frontain and Frances M. Malpezzi. Conway: U of Central Arkansas P, 1995. 324–49.

Puttenham, George. *The Arte of English Poesie*. Ed. Edward Arber, intro. Baxter Hathaway. 1906. Kent, OH: Kent State UP, 1970.

Rollins, Roger B. "John Donne's *Holy Sonnets*—The Sequel: *Devotions Upon Emergent Occasions*." *John Donne Journal* 13:1–2 (1994): 51–60.

Seelig, Sharon. "In Sickness and in Health: Donne's *Devotions Upon Emergent Occasions*." *John Donne Journal* 8.1–2 (1989): 103–13.

Shuger, Debora K. *Sacred Rhetoric: The Christian Grand Style in the English Renaissance*. Princeton: Princeton UP, 1975.

Sullivan, David. "The Structure of Self-Revelation in Donne's *Devotions*." *Prose Studies* 11.2 (1988): 49–59.

Van Laan, Thomas F. "John Donne's *Devotions* and the Jesuit Spiritual Exercises." *Studies in Philology* 60 (1963): 191–202.

White, Helen C. *English Devotional Literature [Prose] 1600–1640*. Madison: [U of Wisconsin P], 1931.

10

Breaking Down the Walls That Divide

Anti-Polemicism in the *Devotions Upon Emergent Occasions*

ELENA LEVY-NAVARRO

Given the volatile history of Donne criticism, I worry that we might be entering a new era where we will now apply our new religio-political terminology to him. Should we import the new terms that recent revisionist history of the period has to offer— whether "avant-garde conformist," "church papist," or "conforming puritan"?[1] This essay explains why I answer "no" to this question. Such terms, coined to characterize the complex political atmosphere of Donne's day, do not sufficiently describe his purposeful anti-polemicism. In my view, Donne reacted to growing divisions in the church, widening in the 1620s, by developing strategies to repair them. Consequently, these new terms are inappropriate because they make him part of a specific faction rather than the anti-polemicist I believe he is.

In this essay, I consider the way that the *Devotions Upon Emergent Occasions*, Donne's account of his illness in late 1623 that he published in 1624, takes an anti-polemicist position in order to renew and revitalize "*true Religion*" in England (*Devotions* 102). Much of his terminology, including the use of the words "true religion" itself, suggests that Donne was committed to the fundamentals of the Reformation heritage of the Church of England. Donne counters an emerging polemicism in the church, evident in the increase of inflammatory pamphlets and sermons in the 1620s, in order to conserve what he sees as the foundation of its Reformation heritage. In a 1624 Easter Day sermon, Donne makes it clear that England as a nation must preserve its Reformation heritage. He uses a strikingly unorthodox version of millenarianism as he describes the Reformation as bringing the second coming of Christ. Now that they have "raigned so with Christ, but 100. yeares," they must "persist in a good use of it" so that their posterity will "make that 100.1000" (6:68). Donne's millenarian account places considerable pressure on his contemporaries by insisting that the Church of England is required by God to remain true to what he conceives of as a doctrinally minimalistic Reformation heritage.

In using terms like "*true Religion*" and even in implying, if not saying, that he is more "moderate" than his contemporaries, Donne undoubtedly participates in the polemics of his day.[2] I am not arguing that Donne rises above politics, since, I believe, his masterful, innovative, and often beautiful imagery emerges as he reacts to what he considers the tense religio-political atmosphere of his day. Surely, Donne's unorthodox version of millenarianism can be explained, for example, by his efforts to redefine the nature of the church settlement. In offering his own version of this church settlement, one that stops further reform in doctrine and discipline of the church, Donne is undoubtedly taking a political position. In fact, any person who wants to push for further reform in either doctrine or discipline is implicitly labeled an extremist. Donne attempts to stop the Reformation at some earlier self-consciously minimalistic settlement in order to prevent, for example, any further specification of Article 17, the controversial and vague article on predestination. Obviously, all such reformers would find Donne to be rather political, indeed.

I use the term "anti-polemicist," then, not so much to suggest that Donne is apolitical as to suggest the type of engagement he had with the polemical wars of the 1620s. Precisely because Donne writes in a purposefully anti-polemicist way in his sermons and the *Devotions*, we cannot define him by turning to any of the religio-political categories used to describe the emerging factions of his day. We can, however, follow the lead of a number of historians (e.g., Peter Lake, Lori Anne Ferrell, and Anthony Milton) to show how Donne responded to the religio-political milieu of his day in a complex and sometimes unexpected manner. In examining Donne in relation to his contemporaries, it becomes clear that he is one of those figures who quite purposefully seems to have refused to take sides in the polemical wars of his day; thus, although he draws on rhetoric used by polemicists, Donne does so in an effort to silence dissent and create a more devout and thus quiescent church membership.

According to Donne's unorthodox millenarian view of history, the present-day Church of England must actively work to persevere in its

Reformation faith. In several sermons, Donne urges his church audience to focus on their shared Reformation heritage rather than on what he defines as less important and potentially divisive religious concerns. For Donne, true religion is facing a crisis in England as it enters the second century of the Reformation because too many people, such as avant-garde conformists and puritans, are focusing on contentious issues surrounding various types of *adiaphora*, things indifferent—that is, those things that are not necessary for salvation.[3] Donne insists that the church needs indifferent practices, thereby closing off any push for further ceremonial reform in the church. For precisely this reason, the church membership should avoid arguing over these practices. All such arguments, Donne insists, focus too much on "speculative divinity" at the expense of "practical divinity."[4] In making such arguments, Donne alternately criticizes both puritans and avant-garde conformists for focusing too much on uncertain points rather than sticking to the fundamentals upon which the church is built.

Donne's anti-polemicism makes it particularly difficult to categorize him, especially if we apply factional terms drawn from his contemporary situation. We could follow his lead and call him by the simple term "Christian," but this term would still be misleading insofar as it might not underscore his true commitment to a broadly defined Reformation faith.[5] Clearly, Donne believes that the Reformation ushered in the "true faith," even though he does not believe that that faith is restricted only to the present-day Church of England. The late-medieval Church of Rome only became a false church when it doggedly refused to allow its people access to Scripture.[6] In his purposefully minimalistic description of the foundation of the Reformation faith, Donne focuses largely on the evangelical role of the church. The church must make Christ available to the people by cultivating a preaching ministry and by making the vernacular Bible available to its members. Typically, Donne speaks fervently about the centrality of preaching in the church.[7] As he states in the *Devotions*, the church offers its people the "means" of salvation where the "*meanes* is preaching" (101). Donne clearly is a Reformation figure, even if he is not a "puritan" one.

The conclusion of the *Devotions* will suffice to demonstrate that Donne is committed to broadly conceived principles of the English Reformation. Donne employs the rhetoric of a militant Protestantism, a rhetorical mainstay of the Church of England since the reign of Queen Elizabeth, yet in a characteristically anti-polemicist way. To put it another way, Donne resists the dualism that had dominated under Queen Elizabeth in the same way that he resists the implicit dualism in the rhetoric of the emerging avant-garde conformists. The militant Protestants saw the world in dualistic terms as a struggle between the true and false religions, embodied sometimes in the nation itself and sometimes in a church. To offer a rough outline, the English nation was seen as God's chosen people, who were locked in a cosmic battle against the enemies of God, alternately characterized as the Whore of Babylon or Antichrist and equated with either the Church of Rome, the papacy, or the Spanish Empire. Such a dualistic worldview was useful under Queen Elizabeth, since it assured that many in the nation would support her war efforts against Spain, but the same worldview became problematic when the national context changed under the reign of King James. Now, this dualistic worldview did lead some in the ministry and populace to attack James's policies as too sympathetic to the Catholic cause.[8]

Donne employs much the same rhetoric, but now in order to encourage the reader to engage in the type of devotional life depicted in the *Devotions*. In section 23, Donne speaks to the English nation as God's chosen people, warning them that they must not relapse into "idolatry," a term that, as Milton explains, is a fairly muted term for popery (187–228). Again employing the seemingly inflammatory language of a militant Protestant, Donne warns the English readership that "*Idolatry* in any *Nation* is *deadly;* but when the *disease* is *complicated* with a *relapse* . . . it is *desperate*" (124). Such rhetoric might suggest in another context that they must stamp out idolatry entirely, but Donne resists such a conclusion, urging readers, instead, to look to their own devotional lives. The duty of England as God's chosen nation is merely to "persist" in their faith, not to enter into combat with idolatrous nations like Spain or to engage in a domestic campaign of iconoclasm. To quote from a 1622 sermon that uses the same terminology as section 23 of the *Devotions*, "True repentance destroyes this Idolatry" (4:140).

In what follows, I resist the assumption that any single religious label, even taken from recent historiography of the Stuart church, could adequately explain a complex devotional work like the *Devotions*. I take as my starting point an article by Richard Strier, on what I think typifies this tendency, which argues that the *Devotions* is an avant-garde conformist text. Strier bases his argument largely on the mere presence of an admittedly papist and extra-scriptural ritual in the work, the ceremony of the bells. While Donne is undoubtedly responding to the polemics of the avant-garde conformists and their "opponents," the puritans, he is doing so not to advance the avant-garde conformist position, as Strier maintains, but rather in an explicitly anti-polemicist manner that undermines this avant-garde conformist position. Thus, to point to the presence of a ritual to establish avant-garde conformism and thereby argue for Donne's support of this position, as Strier does, misses Donne's point. On the contrary, readers of Donne need to examine in-depth the way Donne describes the ceremony.[9] Such an examination will reveal that Donne promotes the ceremony in terms that exceed the exclusionary logic of his present-day polemicist, including the avant-garde conformists. By examining the "devotions of the *Devotions*" (Strier 99), as Strier urges us to do, it becomes clear that Donne recommends a form of worship that can be acceptable to both sides, provided they do not insist on reforming the church so that it promotes their position alone.

If we contrast the *Devotions* with two key documents of the avant-garde conformist faction that was emerging in England in the 1620s, we can see that Donne is neither an avant-garde conformist specifically nor a polemicist generally. The term "avant-garde conformist" was coined by early modern church historian Peter Lake to designate a small group of polemically minded court preachers. Others have preferred the term "anti-Calvinist," "Arminian," "sacramentalist conformist," or "Laudian" (Tyacke, Davies, and Ferrell). No matter what their name, this group clearly gained ascendancy in the 1620s because it supported King James's unpopular foreign policy such as his ongoing negotiations for the Spanish Match and James's refusal to enter into the Thirty Years' War on the side of the beleaguered Protestants.[10] These two policies alone were enough to make many in England question James's commitment to Protestantism. In the 1620s, even preachers would use their pulpits to express their opposition to James's pro-Catholic policies.[11] Under this atmosphere, the avant-garde conformists gained ascendancy with King James because their religious beliefs allowed them to defend James's unpopular policies, disliked by much of the population, including many ministers.

The loose group of insiders and more marginal figures that made up the avant-garde conformists employed exclusionary rhetoric in an attempt to redefine the church settlement in England. Avant-garde conformists characterized as extremists those who were previously considered to be in the mainstream of the church, those whom Donne understood to be invested in the broad principles of "true religion." That the avant-garde conformists were gaining the upper hand is evident in King James's 1620 "devotional" work, *A Meditation Upon the 27. 28. 29 Verses of the XXVII. Chapter of Saint Matthew*. This text is a counterpart to the immensely influential *Basilikon Doron* (1599 and 1603), a work of advice to James's now deceased son, Prince Henry (he died of typhus in 1612), on how to govern a kingdom. The *Meditation*, transcribed by the king's powerful favorite,

George Villiers, duke of Buckingham, and offered as advice for his son, Prince Charles, on how to govern, clearly offered indications of a shift in James's religio-political policy toward the position articulated by avant-garde conformists like Lancelot Andrewes.

The *Meditation* shows just how much James had come to accept the avant-garde conformists' position, which serves to marginalize and demonize those who had once been in the mainstream of the church as dangerous "puritans." The term "puritan," like the terms "church papist" and "papist," is a vexed one in large part because those whom we designate as "puritans" rejected it as a slur. However, the term, like the term "papist," is useful, especially in discussing either polemicism or the politically charged atmosphere of the early seventeenth century.[12] Moreover, the term is particularly useful when one considers James's own religio-political policy, since he seems to alternate between perceiving either "papists" or "puritans" as threats to the church and state. For the first part of his reign, James had been largely interested in the threat posed by the "papist"; thus his *Meditation* signals a significant change in policy when it focuses on the threat posed by the "puritan." After the 1605 Gunpowder Plot, a foiled attempt to blow up Parliament and with it James and his family, James took efforts to assure himself that the papists were loyal. He attempted to do so by requiring many papists to take the Oath of Allegiance. When the papacy insisted publicly that the oath could not be taken by Catholics, James sponsored, and even participated in, a polemical battle between English Protestants and European Catholics, most famously Robert Bellarmine. Those puritans whom James would denounce in the *Meditation* were some of his greatest defenders in this war to control the papists both at home and abroad.

In the *Meditation*, James represents himself as a suffering Christ who is persecuted by these newly coined "puritans." According to this new politically charged rhetoric, the "puritans" consist of all who refuse to offer external proof of their obedience by submitting to the rituals of the church. In the *Meditation*, James presents sacramentality not so much as a visible sign of holiness but rather as a visible sign of political obedience.[13] James condemns "These therefore, that will refuse in any place or at any time to worship *Christ* as well in body as in soule, [for they] are in that point inferiour to those prophane souldiers [who persecuted Christ]: which I wish were well observed by our foolish superstitious *Puritanes*, that refuse to kneele at the receiving of the blessed *Sacrament*" (234). James seems to have thoroughly internalized the exclusionary rhetoric of the avant-garde conformists, a rhetoric that, contrary to recent historiography of the

Church of England, defines all who disagree with them on all points of religion to be outside the boundaries of the English church. For James and his fellow avant-garde conformists, all individuals should submit to rituals to prove their obedience to church and state. Failure to do so excludes them from the Church of England.

As the passage quoted above demonstrates, by the early 1620s King James is already siding with the avant-garde conformists against those "puritans" who had previously been in the mainstream of the church. Now, ceremonial conformity would be required as a sign of obedience to the church, state, and king. According to Lori Anne Ferrell, the avant-garde conformists increased their power as they entered the debate over ceremonial conformity that took place in relation to the Scottish Kirk in its 1617 Perth Assembly (150–53). There, Scottish presbyters angrily decried the Five Articles endorsed by King James and the limited episcopacy he had installed earlier in his reign. The fifth article was especially offensive to many in the Kirk because it required the congregation to kneel at communion, a papist practice. When the debates of the Perth Assembly moved into print, the English avant-garde conformists could now show themselves to be loyal to James by warring with the disruptive and unruly puritans. Thus, avant-garde preachers in England, most notably Lancelot Andrewes and John Buckeridge, could use this foreign debate to characterize their English counterparts as dangerous rebels who, if given the chance, would cause as many problems in England as their Scottish counterparts caused in Scotland (Ferrell 151). In what Ferrell describes as "a new shriller style" of preaching, the avant-garde conformists insisted that those who refused to conform themselves to even the most indifferent practices, such as kneeling at communion, were dangerous rebels. As this implies, the avant-garde conformists were effective in convincing James that those ceremonies that were once deemed indifferent should be imposed on the members.

Where Donne allows individual members to follow their conscience as to whether to conform to such indifferent ceremonies, the avant-garde conformists absolutely require them as a sign of obedience to the church, state, and king. Kneeling to receive communion is required absolutely of the subject as a sign of reverence for, and obedience to, existing authority. One of the numerous tracts that weighed in on the debate over this practice, John Denison's *The Heavenly Banquet* (1619), argues both that "the Church hath power and authority to impose it [kneeling]" and that kneeling, "being so imposed ... is to be imbraced" (293). Denison offers a largely legalistic argument in insisting that ritual conformity is required by law.

"If a Church make a Law, or constitution," he explains, "eyther for sitting, or for standing, or for kneeling, at the receiving of the Lords Supper, the law should be obeyed" (91–92). In this view, individuals do not participate in a ritual primarily because it is helpful to their devotions or because it offers them an opportunity to make the holy visible, but rather in order to show their obedience to the authorities. Such rhetoric makes it clear that the avant-garde conformists were seeking to seize the church and force their opponents into submission. With its focus on law and order, this argument seems designed to appeal to King James because it focuses on the need to impose order on the unruly subjects.

One more text offers us a telling expression of the polemical spirit of the avant-garde conformists—John Buckeridge's 1618 tract defending the practice of kneeling to receive communion. Buckeridge, bishop of Rochester, was a key figure in this group of powerful men that included William Laud, the future archbishop of Canterbury under King Charles and present bishop of St. Davids; Richard Neile, bishop of Durham; and Lancelot Andrewes, bishop of Ely. Buckeridge seems to have been rather shrewd in knowing how to choose his battles, and he worked to promote the innovative doctrinal and ceremonial beliefs desired by the avant-garde conformists (Tyacke 106–24). Buckeridge's sermon certainly shows him doggedly advancing the position of the avant-garde conformists. He follows the much-beloved court preacher Lancelot Andrewes in setting up a stark opposition between "eye" and "ear," sacrament and preaching. Early in King James's reign, Andrewes used his facility with language to offer some of the first attacks on "puritans" even at a time when James proved more interested in the threats posed by papists. In a 1607 sermon preached before the king, Andrewes condemns those "people who stay only for sermons" in terms that seem designed to appeal to the king (5:195). Their refusal to stay for the whole ceremony implies a certain restlessness on their part, implicit in the slur "sermon-gadder" as well. Andrewes seeks in this early sermon to refashion the church so that it centers on the sacrament rather than preaching, where any members interested only in the latter are implicitly characterized as extremists. He even asserts that "godliness is as a sacrament... not the word to be heard, but the word also to be performed: or if it be not a sacrament it is not true godliness" (5:195). In "not to be heard," Andrewes defines holiness in a way that excludes the form of "ear-worship" that is central to preaching; in doing this, he is, of course, developing a polemic meant to control, and even exclude, those sermon-gadders as unruly. Overall, then, Andrewes insists on a binary where it must be either sign or word, sacrament or preaching, eye or ear. To oppose this exclusionary rhetoric, Donne will require both or all.

Buckeridge employs Andrewes's commonplace opposition to attack those sermon-gadders. Even the text he chooses—Psalm 95, "*venite, adoremus*"—foregrounds the opposition between ceremonial worship and preaching. From the very beginning of his sermon, Buckeridge makes the clearly polemical claim that the psalm can "never be fully expressed by words" (1). Obviously, many of those puritans he attacked would disagree with his point, since they were trained in preaching by listening and debating interpretations of Scripture in small study circles.[14] In what follows, Buckeridge attacks the puritans because they are said to desecrate the church: "It is not said . . . Come let us heare, as those doe that turne Oratories into Auditories, and Temples into Scholes, and all adoration and worship into hearing of a Sermon" (10). Buckeridge characterizes the puritans as those individuals who reject all public prayer and worship in favor of preaching alone. Significantly, the tract ends with a direct appeal to King James to impose his authority on these unruly church members. In a striking passage, Buckeridge affirms that "disobedience must be subjected to coercion, who bears not the sword in vain" (5–8). In other words, Buckeridge urges King James fairly directly to use civil power to enforce ceremonial conformity.

The *Devotions Upon Emergent Occasions* works to reverse this type of exclusionary rhetoric predominant among the polemicists described above. Rather than support any specific polemical position, Donne works to stabilize a settlement consistent with what he considers the foundational principles of the Reformation. In typical Donnean style, he refuses to reify the terms of the debate, and when given a choice between sacrament and preaching, Donne invariably chooses both. No one side, then, wins or is even presented with terms that would allow it to win. Donne rejects both positions—that of the avant-garde conformists and that of the anti-ceremonialist puritan—insofar as they are polemical and exclusionary, even as the individuals who hold the divergent views are invited into the church's fold. There is enough in this church, Donne seems to say, to satisfy all members, provided they are the type of people who want to be satisfied.

Despite Strier's opinion to the contrary, as discussed above, the mere presence of this or that ceremony in the *Devotions* does not establish that Donne is an avant-garde conformist. On the contrary, Donne includes the funeral bell in the *Devotions* in a manner that frustrates the exclusionary rhetoric of the polemicist, including the avant-garde conformist. The genre of the work, of course, is not polemical in nature, for at its center it focuses on Donne's private devotional struggles (Frost, Papazian). In this, Donne makes it clear that individuals only come to public worship once they have done their private duty as Christians. If individuals approach public worship in this way, the corporate worship in the congregation will become especially helpful for their private devotions. Such a position clearly places Donne at odds with any polemicist, and particularly with the avant-garde conformists. Donne never argues, as Buckeridge and Denison do, that individuals should simply submit to this practice to show obedience to the church, state, or king. Public worship, instead, is seen as something that helps and follows private worship.

Donne chooses to focus on a ceremony—the ceremony of the bells—that had not been at the center of recent polemical debates. As such, he does not appear to be endorsing one side or another, as he would if he had even recommended briefly the more contentious practice of kneeling to receive communion. The ceremony of the bells *could*, nonetheless, excite controversy in that it was clearly an indifferent ceremony and thus one of those ceremonies that drew suspicion from the godly as a vestige of papist practices.[15] Only in this way can Donne make his larger point that such indifferent ceremonies can be acceptable to all, including the puritan, if they are approached correctly. In the passages that follow, Donne goes to great lengths to show that he has considered all the shortcomings of the ceremony and has chosen, nonetheless, to participate in it because it offers him much-needed comfort and assurance of his future salvation.

Now, we need to consider how Donne embraces the ceremony of the bells in terms that are purposefully anti-polemicist. Neither church nor state requires him to participate in it, nor is it a ceremony required for salvation. As he describes the good and bad use of the ceremony, Donne makes it clear that the Church of England can never impose an indifferent ceremony on its members, as Buckeridge advocates, for it follows the Reformation tradition of protecting the "Christian liberty" of its members. Unlike the corrupt post-Tridentine Catholic Church, the Church of England allows its members to choose whether to participate in many of the most peripheral ceremonies, such as the ceremony of the bells to commemorate the death of a member of the community. In this, Donne aligns himself with the older understanding of indifferent ceremonies evident in the church before the contentious 1620s brought the rise of the avant-garde conformism.[16] In general, the church had followed Calvin's position on things indifferent. As Calvin explains in his *Institutes*, "the third part of Christian freedom lies in this: regarding outward things that are of themselves 'indifferent,' we are not bound before God by any religious obligation preventing us from sometimes using them and other times not using them, indifferently" (3.19.7; as quoted in Papazian, "Bunyan," 325).

Why, Donne asks in the *Devotions*, should he participate in ceremonies some godly members with Calvinist beliefs would reject as "pagan"? He answers this question without appealing to any external authority; instead, he argues, the ceremonies can prove useful for guiding private devotions. Indeed, ceremonies both unite the individual to the community and help promote private devotions. They offer a form of "natural" assistance to battle the "natural man" remaining in all humans. Once again, Donne uses an argument designed to appeal to a broad readership, including the puritan readers, whom the avant-garde conformists try to dismiss and marginalize. He employs the Calvinist doctrine of depravity to recommend a specific ceremonial practice. Such indifferent ceremonies remain in the church because of God's mercy for his fallen people:

> I know the *Church* needed not to have taken in from *Jew* or *Gentile*, any supplies for the exaltation of thy *glory*, or our *devotion*; of *absolute necessitie* I know shee needed not; But yet wee owe thee our thanks that thou has given her leave to doe so, and that as in making us *Christians*, thou diddest not destroy that which wee were before, *naturall men*, so in the exalting of our religious devotions now we are *Christians*, thou hast beene pleased to continue to us those *assistances* which did worke upon the affections of *naturall men* before. (84–85)

God reaches out to his humans from where they are. Aware that they are fallible and corrupt by nature, he offers them through his church "natural" aids that can appeal to them. Such ceremonies can prove helpful to individuals, who often seem to falter in their devotions without any external guidance.[17]

Donne's argument here is purposefully anti-polemicist in insisting that ceremony is simply not that important. As Donne's own words make clear, he refuses to attribute to such indifferent ceremonies the importance given them by any of the contemporary polemicists, whether from the puritans attacking them or the avant-garde conformists requiring them.[18] Now, ceremony is merely something "natural," to be used only insofar as it aids the more important private devotions. His position in the *Devotions* is designed to relieve the growing controversy in the church over ceremonial matters in a way that ideally will forestall any further discord and division.

Donne goes out of his way to expose the ceremony of the bells as one with no doctrinal or scriptural justification. Indeed, he lists all the shortcomings of the ceremonial practice: its pagan and papist origins and its tendency to promulgate superstitious beliefs. The bells are said to ward off evil spirits, and they are similarly associated with the belief that prayers for the dead can be efficacious (83, 93–94). Moreover, in foregrounding these shortcomings, Donne offers an alternative use for such ceremonies; they can serve a useful purpose for individuals provided they accept the bells' status as an indifferent ceremony. In making this point, Donne criticizes all puritans who work so hard to abolish rituals and all avant-garde conformists who work so hard to preserve them.[19]

In expostulation 16, Donne particularly criticizes those puritans who would cleanse the church of these rituals. In doing this, these puritans would be depriving people like Donne himself of useful and necessary aids to difficult private devotions. As he rejects the polemical position of non-conforming puritans, Donne underscores the usefulness of the ceremony, a position that would seem to align him with the avant-garde conformists discussed above. Donne uses the *Devotions* to make indifferent ceremonies, such as the ceremonies of the bells, more appealing to readers so that they will willingly participate in them. In the following passage, Donne focuses on all those reservations that a puritan might be likely to have regarding these ceremonies: "My *God*, my *God*, I doe not expostulate with *thee*, but with *them*, who dare doe that: Who dare expostulate with *thee*, when in the voice of thy *Church*, thou givest allowance, to this *Ceremony* of *Bells* at *funeralls*. Is it enough to refuse it, because it was in use amongst the *Gentiles*? so were *funeralls* too. Is it because some *abuses* may have crept in, amongst *Christians*? Is that enough, that their ringing hath been said to drive away *evill Spirits*" (83). Against all possible objections, Donne describes these ceremonies as merciful "allowances" that God has provided for weak humans; as such, only the most proud and foolish individual would refuse them, let alone seek to abolish them entirely from the church.

Thus far, the passages I have chosen might seem more explicitly directed against the puritan polemicist. Donne certainly dismisses those strident puritan polemicists, who would not allow anyone to participate in these ceremonies. Yet at the same time, he uses language designed to persuade other Calvinists of the possible benefits that indifferent ceremonies can provide. In short, Donne seeks to integrate, rather than to exclude, the puritan reader. In a similar way, he never argues that the individual is *required* by either church or state to conform to such indifferent ceremonies. Clearly an expert rhetorician, Donne describes the "ceremony" in a manner which makes it clear that his allegiance does not lie with the avant-garde conformist position.

Equally important, Donne resists the exclusionary rhetoric of the avant-garde conformist in the way he describes the funeral bell, for Donne describes the "ceremony" of the bell in a way that makes it impossible to use this section of the work for any specific polemical position, whether supporting the avant-garde conformist or puritan. Now, the funeral bell is not just a ceremony, but a ceremony that appeals to the ear; moreover, the tolling of the bell is described on several occasions in the *Devotions* as a "sermon." Contrary to the avant-garde conformists, Donne suggests that those distinctions between the "eye" and "ear" are meaningless. Devoted Christians will bring their whole body to public worship, just as they will willingly and zealously embrace the whole worship, sermon and ceremony together. Donne's description of his own participation undermines the exclusionary rhetoric employed by the polemicists of his day. All believers are invited to participate in the public worship wholeheartedly in a way which demands that they abandon those types of exclusionary categories and allegiances expressed by terms like "eye" and "ear."

What is the effect of dissolving this exclusionary rhetoric? Overall, Donne seems to imply that the church cannot be whole when its members are busy clinging to such divisive categories as those used in polemical works of the day. Both polemicists would end up closing either their ears or their eyes to God because they are too busy clinging to their unimportant and divisive categories. The puritan might refuse the ceremony because it is papist, and the avant-garde conformist might refuse the sermon because it is puritan. The two dimensions of public worship act best, however, when they work in concert. Even the *ceremony* of the bells cannot be divided from other aspects of the public worship; thus the first ringing of the funeral bell is "the *Bell* that rings to a *Sermon*" (86). Here, Donne insists that ceremony is yoked with sermon. Equally important, he continues by showing how the two together invite all members to the church: the bell "calls not upon the *Preacher* onely, but upon the *Congregation* to come; so this *Bell* calls us all" (86). Donne purposefully shows the bell uniting, not just sermon and ceremony, but preacher and congregation.

In a similar way, the tolling bells are able to break a number of other ordinary barriers that, for most of the *Devotions*, have seemed to divide Donne from the church. In the *Devotions*, the tolling bell brings the "sermon" to Donne even as he lies in bed, and in so doing it allows him to commune with the congregation. Donne no longer feels the same sense of devastating loneliness evident in the first five sections of the *Devotions*, where he even began to suspect that his isolation is a sign of his "*Excommunication*" and thus imminent damnation (25; see expostulations 3 and 5). Through the tolling funeral bell, Donne now becomes a participating member of the congregation and its worship service. In a similar way, his meditation on the tolling of the bell seems to break the barrier of time that divides him from God: "The *Bell* doth toll for him that *thinkes* it doth; and though it *intermit* againe, yet from that *minute*, that that occasion wrought upon him, hee is united to *God*" (86–87). The bell unites dead men with God, even as it unites Donne to both himself and God through his meditation on it. As Donne writes, "In that Contemplation I make account that I heare this dead brother of ours, who is now carried out to his *buriall*, to speake to mee, and to *preach* my *funerall Sermon*, in the voice of these *Bells*" (85). This whole section continually requires that we think beyond even the most seemingly apparent barriers of time and place. In so doing, it offers a vision of a larger Communion of the Saints that defies a number of distinctions, including those insisted upon by polemicists of Donne's day.

There is more to be said about this brilliant piece of devotional prose at the heart of the *Devotions*. I could speak of the way it breaks down all sorts of divisions in the larger church, for all Christians past, present, and future are included in this heavenly Communion of the Saints. For our purposes, it is most important to remember that Donne describes this heavenly communion in terms that are within the mainstream of the Reformation tradition. The ideal of the Communion of the Saints is absolutely consistent with a Calvinist belief in election and a Calvinist ecclesiology. That such rhetoric was part of a position recognized as Reformed by others is evident in the reception of the work in the Calvinist Netherlands. Paul Sellin describes the way that the Dutch translation of the *Devotions* was seen as consistent with a Dutch Reformed understanding of the Communion of the Saints.[20] The Communion of the Saints described in the conclusion of this section, prayer 18, is entirely consistent with a Calvinist worldview.

I end here, not because I want to conclude by arguing that Donne is a Calvinist, but because I want to underscore Donne's anti-polemicism. Here, we have considered the way that Donne undermined those exclusionary categories erected by the polemicists of his day. Donne was even more broadly anti-polemicist when it came to his vision of the larger church. The tolling of the bells comforts pious readers with the assurance that they are part of a larger Communion of the Saints. The vision of this larger heavenly communion at the heart of the *Devotions* requires that readers break down all of the numerous categories that divide Christian from Christian. This broad anti-polemicism, directed at the false divisions erected between even Catholics and Protestants, takes us beyond our present topic. Thus I observe only that this anti-polemicism can explain Donne's attitude toward Catholicism too. Donne directs his wrath against those polemicists of the post-Tridentine church—the Jesuits and papacy—while he refuses to condemn the simple recusant or the old-style Catholic.

Donne's desire to see the church in such expansive terms cannot be understood if we rely too heavily on the terms of recent historiography of the Stuart period. Insofar as such terms require us to place Donne in the limiting context of contemporary polemical debates, we will not be able to see the multiple ways he seeks to break down the barriers that divided the church in his day. Donne revels in imagining the moment of the final consummation as one that breaks down all the walls currently maintained and erected in the church by strident polemicists. In the last moment, "puritan" will be united with "avant-garde conformist," Catholic with Protestant, and all with Jesus Christ. That Donne constantly imagines this moment, here in the meditation on the tolling of the bell, suggests that he wants his audience to remember that present-day divisions are arbitrary and transitory. As he promises in an early sermon, "Jesus is amongst us all, and in his time, will break downe this wall too, these differences amongst Christians, and make us all glad of that name, the name of Christian" (2:112).

Notes

Many of the ideas presented in this essay were developed and refined at the 1998 NEH Summer Institute, "Redefining the Sacred in Early Modern England," hosted by the Folger Shakespeare Library, and at the 1999 NEH Seminar, "The English Reformation," hosted by Ohio State University. I would also like to thank Professor John N. King, who generously offered comments on earlier versions of this essay.

    1. The scholarship on Donne's political beliefs broadly conceived is substantial. In recent years, much of the discussion has centered around John Carey's claim that Donne was a careerist, absolutist, and apostate. Since my argument deals primarily with Donne's religious disposition, I refer the reader only to Shami for a broad discussion of the debate over Donne's absolutism. As for his religious disposition, see Papazian ("New Historicism") for a discussion of the *Devotions* in the context of the larger Reformation tendencies, Doerksen for the argument that he is part of a "Calvinist consensus" that is said to characterize the church, and Sellin

for the argument that he is in the mainstream of a more continental Reformed tradition. I am closest to Papazian, who argues in her fascinating article "New Historicism" that the *Devotions* should even be seen as representing Donne's purposeful turning away from a narrowly defined politics.

2. Recent historiography has undoubtedly taught us that terms like *via media*, once viewed as apolitical, were actually politically loaded terms used to bolster specific factional arguments. Peter Lake argues "that the manipulation, for partisan purposes, of even the most calmingly consensual strains of early Stuart discourse often represents a (thinly?) masked form of ideological conflict, the full resonances of which historians can only properly recover by a careful contextual reading of the sources in question" ("Moderate and Irenic Case" 57).

3. Donne consistently argues both to the church as a whole and to the individual that indifferent matters should be given less importance than fundamental ones. Thus, in a 1621 Christmas Day sermon he urges the Christian to develop "a love so perfect in the *fundamentall articles* of Religion, without impertinent additions" (3:375).

4. In a 1619 sermon "Preached to the Lords upon Easter-day, at the Communion, The King being then dangerously sick at New-Market," Donne notes that "nothing becomes a Christian better then sobriety; to make a true difference betweene problematicall and dogmaticall points" (2:203). In the same sermon, Donne criticizes the Council of Trent because it corrupted the Church of Rome by insisting that certain indifferent beliefs and customs must be believed as an article of faith. The Church of Rome proves that "nothing endangers a Church more, then to draw indifferent things to be necessary; I meane of a primary necessity, of a necessity to be beleeved, *De fide*" (2:204).

5. See, e.g., the passage I quote at the conclusion of this article. When Christ comes, all transitory names like "Lutheran" or "Calvinist" will be replaced by the simple term "Christian" (2:111). Significantly, in his earlier text *Pseudo-Martyr*, Donne calls himself by the simple term of "Christian" even as he describes his Catholic upbringing (8).

6. As an anti-polemicist, Donne does not exhibit the rabid antipopery that characterizes many of his contemporaries. When necessary, Donne does offer antipapist remarks, but virtually always in a manner that is directed at the institution rather than the people. His first sermon delivered to King Charles offers a succinct introduction to his particular brand of antipopery directed at the oppressive papacy and its minions, the Jesuits (6:241–61).

7. Doerksen similarly observes that Donne emphasizes preaching. While I agree with this conclusion, I question his overall interpretation of Donne because he describes him as belonging to the "preaching pastors" who are opposed to the "custodians of order" (terms taken from Fincham). Donne self-consciously focuses

on both preaching and ceremony and "order" in church government in a way which suggests that we cannot align him with any one of these factions. In a 1624 sermon delivered at St. Dunstans, Donne carefully endorses preaching in a way that is conciliatory to avant-garde conformists. Initially, he begins with the simple Reformation point "That we are bound to *teach*, and that this *teaching* is to *preach*," only later to insist that this duty "excludes not *Catechizing*" (6:104). Here again, Donne seeks to use his inclusionary rhetoric to settle ongoing divisions in the church, since the practice of catechizing had become a contentious issue ever since James issued the *Directions to Preachers* (1622), which sought to replace afternoon sermons with catechizing.

8. For a discussion of how this type of militant Protestant view altered in the reign of James, see Milton 94–111. For a discussion of the way this worldview could inspire violence in the populace, see Walsham, "Fatall Vesper." Finally, for a discussion of the type of polemical attacks leveled at James in this period, see Wright.

9. Strier purports to respond to "political discussions of the *Devotions*" even though he notably ignores Papazian's "Politics of John Donne's *Devotions*," which takes up the same issue only to come to a different conclusion.

10. See Cogswell for a description of the tense domestic atmosphere of the time.

11. McCullough describes a fascinating instance of such criticism delivered from the pulpit to King James himself (141–47).

12. For a brief introduction into the debate over the term "puritan," see Lake, "Defining Puritanism—again?" and Walsham, *Church Papist* 8–10, 11–15. Donne did not like the term "puritan," because he considered it a slur used to marginalize those in the mainstream of the church. In an undated sermon delivered when he was preacher at Lincoln's Inn, Donne observes, "Let a man be zealous, and fervent in reprehension of sin, and there flies out an arrow, that gives him a wound of a puritan" (2:158). In what follows, Donne levels the same argument at those who insist on calling their brethren who respect ceremony (the avant-garde conformists) "papists."

13. I am focusing on the political and polemical character of the avant-garde conformist position, evident even in the writing of its most prominent practitioner, Lancelot Andrewes. I am not focusing on their ceremonial impulse, described in Lake's "Laudian Style." My argument also suggests that Donne is not a member of the Laudian "cult of holiness" insofar as he refuses the developing dichotomy of the day by focusing simultaneously on public preaching and private devotions.

14. On the education of puritan preachers, both conforming and separatist, see Webster.

15. For a discussion of the controversies over ceremony on the level of the parish, see Cressy. In his discussion of funeral practices generally, Cressy briefly

discusses the objections raised against the practice of tolling the funeral bell (421–25).

16. See Ferrell for a discussion of the shift in the understanding of things indifferent in the radical 1620s from something left up to the member's conscience to something implicitly required.

17. When Donne comes to describe his later choice to accept ritual confession, administered at the hands of a priest, he uses precisely this form of argument: "I know, I am not submitted to such a *confession* as is a *racke* and *torture* of the *Conscience*. . . . If it were meerely *problematicall*, left meerely indifferent, whether we should take this *Physicke*, use this *confession*, or no, a great *Physitian* acknowledges this to have beene his *practise, To minister many things, which hee was not sure would doe good*" (*Devotions* 108). That this ritual is likened to "physicke" underscores the purpose of these indifferent rituals as aids to a weak and fallen human nature.

18. In a sermon delivered at Lincoln's Inn, Donne similarly denigrates ceremony by proclaiming that "I would be loath to put a *Master of Ceremonies* to define ceremony . . . in so constant a thing, as a Definition" (3:111).

19. In "The Crosse," most likely written during Donne's middle period in the late 1610s before his ordination into the Church of England, he similarly denounces those scandalous "puritans" whose institutional reforms would deprive him of potentially comforting, indifferent ceremonies. He writes, "From mee, no Pulpit, nor misgrounded law, / Nor scandall taken, shall this Crosse withdraw" (lines 9–10).

20. For a discussion of the Dutch translation of the *Devotions* and its reception in the Calvinist Netherlands, see Sellin 59–61.

Works Cited

Andrewes, Lancelot. *The Works of Lancelot Andrewes*. Ed. J. P. Wilson and J. Bliss. 11 vols. Oxford: Oxford UP, 1841–45.

Buckeridge, John. *A Sermon Preached before His Maiestie at Whitehall, March 22. 1617 being Passion-Sunday, Touching Prostration, and Kneeling in the Worship of God. To which is Added, A Discourse Concerning Kneeling at Communion*. London, 1618.

Carey, John. *John Donne: Life, Mind, Art*. Oxford: Clarendon, 1970.

Cogswell, Thomas. *The Blessed Revolution*. Cambridge: Cambridge UP, 1989.

Cressy, David. *Birth, Marriage, and Death: Ritual, Religion, and the Life-Cycle in Tudor and Stuart England*. Oxford: Oxford UP, 1997.

Davies, Julian. *The Caroline Captivity of the Church: Charles I and the Remoulding of Anglicanism, 1625–1641*. Oxford: Clarendon; New York: Oxford UP, 1992.

Denison, John. *The Heavenly Banquet: or The Doctrine of the Lords Supper.* London, 1619.

Doerksen, Daniel W. *Conforming to the Word: Herbert, Donne, and the English Church before Laud.* Lewisburg, PA: Bucknell UP; London: Associated UP, 1997.

———. "'Saint Pauls Puritan': John Donne's 'Puritan' Imagination in the Sermons." Frontain and Malpezzi 350–65.

Donne, John. *The Complete Poems of John Donne.* Ed. John T. Shawcross. New York: Doubleday, 1967

———. *Devotions Upon Emergent Occasions.* Ed. Anthony Raspa. New York: Oxford UP, 1987.

———. *Pseudo-Martyr.* Ed. Anthony Raspa. Montreal: McGill-Queen's UP, 1993.

———. *Sermons.* Ed. George R. Potter and Evelyn M. Simpson. 10 vols. Berkeley: U of California P, 1953–62.

Ferrell, Lori Anne. *Government by Polemic: James I, the King's Preachers, and the Rhetoric of Conformity, 1603–1625.* Stanford: Stanford UP, 1998.

Fincham, Kenneth. *Prelate as Pastor: The Episcopate of James I.* Oxford: Clarendon, 1990.

Frontain, Raymond-Jean, and Frances M. Malpezzi, eds. *John Donne's Religious Imagination: Essays in Honor of John T. Shawcross.* Conway: U of Central Arkansas P, 1995.

Frost, Kate Gartner. *Holy Delight: Typology, Numerology, and Autobiography in Donne's "Devotions Upon Emergent Occasions."* Princeton: Princeton UP, 1990.

James VI and I, King. *Political Writings.* Ed. Johann P. Sommerville. Cambridge: Cambridge UP, 1994.

Lake, Peter. "Defining Puritanism—again?" *Puritanism: Transatlantic Perspectives on a Seventeenth-Century Anglo-American Faith.* Ed. and intro. Francis J. Bremer. Massachusetts Historical Society Studies in Early American History and Culture, no. 3. Boston: Massachusetts Historical Society, 1993. 3–29.

———. "Lancelot Andrewes, John Buckeridge, and Avant-Garde Conformity at the Court of James I." *The Mental World of the Jacobean Court.* Ed. Linda Levy Peck. Cambridge: Cambridge UP, 1991. 113–33.

———. "The Laudian Style: Order, Uniformity, and the Pursuit of the Beauty of Holiness in the 1630s." *The Early Stuart Church.* Ed. Kenneth Fincham. Stanford: Stanford UP, 1993. 161–85.

———. "The Moderate and Irenic Case for Religious War: Joseph Hall's *Via Media* in Context." *Political Culture and Cultural Politics in Early Modern England: Essays Presented to David Underdown.* Ed. Susan D. Amussen and Mark A. Kishlansky. Manchester: Manchester UP, 1995. 55–83.

McCullough, Peter E. *Sermons at Court: Politics and Religion in Elizabethan and Jacobean Preaching.* Cambridge: Cambridge UP, 1998.

Milton, Anthony. *Catholic and Reformed: The Roman and Protestant Churches in English Protestant Thought, 1600–1640.* Cambridge: Cambridge UP, 1995.

Papazian, Mary Arshagouni. "Donne, Election, and the *Devotions Upon Emergent Occasions.*" *Huntington Library Quarterly* 55.4 (1992): 603–19.

———. "Literary 'Things Indifferent': The Shared Augustinianism of Donne's *Devotions* and Bunyan's *Grace Abounding.*" Frontain and Malpezzi 324–49.

———. "The Politics of John Donne's *Devotions Upon Emergent Occasions:* or, New Questions on the New Historicism." *Renaissance and Reformation* 15.3 (1991): 233–48.

Sellin, Paul R. *John Donne and the "Calvinist" View of Grace.* Amsterdam: VU Boekhandel, 1983.

Shami, Jeanne. "Donne's Sermons and the Absolutist Politics of Quotation." Frontain and Malpezzi 380–412.

Strier, Richard. "Donne and the Politics of Devotion." *Religion, Literature, and Politics in Post-Reformation England, 1540–1688.* Ed. Donna B. Hamilton and Richard Strier. Cambridge: Cambridge UP, 1996. 93–114.

Tyacke, Nicholas. *Anti-Calvinists: The Rise of English Arminianism, c. 1590–1640.* Oxford: Clarendon; New York: Oxford UP, 1987.

Walsham, Alexandra. *Church Papist: Catholicism, Conformity and Confessional Polemic in Early Modern England.* Woodfield, Suffolk, UK; Rochester, NY: Boydell P, 1993.

———. "'The Fatall Vesper': Providentialism and Anti-Popery in Late Jacobean London. *Past & Present* 144 (1994): 36–87.

Webster, Tom. *Godly Clergy in Early Stuart England: The Caroline Puritan Movement, c. 1620–1643.* Cambridge: Cambridge UP, 1997.

Wright, Louis B. "Propaganda against James I's 'Appeasement' of Spain." *Huntington Library Quarterly* 6.2 (1942–43): 149–72.

11

Reforming Baptism

John Donne and Continental Irenicism

ANNETTE DESCHNER

Living during the period of the Counter-Reformation, John Donne continually faced the effects of the Protestant Reformation and the age of denominationalism, a period of high religio-political debate that involved not only strict orthodox theologians of various denominations but also irenic theologians. The aim of the irenic movement—whose ideas were found among both Catholic and Protestant theologians—was to promote peace and reconcile the warring confessions. As this essay will show, Donne's lyric poetry as well as his prose and his sermons are driven by the idea of irenicism. Donne officially started his life as a Catholic, and his uncles, Jasper and Ellis Heywood, even belonged to the Jesuit order. But as Donne well understood, he could advance his career in Renaissance England only as a Protestant. Donne's concern with various religious conflicts, however, arose not only because of the troubles caused by religion within his family but also as a consequence of his professional ambition. King James was very concerned about religious peace and was even called the British Solomon. Like Donne's, King James's life was multiconfessional: although he was baptized as a Catholic, six months later he was crowned King James VI of Scotland according to the Protestant rite (Ebert 4). Thus Donne was confronted with confessional problems and irenic ideas in a sociocultural as well as in a religio-political context.

The aim of this essay is to locate Donne's work—his lyric poetry, prose writings, and sermons—within the irenic movement. Baptism, a rite that continues to be accepted in all Christian denominations and confessions, provides the perfect guide to help us trace Donne through this dogmatic maze. Baptism has less schismatic tendencies than the Eucharist, as the debates in Donne's time on the eucharistic rite show, and rather tends to integrate people into a congregation, a consequence of the irenic potential of baptism demonstrated in the early history of Christianity.

In earliest Christianity the rite of baptism was the motor of the ecumenical movement: different congregations accepted each other's rite of initiation. Mutual acceptance of this rite led to an accumulation of rites such as baptism by water, exorcism, the administering of salt, the handing over of candles, and anointing or the laying on of hands. Early Christian theologies concurred in establishing the boundaries of each group and agreed about how to define their own religious identity in contrast to other religious systems. Whereas other theological topics could be discussed controversially within the inclusive circle, the initiation rite had to be clearly determined because it constituted who was accepted within a community. Therefore the "name of Jesus" became the criterion of affiliation, for at that early stage of Christianity there did not exist a canon of scriptures, binding texts with a guideline function that could be used as a normative basis for a religious community. Because different theologies legitimatized themselves by the "name of Jesus," baptism, where this performative sentence was used, gained an ecumenical character (Berger 7). In other words, baptism became the universal basis for a congregation.

Early-seventeenth-century irenic thinkers regarded the early Christian church as the role model of Christian unity because it was thought that there had not existed any hardened dogmatic position in the early church and that therefore a united church was able to prosper. For the Dutch jurist and statesman Hugo Grotius (1583–1645), the ideal *ecclesia christiana* was realized in spiritual community. Grotius thought that if the Protestant denominations succeeded in becoming reunited, the Roman Catholic Church would want to imitate the Protestant achievement and thus join the Protestants within a universal church. For Grotius, this spiritual community consisting of Christ and those who believed in him was reinstituted and quantitatively expanded by each act of baptism, a perspective Donne also shared (Wolf 55). Grotius, whose interest lay in the theological harmony of the different denominations, also intended to bring about social and political peace based on harmonious interhuman relations. Consequently, he strove for a *pax dei*, which united not only all Christian confessions and denominations but also all human beings. To accomplish this, Grotius developed a strategy to strengthen the irenic movement. To start, he pushed for realization of a broad Protestant union, for he thought that a *unitas protestantium* could be an incentive to a universal irenicism for those Catholics who were open to reform. In other words, he wanted to unite all Protestants first and then create a unity among all Christians. Because Grotius felt that the early church was the only Christian congregation that had ever performed its actual task of establishing a universal community of love, he turned to it as the basis for the irenic idea that he was developing and for the development of fundamental articles (Wolf 55). By returning historically and ideologically to the basis of Christianity, Grotius was able to consider the diverse articles of faith of each denomination and confession, try to make their foundations clear for contemporary Christians, and thereby create the fundamental articles on which all denominations and confessions could agree. For Grotius, the aim of producing fundamental articles was to purify and harmonize already-existing confessions. Indeed, irenic thinkers of the sixteenth and seventeenth centuries believed that such a newly designed dogmatic catalog would end schismatic factions and enable the constitution of an interconfessional harmony. Taking for granted limited human insight, Grotius suggested concentrating the theological discussion only on *dogmata ad salutem necessaria*, leaving out dogmas that are not necessary for salvation, such as the doctrine of the Trinity or of transubstantiation (Wolf 13).

In a 1622 Lincoln's Inn sermon, Donne embraced the irenic concept of fundamental articles: "Substantial and fundamental points of Religion . . . do not ebb and flow; they binde all men, and at all times, and in all cases" (4:142). Here, he emphasizes that the very substance of religion is binding for everyone. Donne, however, is aware of the danger that these fundamental articles will themselves become dogmatic. Therefore, in the same sermon he strongly advises his audience not to become fanatic worshipers but to be humane even toward heretics, since they are not damned (4:141). In contrast to Donne, Grotius regards the *Tridentine canones* as the very epitome of a pure doctrine (Wolf 60). Like Grotius, representatives of a Christian humanistic irenicism such as Erasmus vehemently supported a purification of rites and sacraments. Looking for generally binding norms, Erasmus and his followers went back to a supposed origin, to a time before the process of denaturation had started (Wolf 98).

The Italian Renaissance poet and scholar Petrarch developed the theory of depravation, according to which Christianity morally and intellectually declined. Looking at the religious decadency of his time, for example, Petrarch wanted to purify religious rites. This attitude forms the basis for what I would like to call a *retrospective normativity*, which describes a backward-bound set of norms. According to this theory, in the sixth century Christianity and its institutions succumbed to decadency that led to their deformation (Wolf 91). Grotius believed, however, that in the Roman Catholic Church, with its sense of community and love for tradition, some features of the true universal church had remained (Wolf 62). The early church's understanding of sacraments was praised as a normative ideal. Grotius, like Donne, appreciated that via the sacraments, and especially via baptism, the ritual community obtained a central sociocultic meaning, which at the same time constitutes and witnesses to an ecclesiastic unity. The Eucharist and baptism, in particular, awaken the spirit of Christ in the faithful. Since different ritual habits should not cause schisms, there should only be an individual ritual form if there does not exist a continual tradition (Wolf 61).

Both Grotius and Donne had high regard for early Christianity, but this is not the only link between them. These theologically knowledgeable men also were strongly influenced by the irenicism of Franciscus Junius the Elder. In his treatise *Irenicum* (1593), the theologian Junius, who during his lifetime had also taught at Heidelberg and Leiden, confined the fundamental articles, the *articuli fundamentales*, to the individual relation between God and each Christian (Neuser 350). Grotius, Donne, and Junius were part of a larger European irenic development; for example, some decades earlier, in 1570, the *Consensus Sedomirensis*—a dogmatic concession between Lutherans, the Reformed Church, and the Bohemian Brothers—was developed in Poland (Neuser 349). It is not only the different national offspring of those irenic thinkers but their academic way of life that led them to various countries and made irenicism a highly international venture.

In Donne's and Grotius's irenicism, the recollection of early Christianity and its texts, as we will soon see, is crucial. This concern about texts stands in the tradition of the *sola scriptura*, the manifesto of the Protestant Reformation. Thus, considering the Counter-Reformation as well as the hardened dogmatics of Protestant orthodoxy, Donne's revivifying of the biblical text can be regarded not only as an irenic possibility but also as a proper administration of the heritage of the Protestant Reformation, since Luther's true intention was reformative but not schismatic. It is a paradox to make Luther responsible for the destruction of ecclesiastical unity, since there had been a schism between Rome and Byzantium in 1045, as well as various papal schisms. Luther, in contrast, aimed at tracing the church back to its pneumatic unity (Sommer 73). According to the theologian and scholar Nathan Söderblom, there cannot be found any confessionalistic polemic within Luther's *Little Catechism* of 1529. Luther is generally regarded as the main founder of the Protestant Reformation, and therefore he is widely made responsible for the separation between the Roman Catholic and the Protestant churches. What I would like to show, however, is that there can be traced irenic features in Luther's theology, which contributed to the irenicism that developed in the later sixteenth and early seventeenth centuries. In an age of denominational quarrels, Luther designed a pneumatic ecclesiology (Söderblom 66) with which he established a framework for a church community that is spiritual and can exist apart from any dogmatic architecture of the church. The irenic potential of Luther's theology can also be seen in the *sola scriptura* principle. According to this principle, it is important not to believe in imposed dogmatics but to go back to the Scriptures and look at the meaning contained therein. Only then can dogmatic sentences be newly formulated. Donne may have understood the irenic intention of the *sola scriptura*. Through the critical impact of this principle, Luther could have traced Christianity back to early Christianity, the common basis of all denominations and religious groups. Luther did not hold the *sola scriptura* principle as an absolute maxim. He also introduced the *solus Christus* and the *sola fide* principles in order to strengthen the radical *sola scriptura* principle against Roman Catholic tradition and to protect it from enthusiastic misuse (Gloege 5: col. 1541). Thus a new authority on texts was established above the Roman Catholic Church that also worked as guideline for those who were going further in their interpretations of the Bible.

In a sermon on the meaning of Scripture, preached at St. Paul's in 1622, Donne refers to Luther's combined principle of Scripture:

> And though the Scripture be inspired from *God* and the conscience be illumined and rectified by the Holy Spirit immediately, yet, both the *Scriptures* and the *Conscience* admit *humane arguments* . . . there is a manifestation of the will of God in certain Scriptures, if we who have not power to infuse *Faith* into men, (for that is the work of the Holy Spirit onely) but must deal upon the *reason* of men, and satisfie that, if we might not proceed *pertestimonia ab homine*, by humane Arguments, and argue, and infer *thus*, That if God will save man for worshipping him, and damne him for not worshipping him, so as he will be worshipped, and that in some visible, in some permanent manner in *writing*, and that that writing is *Scripture*, if we had not these testimonies, these necessary consequences derived even from the *natural reason* of man to convince men, how should

we convince them, since our way is not to create *Faith*, but to satisfie *reason*? And therefore let us rest in this testimony of men, that all *Christian* men, nay *Jewes* and *Turkes* too, have ever beleeved, that there are certain Scriptures, which are the revealed will of God, and that God hath manifested to us, in those Scriptures, all that he requires at our hands for *Faith* or *Manners*. (4:216–17)

Like Luther, Donne based his argumentation on the theory of inspiration and introduced a further principle, conscience, in order to protect Scripture. The Holy Spirit works analogously to Luther's *sola fide* principle; that is, via conscience, the Holy Spirit connects Scripture and the lived faith and thus makes the truth of the Scripture visible. Donne, in contrast to the German Protestant reformer Melanchthon (Gloege 5: col. 1543ff.), did not consider Scripture as absolute truth, pure and without any mistakes. However, Donne understood God's revelation as superior to any mistakes that may have occurred when this revelation was handed down in tradition. While Melanchthon develops a kind of *sola scriptura* dogma in his *Loci*, Donne imitated Luther's method of speaking in favor of an open discourse. In his sermons Donne extends the *sola scriptura* principle and also includes the writings of the church fathers.

This common method of seventeenth-century irenicism employed by Donne was backed up theoretically by Grotius. In *De Imperio summarum potestatum circa sacra* as well as in his letters, Grotius, who was influenced by the *sola scriptura* principle of the Reformation, took the Bible and the conscience of the individual as the basis for faith. In his letters, Grotius states that the consensus of the church fathers can provide a useful corrective to the individual interpretation of the Bible. In *Rivetani apologetici pro schismate contra votum pacis facti discussio*, Grotius remarks that "traditio interpretatur scripturam [tradition interprets the scripture]" (Wolf 58). Contrary to Dieter Wolf, who argues that with this statement Grotius affirms Catholicism, in my view it rather seems that Grotius has the same irenic intention as Luther with his *sola scriptura* principle, which goes back to the origins of Christianity and therefore has the potential to reunite Christianity. Coming from a humanist background and having also in mind Luther and the Protestant Reformation, Grotius newly interprets tradition that used to be labeled Catholic. While Luther adds the *solus Christus* and *sola fide* principles as correctives to the *sola scriptura* principle, Grotius, influenced by humanism, introduces the patristic writings as an additional source for interpretation of the foundations of Christianity. With this idea, Grotius surpasses Luther's *sola scriptura*, a position that later would even impede biblical exegesis. Placing Christianity in its historical context, Grotius attacks a merely cultic and dogmatic Catholicism, which uses tradition only as a witness of the eternal truth of the Roman Catholic Church. For Grotius, in contrast, the *antiqua christianitas* serves as a role model for a reformed Christianity, a perspective that is based on humanistic thought, since the early church and the patristic writings that form the historical core are accepted as normative since they existed before the dogmatic estrangement from original Christianity began. This historical approach to religion, one that opposes traditional Catholicism, embraced by Grotius is also discussed by Donne in one of his 1629 sermons:

> Hence appeares the vanity and impertinency of that calumny, with which our adversaries of the Roman perswasion labour to oppress us, That those points in which we depart from them, cannot be well established, because therein we depart from the Fathers.... And yet, if those blessed Fathers, now in possession of heaven, be well affected with our celebrating, or ill, with our neglecting their works, certainly they finde much more cause to complaine of our adversaries, then of us. Never any in the Reformation hath spoken so studiously in diminution of the Fathers, as they have done. (9:158–60)

While the Jesuits and followers of the Council of Trent discredit the theology of the church fathers, Donne takes this theology seriously and thereby identifies with the humanistic branch of the Protestant Reformation. In Donne's sermon, this identification with the humanistic Protestant reformers is expressed by the pronouns "we" and "us." As we have seen above, there is a close connection between the evaluation of early Christian texts and the normative importance of the early church. The irenic movement depends on discovering the original ritual roots in early Christianity, since the representatives of the irenic movement considered early Christianity to be heavily based on rituals and therefore to execute a strong integrative force. Because baptism was regarded as a primordial ritual, the discussion about baptism became crucial. And, indeed, in his sermons Donne seems to be in a constant dialogue with the Protestant reformers about baptism.

Donne's understanding of baptism in his 1619 "Heidelberg sermon" allows us to place him in the traditions described above. In 1619 Donne arrived with the Doncaster delegation at Heidelberg and gave a sermon in the Holy Ghost Church at the beginning of the Thirty Years' War. He must have been well aware that Heidelberg at this time was religiously and politically explosive, a center of religious quarrels where Catholic and Protestant viewpoints were present not only in academic and theological debate but also influenced everyday life (as can be seen in the architecture of the Counter-Reformation with its newly put up Madonnas, which roused Protestant anger). Therefore, in this sermon Donne focused on neither the doctrine of justification (the question of how sinners can meet the demands of the divine law) nor the topic of the assurance of faith (the belief that because of their faith Christians are accepted by God) as the basis for religion. Rather, he refers to baptism, which is not as centrally located in dogmatic debate and confessional quarrels as are the doctrines of justification and assurance. Baptism, in other words, is not immediately suspicious, and consequently it can fulfill an irenic mission, as it had done in early Christianity. As in the early church, baptism is the lowest common denominator, something shared by all Christian churches. In the context of the seventeenth century, however, Donne does not understand baptism as an instrument to determine the legitimacy of church membership, as had been the case after Jesus' death. After Jesus died, it became important to build categories for the members of a Christian congregation because he could no longer name his followers. In the Heidelberg sermon, Donne transfers the defining of authority through baptism—the institutional power of baptism to constitute a community—from the situation of the early church to the dogmatic stalemate between Protestants and Catholics that was reached in the seventeenth century in order to demonstrate that neither academic skirmish nor military actions could answer the question of religious and thus political legitimacy. As we shall see below, Donne does not plead for academic or military resolution to the problem of religio-political legitimacy but rather turns to baptism, the early church's ritual solution to the problem of creating community.

Baptism is not only a method of constituting a legitimate membership; it also stands for the communal aspect of religion, while at the same time making possible the experience of individual salvation. Because baptism is central to both Donne's theology and his Heidelberg sermon, I would like to give examples from several sermons in order to show their interdependency. In a 1624 sermon, Donne elaborates a guide to Christianity: "Consider a man, as a Christian, his first element is Baptisme, and his next is Catechisme; and in his Catechisme, the first is, to beleeve a Father, Son and holy Ghost" (6:134–35). In this passage, Donne mentions baptism as the first element in the genesis of a Christian and asserts that it comes before any dogmatic lessons. Thus taking this sermon as a constituent part of Donne's theological ideas, I would like to claim that in Donne's theology, people should be baptized before attending any catechismal instructions, because this order, where people first become ritually integrated, seems very promising for a lived irenicism. This kind of theological integration corresponds to Grotius's irenic method, where the strong magic-ritual element in the early church is ranked above later dogmatic discourse. Even the puritans and Presbyterians in Elizabethan times criticized a baptism that was over-ornated by Catholicism and tried to return to the custom in the early church to purify the rite of baptism (Benrath 659). This view of baptism and catechism also refers back to Calvin's *Institutes*, where Calvin argues against the Anabaptists, who rejected infant baptism and spoke in favor of an early baptism before any religious instruction (4.16.23). In the Heidelberg sermon Donne also discredits the schismatic Anabaptists. Justifying the baptism of children, Donne does not refer to Augustine's doctrine of original sin, according to which sin is innate because it is Adam's heritage, a doctrine then taught by the radical wing of the Protestant Reformation. To refer to original sin as an explanation would have been counterproductive to Donne's irenic intentions. Taking baptism as a causative means against original sin, in Augustine's theology the anthropological argument of the early church is superseded by a theological one: since infants are sinners by nature, they must be baptized. As we can learn in the writings of Irenaeus, Cyprian, and Origen, even in the early church it was common to baptize infants (Schmaus 3:2, 112). However, there is no evidence for infant baptism in the Bible, and the ritual regulations in the New Testament are not as detailed as the ones later on in the early church. There are no statements about the age of the person to be baptized. From a Protestant perspective, which is influenced by the *sola scriptura* principle, this leads to the question of whether infant baptism could have been intended in the New Testament. In various exegetical works, the blessing of the children (Mark 10:13) and the fact that whole households were baptized (Acts 10:44, 16:15.33; 1 Corinthians 16:15) were interpreted in favor of infant baptism. However, 1 Corinthians 7:14 serves as a counterexample. Here it is reported that "the unbelieving husband is consecrated through his wife, and the unbelieving wife is consecrated through her husband," and therefore their children are also holy.

In his Heidelberg sermon, Donne also refers to the descent from Christian parents suggested in the passage from 1 Corinthians and not to the doctrine of original sin. Trying to interpret baptism without referring to original sin represents the idea of an irenic mission more than talking about the doctrine of original sin, which was heavily debated among the theologians of different confessional backgrounds. As we can see in the following passage from the Heidelberg sermon, Donne circumvents this religious matter of dispute by linking baptism with the covenant: "a Christian man, his being born of Christian Parents, . . . that makes him of the body of the Covenant; . . . thereby he may make his claim to the seal of the Covenant, to baptism, and it cannot be denied him" (2:262). In the quoted text and the following lines, Donne understands baptism as the seal of the covenant. Within the baptismal act, a soul is bestowed on man; this is a spiritual sign for the covenant, which stands for the possession of grace. Donne states that man is made not only of soul but also of flesh. Therefore, the spiritual part of man must continually be developed; otherwise the grace—which is conceived in baptism—cannot be effective. In contrast to Augustine, Donne in the above-quoted sermon emphasizes that Christian parents pass on Christianity—and not original sin—to their children. This attitude toward original sin also can be found in other sermons by Donne, for example, in his christening sermon on Ephesians 5:25–27: "we argue with an invincible certainty, that because this Sacrament belongs generally to the church as the *initiatory* Sacrament, it belongs to *children*, who are a part, and for the most part, the most innocent part of the Church" (5:129). Although Jeffrey Johnson quotes this passage to show Donne's agreement with the doctrine of original sin (70), in my view the quoted text on children's innocence demonstrates instead that Donne does not support the idea of original sin, wherein infants are considered sinners. In another christening sermon, Donne does not disapprove of the concept of original sin from the start but rather introduces it as an element in his argument against the Anabaptists, who rejected infant baptism. Because Donne needs the doctrine of original sin to produce an argument against the Anabaptist rejection of infant baptism, he only levels a very subtle criticism at the doctrine of original sin in his sermon:

> . . . because if we consider this *washing away of teares*, as Saint *Cyprian* says, *young children*, doe most of all need this mercy of God and this assistance of Man, because as soone as they come into this world, . . . they beg with tears something at our hands, therefore need this abstersion, this wiping. For though *they* cannot tell *us*, what they aile, though (if we will enter into curiosities) *we* cannot tell *them* what they aile, that is, we cannot tell them what properly, and exactly *Originall sin is*, yet they aile something, which naturally disposes them, to *weep*, and *beg*, that something might be done, for the *wiping away of tears from their eyes*, And therefore though the other errors of the *Anabaptist* be ancient, 1000 year old, yet the *denying of baptisme* to children, was never heard of till within

100 year, and lesse. The *Arrians*, and the *Donatists* did *rebaptize* those who were baptized by the true Christians, whom they counted *Heretiques*; but yet they refused not to baptize children; The *Pelegians* denied *original sin* in children; but yet they *baptized* them. All Churches, ... howsoever they differ in the *body* of the Church, yet they meet, they agree in ... the *Sacrament* of *baptisme*, and acknowledge that it is communicable to *all children*, and to *all Men*. (5:100–101)

Although Donne confirms that children fear "something," which is why they cry, there is, however, no one who can actually explain original sin. The theological claim of truth is denied by reducing it to a mere psychological explanation: children fear something. Thus original sin becomes a myth. It seems as if Donne's argumentation aims to convince a jury (the community of the believers) of his client's (the communal sacrament's) innocence. The sacrament of baptism is supported by common sense: baptism is intelligible to anyone. Moreover, any church can witness the communal function of baptism. Even the usual suspects, such heretics as the Donatists, appear as witness against the Anabaptists. In Donne's argumentation, the Anabaptists' denial of infant baptism is framed by the myth of original sin and rebaptism practiced by Donatists and Arians, who denied that Christ was of one substance with the Father. This prominent position is approved by Donne's language in the above-quoted sermon, where the "but yet" indicates that the teachings of the Arians and the Donatists are not as suspicious as those of the Anabaptists.

This aversion to the Anabaptists may have been caused by their antisocial and highly schismatic inclinations, as shown, for example, by John Smyth's congregation. Founding a self-governing and independent congregation, the preacher John Smyth (1554–1612) surpassed even the standards of Robert Browne, the first representative of congregationalism. In exile in the Netherlands, Smyth founded the first Baptist church (Benrath 659). A radical emancipation from ecclesiastic as well as from social norms characterizes Anabaptism as a socioreligious revolutionary movement. Combining Protestant and Catholic features, Anabaptism cannot clearly be assigned to one confessional line. It is based, on the one hand, on a protest against ecclesiastic and social defects, and, on the other hand, on disappointment with the Wittenberg and Zurich Reformation. This disappointment, in particular, may have caused a radicalized search for new forms of piety and social orders, which resulted in a denial of any compromise worked out between the Protestant reformers and the authorities (Klueting 182). Because Anabaptism does not allow for any socioreligious conformity (Dülmen 193), Donne attacks such subversive ideas, which are nourished by the antinomianism of the Anabaptists as well as by the Roman Catholic enthusiasm for martyrdom:

> Gospel is truly . . . a Law of Liberty. . . . Not such a Liberty as they have established in the Roman Church, where Ecclesiastical Liberty must exempt Ecclesiastical persons from participating all burdens of the State, and from being Traitors, though they commit treason, because they are Subjects to no secular Prince: nor the liberty of the Anabaptists, that overthrowes Magistracy, and consequently all subjection, both Ecclesiastical and Laick. (8:349)

In his Heidelberg sermon, Donne exemplifies his understanding of baptism, referring to symbols from the Old Testament. Like Calvin in the *Institutes* (4.16.23), Donne uses the covenantal theology of the Old Testament to illustrate his point. In the *Institutes*, Calvin argues against the Anabaptists that among the Israelites only foreigners were taught about religion before their circumcision. Both Calvin and Donne claim that circumcision and baptism typologically correspond to each other. The foreigner has to be instructed in the Law and the covenant, since he does not from descent participate in the covenant between God and the Israelites. A member of the tribe, however, does not have to be instructed before he is circumcised, since he is already part of the people with whom God made the covenant, a reality that this is only confirmed by the act of circumcision. In the first of four christening sermons, Donne takes up this covenantal approach and backs it up with christological and pneumatological arguments emphasizing that children, because they are born within the covenant, not only have a legal right to be baptized but are also in the possession of the Holy Spirit and led by Christ. According to Donne:

> Well then, they to whom these waters belong, have Christ in his Church to lead them; and therefore they need not stay, till they can come *alone;* till they be of age and years of discretion, as the *Anabaptists* say; for it is *Deducet*, and *Deducet eos*; generally, universally; *all* that are of this government, *all* that are appointed for the *Seal,* all *the one hundred and foure thousand,* all the *Innumerable multitudes of all Nations,* Christ leads them all. *Be Baptized every one of you, in the name of Iesus Christ, for the remission of sinnes; for the promise is made unto you, and your children.* Now all promises of God, are sealed in the *Holy Spirit;* To whom soever any promise of God belongs, he hath the Holy Spirit; and therefore *Nunquid*

> *aquam quis prohibere potest? Can any Man forbid water, that those should not be baptized, which have received the Holy Spirit, as well as we?* says S. Peter. And therefore the *Children* of the Covenant which have the *promise*, have the *Holy Spirit*, and all they are in this Regiment, *Deducet eos*, Christ shall lead *them all*. (5:109)

However, Donne states that although the children who have Christian parents are part of the covenant and are entitled to the seal of the covenant, they are not automatically granted assurance of faith after their baptism. Only when the grace that is conceived in baptism becomes effective is there assurance of faith. With this statement Donne takes up the theology of the Protestant Reformation. The Protestant reformers deny that the sacrament is merely magic (Wenz 93), and to back this up they refer to the connection between faith and baptism in the New Testament. Although the reformers are generally against the Anabaptists, they also think that faith and baptism should come together. This links them to the Anabaptists, who did not acknowledge infant baptism and therefore rebaptized people. In other words, Anabaptists do not baptize anyone before they know that the person to be baptized has faith, a faith that came into existence through the Word that, however, cannot be understood by children. Therefore, only religiously mature people, who can understand the Word, are allowed to be baptized. The Protestant reformers held to the unity of faith and baptism, yet Luther and Calvin opposed the Anabaptist individualization and psychologization of faith and point to the medieval thesis of the hidden faith of children. Although the Reformed tradition rejects the emergency baptism of children and does not regard baptism as necessary for salvation, it nevertheless decided for infant baptism. Calvin, especially, in his *Institutes* tried to prove that infant baptism existed at the time of the New Testament (4.8.16); and Luther emphasized an objective sacramental power of baptism, which results from the validity of God's promise. Although it is hard to harmonize infant baptism with the idea that baptism can only be conceived in faith, Luther defended infant baptism against Anabaptism. In the *Large Catechism*, Luther is of the opinion that through baptism God can cause children to believe. He adds that faith does not cause but conceives baptism, but those who do not yet believe when they are baptized can found their faith on baptism later on.

In the above-mentioned examples from the sermons, Donne's way of interrelating elements of the covenantal theology and baptism—for example, that baptism, like circumcision, can be seen as a seal of the covenant—points to Zwingli's theology in particular. Ulrich Zwingli (1484–1531), the

Swiss leader of the Reformation based in Zurich, defended infant baptism by showing that baptism is a mere sign of duty, which witnesses that God's promises also include children. This argument is strengthened by the conception of the covenant, according to which God makes a covenant not only with Abraham but also with Abraham's descendants (Genesis 17:7). According to Zwingli, what was agreed on in the old covenant also has to be in force for the new one. In comparison to the circumcision of the old covenant, baptism is the sign for membership in the new covenant (Weber 2:670). In sixteenth- and seventeenth-century Reformed theology, covenantal theology is a common element. In Zwingli's theology the conception of the covenant is used to clear up a paradoxical construction in the history of salvation. Thus, looking at the history of salvation, covenantal theology is used to harmonize the conceptions of God's grace and Christ's grace (Neuser 344).

Entirely within the tradition of the Protestant reformers, Donne repeatedly argues against the dismantling of infant baptism and "the madnesse of the Anabaptists" (4:202, 208). Whereas in the Heidelberg sermon, referring to the descent from Christian parents, Donne alludes only to the New Testament, in a sermon from 1624 he gives a christological reason for rejecting Anabaptism: without any catechismal instruction or any knowledge about the sacrament of the Eucharist, Christ was baptized (6:135). In this passage Donne also takes up the counterargument that Christ's baptism, which he received from John the Baptist, has a different quality. Against this Donne argues that it was only a different mode of baptism. The very essence, however, remained the same, since in both cases the souls were washed in Christ's blood. While after the death of Christ people were baptized in the name of Christ who died for man, John the Baptist baptized Christ in the name of Christ who was to die for man, so that Christ was baptized by his own baptism. In a Lincoln's Inn sermon, Donne presents the Anabaptists as a cautionary example of a hostile denomination (2:112). With a good sense of humor, he reports on his journey to Germany. On his way to Germany he stayed in a house together with Anabaptists. Since Anabaptists were convinced that their religious orientation was the only true one, the mutual excommunication of family members was an everyday Anabaptist ritual in this house. Confused by this heretical way of life and concerned about his spiritual welfare, Donne fled from this house very shortly after he had arrived. According to Johnson, Donne's reaction was not motivated solely by a different theological opinion; he was also anxious that the dissociation from each other in the Anabaptist household could also effect the individual's communion with

God (42). Such a lived heresy is anticommunal and destroys any social nexus, as can be seen in the interfamiliar excommunications. Since such behavior also suggests a basically destructive attitude toward authority, Anabaptism, for Grotius, implied political explosiveness. In several sermons Donne mentions that the Anabaptists do not acknowledge authority (see 4:312, 142). In contrast, the sacrament of baptism, where the naming of the child at the center of the ceremony constitutes social connections, stands for a stable social order. Thus the religious ceremony functions as an initiation of the child into society (6:137).

These examples from Donne's sermons illustrate that Donne agrees with the Protestant reformers' views regarding Anabaptism. Although the opposition to Anabaptism is important in the reformers' definition of baptism, the reformers also try to work out their understanding of baptism, which is of course again part of the debate with the Anabaptists. Answering the topical question for the Protestant reformers as to whether baptism is primarily the work of God or of man, Donne emphasizes the theological nexus of grace, which combines God's action and man's faith. In his Heidelberg sermon, Donne connects grace and faith with baptism. A new coming of Christ makes faith grow within the person to be baptized, and this lively faith is expressed in charity (2:263).

According to the Protestant reformers, God's gracious action anticipates any human contribution. They oppose the *sola fide* principle to the *ex opere*—the Catholic idea that a sacrament works as soon as it is performed no matter how spiritually involved the actor is—in order to counteract a magical misunderstanding and a sacramental overactiveness. Luther, however, held to the *ex opere operato*, emphasizing that it cannot take place without faith. The Protestant and Catholic standpoints have in common that they give priority to God's action and the grace offered by God. Tying the investiture of the sacraments to Jesus Christ is to show that the sacraments are merely donations. Neither the words spoken by the priest nor the condition of the person to be baptized constitutes a sacrament. It is only Christ's word that constitutes a sacrament, and it does not at all depend on the dignity of the donator or recipient. In his *Large Catechism*, Luther writes that it is Jesus Christ who, through the power of the Holy Spirit, is the actual baptist, and to be baptized in the name of God does not mean to be baptized by man but by God himself. When the priests perform the sacraments, they do not act without authorization. Rather, they are Christ's appointed spokespersons. Both Luther and Calvin considered sacraments first and foremost a sign of God's grace and only then as a human reaction to this grace. For the external signs, which only confirm and seal God's word and promise, are worthless without this promise, just as the ceremony is worthless without faith. Zwingli, in contrast to Luther and Calvin, understands baptism primarily as a sign of human obedience, a sign of duty, knowledge, and confession. For Zwingli, sacraments are acts of the believer. Having had a look at Luther's, Calvin's, and Zwingli's insights about the position of grace and faith in baptism, we see that Donne is in the same line of argumentation.

Another crucial aspect of baptism during the Protestant Reformation is the question of whether baptism is necessary for salvation. In his sermons Donne also responds to this topic. In one sermon he describes how God, through baptism, admits people to the community of saints and thus proves his grace:

> It was an Act of *mercy*, meerly, that *God* decreed a meanes of salvation; . . . My will was neveer able to *rectifie*, to *justifie* it selfe; But the power of *God's grace* cals in a *forraine Righteinousnes*, to my succour, the *Righteousnesse* of my *Saviour*, and *cals* his, and *makes* his, my *Righteousnesse*. But yet, *Non habitat*, This *Righteousnes dwels* not unremoveable, in mee, here. Though I have put on that *garment*, and it fals from mee, before I am aware, and in my sinnes of *contempt* and *rebellion*, I teare it off, and throw it away my selfe. But in this new *state*, these *new Heavens*, and *new Earth* shall bee his *standing house*, where hee shall *dwell*, and wee with him; . . . And *God* shall say to us *all*, . . . Sit *ye all* on my right hand; . . . And to us *all*, *Hodie genui vos*, This day I have begotten *you all*; begotten you in the *confirmation* of my first *Baptisme*, in the *ratification* of my first *Election*; . . . For *God* shall establish *us* there, *Ubi non intrat inimicus, nec amicus exit*, Where no man shall come in, that troubles the company, nor any, whom any of the company loves, goe out; but wee shall *all*, not onely *have*, but *be* a part of that *Righteousnes* which *dwels* in these *new Heavens*, and *new Earth*, which *we*, *According to his promise look for*. (8:84)

Donne argues that even if people sin after baptism, they keep the status acquired through baptism, because God's justice surpasses man's sins. In addition, the innocence and immaculacy gained in baptism cleanse the gradually acquired stains on the christening robe.

The question as to whether baptism is necessary for salvation, which Donne also addresses, is discussed controversially by the various denominations. In Catholic dogmatics, baptism is regarded as necessary for salvation, since human self-redemption is not possible and salvation is joined to baptism by Jesus Christ. This doctrine is supported by John 3:5 ("Verily, verily, I say unto thee, Except a man be born of water and of the Spirit, he cannot enter into the kingdom of God") and Mark 16:16 ("He that believeth and is baptized shall be saved; but he that believeth not shall be damned"). People who were prevented from being baptized can be saved through a so-called baptism of desire, an aversion to sin, but unlike in the sacramental act, they cannot enter Christ's death, even as they die a symbolic death in the aversion to sin.

Church fathers such as Irenaeus, Origen, and Augustine combine the idea of the necessity of grace with the conception that baptism is necessary for salvation. In the third and fourth centuries, the idea that baptism is necessary for salvation exerted such an influence on people that they postponed their baptism until shortly before their death so that they would not lose the cleansed state and sanctification gained in baptism. In the fourth century, Cyril of Jerusalem and Augustine rejected this custom. In a treatise on baptism, referring to Luke 23:43 ("Verily I say unto thee, To day shalt thou be with me in paradise"), according to Cyprian, Augustine stated that sometimes suffering can supersede baptism. Such an invisible performance, however, can only take place if baptism was not donated because of an emergency or because of religious indifference. In his funeral oration, for example, Ambrosius consoles the relatives of Emperor Valentian by mentioning that he had desired to be baptized. Thomas Aquinas also holds the view that God's power is not confined to visible sacraments and that man can also be sanctified internally.

Although the baptism of desire wipes out original sin, it does not cleanse venial sins or leave an inextinguishable sign. As in the baptism of desire, man does not become an image of Christ. Nor does he become part of Christ's body as he does in the baptism of water. In addition to the baptism of desire, the baptism of water can also be replaced by the baptism of blood, since this resembles Christ's death. Cyprian considers martyrdom the most glorious baptism. And Tertullian understands the water and blood flowing from Jesus' side as a symbol for the baptism of water and the baptism of blood. According to John Chrysostom, martyrs are cleansed by blood, just as people to be baptized are cleansed by water. Referring to Matthew 10:32 ("Whosoever therefore shall confess me before men, him will I confess also before my Father which is in heaven"), Augustine equates martyrdom with baptism in *Civitas Dei* (Bk. 13, ch. 17).

While the Pelagians, who relate to the heretical doctrine that there exists no original sin and the individual can actively acquire salvation, reject the idea that baptism is necessary for salvation, because eternal life can also be attained without baptism, Luther regards baptism as necessary for salvation, since through baptism God admits man to his grace. For Luther the old man was conceived in sin, but the new one will be born in grace, for God takes away sin from man and strengthens man: When man dies, he is redeemed by God from sin. Even if man remains a sinner despite baptism, original sin will be wiped out. Whereas baptism is only the beginning of purification, sin is totally cleansed away by the actual death. Baptism anticipates death and resurrection, through which man is newly created. In baptism the Holy Spirit also wages war against sin and incites the desire to avoid sin (Schmaus 2:105). Because sin is wiped out in baptism, man cannot be damned. In the above-quoted passage from one of his sermons, Donne uses the metaphors of the "*new Earth*" and the "*new Heavens*" as well as the christening robe to illustrate his understanding of baptism. Both Luther and Donne consider baptism necessary for salvation.

In the Reformed tradition, baptism is not regarded as necessary for salvation. Baptism does not cause salvation but is only a constant sign of what God has caused through the Holy Spirit. Yet it is necessary to be baptized in order to obey Christ's instruction. Although baptism is regarded as mediating salvation, Calvin states that no one who was prevented from being baptized is damned (Weber 2:667). With this statement Calvin argues against Anabaptism and its belief that baptism is necessary for salvation. According to Johnson, in *Institutes* 4.15.1 Calvin "argue[s] for the sacraments as necessary for salvation and, therefore, against the view that they are merely signs or tokens" (72n. 30). In the passage from the *Institutes*, Calvin, in contrast to Johnson's interpretation, seems rather to understand baptism as "a sign of initiation" and to describe baptism as "a sign of reminiscence and prove of our purification." To sharpen the term *sign*, Calvin distinguishes baptism from "a sign of reminiscence or marking with which we confess our religion before other people like soldiers have the sign of their general in order to show that they belong to him." The sign of baptism does not merely stand for an external membership, as is used in a battlefield, but is a sign of God's promise. In Calvin's theology, baptism is only a sign that confirms what God causes through his Word and the Holy Spirit. Baptism can be understood as a seal. So baptism has a significative meaning and not an exhibitive one (Joest 2:567).

In his book, Johnson also tries to trace Donne's understanding of baptism directly back to Calvin. However, as can be seen in *Institutes* 4.16.26, Calvin, in contrast to Donne, rejects vehemently the conception that baptism is necessary for salvation. In this passage Calvin emphasizes the importance of baptism but mentions that God has never damned someone who had not been baptized. Concerning Donne's sermons, Johnson's line of argumentation may not be very convincing (72). The examples Johnson quotes from Donne's sermon are the following: "the sacraments are never without *Grace*, whether it be accepted or no, ther it is" (5:147); and "baptisme doth truly, and without collusion, offer grace *to all*; and nothing but baptisme, by an ordinary institution, and as an ordinary meanes, doth so . . . if we speake of reall salvation by it, baptisme is more then a figure" (5:163). As we can see, these passages deal only with grace—they do not argue that baptism is necessary for salvation.

The question of whether baptism is necessary for salvation is superfluous, for the center of baptism is not the individual human being but the person's integration into a community. And as there does not exist any *proprium* of baptism, there does not exist any necessity for salvation, since baptism is only a mode of the dedication to salvation but it is not identical with it. According to Calvin, it is like a vituperation of God if people do not trust that God's promise becomes effective of its own. Luther, too, considers baptism only an external sign that is to remind people of the promise, but wherever there is the gospel there also is baptism. In the Lutheran orthodox tradition, baptism is not understood as a *necessitas absoluta* but as a *necessitas ordinata* (Weber 2:667). Donne, however, thinks that there is a general necessity for baptism, as the following passage illustrates:

> But where's our remedy? Why for this, for this originall uncleannesse, is the water of *Baptisme*. *Oportet nos renasci*; we must be *borne againe*; we *must*; There is a *necessity* of *Baptisme*: As we are the children of Christian parents, we have *Jus ad rem*, a right to the Covenant, we may claime baptism, the Church cannot deny it us; And as we are baptized in the Christian Church, we have *Jus in re*, a right in the Covenant, and all the benefits thereof, all the promises of the Gospel; we are sure that we are *conceived in sinne*; and sure that we are *borne children of wrath*, but not sure that we are cleansed, or reconciled to God, by any other meanes then that, which he hath ordained, *Baptisme*. (8:211)

Apart from the communal and cultic character of baptism, which is of significance for its irenic function, Donne makes baptism theologically indispensable for irenicism. Thus baptism, a religious rite that is dogmatically less problematic than the Eucharist and less bloody than martyrdom, can lead to salvation. This is crucial for the socioreligious situation, for it means that baptism is a peaceful as well as a socially integrative alternative to the politically highly explosive matter of martyrdom. Coming after the Protestant Reformation had reformed the ritual of baptism, Donne and other like-minded thinkers argued for an irenic reformation of baptism, tracing the ritual back to its cultic origins in the early Christian church.

Works Cited

Benrath, Gustav A. "Die Lehre au·erhalb der Konfessionskirchen." *Handbuch der Dogmen- und Theologiegeschichte.* Ed. Bernhard Lohse et al. 3 vols. Göttingen: Vandenhoeck, 1988.

Berger, Klaus. *Theologiegeschichte des Urchristentums.* 2nd ed. Tübingen and Basel: Vandenhoeck, 1995.

Calvin, Johannes. *Ioannis Calvini Opera Quae Supersunt Omnia.* Corpus Reformatorum. Ed. Guilielmus Baum et al. 100 vols. Braunschweig: C. A. Schwetschke & Sohn (M. Bruhn), 1864.

Donne, John. *Sermons.* Ed. George R. Potter and Evelyn M. Simpson. 10 vols. Berkeley: U of California P, 1953–62.

Dülmen, Richard van. "Das Täufertum als sozialrevolutionäre Bewegung: Ein Versuch." *Zeitschift für historische Forschungen* 6 (1979): 185–97.

Ebert, Manfred. *Jakob I. von England (1603–25): Als Kirchenpolitiker und Theologe.* Studia Irenica 12. Ed. Wolfgang Philipp and Axel Hilmar Swinne. Hildesheim: Dr. H. A. Gerstenberg, 1972.

Gloege, G. "Schriftprinzip." *Religion in Geschichte und Gegenwart.* 7 vols. 3rd ed. Tübingen: J. C. B. Mohr, 1986.

Joest, Wilfried. *Dogmatik.* 2 vols. Göttingen: Vandenhoeck, 1989.

Johnson, Jeffrey. *The Theology of John Donne.* Studies in Renaissance Literature 1. Cambridge: D. S. Brewer, 1999.

Klueting, Harm. *Das Konfessionelle Zeitalter 1525–1648.* Stuttgart: Ulmer, 1989.

Neuser, Wilhelm. "Dogma und Bekenntnis in der Reformation: Von Zwingli und Calvin bis zur Synode von Westminster." *Handbuch zur Dogmen- und Theologiegeschichte.* Ed. Bernhard Lohse et al. 3 vols. Göttingen: Vandenhoeck, 1988. Vol 2:167–85.

Schmaus, Michael. *Katholische Dogmatik.* 3 vols. München: Max Hueber, 1941.

Söderblom, Nathan. "Luther im Lichte der Ökumenizität." *Luther in ökumenischer Sicht.* Ed. Alfred von Martin. Stuttgart: Frommann, 1929.

Sommer, J. W. Ernst. "War Luther ein Zerstörer der Einheit der Kirche oder ihr Bahnbrecher?" *Luther in ökumenischer Sicht.* Ed. Alfred von Martin. Stuttgart: Frommann, 1929.

Weber, Otto. *Grundlagen der Dogmatik*. 2 vols. Neukirchen: Neuenkirchner Verlag, 1955–62.
Wenz, Gunther. *Einführung in die evangelische Sakramentenlehre*. Darmstadt: Wissenschaftliche Buchgesellschaft, 1988.
Wolf, Dieter. *Die Irenik des Hugo Grotius.* Studia Irenica 9. Ed. Wolfgang Philipp and Axel Hilmar Swinne. Hildesheim: Gerstenberg, 1972.

12

True Purification

Donne's Art of Rhetoric in Two Candlemas Sermons

MARIA SALENIUS

The nature of Donne's true faith, or his sincere church allegiance, is something that ceaselessly fascinates and/or disturbs almost every Donne scholar. Indeed, Donne's writings provide ample examples of Catholic or Protestant, Calvinist or puritan, doctrinal detail, leading many writers to suggest that Donne's conviction shows signs of one or another of these dispositions; equally numerous accounts favor interpreting Donne as a proponent of the *via media*.[1] The emphasis varies, sometimes depending on the particular interest of the reader/researcher. And surely Donne may have encompassed more than one—or, at different points in time, all—of these inclinations, at least to some extent; this would not be unusual for a convert in times of religious turbulence.

Somehow, however, the search for doctrinal detail has gone too far, for doctrinal details—or even larger issues—are not the main contents of Donne's belief. As Jeanne Shami reminds us, although Donne's writings contain numerous references to the Catholic fathers as well as to Luther, Calvin, and other reformers, "trying to determine Donne's religious alignments by the sources of his quotations doesn't work" (11). As an influential writer with significant connections in highly political times, Donne was compelled, and even obliged, to take up relevant religious and/or political issues in both his sermons and in his other prose writings; as an alert writer, he probably did the same in his poetry. This consummation of detail, however, does not produce an image of a complete faith or systematic theology, whether Catholic or Protestant. It often merely points to issues of interest or usefulness at a particular time or in a particular context.

In order to find Donne's true vocation and his true faith we must look to define a larger context, a larger framework of development, into which we might place Donne and his religion. This larger context should not be constructed by separate elements of doctrine, but by a more holistic view of Donne's religious disposition and its particular evolution. One way of pursuing this religious development is to look at Donne's language, to shift the main attention from the actual doctrinal contents to the presentation thereof, to look at Donne's rhetoric of *presenting* his theology rather than at the *details* of this theology. With a conscious writer like Donne, too little attention has been directed toward his form of expression as a means to reach an understanding of his thought. A study of rhetorical conventions as an expression for thought can open a new angle to the analysis.

This essay will consider two of Donne's Candlemas sermons from the 1620s in order to trace his true faith and to show its realization in and with rhetorical device. Such a consideration will be accomplished by reading Donne's text through the concepts and the philosophy presented in Thomas Wilson's *Art of Rhetoric* (1560), partly to give the text a linguistic framework for the analysis and partly to demonstrate a Protestant theory of language. The aim is to demonstrate how Donne uses rhetorical conventions to discuss his topic from a Protestant viewpoint, how he uses a Protestant rhetoric to redefine his originally medieval and Catholic themes. I will show that beyond Donne's religious references and implications there is deep and strongly convincing rhetoric conveying his Protestant disposition and reaching out to his audience in a powerful way. This point is especially relevant, as a number of scholars have made a point of stressing Donne's weakness in vocation and his disinterest in his congregation.[2]

The choice of Wilson as the framework for an analysis of Donne is based on linguistic as well as theological criteria. Both Donne and Wilson write in a time of solid Elizabethan and Stuart Protestantism, at a time when the Renaissance flourished in England and when the Protestant community was being secured in its position. This is also the time when original writing (as opposed to translations of reformers) dominates and when the English Reformation can be seen as a linguistic phenomenon. Both Donne and Wilson must thus be viewed as writers in the very core of the Judeo-Christian tradition, carrying the concepts of the western European cultural inheritance and presenting them at a point in time when these concepts were reevaluated and their direction reviewed. Moreover, both Wilson and Donne touch upon the evolution of ideas and values that extends through centuries and reaches one of its turning points in the English Reformation as "a religion of words" (Mallette 12). Likewise, the tradition of Christianity is closely linked to language and to words, to the encouragement to preach and to "teach all nations" (Matt. 28:19).[3] Wilson's particular way of rendering, and rewriting, the philosophical aspect of the (originally pagan) classical theories of rhetoric when expressing his Protestant mode of thought makes his text an interesting choice as a framework for Donne's expression of faith.

The two of Donne's sermons where his Protestant disposition is demonstrated in a most striking way through rhetorical device are two preached on "a Candlemas Day." Both sermons are originally undated, only mentioning the feast (which thus refers to February 2, the feast of the purification of Virgin Mary). For the first sermon presented here (no. 3 in vol. 10), Potter and Simpson, the modern editors of Donne's sermons, suggest that the year may have been 1624, a date I also accept. Studies of both Donne's theology (Rissanen) and his language (Salenius, *Dean*) have suggested a shift in Donne's presentation around 1624, and this shift supports the dating of the present Candlemas sermon. The second sermon discussed here is the Candlemas sermon that Potter and Simpson date to 1627 (no. 13 in vol. 7). Both were presumably preached at St. Paul's in London (Potter and Simpson 10:10–14, 7:28–32).

Potter and Simpson claim that both of these sermons show great emphasis on the actual feast of Candlemas (10:12), a day when candles were burned in memory of the Holy Virgin and for spiritual purification. At this time—in the 1620s—the new church order was seeking its form, and there was much debate over whether church ceremonies should be abolished or retained, an issue that touches these particular sermons. However, more than that, these sermons both use the feast itself and its tradition and characteristics as a rhetorical trope and thus as a linguistic starting point for a kind of transformation. This aspect echoes the sacrament of Eucharist and the significant doctrinal discussion of the Reformation, of the relationship between Christ's body and the bread of the communion. Donne's application of this sacrament for a metaphorical purpose in a linguistic setting will be discussed in more detail below.

The Linguistic Dimension of the Reformation

In order to reach a fuller understanding of Donne's use of language, however, it is important to see the Reformation as a linguistic phenomenon.

This is especially important with regard to England, where the Reformation had a much clearer linguistic dimension than on the Continent.[4] In general, the emphasis on the vernacular Bible and liturgy, on the one hand, and the (especially humanist) emphasis on the knowledge of the language of the original when translating the Bible (see Kopperi), on the other, were central arguments in the reshaping of Christianity. The first of these issues stressed man's right to approach, as well as to be approached by, God; the second manifested the Bible literally as God's Word.

The human-centeredness of this vernacularization of religion is also related to the emphasis on reason, where man may—and must—take responsibility for hearing and reading the Word of God and for making his own choices. Everything that resembled superstition and magic in the medieval Catholic tradition now gave way to man's reasonable ability to interpret the Word of God. Faith was to be comprehended, not merely felt as the realization of a riddle. The text of the Bible was a message, a guideline, a rule of conduct, not merely a form or convention of medieval mysticism. In his prologue to *The Art of Rhetoric*, Wilson defines man as a creature with "the gift of speech and *reason*" (emphasis added), and he also links the concept of reason to those of eloquence and perception (42).

This perspective of man's own interpretation of the word of the Scriptures has direct bearings on the idea of metaphor. The nature of the Reformation, of purifying and simplifying religion, emphasized a literal, nonmetaphorical interpretation of the Scriptures, leaving out all symbolic and mystical linguistic explanation; the interpretation of God's Word was to be achieved without any outside—particularly priestly—intervention (see Luxon). God's Word, thus, was aural/oral, and it was primarily transmitted through the Scriptures themselves and by the Holy Spirit in the sermon (Collinson 99). The purpose of the sermon as explanatory to the Word of God merged with the concept of the power of language in general; as the classical good speaker was a good man (*vir bonus*, to be discussed in more detail below), so the good preacher was influenced by the Holy Spirit. Instead of being present primarily in the sacraments, God was now foremost present in his Word. Thus also, as opposed to the mystics (e.g., Augustine and Bonaventure), who considered sight to be the central of man's faculties for religious contemplation, the reformers emphasized the importance of hearing (cf. Rom. 10:17).[5]

This hearing of the literal word was brought furthest by the puritans, who believed that the text of the Bible could not include images or figures of speech. For them, the promise in Christ's Sermon on the Mount (which also is the text of the Candlemas sermon of 1627, to be discussed below) for the "pure in heart" to be blessed in that "they shall see God" (Matt. 5:8) thus denoted a real promise of literal seeing.[6] Donne, too, discusses this point in the context of language in one of his earlier (undated) sermons and, from a purely linguistic point of view, he does not impose these restrictions on the Bible itself as he states: "the Holy Ghost in penning the Scriptures delights himself, not only with a propriety, but with a delicacy, and harmony, and melody of language; with height of Metaphors, and other figures, which may work greater impressions upon the Readers" (6:55).

Due to this view of the Word in the Reformation, language, although not void of figures and images, received a more communicative and functional purpose, with an emphasis on its operation on the level of reason rather than on the level of emotion. Raymond-Jean Frontain has noted, in a discussion mainly of Donne's verse writings, that "it is God's linguistic power—His creation *ex verbo*—that fascinates Donne" above all (14). In my view, this fascination seems even more evident in Donne's sermons. Donne finds in the Scriptures his most inspiring material upon which to elaborate, and the disruption and redefinition caused by the Reformation crystallizes this expression even more, giving Donne both metaphors with which to work and material for creating his own complex metaphors and images.

Finally, it is of greatest relevance to remember that one of the most central theological points of dispute in the Reformation was strongly reflected in linguistic interpretation: the understanding of the Eucharist as an actual distribution of Christ's body and blood rather than as a symbolic, or even metaphorical, event. In England this discussion dates back to as early as John Wycliffe (c. 1330–84) and his followers. Wycliffe generally is associated with the translation of the earliest English versions of the Old and New Testaments made from the Latin Vulgate version, completed in the 1390s, and he has also been named "the morning star of the Reformation," because many of his views were later presented by the reformers and merged with the continental Reformation movement. Wycliffe's main argument, however, was that although he believed in the transubstantiation in the Eucharist (i.e., the actual transformation of the bread and wine into Christ's body and blood), he also claimed that the bread and wine maintain their form in the process (i.e., remain *in the likeness* of bread and wine). In his "Confessions on the Eucharist," as reported in the *Chronicle* of Henry Knighton, Wycliffe explains: "We beleue, . . . that the sacrament of the autere white and ronde, and lyke tyl oute brede or ost vnsacrede, is verray Goddus body *in forme of brede* . . . And right as it is heresie for to trowe [that Crist is a spiryt and no body, so it is heresie to trowe] that this sacrament is Goddus body and no brede, for *it is bothe togedur*"

(Hudson 17–18; square brackets in original, emphasis added). Here Wycliffe presents a view combining a belief in miracle with his more rational view of perception where a bread perceived as a bread must be a bread. Wycliffe's followers (the Lollards), however, drew further conclusions from this interpretation and claimed that no transubstantiation takes place at all.

The discussion more than a century later was still influenced by the Wycliffite and Lollard modes of thought, and it merged with the reformational ideas introduced from the Continent. The concrete and literal reformer saw Christ's ascension to heaven as an actual and indisputable event in which Christ is seated at God's right hand—thus he cannot be bodily present in the bread and wine. Thomas Cranmer (1489–1556), archbishop of Canterbury in the reign of Henry VIII and thus one of the main local theological reformers of the English church when the more substantial reformation took place, distinguished Christ's *carnal* presence in heaven from both his *figurative* presence in the bread and wine and his *spiritual* presence in the soul of the receiver of the bread and wine (Booty 340). Hence the whole concept of Christ's presence in the world receives in the Reformation a metaphorical, figurative dimension. Wilson uses this aspect of doctrine as an example of a "sign," of the trope of "intellection," as he states that by "eating bread at the Communion, we remember Christ's death, and by faith receive him *spiritually*" (200; emphasis added). This does not diminish the power of the presence of Christ in the world of man, but it adds to man's (reasonable) understanding of a new level of perception, which in turn is reflected in the language. Likewise, the allegorical conception receives an additional parallel concept, opening up new dimensions of communication.

In the two sermons discussed below, Donne uses the new dimensions of religious language, granted to him by the new considerations about the function and scope of language, to bring his audience over to a new—and in general Protestant—reading of the Scriptures and of liturgy and traditions.

The 1624 Candlemas Sermon

In the 1624 Candlemas sermon Donne preaches upon a verse from Christ's Sermon on the Mount: "Let your light so shine before men, that they may see your good works, and glorify your father which is in heaven" (Matt. 5:16). In connection to the feast of Candlemas and the theme of purification, Donne states that "all true purification is *in the light*" (10:84;

emphasis added). For Donne, then, "good works" are not as such directly a means of salvation, but they are a means of purification, and thus, eventually, also an element in salvation. Good works, seen by others, add to their faith and thus purify man for/by God. Furthermore, good works, Donne asserts, presuppose faith (10:85): only a man of God can do God's (good) work. Thus the one who has the most good works to be seen has the most (or strongest) faith. "Good works" are the fruit of faith; faith is "the only true root of all" (10:89). Donne refers to Christ the man (as opposed to Christ the God), who "saw" the faith of the woman with the "issue of blood" (Mark 5:25–34). This woman believed that Christ could heal her (i.e., she had the faith, the "true root") if only she touched him (i.e., performed an act, an action—a "good work").[7] This act, Donne points out, was a fruit of her faith: "And so, in divers of those places, where Christ repeats that, *fides tua, thy faith*, we finde it added, *Iesus videns fidem, Iesus seeing their faith*. With what eyes? he looked upon them with his humane eyes, not his divine; he saw not (that is, considered not at that time) their hearts, but their outward declarations, and proceeding as a good man would, out of their good works concludes faith" (10:88–89).

In the Scriptures, "outward declarations" were needed for Christ the man to see. But for Donne these "outward declarations" become the Protestant forms of metaphor—as opposed to, in Wilson's words, the "darkness" of the "quaint proverbs and blind allegories" of the "mystical wise men" (188). Linguistically, the "good works" in this text are metaphors; theologically, they are a relevant part of a doctrine that requires "personall faith" (10:88) and involvement. In the Protestant sense, metaphors, as good works, must be real and genuine to serve the purpose of means of purification and eventually salvation; they cannot be required acts or a set jargon. Men can also not reach salvation through the actual *accomplishing* of "good works." Donne makes it very clear in his sermon that faith is man's only way to salvation, and this faith is granted to man by the grace of God. He states: "[Christ] enlightened all that came into the world, that is, all that were enlightened in the world, were enlightened by him; there was no other light; and so he makes this light to be *the light of faith, and the light of effectuall grace*, which all have not, but *they that have, have it from Christ*" (10:86; emphasis added). Yet, unlike predestination in a Calvinist spirit, Donne emphasizes that this faith is granted to *all*, to "every man that commeth into the world" (10:86; cf. John 1:9). However, man must declare his acceptance of this gift, through action, by doing "good works." In Donne's words: "Our faith is ours as we have received it, our worke is ours, as we are doers, actors in it" (10:88). This is why the good works are so important for Donne also from the Protestant point of view: only by choosing good works can man acknowledged the faith granted. Although the "just shall live by faith" (Rom. 1:17; Gal. 3:11), this faith must be demonstrated in good works; the "only true root of all" (see above) must be shown in the fruit. This also links to the most powerful encouragement *to act* included in the Gospels: "*Go* ye therefore, and *teach* all nations, *baptizing* them . . . / *Teaching* them *to observe* all things whatsoever I have commanded you" (Matt. 28:19–20; emphasis added). The aspect of personal conviction is very important for Donne here; it turns the good works from passive events into active participants in the process of salvation. Responding to the opening for man to approach God individually, prepared by the Reformation, man must make a personal choice of acknowledging his faith and heeding to the call of the Gospels. Yet, salvation, ultimately, is (in the most Lutheran spirit) in faith alone.

When discussing personal faith further in this sermon, Donne refers to the faith of parents, a reference that can be seen solely as a reference to home and previous generations. But knowing that Donne himself was born into an eminent Catholic family (related, e.g., to Thomas More) and that he had converted later in life, and thus the faith of Donne's own parents, and probably the parents of many in his congregation, was that of Catholicism, the personal choice of faith becomes ever more crucial: "His faith must save him; his own, and not anothers, not his parents faith, though he be the son of holy parents, not the Churches faith, (if he be of yeares) though he be within the covenant, but his own personall faith" (10:88).

Quite early in this 1624 Candlemas sermon, Donne also expresses concern for the tradition and liturgy of the burning of candles. He refers to the heathen tradition that originated the use of lights, a "superstitious multiplying of Lamps, and Torches in Divine Service" (10:89). Although quoting authorities who disapprove of these traditions, like the church fathers Tertullian (born c. 150–60) and Lactantius (born c. 250), Donne himself does not condemn the burning of candles in ceremony. Here again he balances carefully between the acceptable and the unacceptable, between the "pure and innocent primitive Church" and Catholicism gone astray. In other words, Donne echoes a Cranmerian spirit when he states: "It is in this Ceremony of lights, as it is in other Ceremonies: They may be good in their Institution, and grow ill in their practise. . . . For, ceremonies, which were received, but for the instruction, and edification of the weaker sort of people, were made reall parts of the service of God, and meritorious sacrifices" (10:90). Here the aspect of "edification" justifies the otherwise condemned celebrations with possibly even pagan (and not only

Catholic) origins. The guideline comes from St. Paul: "Let all things be done unto edifying" (1 Cor. 14:26). This "edifying" aspect of ceremonies had been discussed also, for example, in the Book of Common Prayer (1559) under the title "Of Ceremonies, Why Some Be Abolished and Some Retained" (which Donne clearly had in mind when writing the passage quoted above):

> Of such ceremonies as be used in the Church and have had their beginning by the institution of man, *some at the first were of godly intent and purpose devised and yet at length turned to vanity and superstition,* some entered into the Church by undiscreet devotion and such a zeal as was without knowledge. And forbecause they were winked at in the beginning, they grew daily to more and more abuses, which not only for their unprofitableness but also because they have much blinded the people and obscured the glory of God are worthy to be cut away and clean rejected. Other there be which although they have been devised by man, yet it is thought good to reserve them still, as well for a decent order in the Church, *for the which they were first devised, as because they pertain to edification,* whereunto all things done in the Church, as the Apostle teacheth, ought to be referred. (Booty 18; emphasis added)

In the present Candlemas sermon, Donne has a very strong emphasis on the aspect of edification and instruction, and that lets him move on to presenting the ceremony, or the feast, as a metaphor.

The Feast as Metaphor

Donne's concern about ceremonies is realistic and understandable, given Protestant reformers' dislike of medieval superstition and magical liturgy. However, rather than pursuing a lengthy attack on (hidden) Catholicism, Donne uses the phenomenon to his advantage: he transforms the burning of candles from a liturgical issue into a linguistic one by shifting his focus to the metaphorical aspects of the event. In the medieval (and thus, in this discussion, Catholic) context, the burning of candles was a sacrifice, an effectual phenomenon—a ceremony to which "was attributed an operation, and an effectuall power" (10:90), "as though [God] were to be supplied by [man]" (10:91). This is what Wilson calls "blind custom," devised "by the fantasy of man" (75). Here Donne, however, reads the text of the Bible from its metaphorical point of view, where the "light" shining denotes "good works," "the true shining of our light, the emanation from us, upon others" (10:92), and thus also the event of burning candles at this feast becomes metaphorical of the works—symbols of the faith presupposed by the good works.

There are further examples of this shift from effectual to symbolic use of text in the present sermon; Donne takes topics (e.g., "light," "candle") from the context of the sermon text and gives them metaphorical, or symbolic, values. He employs different mental images to strengthen his metaphor and to "amplify" his oration (Wilson's term referring to both augmenting and diminishing where appropriate; 146ff.). For example, Donne draws an extension of and elaboration to his metaphor from a reference to a verse in Genesis[8] and states: "God calls the Sun, and the Moone too, Great lights, because though there be greater in the Firmament, they appear greatest to us; those works of ours are greatest in the sight of God, that are greatest in the sight of men, that are most beneficiall, most exemplary, and conduce most to the promoving of others to glorifie God" (10:91–92). Here the metaphor of "light" is concentrated ("diminished") to the linguistic vehicles of "sun" and "moon" versus "other," "greater," and thus the image is made more precise. At the same time, the shift to lights in the firmament, as opposed to candles burning in church, expands ("augments") the metaphor onto a new level of perception. This opens up for the audience a new framework, a new context for understanding the relations of the topic discussed (i.e., "good works").

In the metaphor quoted above, Donne uses the image from the "new philosophy," the knowledge that there are "greater [lights] in the Firmament" than the sun and the moon, as opposed to more biblically correct views of the universe, where the earth is central and still and the sun, moon, and stars are secondary planets created by God after earth, to circle around it, with the mere function to bring light to man.[9] This usage indicates as such Donne's choice of the new (Reformed) world order before the old (medieval, Catholic) world and its traditions. Donne's choice of metaphor reflects his worldview, and the impact is even stronger when he decides to use this image to address his congregation: Donne not only indicates his own conviction but also attempts to assure his audience that the new religion is part of the new world order.[10]

Protestantism in the Terms of Rhetoric

Donne's shift from an effectual reading to a metaphorical (or symbolic) one is also purely rhetorically a shift from a medieval framework to a more linguistically oriented view emphasized by the Reformation, where the nature and character of God's Word was much discussed. As such, a metaphorical reading is, of course, highly unpuritan and to that extent *anti*-reformational. However, the metaphor, for Donne, is clearly a tool for precise expression and apt argumentation—and a central form of linguistic amplification, for which purpose, Wilson states, such words must be used "as be of great weight, wherein either is some metaphor, or else some large understanding is contained" (146). Wilson also states that "[v]ehemency of words full often help the matter forwards, when more is gathered by cogitation than if the thing had been spoken in plain words" and that "the knowledge of a metaphor shall bring men to much knowledge" (158). This is a shift from a basically Catholic way of expression of a rather comprehensive allegory (cf. the *Pilgrim's Progress*, Chaucer, etc.) to a more Protestant rhetoric of interpretative symbolism, applied by less puritan reformers on the Gospels and elaborated upon especially in the language of the more baroque reformational writers.

When discussing the purpose of rhetoric in the first place, Wilson also stresses the importance of following the good example of "the learned and wise men" who have compiled this art: man must "labor . . . to follow their works" (49). Wilson also emphasizes knowledge as a God-granted means to distinguish right from wrong (67). This is a clear Protestant reading of the Gospel as it stresses man's faith as an act of reason. Again, as opposed to the Catholic view of faith as passed on to man by the clergy, the Protestant view requires man to make a choice, to perform an active mental act.

The shift presented by Donne, from an effectual reading of words to a metaphorical presentation, and, with that, his emphasis on the aspect of good works, not so much as a means toward salvation as an indication thereof, is here foremost a rhetorical phenomenon. Donne's framework is linguistic rather than doctrinal. However, at the end of his sermon Donne refers to the especially Protestant aspect of his reading of the text of the sermon, to how man can "doe good works without relying upon them, as meritorious" (10:102). The "good works" are not acted as a payment for a salvation to come but rather as a result, the "fruit," of the faith already obtained. A man of true faith does good works, not to buy salvation, but because he *already has* faith.

The 1627 Candlemas Sermon

Donne's Candlemas sermon of 1627 is preached upon another verse from the Sermon on the Mount: "Blessed are the pure in heart: for they shall see God" (Matt. 5:8). The theme of this sermon is that of "purity" (as the emphasis in the 1624 sermon was on the character and identity of the "light" of the candles), and the emphasis in the text is on the "pure in heart." Donne finds examples of different interpretations of purity from the early church as well as from the medieval church (7:333–35), and like the sermon of 1624, the present one contains several instances of official criticism toward the corruptness of Catholicism. Especially the puritans of the time saw the original primitive church, still unspoiled by later Catholicism, as an ideal form of the church and as a model for the church of the Reformation.

However, first in this sermon Donne again discusses the origins of the feast of Candlemas. The link between the heathen tradition of burning lights for the god of darkness (Februus) and lighting candles to celebrate the purification of the Mother of Christ is by Donne explained in the terms of "re-formation": "We dealt in the reformation of Religion, as Christ did in the institution thereof; . . . Christ borrowed nothing of the Gentiles, but he *took his own* where he found it: Those ceremonies, which [God] himself had instituted in the first Church of the Jews, and the Gentiles had purloined, and prophaned, and corrupted after, he returned to a good use again. And so did we in the Reformation, in some ceremonies which had been of use in the Primitive Church, and depraved and corrupted in the Romane" (7:325–26; emphasis added). Thus, for Donne, the old traditions, some pagan in origin, others corrupted by the Catholic Church, can be made holy again by reinstituting them for a good cause, in good faith. This parallel between the two acts of reinstitution forms the framework of Donne's metaphor in this sermon: the reshaping, re-forming, of an existing tradition, from a corrupted state into purity.

Wilson establishes the concept of the "translation" of words as a means by which "the hearer is lead by cogitation upon rehearsal of a metaphor, and thinketh more by remembrance of a word translated than is there expressly spoken" (196–97). It is of great importance to note that, in Wilson's terms and in accordance to especially the classical rhetoricians Aristotle (384–322 B.C.) and Quintilian (c. 35–95 A.D.), "translation" here refers to, and implies the idea of, metaphor, the "alteration of a meaning" (198) where the substance is the same but the item or idea referred to has been altered. Thus, in the process of "translation" there is a transformation of meaning from one event or phenomenon to another, as such different but related in nature and/or form. As in reference to Wycliffe and the Eucharist above, in the "translation" the item remains "in the likeness" of the original. Donne employs this method on two levels: first, in his amplification by comparison and examples (e.g., he changes his framework from pureness of the heart to pureness of the mind; see Wilson 154–55), and second, in his use of metaphor.

Learning is a way of re-forming, and thus a way to pureness of heart, Donne states, as the "Wisdome that accomplishes this cleannesse, is the knowledge, the right valuation of this world, and of the next" (7:336). In this world man must actively partake of the information granted (through Scriptures in the vernacular, sermons, and comprehensible liturgy) and make his choice. Donne refers to the apostle Paul's encouragement to active action on the question of purity, to man "cleansing himself from all filthiness."[11] Donne states:

> Since God, by breeding us in the Christian Church, and in the *knowledge* of his word, by putting that balance into our hands, *to try* heavenly, and earthly things, by which we may *distinguish* . . . what is leprous and sinful, what is indifferent, and cleane action, let us be content to put the ware, and the waights into the balance, that is, *to bring* all objects, and all actions *to a consideration, and to an examination,* by that tryall, before wee set our hearts upon them: for God leaves no man, with whom he hath proceeded so far, as to breed him in the Christian Church, without *a power to doe* that, *to discerne his own actions,* if he do not winke. (7:337; emphasis added)

As in the Candlemas sermon of 1624, here, too, readers can distinguish a clear division into, and balance between, that which is granted by God, with no merit of man, and that in which man must actively respond in order for the equation to be fulfilled, for salvation to be completed. The first part comes from the grace of God, granted to all men; the second part comes through the Reformation. The whole image of two parts, or levels, is metaphorical of Donne's Protestant disposition. This image is developed further in the present sermon when Donne introduces a house with two rooms as the metaphor of blessedness to those "pure in heart": "The pure in heart are blessed already, not onely comparatively, that they are in a better way of Blessednesse, then the others are, but actually in a present possession of it: for this world and the next world, are not, to the pure in heart, two houses, but two roomes, a Gallery to passe thorough, and a Lodging to rest in, in the same House, which are both under one roofe, Christ Jesus" (7:340).

Here again, it is action, movement, that characterizes also the present sermon in its pursuit of purity. Having received faith, man must himself acknowledge the gift with his action, with "outwards declarations" (see reference to 10:88–89 above), and for this purpose the Protestant Reformation provides means in its emphasis on choice and personal conviction.

Donne's Protestant Metaphor

When we look at both Candlemas sermons from the point of view of Donne's Protestant rhetoric, it is of interest to note that Donne spends a considerable amount of the second part of his 1624 Candlemas sermon on emphasising the *end result* of man's action (10:94ff.). He notes that there is action to be hidden as well as action to be seen. He refers to Christ's instruction that man must not give alms "before men," "to be seen."[12] The contradiction between this, on the one hand, and the encouragement in the text of the sermon to let one's light—one's "good works"—"shine before men," on the other, is explained by Donne in that the actual giving of alms is the end result itself and making it seen would only glorify the giver; yet, the end result of the "good works" as discussed here is that "men will be mov'd to *glorifie your Father which is in Heaven*; which is the true end of all" (10:96). Here Donne makes a further elaboration on acting out the metaphor of his own text: because, as man's "good works" must "move" men to glorify God, so must Donne (following Wilson) as a speaker (preacher) also "move the affections of his hearers in such wise that they shall be forced to yield unto his saying" (Wilson 48).

On a further level, Donne's own presentation, the wording of his sermon, is a metaphor of the text upon which he preaches. Wilson states that God's grace is granted "so to work in the hearts of all men, that they may as well practice well-doing in their own life as they would that others should follow justice in their life" and that "if through [Wilson's] words God shall work with any man, then may [he] think [himself] in happy case and rejoice much in the travail of [his] wit" (66). Likewise, Donne's sermon, his act of rhetoric, becomes his "good works" shining upon the congregation and glorifying God. In Wilson's terms, Donne's "knowledge of learning" is "for the goodness sake," and his "trade of life" is "most necessary for the advancement of God's glory" (77).

Following Donne's reasoning in the 1624 sermon, then, also his "good works" (or: good *words*) presuppose faith. This echoes the *vir bonus* concept from classical rhetoric (Fafner 107). According to this concept, first introduced by Quintilian, only a good man can be, or become, a good speaker. With this concept the art of oratory was linked to an old Roman ideal as well as to the Greek heroic tradition, giving oratory a moral as well as a functional purpose. These originally pagan aspects were readily adapted by the early Christian church in its effort to give power and authority to the preacher of God's Word, and in the Reformation this became even more important. Wilson turns the rhetorical concept into a philosophy of religion and of his personal faith by stating that "where honesty is called in to establish a cause, there is nature and God himself present, from whom cometh all goodness" (71). As a preacher in this tradition, Donne is by definition a good man, a man of God and of sincere conviction.

In the Candlemas sermon of 1627, it is clear that Donne considers himself, as a preacher, first and foremost a vehicle of God; it is God who "directs the tongue of his Ministers, as he doth his showres or rain" (7:328).[13] The *vir bonus* preaches the truth because his voice is a gift of God, not an invention of man. Again, it is the end result, the edification of the congregation, that is the purpose of the preacher's work: "A preachers end is not a gathering of fame to himself, but a gathering of soules to God: and his way is not novelty, but edification" (7:329).[14] Wilson calls for "wit" and "aptness," "knowledge" and "learning," if man wishes to excel in "the *gift* of oratory" (48; emphasis added).[15] Donne also states that "reason is the face of God to the naturall man, the Law to the Jew, and the Gospell to us" (7:344).

Throughout the final part of the 1627 Candlemas sermon (7:342ff.), Donne engages in a detailed discussion on the aspect of those pure in heart actually "seeing" God. This is an important discussion from the point of view of the metaphorical versus literal interpretation of God's Word: the puritans, as mentioned above, claim a most literal reading of this promise recorded by the evangelist (Matt. 5:8; quoted above). From the point of view of a rhetorical framework, it is interesting to follow Donne's argumentation in this sermon, ranging from a seemingly literal presentation ("they shall see God, and be glad to see him"; 7:341), yet questioning this ("but with what eyes I shall see him"; 7:342), considering interpretations of the word ("the words must be understood thus, *In my flesh*, that is, when my soule shall re-assume this flesh in the Resurrection, In that flesh I shall see God"; 7:345), and finally settling on a metaphorical reading ("Every sense is called sight"; 7:346). Donne elaborates upon the metaphor further: "Heare him in his word, and so see him; Speak to him in your prayers, and so see him; *Touch him in his Sacrament, and so see him; Present holy and religious actions unto him, and so see him*" (7:346; emphasis added). Here Donne associates the actual touching of Christ in the sacrament to the "touching" of him in the acknowledging act of "good works" and "outward declaration" (cf. above the discussion of the woman with the "issue of blood" touching the garment of Christ, Mark 5:27–28). Not only does Christ touch man in the sacrament, but man can touch Him; according to Donne, Christ "is otherwise present at the Sacrament, then at any other act of Divine Service" (7:333). However, man can only see (and touch) Christ if man presents rightful "holy and religious *actions* unto him" (see the longer quotation above), that is, if man acknowledges his faith in outward declarations. Christ, then, comes within the reach of man (to be touched in the sacrament) through a process of Wilsonian (or Quintilian) "translation," of an alteration of the "meaning," the reference, of the bread and wine (see above), which is activated, or realized, upon the deliverance of the "good works" and "outward declarations."

This argument has some implications relevant for the rhetorical framework. First, the metaphorical aspect of "seeing" God in "touching" Christ's body and blood in the sacrament includes a second level of metaphor, as the bread and wine also have a translated meaning. Thus the "pure in heart" are raised through two metaphorical levels in the sacrament, from receiving the bread and wine, through touching Christ in this bread and wine, to seeing God. This is far from the literal puritan interpretation. However, second, the emphasis is, again, on man's *action:* "to present holy and religious actions" (see the longer quotation above) and to serve God. Also, the fruit, which in the 1624 sermon denotes the "good works" that presuppose faith, here, too, is related to salvation.

Conclusions: Donne's Art of Protestant Rhetoric

The theological, political, and social references in Donne's texts, and in particular in such public texts as sermons, include elements of the times, of the context in which Donne lived and acted, and they are indeed good indicators of social development and public opinions and trends. Donne worked close to court, and his voice was often harnessed for higher earthly purpose—especially to serve King James's aims. However, the image of Donne's personal vocation and faith in this context may become blurred and confused with the public picture. It is of interest to hear Donne's own voice when reflecting, and distributing, his own true conviction—and when only harnessed for a higher *heavenly* purpose.

I have suggested above that reading Donne's text within the framework of rhetoric (and here especially Thomas Wilson's form of the *art*) gives us a new dimension to Donne's thinking. Looking at the linguistic aspects of Donne's text, as opposed to the purely theological details, reveals an element of communication that can easily go undefined but that has strong impact on the final text and its intended effect on the audience. Donne uses his rhetoric to demonstrate a shift in thought, a movement in time and attitude.

These sermons show that Donne is taking his framework from the theory of rhetoric, as realized in a Protestant philosophy and in the terms of Protestant doctrine. Donne is working with, and elaborating upon, the same concepts that are presented in Wilson's writing; the two clearly share a view of language and a philosophy of rhetoric. Wilson presents his Ciceronian concepts and the logic of/in language in the context of a strong Protestant disposition. Likewise, for Donne, the framework is a concept of the metaphor as a linguistic device *and* a frame of mind, and he uses rhetorical conventions to discuss his topic from a Protestant viewpoint, thus employing a Protestant rhetoric to redefine his (originally medieval and Catholic) themes.

The starting point in both sermons discussed above is that of the "old," the unreformed: in the 1624 sermon the emphasis is on the Catholic tradition as developed throughout the Middle Ages, and, even further back in time, on the primitive church; in the 1627 sermon Donne begins with an elaboration on the heathen custom leading to the feast of Candlemas. In the first of these texts the actual, effectual carrying of lights becomes metaphorical of the act of "good works," and the discussion is developed through this metaphor of an active declaration of faith (vs. passive, undeclared faith). In the second text the state of purity is accomplished through reshaping and re-forming, again active processes involving the believer and preacher alike.

This aspect of movement and development is crucial to Donne's art. He does not merely present his faith, and the conviction he wishes to convey to, or impose upon, his audience, as a static conception, but he shows his view as a result of an evolution. Donne uses the metaphor, and the whole aspect of metaphorical thinking, to "translate" the words of his thoughts into a form in which "the whole matter seemeth by a similitude to be opened" (Wilson 197). Yet, more than this linguistic translation, Donne also performs a "translation" on the level of matter when he moves from a presentation of the old tradition into the new. Donne's strength is in comparison, in the transformation of one state (an effectual burning of candles) into another (a demonstration of good works) within one phenomenon (the feast), and the transformation is accomplished through the turning of the phenomenon itself into a metaphor.

This turning of the phenomenon into a metaphor, apart from being a linguistic and rhetorical act, is an active reaction to the Reformation—like the "good works" are an active reaction to the infusion of faith, and like the "true purification" requires a re-formation in the form of God's blessing. Thus, by transforming the words, Donne also transforms the matter, and he performs a reshaping, a re-formation, of the faith he is illustrating. Donne is creating his own form of the rhetorical process, which includes as a crucial element the aspect of change, of movement and development, of transformation and re-formation.

Here we are back to reading Donne's own act of preaching as a metaphor for his text. Donne uses his own art of rhetoric both as a demonstration of his sincere vocation (as a *vir bonus*, a preacher by the grace of God and under the direction of the Holy Spirit) and for the edification of his hearers, to "move men to glorify the Father." He is using his art both as an application into practice, that is, in his use of the rhetorical device in his argumentation, and as a metaphorical presentation in the form of his own action, that is, in demonstrating his own good works as a preacher of God's Word. Just as the act of transformation replaces the old (Catholic) tradition with the new (here Protestant) framework, likewise Donne's translation into metaphor is his act of "good works" (good *words*) and his personal form of "true purification."

Notes

1. See, e.g., Scodel, Klawitter, and Young, to name examples from but a few categories.

2. E.g., Carey, and more recently Oliver.

3. All quotations from and references to the Bible, when not specifically included in a quotation by Donne, use the Authorized Version.

4. Discussed in detail, e.g., in Mallette.

5. "So then faith cometh by hearing, and hearing by the word of God."

6. In one of his sermons, Donne, too, reflects this "puritan" view by stating: "*No man ever saw God and liv'd;* and yet, I shall not live till I see God; and when I have seen him I shall never dye. . . . We shall se the Humanity of Christ with our bodily eyes, then glorifyed" (3:111–12). However, in his Candlemas sermon of 1627, discussed below, Donne maintains that the "bodily eyes of no man, in the highest state of glorification in heaven, can see the Essence of God" (7:345). All references to and quotations from the sermon texts are here made stating the volume of the Potter and Simpson edition and the relevant page number.

7. "And when our blessed Saviour sayes to the woman with the bloody issue, *Fides tua, Daughter, thy faith hath made thee whole*, it was said then, when he had seen that woman come trembling and fall down at his feet; he saw outward declarations of her faith, he saw works" (10:88).

8. "And God made two great lights; the greater light to rule the day, and the lesser light to rule the night: he made the stars also" (Gen. 1:16).

9. Cf., e.g., Psalm 104:5 ("[God] laid the foundations of the earth, that it should not be removed for ever") and Job 9:6–7 ("Which shaketh the earth *out of her place*, and the pillars thereof tremble. / Which commandeth the sun, and *it riseth not*; and sealeth up the stars"; emphasis added).

10. This aspect of Donne's language in general will not be elaborated upon in the present article, but it is discussed further in other contexts (e.g., Salenius, "The Circle and the Line" and "Kopernikaaninen.")

11. "Let us *cleanse ourselves* from all filthiness of the flesh and spirit" (2 Cor. 7:1; emphasis added).

12. "Take heed that ye do not your alms before men, to be seen of them" (Matt. 6:1).

13. Johnson discusses in detail Donne's "Trinitarian theology" and his emphasis on the workings of the Holy Spirit (28–32).

14. Oliver suggests (9) that edification was not one of Donne's aims in his poetry; however, it is clear that edification certainly was Donne's aim, as a part of his Protestant rhetoric, in his sermons.

15. Likewise, the reformational aspect of man's own knowledge and reason is reflected when Donne appeals to the preacher's choice for his own positive action, saying that being the mediator of God's Word "excuses no mans ignorance, that is not able to preach seasonably, . . . Nor any mans vain-glory, and ostentation, who . . . having made an Oration of Flowres, and Figures, and Phrases without strength, sings it over in every Pulpit" (7:329).

Works Cited

Booty, John E., ed. *The Book of Common Prayer, 1559*. Washington, DC: Folger Shakespeare Library, 1976.

Carey, John. *John Donne: Life, Mind, Art*. New ed. London: Faber and Faber, 1990.

Collinson, Patrick. *The Birthpangs of Protestant England: Religious and Cultural Change in the Sixteenth and Seventeenth Centuries*. London: Macmillan, 1988/1992.

Donne, John. *Sermons*. Ed. George R. Potter and Evelyn M. Simpson. 10 vols. Berkeley: U of California P, 1953–62.

Fafner, Jørgen. *Tanke og tale: Den retoriske tradition i Vesteuropa* [Thought and Speech: The Rhetorical Tradition in Western Europe]. København: C. A. Reitzels forlag, 1982.

Frontain, Raymond-Jean. "'Make all this All': The Religious Operations of John Donne's Imagination." Frontain and Malpezzi 1–27.

Frontain, Raymond-Jean, and Frances M. Malpezzi, eds. *John Donne's Religious Imagination: Essays in Honor of John T. Shawcross*. Conway: U of Central Arkansas P, 1995.

Hudson, Anne, ed. *Selections from English Wycliffite Writings*. Cambridge: Cambridge UP, 1978.

Johnson, Jeffrey. *The Theology of John Donne*. Cambridge: D. S. Brewer, 1999.

Klawitter, George. "John Donne's Attitude toward the Virgin Mary: The Public versus the Private Voice." Frontain and Malpezzi 122–40.

Kopperi, Kari. *Renessanssin Luther* [Luther of the Renaissance]. Helsinki: Helsinki UP, 1994.

Luxon, Thomas H. *Literal Figures: Puritan Allegory and the Reformation Crisis in Representation*. Chicago: U of Chicago P, 1995.

Mallette, Richard. *Spenser and the Discourses of Reformation England*. Lincoln: U of Nebraska P, 1997.

Oliver, P. M. *Donne's Religious Writing: A Discourse in Feigned Devotion*. London: Longman, 1997.

Potter and Simpson. See Donne, *Sermons*.

Rissanen, Paavo. *John Donne's Doctrine of the Church*. Helsinki: Missiologian ja ekumeniikan seura r.y., 1975/1983.

Salenius, Maria. "The Circle and the Line: Two Metaphors of God and His Works in John Donne's *Devotions Upon Emergent Occasions*." *Neuphilologishe Mitteilungen* 2 CII (2001): 201–10.

———. *The Dean and His God: John Donne's Doctrine of the Divine*. Helsinki: Société Néophilologique, 1998.

———. "Kopernikaaninen vallankumous ja retoriikan reformaatio: Maailman kaikkeus Jumalan kuvana John Donnen uskonnollisessa proosassa 1600-luvun Englannissa" [The Corpernican Revolution and the Reformation of Rhetoric: The Universe as an Image of God in John Donne's Religious Prose in Seventeenth-Century England]. *Kielen ja kirjallisuuden hämärä* [Obscurity in Language and Literature]. Ed. Päivi Mehtonen. Tampere: Tampere UP, 2001. 60–86.

Scodel, Joshua. "John Donne and the Religious Politics of the Mean." Frontain and Malpezzi 45–80.

Shami, Jeanne. "'The Stars in their Order Fought Against Sisera': John Donne and the Pulpit Crisis of 1622." *John Donne Journal* 14 (1995): 1–58.

Wilson, Thomas. *The Art of Rhetoric (1560)*. Ed. Peter E. Medine. Pennsylvania State UP, 1994.

Young, Robert V. "Donne's Holy Sonnets and the Theology of Grace." *"Bright Shootes of Everlastingnesse": The Seventeeth-Century Religious Lyric*. Ed. Claude J. Summers and Ted-Larry Pebworth. Columbia: U of Missouri P, 1987. 20–39.

13

"Not upon a Lecture, but upon a Sermon"

Devotional Dynamics of the Donnean Fisher of Men

GALE H. CARRITHERS, JR.,
AND JAMES D. HARDY, JR.

Donne's remark which stands as our title was made early in his ministry. It may be taken with a later self-definition as emblematic of his characteristic sermonic practice: we are, he said, "not in the School, but in the Pulpit, not in Disputation, but in Application."[1] This Donnean position, broadly consistent through his preaching career, has several implications for critical discourse. First, genre matters; hence the most immediately relevant concept for appraising any element or aspect of his preaching is the whole sermon, especially its dynamism, and its generic emplacement in the liturgy of the Book of Common Prayer. Taxonomy and propositional particularity, however essential to criticism, conflict with the dynamism crucial to the whole Donnean sermon, and conflict with the profundity of its movements from abstractly propositional language to more personalized expression. An equally relevant historical context for many a feature of Donne's sermons, because implicit in their dynamic unfolding, is the bewilderingly rich tradition of Augustinian biblicism. Less obviously implicit, but equally important: quality matters. Donne and Lancelot Andrewes were the most celebrated preachers in England in their generation, and critical and editorial attention in the twentieth century has seconded that judgment.

Accordingly, we propose a middling conceptual generality, a level between the height of "Protestant Reformation" and the allusions to singular and parochial, earthbound times or places.[2] At this middle level we focus on three concepts: liturgy—what one was to do in worship, literally the "people's work"; ecclesiology—wherein one was to do it; and justification—the ontology of the believer's status in church and liturgy. By keeping these familiar, powerful framing concepts in play against the movements of a rich but not uncharacteristic sermon, in a hermeneutic succession of approximations, we seek some of the clarity of taxonomy without unduly reducing or degrading what Donne insisted on, the "Sermon of the Sermon."[3]

The most obvious distinction to those who went to church, and all in England were supposed to go to divine services, resided in the form and substance of the liturgy. The Book of Common Prayer described a sacramental Eucharist, while Calvinist books of public worship were fundamentally memorialist in liturgical theology and accordingly emphatic of the ministry of the Word.[4] One could hear and see and taste the implications of this difference every Sunday, even if the entirety of the theology remained obscure. A second difference, also experienced albeit less dramatically and concretely, lay in the area of ecclesiology. Should the church include the whole social community and be governed by kings and prelates, or should much (though certainly not all) authority reside in the congregation of the saints who had been baptized again by the Holy Spirit? Such differences went beyond rationalized doctrine to general inclinations as to how the Christian might relate to God: through intermediaries of priest and sacrament, or directly as one of the priesthood of all believers. The third difference dealt with justification. Justification by faith had been the original Lutheran stand, and it was opposed at Trent by a doctrine of justification by faith and works, while Calvinists espoused yet another way, justification by grace.[5] Doctrine concerning salvation, as well as liturgy and church order, set the competing denominations into formulae that must have been supposed to distinguish true from false doctrine.

So viewed, three general categories emerge, and these apply to the cleavages that then divided Roman Catholic from Protestant and would come increasingly to separate Calvinists (Baptists, Congregationalists, Presbyterians, and puritans generally) from what we will (conveniently but a little anachronistically) call Anglicans, meaning the range of those conforming to Prayer Book worship from catholic (but not papist) to reformers willing to tolerate bishops and sacraments. Cleavages along these lines after 1630 would increasingly manifest themselves in the positions of institutionally and liturgically conservative Laudians and such radical sectarians as John Lilburne and John Wharton.[6]

Donne's own double sermon on Matthew 4:18–20 touched in his individual way on all of these cardinal Christian matters, notwithstanding its ambiguous time setting, 1619/1630. It directly addressed church polity, community, and calling as well as justification, and by implication (especially through his assault on Pelagianism) entailed a sacramental liturgy. With Donne—poet, controversialist, preacher, Reader in Divinity at Lincoln's Inn, and dean of St. Paul's—a major question has been where to place him. This is not because Donne's religious beliefs were concealed. His religion was constantly being made public vocally in sermons, 6 contemporaneously and 160 posthumously preserved by publication and others not, in religious poetry (mostly earlier), and in early polemical tracts such as *Pseudo-Martyr* and *Ignatius His Conclave*. Modern perplexities concerning his religious position have arisen from confusion of religion with secular power politics, from the deliberate murkiness of the Elizabethan Articles of Religion for the Church of England, and from the sheer density of the sermons. Not that Donne spoke with clarity and rigor for all his co-religionists, but Donne, joined with Richard Hooker, did adumbrate a moderate institutional Anglican adherence, obviously Protestant, attached to preaching (the word), the Bible (the Word), and conversion, obviously not puritanically attached only and fiercely to preaching and the Bible and adult conversion. Donne's double sermon illustratively and his other sermons collectively supported Protestant moderation in a time of increasingly radical Calvinist sectarianism and Roman Catholic defense of the papacy as the foundation of the Church.[7]

In the second part of his sermon on Matthew 4:18–20, delivered in 1619 "at the Haghe" and amplified to two sermons in Essex in 1630, in connection with Christ's call to the fishers Peter and Andrew to "follow Me," Donne urged upon the beloved faithful a central Pauline dictum: "For here we have no continuing City, but we seek one to come" (Heb. 13:14). The merely earthly city is comprised of the "materials, the living stone, and timber, for his Militant Church, from all places, from Cities, from Deserts, and here in this Text, from the Sea" (2:270). Augustine in the *City of God* had understood the earthly city as *properly* a "pilgrim Church," not ultimately of this world, but nonetheless a community within this world, to be a "passage to our habitations."[8] While the continuing city is elsewhere, Christian life and doctrine demand that "we seeke it not here, but we seeke it whilest we are here, els we shall never finde it" (2:307). Donne informed his hearers (and readers) that "the very name of Church implies company . . . it is a congregation, a meeting, an assembly" (2:279).

Community existed as part of a Christian calling and not merely a secular amenity; "whose feet will you wash?" asked Athanasius of the Egyptian anchorites, and Donne repeated this idea with his reference to the commandment to love thy neighbor.[9]

But if the trope of calling necessarily led the pilgrim through community, this was not an end in itself but rather a station on a longer journey to a higher *telos* based in *kairos*. Donne advised his audience "that this world is not our home," and Christians were instructed to "Arise ye, and depart; for this is not your rest: because it is polluted, it shall destroy you, even with a sore destruction" (Mic. 2.10; *Sermons* 2:307). For Donne this command of the Old Law was understood to be fulfilled in the New Testament's "follow Me" (Matt. 2:19). Such a command, Augustine commented, is to love the greater thing (God) the more, and love the lesser thing (the world) less (2:284). Donne elaborated: "Not to be too diligent toward the world, is the diligence that God requires. S. *Augustine* does not say, *sua relinquere*, but *sua imperfecta relinquere*, [not] that God requires we should leave the world, but that we should leave it to second considerations" (2:284). Later in the sermon, Donne would recapitulate: "Those meditations, and those endeavors which must bring us to heaven, are removed from this world, and fixed entirely upon God" (2:307). The command "follow Me" directed loves into their proper relationships and pointed the pilgrim "ad regnem caritatis."[10]

Community emphasized the worldly and the Church militant, because that alone was where the community in a fallen world could exist. But the trope of calling emphasized a preparation for and concentration upon heaven, which, if taken to extremes, could be held to imply a *contemptus mundi*. Donne avoided that extreme and insisted that pastoral care could not exclude community in its role of ambassadorship, looking beyond the *civitas terrena* to the *civitas Dei*. The tension between these two obligations, the location of the journey among the "creatures here below" though directed "ad regnem caritatis," could not be resolved, as Donne was clearly aware, by any secular formula or expedient. If the *civitas Dei* was considered only in terms of attainment by the individual, a dangerously Pelagian view, then a continuous tension existed between the demands of community and the fulfillment of calling. Taken to its logical conclusion, this tension rose to the level of a discontinuity; indeed, as early as the Egyptian anchorites it seemed that participation in a necessarily fallen but perhaps still loving Christian community endangered the individual soul. But such an antinomy only existed if the divine command to "follow Me" instructed the believer to abandon the world rather than to illuminate it. Donne preached inclusiveness and engagement in the world, though with "second considerations," rather than withdrawal to pretended perfection. He felt no contradiction or even tension between the "first and greatest commandment" and the second which was "like unto it": "God hath manifested his will . . . and . . . digested it into two Commandments, 'Love God, love thy neighbor'" (2:279). Calling and community in that context, which Donne, like Rabbi Hillel before him, thought the heart of the way, became each a part of the other and both a function of love rightly ordered toward God.

Considered within the limits of the *civitas terrena*, religious communities may be lumped together within the sociology of religion; when considered in connection with the *civitas Dei*, however, enormous differences emerge at once. Donne was at some pains here to define his understanding of a Godly *congregatio*, an understanding usually less explicitly described; indeed, the definition of community as he understood the Bible to express it was a fundamental goal of this double sermon. The biblical text invited such examination; as the Folio prints it:

> MAT.4.18,19,20. AND JESUS WALKING BY THE SEA OF GALILE SAW TWO BRETHREN, SIMON CALLED PETER, AND ANDREW HIS BROTHER, CASTING A NET INTO THE SEA, (FOR THEY WERE FISHERS,) AND HE SAITH UNTO THEM, FOLLOW ME, AND I WILL MAKE YOU FISHERS OF MEN; AND THEY STRAIGHTWAY LEFT THEIR NETS, AND FOLLOWED HIM.

Donne divided the text broadly into a "twofold consideration" of Peter and Andrew, thus called to the community of apostles: "What their present, what their future function was, what they were, what they were to be" (2:270). And these two were in some sense one; they had been fishers and they would be fishers, "but there is an improvement, a bettering, a reformation, (They were *fisher-men* before, and now they shall be *fishers of men*;)" (2:287). The first sermon of the two (*Sermons*, vol. 2, no. 13) explored the "many circumstances, in and about their calling" (2:270), notably the symbolic implications of place, causalities, and corollaries of vocation and of familial closeness and distance. The second (vol. 2, no. 14) explored the command to follow, with regard to humility and cautionary straightness, and explored the promise in anti-Pelagian terms as reformation, world/sea, gospel/net, and grace (2:287).

The emblematic fishers' community had been changed by grace beyond purely human recognition and from a purely human association, though their vocation remained ostensibly the same. Having obeyed the call "sequere me," they had become "very members incorporate," and among the first such members of the Church militant, which incorporated elements both of *chronos* (physical time) and *kairos* (divine presence). As Donne would finally imply, Peter and Andrew, by leaving their nets, left also the tychastic time of vicissitude known to all fishers everywhere ("Having any luck?") for the linear time of new covenant and *telos*.

Donne further noted that Christ "provided at first against singularity." He called two men, neither of whom was of his house and lineage. Only the second "payre of Brethren," James and John, were kinsmen. Donne argued that by calling strangers to community Christ "provided at first against partiality" (2:270), signifying the ecumenical call of inclusiveness, of going into all the world. The second call indicated that those who are close may not be ignored. The Roman formula, that the church works "urbi et orbi," seems apposite. But Donne did not direct his comments on community toward a Roman Catholic conclusion, but rather toward a catholic one.

Donne's examination of community was not merely directed narrowly toward parsing details from the text. As was usual in Donne's pastoral theology, he more largely emphasized the general and salvific journey of what Augustine had called the "society of Pilgrims" moving toward the *civitas Dei*. This initial examination of the first *res publica Christiana*, already in some measure the *Corpus Christi*, dealt with the fundamental duty of those apostles who were called to be fishers of men. He exhorted his listeners (and readers): "Thinke not thy selfe well enough preached unto, except thou finde a desire, that thy life and conversation may preach to others" (2:271). The Christian's duty, as symbolic fisherman, was "to gather all Nations to one household of the faithfull, and to constitute a Communion of Saints" (2:273), a transcendence of class and sect in catholicity. Christ chose some apostles from among the poor and ignorant of the world and the world's judgment, exalting—as Luke had observed and Donne implicitly concurred—"those of low degree": "Christ needed not mans sufficiency, he took insufficient men; Christ excuses no mans insufficiency, he made them sufficient" (2:274). The community was at once "all Nations," and the *ecclesiola* of the "Communion of Saints," at once those seemingly "sufficient" and those esteemed not to be so, at once both of this world and beyond it, at once both a pilgrim and a promise, and always a calling.

Donne in this double sermon had a double meaning for "calling": the familiar contemporary usage of calling as personally fitting profession or craft or trade or station, and the more general application of calling for each to be fit ambassador of truth, love, and repentance for the whole *res publica Christiana* as proclaimed by Matthew (5:14–16), Paul (2 Cor. 5:21), and the Book of Common Prayer. The common meaning of "calling" lay in the pastoral requirement that all perform their daily tasks well and with (at least implied) devotion. It became an *imitatio Christi* on a quotidian level, not unimportant but also not everything.[11] The designation of calling as ambassadorship instructed the faithful that they were, both by their lives and doctrine, preachers to the whole community of saints (2 Cor. 5:21). Both doctrines of calling—ambassadorship and the daily tasks of life—were part of ordinary Christian duty, and Donne regarded them as complementary in the devotion of daily life that Paul had described as prayer without ceasing.[12]

The ordinary calling here was fishing, which Andrew and Peter practiced before their greater calling and followed again after the Crucifixion. This was an honest calling, not to be despised except through "*appetitus celsitudinis perversus,*" the "inordinate desire of being better than we are" (2:291). The two first apostles had followed only their own rough and lawful calling, avoiding "intrusion into other mens callings," which Donne called "an unjust usurpation; and, if it take away their profit, it is a theft" (2:278). Christ found Peter and Andrew casting their nets into the sea: "That they did it because they were fishers; It became them, it behoved them, it concerned them to follow their trade; And then they did it as they were fishers, If they had not been fishers they would not have done it, they might not have usurped upon anothers Calling" (2:270). The copiousness of Donne's reiteration of the same simple point presumably ministers to the residual orality of much of his audience (their expectation of redundancy), but it also emphasized the role that Donne accorded the dignity of ordinary work. *Laborare est orare*, proclaimed the Western monastic tradition from Benedict onward, and these two sermons show Donne in general agreement with that view of raising the ordinary from vicissitude to journey.[13]

Calling, most particularly in the role of ambassadorship, was one of the four basic tropes of the habitually religious thought characteristic of the English Renaissance (journey, moment, and theater were the others), and Donne did not deal with so important an aspect of the faith lightly.[14] Calling was not merely what one did; it also encompassed how one did it. The world was not utterly to be despised, nor its requirements totally ignored. The Pauline doctrine was abundantly clear: "Now then we are ambassadors for Christ" (2 Cor. 5:20), meaning ambassadors for and in this world, not against this world. Donne regarded this aspect of calling as one that all who were of the faith and church of Christ would and must joyfully heed. Ambassadorship was explained in the Gospel of Matthew: "Neither do men light a candle, and put it under a bushel, but on a candlestick; and it giveth light unto all that are in the house" (Matt. 5:15). Donne glossed this further in an Augustinian direction, employing a crucial distinction between his own theology and the austerity of the monastic (latterly puritan) tradition: "*Perfecta obedientia est sua imperfecta relinquere*, not to be too diligent toward the world is the diligence that God requires" (2:284). He explained with compassionate trenchancy: "there is no example of forsaking a calling, upon the pretence of following Christ; no example here, of devesting ones selfe of all means of defending us from those manifold necessities, which this life lays upon us, upon pretence of following Christ; It is not an absolute leaving of all worldly cares, but a leaving them out of first consideration; *Primum quaerite regnem Dei*, so, as our first businesse be to seeke the kingdome of God" (2:284). The humble and earthly calling merged without discernible boundaries into the higher ambassadorship for Christ, but both were performed within the Augustinian "pilgrim church" in the *civitas terrena*. The two elements of calling were not to be distinguished but rather combined into a continuing profession of faith that was to be lived rather than merely asserted.

A requisite of calling as ambassadorship, Donne argued, was a humble and contrite heart. Without this, a person loved the lesser thing, this world, the more. It was not the pride that "goeth before a fall" that mattered; it was the pride that resulted from the Fall that kept the faithful from turning daily tasks into calling and calling into ambassadorship: "Pride is so contrary to God, as that the proud man, and he can meet in nothing. And this consideration hath kept us thus long, from that which we make our first and principal collection, that this commandment of Humility, was imprinted in our very first word, *Sequere*, follow, be content to come after, to denote how early and primary a sin Pride is, and how soone it entered the world, and how soone into us" (2:293–94). The sin of pride was to be understood as standing athwart the most essential transformation in the lives of the beloved faithful, from love misdirected toward intermediate goods to love properly directed through grace toward God. Such an "*imperfecta relinquere*" placed one in God's way, and Donne reiterated that "He does not call them from their calling, but he mends them in it. It is not an Innovation . . . But it is a Renovation" (2:305). Such a renovation would combine community and calling into a life of love and service toward which Donne's pastoral efforts and theology so obviously directed the beloved faithful.

In discussing the pastoral relationship between the believer and the Shepherd, Donne in Protestant fashion mentioned only Christ and not bishops as the Shepherd. The command "Follow Me," uttered by Christ more than once, Donne understood in two ways: "how we are to follow Christ in beleeving, and then how in doing, in practising" (2:298–99). "Beleef" was a gift of grace, but Donne warned against willful misdirections into heresy. Doctrine must be centered on Christ, "to embrace those Doctrins, in which his Church hath walked from the beginning, and not vex thy selfe with new points, not necessary to salvation" (2:299). Perseverence to the end in the road laid out by the gospel constituted following "Christ in Doctrinall things."

The command "sequere me" in matters of doctrine and faith meant for Donne a moderate though distinctly Protestant journey. We, like Holmes, are struck by the dog that did not bark. There was no mention of the cure of souls, that distinctly Catholic description of institutionally based pastoral theology. Rather, the Protestant conception of the priesthood of all believers appears to us as a clear implication of the repeated injunction to follow "the whole Gospel, and nothing but Gospel for Gospel" (2:299).[15] Moreover, Donne's emphasis upon the Augustinian journey toward rest and *conversio* (*Confessions* 1.1, 8.39) placed him in the Protestant tradition of personal responsibility for one's soul, with "no dependance upon any great person" (2:299). Doctrine appeared here as a pastoral concern, not a matter of the theology of salvation or the Eucharist, both areas of intense contemporary dispute. Donne's injunction "to persevere to the end in the whole Gospel" treats doctrine as the Word lived and not just spoken: "to the end (journey) *in*, not *with*, not even *by*"; like Christ as "the way, the truth, and the life." It recalls the *imitatio Christi* of Thomas à Kempis, as well as Geert Groote and the whole *devotio moderna*.[16]

This sense of doctrine does not much distinguish the "Doctrinall" from the "practicall"; both operate (*ex opere operandis* in this case) not within themselves but as complements, as journey-like activity, not as miracle or mystery. One thing was distinguishable, however, and it was Christ's command: "Hee that will follow me, let him take up his crosse, and follow me" (Matt. 16:24). For Donne, evidently, the way of the cross was not necessarily a path of affliction, though of course it might be, and he did not consistently regard affliction as sweet in itself, but a thing to be borne with "not only patience, but cheerfulnesse; more, thankfulnesse" (2:299). For Donne afflictions did not, in themselves, signify a cross that one must carry to Christ. Rather, in a sermon on Galatians 3:27, he glossed "putting on Christ" as experiencing any sufferings that might befall the baptized in terms of Christ's sufferings (5:157). Affliction, that cherished puritan metaphor for grace, was neutral, subject to the believer's use: "for every man hath afflictions, but every man hath not crosses. Onely those afflictions are crosses, whereby the world is crucified to us, and we to the world" (2:300).

Following Christ in "practicall" things required a cross that informed a journey of *conversio* to Christ. The way of the cross consisted of four distinct elements, each coming from the biblical text. There must "bee a crosse, And it must be my crosse, And it must be taken up by me, And with this crosse of mine, thus taken up by me, I must follow Christ" (2:300). The Christian, however strong the requirement to take up the cross, was obliged to take up only one's own cross. *Tollat crucem* was a general command only with regard to people, not to crosses, that is, to situations, circumstances, events, and journey: "Other mens crosses are not my crosses; no man hath suffered more then himselfe needed" (2:300). Superfluous sufferings were, either in themselves or as a road to salvation, of no value, because "Beloved, Christ puts no man out of his way, (for sinfull courses are no wayes, but continuall deviations) to goe to heaven" (2:305).

The cross that was one's own must come from God; otherwise it would lack "a good title." This referred not only to works of supererogation, but to the crosses of others, and to the crosses that have come from nature: "Alas, that crosse of present bodily weakness, which the former wantonnesses of my youth have brought upon me, is not my crosse" (2:301). The problems of prodigality, in body or estate, were "Nature's crosses, not Gods," and were not to be taken up (as in the twin commands of *Tollat crucem* and *sequere me*) as the true vocation and journey of the penitent Christian. These were only "spontaneous and voluntary crosses, contracted by mine owne sins" (2:301), and are necessarily created. Since the cross to be borne to Christ truly fit only the person for whom it was meant, there was no general obligation to bear every cross or seek to repair every sin. The general cross, the general obligation, could belong to Christ alone. To suppose otherwise would, Donne implies, be presumption redolent with the pride of "our first parent." The true way of the cross arose from the "tentations or tribulations in my calling": "I must not go out of my way to seeke a crosse; for, so it is not mine, nor laid for my taking up. I am not bound to hunt after a persecution, nor to stand it, and not flye, nor to affront a plague, and not remove, nor to open my selfe to an injury, and not defend" (2:301). The Jesuits' search for martyrdom had been condemned as a false cross in *Pseudo-Martyr*. It was also a common feature of some "gathered churches," particularly those that envisioned an imminent end of the world and the thousand-year reign of the saints.[17] One little push, one great cross taken up, and the way would be clear and the time would be right for Christ's second coming. Such searching for the greatest cross in the world, Donne suggested, leads away from God, since God alone can provide the cross and "Christ puts no man out of his way."

Donne had no difficulty in asserting that the cross given by God must be "voluntarily embraced." All, of whatever Christian persuasion, would agree with that. But Donne does not take the next and theologically dangerous step of identifying what the cross given by God might be, exactly. The endless search for divine hints—we would see a sign, say the people—psychologically so attractive, was theologically dangerous, for it confused the vicissitudes of the *civitas terrena* with the journey of *conversio* toward the *civitas Dei*.

The true cross, which "put no man out of his way" (the way, the journey of his calling), while carried within the *civitas terrena*, was not discoverable by purely earthly signs; indeed, it could be discerned and carried only by grace, faith, and prayer. Thus, cross and calling would be mutually implicated, both given by Christ to individuals, and not in their essential interiority matters for communities. Only God completely understood both cross and calling. For individuals this meant piety, prayer, and duty; for communities it meant religious toleration, a difficult concept for Catholic and nonconformist alike but entirely accordant with Hooker's middle way.

Although the main action of this double sermon was instructing the beloved faithful in the microcosmic journey of conversion by *applying* the response of the first apostles to the command "Follow Me," Donne also included doctrinal instruction to the end that the true Word of God might be rightly "understood of the people." Implicit in the foregoing and the following are the simultaneously Catholic and Protestant roots of Donne's relation to this biblical text from Matthew as to the other texts he chose for sermons. Preeminent is the fact of so lawyerly and lovingly parsing the text. It betokened a sensibility more Protestant than Catholic in its implicit sense of what might be called real verbal presence. That is, the preacher could without *necessary* reliance on ecclesiastical or patristic mediation, on "Eloquence" or "Traditions of men" (307)—though presumably with dependence on grace and the Holy Spirit—directly apprehend divine Scripture and communicate it.

If Donne's analyses of his texts sometimes suggest the rigor of a fine legal mind, the fact of analysis needs to be put in the context of faculty psychology[18] and devotional meditative practice. Louis Martz virtually gave awareness of this to the scholarly community with *The Poetry of Meditation*, which privileged Catholic continental sources and especially the Ignatian spiritual exercise moving formally through successive engagements of the memory, the analytic intellect, and affections of the will. Barbara Lewalski enlarged the realm of source discourse, and with a complementary privileging, in *Protestant Poetics*.[19] The exact trail of Donne's reading, marking, learning, and inwardly digesting native and continental Catholic and Protestant texts of devotional practice seems so largely effaced as to puzzle conjecture. But, with regard to this double sermon and Donne's sermons generally (and sermons were not the focus of either the Martz or the Lewalski study), two things are observable. The first is what looks like a characteristic Donnean inclusive position: with regard to Catholic and Protestant meditative practice, he has internalized it and made it his own. Elements, moves, and variants of the word *meditation* recur throughout the sermons. The second point is obvious to all readers of the sermons: the animating presence in Donne's religious imagination of many writings of Augustine.

An Augustinian hermeneutic meditation suggests the priesthood of all believers in exemplary action, and with this, as was quite usual, Donne began analytically, not only with his *Divisio* but in passages intermittently in both sermons marked with the *buts, therefores, yets, becauses, ifs*, and *considers* of analytic discourse. In the first sermon, there were fervent identifications of blessings and a feeling general declaration about any "not" in "my life" to be cast aside (2:286). The second sermon turned quickly, in its second paragraph, to memory of pride, and a series of fervent exclamations, "so early... O the earlinesse!" (2:294–96). With an Augustinian hermeneutic flexibility, Donne moved between general and particular, part and whole, middle and end, negative or indeed satiric (as of "Minimes, and Nullans," 2:298) and affirmative, but always within the context of loving pastoral instruction. This hermeneutic recirculation rose to a lyrical vision at the end, suggestive of sacred parody of Donne's own "The Baite" and anticipative of Herbert's "Love III," of fishers and "fish" as alike fare and guests at the "great Mariage-feast, which is the Kingdome of Heaven" (2:310).

While the double sermon was Protestant in its general character, tone, and orientation, the exact nature of Donne's Protestant doctrine requires inference as much as citation. The distinctions between Donne's pre-Laudian Church of England and an increasingly separatist Calvinism are less obvious than attacks on Roman Catholicism, especially papal authority. But Donne's disdain for the Calvinist preoccupation with "Election and Reprobation" struck at the core of Calvinist systematic and pastoral theology, and this seems to us to be no less doctrinally serious than his sustained criticism of Roman papalism.

Donne denied papal *plenitudo potestatis* from two general directions: the primacy of Peter and scope of consequent apostolic papal authority, and the workings of the treasury of merits. He specifically rejected papal supremacy, a controversy that was in Donne's time both old, with the conciliarist movement, and new, with the writings of Cardinal Robert Bellarmine.[20] Donne, a legally trained controversialist, presumably understood that the denial of the primacy of Matthew 26:18–19 *(tu es Petrus et super hanc petram)* was implicit in the whole discussion of community of the apostolate and the saints.[21] Certainly, contemporaries familiar with the ongoing arguments concerning the direct and indirect authority of the pope (James I had written on this point) would have understood the community envisioned by Donne as hostile to the Roman Catholic conception of the Church militant.[22]

As early as the third paragraph of this double sermon, Donne explained his views on apostolic primacy. Andrew was presented as the first of the New Testament apostles, for which reason the Church celebrated St. Andrew as "the first that hath a particular day" (2:272). It was Andrew who "drew Peter," who would become the greater but not the sole apostle. By slighting the *double* calling of Peter and Andrew by Christ, "the Romane heresie *distill* and racke every passage of Scripture, that may drop any thing for the advantage of S. *Peter*, and the almightiness of his Successor" (2:272).

The role of apostle not having fallen upon one man, it was not carried forth by one man either, for "God loves not singularity; the very name of Church implies company; It is *Concio, Congregatio, Coetus;* It is a Congregation, a Meeting, an assembly; It is not any one man; neither can the Church be preserved in any one man" (2:279). For the Church to be reduced to one man, "where all infallibility, and assured resolution is in the breast of one man" (2:280), it must then lose the name "Catholique," which Donne called "a glorious and harmonious name." A catholic church required universal and fundamental doctrines that were true in all times and in all places *(quod ubique, quod semper)*, else the very name catholic "is such a solecisme, as to speak of a white blacknesse, of a great littlenesse" (2:280). In a clear irony, Donne implied that Roman Catholic papal doctrines led to the same end as did Protestant particularity, an end to true catholicity and the endless multiplication of sects, conventicles, and separatists.

The assault on the apostolic authority of the pope begun in the first sermon continued as a doctrinal theme in the second, but more zealously:

> it is an usurpation, an imposture, an illusion, it is a forgery, when the Bishop of Rome will proceed by Apostolicall dignity, and Apostolicall

jurisdiction; If he be S. *Peters* Successor in the Bishopricke of Rome, he may proceed with Episcopall authority in his Dioces . . . yet when they will constitute matter of faith out of matter of fact, and because S. *Peter* was (de facto) Bishop of Rome, therefore we must believe, as an Article of faith, such an infallibility in that church, as that no Successor of S. *Peters* can ever erre, when they stretch it to matter of faith, then for matter of faith, we require Scriptures; and then we are confident . . . the present Bishop of Rome . . . is not S. *Peters* Successor in his Apostleship; and only that Apostleship was a jurisdiction over all the world. (2:302–3)

What Donne denied was not the historical (albeit non-scriptural) tradition concerning Peter's death in Rome, but instead the expansion of tradition into faith, and what he saw as racking, distilling, and forging the Word of God. In these matters, Donne exhibited a profoundly Protestant sensibility.

The second matter on which Donne attacked Roman doctrine and practice concerned the treasury of merits, one of the theological foundations for the use of indulgences. Described doctrinally by the papal bull *Unigenitus Filii* in 1343, indulgences were designed as a substitute for auricular confession to a priest, by confession of sins to God.[23] The same true act of contrition was required, and payment for the indulgence was the needed penance. In accordance with the observation of the American political scientist John Roche, that every reform begins with ideals and ends as a racket, indulgences and the treasury of merits became first an object of protest and rebuke, then of derision. Donne's comment was moderate for a Protestant, more wry than zealous. He stated that it is "a poore treasure, which they boast of in the Romane Church, that they have in their Exchequer, all the works of supererogation, of the Martyrs . . . that suffered so much more than was necessary for their owne salvation, and those superabundant crosses and merits they can apply to me." Donne then added the quintessential Protestant question about the treasury of merits: "If the treasure of the blood of Christ Jesus be not sufficient, Lord what addition can I find?" (2:300). The remedy, for all Christians, was to "professe the whole Gospel and nothing but Gospel" (2:299), that is, the true Word of God followed to the end of the Christian journey of life.

The distinctions between Donne and the more rigorous Calvinists were more discreetly present, though they were not less serious for that. That discretion was certainly decorous when the single sermon was delivered to a Calvinist audience in the Netherlands in 1619 (to whatever degree it may then have been apparent). Back home, the only constraining decorum would seem to have been his sense of his English congregation's needs. Donne demurred from Calvinism in three areas, with the most serious criticism, and the one most delicately expressed, resistance to the doctrine of predestination, saved for last. In the next-to-last paragraph of the second sermon, after having denied any Pelagian tendency ("the Apostle does not say . . . that eternall life is the wages of any good worke of ours," 2:308), Donne discounted supralapsarian predestination by appealing to Christ's promise and God's love. Not only did Christ promise redemption through himself, but "neither did God meane ill to any man, till that man was, in his sight, a sinner. God shuts no man out of heaven, by a lock on the inside, except that man have clapped the doore after him, and never knocked to have it opened againe, that is, except he have sinned, and never repented" (2:308). The choice of heaven, of election, depended upon our repentance and "resolve to lead a new life" as necessary though never sufficient cause, however it may have been kept and always dependent on prevenient grace. Donne argued that human free will, given by grace, was the complement, in the *civitas terrena*, of God's love. This was not a puritan sensibility, as the puritan treatises warning against despair indicated.[24]

The notion that earthly success was indicative of heavenly grace functioned as a psychological necessity, perhaps, in a denomination that sought assurance of election leading to the search for a cross as the means of flight from despair. For Calvinists the "comfortable words" could become the earthly works, a Pelagian tendency that Donne always avoided. Herbert Schneidau has called this tendency to see anything like election in mere human success "vulgar Calvinism," and no part of this was so vulgar as the *idée fixe* that earthly prosperity was a sign of divine grace.[25] The true sign of election for Calvinists was an interior confidence in having been predestined. The outward and visible priggishness and self-righteousness so scorned by adversaries such as Ben Jonson in *The Alchemist* and *Bartholomew Fair* presumably arose in Calvinists from some inward and spiritual mixture of fear, doubt, certainty, hope, faith, and desperation.[26]

Donne was firmly pastoral in dismissing what he evidently saw as (so to speak) a Pelagianism of the right in overvalued Roman Catholic works and observances and a Pelagianism of the left in separatist signmongering. In a sermon on Genesis 1:26 (before King Charles) he was more schematic:

> *Whole-pelagianisme*, to thinke nature alone sufficient; Half-pelagianisme, to thinke grace once received to be sufficient; Super-pelagianisme, to thinke our actions can bring God in debt to us, by merit, and supererogation, and

Catharisme, imaginary purity, in canonizing ourselves, as present Saints, and condemning all, that differ from us, as reprobates. All these are white spots, and have the colour of goodnesse; but are indications of leprosie. (9:67; see also 7:159)

Schematic and explicit, this was also characteristic of his profoundly receptionist (and thus much Protestant) and Augustinian (and thus much old Catholic) theology and symbology. Fire was lustful or refining, red angry or redemptive, white leprous or good, depending on the orientation of the recipient's loves. Two months earlier, he had implied the scheme in preaching that seeing God only "in his Works" is "but the godliness of the natural man," while "hearing many Sermons" is but "a new way of making Beads"—Pelagian work/sign-mongering by "the Papist" and (implicitly) the puritan alike (9:175–76). The positive alternative to Pelagianism (as to hedonism) was of course calling, calling recognized in terms of grace and embraced: "no man can renew himselfe, regenerate himselfe; no man can prepare that worke, no man can begin it, no man can proceed in it of himselfe" (2:305). Calling was exemplified by Donne's own presence in the liturgy of the pulpit.

A third comment on Calvinism involved the politics of denomination, an issue in all countries with an established church, including the Netherlands. Donne linked separatists with libertines, as "persons whom the Devill kept from Church all their lives" (2:296). At a time when numbers of Calvinists were beginning to leave the Church of England in opposition to bishops, liturgies, and doctrines they thought contrary to the Word of God, this was a strong condemnation. Donne did not dwell upon this issue, speaking instead of the primal sin of pride, but enough had been said to indicate that he considered separatism itself a sin of pride.

Separatism in England involved not only differences in ecclesiology but also disagreements concerning doctrines of salvation, more particularly the interrelationships of grace, faith, works, baptism by the Holy Spirit, journey, and calling, along with their concomitant liturgical differences.[27] It was spiritual pride (and sloth?) and intellectual reductionism, presuming to the special calling of the preacher, when Calvinist separatists "are weary of hearing any other thing, than Election and Reprobation, and whom, and when, and how, and why God hath chosen, or cast away" (2:279). People had "liberty enough" to follow the salvation of their souls; further wrangling over "God's eternall Decrees, and unrevealed Councels" would yield nothing for those not called to be "fishers there" (2:279). We are reminded of Hooker's judicious comments concerning the sacraments in general which entered "into the souls of man we are not able to apprehend or expresse how," and, therefore, the appropriate attitude toward the mysteries of sacrament and salvation ought to be: "Take therefore that wherein we all agree, and then consider by it selfe what cause why the rest in question should not rather be left as superfluous than urged as necessarie."[28] For a century or more after Donne, this would be vain advice.

Toward the end of the second part of the double sermon, Donne emphasized the theology that all English denominations held in common. Although English Protestants were divided on the precise role of grace in salvation, all agreed, and agreed with Roman Catholicism, on the necessity of grace.[29] Donne followed the "no man" passage quoted above with an Augustinian description of grace. The beginning of personal "Renovation," even the desire to begin that work, came "from the preventing grace of God, and the constant proceeding is from the concomitant, and subsequent, and continuall succeeding grace of God" (2:305).

As was appropriate in a society of complete orality in many and secondary orality in others, Donne copiously reiterated (as we have) this unifying doctrine of grace as the foundation of Christian life and hope, of Christian faith and fear. The salvation Christ promised was not "in the nature of wages due to our labour, and our fishing. There is no merit in all that we can doe" (2:308). Redemption came through Christ, "who is a Saviour, a Redeemer," and human efforts, mired in original sin, could never cross the gap Augustine had identified as between distress and rest. For Donne, the self (never for him reducible to a function of discourse, economics, or biology) was the problem: "If I would not serve God, except I might be saved for serving him, I shall not be saved though I serve him; My first end in serving God, must not be my selfe, but he and his glory. It is but an addition from his own goodnesse; Follow me, and I will doe this" (2:309). The faithful belief of Andrew and Peter in obeying the command "sequere me" would, in the nature of things, lead to acts of calling and ambassadorship, to the right journey of *conversio*, and to such actions of goodness informed by grace as people may do. Donne's salvific theology, at the heart of this great double sermon, was graciously and hermeneutically sequential and re-circulatory rather than what he evidently adjudged the more simplistic logical stasis of extreme Calvinism or the legalism of Rome. Perhaps this accounts for the difficulty in *placing* Donne in the Roman or the Calvinist camp. The searching Donne, who echoed the judicious Hooker, recognized, in the apt phrase of J. Sears McGee, "the graciousness of many graces and the sinfulness of many sins" (69), and understood that at Christianity's core lay neither harsh predestination nor reductive explanation, but mysteries of love and transcendence.

Notes

1. We quote from the *Sermons* by volume and page, occasionally with date or place. The title quotation: 2:320, at Lincoln's Inn in 1620; "not in the School" (1:234), at Whitehall in 1617. Note also his caution at St. Paul's, Christmas 1626, that "He that brings in any collateral respect to a sermon . . . heares but the Logique, or the Rhetorique or the Ethique, or the poetry of the Sermon, but the Sermon of the Sermon he hears not" (7:293). Sermons and homilies were not the only form of oral exposition in essay form available to the British during the Jacobean period. There were also lectures, which developed a decidedly Calvinist cast during the late 1620s and which were the occasion for a lawsuit against the puritan (not too strong a word here) Feoffees for Impropriations by Laud in 1632. See Seaver, *Puritan Lectureships*. See also brief comments by Sharpe and Collinson. We suggest that lectures were not dissimilar in importance to sermons as a mode for theological and ecclesiological discourse during Donne's period in the Church of England.

2. The analogy of aerial survey, and by extension to maps of diverse scales and subject focuses, is not casual. But (the taxonomic point) no map or even aerial photograph can tell much about the quality of the journey. So no proof text from Donne or others can give deductive certainty in the dynamic and inductive world of a Donnean sermon or "the" Donnean sermon. No compilation from run-of-the-mitre bishops or common-placing sermonizers or *(a fortiori)* cannonading polemicists is likely to gloss Donne's practices as well as his sermon is. On the religious polemics of Jacobean England see Milward, which shows the pamphlets to be extensive in number and dreary in content.

3. The Thirty-nine Articles of Religion may be found in the Book of Common Prayer. See Johnson, an acute general examination of many sermons arriving at persuasive characterizations (e.g., on Donne's Trinitarianism), not seriously at odds with our arguments. At a similar level of generality and abstraction but with a less theological and more rhetorical focus is Carrithers. The essential cautionary note about the risks and limitations of selective quotation is sounded by Shami, "Donne's *Sermons*."

4. See Thompson, esp. sections VII–XI, and Booty. For Church of England liturgy in its various permutations and contexts, see Dix, which remains essential. But a caution: the sermons on Matthew 4:18–20 were conceived in 1619 and elaborated in 1630, while much Calvinism was ostensibly conformist, while separation

was widely thought radical, and before Laud and his henchmen and adversaries had exacerbated every division.

5. On the general English religious conflicts during the half century before the gates of Hull were closed against the king, see, diversely, Shugar, Cressy, importantly New, and (particularly useful) McGee. See also Tyacke, White, and Julian Davies. On Donne, the Book of Common Prayer, and English habits of religious thought, see Carrithers and Hardy; see further Fincham, *The Early Stuart Church* and *Prelate as Pastor*, the latter an institutional, pastoral, and political study of the church in which Donne served.

6. On the origins of English political/religious radicalism, the scholar will wish to consult Russell and Sharpe. For poetic strictures on critical appraisal of religious radicalism, see Marvell, esp. lines 239–315. But see *The Trial of John Lilburn and John Wharton*, in which they spoke eloquently against self-incrimination. For the truly determined: Haller and Davies. See also the useful comment by Hamilton and our comment thereupon on pp. viii and ix of *Age of Iron*.

7. See Hooker, *Of the Lawes of Ecclesiaticall Politie*, V. On the crucial issue of the nature of the Eucharist, see McNees, in which Donne's position is described in quasi-receptionist terms. On Roman Catholic papalism, see Canon 5, Session 24 (November 11, 1563), and "Decree . . . seeking confirmation from the Pope," Session 25 (December 3–4, 1563), from the Council of Trent (Tanner 2:763, 799). For Donnean passages rhetorizing various theological topics, out of context but conveniently marshaled, see Stanwood and Asals. See also Ferrell, which states that the "early seventeenth century English church can no longer be seen primarily as the purveyor of some golden mean" (2). For a further comment on the "mean" see Scodel. On the issues of Eucharistic and Ecclesiological doctrine, see Milton; see also Lake, who describes English Protestant views of "popery as an anti-religion" (73) and the hostility to the Roman Catholic Church and faith as speaking to English "fears and anxieties" (97). See also Shami, "Anti-Catholicism."

8. Augustine, *City of God*, 2:326–28.

9. Athanasius of Alexandria; on work, chap. 53, on works and wonders, chaps. 57–65, 71, 84, 87. See Johnson 39–43 on public prayer "of the Congregation" (7:311) as (for Donne) transcending sectarian allegiances. At 5:223–24, Donne stipulates both public and private prayer as necessary (and reciprocal?).

10. Augustine, *De Doctrina Christiana*, III, xv, XXXIV, 157. The whole phrase was "ad regnum caritatis interpretatio perducatur" (interpretation ought to incline to the kingdom of love). Donnean elaboration on the call to move on appears notably in the double sermon at the "churching" of the countess of Bridgewater, on Micah 2:10, "Arise and depart, for this is not your rest" (5:184–215).

11. On life understood as a daily following of Christ, for more by Donne, see esp. the entire sermon "Preached at Christning" on Galatians 3:27, "all . . .

baptized ... have put on Christ" (5:151–67), wherein baptism is said to seal election (5:160).

12. On the sense of personal sin that underlay much of the Reformation and the lengths people went to assuage the resulting guilt, fear, and despair, see Seaver, *Wallington's World*, and Stachniewski. On the institutionalization of prayer without ceasing, see Seaver, *Puritan Lecturships*. Popular piety and pastoral needs formed a substantial part of contemporary religious administration, and Donne clearly addressed these concerns with the good news of calling and salvation rather than the bad news of sin and reprobation. For an exemplary depiction of popular piety, see Ben Jonson's "To Penshurst," wherein caritas palpably animates the lives and calling of the family.

13. *The Rule of St. Benedict*, particularly prologue and nos. 20, 48, 73; cf. Milton's "Man hath his daily work of body or mind/Appointed, which declares his dignity," *Paradise Lost*, IV, 618–19; cf. indeed Milton's long series of variations on calling, from "How soon hath time" through "Lycidas," and the ambiguously expiatory labor of Samson "eyeless in Gaza," to the Messiah's triumphant following of call in *Paradise Regain'd*. Secondly, the implications concerning the profound and consequential relation of work and prayer to orality is a matter we can only acknowledge within the scope of this article. But see Ong.

14. See our *Age of Iron*, chap. 1.

15. On the priesthood of all believers, and the "gathered churches" that viewed themselves as the true remnant *(shearith)* of Israel, see Williams. Cf. Donne: "A good hearer becomes a good Preacher, that is, able to edifie others" (5:50).

16. On the *devotio moderna* see Hyma, esp. chaps. 1 and 5. See also Jacob, chaps. 7 and 8; see also Oakley, chap. 2.

17. Donne, *Pseudo-Martyr*; see also Capp, and Marvell, esp. 311–15.

18. Faculty psychology: a doctrine of Aristotelian psychology from Petrus Ramus (Pierre de La Ramée, 1515–1572).

19. See Martz, *The Poetry of Meditation*, thoughtfully revisited in his "The Poetry of Meditation: Searching the Memory." See also the important book by Low.

20. Cardinal Bellarmine, *De potestate summi pontificis*. For an instance of explicit opposition by Donne, see 8:73.

21. See Ullmann, *Medieval Papalism*, esp. chaps. 4 and 5; see also his *Principles of Government*, especially the intro. and chaps. 2 and 3. See also the "Tome" of Leo the Great (451 A.D.) in Tanner 1:77–82; it, and the letter of Gelasius I, had placed the *plenitudo potestatis* for the Church militant in the pope.

22. See James I, *Basilikon Doron*, esp. Book V. See also the famous comment from III, 43: "A King is as one set on a stage, whose smallest actions and gestures,

all the people gazingly doe behold." This gives a clear picture of James's view of royal power, and, accordingly, his rejection of papal power.

23. The bull *Unigenitus Filii* (1343) can be found in Kidd, no. 1. On confession generally, see Lea. On the Roman Catholic view of sacramentalism in general, to which, we suggest, Donne at least partially inclined, see the decrees and canons of the Council of Trent, particularly session VII, canon 8: "Si quis dixerit, per ipsa novae legis sacramenta ex opere operato non conferri gratiam, sed solam fidem divinae promissionis ad gratiam consequendam sufficere: a.s." (If anyone says that grace is not conferred by the sacraments of the new law through the sacramental action itself but that faith in the divine promise is by itself sufficient for obtaining grace: let him be anathema), Tanner 2:685; on confession see Session XIV, chaps. 5 and 6, Tanner 2:705–8. See esp. Scodel.

24. See Seaver and Stachniewski (cited in note 12).

25. See, of course, Weber for the origins of the discussion of Calvinism vulgarized and secularized.

26. See, e.g., the character "Zeal-of-the-Land Busy" in *Bartholomew Fair* (1614) and "Tribulation" in *The Alchemist* (1610). In both cases, self-righteousness combined with hypocrisy into an antisocial censoriousness that denounced the mote and ignored the beam. Donne's literary *tone* could rise to zeal, and his delivery could be fervent (to judge by the elegies appended to *Poems*, 1633), but Jeanne Shami argues that his *position* was not ("Donne on Discretion").

27. Although much scholarship has been produced on English Calvinism since the 1960s, the books of New and of Charles and Catherine George give a good overview.

28. Hooker, *Ecclesiasticall Politie*, Bk. V, Par. 67.

29. Calvin, *Institutes*, 3.2.15, in Calvin 10:561: "There is a far different feeling of full assurance that in Scripture is always attributed to faith. It is this which puts beyond doubt God's goodness.... This is so true, that the word 'faith' is very often used for confidence." But, the reprobate might also feel this faith and assurance; "the reprobate are sometimes affected by almost the same feeling as the elect, so that even in their own judgement they do not in any way differ from the elect" (3.2.11; in Calvin 10:555). Thus, "predestination" both caused and identified these feelings. See *Institutes*, 2.3.13–14 and 3.21. For the Roman Catholic position on assurance of salvation, see *Decrees and Canons of the Council of Trent*, Session VI, Canon 14. On Calvinism in England, see, in addition to works already cited, Horton Davies and Cremeans. Calvinist doctrine was elaborated at the Synod of Dort, 1618–19. It is often signified by the acronym TULIP: *T*otal depravity of humanity from the Fall, the *U*nconditional election of the saved by God, *L*imited atonement for sin, *I*rresistible grace of God for the elect, and the *P*erseverence of saints who have been predestined for salvation. Daniel Doerksen sees a less Hookerite,

less *contingently* (i.e., infralapsarian) predestinarian Donne than do we. Sellin learnedly and plausibly conjectures that the original "fishers of men" sermon would have been heard with approval by its Contra-Remonstrant, infralapsarian Dutch Calvinist audience in *John Donne and "Calvinist" Views of Grace;* see also Doerksen's later book *Conforming to the Word.*

Works Cited

Athanasius of Alexandria. *Life of Anthony and the Letter to Marcellinus (356–362).* Trans. and intro. Robert C. Gregg. New York: Paulist Press, 1980.

Augustine, Bishop of Hippo. *City of God.* 2 vols. Trans. Marcus Dodds. Edinburgh: T & T Clark, 1871.

———. *De Doctrina Christiana.* In *Patrologia Latina,* ed. J. P. Migne. 221 vols. Paris: 1844–64.

Bellarmine, Cardinal Robert. *De potestate summi pontificis.* Trans. George Moore. Chevy Chase, MD: Country Dollar Press, 1950.

Booty, John E., ed. *The Book of Common Prayer 1559: The Elizabethan Prayer Book.* Washington, DC: Folger Shakespeare Library, 1976.

Calder, Isobel M. *The Activities of the Puritan Faction of the Church of England, 1625–1633.* New York: S.P.C.K. Press, 1957.

Calvin, Jean. *Institutes of the Christian Religion.* Trans. and ed. Ford Lewis Battles (Philadelphia, 1954), in *The Library of Christian Classics,* ed. Baillie, McNeill, and Van Dusen, 26 vols. Philadelphia: Westminster Press, 1953–77.

Capp, B. S. *The Fifth Monarchy Men: A Study in Seventeenth-Century English Millennarianism.* Totowa, NJ: Rowman and Littlefield, 1972.

Carrithers, Gale H., Jr., *Donne at Sermons: A Christian Existential World.* New York: State U of New York P, 1972.

Carrithers, Gale H., Jr., and James D. Hardy, Jr. *Age of Iron: English Renaissance Troplogies of Love and Power.* Baton Rouge: Louisiana State UP, 1998.

Cohn, Norman. *The Pursuit of the Millennium.* New York: Harper, 1970.

Collinson, Peter. "Lectures by Combination; Structures and Characteristics of Church Life in Seventeenth-Century England." *Godly People: Essays on English Protestantism and Puritanism.* Ed. Peter Collinson. London: Hambledon Press, 1983. 467–98.

Cremeans, Charles Davis. *The Reception of Calvinist Thought in England.* Urbana: U of Illinois P, 1949.

Cressy, David. *Bonfires and Bells: National Memory and the Protestant Calendar in Elizabethan and Stuart England.* Berkeley: U of California P, 1989.

Davies, Horton. *The Worship of English Puritans.* Westminster: Dacre P, 1948.

Davies, Julian. *The Caroline Captivity of the Church: Charles I and the Remolding of Anglicanism, 1625–1641.* Oxford: Oxford UP, 1992.

Dix, Dom Gregory. *The Shape of the Liturgy.* Westminister: Dacre Press 1944.

Doerksen, Daniel. *Conforming to the Word: Herbert, Donne, and the English Church before Laud.* Lewisburg, PA: Bucknell UP, 1997.

Donne, John. *Pseudo-Martyr* (1610). Ed. Anthony Raspa. Montreal: McGill-Queen's UP, 1993.

———. *Sermons.* Ed. George R. Potter and Evelyn M. Simpson. 10 vols. Berkley: U of California P, 1953–62.

Ferrell, Lori Ann. *Government by Polemic: James I, the King's Preachers, and the Rhetoric of Conformity, 1603–1625.* Stanford: Stanford UP, 1998.

Fincham, Kenneth, ed. *The Early Stuart Church, 1603–1642.* Stanford: Stanford UP, 1993.

———. *Prelate as Pastor: The Episcopate of James I.* Oxford: Clarendon, 1990.

Frontain, Raymond Jean, and Frances M. Malpezzi, eds. *John Donne's Religious Imagination: Essays in Honor of John Shawcross.* Conway: U of Central Arkansas P, 1995.

George, Charles, and Catherine George. *The Protestant Mind of the English Reformation, 1570–1640.* Princeton: Princeton UP, 1961.

Haller, William B., and Godfrey Davies. *The Leveller Tracts, 1647–1653.* New York: Columbia UP, 1944.

Hamilton, Donna. *Shakespeare and the Politics of Protestant England.* Lexington: U of Kentucky P, 1992.

Hooker, Richard. *Of the Lawes of Ecclesiaticall Politie*, Vol. V, *The Folger Library Edition of the Works of Richard Hooker.* Ed. W. Speed Hill. Cambridge: Harvard UP, 1977–90.

Hyma, Albert. *The Christian Renaissance: A History of the "Devotio Moderna."* Hamden, CN: Archon Books, 1965.

Jacob, E. F. *Essays in the Conciliar Epoch.* Manchester: Manchester UP, 1952.

James I. *Basilikon Doron. The Political Works of James I.* Ed. Charles H. McIlwaine. Cambridge: Harvard UP, 1918.

Johnson, Jeffery. *The Theology of John Donne.* Cambridge: Boydell & Brewer, 1999.

Kempis, Thomas à. *The Imitation of Christ.* Ed. William Creasy. Macon, GA: Mercer UP, 1989.

Kidd, B. J. *Documents Illustrative of the Continental Reformation.* Oxford: Clarendon, 1911.

Lake, Peter. "Anti-popery: The Structure of a Prejudice." *Conflict in Early Stuart England.* Ed. Richard Cust and Ann Hughes. New York: Longman, 1989. 72–106.

Lea, Henry Charles. *A History of Auricular Confession and Indulgences in the Latin Church.* 3 vols. London: Swan Sonnenschein, 1896.

Lewalski, Barbara Kiefer. *Protestant Poetics and the Seventeenth-Century Religious Lyric*. Princeton: Princeton UP, 1979.

Low, Anthony. *Love's Architecture: Devotional Modes in Seventeenth-Century English Poetry*. New York: New York UP, 1978.

Martz, Louis L. *The Poetry of Meditation*. New Haven: Yale UP, 1954.

———. "The Poetry of Meditation: Searching the Memory." *New Perspectives on the Seventeenth-Century Religious Lyric*. Ed. John R. Roberts. Columbia: U of Missouri P, 1994. 188–200.

———. Review of Lewalski. *Modern Philology* 80 (1982): 168–74.

Marvell, Andrew. "The First Anniversary of the Government Under His Highness the Lord Protector" (1655). *Poems*. Ed. George deF. Lord. New York: Random House, 1968.

McGee, J. Sears. *The Godly Man in Stuart England: Anglicans, Puritans, and the Two Tables, 1620–1670*. New Haven: Yale UP, 1976.

McNees, Eleanor. "John Donne and the Anglican Doctrine of the Eucharist." *Texas Studies in Literature and Language* 29 (1987): 94–114.

Milton, Anthony. *Catholic and Reformed: The Roman and Protestant Churches in English Protestant Thought, 1600–1640*. Cambridge: Cambridge UP, 1995.

Milward, Peter, ed. *Religious Controversies of the Jacobean Age: A Survey of Printed Sources*. Lincoln: U of Nebraska P, 1978.

New, John F. H. *Anglican and Puritan: The Basis of Their Opposition, 1558–1640*. Palo Alto: Stanford UP, 1964.

Oakley, Francis. *The Western Church in the Later Middle Ages*. Ithaca: Cornell UP, 1979.

Ong, Walter, S.J. *Orality and Literacy*. London: Methuen, 1982.

Ozment, Steven E. *The Reformation in the Cities: The Appeal of Protestantism to Sixteenth- and Seventeenth-Century Germany and Switzerland*. New Haven: Yale UP, 1975.

The Rule of St. Benedict. Trans. and ed. Anthony C. Meisel and M. L. del Mastro. New York: Image Books, 1975.

Russell, Conrad. *Parliaments and English Politics, 1621–1629*. Cambridge: Cambridge UP, 1979.

Schneidau, Herbert. "Gatsby's America." Paper presented at the 12th *Arizona Quarterly* symposium, University of Arizona, March 2000 (forthcoming as an article).

Scodel, Joshua. "John Donne and the Religious Politics of the Mean." Frontain and Malpezzi 45–80.

Seaver, Paul R. *The Puritan Lectureships: The Politics of Religious Dissent, 1560–1662*. Stanford: Stanford UP, 1970.

———. *Wallington's World: A Puritan Artisan in Seventeenth Century London*. Stanford, Stanford UP, 1985.

Sellin, Paul R. *John Donne and "Calvinist" Views of Grace.* Amsterdam: VU Boekhandel, 1983.

———. *"So Doth, So Is Religion": John Donne and Diplomatic Contexts in the Reformed Netherlands, 1619–1620.* Columbia: U of Missouri P, 1988.

Shami, Jeanne. "Anti-Catholicism in the Sermons of John Donne." *The English Sermon Revised.* Ed. Lori Ann Ferrell. Manchester: Manchester UP, 2000. 136–66.

———. "Donne on Discretion." *English Literary History* 47 (1980): 48–66.

———. "Donne's *Sermons* and the Absolutist Politics of Quotation." Frontain and Malpezzi 380–412.

Sharpe, Kevin. *The Personal Rule of Charles I.* New Haven: Yale UP, 1992.

Shugar, Debora. *Habits of Thought in the English Renaissance: Religion, Politics, and the Dominant Culture.* Berkeley: U of California P, 1990.

Stachniewski, John. *The Persecutory Imagination: English Puritanism and the Literature of Religious Despair.* New York: Oxford UP, 1991.

Stanwood, Paul G., and Heather Asals. *John Donne and the Theology of Language.* Columbia: U of Missouri P, 1986.

Tanner, Norman P., S.J., ed. *Decrees of the Ecumenical Councils.* 2 vols. Washington, DC: Sheed & Ward and Georgetown UP, 1990.

Thompson, Bard, ed. *Liturgies of the Western Church.* New York: Meridian, 1962.

The Trial of John Lilburn and John Wharton, 3 How. State Trials, 1315 (1637).

Tyacke, Nicholas. *Anti-Calvinist: The Rise of English Arminianism, c. 1590–1640.* Oxford: Oxford UP, 1987.

Ullmann, Walter. *Medieval Papalism: The Political Theories of the Medieval Canonists.* London: Methuen, 1949.

———. *Principles of Government and Politics in the Middle Ages.* New York: Barnes and Noble, 1961.

Weber, Max. *The Protestant Ethic and the Spirit of Capitalism.* 1904. New York: Scribner, 1958.

White, Peter. *Predestination, Policy, and Polemic: Conflict and Consensus in the English Church from the Reformation to the Civil War.* Cambridge: Harvard UP, 1992.

Williams, George H. *The Radical Reformation.* Philadelphia: Westminster P, 1962.

CONTRIBUTORS

GALE H. CARRITHERS, JR., who recently passed away, was Professor Emeritus of English and sometime Sternberg Professor of Honors at Louisiana State University. He is the author of *Donne at Sermons: A Christian Existential World* (1972) and *Mumford, Tate, Eiseley: Watchers in the Night* (1991). With James D. Hardy, Jr., he is coauthor of *Milton and the Hermeneutic Journey* (1994), *Age of Iron: English Renaissance Tropologies of Love and Power* (1998), and *Shakespeare and the Tropes of Love* (in progress).

ANNETTE DESCHNER studied English literature and linguistics and theology at Heidelberg University, receiving her M.A. in 1998. Currently she is working on her Ph.D. thesis on John Donne at Heidelberg University.

DANIEL W. DOERKSEN, Honorary Research Professor of English at the University of New Brunswick, is the author of *Conforming to the Word: Herbert, Donne, and the English Church before Laud* and of articles on Donne, Herbert, Spenser, and Milton. Together with Christopher T. Hodgkins, he has edited essays for a book to be entitled *Centered on the Word: Literature, Scripture, and the Tudor-Stuart Middle Way*. He is also working on a study of Donne and the Bible.

RAYMOND-JEAN FRONTAIN is Professor of English and Director of the Humanities and World Cultures Institute at the University of Central Arkansas. A commentary editor for the *Divine Poems* volume in the John Donne Variorum (in progress), he coedited *John Donne's Religious Imagination: Essays in Honor of John T. Shawcross* (1995) and at present is completing a book to be titled *The Art of Knowing Heaven: John Donne's Biblical Self-Fashioning*.

CHANITA GOODBLATT is a Senior Lecturer in the Department of Foreign Literatures and Linguistics at Ben-Gurion University of the Negev, Israel. Her research interests include Christian Hebraism in sixteenth- and seventeenth-century England (particularly in Donne's sermons and in the Sidneian Psalms), the cognitive study of poetic metaphor, and poetry and discourse. She has published articles in *Mosaic, Style, Renaissance and Reformation, Exemplaria, Poetics Today, Journal of Literary Semantics, Prooftexts,* and *Language and Literature*. She is currently working on a book to be titled *Written with the Fingers of Man's Hand: John Donne and the Hebraic Tradition*.

JAMES D. HARDY, JR., is Professor of History, Associate Dean of the Honors College, and sometime Sternberg Professor of Honors at Louisiana State University. He is the author or coauthor of seven books, most recently, with Gale H. Carrithers, Jr., *Milton and the Hermeneutic Journey* (1994), *Age of Iron: English Renaissance Tropologies of Love and Power* (1998), and "Shakespeare and the Tropes of Love" (in progress). Additionally, he has published *The New York Giants Base Ball Club: 1870–1900* (1996) and, with coauthor Leonard J. Stanton, the introduction to the Signet edition (2000) of Dostoevsky's *Crime and Punishment*. Currently, also with Professor Stanton, he is completing a book on Nikolai Gogol.

JEFFREY JOHNSON is Professor of English at Northern Illinois University. In addition to the articles he has published on Donne, Henry Vaughan, George Herbert, and Richard Crashaw, he is the author of *The Theology of John Donne* and coeditor of *Discovering and (Re)Covering the Seventeenth-Century Religious Lyric*. He is also a contributing editor for *The Variorum Edition of the Poetry of John Donne*.

ELENA LEVY-NAVARRO is Associate Professor of English at the University of Wisconsin–Whitewater. She has been working on issues related to the English Reformation since her graduation from Yale University in 1993 with a degree in English literature. She has published articles on the religio-political milieu of the seventeenth century as well as on John Donne.

CATHERINE GIMELLI MARTIN directs the English Honors Program and the Literature Concentration at the University of Memphis. Besides three essays on Donne (one forthcoming in *Studies in English Literature*) and many more on other major poets of the period, she has published a book-length study of Miltonic allegory. This book—*The Ruins of Allegory: "Paradise Lost" and the Metamorphosis of Epic Convention*—won the Milton Society of America's James Holly Hanford Award in 1999. She is currently completing an edited collection entitled *Reading Milton Writing Gender* as well as a full-length study of Bacon's contributions to the episteme of early modernity: *Proteus Unbound: The Poetics of the Baconian Revolution*.

BRENT NELSON is Assistant Professor of English at the University of Saskatchewan. He is the author of articles on Roger Ascham, John Hoskyns, and "The Social Context of Rhetoric, 1500–1640." He has recently completed a book entitled *"Holy Ambition": Rhetoric, Courtship, and Devotion in the Sermons of John Donne.*

MARY ARSHAGOUNI PAPAZIAN is Associate Professor of English and Associate Dean of the College of Arts and Sciences at Oakland University, Rochester, Michigan. She is the author of numerous articles on Donne and the seventeenth century and a contributing editor for the *Songs and Sonnets* volumes of *The Variorum Edition of the Poetry of John Donne*. She also is completing a book on Donne's *Devotions*, entitled *"Shipwrecked into Health": The Experience of John Donne's "Devotions Upon Emergent Occasions."* She has been secretary/treasurer of the John Donne Society since 1990.

MARIA SALENIUS is Lecturer in British Literature at the University of Helsinki. Her work has appeared in many publications, including *Neuphilologische Mitteilungen,* and her research interests include Donne's religious prose, the Reformation, aspects of worldview and exploration in the Renaissance period, the concept of language and/in religion, and the metaphor. Within modern literature and language her topics of interest are Evelyn Waugh, language and religion/ideology, political rhetoric, and intercultural communication/ translation.

PAUL R. SELLIN is Professor Emeritus, Department of English, UCLA, and Oud-hoogleraar, De Vrije Universiteit, Amsterdam, the Netherlands. Relevant publications include *John Donne and "Calvinist" Views of Grace* (1983) and *"So Doth, So Is Religion": John Donne and Diplomatic Contexts in the Reformed Netherlands, 1619–1620* (1988), as well as a variety of essays on Donne. His current work deals with Milton's *De Doctrina Christiana,* Alexander Morus, Michel Le Blon, Sir Walter Ralegh and the Orinoco, and Donne's *Conclave Ignati.*

JEANNE SHAMI, Professor of English at the University of Regina, Saskatchewan, Canada, discovered a manuscript of a sermon by Donne including his holograph corrections, which she published in 1996. She has just completed a book on the late Jacobean pulpit, with a focus on Donne, presently titled *Active Discretion: John Donne and Conformity in Crisis in the Late Jacobean Pulpit.* She is the current (2002–3) President of the John Donne Society.

INDEX

Abbot, George, 15, 16, 22, 24, 27, 35
Abrahamson, R. L., 253, 261
Act of Succession, 1–2
Act of Supremacy, 1–2
Acts 10:44, 301
Acts 16:15.33, 301
Adams, Thomas, 26
Addled Parliament, 157
Affliction: and Augustine, 83; and Donne, 76–77, 257–58, 267, 343–44; and Puritans, 343
Alexander, William, 148
Allegory, 222, 235, 319
Allen, Don Cameron, 222, 224, 226
Alsted, Johann-Heinrich: *Oratorê*, 250
Ambrosius, 309
Ames, William, 163, 172
Anabaptists, 302, 303–5, 306–7
Ancrum, Sir Robert Ker, earl of, 147, 148, 156
Andreasen, N. J. C., 248–49
Andrew, St., 339, 341, 347, 351
Andrewes, Lancelot, 26, 38–39, 167, 278, 280–81, 335
Anglicans, 6, 12, 13, 47, 166, 206, 336
Aristotle, 325
Arminians/Arminianism: and Andrewes, 38–39; Anglican, 47; background of, 277; beliefs of, 60n. 6; and Donne, 21, 48–49, 51, 53–54, 58, 59; and Douglas, 169; and Dutch Republic, 146; and election, 54; and free will, 84n. 6, 86n. 11; and Hughes, 159; and Laud, 6, 47, 277; and Maurits, 149; and Montagu, 38, 40, 45, 53; and Ogle, 167, 170; and predestination, 60n. 6; and Remonstrants, 61n. 23; rise of, 3, 79; and Ussher, 39; and Utrecht, 157–58; and Uytenbogaert, 170; and York House Debates, 36, 42, 57

Arminius, Jacobus, 60n. 6
Arndt, Murray, 248
Article 17. *See* Thirty-nine Articles of the Church of England
Articles of Religion. *See* Thirty-nine Articles of the Church of England
Articles of the Synod of Dort, 80
Atonement, 48, 53, 198, 205, 206, 267
Augsburg Confession, 46, 48
Augustine: and affliction, 83; and baptism, 309; and Calvin, 68, 79; and Church of England, 73, 74–75, 79; *City of God*, 337; and City of God, 340; and confession, 77; *Confessions*, 7, 66, 67, 68, 69–70, 71–73, 76, 77, 78, 79, 84; *De Correptione et Gratia*, 70–71; *De Praedestinatione Sanctorum*, 69–70; and Donne, 6–7, 21, 44, 48, 66–67, 68–69, 71, 76–84, 86nn. 12, 15, 252, 301, 302, 335, 337, 338, 342, 343, 346, 350, 351; and election, 67, 69, 70–71; and English Reformation, 84n. 4; and free will, 69, 74–75; and grace, 67, 68, 69, 70, 74–75, 82; and human nature, 79, 83; and humility, 69, 78, 82; and Luke 23:43, 309; and Luther, 1, 68, 79; and Manichaeans, 48; and *pathopoeia*, 249–50; and Paul, 68; and Pelagianism, 44, 48, 67, 68, 69–70, 71, 84n. 6, 86n. 11; and perseverance, 67, 69; and pope, 73–74; and predestination, 7, 21, 66–67, 68, 69, 70, 75, 81, 86n. 15; and pride, 69, 70, 78; and Protestantism, 67–68, 71, 75, 79, 85n. 10; and Protestant Reformation, 67–68,

365

Augustine *(continued)*
79, 85n. 10; and Reformed churches, 84n. 5; and reprobates, 74; and Roman Catholic Church, 67–68, 73, 75, 79, 84n. 5; and salvation, 70, 79; and sin, 66–67, 69, 70, 77, 78, 80, 301; and Thirty-nine Articles of the Church of England, 84n. 4; and works, 75

Avant-garde conformists, 13, 14, 16, 24, 27, 275, 276–77, 278, 279–80, 283, 284, 285. *See also* Conformism

Ayton, Sir Robert, 148

Bacon, Francis: "Of Atheism," 194
Baker-Smith, Dominic, 201
Bald, R. C., 3, 35, 36, 79, 90, 91, 238n. 11
Balen, Godard van, 154
Balfour, Henry, of Pitcullo, 151
Balfour, Sir William, 151–52
Bancroft, Archbishop, 16
Baptism, 299–311; of blood, 309; and Calvin, 22–23, 301; and Catholic Church, 308–9; of children, 22–23, 301, 302, 303, 304–5, 306; and community, 300, 303; and Donne, 10, 24, 30n. 35, 50, 102, 105, 106, 198, 293–94, 296, 299–307, 308, 310–11; and Luther, 305, 307, 310, 311; and salvation, 308–11, 310; and sin, 310; and Zwingli, 306. *See also* Sacraments
Baptist church, 303
Baroque, 196, 200
Bawcutt, Nigel, 35–36, 38, 40
Bax, Sir Marcelis, 169
Bedford, Lucy, countess of, 156, 165, 171, 172
Bellarmine, Robert, 104–6, 107, 278, 347
Berkeley, Maurice, 160
Beza, Theodore, 22
Bible: and Anabaptists, 304; and baptism, 301, 305, 309; and Bellarmine, 104; and Calvin, 21–22; and Calvinism, 22; and Catholic Church, 275; and church fathers, 105; and Council of Trent, 97, 98–99, 103; and Dante, 115; and Donne, 9, 14, 15, 21, 22, 26, 43–45, 49–50, 51, 53–54, 55, 67, 96, 97, 101–10, 103, 104–6, 107–8, 113, 118, 119, 135n. 8, 194, 200, 208, 209, 221–23, 224–36, 253, 254, 255–56, 259, 262, 264, 267, 275, 296, 297–98, 318, 320, 322–23, 324, 326, 328, 345; Geneva translation of, 222, 226, 228, 229, 235, 236; and interpretation, 37, 96, 104–6, 108, 317, 328; and James I, 277–78; King James translation of, 222, 223, 224, 226; and Melanchthon, 298; and Protestantism, 229, 301; and Protestant Reformation, 296; and puritans, 317–18; Rabbinic, 239nn. 18, 19; and sacraments, 317; and Sarpi, 98–99, 100; and sermon, 317; and *sola scriptura*, 296, 297, 298, 301; translation of, 73; vernacular, 275, 317; Vulgate translation of, 99. *See also specific books*
Boetzelaars family, 169
Bolduc, Jacques, 225, 226, 239n. 16
Boleyn, Margaret, 180
Boniface VII, 131
Book of Common Prayer, 2, 25, 194, 322, 335, 336, 341
Bouwsma, William, 83, 92, 93, 97, 100–101, 110n. 13
Bray, Gerald, 36
Brog, Sir William, 147, 148, 151
Brooke, Christopher, 178
Brown, Peter, 69
Browne, Robert, 303
Browne, William, 172
Bruce, Walter, 152–53
Buccleugh, Lord (the elder), 149, 150
Buccleugh, Lord (the younger), 149
Buckeridge, John, 42, 280, 281, 282
Buckingham, George Villiers, Duke of, 36, 40, 43, 44, 45, 60n. 5, 152
Bunyan, John, 200; *Grace Abounding*, 79
Burgess, John, 163

Calvin, John, 239n. 16; and Anabaptists, 304, 305; and Augustine, 68, 79; and baptism, 22–23, 301; and Bible, 21–22; and compromise, 47; and depravity, 206; and Donne, 15, 21, 22, 23, 29nn. 19, 20, 22, 47–48, 69, 72, 201, 216n. 5, 225, 226, 235, 282–83, 304; and election, 198; and Eucharist, 47; *Institutes*, 206, 252, 301, 310; and Laudians, 47; and Lord's Supper, 23; and Paul, 68; and prayer, 252–53; and predestination, 18, 68; and sacraments, 307; and Sarpi, 92; and supralapsarianism, 21; and things indifferent, 282–83; and 1 Timothy 2:3-4, 21

Calvinism: and Arminianism, 60n. 6; and baptism, 310–11; and Bible, 22; and ceremony, 284; consensus of, 13, 27; and depravity, 283; and Donne, 5, 6, 12, 14, 15, 16, 21, 27, 53–54, 55–56, 58, 198, 283, 314, 320, 348–50; English, 21, 22–23; and English delegation to Dort, 62n. 32; Gomarist, 43, 53; and grace, 212, 336; and iconoclasm, 197; and James I, 3, 14; and Laudians, 50; and liturgy, 336; and Matthew, 72; and military, 154; and Montagu, 50; and Ogle, 167; and predestination, 21, 22–23, 320, 349; and puritans, 13; and salvation, 310–11; and Sarpi, 92; and success, 349; and supralapsarianism, 29n. 22

Candlemas, 316, 325, 330. *See also* Donne, John, works/sermons

Careuw, Sir Henry, 174–75
Carew, Sir George, 174
Carey, Ferdinand, 174
Carey, John, 287n. 1
Carey, Lady Elizabeth, 180
Carey, Lettice, 175
Carey, Sir George, 175, 180
Carey, Sir Robert, 173–74, 178
Carey family, 175
Carey-Throckmorton, Sir Nicholas, 175
Carie, Sir Lucius, 175

Carleton, Bishop, 38, 56, 60n. 9
Carleton, Lady, 172
Carleton, Sir Dudley, 149, 151, 159, 172
Casimir, Count Ernst, 168
Catharists, 26
Catholic, as term, 25
Catholic Church: and Augustine, 67–68, 73, 75, 79, 84n. 5; and baptism, 308–9; and Bible, 275; and Book of Revelations, 123; and ceremony, 280; and 1 Corinthians 15:29, 101; and Donne, 23–25, 30nn. 31, 36, 38, 31n. 40, 49, 50, 95, 96–97, 102, 104–6, 107, 136n. 10, 195, 198, 201, 205, 207, 229–30, 275, 282, 288n. 4, 293, 346–48; and dualism, 276; and election, 54; and Grotius, 294, 295, 296; and indulgences, 102, 107; and interpretation, 50; and James I, 276, 293; and Luther, 297; and Matthew, 71–73; and preaching, 251; and purgatory, 101; and sacraments, 307; and salvation, 79, 308–9; and Sarpi, 92. *See also* Pope

Catholicism: and Anabaptists, 303; and baptism, 300, 301; and Donne, 3, 4, 7, 15–16, 21, 24, 42, 117, 129, 131, 194, 226, 227, 233, 235, 236, 248, 282, 284, 287, 300, 314, 315, 321–22, 323, 324, 325, 330, 343, 345, 346; and English Reformation, 317; and grace, 124, 307; and Grotius, 298, 299; and Heidelberg, 300; and superstition, 317

Catholics: and Donne, 25, 26; English, 2; and Oath of Allegiance, 278
Causaubon, Meric, 183
Cecil, Sir Edward, 154–56, 157, 158, 159, 161, 162, 166, 168, 173, 181
Cecil, Sir Robert, 154
Cecil, Thomas, 154
Cecil, William, 154
Celestine V, 130–31, 139n. 26
Ceremony, 278, 279–84; and Burgess, 163; and Cranmer, 194; and Donne, 14–15, 275, 276–77, 279, 281–84, 290nn. 17, 18, 19, 321–22; and

Ceremony *(continued)*
    faith, 308; and Petrarch, 295; and Protestantism, 195, 196
Chandos, Grey Bridges, Lord, 155
Charles I, 27, 38, 39, 102–3, 144, 150, 151–52, 173, 174
Cheeke, Hatton, 154
Cheeke, Mary, 154
Christ. *See* Jesus
Christian Hebraism, 9, 230, 232, 233
Church, 336; and baptism, 300; and Buckeridge, 281; and community, 108; corporate body of, 102; and Donne, 91, 95, 101, 103, 107, 108, 206–7, 214, 215, 273, 285, 286, 287, 299, 321, 325, 337–38, 340, 347; early, 294, 295, 296, 299, 300, 301, 321, 325, 328; government of, 336; and Grotius, 294, 295, 296, 299; and Luther, 297; and Sarpi, 100–101, 107, 108. *See also* Catholic Church; Church of England
Church fathers, 96, 97, 103, 105, 106–7, 221, 225, 298, 299
Church of England, 23, 24, 25; and Augustine, 71–72, 73, 74–75, 79; diversity in, 24; and Donne, 3–4, 16, 23, 24, 25, 27, 30n. 35, 37, 53–54, 69, 273–76, 281, 282, 286, 287; and Elizabeth I, 2; and Henry VIII, 1–2; and interpretation, 54; and James I, 3; and Matthew, 84n. 8; and Melanchthon, 46; and moderation, 58; and Montagu, 36; and predestination, 46, 81; and Reformation, 1–2; and reprobates, 74; and Synod of Dort, 37, 38, 43, 45, 46, 48, 49, 51, 53, 54–55, 56, 59, 62n. 32. *See also* Thirty-nine Articles of the Church of England
Church settlement, 274, 277, 281
Chute, Sir Walter, 90
Cicero, 330
Circumcision, 304, 305, 306
Clare, Sir John Hollis, earl of, 162
Clarke, Samuel, 163
Cobham, Lord, 167

Cokayne, Sir William, 258
Communion, 279–80, 282. *See also* Eucharist
Community: and baptism, 300, 303; and church, 108; and Donne, 11, 108, 208, 282, 286, 300, 311, 337–38, 339–40; and grace, 108; and Luther, 297. *See also* Individual
Conciliarism, 91, 93, 97, 100–101, 108
Confession, 77, 210, 248, 264, 290n. 17
Conformism, 13, 14, 15, 16, 277. *See also* Avant-garde conformists
Congregationalism, 303
Consensus Sedomirensis, 296
Contra-Remonstrant Calvinism, 56
Convocation of English clergy, 37, 39
Convocation of English clergy (1624), 36
Convocation of English clergy (1626), 6, 35, 37, 40, 41, 56; eyewitness to, 35, 36, 40–41
Convocation of English clergy (1628), 35
Convocation of English clergy (1629), 36
Conway, Sir Edward, 160, 164–65, 166, 176
Conway, Sir Edward (son), 176
Conway, Sir John, 164; *Poesie of Floured Praiers*, 165
Conway, Sir Thomas, 176
Corbet, Miles, 160
1 Corinthians: 7:14, 301; 14:26, 322; 15:29, 49–50, 101–6, 107–8; 15:51–55, 121; 16:15, 301
2 Corinthians: 5:20, 254; 5:21, 340
Council of Trent: and Bible, 97, 98–99, 103; and church fathers, 103, 105, 299; and Donne, 7, 24, 37, 43, 49, 58, 91, 94–97, 103, 105, 106, 108, 109n. 7, 288n. 4, 295; and faith, 336; and Grotius, 295; and Sarpi, 7, 91, 93, 95, 97, 98–99, 108; and works, 336
Counter-Reformation, 97, 197, 296
Coutts, Allan, 148
Covenant, 57–58, 302, 304, 306

Cranfield, Sir Lionel, 175
Cranmer, Thomas, 2, 194, 319, 321
Crompton, William, 76, 84n. 8; *Saint Augustine's Religion*, 72–73, 74–75
Cromwell, Edward, 174
Cromwell, Oliver, 152
Curll, Walter, 36
Cyprian, 301, 309
Cyril of Jerusalem, 309

Daiches, David, 223, 224, 227
Dale, Sir Thomas, 179
Dante: and Book of Revelations, 115, 116, 118; *Divine Comedy*, 196; and Donne, 113, 114, 117–18, 121, 123, 124, 125, 127, 128, 129, 130, 131–32, 134nn. 1, 2; and Elisha, 115; and Ezekial, 115, 116; and inspiration, 139n. 29; and Isaiah, 115; and journey, 114, 117, 123, 124, 196; knowledge of, 134n. 1; letter to Can Grande della Scala, 116–17; and Mary, 117, 123; *Paradiso*, 113, 114–18, 121, 123, 124; and Paul, 116, 117; and pope, 130, 131; and prophecy, 114, 115, 117, 135n. 5, 136n. 10; and solipsism, 139n. 27; and witnessing, 116, 132, 135n. 7
Danvers, Magdalen, 19
Davenant, John, 20, 38
Denison, John, 282; *The Heavenly Banquet*, 279–80
Depravity, 91, 100, 206, 208, 252, 283, 295. *See also* Sin
Desiderius Erasmus, 295
Desire, 194, 196–97, 200, 202, 255, 261, 263
Diodati, Giovanni, 92
Doerksen, Daniel W., 27, 62n. 30, 78, 287n. 1, 288n. 7
Dominicans, 54
Donaldson, Andrew, 148
Donatists, 303
Doncaster, John Hay, Viscount, 145, 146, 147, 153, 155, 170, 171, 172, 177, 178, 181, 184

Donne, George, 147, 183–84
Donne, John: and Abbot, 16, 24; and accommodation, 50; and action, 132, 321, 326–27; and Addled Parliament, 157; and *adiaphora*, 10, 103, 275, 282–83; and adoption, 28n. 15; and affliction, 76–77, 257–58, 267, 343–44; and agitation, 255, 258; and allegorical interpretation, 222, 235; and ambassador, 340, 341–42; and Ames, 163; and amplification, 323, 324, 325–26; and Anabaptists, 302, 303–5, 306–7; and *anaphora*, 263, 266; and Andrew, 339, 341, 347, 351; as Anglican, 12; and apostles, 339, 340; and Apostle's Creed, 31n. 39; and *apostrophe*, 261, 263; and Arminianism, 6, 21, 48–49, 51, 53–54, 58, 59; and Article 17 of the Church of England, 17, 18, 20, 274; and assurance, 80, 81; and atonement, 48, 53, 198, 205, 206, 267; and audience, 9, 165–66, 186n. 9, 248, 249, 267, 330; and Augsburg Confession, 46, 48; and Augustine, 6–7, 21, 44, 48, 66–67, 68–69, 71, 76–84, 86nn. 12, 15, 252, 301, 302, 335, 337, 338, 342, 343, 346, 350, 351; and authority, 300; and *auxesis*, 263; and avant-garde conformists, 16, 24, 27, 276–77, 279, 281, 282, 283, 284, 285; and baptism, 10, 24, 30n. 35, 50, 102, 105, 106, 198, 293–94, 296, 299–307, 308, 310–11; and baptism for the dead, 106; and baptism of children, 301, 302, 303, 304–5, 306; and basilisk, 45; and beauty, 198; and Bellarmine, 104–6, 107; and Bible, 9, 14, 15, 21, 22, 26, 43–45, 49–50, 51, 53–54, 55, 67, 96, 97, 101–10, 113, 118, 119, 121–22, 123, 124, 125, 127, 128–29, 135n. 8, 137nn. 15, 16, 194, 200, 208, 209, 221–23, 224–36, 253, 254, 255–56, 259, 262, 264, 267, 275, 296, 297–98, 318, 319, 320, 321, 322–23, 324–25, 326, 328, 337, 340, 341,

370 · Index

Donne, John *(continued)*
342, 343, 345, 347; and body, 209, 259, 270n. 14; and calling trope, 11, 338, 339–45, 351; and calling *vs.* meeting, 55, 56; and Calvin, 15, 21, 22, 23, 29nn. 19, 20, 22, 47–48, 69, 72, 201, 216n. 5, 225, 226, 235, 282–83, 304; and Calvinism, 5, 6, 12, 14, 15, 16, 21, 27, 37, 53–54, 55–56, 58, 198, 283, 314, 320, 348–50; and candle-burning, 321–23; and Candlemas, 316, 325, 330; and Carey, 175; and catechism, 301; and Catharists, 26; and catholic as term, 25; and Catholic Church, 23–25, 30nn. 31, 36, 38, 31n. 40, 49, 50, 95, 96–97, 102, 104–6, 107, 136n. 10, 195, 198, 201, 205, 207, 229–30, 275, 282, 288n. 4, 293, 346–48; and Catholicism, 3, 4, 7, 15–16, 21, 24, 42, 117, 129, 131, 194, 226, 227, 233, 235, 236, 248, 282, 284, 287, 300, 314, 315, 321–22, 323, 324, 325, 330, 343, 345, 346; and catholicity, 340, 347; and Catholics, 25, 26; and Cecil, 156; and Celestine V, 130, 131, 139n. 26; and ceremony, 14–15, 275, 276–77, 279, 281–84, 290nn. 17, 18, 19, 321–22; and chain, 57–58, 59; and Charles I, 102–3; and Charterhouse in London, 58; and Christ, 57; and Christian Hebraism, 9; and church, 91, 95, 101, 103, 107, 108, 206–7, 214, 215, 273, 285, 286, 287, 299, 321, 325, 337–38, 340, 347; and church fathers, 96, 97, 103, 106–7, 221, 225, 298, 299; and Church of England, 3–4, 16, 23, 24, 25, 27, 30n. 35, 37, 53–54, 69, 273–76, 281, 282, 286, 287; and church settlement, 274, 281; and circumcision, 304, 305; and city of God *vs.* earthly city, 207, 337, 338–39, 345; and *climax,* 257; and communion, 200, 282; and Communion of Saints, 340; and community, 11, 108, 208, 282, 286, 300, 311, 337–38, 339–40; and compromise, 47; and conciliarism, 91, 108; and confession, 77, 210, 248, 264, 290n. 17; and conformism, 14, 15, 16, 24, 26; and conformity, 13; and congregation, 315, 328; and conscience, 298; and consolation, 263; and contemplation, 261; and contrition, 265, 342; and controversialists, 208; and conventicles, 16; and conversion, 3–4, 79, 197; and Convocation of English clergy, 6, 35, 36, 37, 38, 39–40, 56; and Conway, 160, 164, 165, 176; and 1 Corinthians 15:29, 49–50, 101–6, 107–8; and 1 Corinthians 15:51–55, 121; and 2 Corinthians 5:20, 254; and 2 Corinthians 5:21, 340; and Council of Trent, 7, 24, 37, 43, 49, 58, 91, 94–97, 103, 105, 106, 108, 109n. 7, 288n. 4, 295; and councils, 44, 45, 49, 91, 108; and covenant, 57–58, 197, 200, 211, 302, 304, 305; and cross, 343–45; and crucifix, 197, 198; and damnation, 17; and Dante, 113, 114, 117–18, 121, 123, 124, 125, 127, 128, 129, 130, 131–32, 134nn. 1, 2; and death, 81, 102, 107, 139n. 24, 200, 261–62, 268, 282, 284, 286; and debate, 36–37, 38, 39, 41–42, 43–46, 47–49, 58, 61n. 24; and decorum, 44; and decrees, 20; and *de fide* rulings (Trent), 95–96; and dependence, 77, 195, 252; and depravity, 208, 252, 283; and desire, 194, 196–97, 200, 203, 204, 207, 213, 214, 255, 261, 263; and despair, 17, 83; and devotion, 247, 249, 252, 260, 276, 282, 283, 284; and *Directions to Preachers,* 45; and divinity, 275; and Doncaster, 155; and double, 203, 209, 210; and double bind, 202, 203, 207, 211; and doubt, 194, 199; and Douglas, 170; and Drake, 145;

and Drury, 155; and dualism, 275–76; and eagle, 45, 251; and early church, 296, 299, 321, 325; and Ecclesiasticus 43:24[26], 267; and *ecphonesis*, 260–61; and edification, 321, 322, 328, 332n. 14; and Egerton, 178; and election, 17, 18–19, 28n. 15, 43, 48, 51–56, 59, 80, 81, 82, 194, 198, 215, 286, 349; and emotion, 82, 251; and England, 276; and Ephesians 5:25–27, 302; and *epiplexis*, 261; and Eucharist, 47, 198, 203, 209, 316, 328–29, 343; and evangelism, 275; and example, 249, 258, 261; and experience, 57, 59, 248, 261; and experimental predestinarians, 19; and extreme unction, 196; and *exuscitatio*, 258; and Ezekial, 53, 120, 128, 254; and faith, 51, 57, 58, 95–96, 102, 103, 197, 201, 206–7, 264, 275, 300, 305, 320, 321, 326, 327, 329, 330, 331, 343; and fall/redemption pattern, 252, 253–54, 255, 258, 260, 263; and father, 203–4; and fear, 80, 81–82, 83, 197, 199, 200, 201, 260, 263; and figurative sense, 49, 50, 104–5, 106, 221, 222; and first-second person perspectives, 258; and fishers, 339, 340; and free will, 49, 54, 55, 349; and funeral bells, 281, 284, 285, 286, 287; and Galatians 3:11, 321; and Gates, 178; and Genesis, 323; and Geneva Bible, 222, 226, 228, 229, 235, 236; and God, 18–19, 51, 57, 77, 195, 199–201, 203, 204, 209, 227–29, 231, 248, 252, 253, 258, 260, 263, 283, 318, 320, 328, 329, 342, 345, 349; and Goodyer, 197; and grace, 15, 20, 49, 52, 54, 55, 56, 76, 78–79, 80, 82, 101, 108, 195, 197, 198, 199, 200, 201, 210, 252, 302, 305, 311, 343, 349, 350, 351; and Grotius, 294, 296; and guilt, 82; at Haarlem, 146; and Habakkuk, 113, 128–29; at The Hague, 145, 147, 148, 178; and Hall, 24; and Harwood, 172; and hearing, 52–53; and Hebraism, 223–27, 238n. 11; and Hebrews 13:14, 337; and Herbert (George), 201; and Herbert (Magdalen), 197; and Herbert (Sir Edward), 145, 155–56; and Herbert (Sir Gerard), 177; and heresy, 44, 45, 106, 295, 343; and Hezekiah, 253; and historical sense, 221, 222; and holiness, 15; and holiness cult, 289n. 13; and Hollis, 162; and Holy Spirit, 96, 206, 298, 318; and Hosea, 120, 137n. 16; and Howard, 157; and human condition, 261; and human nature, 77; and humility, 11, 78, 82, 83, 342; and Hunsdon, 175; and *hypotyposis*, 255, 256, 258, 261; and iconoclasm, 197; and idolatry, 198, 204, 276; and illness, 77, 253, 258, 261, 265, 266; and *imitatio Christi*, 200, 210, 341, 343; and incarnation, 198; and inclusion, 340, 346; and individual, 102; and indulgences, 102, 107, 348; and Inquisition, 55; and inspiration, 124, 129, 131, 298; and intellect, 248; and interdict, 94; and interpretation, 43–45, 49, 50, 96, 104–6, 108, 221–23, 224–36, 318, 324, 328, 329; and irenicism, 10, 24, 50, 295, 296, 297, 300, 301, 311, 312; and irony, 81, 82, 194; and irresolution, 194; and Isaiah, 113, 120–21, 128; and *isocolon*, 257; and Jacob, 194, 207; and Jeremiah, 120; and Jerome, 235, 256; and Jesuits, 4, 24, 30n. 31, 50, 95, 201, 207, 287; and Jesus, 194, 195, 196, 197, 198, 199, 200, 203, 204, 206, 207–8, 210, 211, 212, 214, 215, 216n. 3, 228, 306, 320, 341, 343, 349, 351; and Jews, 194, 223, 227, 229–30, 231, 233, 236, 240n. 27; and Joel 2:1, 120; and John 14:2, 53–54; and John of Patmos, 119, 127, 209; and John the Baptist, 306; and journey, 123–24, 128, 196, 255,

Donne, John *(continued)*
256, 257, 265, 266, 267, 338, 340, 343, 345, 348; and justification, 57–58, 201, 211, 300, 337; and Killigrew, 177–78; and King (Henry), 16; and King (John), 16; and knowledge, 332n. 15; and labels, 22; and language, 196; and Laud, 16, 27; and Laudians, 23, 289n. 13; and law, 212, 213; and light, 319, 320, 322, 323, 327; and literal sense, 49, 50, 104–5, 106, 221, 222, 328, 329; and liturgy, 102, 321, 322, 337; and Lord's Prayer, 56; and love, 342, 349; and Luke 12:50, 104; and Luther, 23, 25, 46, 48, 50, 51, 72, 298; and Mark 5:25–34, 320; and martyrdom, 207, 344; and Mary, 114, 138n. 19, 325; and *massa damnata*, 69, 81, 82; and Matthew, 76, 197; and Matthew 2:19, 338; and Matthew 5:8, 324–25; and Matthew 5:14–16, 340; and Matthew 5:15, 342; and Matthew 5:16, 319; and Matthew 9:13, 55; and Matthew 11:28, 21; and Matthew 16:24, 343; and Matthew 20:22, 104; and Matthew 26:18–19, 347; and Matthew 28:19–20, 321; and mediator/mediation, 203, 204, 206, 207, 209, 210, 214; and medieval framework, 323; and meditation, 114, 117, 122, 125, 128, 129–30, 131, 132, 197, 200, 247, 253, 259, 261, 263, 269n. 6, 270n. 7, 345, 346; and melancholy, 201; and Melanchthon, 46–47, 48, 50, 133, 298; and metaphor, 196–97, 322–23, 324, 325, 326, 327–29, 330–31; and militancy, 275–76; and military, 8, 145–46, 147, 150, 152, 153, 154, 160, 165–66, 176, 183, 184, 185n. 1, 186n. 9; and millenarianism, 274–75; and moderation, 5, 6, 15, 21, 36, 37, 45, 49, 51–52, 56–57, 58, 195, 198, 314, 337; and monasticism, 341, 342; and Montagu, 58, 59; and Morgan, 168; and mother, 3, 24; and motivation, 251; and Mountford, 16; and neosacramentalism, 197; and new philosophy, 323; and nonconformity, 25; and Northumberland, 171; and Numbers 10, 119, 137n. 15; and Ogle, 170; and opinion *vs.* dogma, 48; ordination, 3, 24; and paganism, 284, 325; and paradox, 196; and parental faith, 321; as pastor, 17, 18, 19, 26, 27; and pastoral theology, 343; and Paul, 67, 107, 135n. 8, 200, 208, 209, 253, 326, 337, 341; and Pelagianism, 39, 44, 56, 58, 337, 338, 349–50; and penance, 104, 198, 211, 215; and perseverance, 48, 55–56, 59; and persona, 195; and Peter, 339, 341, 347, 348, 351; and piety, 56; and Piscator, 29n. 21, 50; and polemic, 9, 10, 12, 13, 19, 23, 24, 25, 229–30, 274, 275–76, 277, 281–82, 283, 284, 285, 286, 288n. 6; and politics, 273, 274, 287n. 1, 314; and pope, 43, 94, 97, 108, 130, 131, 276, 287, 288n. 6, 346–48; and prayer, 255; and prayers for dead, 102, 107; and preaching, 6, 9, 11, 12, 13, 23, 26, 55, 134, 140n. 30, 247, 249, 251–59, 275, 285, 288n. 7, 315, 327, 331, 335; and predestination, 5, 6, 15, 16–21, 49, 53, 66–67, 76, 78–79, 80, 81, 86n. 15, 274, 320; and press, 49; and pride, 78, 342; and private, 248; and private devotion, 282, 283, 284; as prolocutor, 6, 35, 36, 37, 42, 58; and prophecy, 113, 119, 120, 123, 124, 127, 128, 129, 137n. 14, 140n. 30, 209; and Protestantism, 3, 80, 194, 198–99, 207, 226, 227, 233, 236, 248–49, 275–76, 287, 300, 314, 315, 321, 324, 326, 330, 343, 345, 346; and Protestant Reformation, 23, 91, 95, 273–76, 282, 286, 299, 305; and Proude, 158; and Proverbs, 26; and

Psalm 6, 222, 227, 233; and Psalm 24:4, 264; and Psalm 51:7, 106; and Psalm 90, 255–56, 259; and public, 248; and public worship, 282, 285, 286; and purgation, 263, 264; and purgatory, 42, 49, 50, 101, 102, 103, 104, 105, 107, 132, 209; and purification, 319, 320; and puritans, 12, 15, 16, 25, 26, 28n. 9, 29n. 18, 197, 275, 281, 282, 283, 284, 285, 289n. 12, 314, 331n. 6, 342, 349; and purity, 26, 325–26, 328, 329, 330; and Rabbinic Bible, 239n. 19; and Real Presence, 203, 215; and reason, 102, 248, 249, 332n. 15; and redemption, 211, 216n. 4; and reform, 274; and reformation, 325, 330, 331, 339; and religion, 273, 274, 275, 277; and religious alignments, 314–15; and religious history, 299; religious upbringing, 3; and repentance, 50, 55, 56, 264; and repetition, 255; and reprobation, 17, 52, 53, 55, 82, 83; and *ressentiment*, 204, 213; and restlessness of mind, 253, 254; and resurrection, 101, 102, 105, 107, 108, 121, 123, 196, 200, 203, 209, 211, 256, 260, 262; and revelation, 298; and Revelations, 113, 118, 119, 121–22, 123, 124, 125, 127, 129; and rhetoric, 196–97, 247–68, 315, 316, 319–23, 324–31; and righteousness, 56; and ritual, 14–15; and ritual murder, 230; and rival, 203, 204, 206, 212, 213, 214; and Rols, 209; and Romans 1:17, 321; and Rudd, 22; and Sackville, 180; and sacraments, 10, 15, 24, 30n. 35, 47, 50, 102, 105, 106, 196, 197, 198, 201, 203, 208, 209, 215, 293–94, 296, 299–307, 308, 310–11, 316, 328–29, 337, 343; and saints, 129; and salvation, 10, 58, 59, 193, 194, 200, 207, 215, 216n. 2, 228, 252, 275, 308, 310–11, 320, 321, 324, 329, 340, 343; and Sarpi, 7, 90–92, 93, 94, 95, 97, 101, 102, 107, 108; and schism, 25; and separatism, 16, 25, 350; and Sermon on the Mount, 324; and service, 58, 59; and shepherd, 342–43; and Sidney, 170, 173; and sight, 285, 320, 327, 329, 332n. 15; and sin, 17, 44, 66–67, 76, 77, 78–79, 80, 81, 82, 107–8, 198, 199, 200, 208, 211, 215, 252, 253, 258, 264–65, 300, 301, 302–3, 349, 351; and singularity, 16; and sobriety, 39, 54; and *sola scriptura*, 297; and solipsism, 139n. 27; and Son, 199, 204, 206, 207, 210; and son, 203, 204; and Song of Songs, 233–34, 235; and soul, 29n. 22, 123–24, 126, 128, 200, 208, 209, 259, 260, 268, 270n. 14, 302; and stars, 40–41; and submission, 253, 260; and suffering, 209–10; and superstition, 284; and supralapsarianism, 21, 29n. 22, 349; and symbols, 323, 324; and Synod of Dort, 6, 23, 37, 39, 43–44, 48, 49, 51, 55, 56, 59, 60n. 9, 77, 86n. 16; and *synonymia*, 263; and *tertium quid*, 195; as theologian, 6; and things indifferent, 10, 103, 275, 282–83; and Thirty-nine Articles of the Church of England, 6, 17, 18, 20, 47, 274; and 1 Timothy 2:3–4, 21; and tradition, 96, 321, 325, 348; transformation of, 66, 86n. 12; and translation, 325–26, 330–31; and transubstantiation, 197, 198, 200, 209, 213; and treasury of merits, 347; and triangulation, 203, 204, 207, 209, 212, 213, 215, 217n. 14; and Trinity, 91, 108; and tripartite mind/body/soul, 209; and trumpet, 119–23, 124, 134, 137n. 15; and understanding, 261; and upwardness/downwardness, 255, 261, 262, 263, 264–65; at Utrecht, 153, 170; and Van Meetkerken, 182, 183; and Venice, 90; and Vere, 161; and *via media*, 195, 198, 314; and Virginia Company, 170, 172, 178, 179; and vision, 113,

Donne, John *(continued)*
119, 124, 125–28, 138n. 19; and watchtower, 124, 128–29; and wife, 203, 213; and Wingfield, 160, 186n. 9; and witness, 124; and Word, 15; and works, 57, 58, 201, 264, 319, 320–21, 322–23, 324, 327, 328, 330, 331; and world order, 323; and Zwingli, 305;

—WORKS: "The Canonization," 210–11; Convocation of English clergy (1626) address, 35, 38, 39–40; *Death's Duell*, 195; *Devotions on Emergent Occasions*, 9, 69, 71, 77, 78, 79, 80, 83, 247, 248–49, 250, 253, 257, 259–68, 269n. 2, 273, 274, 275, 276–77, 281–87; divine poetry, 68, 77, 78; "Elegy on the L. C.," 175; *Essays in Divinity*, 4, 221, 222, 227, 229, 230–31, 237n. 5; "The Extasie," 139n. 29; "Fall of a Wall," 168; *First Anniversary*, 7–8, 119, 121, 125–26, 127, 133, 134, 137n. 14, 139n. 24, 157, 193, 194–95, 196, 199, 208; "Good Friday, 1613: Riding Westward," 209, 217n. 14; "Here where by All All Saints invoked are," 175; "His Picture," 183; *Holy Sonnets*, 7, 24, 71, 79–83, 86n. 14, 165, 180, 193, 194, 199, 201, 203, 204, 205, 252; "As due by many titles I resigne," 82–83; "At the round earths imagin'd corners," 81–82, 122, 199; "Batter my heart," 211–12; "Death be not proud," 80, 81; "Father, part of his double interest," 209, 212–13; "If faithfull soules be alike," 204, 207; "Oh might those sighs and tears," 211; "Oh my black Soule!," 83, 199; "Oh to vex me, contraryes meete in one," 194, 214–15; "Show me dear Christ, thy spouse," 213–15; "Since she whom I loved," 213; "Spit in my face you Jewes," 194; "What if this present were the worlds last night?," 80, 197–98, 209; "Why are wee by all creatures waited on?," 80; "A Hymn to God the Father," 199–200, 203; *Ignatius His Conclave*, 132, 135n. 8; "I know not how Desert more great can rise" (disputed), 179; *Letters* 51, 200; letter on Sir Edward Herbert, 145; letter on Sir Gerard Herbert, 177; and *Overburian Characters*, 156; *Pseudo-Martyr*, 3–4, 7, 23, 94–95, 197, 344; *Satyres*, 208; "Satyre 2," 132; "Satyre 3," 164, 194, 203–4; "Satyre 4," 132; *Second Anniversary*, 7–8, 113–14, 117–19, 120, 121, 122, 123–28, 129–30, 132, 133, 134, 137n. 14, 138n. 19, 139n. 24, 157, 193, 194–95, 196–97, 199, 208, 209; "To Sir Edward Herbert, at Julyers," 155–56; "To the Countess of Salisbury, August, 1614," 157;

—SERMONS: 1615, (first extant sermon) (1:164), 20; 1616/1617, at Paul's Cross (1:183), 25–26; 1617, December 14, before Queen Anne, at Denmarke-house (1:249–250), 76; 1618, April 19, at White-Hall (1:292–293), 78–79; 1618, at Lincoln's Inn (2:51–52), 76–77; 1618/1619, February 12, at Whitehall (2:164–178), 140n. 30; 1618/1619, February 12, at Whitehall (2:167–168), 251; 1619, at Heidelberg, 10, 299–302, 304–5, 306; 1619, at Lincoln's Inn, Sermon of Valediction, 29n. 26 (23); 1619, December 19, at The Hague (2:295), 77–78; 1619, Easter (2:203), 288n. 4; 1619 (2:248–249), 23; 1619/1630, on Matthew 4:18–20, on Fishers of Men, 11, 337–52; 1620s, at St. Paul's (5:273), 255–56, 259; 1621, Christmas (3:369), 96; 1621, Christmas (3:375), 288n. 3; 1621/1622, at St. Paul's (10:123), 253; 1621/1622 (3:377), 17; 1622, Ascension Day (4:139), 95–96; 1622, At Lincoln's

Inn (4:142), 295; 1622, At St. Paul's (4:216–217), 297–98; 1622, before the Earle of Carlile (5:255), 22; 1622 (4:140), 276; 1622 (4:179), 41; 1624, at St. Dunstans (6:104), 288n. 7; 1624, Easter Day (6:68), 273–74; 1624, February 2, Candlemas (v. 10, no. 3), 10–11, 316, 319–24, 325, 327, 329, 330; 1624, on Anabaptism (6:135), 306; 1624 (6:134–135), 300; 1625, Christmas Day, at St. Paul's (6:31–35), 230; 1625, Christmas Day, at St. Paul's (6:347), 19; 1626, 36–37, 45, 49, 51, 57; 1626, April 30 (7:155–156), 55; 1626, April 18, at Whitehall (7:119), 49; 1626, April 18 (7:123), 53–54; 1626, April 18, before Charles I, at Whitehall (7:124–125), 96–97; 1626, April 18 (7:127), 43; 1626, April 18 (7: 206–7), 46; 1626, before Charles I (7:127), 18; 1626, Easter, at St. Pauls (7:95), 101–2; 1626, Easter (7:116), 53; 1626, February 24, before Charles I, at Whitehall, 41–42; 1626, February 24 (7:74), 52; 1626, for Sir William Cokayne (7:264–265), 258; 1626, January 29 (7:62–63), 52; 1626, June 18 (7:190), 103–6, 107–8; 1626, May 21, at St. Paul's (7:164), 102, 103; 1626, May 21 (7:166), 42–43; 1626, Whitsunday (7:228), 57; 1627, at St. Dunstan's church (8:43,44), 251; 1627, at St. Paul's (8:117), 23; 1627, February 2, Candlemas (v. 7 no. 13), 10–11, 316, 324–27, 328, 330; 1627 (7:433), 15; 1629, at St. Paul's (8:331), 14; 1629 (9:158–160), 299; 1630, before Charles I (9:214), 25; 1630, Easter Day, at St. Paul's (9:204), 19–20; 1630, Sermon 13 (9:221–222), 225; 1631, before Charles I, "Death's Duell," 20; sermon (2:169), 134; sermon (5:184), 254–55; sermon (7:222), 206; sermon (7:368), 201; sermon (8:84), 308; sermon (8:168), 200; sermon 50, on Psalm 6:1 (5:324–325), 227, 231, 232; sermon 52, 228; sermon 54 (8:197–198), 233–34; sermon at Denmark House, after James I's death (6:286), 19; sermon at Lincoln's Inn (2:58), 25; sermon at Lincoln's Inn (2:102), 77; sermon at Lincoln's Inn (2:112), 306; sermon at Lincoln's Inn (2:158), 289n. 12; sermon at Lincoln's Inn (3:111), 29018; sermon before Charles, on Genesis 1:26 (9:67), 349–50; sermon on baptism (5:100–101), 302–3; sermon on baptism (5:109), 304–5; sermon on baptism (5:129), 302; sermon on marriage (8:94), 254; sermon on preaching (2:199), 254; *Sermons*, 71, 194–95, 200, 223, 247, 249–59; *Sermons* 50–53, 222

Donne, John, Jr., 183
Dorset, Edward Sackville, fourth earl of, 153, 180
Dorset, Robert Sackville, second earl of, 180
Dorset, Thomas Sackville, first earl of, 180
Double, 203, 205, 209, 210
Double bind, 202, 203, 205, 206, 207, 211
Douglas, William, 169–70
Drake, Sir Francis, 145, 164, 182
Drummond, Alexander, of Midhoop, 148
Drummond, Sir John, 148, 149
Drummond, Sir William, of Hawthornden, 148–49
Drummond, William, 148
Drummonds of Hawthornden, 153
Drury, Diana, 157
Drury, Elizabeth, 113, 119, 120, 121, 124, 125, 126, 127, 128, 132, 137n. 14, 138nn. 19, 21, 145, 157, 196, 209, 216n. 3
Drury, Sir Robert, 113, 145, 155, 157, 162, 166, 168, 175, 182
Drury, Sir William, 157

Duffy, Eamon: *The Stripping of the Altars*, 193
Durham House, 38, 60n. 12
Duxberry, Joseph, 178–79
Dyer, Sir Edward, 164

Ecclesiasticus 43:24[26], 267
Edward VI, 2, 193
Egerton, Alice, 180
Egerton, Sir Thomas (father), 178, 180
Egerton, Sir Thomas (son), 155, 178
Election: and Augustine, 67, 69, 70–71; and Calvin, 198; and Donne, 17, 18–19, 28n. 15, 43, 48, 51–56, 59, 80, 81, 82, 194, 198, 215, 286, 349; and Roman Catholic Church, 54; and success, 349
Elizabeth I, 2, 143, 144, 155, 161, 176, 186n. 9, 193, 275, 276
Emotion, 82, 247, 249–59, 260–68. *See also* Pathopoeia
Empson, William, 216n. 3
England, and Reformation, 2, 84n. 4, 315–16, 317
Ephesians 5:25–27, 302
Erskine/Arskin, Thomas, 152
Essex, Frances Howard, Lady, 156
Essex, Robert Devereux, second earl of, 171
Essex, Robert Devereux, third earl of, 171
Eucharist: and Book of Common Prayer, 336; and ceremony, 279–80, 282; and debate, 294, 311; and Donne, 47, 198, 203, 209, 316, 328–29, 343; and spirit of Christ, 296; and translation, 325; understanding of, 318–19. *See also* Communion; Sacraments; Transubstantiation
Evans, Robert, 58
Everard, Thomasin, 175
Everarts, Sir Michiel, 175
Ezekial, 53, 120, 128, 254

Fairfax, Sir Charles, 166, 168
Faith: and ceremony, 308; and Council of Trent, 336; and Donne, 51, 57, 58, 95–96, 102, 103, 197, 201, 206–7, 264, 275, 300, 305, 320, 321, 326, 327, 329, 330, 331, 343; and English Reformation, 317; experiential, 51; and Grotius, 298; and justification, 336; and Luther, 1, 336; matter *vs.* manner of, 103; and Micanzio, 92; and Protestantism, 195; and Protestant Reformation, 307; and Sarpi, 92; works of, 58. *See also* Justification; Works
Fall/redemption pattern, 247–48, 252, 253–54, 255, 258, 260, 263
Featley, Daniel, 85n. 9
Ferrell, Lori Anne, 13, 16–17, 26, 274, 279
Figure/figurative sense, 49, 50, 104–5, 106, 221, 222, 318. *See also* Interpretation
Fincham, Kenneth, 16, 27
Fish, Stanley, 195, 198, 203
Fletcher, John, 167–68
Flynn, Dennis, 30n. 34, 90, 94
Forty-two Articles of Religion, 2. *See also* Thirty-nine Articles of the Church of England
Frederick Henry, Prince of Orange, 150, 156
Free will, 46, 49, 54, 55, 69, 74–75, 84nn. 6, 11, 349
Frontain, Raymond-Jean, 318
Frost, Kate Gartner, 249, 253
Fuller, Thomas, 36

Galatians 3:11, 321
Gardner, Helen, 23
Garrard, George, 157
Gates, Sir Thomas, 178
Genesis, 323
Geneva Bible, 222, 226, 228, 229, 235, 236. *See also* Bible
Gilman, Ernest, 132–33
Gilpin, Emmanuel, 176
Girard, René, 202–3, 204, 207; *Deceit, Desire*, 205; *Violence and the Sacred*, 204–5, 215

God: and Augustine, 69; and ceremony, 283; dependence on, 77, 79, 195, 248, 252; and Donne, 18–19, 51, 57, 77, 195, 199–201, 203, 204, 209, 227–29, 231, 248, 252, 253, 258, 260, 263, 283, 318, 320, 328, 329, 342, 345, 349; as Essence and Being, 231, 232–33; and grace, 124; and justification, 57; and language, 318; and mercy, 80, 81; name of, 227–29, 231, 240n. 22, 241n. 32
Goldberg, Jonathan, 253
Goldish, Matt, 224
Gomarist Calvinism, 43, 53
Goodyer, Sir Henry, 165, 178, 197
Grace: and Augustine, 67, 68, 69, 70, 74–75, 82; and Calvinism, 212, 336; and Catholicism, 124, 307; and community, 108; and covenant, 200, 306; and Crompton, 74–75; and Donne, 15, 20, 49, 52, 54, 55, 56, 76, 78–79, 80, 82, 101, 108, 195, 197, 198, 199, 200, 201, 210, 252, 302, 305, 311, 343, 349, 350, 351; and Herbert, 201; and Luther, 1; and Matthew, 74; and Paul, 68; prevenient, 76, 252, 351; and Protestantism, 124, 195, 199, 307; Real Presence of, 202; and Sarpi, 100, 108; and soul, 206; and success, 349; and Sutcliffe, 74
Grant, Patrick, 86n. 15
Gregory I, 225, 226
Greville, Eleanore, 164
Grey, Lady Jane, 2
Grey de Wilton, Thomas, Lord, 167
Grotius, Hugo, 10, 294–95, 296, 301; *De Imperio summarum potestatum circa sacra*, 298; *Rivetani apologetici pro schismate contra votum pacis facti discussio*, 298
Guibbory, Achsah, 28n. 6, 48
Guilpin, Everard, 175, 176
Guilpin, George, 175–76

Habakkuk, 113, 128–29

Hakewill, George, 22
Halewood, William, 68, 80, 83, 84nn. 3, 5, 85n. 10, 86n. 13, 252
Halkett, George, 150
Halkett, Sir John, 150
Hall, Joseph, 24, 27, 39, 47, 248
Hamilton, Hugh Hamilton, First Baron, of Glenawley, 153
Hamilton, marquis of, 147
Hamilton, Mongo, 153
Harsnett, Samuel, 35
Harvey, Gabriel, 118
Harwood, Sir Edward, 171–72, 174
Hassel (Hessel), John, 163
Hay, Sir George, of Kinfauns, 147
Hay, William, 147
Hearing. *See* Preaching
Hebraism, 223–27
Hebrews 13:14, 337
Heidelberg, 299–300
Henderson, James, of Fordell, 149
Henderson, Sir Francis, 150
Henderson, Sir Robert, 149–50, 161
Henry IV, 174
Henry VIII, 1–2, 193
Herbert, George, 28n. 6, 201
Herbert, Henry, 172
Herbert, Magdalen, 197
Herbert, Sir Edward, Baron, of Cherbury, 145, 155–56
Herbert, Sir Gerard, 177
Herbert, Sir Henry, 177
Herz, Judith Scherer, 224
Hexam, Henry, 163–64, 165, 182
Heywood, Ellis, 3, 293
Heywood, Jasper, 3, 293
Hezekiah, 253
Higham, Thomas, 166
Hill, Robert, 13, 29n. 18
Hillel, Rabbi, 339
Historical sense, 221, 222. *See also* Interpretation
History, 299
Hoby, William, 162
Hollis, Sir George, 161, 162, 168
Holy Spirit, 96, 206, 298, 310, 317, 318, 336

Hooker, Richard, 14, 194, 203, 216n. 5, 248, 337, 345, 350–51
House of Habsburg, 144
Howard, Catherine, 157
Howard, Frances, 156, 171
Hughes, Jacobus, 159
Hughes (Hewes), Adrian (Andrew), 159
Humanism, 298, 299
Humility, 11, 69, 78, 82, 83, 342
Hunsdon, Henry, Lord, 175
Hunter, Andrew, 153
Huygens, Christiaan, 176
Huygens, Constantijn, 150, 167, 176, 177–78; *Heylige Dagen*, 166
Huygens family, 169
Hyperius, D. Andreas, 251, 253, 258; *De formandis concionibus sacris*, 250
Hypotyposis, 247, 250, 255, 256, 258

Ibn Ezra, 225, 226, 239n. 19
Ignatius of Loyola, 345–46; *Spiritual Exercises*, 248
Imagination, 250
Individual, 100–101, 102, 107, 298, 309–10. *See also* Community
Indulgences, 102, 107
Inquisition, 55
Interpretation, 37, 43–45, 49, 50, 54, 96, 104–6, 108, 221–23, 224–36, 317, 318, 324, 328, 329. *See also* Rhetoric
Irenaeus, 301, 309
Irenicism, 10, 294, 296, 297, 298, 299, 300, 301, 311, 312
Isaiah, 113, 120–21, 128

Jackson, Robert, 194
Jacob, 194, 207
James I, 25, 180, 185n. 1; and avant-garde conformists, 277–79, 280; *Basilikon Doron*, 277; and Bible, 277–78; and Brog, 148; and Calvinism, 3, 14; and Catholic Church, 276, 293; and Church of England, 3; conspiracy against, 167; *Directions to Preachers*, 41, 42, 45, 288n. 7; and Drummond, 149; and Henderson, 150; *A Meditation Upon the 27. 28. 29. Verses of the XXVII. Chapter of Saint Matthew*, 277–78; and military, 144, 155; and Ogle, 168; and Packenham, 158; passing of, 102; and peace, 293; and polemic, 278; and Protestantism, 277, 293; and puritans, 278, 279, 281; and Scot, 159; and Scottish Kirk, 279; and Sutcliffe, 84n. 8; and Synod of Dort, 18, 46
Jeremiah, 120
Jerome, St., 235, 256; *Homilies on the Psalms*, 129
Jesuits, 3, 4, 24, 30n. 31, 50, 54, 95, 201, 207, 287, 299, 344
Jesus, 307, 344; ascension of, 319; and baptism, 294; and Donne, 194, 195, 196, 197, 198, 199, 200, 203, 204, 206, 207–8, 210, 211, 212, 214, 215, 216n. 3, 228, 306, 320, 341, 343, 349, 351; and justification, 57–58; presence in the world, 319; and sacraments, 307, 328–29
Jews, 194, 223, 227, 229–30, 231, 233, 236, 240n. 27
Joel 2:1, 120
John 3:5, 309
John 14:2, 53–54
John Chrysostom, 106, 225, 226, 239n. 15, 309
John of Patmos, 115, 119, 121–22, 127, 209
Johnson, Jeffrey, 62n. 30, 302, 306, 310–11
John the Baptist, 306
Jonson, Ben, 123, 160, 172
Journey: and Dante, 114, 117, 123, 124, 196; and Donne, 123–24, 128, 196, 255, 256, 257, 265, 266, 267, 338, 340, 343, 345, 348
Judä, Leo, 223, 237n. 8
Junius, Franciscus, the elder, 296
Justification, 1, 57–58, 92, 201, 206, 211, 300, 336, 337. *See also* Faith; Works

Kelliher, Hilton, 35–36, 38, 40
Kendall, R. T., 19

Kerr, Sir Robert, 260
Kilbye, Richard, 183
Killigrew, Peter, 177
Killigrew, Sir Henry (father), 177, 179
Killigrew, Sir Henry (son), 177
Killigrew, Sir Robert, 177
Kimhi, David, 235, 237n. 6
King, Henry, 16
King, John, 15, 16
King James Bible, 222, 223, 224, 226. *See also* Bible
Kinloss, Edward, Lord, 153
Knightely, Sir Richard, 176–177
Knowledge, 92–93, 97, 98, 99, 100, 324, 332n. 15. *See also* Reason

Lactantius, 321
Lake, Arthur, 16, 20, 27
Lake, Peter, 14, 16, 27n. 1, 51, 62n. 32, 274, 277, 288n. 2
Lake, Sir Thomas, 151
Language, 316–19. *See also* Interpretation; Rhetoric
Laud, William, 3, 6, 16, 27, 173, 280
Laudians, 13–15, 16, 23, 27, 47, 50, 84n. 6, 277
Layfield, John, 224, 238n. 11
Ledenberg, Gillis van, 167
Leicester, earl of, 171, 174
Leicester, Robert Dudley, earl of, 151, 181
Leicester, Sir Robert Sidney, second earl of, 170, 178
Lennox, duke of, 151
Lewalski, Barbara, 123, 247; *Protestant Poetics*, 216n. 4, 346
Lindsey, David, 152
Lindsey, John, 152
Lisle, Sir Robert Sidney, Viscount Lord, 170–71, 172
Literal sense, 49, 50, 104–5, 106, 221, 222, 317, 318, 328, 329. *See also* Interpretation
Liturgy, 317, 336, 337. *See also* Ceremony
Livingstone, James, 153
Loe, William, 38

Lollards, 319
Lord's Supper. *See* Eucharist
Lovelace, Richard, 176
Lovelace, Sir William, 176
Low, Anthony, 261, 269n. 6
Ludham, John, 250
Luke 12:50, 104
Luther, Martin: and Anabaptists, 305; and Augsburg Confession, 46, 48; and Augustine, 1, 68, 79; and baptism, 305, 307, 310, 311; and Catholic Church, 297; and Donne, 23, 25, 46, 48, 50, 51, 72, 298; and faith, 336; and interpretation, 50; and irenicism, 298; *Large Catechism*, 305, 307; *Little Catechism*, 297; and Paul, 68; and predestination, 68; and sacraments, 307; and salvation, 321; and schism, 296–97; and *sola scriptura*, 298–99; tenets of, 1
Lutherans, 92, 99

MacCulloch, Diarmaid, 79
Magic, 317, 322
Manichaeans, 48
Manley, Frank, 124, 128
Mark 5:25–34, 320
Mark 10:13, 301
Mark 16:16, 309
Marnix, Elizabeth van, 168, 169
Marnix, Philips van: *Byencorf der Heilige Roomsche kercke*, 168–69, 176
Marotti, Arthur F., 237n. 5
Marre, Sir James Erskine, earl of, 150
Marston, John, 176
Martin Marprelate, 176, 177, 181
Martyrdom, 309, 311, 312, 344
Martz, Louis: *The Poetry of Meditation*, 86n. 13, 345–46
Mary, 72, 114, 117, 123, 138n. 19, 325
Mary Tudor, 2, 193
Massa damnata, 69, 70, 81, 82
Massinger, Philip, 167–68
Matthew: 2:19, 338; 5:8, 324–25; 5:14–16, 340; 5:15, 342; 5:16, 317–18, 319; 9:13, 55; 10:32, 309;

Matthew *(continued)*
11:28, 21; 16:24, 343; 20:22, 104; 26:18–19, 347; 28:19–20, 321
Matthew, Sir Tobie, 84n. 8, 85n. 9, 197; translation of Augustine's *Confessions*, 7, 71–73, 74, 76
Maurits, Prince of Orange, 144, 146, 148, 149, 150, 151, 154, 155, 161, 162, 166, 167, 168, 172, 176, 179, 182
Mawe, Leonard, 35, 36, 40, 41
McCulloch, Peter, 48–49, 61n. 24
McGee, J. Sears, 351
Mediator/mediation, 202, 203, 204, 206, 207, 209, 210, 214
Melanchthon, Philip: and Bible, 298; *De modo et arte*, 250; and Donne, 46–47, 48, 50, 133, 298; and interpretation, 50; and preaching, 250, 251–52; and predestination, 61n. 25
Metaphor, 196–97, 317, 320, 322–23, 324, 325, 326, 327–29, 330–31. *See also* Rhetoric
Micanzio, Fulgenzio, 90, 92
Military, 143–84
Milton, Anthony, 13–14, 15, 16, 21, 24, 25, 27n. 1, 30n. 38, 46, 47, 84n. 8, 274
Milton, John, 134, 134n. 1, 180; *Paradise Lost*, 118–19
Monasticism, 341, 342
Montagu, Richard, 36, 37, 39, 40, 42, 43, 44, 45, 46, 48, 50, 51, 53, 56; and Arminianism, 38; and Donne, 58, 59; and election, 54; and Pelagianism, 58; and Thirty-nine Articles of the Church of England, 51
Montaigne, George, 35
Moore, Sir George, 26
More, Ann, 175, 178, 181
More, Sir George, 171
Morgan, Sir Charles, 168, 169
Morgan, Sir Thomas, 169
Morton, Abraham, 152
Morton, Sir Albertus, 152
Morton, Thomas, 42
Morton, William Douglas, earl of, 152

Mountford, Thomas, 16
Mueller, Janel, 247
Murray, Sir David, 148

Narveson, Kate, 13, 14, 29n. 18, 249
Nassau, Justinus van, 169
Neile, Robert, 42, 280
New Model Army, 152
New Testament. *See* Bible; *specific books*
Nonconformism, 25, 162, 163
Norbrook, David, 13
Northumberland, Algernon Percy, tenth earl of, 173
Northumberland, Henry Percy, ninth earl of, 171

Oath of Allegiance, 278
Ogle, Lady, 168
Ogle, Sir John, 166–68, 169–70, 172, 176
Ogle, Thomas, 166
Ogle, Thomas (nephew), 168
Ogle, Trajectina, 167
Ogle, Utricia, 167
Oldenbarnevelt, Johann van, 161, 167, 168, 181
Old Testament. *See* Bible; *specific books*
Oratory, 327–28. *See also* Preaching
Origen, 301, 309
Overbury, Sir Thomas, 156; *A Wife*, 171

Packenham, Sir Philip, 158
Paganism, 284, 325, 328
Paget, John, 163
Pagninus, Santes, 223, 237n. 7
Panton, Thomas, 169
Papazian, Mary Arshagouni, 29n. 26, 62n. 30, 84n. 7, 145, 217n. 7, 253, 269nn. 2, 7, 287n. 1, 289n. 9
Papist, as term, 278. *See also* Catholic Church; Pope
Pathopoeia, 9, 247, 249–59, 260–68
Patterson, W. B., 46, 56
Paul, St., 105; and Augustine, 68; and Calvin, 68; 1 Corinthians 15:51–55, 121; and Dante, 116, 117; and dependence on God, 79; and

Donne, 67, 107, 135n. 8, 200, 208, 209, 253, 326, 337, 341; Galatians, 68; and grace, 68; and Luther, 1, 68; and Reformation, 85n. 10; and resurrection, 107; and salvation, 79; and trumpet, 121, 122
Pelagianism: and Augustine, 48, 67, 68, 69–70, 71, 84n. 6; and Buckingham, 45; and Convocation of English clergy, 38; and Donne, 39, 44, 56, 58, 337, 338, 349–50; and Luther, 1; and Montagu, 36, 51; and salvation, 309–10; and sin, 309–10; and Synod of Dort, 37, 86n. 11
Pelagius, 69, 70
Pembroke, William Herbert, earl of, 159, 160
Percy, Dorothy, 171
Percy, Lucy, 171
Perseverance, 48, 55–56, 59, 67, 69
Peter, Hugh, 172
Peter, St., 19, 339, 341, 347, 348, 351
Petrarch, 295
Pigott, John, 177
Piscator, Johannes, 29n. 21, 50, 226
Placher, William, 68
Plato, 232; *Timaeus*, 230–31
Pocahontas, 179
Politics, 8, 273, 274, 278, 287n. 1, 314
Pope, 278; and Augustine, 73–74; and Dante, 130, 131; and Donne, 43, 94, 97, 108, 130, 131, 276, 287, 288n. 6, 346–48; and polemic, 24; and Sarpi, 92, 93, 97, 108. *See also* Catholic Church
Potter, George R., 23, 28n. 9, 66–67, 69, 79, 101
Preaching: and Donne, 6, 9, 11, 12, 13, 23, 26, 55, 134, 140n. 30, 247, 249, 251–59, 275, 285, 288n. 7, 315, 327, 331, 335; and ear *vs.* eye, 280, 285, 317; and James I, 41, 42, 45, 288n. 7; and Protestantism, 250, 251–52, 317; and puritans, 281
Predestination: and Arminianism, 60n. 6; and Augustine, 7, 21, 66–67, 68, 69, 70, 75, 78, 81, 86n. 15; and

Calvin, 18, 68; and Calvinism, 21, 22–23, 320, 349; and Church of England, 46, 81; and Donne, 5, 6, 15, 16–21, 49, 53, 66–67, 76, 78–79, 80, 81, 86n. 15, 274, 320; and English Calvinism, 22–23; and Melanchthon, 61n. 25; and Sarpi, 91, 100; supralapsarian, 17, 21, 29n. 22, 349
Presbyterians, 153, 301
Prichard, Edward, 172
Pride, 69, 70, 78, 342
Prideaux, John, 16
Protestantism: and Anabaptists, 303; and Augustine, 67–68, 79; and baptism, 300; and Bible, 229, 301; and ceremony, 195, 196; conflict in, 194, 198–99; and desire, 261; and Donne, 3, 80, 194, 198–99, 207, 226, 227, 233, 236, 248–49, 275–76, 287, 300, 314, 315, 321, 324, 326, 330, 343, 345, 346; and doubt, 194; English, 92; and faith, 195; and fall/redemption pattern, 247–48, 252; and grace, 124, 195, 199, 307; and Grotius, 294, 295; and Heidelberg, 300; and insecurity, 199; and James I, 277, 293; and Luther, 1; and Matthew, 71–72; and melancholy, 195; and metaphor, 320; militant, 275–76; and military, 145; and preaching, 250, 251–52, 317; and rhetoric, 315, 328; and sacraments, 195–96, 216n. 5; and salvation, 198–99; and Sarpi, 92; and sin, 252; and transubstantiation, 196. *See also* Calvin, John; Calvinism; Luther, Martin; Melanchthon, Philip
Protestant Reformation: and Anabaptists, 307; and Augustine, 67–68, 71, 75, 79, 85n. 10; and baptism, 308–11, 310; and Bible, 296; and covenant, 306; and Donne, 23, 91, 95, 273–76, 282, 286, 299, 305; and England, 84n. 4, 315–16, 317; and faith, 307; and language, 316–19; and Luther, 1, 297; and Matthew,

Protestant Reformation *(continued)* 71–73; and Paul, 85n. 10; and predestination, 75; and salvation, 310; and Sarpi, 91; and *sola scriptura*, 296, 301; and works, 307
Proude, William, 158
Psalm 6, 222, 227, 233
Psalm 24:4, 264
Psalm 51:7, 106
Psalm 90, 255–56, 259
Psychoanalysis, 202
Purgatory, 42, 49, 50, 101, 102, 103, 104, 105, 107, 132
Puritans: and affliction, 343; and Andrewes, 280; and Bible, 317–18; and Buckeridge, 281; and Calvinism, 13; and Donne, 12, 15, 16, 25, 26, 28n. 9, 29n. 18, 197, 275, 281, 282, 283, 284, 285, 289n. 12, 314, 331n. 6, 342, 349; and early church, 325; and Henderson, 149; and interpretation, 324, 328; and James I, 278, 279, 281; and military, 154; and preaching, 281; and Sidney, 173; as term, 278, 289n. 12; and Thirty-nine Articles of the Church of England, 25; and Veres, 162
Puttenham, George: *The Arte of English Poesie*, 268

Quinn, Dennis, 222
Quintilian, 325, 327, 329

Rabbinic Bible, 239nn. 18, 19
Radcliffe, Robert, 160
Radcliffe, Sir John, 178
Ralegh, George, 177
Ralegh, Sir Walter, 160, 167, 174, 177
Ralegh, Walter (son), 177
Randolph, Thomas, 172
Raspa, Anthony, 94, 224, 261, 270n. 7
Reason, 102, 319, 324, 332n. 15. *See also* Knowledge
Recusants, 3
Redemption, 211, 216n. 4
Remonstrants, 44, 56, 61n. 23, 149, 157, 161, 167, 170, 172, 181

Reprobation, 52, 53, 55, 74
Ressentiment, 195, 203, 204, 213
Resurrection, 101, 102, 105, 107, 108, 121, 123, 196, 200, 203, 209, 211, 256, 260, 262
Reuchlin, Johannes: *De Verbo Mirifico*, 230–31
Revelations, 113, 118, 119, 121–22, 123, 124, 125, 127, 129
Rhetoric, 196–97, 247–68, 314–31. *See also* Interpretation
Rival, 203, 204–5, 206, 212, 213, 214
Rolfe, Thomas, 179
Rollins, Roger B., 249
Roman Catholic Church. *See* Catholic Church
Romans 1:17, 321
Rudd, Anthony, 22
Rudnytsky, Peter, 216n. 2
Russell, Conrad, 60n. 5

Sackville, Anne, 180
Sackville, John, 180
Sackville, Sir Christopher, 180
Sackville, Sir John, 180
Sackville, Thomas: *Gorborduc*, 180; *A Mirror for Magistrates*, 180
Sacraments, 280; and Bible, 317; and Catholic Church, 307; and Donne, 10, 15, 24, 30n. 35, 47, 50, 102, 105, 106, 196, 197, 198, 201, 203, 208, 209, 215, 293–94, 296, 299–307, 308, 310–11, 316, 328–29, 337, 343; and early Church, 296; and Herbert, 201; and Hooker, 351; and Jesus, 307, 328–29; and Protestantism, 195–96, 216n. 5; and Zwingli, 308. *See also* Baptism; Eucharist
Salisbury, Robert Cecil, Lord, 154
Salvation: and Anglicans, 206; and Augustine, 70, 79; and baptism, 308–11, 310; and Catholic Church, 79, 308–9; and Crompton, 74; and Donne, 10, 58, 59, 193, 194, 200, 207, 215, 216n. 2, 228, 252, 275, 308, 310–11, 320, 321, 324, 329,

340, 343; and fear, 206; and Luther, 321; and Paul, 79; and Pelagianism, 309–10; and Protestantism, 198–99; and separatism, 350
Sanders, Wilbur, 198
Sanderson, Robert, 16, 47
Sandilandis, Jacques, 152
Sarpi, Paolo, 7; and Bible, 98–99, 100; and Calvin, 92; and Church, 100–101, 107, 108; and conciliarism, 91, 100–101; and Council of Trent, 7, 91, 93, 95, 97, 98–99, 108; and depravity, 91, 100; and Donne, 90–92, 93, 94, 95, 97, 101, 102, 107, 108; and grace, 100, 108; and history, 110n. 13; *History of the Council of Trent*, 7, 93, 97–100; and individual, 100–101, 107; and interpretation, 108; and knowledge, 92–93, 97, 98, 99, 100; *Pensieri*, 98, 108; and pope, 97, 108; and predestination, 91, 100; and Reformation, 91; and sin, 100
Scheler, Max, 195
Schneidau, Herbert, 349
Schot, Robert, 153
Scodel, Joshua, 27, 28n. 4, 195
Scot, Sir John, 153; *A Tongue Combat*, 163
Scot, Thomas, 159
Scott, Walter, 148
Scottish Kirk, 279
Scottish military, 146–53
Seelig, Sharon, 268
Sellin, Paul, 13, 28n. 13, 29n. 28, 62n. 30, 80, 82, 86n. 16, 286, 287n. 1
Semi-Pelagianism, 38, 45
Sermon-gadder, 280, 281
Sermon on the Mount, 317–18, 319
Seton, Sir John, of St. Germain, 152
Shakespeare, William, 178, 180
Shami, Jeanne, 23, 24, 30n. 38, 31nn. 40, 45, 96, 103, 109n. 7, 222–23, 314
Shapiro, James, 230
Shawcross, John T., 128
Sherwood, Terry, 102

Shuger, Debora, 206, 247; *Sacred Rhetoric*, 249–50
Sibbes, Richard, 13, 163
Sidney, Edmund, 174
Sidney, Sir Philip, 124, 154, 164, 170, 176, 181
Sight, 280, 285, 317, 318, 320, 327
Simpson, Evelyn M., 23, 28n. 9, 66–67, 69, 79, 101, 222
Sin: and Augustine, 66–67, 69, 70, 77, 78, 80, 301; and baptism, 310; and Crompton, 74; and Donne, 17, 44, 66–67, 76, 77, 78–79, 80, 81, 82, 107–8, 198, 199, 200, 208, 211, 215, 252, 253, 258, 264–65, 300, 301, 302–3, 349, 351; and Luther, 1; original, 66–67, 69, 77, 198, 252, 301, 302–3, 351; and Pelagianism, 309–10; and Protestantism, 252; and Sarpi, 100. *See also* Depravity
Smith, John: *True Travels*, 178–79
Smith, Lady, 172
Smyth, John, 303
Söderblom, Nathan, 297
Somerset, Sir Robert Ker, earl of, 156
Son, 199, 204, 206, 207, 210. *See also* Jesus
Spain, 143, 144, 145, 155
Spencer, Sir John, 180
Spencer, Sir Richard, 180
Spenser, Edmund, 164; *Colin Clout's Come Home Again*, 180; *Muiopotmos*, 180
Spinola, commander, 149, 150
St. Leger, Sir Warham, 177
Stachniewski, John, 67, 81, 84n. 3, 216n. 5
Stanwood, Paul, 106–7
Steinmetz, David, 67
Stone, Lawrence, 193
Strier, Richard, 13, 16, 276, 277, 281
Superstition, 284, 317, 322
Sussex, Sir Robert Radcliffe, earl of, 178
Sutcliffe, Matthew, 75, 76, 84n. 8; *The Unmasking of the Masse-monger*, 73, 74
Synod of Dort, 149, 159; articles of, 80;

Synod of Dort *(continued)*
and Donne, 6, 23, 37, 39, 43–44, 48, 49, 51, 55, 56, 59, 60n. 9, 77, 86n. 16; and election, 54–55; English delegation to, 6, 37, 38, 43, 45, 46, 48, 49, 51, 53, 54–55, 56, 59, 62n. 32; and Pelagianism, 86n. 11; and predestination, 17–18, 52; and Vere, 163

Tertium quid, 195, 202
Tertullian, 106, 309, 321
Theodoret, 106
Theophylact, 106
Thirty-nine Articles of the Church of England, 2, 3, 6, 25, 47, 51, 71, 84n. 4; Article 17 of, 17, 18, 19, 20, 274. *See also* Church of England; Forty-two Articles of Religion
Thirty Years' War, 71
Thomas Aquinas, 106, 309
Throckmorton, Arthur, 160
Throckmorton, Elizabeth, 181
Throckmorton, George, 181
Throckmorton, Job, 181
Throckmorton, Sir John, 180–81
1 Timothy 2:3–4, 21
Tophichen, Sandilands of Calder, First Lord, 152
Tourneur, Cyril: *The Atheists Tragedy*, 164
Tracy, Dorothy, 165
Tradition, 96, 299, 348
Translation, 325–26, 330–31. *See also* Metaphor; Rhetoric
Transubstantiation, 196, 197, 200, 209, 213. *See also* Eucharist
Treaty of Nonesuch, 144
Tremellius, John Immanuel, 226, 237n. 6
Triangulation, 202, 203, 204, 206, 207, 209, 212, 213, 215, 217n. 14
Trinity, 91, 108
Twelve Years' Truce, 145
Tyacke, Nicholas, 21, 28n. 17, 42, 280

Understanding, 319. *See also* Knowledge; Reason

United Provinces, 144, 145
Urrie, Sir William, 151
Ussher, James, 39
Utrecht, 168
Uytenbogaert, Johannes, 170

Van Meetkerken, Anthony, 181
Van Meetkerken, Boudewijn, 182
Van Meetkerken, Edward, 182
Van Meetkerken, Guido, 182
Van Meetkerken, Nicholas, 182
Van Meetkerken, Sir Adolf (father), 181
Van Meetkerken, Sir Adolf (son), 181, 182
Venice, 90, 91, 92, 94
Vere, Lady Mary, 162–63, 165
Vere, Sir Edward, 161–62
Vere, Sir Francis, 160, 161, 166, 171, 182
Vere, Sir Horace, 154, 155, 160, 161, 162, 163, 164, 165, 166, 168, 173, 181, 182
Vessey, Mark, 106
Villiers, George, 278
Virgil: *Aeneid*, 116, 117
Virginia Company, 170, 172, 178, 179

Wallace, Dewey, 46–47, 61n. 25
Waller, Marguerite, 115
Walton, Isaak, 79; *Life of Donne*, 66, 67
Ward, Samuel, 20
Ware, Tracy, 86n. 15
Watts, William, 84n. 8
Wendel, François, 21
Whetston, Bernard, 172
Whetston, George, 172–73
White, Francis, 57
White, Peter, 27n. 1, 60n. 8
Whitgift, John, 15, 16
Will. *See* Free will
William of Orange, 169
William the Silent, 144
Willoughby, Francis, 179
Willoughby, Robert Bertie, Baron, 179
Willoughby de Eresby, Peregrine Bertie, Lord, 179

Wilson, Thomas, 319, 320, 322, 323, 324, 325, 327, 328, 329, 330; *The Art of Rhetoric*, 10, 315–16, 317
Wingfield, Sir John, 160, 186n. 9
Winniffe, Thomas, 36, 58
Winwood, Sir Ralph, 180
Wishart, Alexander, 151
Wittenberg, 303
Wittreich, Joseph Anthony, 118
Wolf, Dieter, 298
Wollman, Richard, 216n. 2
Wootton, David, 93, 100
Work, 341
Works: and Augustine, 75; and Council of Trent, 336; and Crompton, 74, 75; and Donne, 57, 58, 201, 264, 319, 320–21, 322–23, 324, 327, 328, 330, 331; and Protestant Reformation, 307. *See also* Faith; Justification
Wotton, Sir Henry, 90–91, 92, 94, 130
Wycliffe, John, 318–19, 325
Wytston (Whetston), Walter, 172

Yates, Frances, 91, 134n. 4
York House Debates, 36, 42, 54, 57
Young, John, 36
Young, Robert V., 197

Zouche, Allan, 172
Zouche, Edward, eleventh Baron, 172
Zouche, Richard, 172
Zouche, Sir William, 172
Zurich Reformation, 303
Zwingli, Ulrich, 100, 305–6, 308